RACE TO REVOLUTION

RACE ᴛᴏ REVOLUTION

*The United States and Cuba during
Slavery and Jim Crow*

GERALD HORNE

MONTHLY REVIEW PRESS

New York

Library of Congress Cataloging-in-Publication Data

Horne, Gerald.
  Race to revolution : Cuba and the United States during slavery and Jim
Crow / Gerald Horne.
    pages cm
ISBN 978-1-58367-445-1 (paperback : alkaline paper) — ISBN
978-1-58367-446-8 (cloth : alkaline paper) 1. United States—Relations
—Cuba. 2. Cuba—Relations—United States. 3. Slavery—Cuba—History.
4. Slavery—United States—History. 5. African Americans—Segregation
—History. 6. Blacks—Segregation—Cuba—History. 7. Cuba
—Race relations. 8. United States—Race relations. 9. Blacks—Cuba
—Politics and government. 10. African Americans—Politics and
government. I. Title.
  E183.8.C9H65 2014
  327.7307291'09034—dc23
                        2014011580

Typeset in Eldorado

Monthly Review Press
146 West 29th Street, Suite 6W
New York, New York 10001

www.monthlyreview.org

5 4 3 2 1

Contents

Introduction

THE AFRICANS[1] WERE APPREHENSIVE—with good reason.

It was early in 1862 and the nation in which they resided, the United States, was embroiled in a bloody civil war. As such, the Washington authorities sought to send hundreds of them to Key West to work on fortifications, as this small town was well behind the lines of the so-called Confederate States of America—which dominated most of Florida—and had sought secession precisely on the grounds of continuation of enslavement of Africans. But the Africans asked to take on this important task balked, assuming this might be a prelude to selling them into slavery in Cuba, just across the Florida Straits.[2] Their nervousness was understandable, since, for the longest period, there had been a robust slave trade—licit and otherwise—between the republic and the Spanish colony.[3]

Thus by 1862 the republic, which had countenanced this odious commerce for so long, was now ironically placed in jeopardy because Africans had long memories of being shipped to one of the world's most significant slave emporia.[4] These were not unreasonable fears given that some Confederate rebels were then in the process of transferring or liquidating their human assets by sending them to or selling them in Cuba.[5] Though in the long run the demise of slavery in the republic spelled doom for its counterparts in Cuba, in Barbados in 1863 sugar planters complained that the increase in slaves delivered to Havana by fleeing rebels and increased traffic from Africa (often captained by comrades of these rebels) was providing "unfair competition."[6]

In short, given the intense traffic between Havana and the mainland, slaveholders taking their slaves with them to Cuba were not uncommon.[7] Africans resisting their dispatch to Florida may also have heard about the rude reception those like them had received by colonial authorities in Cuba. In 1837, George Davis, a tailor—and U.S. Negro—was traveling in Cuba where he was suspected of being a dreaded abolitionist. He was arrested and almost immediately condemned to death. As an antislavery journal put it, he was "executed by being screwed to death"—and this was not the first incident of this type. "Colored seamen" particularly from the republic were persecuted; generally they were barred from landing and if somehow they managed to evade this proscription, they were jailed, then tried, and if convicted were slated for execution or enslavement. [8] "God only knows when we shall get out," said a U.S. detainee in a prison in Santiago de Cuba in 1841, since "it has often happened that free colored persons put in prison here have been sold into slavery to defray the jail fees." [9]

In 1849 the periodical published by Frederick Douglass, the leading Negro abolitionist, excoriated Cuba as the "great Western slave mart of the world" and "the channel through which slaves are imported annually into the United States."[10] Like others, Douglass saw the supposed ban on slave importations into the republic as being as effective in halting this practice as bans on illicit drugs were in halting ingesting of such substances.

Unfortunately, the impressment of U.S. Negroes into slavery in Cuba continued after the Civil War's end in 1865, suggesting that ill conditions on one side of the Straits could have contagious effects on the other side.[11] In 1872 Margaret Ray of Owensboro, Kentucky, complained directly to President Ulysses S. Grant that "100 colored [sic] freedmen" were "decoyed to Cuba" after being offered "fabulous wages" but found themselves "forced into slavery more terrible than of which they could ever have conceived." Adequate recourse seemed unavailing so she demanded that Grant "go and take Cuba and wipe out the stain" of "slavery," so such a tragedy would not recur.[12]

THIS IS A BOOK ABOUT U.S.-Cuban relations in the bitter context of slavery and Jim Crow. It focuses heavily on the words and deeds of U.S. Negroes— and their "white" counterparts.[13] This book engages the question of racism with an emphasis on the United States—which should not be interpreted to excuse Spain's depredations in this conflicted realm: on the other hand, exploring race and racism in Cuba without reference to the gravitational pull exerted by the mainland seems shortsighted. U.S. slave traders were heavily responsible for the presence of so many Africans in Cuba and U.S. nationals were a potent presence there almost from the moment of independence. The U.S. Negro abolitionist Martín Delany was among those who crusaded against slavery in Cuba, seeing the eradication of this system as a precondition for freedom in the Americas. Like the Africans in Florida in 1862, U.S. Negroes came to understand that their freedom would be imperiled as long as bondage existed ninety miles from the mainland. Delany famously argued in 1852 that "in almost every town where there is any intelligence among them, there are some *colored persons* of both sexes who are studying the Spanish language," not least because of fervent interest in Cuba.[14] This was followed in the twentieth century when U.S. Negro Communists and Reds of African descent in republican Cuba campaigned relentlessly against U.S. hegemony in Cuba—notably against the Jim Crow that predominated on both sides of the straits, which supplanted a different and, according to many commentators, milder form of racism that had prevailed in Cuba for centuries. Actually, slavery in the republic was so horrific that it tended to make Spanish slavery seem mild by comparison, according to many commentators of that era. And, as we shall see, repugnance toward the heightened racism imposed by Washington in Havana paved the way for the revolution that climaxed on 1 January 1959.

Yet even before independence, colonial Cuba often intimidated the slave South, as arming Africans had been the practice on the island since the sixteenth century[15] and by the early eighteenth century St. Augustine in Florida had become notorious for its forays into the Carolinas featuring Spanish-speaking Negroes with guns. [16] This was of significance when the republic and Spain jousted over control of Florida almost 200 years ago: Washington seemed to think that deploying armed Africans from Cuba to engage in combat was akin to a crime of war. [17]

After breaking from rule by London, the republic was hampered in trading with its neighbors—including Canada and the Caribbean—which left few options beyond commerce with Spanish possessions,[18] including Cuba; hence, as early as the 1790s, aggressive Yankee merchants were dominating the slave trade to Havana.[19] The arrival of these merchants coincided with a quantum leap in Cuba's African population.[20] Surely Cuba represented a lush opportunity—but it also represented danger, which dialectically gave impetus to the republican desire to penetrate the island, for early in the nineteenth century Governor William Claiborne of Louisiana limned the consensus of the U.S. ruling elite when he claimed that Cuba was "the real mouth of the Mississippi [River]," the serpentine spine of the mainland, and until the island was controlled by the United States, the republic itself would be imperiled.[21] "We must have the Floridas and Cuba," echoed Thomas Jefferson.[22]

By bringing more Africans to Cuba and seeking to control more territory there, republicans could also attain a strategic goal, even without annexation. Constantly in search for new markets, by 1806 these creative entrepreneurs had veered from the traditional hunting ground for the enslaved—West Africa— and had headed southward, rounding the Cape toward Mozambique in search of human chattel destined for Cuba.[23] By 1838 Captain Brunswick Popham of the Royal Navy, then sailing off the coast of Africa, rued the "active and undisguised assistance given to the Slave Trade by citizens of the United States of America," which was "as notorious as it is disgraceful"; in fact, he continued, "were it not for the active co-operation of the Americans, the Slave Trade would very materially decline," which would have had a salutary impact on "Havana and Brazil." [24] By 1839 one U.S. Negro journalist was dumbfounded to find that "out of 177 slave ships which arrived at Cuba every year, five-sixths are owned and fitted out from ports in the United States," with profits fueling robust development within the republic, as this filthy lucre was going disproportionately to Boston, New York, and Baltimore. [25]

By 1840, a British diplomat estimated that U.S. nationals owned thousands of slaves in Cuba and often held property jointly with Spaniards: there had been a "great increase" in these categories "within the last ten or twelve [years]," it was reported. [26] That same year Joel Poinsett, a leading U.S. emissary in the region, had reason to believe that his fellow citizens controlled a "third of all the wealth of the island." [27] By 1841, another Negro analyst opined that since 1808, when the slave trade was thought to be in remission, there had been "kidnapped and carried away from Africa to . . . Cuba and Porto Rico 1,020,000" unlucky souls. [28] As early as 1841, London had concluded that Spanish complicity in the dramatically extraordinary increase in the enslaved population was a desperate roll of the dice by Madrid whereby it would free and unleash Africans in order to foil U.S. annexation or a revolt by the Creoles, the Cuban-born population of Spanish ancestry. This phenomenal increase was also a kind of planned deflation, it was said, to drive down the price of Africans to the detriment of the U.S. nationals then flooding the island. [29]

By 1849, London concluded that "those who are most active in encouraging the slave trade are the American settlers, who have bought land and wish to bring new land into cultivation, or extend the cultivation of existing estates." [30] By the mid-1850s Cuba sold over 85 percent of its sugar to its northern neighbor—overwhelmingly produced by slave labor—as it slid uneasily into the role of becoming a de facto appendage of the republic. [31]

It was also during this time that a U.S. emissary in Trinidad, Cuba, estimated "at least nineteen-twentieths of the present slave population" had been imported since 1820. Though he did not add that his compatriots played a major role in this dastardly process, he did say that since London had pressured Madrid into anti-slave-trade provisions that suggested that Africans imported after 1820 were in Cuba improperly, it could mean a massive emancipation that "would be seriously injurious"—notably to the republic—since this "would amount very nearly to a total abolition of slavery." And since the importation "has been almost exclusively confined to males, and that at this moment at least four-fifths of the whole number of slaves on the estates of the planters [are] composed of that gender," this could augment the already formidable Cuban military. [32] Correspondingly, by 1850 William Hunt, formerly of Philadelphia, was billed as "the most extensive sugar planter in the island of Cuba" and, as a result, "probably the richest man of his age in the Union." [33]

By 1858 there were so many Africans flooding into the mainland region abutting the Gulf of Mexico—a process driven by the seemingly insatiable appetite of Cuba for slaves—that the African slave trade, thought to be on the decline, had actually surged with a vengeance, a U.S. journalist claimed: this was evidenced by the depot for arriving Africans he had espied in the Pearl River delta in southern Mississippi.[34] It was with disgust during that same year that a British delegate in Havana denounced the "abuse of the flag of the United States in carrying on the Slave Trade." "Indeed," he averred mournfully, "it is only under that flag that slave-trading in this island is carried on" in what amounted to a "prostitution" of the Stars and Stripes.[35] As late as 1876, British officials were astonished to find the continuing involvement of U.S. flagged vessels in transporting enslaved Africans.[36]

In short, the considerable role of U.S. nationals in promoting enslavement of Africans in Cuba was a poisoned chalice because Washington's influence in Havana brought the abolitionist gaze of London, which had demonstrated previously that its antislavery stance could attract mass support from U.S. Negroes to the detriment of the republic.[37] As some fire-eaters in Dixie clamored for forcible annexation of Cuba, the dovish Congressman Joshua Giddings of Ohio warned pointedly in 1854 that these warmongers should be careful since a war for the island could paradoxically mean "the overthrow of slavery in Cuba," which could easily spread to Dixie itself.[38] When Congressman William Boyce of South Carolina spoke balefully in 1855 about "two hundred thousand Spanish Free Negroes" in Cuba who "strike me more like two hundred thousand half-lit torches, which a single flash may light up and set the whole island in a flame at any moment," he suggested how and why the republic would find it difficult to swallow and digest Cuba. "It was the same Free Negro race," he argued, "under the workings of Spanish and French ideas, which upturned the entire social fabric in St. Domingo [*sic*] and wreaked infinite slaughter on the white race."[39]

Nonetheless, the importance of Cuba was signaled when Washington posted as its top diplomat there, Nicholas Trist, married to a granddaughter of Thomas Jefferson and maintaining varying ties of intimacy to four other U.S. presidents. Trist boasted of his tie to Jefferson as reflecting an "intimacy as close, a familiarity as unreserved," as could be imagined. Andrew Jackson appointed him in 1833 and he served in Cuba for eight years, then resided in Cuba for over three more years and distinguished himself for his pivotal role in the slave trade.[40] He was "most unfit," sniffed London's man in Havana in 1839, this after the U.S. citizen had taken on the added assignment of consul in Portugal, a declining European power renowned for its prowess in the slave trade. Trist, it was said, was an "apologist for the Slave Trade" and "an abetter of slave dealers," eager to "partake of the blood money of the slave."[41]

To be sure, as suggested by the abolition of slavery in Cuba not taking effect until years after the Emancipation Proclamation, Madrid was able to teach Washington a thing or two about how best to maintain slavery, particularly in the training of fearsome dogs trained to capture—and mangle—runaways.[42] As early as 1839, Zachary Taylor, a future U.S. president, thought it would be a grand idea to import these animals to the mainland to check an increasingly rambunctious population of Africans.[43] When in 1836 a New Yorker spoke movingly about how in Cuba "fat" Africans were killed and converted to "sausages," the unwary would have been excused if they took this story seriously.[44]

Still, given an antebellum Hobson's choice, Africans tended to favor residing in Cuba rather than the republic, perhaps because escaping to the island generally meant gaining freedom and escaping mainland enslavement. This became clear during the tortuous transition from Spanish to U.S. rule in Florida. Africans fled en masse to Cuba during this era, not least because options for free Negroes were broader there. An illustrative case was that of Antonio Proctor, who because of his service to His Catholic Majesty, not least during the "Patriot War" of 1811 when Washington sought forcibly to annex Florida, received a land grant of 185 acres near St. Augustine around 1816, but by the late 1840s, with Florida firmly under U.S. rule, his family had been sold into slavery.[45] The case of the Proctors exemplifies a major theme of cross-straits history: the rise in influence of Washington was a catastrophe for Africans.

On the other hand, the case of the slave ship *Amistad* and its enslaved Africans who revolted in Cuban waters, then found themselves ensnared on the mainland,[46] is now part of U.S. lore. Less renowned is a case a couple of decades later in 1861 when a crew of African seafarers from Cuba sailed northward but rebelled on the open seas when they found their destination was to be Baltimore where they feared they would be sold into bondage. [47]

The determined avoidance of U.S. jurisdiction by Africans of all stripes was a reflection of the fact that when Washington replaced Madrid as the sovereign in Florida, what one scholar has described as a "mild and flexible system of race relations" was supplanted by a different system "with a severe definition of slavery" that "viewed [Africans] as degraded members of a despised race and which erected institutional and social barriers between whites and all persons of African descent. . . . The United States brought a harsh two-caste system of slavery with rigid racial dimensions to the new Florida territory."[48] To a degree, when Washington replaced Madrid in Cuba in 1898 there was a similar replacement in "race relations" which, I contend, contributed to the Cuban Revolution in 1959.

Nonetheless, as suggested by the rough treatment accorded to U.S. Negroes who found themselves in Cuba during the era of slavery, Havana watched the activities of the slave South with a keen eye focused on Negro unrest, as if it were a contagion that could easily spread across the straits.[49] Beyond bilateral relations, this was understandable given the deep and liquid nature of the market in enslaved Africans, and Havana was wise to ascertain if any of those imported had reputations for obstreperousness. Thus it seemed almost routine in 1823 when Havana received a report from Charleston that Africans involved in a recent significant conspiracy were designated for expulsion.[50] Quite naturally, Havana watched carefully the unfolding 1830s war in Florida between indigenes—thought to be led by Africans—and federal troops.[51] Colonial Cuba had become so leery of the republic that it had become nervous about the presence on the island of men of color who had roots in St. Augustine, a policy that befell Juan Romero in 1844[52] and Juan Bernardo Marrero during that same year.[53] Havana may have known that as the slave trade to Cuba increased, driven by events in Texas, U.S. Negroes took an ever more determined interest in the island, leading to increased visits by them to Havana. [54]

On the one hand, the republicans seeking to annex the island may have been enthusiastic about the unrest generated in Cuba in the 1840s, which was driven in part by the flux generated with their Stakhanovite labors in enchaining Africans for the island: Cuba was rocked by major slave revolts during this time. On the other hand, as their investments grew in Cuba, republicans had to be concerned about their holdings being destroyed by rebellious Africans. By April 1844, John C. Calhoun, the hawkish doyen of Dixie, was bemoaning the "great outrages" inflicted on "white residents, especially of our citizens"[55] near Cardenas at the instigation of Africans and sought to dispatch "one of our ships of war" there.[56] If Calhoun and his ilk had been paying attention to the views of U.S. Negroes about tumultuous events in Cuba, they might have been even more sobered when Martín Delany seized the opportunity provided by this commotion to pen one of the more profound novels of the entire antebellum oeuvre, which suggested that a revolt of the enslaved in Cuba would lead to the downfall of that peculiar institution in the republic. Delany imagined a U.S. Negro protagonist who became embroiled in a plot to overthrow the illicit slave trade to Cuba and assisted Africans there in routing wealthy U.S. nationals who dominated the economy of the island.[57]

Inspired by an actual revolt of enslaved Africans in Cuba in the early 1840s, Delany named one of his children after the renowned Cuban poet of that era, Placido.[58] His novelistic conjoining of the fates of Africans on either side of the straits was redolent of thinking among Africans in the Republic,[59] a reflection of the tragic reality that kidnapping and illicit commerce could often transform a U.S. Negro into an African residing in Cuba. Delany, like most Africans of the era, had a sour view of the fruits of 1776 and saw the militant overthrow of slavery on both sides of the straits as a necessary corrective to the establishment of the United States itself.[60] It was Delany, speaking in Pittsburgh in 1855, who saw the presence of armed Africans in Havana as the surest guarantor that the island would not be taken by the slaveholders' republic.[61]

Surely Washington played an instrumental role in the development of Cuba as a slave society. And this process was accelerated with the secession of Texas from Mexico in 1836—encouraged by Washington—and its annexation by 1845. Texas, whose independence was driven in no small part by a desire to escape an abolitionist Mexico, quickly developed a major slave trade with Cuba, and in that sense the Lone Star on the flags of both was more than coincidental, for the astonishing increase in Cuba's African population during the decades leading up to 1865 was a function to a sizable degree of its tie to Texas. In December 1836 a U.S. abolitionist found that the price of enslaved Africans in Cuba was "considerably higher now than it was two years ago"; this "advance in price was attributed" to the "market that was found for them in Texas."[62] By 1840, the British emissary in Cuba, David Turnbull, found a large exportation of slaves from the island of Cuba to the new Republic of Texas, perhaps "as high as 15,000 in a single year. . . . the price of a slave at Houston or Galveston is three or four times as great as it ever is at the Havana."[63] By 1841 U.S. abolitionists were moaning about the "large number of slaves who had been illegally smuggled from Cuba into Texas."[64]

In a sense Spanish Cuba was trapped with an abolitionist London pressuring from one side and the slaveholders' republic from another. Spanish Cuba was also facing pressure from abolitionist Haiti and a growing abolitionist movement in the United States that was centered among U.S. Negroes, a trend that led to Havana seeking to bar virtually any other foreign Negro from its territory, which complicated relations not only with Britain and Haiti (and U.S. Negroes) but with some of its more influential neighbors, including Mexico, whose election of Vicente Guerrero (who happened to be of African descent) to the highest office in the land had helped to spur Texas to secede.[65] When the famed abolitionist writer from the United States Harriet Beecher Stowe turned up in London in 1853, Madrid's man there seemed to be having a nervous breakdown, worrying about the implications for Cuba.[66]

As in the republic, Haiti was a frightful reality for colonial Cuba, representing the successful revolt of the enslaved and the liquidation of the slaveholding class.[67] As early as 1802 when the result of the turmoil in Hispaniola was still unclear, Cuba moved to bar African "insurrectionists" from neighboring—and French-controlled—Guadalupe seeking to visit the island.[68] In 1812 an English-speaking African named Hilario Herrera visited Cuba just before the launching of one of the more profound revolts in the island's history—apparently inspired by Haiti—and was accused of seeking to ignite an uprising of the enslaved by colonial authorities who thought they had reason to be wary of visiting Africans.[69] The worst fears of Havana and Washington were realized when furious Africans in 1849 attacked the palace of the governor in St. Lucia and burned several homes while chanting "Viva Soulouque!," reciting rhythmically the name of Haiti's leader.[70]

During this same decade, Cuba was seized with the notion of a widespread revolt of the enslaved with some thinking that London was behind it all. Some Cubans in the United States hostile to Madrid's rule argued that the Spanish colonizers were winking at the importation of more Africans on the premise that if the United States invaded, the enslaved would be freed and unleashed, which could have far-reaching repercussions on the mainland. "It is desirable that a Negro empire should not be consolidated by hostile power within a few days' sail by steam," argued a group of Cubans in the United States in the late 1840s; these "ferocious hordes," it was said, would "burn and slaughter" until exterminated: Haiti was the negative example proffered.[71]

Havana and Washington were united in opposition to the rise of Haiti, which was thought to represent a breach in the pro-slavery wall in the hemisphere. This could have brought them together, except that Washington continued to lust after Cuba and the republic and colony were apprehensive that they both would be outflanked by the abolitionism then surging in London. Madrid's dilemma was illustrated during the U.S. Civil War when the administration of Abraham Lincoln was frantically seeking a new homeland for the African population of the republic and contemplated, among other sites, what is now the Dominican Republic, where Haitian influence was waning and Spanish influence was rising. In July 1862 Madrid's representative in Haiti worried anxiously that the arrival from the mainland of an even more substantial population to reside in eastern Hispaniola would bolster the Negro republic and could mean the possibility that a "Garibaldi" that was a "Negro" would disrupt altogether Spanish interests in the region.[72] This fear was part of a preexisting anxiety in Havana that tended to conflate the interests of Africans in the republic with the interests of Haiti. The Haitian Revolution that led to a surge in British abolitionism led to the demise of U.S. slavery,[73] which in turn undermined slavery in Cuba.

Inexorably, the end of slavery in the republic had direct repercussions in colonial Cuba. "I was happy but not surprised," said Frederick Douglass in February 1863, "to learn that the price of slaves declined in Cuba as soon as the news of the President's [Emancipation] Proclamation reached the island. She would be able to maintain her Slavery scarcely a year after ours had ceased,"[74] he opined wrongly but understandably. Actually, as an outgrowth of the blockade of Southern ports during the war, a more intense relationship developed between Dixie and Cuba, as if the long-standing mainland desire for annexation was occurring indirectly.[75] But annexation did not occur. Previously this was because of a standoff between London, Washington, and Madrid, with

the former two willing to accept the status quo rather than see the other prevail. Yet even within the United States there was a standoff. Visiting the island
in 1860 the republican visitor John Abbott acknowledged that taking Cuba
"would strengthen slavery in the Senate and the House" and would also "be
the instant destruction of every sugar plantation in Louisiana."[76]

Then Dixie lost: Washington's relations with London that had been vexed
and had stayed the hand of the republic to a degree in its desire to annex Cuba,
was eroding: and then from 1868 to 1878 the island erupted in turmoil against
both colonialism and slavery, creating an opportunity for a republic that was
supposedly opposed to both. Yet U.S. economic interests were affected and
not always positively,[77] creating the possibility that a Cuba free from Spanish
rule would not necessarily be a gift to the republic.

Inevitably, this turmoil on the island accelerated an ongoing trend—
Cubans moving to Florida. There a number of them fit smoothly into the
population of U.S. Negroes with some becoming leaders of this community,
particularly in Key West, Pensacola, and Escambia County, not far from
Mobile, which had long been a center of Negro unrest, a trend that was mul-
tiplied after the republic banned slavery in 1865.[78] The rank and file of the
Republican Party in Key West, for example, which sought to extend the anti-
slavery that helped give birth to this organization, consisted heavily of U.S.
Negroes and Cubans of African descent.[79] Traveling in the opposite direction under foul means were U.S. Negroes headed to enslavement in Cuba;
simultaneously, the fabled Jose Martí of Cuba was among those who objected
strenuously to the plan bruited in Washington of dumping newly freed slaves
on the island.[80]

As Cuba strained under the Spanish yoke in the years following the end
of the U.S. Civil War, there were those who felt that U.S. Negroes would
be a natural ally of the island. Henry Turner, a militant Negro from Georgia,
concurred. In 1873 he informed President Grant about "an enthusiastic mass
meeting of the colored citizens held last night to express indignation at the
butchery of our fellow citizens in Cuba" and that it was agreed "unanimously"
that "5,000 colored citizens are ready to enlist for Cuba to teach the Spanish
authorities respect."[81] Another group of Negroes from Williamsport, Pennsylvania, sought to "furnish" up to "one hundred men" to fight in Cuba.[82] By the
same token, Antonio Gallenga in this same year informed his London audience correctly that "there is a great stir" extant "among the Negroes in the
United States, thousands of whom could be easily enlisted in any enterprise
intended to liberate their African brethren" in Cuba; this weighty possibility,
he added, "does not preclude the possibility of an eventual rise of the whole
Negro race at some future period, if political agitators and especially colored
men from the States, are sent as apostles of freedom among them."[83]

This was precisely the fear held by some mainlanders, one of whom informed Senator Charles Sumner of Massachusetts in 1873 that "should the insurgents succeed in overthrowing Spanish rule" that the "162,983 whites of foreign birth, together with those among the Creoles who are loyal" could be "massacred by the now subject classes" leading to another Haiti. Since Cuba was "within five days' sail of New York," what would "Negro insurrection" mean for the republic? "Will it not lead to the total extinction of the power of the whites and the establishment of another black republic?"[84] The "Black Scare" was designed to appeal to Washington's tastes and was quickly taken up by Madrid, which informed Grant's secretary of state that those they were fighting "consist of Negroes, Mulattoes, Chinese" and the like in a "war of races"; if this motley coalition prevailed, "power would be in their hands," meaning "the end of all civilization." Thus, said Fernando Calderon y Collantes, it was in "the interests of all Europe and America"—not to mention "the white race in Cuba"—to subdue these rebels. Spain's triumph, he reassured, would mean abolition, so there was less compulsion for aid to the insurrectionists, who were like "birds of prey, pillaging and applying the torch of the incendiary."[85]

Congressman Josiah Walls of Florida, a prominent Negro leader in Florida, contradicted Madrid in December 1873 when he introduced a joint resolution demanding the recognition of Cuban belligerency, and then a few weeks later took to the floor of the House of Representatives in Washington to bolster his démarche with militant and impassioned words.[86] John Willis Menard was the first Negro to be elected to the House (though he was not seated); part of the opposition to him stemmed from the allegation that he was much too close to revolutionaries in Cuba. Actually, he did attend their meetings in Key West and wrote poetry hailing them.[87]

Unfortunately, the activism at the highest level of Negroes like Walls and Menard was soon to be evanescent and their absence was a blow to Cuban independence and to those still struggling to eradicate slavery on the island, which did not end effectively until 1886. With the termination of Reconstruction—effectively in 1876—Negroes on the mainland found they had shed blood profusely during the war in order to erect an apartheid state, which also proved to be a baneful influence on Cuba. Traveling in Charleston in 1886, Jose Martí was struck by the Jim Crow he witnessed; still, it is possible that such experiences steeled the growing revulsion toward the republic in Cuba and instilled a deeper Cuban patriotism and nationalism.[88]

Certainly, the burgeoning Cuban population in Key West had difficulty in adjusting to Jim Crow. "Key West is the freest town in the South," reported one Negro journal in Manhattan in 1888. "The Ku Klux Klan," the notorious terrorist wing of the Democratic Party, "would be unceremoniously run into the Gulf of Mexico or the Atlantic Ocean" if they were to appear in this growing town. In contrast to even other sites in the Sunshine State, "no Negroes are murdered here in cold blood," while "in public places colored people experience better treatment than they get in Washington." Why the difference? "The presence of foreigners," including the Cubans, since a "white Cuban gentleman will treat a colored Cuban gentleman or a colored American gentleman" appropriately, unlike "a white American gentleman." Besides, Key West was not exactly on the mainland but part of an archipelago and "should the governor order out the militia" it would "take a day or two to get over here" and "the boat only makes two trips a week," giving the city a healthy distance from the pestilence that pervaded the republic.[89] By the pivotal year of 1898, Key West had a population of about 18,000, making it one of the largest cities in the then sparsely populated state, with Cubans comprising about a third of the total, which—said another Manhattan journal—consisted of about 4,000 of African ancestry.[90]

Though their thrust toward democracy was aborted, U.S. Negroes, perhaps in compensation, did not stint in their support for Cuban freedom. "All hail Cuba libre!" was the cry heard in the republic. A Negro physician, Dr. L. A. Hinds of South Bend, Indiana, served on the staff of Antonio Maceo in Cuba and regularly sent home reports on this "army of colored men." Another Negro physician, Allen A. Wesley of Chicago, was in frequent touch with Maceo and a lobbyist on behalf of his cause. After Maceo's untimely death, it is estimated that 50,000 U.S. Negroes went to fight in Cuba.[91] Charles Strachan, a Negro who was born in Nassau but whose family subsequently migrated to the United States, secretly transported Martí to Cuba in 1895.[92] James Floyd of Jacksonville was acclaimed for years by his fellow U.S. Negroes for his heroic role in smuggling arms to Cuban insurgents in the 1890s.[93] While touring the republic, Maceo met frequently with Negroes, including the writer Frank Webb.[94] This activism was suggestive of the point that in the 1890s mass meetings among U.S. Negroes in support of a free Cuba had become commonplace.[95] The growing list included the famed anti-lynching crusader Ida B. Wells-Barnett: in 1896 she addressed a sizable gathering in Chicago's Bethel Church lamenting the killing of Maceo.[96]

This collaboration had not escaped the attention of Washington, and in 1896 the U.S. consul in Cardenas, Cuba, warned that "should Maceo the leader of the Negro element, who has done the most effective fighting" not be satisfied "he could maintain a warfare for years" and possibly threaten U.S. interests.[97]

Continuing a long-term trend, the republic was taking an ever-increasing interest in Cuban affairs. Interrogated by Congress in 1896, the Reverend A. J. Diaz of Cuba was asked bluntly, "What proportion of Negroes and whites" are in "Maceo's army"? "One-third Negroes," he responded. "Are the

Negroes and whites in separate companies and regiments or are they all mixed up together?" Aware of his audience's preferred response, the witness hedged, averring, "I do not know very well," though conceding "they mingled." Pouncing, the U.S. senator asked querulously, "In the same organization?" which the witness then confirmed.[98]

These legislators were concerned about the impact of the 1898 war on domestic race relations. Exposing U.S. Negroes to the differing racial climate led many to question the more severe clime in the republic;[99] besides, many U.S. Negroes recruited by Washington questioned why they should fight in Cuba, supposedly for a liberty they themselves did not enjoy.[100] The experience with Cuba engendered more militancy among U.S. Negroes, leading more to arm, organize, and forcefully resist racism, which led to bloody confrontations in Darien, Georgia, and Tiptonville, Tennessee, among other sites. The symbol of this era was the Negro David Fagen of Tampa, who after being sent to fight in the Philippines, wound up defecting to the side of the indigenes and confronting U.S. forces.[101]

As the war was unfolding, U.S. Negroes began to flock to Cuba because of the perception that racism there was not as intense as on the mainland. Arguably, the more intimate relationship with Cuba lubricated the path for the rise of the music known as jazz, then developing in New Orleans, whose ties to the island stretched back decades.[102] Similarly, ties in baseball were reflected in the number of U.S. Negro teams who took the name "Cuban." This naming symbolized how the island had garnered a reputation for being more racially tolerant, just as the increasing number of Cubans who played on U.S. Negro teams on the mainland represented a growing tie.[103] A number of these U.S. Negro athletes learned Spanish as an outgrowth of their lingering presence on the island, thus increasing the depth of the relationship.[104]

Some of the Negro soldiers who went to fight in Cuba in 1898 stayed on and took Cuban brides; at times, they returned to the mainland with their new family. Others simply chose to stay on the premise since, according to one corporal, "there is no discrimination in Cuba. Everybody looks alike," [105] a distortion that reflected a state of mind among many U.S. Negroes. Arriving from Hispaniola (where he had resided) in Cuba was the Philadelphia Negro attorney John Durham, who wound up investing in sugarcane; he was light-skinned, which was a demerit on the mainland but afforded mobility in the Caribbean, and at his death in 1919 he left a hefty estate of $150,000.[106] But what these Negroes did not take fully into account was the fact that also moving to the island were a number of their "white" erstwhile compatriots who strove to impose a form of Jim Crow akin to what they enjoyed in Dixie. This led to a difficult transition, notably in the hinge year of 1898 when violent fracases featured U.S. nationals from opposite sides of the color line.[107]

To that juncture, a number of Cubans residing in Dixie had been integrated into the elite—assuming that they could easily pass the test for "whiteness"—but here too a turning point was reached in 1903 when Narciso Gonzalez, whose family had served the cause of slavery and Jim Crow faithfully,
was slain in the streets by the nephew of the rising Dixie politician "Pitchfork"
Ben Tillman as a result of a fierce political dispute (though the deceased was
seen as not being as rigid in his racism as Tillman).[108] Ultimately, the forcible
imposition of a heightened Jim Crow helped to undermine the U.S.-backed
regime in Havana, lubricating the path for its overthrow in 1959.

The untidy fit between U.S. Jim Crow and Cuba manifested most dramatically in 1912 when hundreds—perhaps thousands according to Spanish observers[109]—of Cubans of African descent were slain in a confrontation
with the U.S.-backed regime. Opinions have varied as to who—or what—
was responsible,[110] but not among the U.S. Negroes of that era. They blamed
Washington and its hateful Jim Crow; one writer was appalled that "photographs of such [slain] Negroes have been made and distributed throughout the
United States" for purposes of intimidation,[111] confirming the apprehension
that the taking of Cuba was yet another maneuver designed to enhance racism.
Another tied the slaughter to the desire to intimidate Africans regionally—and
not just in the United States—in light of the building of the Panama Canal, a
strategic chokepoint deemed essential to Washington's security: this construction was heavily dependent on black labor.[112] Washington was responsible,
said the *Baltimore Afro-American*, for the "recent revolt" in Cuba, adding that
"if American control of Cuba is to mean to the Cuban Negro what has happened to the American Negro in the South, it is not improvement of his condition that Spanish rule is gone."[113]

This intimidation was manifested further by the U.S. intervention in
neighboring Haiti, where by 1916 one U.S. soldier was comparing his comrades to the terrorist Ku Klux Klan, suggestive of the racist poison spreading like an oil spot regionally.[114] This enhanced Jim Crow, which arrived with
increased influence from Washington, clashed with the predilections of some
Cubans. Thus Manuel Cabeza, then residing in a now different Key West,
was tarred and feathered in 1921 because of objection to what was described as
his "mulatto mistress." In turn he shot and killed one of his attackers—and he,
in turn, was then shot and hanged on Christmas morning at the behest of the
same KKK that had been recently hailed in Haiti.[115]

Yet during that same time, Robert Robinson—a U.S. Negro—was headed
on a bus to Key West where he was forced to endure racist harassment. But
like so many U.S. Negroes during that era, he sought to foil his tormentors by
rising from his seat, beating his chest and saying in Spanish—"I do not want
to be lynched! Because I am Cuban! I am Cuban! I am Cuban!" "Leave him

alone," was the response. "He's not an American. He's a Cuban; leave him alone."[116] He escaped pulverizing because mainland white supremacists had a unique and special animus toward those perceived as descendants of enslaved Africans from Dixie, which, as Cabeza could have attested, did not mean that Cubans escaped attention altogether. In other words, though an accelerated Jim Crow was being imposed on the island, mainland Negroes still felt they could escape the harshest persecution by masquerading as Cuban.

Thus, in the 1950s the Puerto Rican pitcher Ruben Gomez commented scornfully on "how crazy the whole question of race is in [the United States]— if you speak Spanish you're somehow not as black."[117]

What befell Cabeza was not particularly unique for Dixie, though it represented a divergence for Key West. It was part of a process that followed in the wake of 1898, which saw the growth of a more muscular presence of Jim Crow generally, not only in Florida but, as ever, its cross-straits neighbor: Cuba. The island had a steeper climb to accommodate itself to this ethos than the mainland, which mandated more aggressive methods. Simultaneously, Florida was beginning to experience increased development and population, which brought with it a certain flux providing fertile soil for unrest. During the pre-1959 Jim Crow era, Florida was the per capita leader in lynching, tripling Alabama's rate and doubling that of such mighty competitors as Mississippi, Georgia, and Louisiana. Some of the last lynchings on the mainland occurred in Florida even as the practice was grinding to a halt elsewhere.[118]

The flight of U.S. Negroes from terror also meant a departure from Florida. This trail of tears was traversed by James Weldon Johnson, who became one of the leading intellectuals and activists of his era, serving for a time in the top slot of the NAACP. His ties to Cuba were long-standing, and he spoke fluent Spanish as an emblem of this tie. He was born in Florida in 1871 where his father learned Spanish, then, as was the custom, invited a Cuban family to send a son to reside with them in Jacksonville. Johnson thus picked up the language before residing in Nicaragua and Venezuela.[119]

The rise of Johnson's NAACP signaled a new militancy on the part of U.S. Negroes, and the Bolshevik Revolution of 1917 served to give rise to Communist parties on both sides of the straits auguring a fierce pushback against Jim Crow that—simultaneously—helped to erode the U.S. regime in Havana. A turning point in this process was the Scottsboro case, ignited in 1931 when nine Negro youths in Alabama were falsely accused of sexual molestation of two non-Negro women and were headed, like so many others previously, for the electric chair before the intervention of the Communist-led International Labor Defense, which converted this matter into an international concern, leading to a global crusade against Jim Crow, marking the beginning of the end of this system of bigotry.[120] This case led to increased collaboration between and among activists of all sorts across the straits, with Cubans particularly vigorous in protesting this injustice, which allowed them to forge cross-straits bonds while protesting Jim Crow on the mainland and the island.[121]

This protest was also an outgrowth of increasing ties between the Communist parties of the United States and Cuba, with the latter sending cadre to Manhattan to be trained and the former sending funding to the island.[122] The National Maritime Union of the United States, whose leader for a good deal of the 1930s and most of the 1940s was a Jamaican-born Communist, had close ties to seafarers and maritime workers of a similar ideological persuasion in Havana.[123] In 1945 Esther Cooper Jackson, a leading Negro Communist and spouse of one of the party's highest-ranking leaders, conferred with future Cuban president Raul Castro at an important gathering of progressive forces in London.[124]

During the 1930s and 1940s both parties, but particularly that of Cuba, were ascending to the point that by 1947 one Negro periodical in Pittsburgh was musing about the "high incidence of communism in Cuba" and observing that "a high percentage of all Cubans are colored."[125] George Schuyler, the leading U.S. Negro conservative, was struck that same year by the fact that the "Four Bigs" of this party were "all Negroes."[126] One bedazzled U.S. Negro writer asked agog in 1947, "Will Cuba be the first Communist republic in the new world?"[127]

The "most powerful Negro labor leader in the world," claimed the *Atlanta Daily World*, was a Cuban, Lázaro Peña: "Rich Cubans insist he is the real ruler of the island republic," their Negro readership was informed in 1947. [128] Who was—and was not—defined as a Negro was not just a function of the black press on the mainland. At the same time the Truman administration, then involved in an agonizing retreat from Jim Crow, was informed which Cuban leaders could be so categorized.[129]

Unfortunately for Dixie, Jim Crow was not very popular in Cuba at a time when the Cold War dictated winning "hearts and minds" globally. This led to a retreat of Jim Crow, a calcified system of bigotry that was both unpopular in Cuba and undermined those on the island that had been close to those that supported this system. Thus when Truman moved against Jim Crow, the influential Cuban Pedro Portuondo Cala saluted him. He forwarded a complimentary resolution from the Federation of the Societies of the Race adopted "unanimously" in Santa Clara, Cuba, on 9 November 1947.[130]

Naturally, it was not just Negroes and elites who were comparing notes across the straits for it was during this time that non-Communist Negro leaders began to deepen ties. This was realized when Congressman Arthur Mitchell of Chicago arrived on the island in 1937 and, as was now the custom, was subjected to Jim Crow. He took adamant exception—and was backed by a broad array of forces on the island, who were not only able to curry favor with an important mainland constituency but express disgust with what had been imposed on their nation by Washington.[131] An indication of this relationship was the fact that by the 1950s the leading NAACP attorney in Florida was a Cuban of African descent, Francisco Rodriguez of Tampa.[132]

As Cubans of African ancestry played a larger role in the mainstream desegregation movement, this opened new vistas for U.S. Negroes. Thus the *Atlanta Daily World* took note of the 1948 meeting in Jim Crow Washington where the leading civil rights attorney—Charles Hamilton Houston, the mentor of future U.S. Supreme Court Justice Thurgood Marshall—addressed a group that "represented Cubans with darker complexions" in fluent Spanish: "Because they were Spanish-speaking people they [had] no difficulty in [assembling] at the downtown Willard Hotel."[133] Just as Key West in 1862 and 1888 was an oasis of sorts in Dixie, by 1951 one visitor at the airport in Miami was surprised to observe that toilets were not "Jim-Crowed" and on buses to the airport there was no "enforcement of the sign 'White Passengers Seat from the Front." Why? There was nervousness about "antagonizing" Caribbean visitors "who are also black."[134]

At the same time, when the U.S. Negro journalist Lucius Harper visited Cuba in 1949, the relative absence of Jim Crow, compared to the mainland, convinced him that "prejudice and discrimination can be wiped out completely,"[135] hardening him for future battles. Conversely, the father of talented baseball pitcher Luis Tiant of Cuba, who had endured earlier difficult racist experiences on the mainland, did not want his son to pursue his craft there: "I didn't want him to be persecuted and spit on and treated like garbage like I was," he observed acerbically in 1975.[136] The concentrated racism of Jim Crow was being assailed from both sides of the straits, shortening its shelf life: this was to lead to formal desegregation in Dixie and an undermining of U.S. surrogates in Havana, creating conditions for a radically different regime.

As was the pattern since 1898, a U.S. development, the onset of the Red Scare in Washington, resonated on both sides of the straits as Communists retreated. Howard Johnson, a Negro Communist from Harlem, like many of his comrades felt compelled to go underground and retreated to Cuba in the early 1950s where he found solace with Reds and other forces of the left including, he says, "many of the people who later became the power behind the Castro throne in Cuba after 1959. . . . People like Juan Martínello, Blas Roca, Lázaro Peña . . . Nicolás Guillén." He viewed this opportunity as a "tremendous resource for the Afro-American movement in the United States."[137] Cuba had been in the vanguard in the international community clamoring against Jim Crow, which weakened the most retrograde forces in the United States and helped to empower more U.S. Negroes who could then ally with Cubans in a virtuous circle of liberation.

An essential part of this process was the Harlem congressman Adam Clayton Powell, Jr., one of the few Negroes in this august body and a powerful member because of his seniority. By 1958 he was in the forefront in demanding an "immediate stoppage of the flow of arms and ammunition from this country" to Cuba—"and there should be an immediate withdrawal of the mission" he added for good measure.[138] After the triumph of the revolutionaries one high-level Washington spokesman noted confidentially—with the now casual racism for which those of his ilk were notorious—that Powell "will emerge as an important you-know-what in the woodpile" in Havana. "The question of Castro's picking up Powell's sizable hotel tab in Havana has not yet been satisfactorily cleared up." As Washington saw itself in a fight to the death with the Reds, he was distraught that the "hardest nut to crack will be the business of the U.S. financial support" along with "the degree of Communist infiltration and the details of how the whole thing works."[139] Certainly, lessening the odoriferous Jim Crow then in place could reduce Negro support for radicalism, though it would upset Dixie, perhaps weakening its retrograde resolve to the detriment of the anticommunist cause.

This ongoing trend had been detected in Dixie early on. "So close in ties to our country" was Cuba, chortled a Jim Crow periodical in Charleston in 1957, "it has been called 'the 49th state.'"[140] As such, by 1958 the editorial writer was furious that "bayonets" were drawn to enforce desegregation of public schools, though, it was claimed, no such response met "arson, murder and defiance of federal authorities by Cuban rebels. Public schools in Cuba," it was noted wondrously, "are mixed," contradicting sacred tenets and evoking not a murmur from Washington.[141] What had happened was that by the 1950s, Jim Crow was in a death spiral, sharpening the attention of policymakers while disorienting the powerful Dixie bloc, all creating an opening for change in Cuba. As the anti-Jim Crow movement in the United States gained traction and forced the ultra-right wing to backpedal, progressive change on the island also proceeded apace.

As Washington became anxious about being crippled in charging Moscow with human rights violations while countenancing Jim Crow, this created favorable conditions for the erosion of this system of discrimination.[142] The price paid, however, was an intensified attack on Communists—hence Johnson's presence in Cuba. At the same time, though Washington felt Johnson's comrades in Havana had been suffocated, by 1959 revulsion toward U.S. rule, including the racial regime imposed in 1898, led to a new order. [143] Surely, the fierce focus on Communists in Cuba led Washington to overdetermine the role of those men of African descent that had so captivated the Negro press[144]— combining their worst nightmare: Black and Red, creating an opening for Fidel Castro and his movement.

BY 1960, CUBAN COMMUNIST leader Blas Roca was asking why it was that "20 million North American Negroes are in a situation that is in many respects worse than that suffered by millions in Latin America."[145] He had a point—then. But just as the relatively late abolition of slavery in Cuba and then the attempted implantation of Jim Crow served to induce a radical counterreaction in 1959, the horrific conditions to which Roca alluded—combined with immense global pressure, propelled by Washington's emerging role as a superpower—created conditions for significant advance by U.S. Negroes by the dawn of the twenty-first century. Still, Roca's larger point remains worthy of interrogation. How did conceptions of racism differ on either side of the straits?

Of course, though slavery had existed in Dixie and Cuba, conceptions of race and racism varied. U.S. nationals tended to think that Spaniards were "not quite white," given the lengthy occupation of the Iberian peninsula by Arabs and Africans and, inter alia, this disqualified them from holding the prize that was Cuba. In 1815 presidential hopeful William Crawford was reminded that their Iberian competition had a "tinge of the political institutions as well as of the manners & complexion of the Saracens and Moors with whom they were so long connected–traces of the sloth" and the "intolerance in religion and of the despotism & loyalty of the East still follow them in all their migrations & into all their establishments."[146] U.S. nationals, many of whom were anti-Vatican, took umbrage at the Catholicism that prevailed in Cuba.[147] Tellingly denoted as the "Black Legend," there was an angry rejection of the Spanish role in the hemisphere,[148] which had the added advantage of providing momentum in the republic for the ouster of Madrid and its replacement by Washington. Arriving in Cuba in 1834, it was with disgust that Nicholas Trist was distraught to "think that such a paradise should be in the hands of such animals."[149] Earlier, a visiting republican found the "morals of the people" to be "very depraved, the natural consequence, I am informed, of a warm climate."[150]

An unnamed visitor in 1849 to the island from Massachusetts summed up the racial fears of many mainlanders, observing with irritation that "after residing here five or six weeks, I became a greasy bronze color, like the natives, and probably it will take me as much more after leaving to scour it off again, besides being subject to the constant remarks of my friends." He was prepared for the defining insult—"Why, how black you look!"[151]

By 1856 one republican scribe observed archly that Spaniards tend to "indulge in the belief" that "Creoles are mulattoes," unlike themselves who were "*white*" [emphasis in original]—though, he said, the "complexion of the greater part" of the Spaniards was "nearer that of Negroes than of white people," since "much African blood flows in their veins" given the Moorish "armies that invaded Spain in the eighth century," which included "four thousand Negroes from Ethiopia, who never were known to have left the country," as suggested by the "features" and the "quality of their hair," the "origin of many Spaniards can be confidently traced to the African race"—rendering them wholly undeserving of Cuba. That these Spaniards had a "hatred" of his homeland increased his ire in return.[152] By 1856, Alexander Humboldt had agreed that "the Spanish character has been . . . Orientalized by the seven hundred years of Moorish domination in Spain."[153]

By 1859, a U.S. visitor to Cuba, Joseph J. Dimock, was quick to adopt the characterization of Spaniards as "dirty whites" (sucios blancos), as if their purported melanin content made them suspect. As for the Creoles, island-born Spaniards, he admitted that before his arrival, he thought this descriptor (as was the case in certain parts of Louisiana) was meant to "imply Negro or mixed blood," disqualifying them from the sweetest fruits of exploitation.[154] By 1861, the visiting republican Mary G. Davis was taken by the coloration of "tawny Spaniards" and "Creole women as yellow as bar soap," not to mention the "greasy young men," a term signifying a dearth of endearment usually reserved for Mexicans.[155] Near the same time, the leading Negro abolitionist Martín Delany, in his roman à clef about Cuba, inserted monologues for his villainous characters intended to indict the offensive racial discourse that pockmarked the mainland.[156]

Though Havana was no slouch when it came to bedeviling Africans, even pro-U.S. analysts conceded—as did Maturin M. Ballou in 1888—that Cuba's laws in this realm were "far more favorable and humane towards the victims of enforced labor than were those established in our Southern States."[157] It was in 1933 that the visiting U.S. journalist Carleton Beals noticed that in Cuba one could be "classified white" if there was a "drop of white blood" whereas in the United States a "man is colored if he has a drop of black blood," making the island then—according to U.S. calculations—"70 percent black."[158] The renowned Negro sociologist Oliver Cromwell Cox asserted in 1941 that "a white man in Cuba who is called a Negro when he comes to the United States, is white in Cuba and black in the United States."[159] Fernando Ortiz, the leading Cuban scholar, speaking to a U.S. audience in 1943, argued that his homeland was more advanced in the realm of antiracism than the United States—though it too had difficulties in this realm—which was "more retarded than Cuba in the field of inter-racial relations."[160]

Yet Bernardo Ruiz Suarez, a Cuban analyst of partial African ancestry, argued paradoxically in 1922 that since U.S. Negroes were treated worse than any other group of Africans in the hemisphere, this dialectically provided an advantage in providing them with cohesiveness, skepticism of their homeland, and group militancy.[161] This helped to convert U.S. Negroes into a battering ram against their sworn foes, and against the staunchest anticommunists, which were often the same thing, and in turn created space for maneuver for

Cuban radicals who then triumphed in 1959 as Jim Crow was on the ropes. Moreover, because of the exceedingly skeptical attitude taken by the United States to the "white" bona fides of Cubans as a whole, it was difficult to forge a stable and enduring base for Washington's rule, of which Jim Crow was a constituent element. Ultimately, these interlinked processes caused both—Jim Crow and U.S. hegemony in Cuba—to come crashing down. The following pages trace the long road leading to this result.

CHAPTER 1

Spanish Florida Falls, Cuba Next?

T HERE WAS A CRY AMONG THE PEOPLE. *"The Spanish Negroes; the Spanish Negroes; take up the Spanish Negroes."*[1]

This was the anguished response in Manhattan in 1741 when one of the more significant uprisings among the enslaved erupted—and Africans from Cuba, who were in and out of this rapidly growing port town regularly, were blamed. This created numerous complications.[2] This finger-pointing was an aspect of the larger competition between London and Madrid for hegemony in the hemisphere and a reflection of the fact that Spain stole a march on its competitor by militarizing Africans more consistently. Africans were a ubiquitous and pivotal part of the Spanish conquest, virtually from its inception.[3] The same was not so for the colonists who were to form the United States. Thus a similar outcry erupted earlier—in 1739—when yet another revolt of the enslaved unfolded in South Carolina and, again, Africans from St. Augustine and Havana were fingered as the instigators.[4] The point is that British colonists and their successors on the mainland came to see Cuba and its differing approach to Africans as a threat to their projects. This conflict was embodied notably in the relatively larger free Negro population on the island, which not only carried arms but whose presence on vessels from Cuba to the mainland also became an irritant between the two rising powers.[5]

Ultimately, the conflict between London and Madrid led to the redcoats seizing Havana in 1762,[6] a tenure that lasted for months and was in many ways a turning point: it did not sufficiently intimidate the Spaniards, encouraging them to ally with mainland rebels in ousting London from a good deal of North America, creating the United States, and this brief occupation also led to a spurt in the African slave trade to Cuba,[7] which became a preoccupation for mainlanders for decades to come, utilizing Havana as a base of operations.[8] Eventually a bludgeoned Spain was able to wrest back Cuba but in 1763 had to relinquish Florida after centuries of rule. In a telling coda, Africans fled en masse to Havana,[9] well aware that the model of development emerging on the mainland gave pride of place to a kind of racist despotism targeting Africans particularly.

Still, the compelled marriage between Spaniards and self-styled North American "patriots" was a poisoned chalice for the latter—to a degree—since as more of the mainland came under control of London's opponents, His Catholic Majesty dispatched to his realm more armed Africans from Cuba. Thus in 1769 as Louisiana came under Spanish control, of the 1,847 troops and 240 militia dispatched there, at least 160 of the latter were of African ancestry, hailing from Havana.[10]

Spain aided immeasurably in the creation of the United States in pursuit of its long-standing animus toward London,[11] but as evidenced by the fact that California, Texas. and Florida, three of the largest states in the republic today, (and numerous territories), were once under Madrid's rule, it is questionable if this was a wise investment. Shortly after the formal creation of the republic, the prominent U.S. politician Oliver Wolcott, Jr.. already was eyeing Cuba hungrily—though strikingly, U.S. emissaries seemed to be unnerved by the sight of armed Africans guarding Havana. At the same time, it was felt on the mainland that Cuba could absorb many more enslaved Africans than those already enchained, and the republicans were well positioned to make sure this happened.[12]

Shortly thereafter, the republicans were the major force in the slave trade to Cuba,[13] a process facilitated by Spain's decision in 1774 to rescind all duties on Cuban imports, followed in the next decade by the decision to initiate free trade in enslaved Africans, a virtual invitation for intensified mainland influence.[14] In some ways, Havana was a waystation before enslaved Africans were deposited on the mainland.[15] Spaniards in Louisiana smoothed the way for this development, since by the 1790s it seemed that New Orleans and Havana were sister cities, particularly in terms of the slave trade. After the unsettling Point Coupee uprising of the enslaved in 1790s Louisiana, numerous Africans were exiled to Cuba, though forwarding rebels to the island was not necessarily in the long-term interests of slavery there.[16] Yet this was part of a continuing trend for in the late eighteenth century an increasing number of the enslaved arriving in Havana had departed from Charleston, Baltimore, and the mainland[17] and vice versa, as by 1796 the enslaved arriving in Louisiana were departing increasingly from Cuba.[18]

This flux was driven in part by the slave insurrection that came to be denoted as the Haitian Revolution. Yet it was not as if these arriving Frenchmen fleeing this island of unrest were being greeted with warm abrazos, for the leading Havana official—the Captain General—warned as early as 1796 that precautions should be taken to screen these exiles and in particular free persons of color.[19]

Despite the alliance with Spain that led directly to the birth of the new republic and as evidenced by the early interest displayed by Oliver Wolcott, Jr., relations between the two nations were not a model of concord. John Adams was not singular in reasoning that if Cuba or Puerto Rico became independent, Africans would dominate the emerging governments and might try to turn the islands into havens for runaway slaves; therefore the republic tended to take a more forthcoming stance toward many Latin American nations that could be encouraged to gain independence (thereby eroding Madrid's influence), as opposed to the Caribbean.[20]

Because capital was so heavily invested in enslaved Africans, the republic was quite sensitive about the matter of slave flight to Florida, leading to a carefully negotiated treaty that hardly resolved the matter.[21] With Florida reverting to Spain by 1783,[22] Africans once more began departing the Carolinas and Georgia in droves, heading southward,[23] adding to an already complicated relationship. Spain had its own problems with Africans,[24] but they paled in comparison to those of the Anglo-Americans: Jamaica was an analogue to the Carolinas in that Africans from there also sought to flee to Cuba.[25]

William Carmichael—the republic's emissary in Madrid, whose authorization was signed by both George Washington and Thomas Jefferson[26]—sought to focus Spain instead on the "machinations of the common enemies" of the two,[27] so as to distract attention away from issues of contention. Adroitly, Carmichael, to foil a Spain that could make life even more difficult for the republic, maneuvered to steer Madrid away from aligning with militant mainland indigenes, an alignment that was inimical to the health of the toddling republic. He sought to influence Madrid to intensify its own conflict with indigenes in "Spanish colonies," for example, Texas and Florida, and denied that his nation was "exciting the Chickasaws to war on the Creeks." Strikingly, he appealed to Spain as a fellow "white nation" and sought to stress their common hostility toward indigenes.[28] This was even more ironic, given that arriving U.S. nationals would be questioning the racial integrity of Spaniards in Cuba particularly, which provided a rationale for ousting Madrid altogether. And, in any case, conflict between the two powers was not abated easily.[29]

Spain had leverage over the republic, particularly control of the Mississippi River, and Carmichael charged repeatedly that Madrid was "exciting among the Indian tribes animosity" toward his nation, "furnishing" them with "arms & ammunition."[30] Naturally, this only encouraged the republic to more aggressively seek to seize Louisiana, Florida, and Cuba. But as evidenced by his emphasis on who was "white," the republic had a trump card in confronting Spain, for it was not long before Baron de Carondelet, Spain's chief representative on the mainland, was complaining about an influx onto lands he ostensibly controlled of "many refugees" from various parts of Europe who could more easily fit in the republic's expansive "whiteness" than as Spanish subjects (particularly if they were not Catholic). [31]

The republic thought that Cuban authorities handled its diplomats much too roughly and that Spain in collaboration with North Africans detained its seafarers to the point of bondage.[32] Nonetheless, with the complexity that inexorably enveloped two nations—one rising, the other headed toward decline—Spain found that the danger presented by mainland republicans may not have been its most severe challenge. As unrest began to rock Hispaniola, it became evident that this contagion could spread to neighboring Cuba—then, perhaps, the republic itself.[33] That Cuba—not least due to the ministrations of republicans—continued to bring in massive cargoes of humans[34] only under-scored this concern, as it hampered the ability of Havana to focus its external energy on its neighbor to the north.

When finally the republic obtained Louisiana in 1803, it included what well could have been considered a poisoned pill: Days after taking control the new governor expressed mordant concern about the presence of "two Negro companies contained in the Spanish militia"; though he knew there was a "scarcity of troops," this was no tiny issue given the fearsome presence of indigenes in the vicinity. New Orleans resembled Havana, it was said, in that "all free Negroes and persons of color in the territory" were "suspect because of their seeming attachment to the comparatively liberal laws of their former motherland."[35] When Madrid's men exhibited reluctance in returning Negro fugitives from Louisiana who had fled to Texas, the republic's worst fears materialized.[36] Spain made it plain that their colonies had little interest in returning Negro fugitives to the republic, emphasizing that since 1789 they had made this firm decision, particularly since their enslaved population in this vicinity was so much smaller than the republic's, a treaty based on equal-ity of return would disadvantage Madrid. Besides, this was leverage against a growing rival, a strategic consideration given the republic's desire for Cuba.[37] Moreover, the republicans had taken enslavement of Africans as the paragon of development to such a heightened level that Spain began to cast a jaundiced eye on republicans arriving in their colonies with bonded laborers, [38] sensing that such an influx was just a prelude to a republican takeover.

The presence of these African militias in New Orleans may have been even more worrisome because Hispaniola was in the process of undergoing a revo-lutionary transformation that was to change the calculus—forever—on slavery. Coincidentally, in 1791 as what came to be called the Haitian Revolution was ignited, officials in Santiago de Cuba were busily soliciting troops to smother a similar uprising of the enslaved.[39] Apparently, uprisings of the enslaved in Hispaniola contributed to the same in Cuba,[40] which was unsettling and pointed to the long-term problem the authorities in Havana would have in controlling this increasingly restive island. Unrest in Hispaniola also increased the importance of Cuba, particularly its sugar, and now enslaved Africans who might have been sent to Hispaniola would now head to Havana. But more than this, the entrance of Haiti onto the world stage meant that Havana, then Washington, had to engage diplomatically and strategically from that point in a radically different context.

As I have written elsewhere,[41] the existence of a new Haiti helped to push London more decisively toward abolition, which was to shape the actions of Madrid, then Washington. In a sense this brought the republic and Spain closer together. This realization arose in 1804—the same year that Haiti's reinvigorated tricolor first fluttered triumphantly—when a U.S. seafarer was decorated and hailed by His Catholic Majesty himself after aiding in suppressing a revolt of the enslaved on a Spanish vessel, in an echo of the more renowned case of the *Amistad*.[42]

The bad news for Spanish Cuba was that as it was being rocked from one side by the convulsions delivered by Haiti, it was being socked on the other side by the rise of Napoleon Bonaparte, whose ascension challenged His Catholic Majesty's rule at home and provided propulsion for independence movements that soon were to prevail in Mexico and throughout the Americas.[43] This trend allowed the republic to appear to be on the side of the angels in supporting these movements, which weakened Madrid, and gave added impetus for the attempt to take Cuba. At the same time—if it had not already—it alerted Havana to the reality that the fate of the island could be determined elsewhere, Europe not least.[44]

When fleeing French arrived in Cuba with their enslaved,[45] who then proceeded to revolt, the U.S. emissary in this Spanish realm instantly spread the news to the mainland, for this could complicate mightily the heretofore deep and liquid market in slaves and sent a signal that, perhaps, a new epoch had opened.[46]

At this juncture the republican realm may have seemed to be a safer sanctuary for slavery. Thus, within a period of two months—mid-May to mid-July 1809—thirty-four vessels arrived at New Orleans from Cuba (overwhelmingly from Santiago) bringing 5,754 refugees, including about 2,000 enslaved persons and a like number of free persons of color.[47] Though many of the latter were not necessarily hostile to slavery—as suggested by their flight—the authorities in New Orleans were not necessarily pleased with their arrival, since even a hint of African ancestry combined with freedom disrupted their model of development. However, their arrival and their joining the militia proved decisive when redcoats invaded in December 1814, though understandably the republicans remained concerned that these new arrivals would be sympathetic to Spanish Cuba in the event of a confrontation.[48]

The U.S. emissary, Maurice Rogers, was posted in Santiago de Cuba and thus had a front-row seat as tempestuous history unfolded. He warned his superiors on the mainland that "in some instances [the refugees'] sole property consists of their Negroes," who they were "reluctant to abandon" but he cautioned against the "difficulty" and "impracticability" of "introducing that kind of property"—who had seen Europeans flee in fear—"among us." Nonetheless, these "reputable planters" were "preparing to embark for the continent, principally to Louisiana,"[49] to introduce their problematic presence in the republic. All the while, U.S. planters were pouring into Havana,[50] at times with their human property, as the sugar market accelerated in Cuba due to the upending of Hispaniola.[51] And with their presence came a trade in Africans that expanded tremendously.[52] The trade in sugar became so tremendous that before long U.S. planters in Cuba were shipping the valuable commodity to faraway St. Petersburg, Russia.[53]

Yet the doggedness of the republicans in avidly pursuing the enchainment of Africans carried the seeds of its own destruction. The 1792 census marked the first time in Cuban history that the combined populations of slaves and free people of color outnumbered those thought to be "white," and this massive demographic shift could easily make the island subject to gravitational pull from Hispaniola, already experiencing the joyful birth pangs of antislavery. Like falling dominoes, this force could then reach the North American mainland. Many of these present (and past) slaves had been born in Africa, crossed the Atlantic, resided in various colonies ruled by various Europeans, and thus were in many ways more sophisticated and cosmopolitan than those thought to be their betters. Havana's penchant for exiling dissident Africans in Cuba to Florida placed those with records in rocking the boat even closer to republican slavery.[54]

First things first, however, and republicans ousting Spain from Florida took precedence over Cuba, which led to the so-called Patriot War of 1811, which may have succeeded but for the staunch opposition of Africans and those deployed from Cuba, not to mention the rough tactics employed by the "Patriots" against indigenes, causing a number to flee to Cuba.[55] The presence of armed Africans on the mainland was the materialization of a dystopian fantasy that had haunted the republic for years and when the "Patriots" were routed, these apprehensions took flight.[56] In fact, the presence of these armed Africans in Florida contributed to the U.S. desire to oust Madrid from the peninsula,[57] and a similar impulse drove the desire to take Cuba. The republicans could not ignore that St. Augustine, Florida, was supplied from Havana[58] which suggested that weakening Spanish Cuba was critical to taking what came to be called the Sunshine State. Still, the modus operandi—Euro-Americans streaming across the border from Georgia, gaining a toehold, then clamoring for "independence"—was to form the template for what prevailed in Texas a few years later, which led to Madrid seeking to stem the flow of U.S. nationals into Cuba, and posting a consul in Charleston in 1809 with oversight of Georgia as part of this plan.[59] That same year detailed instructions were promulgated to impede the entry of foreigners.[60]

This attempted blockade was even more pronounced when it came to the arrival in Cuban ports of foreigners of African ancestry,[61] some of whom were also fleeing Hispaniola.[62] The problem for Havana was that this ban did not necessarily apply to the arrival of enslaved Africans,[63] often brought in vessels captained by U.S. nationals, which defeated the essence of the finely wrought bar, just as the increased presence of republicans in Florida led to an increase in the arrival of enslaved Africans.[64] Pressure from the United States also led Havana to adopt measures that could just as well have emerged in Philadelphia, for example. seeking to hinder marriages across the color line,[65] which could only serve to increase the republic's encroachment. When Spanish rule in Mexico eroded in 1810, Havana's hysteria increased all the more.[66]

The combination of these events unfolding simultaneously—the U.S. takeover of Louisiana; the Haitian Revolution; the weakening of the Crown in Madrid that accompanied the rise of Napoleon; the fleeing of refugees to Santiago and New Orleans; the Patriot War—all contributed to an increase in the African slave trade to both Havana and the republic (and between the two), though it was thought that 1808 marked a decline in this baneful commerce.[67] Charleston was no more than a fortnight from Havana and the increased commerce between the two also led directly to increased republican interest in Vera Cruz and Cartagena where ties with Cuba had evolved over centuries.[68] By 1812 one scion of a prominent republican family was boasting that a "mercantile house" in Havana "wishes to have me undertake an agency for them," which would provide "something handsome."[69]

As Florida began its grinding transition from Spanish to republican rule, slaveholders and slave dealers on the peninsula—who were to become aligned with Washington—hedged their bets by moving aggressively into the lucrative Havana market.[70] Facilitating the move of these men toward outright hostility to London was the action of the British in Pensacola during the 1812 war when the redcoats lured their slaves away—without adequate compensation—and at times armed and unleashed them, which was viewed as dangerously seditious, if not a violation of the laws of war. James Innerarity, who was to develop extensive holdings in Cuban slavery, denounced Redcoat officers since they believed "Negro stealing is no crime but rather the chief of virtues."[71] Indeed, by 1816 some Floridians were demanding that London's chief operative in Florida be hanged in Havana in light of his ever more insistent appeals to the enslaved.[72]

In Cuba—and Florida under U.S. rule—Innerarity did not have to worry about this species of property being expropriated rudely: by 1817 his brother and partner, John, expressed the desire to move to Cuba altogether.[73] With Florida's fate unclear, these major slave dealers began transferring some of their chief human assets to Matanzas, Cuba.[74] Their comrade in slave dealing, James Forbes, resided in Florida until 1817, then—as the situation deteriorated—moved to Cuba to administer his sugar plantation, before dying in New York in 1823.[75]

Increasingly, the realization that Florida's destiny was clouded (given British sedition in Pensacola), while Cuba's—as far as slavery was concerned—was not, fomented a kind of slave imperialism, with Rhode Islanders most notably investing heavily in Cuban slavery.[76] This was to mean that as abolitionist London pressed Havana, republicans' preexisting Anglo-phobia—spurred by the 1776 revolt on the mainland—accelerated. Surely, the growth of abolitionist sentiment in the British isles predisposed republican and Cuban slaveholders alike to despise London. Though under British rule in 1776, Florida did not join its neighbors to the north in revolt and, thus, by the early 19th century still contained a modicum of Tories and Loyalists. London's presumably cavalier attitude toward human property eased the way for the rise of the republicans in Florida, as British influence on the peninsula was increasingly outweighed by the arrival of a steady stream of slaveholders from the region north of St. Augustine.[77] By 1820 Moses Levy of a Florida that was rapidly on its way to U.S. rule was in Havana shopping for "40 or 50 Negroes."[78] By 1821, as Florida was falling into the hands of the republicans, slave dealers like Innerarity were heavily involved in this awful business on both sides of the straits, as Africans were enmeshed in a circle of misery.[79]

The debilities of Spain that led to the cession of Florida also placed Cuba in jeopardy, and slavery was a major reason why. For as Africans descended in greater numbers on the island, the resultant demographic imbalance meant the specter of Haiti rose along with it. What to do? What the Spanish consulate in Norfolk, Virginia, did was solicit Euro-Americans there to migrate to Cuba, but this was like asking the fox to take up residence in the hen house. But the consulate spoke in terms that the Euro-Virginians could well understand, observing that it was necessary that "colonists" be "armed" in order "to keep their slaves in subjection and to be prepared to resist invasion"—though the bias expressed for Catholics limited this appeal.[80] Nor could these potential migrants bring "slaves of any sex or age whatsoever," warning that "if any slaves are discovered" and "introduced" to Cuba, "they shall immediately be declared free."[81] The republic should not have felt that special since simultaneously Madrid was beckoning to French families in Louisiana—many of whom had fled Hispaniola—to settle in Cienfuegos, Cuba.[82]

Yet Spain's own actions acknowledged that it was aware of the dilemma it faced when appealing to republican migrants. John Quincy Adams was among those carping about the frequent detention of his compatriots in Cuba with some—in the ultimate indignity for the racist despotism that prevailed in the republic—transported to serve time in dank cells in Ceuta, Spain's African colony.[83] In sum, while one branch of His Catholic Majesty's government was appealing for U.S. nationals to migrate to Cuba, another branch was imprisoning them and shipping them to Africa upon their arrival. This bipolar policy was a reflection of how Madrid was torn by the challenge from Washington: seeking aid to confront London, while being revolted by the republican challenge.[84] The scion of a founding family was well aware of the meaning of the latter point since it was he who argued that Cuba was "the keystone to our Union. No American statesman ought to ever withdraw his eye from it."[85]

Nonetheless, this desperate appeal was suggestive of the underlying problem Madrid would have in holding on to this valuable colony. Spanish Cuba was trapped between (and among) Haiti and the United States and Britain, all with dreams of their own as to how this pistol-shaped island should evolve. That Madrid felt compelled to appeal to U.S. nationals was emblematic of the reality that Cuba was far from Spain but close to the mainland republic, and like metal filings to a magnet Havana seemed to be drifting inexorably toward the Stars and Stripes. Also telling was the point that the Spanish consul in New Orleans expressed concerned about the prospect of free Negroes, with roots in Hispaniola, moving to Cuba from this port town.[86] Above all, it seemed that the Captain General in Havana was mortified by the prospect of what he called seditious ideas of rebellion being introduced,[87] which allowed for a precursor of racial profiling to sweep those with any hint of African ancestry into his dragnet.

Haiti was also close to Cuban shores and events on this revolutionary island continued to reverberate in Havana.[88] Republicans had to consider that if the example of Haiti spread to its neighbor, then hundreds of millions of dollars in slave property in Dixie could eventually be jeopardized. In that context, it was hardly reassuring when in 1811 the Captain General in Havana informed the authorities in Santiago—the main port of entry for those fleeing Hispaniola—of a plan presented to the authorities in Madrid about abolishing slavery.[89]

The republic, however, was diverted into a war with London from which it barely escaped with sovereignty intact. and while that war was grinding on, Africans continued to flee to Spanish Florida from Georgia and the Carolinas, thus making the attempt to oust Madrid from the peninsula that much more difficult.[90] In 1813 when it became apparent that republican plans to seize the whale that was Canada were coming a cropper, Senator William Hunter of Rhode Island, who represented constituents with vast interests in both the slave trade and Cuba, addressed his fellow solons in a secret session on matters deemed essential to a fraying national security. He feared that London and Madrid would see the value in allying against their common republican foe, thus blocking the plan to take Florida, then pushing on to threaten Georgia and points northward. "Spain [will] seduce the Negroes" in the Peach State, then spur an "invasion of Southern States." Here the ebony troops of Cuba would prove essential as he reminded of their deployment in Georgia in 1739, which could inspire slaves in the republic. In turn this could cause Haiti to join in the fray, leading to a catastrophe for the United States.[91]

Thinking along parallel lines was Britain's Sir John Beresford, who a few months after Senator Hunter's portentous words sought to enlist Madrid and Havana in his nation's war against the republic. The "Spanish nation," he said, was open to this démarche since the republic "not only swindled them out of Louisiana" but now "great numbers of them are engaged with the rebellious subjects of Spain in Mexico & endeavouring to revolutionize that country." Yet he may have strayed too far by arguing that "emancipation of the slaves" was to be an essential element of this far-reaching plan, which was a bridge too far for Havana. Sir John also thought that "the power of the Southern States" of the republic "ought if possible to be broken down & they richly deserve it"[92]— and since this too might have envisioned abolition or empowering of African dissidents, it would receive a mixed reaction in Havana. The problem for Sir John's ambitious plans was that it was no secret that London, whose rising abolitionism presented a clear and present danger to Havana, had schemes of its own for Florida and already was collaborating with the peninsula's large African population.[93]

Moreover, Sir John had made these controversial assertions in the aftermath of what was called the Aponte Rebellion in Cuba, one of the more significant revolts of the enslaved, and a typically skittish Spanish Cuba was in no mood to heed a spokesman for a power well on the road to abolition and enhanced alliances with Negroes. Just before this—and quite suspiciously— an English-speaking African (possibly from Sir John's own Jamaica) had been detained as a suspect in a planned uprising of Africans.[94] Hilario Herrera was detained[95] and deported to Santo Domingo,[96] but anxieties about African intentions could not so easily disappear.

It was not long before London sent agents into Florida, which could only cause mixed feelings in Cuba—heartening in that the rapacious republicans might be blocked but nervous about the presence of an increasingly abolitionist power. The Havana authorities filed away a Boston newspaper account that maintained that London's purpose was stirring up indigenes and Africans against republican incursions, though their activities could easily spill over into Georgia. This was in January 1815 and though the war between the Union Jack and the Stars and Stripes was seemingly ending, the battle for Florida— and ultimately Cuba, which this struggle presaged—was still under way. The journalist who recounted this episode railed against the "Negro-Indian war against our border" by "Negro Indian banditti" and made reference to the "Negro Fort," one of the most heavily armed encampments in the southern mainland,[97] which already had attracted the angry attention of Andrew Jackson, a future president.[98] Confirming their worst fears was a similar report from this same periodical from December 1815 that reported warily that "Negroes here are becoming very unruly," speaking of faraway Peru, as many of the wealthy fled—though it would be simple to surmise that a hemispheric contagion was at play that could easily reach Cuba.[99] Closer to home, the Captain General was paying attention to spreading Negro unrest in Barbados and the Virgin Islands.[100]

If anything, Sir John may have underestimated the situation, because as the republic was battling London, it was aiding those seeking to oust Spain altogether from the hemisphere—and not just in Mexico. This included purveying armed vessels built to specification in New York.[101] As early as 1810, the experienced U.S. leader Joel Roberts Poinsett was told of the "great changes in the situation of Spanish America" then afoot, which would impact the "geographical position" of the republic; thus he was told to "proceed without delay to Buenos Ayres [sic]," then Lima, in an attempt to influence developments.[102] By 1815 Havana detected a planned expedition from Louisiana with Mexico as the target.[103]

By this point Havana could feel the noose tightening, for it was not only the republic that was hungering to oust Spain from the hemisphere. At the same time a peppy Haiti was conferring with the South American revolutionary Simon Bolívar with a like intent—at least that is what a confidential agent reputedly said.[104] Havana's ire was inflamed when it ascertained that Bolívar's capacious plans not only included expeditions from Hispaniola to the northern coast of South America in a fleet of armed corsairs but Jamaica—where London ruled—was also implicated.[105] Cartagena was the destination for some of these revolutionaries and they were assisted by Haitians at the highest level—or so concluded the Captain General in Havana.[106] The Spanish consulate in Norfolk reported anxiously that vessels for anti-Madrid insurgents were being constructed in Baltimore and that the Venezuelans involved would be embarking for Cuba after liberating their homeland.[107] As if that were not enough stress to handle, by 1819 the Cuban authorities were apprised of the growth of African maroons at the eastern end of the island, not that far from Haiti.[108] In response, Havana accelerated its already close surveillance of Hispaniola.[109]

Thanks in large part to armed men of color, viewed suspiciously in New Orleans, the republicans managed in 1815 to administer a rebuff to the red-coats—who included a substantial complement of armed Africans themselves. But if London and Washington were not ensnared in warfare, they could more easily turn their attention to Cuba. To the detriment of Madrid, a rebuff of the republicans in Canada meant their return to Cuba with a vengeance. As the Treaty of Ghent ending the 1812 war was being inked in 1815 a well-placed republican then residing in Rio de Janeiro distilled the thinking of his class by beginning to talk of ousting Madrid and Lisbon from the hemisphere. Thomas Sumter, who bequeathed his name to the site where the U.S. Civil War was launched, denigrated the Iberians as not worthy of their immense holdings: "They have been the last people in Europe to think of religious toleration," he told presidential aspirant William Crawford, "as well as the last to think of personal & political freedom"; which was why they—and particularly Spain—presided over a "miserable colonial system." This was not mere blather; while in Brazil he had conferred with anti-Madrid activists from nearby Buenos Aires.[110]

The conclusion of the 1812 war with its challenge to the very existence of the republic ultimately led to an increase in the number of chained Africans dragged to Cuba on U.S. vessels. In 1816 Philadelphia was the port that seemed to be twinned in this regard with Havana.[111] In one voyage, said U.S. prosecutors, "force and arms" were enlisted to transport Africans from the then Danish West Indies to Cuba.[112] By 1817 Spanish officials in Pensacola were being besieged by pirates hailing from New Orleans and its environs, a category that often included freelance slave traders. Galveston[113] was also pointed to as a site of sedition and in a repetitive pattern Spain's minister in the United States in 1817 was warning about designs on Texas, an advisement that understandably made its way to Havana.[114]

The rise of Haiti and the conclusion of the 1812 war, which led to a Ghent Treaty that sought to circumscribe slave trading, and the parlous nature of Florida led to a Spanish enhancement to their approach to Africans on the peninsula. By the spring of 1815 Spanish negotiators were dickering with the powerfully armed Africans along the Apalachicola River, seeking to entice some to move to Tampa Bay.[115] St. Augustine had been established as a bastion for Africans decades earlier and had effectively harassed Georgia, and by late 1815 the Spanish were seeking to fortify this encampment, bringing in even more free Negroes[116]—not good news for the republic.

But Spain was in a crushing pincers—which sheds light on their attempted entente with Africans on the peninsula—for by 1818 Madrid turned hurriedly back to Florida and territorial violations by U.S. nationals.[117] By 1819 Havana received word that Galveston had been occupied by the notorious Louisiana pirates Pierre and Jean Lafitte, known to be heavy traffickers in slaves.[118] That same year the Captain General received news that U.S. nationals were preparing to invade Texas.[119] Taking the hint, in 1819 the Captain General ordered the strengthening of Havana's defenses,[120] while his comrades were busily preparing plans to frustrate the plans of those who desired Spanish possessions.[121] But Spain was flatfooted as mainland pirates raided its shipping, a point its representative conveyed to James Monroe; yet when Luis de Onis y Gonzalez conceded that Pensacola was the "key of the Gulf of Mexico," he exposed why his nation was being pressed from all sides.[122]

Florida presented its own challenges to the republic. Invoking Haiti, as Senator Hunter had bruited, was not far-fetched; as a result of the turmoil on the island numerous persons of African ancestry had fled not only to Cuba but to St. Augustine, dangerously close to Georgia. The problem for the republic was that some of these new Floridians were battle-hardened, pro-Madrid, and willing to collaborate with troops of African ancestry dispatched from Cuba. This group included—but was not limited to—Jorge Biassou who had launched Toussaint's career in Hispaniola before departing the island for Florida where he became the second-highest-paid official in the Spanish colony and where he commanded the militia of free Negroes.[123] Biassou brought with him a reputation as a fierce fighter, having slaughtered Frenchmen in Hispaniola during the abolitionist revolt.[124] His militia worked hand-in-glove with armed Africans from Cuba at the time of the Patriot War,[125] as both Havana and counterparts in St. Augustine realized that few sights were as intimidating to republicans as armed Africans.[126] As things turned out, men of African ancestry formed the majority of those in arms in St. Augustine, though they were joined by indigenes in harassing the invaders.[127] When Havana complained in 1820 about the deplorable state of the army in Florida, this was not only a signal that Cuba itself might be threatened, it also indicated why His Catholic Majesty had to depend so heavily on Africans.[128]

The republicans took particular umbrage at the use of Negro troops, as if this were a kind of crime against humanity. Addressing Congress in 1819, James Monroe condemned the "great losses" that Spanish "cruisers" had inflicted on his nation's shipping—stretching back to 1802, he claimed. In any case, the territory he demanded that Spain renounce was "of no value to her," while he denied flatly any U.S. interest in Texas. As for the wars of liberation then in motion in the hemisphere, he said bluntly that Washington was neutral and, in any case, Madrid did not have backing from London, Paris, or St. Petersburg, meaning it was terribly exposed. But he kept returning to the question of Negro fugitives fleeing to neighboring lands, which served as an impetus for the republic to gobble up Florida,[129] providing momentum for a similar desire to absorb Cuba.

Though Cuba did not send troops to join the redcoats during the 1812 war, afterward London and Madrid did collaborate in seeking to keep Florida out of republican hands—or so thought Thomas Sidney Jessup of the United States: actually, he thought these "secret negotiations" involved not just Florida but Cuba, which once again would place New Orleans and "all western America" in the crosshairs, he argued.[130] As early as 1816 Jessup, a leading U.S. military figure, linked Florida and Cuba and warned Madrid—and London implicitly—that the island was the "key, not only of all the western states and territories but also of the Spanish main and the West Indies" and war was a small price to pay for taking Havana,[131] a provocative idea he shared with future U.S. president Andrew Jackson.[132] These were not empty threats; by September 1816—reporting from New Orleans—Jessup was detailing armed clashes between Spanish and U.S. vessels.[133] A few days later he was informed of "active preparations" at Havana "for a military enterprise...probably intended for the city of New Orleans."[134]

The only thing misleading about Jessup's words was the term "secret," since it was well known that London lusted after Florida and was not averse to taking Cuba in the bargain.[135] Sir John had opined that London had "not so bitter & dangerous an enemy" as the republic, and thus "this naval hydra ought to be strangled in its infancy & before another season elapses."[136] Ending inconclusively, but with the republic battered though largely intact, the 1812 war did not accomplish his goal. Would not transferring Florida and Cuba to London constitute payback for the "swindling" that accompanied the deal for the Louisiana Territory?

Still, Sir John was on the same wavelength as Lord Castlereagh, instrumental in bringing Napoleon to account after he had threatened the long-term viability of His Catholic Majesty. London, it was said, either had to "support Spain" in its attempt to retain Cuba and particularly Florida—or move to "annex" the latter—but by all means keep new territory out of U.S. hands or face "fatal consequences," particularly in the Caribbean. Do not be so consumed with Europe so as to miss out on the larger prize in the Americas was the message conveyed ominously to Lord Caslereagh.[137]

Thus London emulated Madrid in arming Africans in Florida so as to resist republic encroachment. In some ways, the battle for Florida represented a burst of Pan-Africanism, as runaways from Georgia joined with Africans aligned with indigenes (Seminoles) and Africans from Cuba and the Bahamas in fighting the United States.[138] Painful experience with the United States, the most tenacious of the slaveholding powers, convinced the enslaved that republican victory in Florida would be a defeat for Africans. This placed them in objective alliance with London and, to a degree, Madrid, as Sir John had prophesied and as Lord Castlereagh had been informed. Another articulate

Londoner wrote at length about the necessity of blocking the republicans from taking Florida, for this would only be a stepping stone to taking Cuba, a "beautiful island" that was "the most important in the Western Hemisphere."[139]

But there was a yawning contradiction in this anti-republican alliance because London was pressing Havana on the matter of anti-slave trading, which Madrid resisted, thus complicating the possibility of a full-blown relationship.[140] Besides that, slave traders on the peninsula, who had profited handsomely under Spanish administration and had also developed extensive holdings in Cuba, were unhappy with the ongoing relationship between London and armed Africans and their militant indigenous allies.[141] Though Andrew Jackson thought he had destroyed the Negro fort in 1816, by 1818 he was receiving disturbing reports about yet another encampment featuring armed Africans in the hundreds.[142]

So menacing was this African presence, said Jackson, that it provided sufficient rationale for ousting the Spanish from Florida. It was evident that the Spanish either could not or did not want to extirpate this intimidating reality and thus U.S. settlements in Georgia and Alabama and beyond could be jeopardized.[143] His erstwhile opponent, John Quincy Adams, concurred, indicating that the republicans found the status quo wholly unacceptable.[144]

So bad were relations between the republic and Madrid that by 1818, Havana was charging that Washington had plans to use pirates to intervene in the island's internal affairs, sparking a slave uprising on the pretext of a precursor of humanitarian intervention. Supposedly men in Hispaniola were part of this conspiracy. That the empire of slavery headquartered on the mainland would be accused of using stratagems that could so easily backfire was indicative of a larger bilateral crisis. Intense discussions in Havana followed involving the deployment of their own agents in New Orleans and Galveston—the presumed source of the sedition. There was even suspicion that Madrid's leading diplomat on the mainland, Luis de Onis, might be a double agent since it seemed that his office had difficulty in keeping secrets.[145] These suspicions—at least of an antislavery plot involving U.S.-Haitian collaboration—were, more than anything else, indicative of the deep crisis faced by Madrid as it saw Florida slipping away and Cuba under constant threat from all sides.

Still, these suspicions were not totally awry because the British diplomat, James Buchanan, contemporaneously warned of U.S. "aggression" against Cuba.[146] Like others, he sensed the importance of Cuba as a staging ground for attack on the mainland during the just concluded 1812 war. Cuba was a strategic chokepoint, controlling commerce east and west of the mainland and acting as a plug for the basin of the Mississippi River, the circulatory system of a good deal of North America. He who held Cuba potentially also had a firm grip on the throat of the mainland.[147]

Thus early in 1819 Buchanan worriedly declared that "measures" to oust Spain from Cuba were "in full operation" though he foiled future historians by adding that he would not "commit to paper my informant's name or office."[148] The emissary of Spain in Washington did not seem pleased when the republic peremptorily rejected London's attempt to mediate over Florida.[149]

Andrew Jackson was informed by President James Monroe in 1818 that ousting Spain from the neighborhood was a high priority and Florida and Cuba were major steps to that end—this would facilitate U.S. domination in the hemisphere—and denounced Madrid's "pertinacious refusal" to comply. He warned that a weakened Madrid would even attempt "war against the United States" rather than yield.[150] Monroe was old enough to recall that during the 1812 war the Royal Navy had preyed upon U.S. shipping in the waters off Havana, with little outcry from the Spanish authorities,[151] leading some to surmise that Madrid was allied with London to bring down the republic.[152]

John C. Calhoun, the most insistent proponent of Dixie expansionism, concurred, adding that there were two major challenges to U.S. foreign policy then, both implicating Cuba: "the island should fall into the hands of Great Britain; the other that it should be revolutionized by the Negroes."[153]

But these men of African descent did not prevail. Part of the reason why can be gleaned from the reminiscences of Susan L'Engle, who was related by marriage to George Washington and had relatives who had fled the French Revolution, the Haitian Revolution, British Florida (returned to Spain in 1783), then Spanish Florida. Her family over the decades had been inured to warfare most foul and were sufficiently determined not to flee again.[154]

In 1821 when the Stars and Stripes was hoisted over Florida, a steady stream of vessels jammed with Africans and free Negroes headed southward to Cuba, unwilling to see if the racist despotism that prevailed north of St. Augustine would now be imposed—as it was.[155] The republic swallowed Florida and, quite wisely, Cuba absorbed a massive influx of free Negroes who fled as a result.[156] But this influx also included a considerable number of runaway slaves fleeing Georgia and points northward.[157] Cuba was strengthened militarily by the arrival of this African manpower,[158] for also arriving in Havana were two companies of Negro militia, as Spanish officials took pains to ensure that they and their families would reach the island.[159]

The arriving refugees were prescient, for unlike the Spaniards, the republicans in Florida were hardly disposed to permit persons of color to serve in military units as commissioned or non-commissioned officers, nor did they permit separate Negro military units. The Spaniards had sponsored quasi-integrated schools while the republicans displayed a general indifference to the idea of free education. Spanish slave codes—in Florida and Cuba—encouraged manumission, which fed the growing population of free Negroes, anathema to the republicans. Under Spanish law a bonded laborer could take his "master" to court; the republicans disagreed vehemently with such a measure.[160] In 1821, according to one historian, "a mild and flexible system of race relations" left by the departing Spaniards was supplanted by a "severe definition of slavery."[161]

By 1821 Florida was festooned with various encampments of armed Africans and Negro militancy of various sorts. With the arrival of the republicans, slave raids into Florida became more prevalent with marauders descending on the state from Georgia and the Carolinas. The site known as Angola—reflective of the West African origins of the inhabitants on the Manatee River near the Gulf Coast and present-day Bradenton—was a juicy target. Andrew Jackson was accused of sending his officers there to capture and sell any person of color they could collar. Since importation of Africans was supposedly verboten, this increased the value of their prey, as the price for one African soared to a frothy $1,000. Many of these Africans managed to flee to Cuba, bringing with them an anti-Washington attitude that came to define the entire island. Decades later, according to one scholar, their descendants "were the supporters of Fidel Castro when he came out of Matanzas Province" on his triumphant march to Havana in 1959.[162] After Angola was destroyed and hundreds of Africans were captured and returned to enslavement, another settlement arose known as "Negro Point." Some escaped to the Bahamas, where their descendants continue to reside and where they helped to reinforce anti-U.S. sentiment that complicated bilateral relations with London for years to come.[163]

Having tasted the bitterness of republicanism, these migrants were in no mood to stand idly by as their new home was compelled to endure the destiny that was Florida's where those of African ancestry were at times driven from an elevated status to virtual—or actual—enslavement. Certainly, the republican absorption of Florida was a massive and historic setback for Africans on both sides of the straits, though in the long run it strengthened a growing attitude in Cuba that was hostile to the republic.

CHAPTER 2

Texas, Cuba, and the African Slave Trade

A LEXANDER HILL EVERETT WAS DISPLEASED.
This Harvard man and U.S. ambassador to Spain was considering Cuba and was not happy with what he envisioned. It was November 1825, a few years after Spain's abrupt ouster from Florida and the racist reign of terror engineered by the republicans that soon followed. Yet that was not what had focused his attention. "The white population" of Cuba, he said, "form too small a proportion of the whole number to constitute themselves as an independent state," and considering that both Mexico and Colombia— where those of African descent played leading roles—were considering annexing Cuba, this could provide an existential threat to one of the most significant investment opportunities in the republic: slavery. The other alternative—Cuba to "become an independent [state] principally of blacks"—was too ghastly to contemplate. "Neither part of this alternative"—annexation by neighbors or independence with African leadership—"can be considered as admissible," he sniffed.[1] Perhaps worse, he said, was "British intrigue for revolutionizing the island" and "protection" of London.[2]

By extending its boundaries to the Florida Keys, the republic, perhaps advertently, yoked its destiny even closer to that of Cuba. Yet, as Everett and his cohort well knew, the island was not exactly stable and, besides, was under constant threat from an increasingly abolitionist Britain, often in league with the very symbol of that creed—Haiti—within hailing distance of Santiago de Cuba, the island's second city. By mid-1823 Havana was hurriedly arranging military reinforcements for Santiago in light of a rumored military assault by Haiti;[3] a few months later fear was expressed about what appeared to be revolutionary unrest in Jamaica.[4] Thus Everett would not have been surprised to know that Londoners at the highest level were informed that "the United States would risk war" to gain the island because of apprehension about

Cuba's impact on slave prices—all-important in Dixie—and the strategic threat it posed to the mainland.[5] This London consensus reflected a parallel consensus in Washington where John Quincy Adams asserted, also in 1823, that just as certainly as an apple parted from its parent limb gravitated to the earth, just as certainly would Cuba fall into the lap of the United States once Spain departed,[6] as it had from a good deal of its hemispheric empire.

Spanish Cuba was also ensnared in contradictory dilemmas. Pressed by a growingly abolitionist London, the natural instinct was to align with the pro-slavery mainland, but that was akin to inviting the poacher to take up residence in the game park. In the 1820s the influential James Monroe ascertained that Havana felt it could not maintain its independence alone for fear of being overwhelmed by foreign powers—given weaknesses in Madrid—and, in any event, in case of separation from Spain the Africans could seize power, à la Haiti. At that juncture, Monroe's reputed advice to Havana was to cling to Madrid as long as possible, but that view too would change, leaving in doubt the island's fate and the closely related issue of "Africanization." Even London, not fully committed to abolition by any means, reportedly discouraged a Mexican-Colombian intervention in Havana due to apprehensiveness as to what it might mean for a slave insurrection that could easily spread to Jamaica. Better still for London was Cuban independence under London's protection, but this was impossible for Washington to accept and Madrid was not exactly gung-ho about this idea either.[7] In coming years, authoritative voices in Madrid argued that a free Cuba must of necessity become a twin of Haiti: the latter island was repeatedly accused of seeking to disturb the supposed tranquility in Havana. [8] Cuba twinned with Haiti was a scenario that was guaranteed to foment angst in Washington.[9] The actual reality was the opposite, according to the rapidly growing U.S. abolitionist press, which had come to take a decided interest in the island: Cuba was seen as a bulwark of enslavement that jeopardized the existence of the constituency they were sworn to serve.[10]

The republic had clashed famously with London and with Madrid to a lesser degree in the messy transition in Florida, and both powers had reason to resent the United States. Washington refused to recognize Haiti while encouraging anti-Madrid independence movements in the hemisphere, though blanching at the sight of the ebony-hued leaders then emerging in places like Mexico and Colombia. The republic's energetic emissary in the region, Joel Poinsett, adamantly averred that his nation "never did entertain designs against the island of Cuba"—but this hardly passed the giggle test. Evidently he had forgotten that just before the enunciation of the renowned Monroe Doctrine (which in retrospect can be seen easily as an attempt to reduce competition for hegemony in the hemisphere) he had offered to enter Havana surreptitiously—though he

found it to be "the sickliest and the filthiest place in Christendom"—in order
to foil an alleged takeover plot by London.[11]

More seriously Poinsett objected to "designs of Mexico and Colombia
against the island of Cuba," echoing Everett.[12] Ironically, what Poinsett had
foreshadowed was a "Mexican standoff" that would preserve Spanish sovereignty over the island virtually to the end of the century. Further, the numerous suitors of Cuba allowed Havana to engage in a simple form of arbitrage
keeping them all slightly off-kilter. Filed away in Havana was an 1826 message
from Washington warning of the danger of Cuba falling into the hands of a
foreign power that basically confirmed the validity of Havana's balancing strategy.[13] The status quo was preserved because the chief pro-slavery power—the
United States—could not overcome those nations that leaned toward abolition
(and vice versa).

The republic did not stand still in the face of this stalemate, however, as it
sought forcefully to alter the underlying dynamic to the benefit of slavery and,
ultimately, U.S. suzerainty over the island. In 1825 Poinsett's ally Ben Milam
was to be found on "the frontiers of Texas," where their fellow nationals were
continuing to flock with apparent intentions of overturning Mexican rule, a
point that Milam's observations would have corroborated. Milam was irate
that Louisiana had "lost a grait [sic] many Slaives [sic]" who had fled to Texas,
which was "evill [sic]," particularly since this former Spanish colony, whose
vast territory rivaled that of the republic, chose to "encourage and harbour
such delinquents or refugees."[14]

In light of the republic's plans for Mexico and Cuba, it was a foregone
conclusion that Poinsett would deplore what had attracted Everett's ire: the
idea that Mexico and Colombia would combine to liberate Cuba from Spanish rule. Poinsett was in Mexico City in early 1826 and listened intently as
this measure "to send troops" to Cuba was debated in the Senate. That it
was to be conducted "jointly with the Republic of Colombia" and was to
be raised at a forthcoming Congress of Panama,[15] a historic and trailblazing
gathering of mostly independent former Spanish nations, seemed to drive
Poinsett into the depths of hysterical depression. In retrospect, it is easy to
infer that Washington's burgeoning desire to dismember Mexico was driven
in part by the latter's abolitionism and its allied plans for Cuba. There was a
"feverish anxiety on this subject," said Poinsett, speaking from Mexico City
to the U.S. president, a fervent "desire to emancipate that people" of Cuba,
"to deprive Spain of that advantageous 'place d'armes,' to annex that island
to these states." But fortunately there was "no fixed plan" to liberate Cuba—
"It is an enterprise beyond their force." On the other hand, he floated the
idea of Texas seceding from Mexico—years before the event—which would
serve as a fitting rebuke to Mexico City.[16] This would transmit a disturbing

signal to the hemisphere: cross Washington, back abolition, and run the risk of dismemberment.

Surely Washington was dissatisfied with the diplomatic drift in the hemisphere, notably the Panama Congress that so upset Poinsett. Dr. Thomas Cooper of Columbia, South Carolina, expressed the settled view of his elite class, when he announced in 1826 that if a delegate from his nation was sent there, "I hope his hands will be well tied." Why? He feared that it could lead to Cuba being "placed in a revolutionary state" which—following Everett—would mean a "black government," a dangerous trend since it seemed that the "British West Indies" was heading "into the hands of the blacks."[17]

During the 1812 war and the struggle over Florida, London quite deftly had deployed armed Africans against the republic, and during the 1820s Washington feared that Cuba would become a twin of Haiti in the threat it posed to the continued viability of slavery in Dixie—then joined by Mexico and Colombia. This London knew well for in 1825 a nervous Henry Clay, one of the republic's most eminent statesmen, confided as much to a top British diplomat, implying that the "black population being let loose upon the whites" on the island would have consequences difficult to contain.[18] By 1827 Havana was crawling with republican "confidential" agents, tasked by Secretary of State Henry Clay to report on "insurrectionary movements" and the reputed plans of Mexico and Colombia.[19] (Havana knew of the arrival of the chief U.S. agent, Daniel Cook, and in response ordered that special vigilance should be exercised with regard to the arrival of all foreigners, but particularly those from the mainland.)[20] Days later Clay found it necessary to tell his Spanish counterparts that his nation had no interest in perturbing Cuba with an invasion or a London-aligned blockade. Havana rather boldly assured him that whatever the case they had the strength to repel either.[21] Nevertheless, in the 1820s the repeated mobilizations in Cuba to brace against a possible U.S. incursion drained resources that could have been devoted elsewhere, stunted the island's development, and further engendered anti-Washington sentiments.[22]

The republic's appetite had been whetted by the cession of Florida, and on the heels of this coup John C. Calhoun also pushed for annexation of Cuba. He pointed to the similarities between the island and Virginia and assumed that annexation would add at least two more slave states to the Union. Unlike Adams, his preferred fruitful metaphor for Cuba falling into the republic's lap was the pear not the apple, though the result would be exactly the same.[23] More characteristically—and with the bellicosity that had become typical in Dixie—it was Calhoun who in 1823 proclaimed that he was willing to wage war "to prevent [London] from taking Cuba."[24]

A de facto invasion of Havana by U.S. nationals was in motion, though the racial attitudes brought by these new arrivals were not altogether in accord with those of Cubans, leading to flashpoints of resentment and unpredictable long-term consequences.[25] When in 1823 a "rumour of a war between England and Spain" erupted, this "place[d] the Americans on a more forward footing,"[26] according to the consul there, with the least terrible result U.S. nationals might hope for was simply to be caught in the crossfire. But that was to change: by 1826 John Quincy Adams was reserving special words of anger for London—particularly given the closed nature of the imperial trading system, which hampered U.S. expansion in the Caribbean and their incipient abolitionism—while softening his tone when addressing Madrid.[27]

Quincy Adams, who may have had more international experience than any within the republic at his level—including a tour of duty in Russia, Washington's partner in bondage and frequent global ally[28]—paid close attention to Cuba, pointing worriedly in 1822 about instability in Spain that might lead Paris or London to seize the island. But like some Europeans, Adams knew that Havana was "terrified by premonitory symptoms of Negro insurrection and [was] looking around for a protector"—in Madrid, of course, London, and the rising power Washington. Some crafty Cubans had sent a "secret agent" to confer with Monroe, said Adams, to discuss the possibility of the island joining the Union if Spain were to be booted out. Like the Louisiana Territory earlier or Texas later, the possibility was held out that Cuba could then be carved up into more than one state. Already smarting from a bruising administered by London during the 1812 war, Monroe demurred, fearing London's reaction. Tellingly, Adams did not reveal this episode until May 1836— when London had moved to abolition—and anxiety and itchy trigger-fingers twitched accordingly in Dixie in order to shoo away British expansionists from taking Texas with the prospect of war with London hanging in the balance. The sensitivity of Adams's words were underscored by the fact that it was not until the 1930s that they were revealed publicly.[29]

Along that same line, another U.S. national reported in 1830 from Havana that "the sugar crop is abundant, also coffee—the former in active demand, for Spain and Russia."[30] An outgrowth of this U.S. incursion was boosting Cuba's role as a trade partner with the republic—the third most important behind Britain and France, according to one account.[31] By 1823, Thomas Jefferson's enthusiasm showed no signs of waning, as he termed the island "the most interesting addition which could ever be made" to the republic. He was simply reflecting the reality that, for example, Philadelphia and Havana had become (seemingly) inextricably linked in commerce most notably.[32] Nevertheless, the City of Brotherly Love was hardly unique: by 1840 reports from relatively small New London, Connecticut, indicated that forty to fifty vessels regularly plied the waters from there to New York, then Dixie—then Cuba.[33] That the U.S. authorities proved lethargic in prosecuting those involved in illicit slave trading to Cuba only encouraged more such activity.[34]

Martín Van Buren, also presidential timber, asserted in 1829 that the European derived population of Cuba was petrified with the notion of independence, the "first effect of which would be the sudden emancipation of a numerous slave population, the result of which could not but be very sensibly felt upon the adjacent shores of the United States."[35] This helped to create a dynamic that could lead to a de facto cession of the island to the republic, à la Florida—or annexation, à la Texas, in 1845.

Part of the problem that Everett did not acknowledge was that enslaved Africans were flooding into Cuba, not least because of the activity of his own countrymen. The republic was entangled in a contradictorily anomalous situation: some U.S. nationals were bringing Africans to the island by the boatload while other U.S. nationals were fretting about the resultant demographic imbalance created, suggesting either an avoidance of difficulty realities or a stubborn reluctance to confront enslavement.

Florida at this point was hardly as developed as Cuba; there was no equivalent on the peninsula to Havana. Hence, as citizens began heading southward to sample the enhancing climate of warmth, they were more likely to head to the island. Becoming acquainted with its assets brought both more visitors and more opportunities for republican investment in Cuba.

Among those enjoying a lucrative life in Cuba, presiding over a sugar plantation heavily dependent on a labor force of enslaved Africans, was Philip Chartrand of Charleston, South Carolina.[36]

He was not alone, though; investors in slavery were arriving from New England, particularly Rhode Island. This was nourishing and benefiting a well-compensated pro-slavery lobby beyond the confines of Dixie, complicating the idea of a sectional divide on this burning matter. As the Spanish standard was being lowered for the last time in Florida,[37] the republicans advanced southward. Joseph Goodwin was hired by George DeWolf of Connecticut to administer his plantation in Cuba. This was an enervating experience for him, providing a microcosm of how the virus of slavery was not precisely limited to Dixie; that is, New England investment in Cuban slavery gave some in that region a vested interest in enslavement of Africans. Goodwin thought that DeWolf had possibly raped enslaved females while the acclimated Goodwin beat slaves for laughing at prayers.[38] The Boston merchant who in the 1830s spent a whopping $200,000 for a plantation in Cuba, which, said abolitionists, "he had 'stocked' by direct importations from the coast of Africa," was all too typical.[39]

Early in the same decade, another well-placed Bostonian found that "prices of sugar are so enormously high" that it seemed he could hardly find the time to count his mounting earnings.[40] Mary Gardner Lowell—related by marriage

to the Cabots of Massachusetts, an eminent family, along with the Lowells—
was among those who spent considerable time in Cuba, where she was deeply
acquainted with republican planters who owned sprawling estates and hundreds of enslaved Africans. It was estimated that when she arrived in 1831 there
were about 1,000 U.S. nationals on the island, though they were overrepre-
sented at the top of the socioeconomic pyramid. She took note quickly of the
"ferocious" dogs who kept Africans in line—soon to be imported to the mainland—and the coupled reality that there were few elderly Africans in Cuba:
she spoke bluntly of how "a Negro had been torn to pieces by the dogs set on
him." She knew that such bestiality roused the Africans to "vengeance." She
knew the enslaved often were incapable of doing anything radically transformative about their plight, which perhaps helped to account for the mounting
suicide rates among them. Like subsequent visitors, she found the Africans
unattractive, probably a comment on the unattractive circumstances in which
they were entangled.[41] The spouse of Nathaniel Hawthorne was among the
sojourners in Cuba.[42]

This unattractiveness included astonishing health problems. The visiting
New Englander Thomas Fales found in 1831 that "near ten thousand persons
mostly Negroes" had perished due to cholera,[43] mortality that served to engen-
der the need for more bonded labor. The constant turnover of population was
not a recipe for harmony, as one 1830s visitor from the United States found in
ascertaining that "travelers in the country generally go armed, not for fear of
robbers but to keep the slaves in awe: a very prudent precaution, where they
are so much more numerous than the whites."[44]

In Cienfuegos, the British writer David Turnbull found an estate owned
by "a certain Mr. Baker from the United States" that featured "no less than
700 male Negroes, to the exclusion of a single female, locking up the men" in
what was "to all intents and purposes, a prison."[45] By 1838, this plantation was
rocked by a revolt of the enslaved.[46] By 1839, U.S. abolitionists were complaining that "great numbers of the citizens of the [republic] have established slave
plantations in Cuba" and "the annual increase of slave plantations opened by
American settlers is twenty."[47]

U.S. nationals had established more than a toehold in Matanzas. This
process was quickened when in 1818 Havana issued new regulations facilitating their arrival—and others defined as "white." Perhaps the brutal approach
to slaving that had inhered in mainland culture sheds light on why Matanzas in 1825 was the scene of one of the island's most profoundly disruptive
slave rebellions in its history. Among those murdered was Joshua Armitage
and his family, most recently of St. Louis, Missouri. Matanzas garnered the
reputation as the site where rebellions of the enslaved were most likely to
erupt—and the place where mainlanders were likely to settle—with the two

possibly connected. For the Armitages, it was a reunion of sorts, since one of the leaders of the revolt of the enslaved also hailed from the mainland, New Orleans in his case.[48]

Reporting from there in 1829, the New Englander John P. Story noted that the population "has increased greatly within these few years past, it contains now about 10,000 inhabitants [and] it is thought be many in twenty years from now the population will surpass that of Havannah [sic]."[49] Matanzas, said U.S. official Nicholas Trist, was "crowded with Americans."[50] There were so many U.S. nationals in Cuba that their offspring were being born there— then becoming leaders of the illicit slave trade.[51] A well-informed British subject in 1839 found that "not less than forty plantations" had just come under U.S. ownership, leading some to conclude that "the island will, doubtless, be wrested from the Spanish and join in a partnership with [the republic]."[52]

This growth in the number of enslaved—and inevitably furious—Africans in the Caribbean in turn was enraging Haiti,[53] which in the same year that Everett had expressed his reservations about Cuba's future began more aggressively seeking to capture Spanish slavers. At this point, according to one source, Cuba had a population deemed to be 44 percent "white"—but in 1775 it was said to be 56 percent and if present trends continued, this portion would decline, further raising the specter that haunted the antebellum republic: Africanization.[54]

Visiting the island near this same time, like so many of his compatriots, the Massachusetts-based writer the Reverend Abiel Abbot paid careful attention to this phenomenon, particularly that Africans seemed to outnumber Europeans. "The free blacks are considerably numerous," he said, coming "to exceed 100,000," and given how dangerous this group was thought to be on the mainland—not to mention their role in the Cuban militia—this was particularly worrisome.

But even Reverend Abbot had detected that of the "355,000 whites" said to reside in Cuba then, there was a growing number of "[Euro]-Americans," thought to be "more numerous than the French" and thus slowly gaining in number on the reigning Spaniards.[55] Most of this group were in Havana and Matanzas, but a few years earlier, the republic's representative in Santiago found that "emigration" from Louisiana had become a "frequent occurrence," though these were mostly "indigent individuals" and, not coincidentally, this had been accompanied by a growth in the slave trade; it was a "subject of notoriety," it was said.[56] According to a sojourner, who visited Cuba in the early nineteenth century, the island had a free Negro population of 130,000—compared to the U.S.'s 285,000 in a much larger overall population but the latter hardly enjoyed the rights of the former.[57] A number of this swelling population had just crossed the straits fleeing St. Augustine and the republicans.[58]

The rise in slaving, ostensibly in violation of Spain's agreements pains-takingly negotiated with Britain, was of concern in London. Thus London began to press Madrid forcefully on this matter, demanding more discretion-ary power to control this commerce, which would mean a reduction of Spanish sovereignty over Cuba—a signal to that other slaving power with interests in Cuba: the republic.[59]

Some of these slaving cases were quite horrific,[60] meaning London would only press harder—and that would probably eventuate in the republic, stron-ger than a debilitated Madrid, taking an ever larger role in this commerce. Some of the Spanish slavers were encountered in the waters of the Bahamas and Florida,[61] which was virtually guaranteed to induce conflict between London and Washington, given the former's aggressive tactics in patrolling the waters. As Reverend Abbot was arriving in Cuba, London's patience with Madrid in the face of its blatant smuggling of Africans was about to snap; one noticeable 1828 case involved a ship found near Florida with hundreds of Afri-cans aboard,[62] which raised obvious questions about republican complicity, given continuing U.S. lassitude in confronting slavers. London had evidence that U.S. nationals were complicit in Spanish slave trading in the 1820s, a field they were to dominate in coming years.[63] More U.S. slavers meant the arrival of U.S. pirates—whose penchant for slaving was well known[64]—as more ban-dits in boats began infesting the waters off Havana.[65] When U.S. authorities began sending ships to pursue pirates, Havana could not be sure if this official response was simply a cover for more piratical hijinks.[66]

Worse from London's perspective was that U.S. nationals were enticing British subjects with the prospect of high wages if they joined slaving expedi-tions in Africa: this was at odds with international accords against the slave trade that the Royal Navy was seeking to uphold and drained the Crown of subjects on behalf of a rising republican rival as well. Devilish induce-ments meant "frequent desertions" to London's detriment,[67] it was said in 1829. The republican navy, complained British abolitionist David Turnbull, "is manned to a large extent by foreigners; and that of these the majority are British seamen."[68] Eventually, British subjects would masquerade as U.S. nationals in order to better participate in the illicit slave trade.[69] As the 1820s unwound, more and more U.S. slaving vessels were detected in Africa, as if the fall of Florida had now led republicans to concentrate on bringing Africans to Cuba.[70] U.S.-flagged ships were sailing from Havana to Africa and U.S.-built ships were being captained by Spanish nationals to that same end.[71]

London was quite distraught when a Spanish schooner arrived at the "American Settlement at Liberia," "took on board 198 slaves," then headed for Cuba, since this part of Africa had been thought by some to be exempt from the travesties of this woebegone commerce.[72] Alarmingly, soon British subjects in Sierra Leone found themselves enslaved by the kinetically inclined republicans.[73] Revealingly, Washington rebuffed London's initiatives to cooperate on suppressing the slave trade.[74]

Why? In 1830 James Baker, London's consul in Mobile, journeyed to St. Augustine, Key West, Pensacola, and the vicinity—and left disgusted. Africans in droves were arriving there, not least as an overflow from Havana. He found official complicity in this illegality and it was a small leap to conclude that this was part of a larger republican scheme to seize the island. Baker found it curious that U.S.-flagged vessels tended to "hover around the back of the island of Key West, from which place they receive instructions," then sail gleefully into Havana, the enslaved in tow.[75] Ever more insistent voices in northern Florida were demanding an official imprimatur on slave imports from Cuba.[76] U.S. abolitionists saw the alleged ban on importation of Africans being shredded because of the Cuban connection,[77] and a journalist in 1831 uncovered a company in Nantes, France, that was "contracted to supply the island of Cuba with 30,000 slaves annually. How many of these will be smuggled into the United States?" he wondered.[78]

This trend of U.S. nationals' heavy role in slavery and the slave trade to the island—which was to pockmark Cuba virtually to the day of abolition in the 1880s—eroded the north-south sectional divide that was said to characterize the republic's stance on slavery.[79] In a contradictory sense, this trend worsened sectionalism, for New England's growing interest in Cuba to a degree undermined the sugar economy of Louisiana and the slave export market of Virginia. Moreover, by deepening New England's ties to slavery, Cuba bolstered Dixie while the proliferating slavery there helped to coarsen a republic that hardly needed more of it. Just as Jim Crow hastened the onset of revolution on the island, slavery on the island hastened the onset of civil war on the mainland.

The republic was playing a dangerous game. With a prodigiously ample fortitude U.S. nationals were shipping Africans to Cuba, while politicians in Washington were gnashing their teeth about the threat this presented. The republic was imposing its crude two-caste racial system on Florida, which in turn was causing revenge-seeking Africans to flee to the island and throwing kindling on the fire of a growing insurgency by indigenes—allied with Africans who chose to stay and fight.[80] As these flames were leaping, a formidable residue of the intensified slave trade to Cuba was washing up on Florida's shores, as Africans through various means were arriving—particularly in the Keys—further alienating resident Negroes.[81]

The republic's interest in the island heightened after the Florida cession and as Mexico (and London too) seemed to threaten Cuba. It was in 1832 that Secretary of State Edward Livingston sought a detailed portrait of administrative power in Cuba—as if he were contemplating its replacement. He also sought racial statistics, along with the "number of American residents," as if his purposes were not benign.[82]

As if it were anticipating Livingston's démarche, Havana resolved the anomaly of the Spanish consul previously encouraging U.S. migrants to the island by seeking to stymie this escalating trend.[83] This included seeking to limit Cuban families from sending their children to the mainland for education, which had become popular,[84] and curbing supposed subversive literature arriving from New York.[85] Special venom was reserved for the priest Felix Varela, then residing in the United States and thought to be seditious—and an abolitionist. [86]

If it was any consolation to him, it was not only the message embodied by Father Varela to which Havana took strident objection. As U.S. nationals invested more heavily in Cuban slavery in the wake of the cession of Florida, they were shadowed by their harassing complement: U.S. abolitionists. Havana and Madrid may have welcomed the former or felt ambivalently about them; there was no such ambiguity toward the latter, particularly if they were encased in an ebony hue. This dragnet extended willy-nilly to U.S. Negroes,[87] even when they had evinced no articulated view on slavery, for their very presence as travelers on the island associated them in officialdom's mind with the slaveholder's bugaboo, the Haitian Revolution—and this was to remain so long after 1804. By 1837 U.S. abolitionists were warning all "free black or colored persons" arriving on the island that they were subject to immediate imprisonment upon arrival. Havana had the notion, according to *The Liberator*, that "the abolitionists of the North had hired certain blacks" to "circulate tracts and other papers amongst the slaves." The "idea is absurd," was the abolitionist response—but Havana begged to differ.[88]

George Davis, a U.S. Negro and tailor, was an exemplar: arriving in Matanzas, a seat of republican influence, he was charged with being an abolitionist, then arrested and jailed. His effects were searched—and lo and behold, abolitionist literature was found. He was tried instantly, immediately condemned to death, and promptly executed by—as was said—"being screwed to death, a most inhuman torture." The only thing unusual about this travesty was that—typically—Negro seafarers, not tailors, were targeted. Routinely, they were imprisoned upon arrival, at times executed or sold into slavery.[89] Davis fell victim to what the prime minister in Madrid had announced, when he warned scornfully and stressfully of "*Abolitionists* coming chiefly from the United States" who "avail themselves of all opportunities for creating insubordination among the black slaves" of Cuba.[90]

Spain's delegate in Washington in late 1836 was virtually hysterical about the growth of abolitionism within the republic,[91] though his distress seemed mild in comparison with the attitude in Havana.[92] As ever, Madrid engaged in surveillance of U.S. abolitionists, with one of their agents becoming almost apoplectic when he thought he had found one in Mobile in 1839.[93]

Again,[94] this concern with visiting U.S. Negroes arose in concert with ongoing concern about Haiti, turbocharged by the advent of British abolition and secession in Texas, all of which seemed to be linked. This linkage proved the policy's undoing for it was not just U.S. Negroes who were victimized, but all visitors of African ancestry,[95] including British subjects: and London was not predisposed to accept supinely such harassment in the aftermath of abolition on 1 August 1834 and the presumed enhanced status of Africans under the Union Jack. With the assumed backing of London,[96] the stern reprimands of this policy by U.S. Negroes had to be taken more seriously, which could only deepen Havana's crisis.[97]

The skewering of Father Varela—and those thought to be like him—was one piece of a broader mosaic. U.S. nationals were arriving regularly to reside and invest in Cuban slavery, which allowed Havana, at least for the time being, to blunt London's abolitionist challenge, though in the long term it was laying the basis for an Anschluss by Washington. This had caught the attention of U.S. abolitionists who in early 1831 noticed that "from the first of February to the middle of March," a whopping 2,000 enslaved Africans had landed at Cuba.[98] Weeks later, a visitor to Cuba informed U.S. abolitionists that "the slave trade" was "never carried on more vigorously than now." Unsurprisingly, these merchants of hate were not deterred by the appearance of U.S. authorities "but when John Bull's cross was seen, they *looked wild*."[99] At Norfolk and Richmond, said U.S. abolitionists, there were agents advertising and purchasing Africans for the Cuban market, which was part of a wider Virginia market, involving "hundreds of whites," who were involved in dealing in Africans, "as they would cattle"—including breeding.[100]

The broader picture was that Cuba had become entangled in a U.S.-Mexico conflict that would explode in war in 1846. Washington did not remain passively inert as an increasingly abolitionist Mexico threatened Cuba—instead, it proceeded with its support of U.S. nationals who were then decamping in the Mexican province that was Texas, which would eventuate in independence for this secessionist slaveholders' republic in 1836. Galveston was just a short hop from Havana and as the declaration of independence was being formulated in what became by 1845 the Lone Star State, a brisk trade in Africans accelerated traversing the Gulf of Mexico.[101] "There can be no doubt," *The Liberator* observed sadly in 1836, that "thousands of the victims of this [slave] traffic are annually imported into this country, most of them via Cuba."[102] And Galveston too, it could have added.[103] The growing role of Texas in providing a new lease on life for the slave trade—which was hardly in danger of expiring in any case—had received the anxious attention of British diplomats in Cuba, which was the other end of this chain of iniquity.[104]

The traffic amounted to 15,000 Africans passing from Cuba to Texas annually, according to one account (probably an undercount), since the price of a slave in Galveston was almost four times than that in Havana—a commerce facilitated by the reality that the two sites were within a few days sail of each other. That U.S. naval men sent to Cuba supposedly to curb this traffic were reputedly pro-slavery themselves was hardly soothing.[105]

Still, according to one source in position to know, as the so-called Second Seminole War was ignited at the same time as Texas was surging to independence, Spaniards were bulldozing the republicans by backing the indigenes and their African allies,[106] as if revanchist dreams were at play. Of course, even if accurate, this may have not been official Spanish support—though not less disconcerting for Washington.

Whatever the case, the problem for Washington, Havana, and all those devoted to enslavement of Africans forevermore—including their allies in Texas—was that London, the reigning superpower, was moving steadily toward abolition, which was bound to discombobulate the already rickety carriage that was slavery. London was quicker to absorb the unavoidable antislavery lesson delivered by Haiti and what that meant for Jamaica, Bermuda, the Bahamas, and its other possessions. The resident planter class in these islands was known to be sympathetic to Washington, in any case, and hardly a model of patriotism. Abolitionism would mean allying with Africans, whose martial skills were unparalleled as they attained the high moral ground in its ongoing battle with the republic, which—despite its soaring rhetoric—was bogged down in an ugly oppression. Perhaps adopting abolitionism, even stirring up the Africans on the island, could be a prelude for taking Cuba, then moving on to the mainland itself.[107]

The ground was moving beneath the feet of all parties, mandating nimbleness. London had few options. Madrid monitored Jamaica in 1831 and nervously kept track of a major slave revolt—against "whites," it was said, with "repercussions" for Cuba; simply barring Jamaican Africans from entering Cuba—Madrid's recommendation—seemed inadequate to the moment.[108] Havana's room for maneuver was constrained, pressed as it was by Jamaica, Haiti[109]—and the United States.

Visiting Cuba from his residence in Londonderry in 1836, one visitor opined that "the Spanish laws are more favorable to the slaves than the laws that obtained in the English West India colonies." If so—and this was hardly inaccurate—London moving to abolition gave Britain an obvious advantage in its contestation with Madrid and Washington for influence in a region where Africans predominated.[110]

The altered correlation of forces in the region had struck the U.S. consul in Puerto Principe in Cuba in 1833, when the notion of abolition had been announced. The "serious attention" of Washington was now demanded: London "is about to give freedom to the slaves" he announced morosely, and Cuba "should be the bulwark between those colonies and our Southern States." But would this be the case if Africans kept arriving in gross numbers on the island? The consul did not think so—"should a revolution break out again in Spain," not far-fetched given what seemed to be congenital instability there, then a "representative government" could be "established" and "all slaves introduced into the island in contradiction to that [earlier London-Madrid] treaty will demand and of course will receive their freedom, as there are an immense number of free people of color here" and "many of them are enlightened who will advise and assist their brethren." What to do? The slave trade must be ended forthwith, otherwise a "vortex" was opening that "must destroy the island." This was part of the deviousness of Perfidious Albion which desired to see its "colonial contagion spread."[111] When after abolition London sent emissaries to Cuba and Puerto Rico to report on the state of the slave trade, noisy rumors were raised suggesting that this was just the advance guard for an invading army that intended to occupy these islands, as part of an abolitionist crusade.[112]

These seemed to be unreasonable suppositions—though it was evident that London worried that contestation over Cuba could unleash what the Earl of Aberdeen in 1830 termed "a spirit of insurrection and revolt . . . amongst the black population," meaning a "servile war" with "horrors" hard to imagine, which could then threaten the Crown's territories in the vicinity: in this context, abolitionism was a desperate attempt to avoid being overtaken by events. But this "servile war" could also mean U.S. intervention, which could not just stare in "indifference upon the approach of calamities" and disruption of "tranquility."[113]

The very next year U.S. abolitionists reported breathlessly about an "insurrection among the blacks" in Cuba, with a resulting bloody suppression leading to the slaying of "4,000!"—an astonishing figure, which if nothing else, would give impetus to more importations to make up for the assumed shortfall.[114] A few years later, these fears were confirmed when almost 600 enslaved Africans, just arrived from Africa, rebelled in Cuba, just thirty miles from Havana. Almost 500 were slain—along with about forty Europeans, a significant loss since according to one account, the Africans "had no weapons but clubs and stones."[115] A few years after that, U.S. abolitionists reported on yet another slave revolt in Cuba, this time near Trinidad with scores "either killed or dangerously wounded" and with "ten to twenty of the revolters [sic] . . . shot every day" until the unrest was suppressed.[116] The tumultuous Trinidad "alarmed" a U.S. resident there, as it created "much excitement and anxiety" with Africans still "skulking in the mountains."[117]

But would Washington be willing to confront its own slave traders who were profiting so garishly from what the U.S. consul in Puerto Principe thought should be curtailed in order to forestall future bloody rebellions?

The answer was not long in coming. "Never," said the British diplomats W. S. MacLeay and Edward W. H. Schenley, then posted in Havana, had the slave trade "reached such a disgraceful pitch as during the year 1835." Why? "Great Britain in vain labours to extinguish this commerce as long as the American Government refuses to aid in the cause of Abolition and while American vessels are ever ready to assist the Spanish Slave Trader in his various schemes." Just that spring, "an American agent from Texas purchased in the Havana 250 newly imported Africans at 270 dollars per head and carried them" back to Galveston, "having first procured from the American consul here certificates of their freedom"—and this was just one among incidents too numerous to recount. This approach—Cuba to Texas and perhaps on to the republic—had given a "great impulse" to this destructive commerce.[118]

What was happening was that instead of retreating in the adamant face of British abolitionism, the republicans and their allies—particularly in Texas— had doubled down on enslavement and had accelerated the process of converting Cuba into an ally in this process: heedlessly, they ignored the counsel that they were laying the basis for a replay of what had overtaken Haiti in 1804 as they tipped the exquisitely maintained demographic balance. Washington, rarely timorous in the face of a stiff challenge, imbued as it was with the messianic idea that its version of republicanism was the inexorable wave of the future, and Havana, as fecklessly frightened as any of London, its longtime antagonist, was hardly in a position to resist.[119] Washington—dominated by slaveholders, whose peculiar form of capital in turn dominated the republic— believed it could countervail the power of London by aligning with Madrid and Havana (and Brazil too), though the republic's obvious lust for Cuba compromised this approach.[120]

It just so happened that 1836, the year of Texas independence, was a critical turning point for London: it was then that Spain's role in the slave trade showed a noticeable "decrease" while U.S. participation was skyrocketing, with Texan "agents" "in constant communication with the Havana slave-merchants." Even when Spanish slave traders were convicted criminally—as occurred in Boston in 1835—they were able to obtain a reprieve and return triumphantly to the island, poised to sail once more to Africa with ill intentions.[121]

As time passed, Spanish slave traders were collaborating more and more with their better capitalized and more diplomatically potent U.S. counterparts.[122] Spaniards were purchasing slave ships in the United States, then sailing under U.S. colors to Africa[123] or Spanish-flagged ships were sailing to New Orleans and returning as U.S. vessels.[124] Conveniently, U.S. ships were sailed to Havana for inspection—and sale—and Washington's stubborn refusal to participate in multilateral conventions against this dirty business brought the unscrupulous into concord with the republic.[125]

Late in November 1839 Joseph John Gurney, the English banker and minister-cum-abolitionist, sailed into Havana where he was distressed to find that 90 percent of the ships engaged in the slave trade were built in the republic, and though sold to Spaniards, sailed under U.S. colors to escape harassment by the Royal Navy, given Washington's reluctance to accede to London's scrutiny of slavers. "In short," he lamented, "American citizens (most unworthy men to be sure) are the principal facilitators or even agents of the Cuba trade."[126] This London well knew, and more pointedly it knew of the role of secessionist Texas in this process, which made it difficult to extend diplomatic recognition to yet another slaveholders' republic.[127]

Coincidentally, this great leap forward in the U.S. role in the slave trade to Cuba took place as Nicholas Trist arrived in Havana as a diplomat.[128] Trist, said the British analyst David Turnbull, was "closely allied to the republican aristocracy of America, having married a grand-daughter of President Jefferson and established a little colony of that illustrious stock at Havana."[129] This was also a moneymaking job, which he well knew, given Trist's role in providing authorization for vessels in return for substantial fees. The importance of his role was underlined when he arrived in Havana in March 1834 as the specter of British abolition loomed. An official rowed out to sea to meet his vessel and bring him personally ashore, "where I was received with all kindness," said the beaming republican.[130]

It did not take long for him to make a provocative tour of the waters surrounding Hispaniola while regretting "fifty times a day" that "our flag does not wave over at least one of these numberless islands right under our nose."[131] Soon the adventurous Trist was venturing to Central America, poking into the affairs of Belize, where the Union Jack fluttered.[132] After the important date of abolition—1 August 1834—Trist's antenna seemed to vibrate even more tremulously, as he detected a "contemplated insurrection among the Negroes," a possibility that was seemingly inescapable given the numbers of Negroes arriving with the resultant flux. Spooked, a number of U.S. nationals—mere "panic-stricken" women, he said dismissively, driven by "alarm,"—instantly fled to New Orleans.[133] Luckily, ships departing frequently from Pensacola to Cuba were common,[134] not to mention Charleston, with connecting voyages to Norfolk, which had the added benefit of facilitating slave smuggling.[135]

A ruffled Trist conceded with emphasis that "I am worried out of mind by the duties (not the moneymaking part) of my office,"[136] which roughly was an accurate objective assessment. The pecuniary advantages of his post were revealed when he began looking into the charms of obtaining real estate—"houses in Guanabacoa" near Havana in his case.[137] It was a "delightful residence which I have secured," he chortled.[138] Trist was taken with his neighborhood: "I was carried back to my walks on the terrace at Monticello," he enthused at one point after an evening stroll buoyed by a "delightful breeze."[139] Cuba proved to be so pleasurable that Trist was apparently debating whether it or Louisiana offered the best long-term prospects (particularly in the slave-intensive realm of sugar cultivation), with the island seemingly winning out.[140] A consensus was gathering that over time Cuba provided better prospects than the Pelican State, particularly given its advantage in slave-labor costs.[141]

Even Madrid well knew that as early as 1832 enslaved Africans were three times as costly in New Orleans as in Cuba.[142] Getting carried away, one Trist correspondent exulted that "there is no country like Cuba in the world," notably with "beauty" and "fertility" being "unsurpassed."[143].

This Texas-size exuberance was causing fearful concern in Louisiana, raising the apprehension that Cuba's growth was shriveling their state that included New Orleans. For if the vastness of Texas could be cultivated by Africans purchased for less than $500 in Cuba, how could Louisiana compete when bonded labor cost almost $1,500? And what would that mean for Virginia, which was busily exporting Africans at New Orleans—not Havana—prices? A Texas beyond the federal union provided too many arbitrage opportunities to the detriment of states already in the union. The remedy? Annex Texas, then Cuba. "Otherwise," said one commentator, "the culture of sugar and cotton in Louisiana will suffer greatly by the cheaper labor which planters of Cuba and Texas can and will employ."[144]

The threats to Cuba—real and imagined—were palpable in Trist's mind, as he worried not only about London but France, too.[145] That London "offered mediation" between Paris and Washington was not reassuring since it placed the Crown in a leveraging stance.[146] As the first anniversary of the date of abolition approached, his "heart bounded" when he heard "two boys cry out" that a republican battleship was approaching Havana.[147]

Trist's dedicated interest in Cuba zoomed far beyond normative diplomatic concerns or even the price of local real estate. For he was not only a slave-master there, presiding over human chattel who seemed to be as uproarious as most,[148] he also was accused repeatedly of being deeply complicit in the slave trade that was quickening throughout his tenure, a commerce that was to change the face of the island dramatically while increasing the possibility for a clash between Washington and London as a result, with Madrid managing to hang on due to the resultant standoff.

As London saw things, Trist's arrival in Havana, the rise of a secessionist movement in Texas, and the growth of the slave trade between the two territories were all connected. Trist's arrival marked a grand transition when the trade in Africans shifted decisively away from Spaniards and Portuguese to mainlanders. The brazen Trist in the instrumental year of 1836 blatantly notified one and all: "Several American vessels have lately been chartered for the transportation of Africans or black men from this island to Texas."[149] When London's delegates in Havana began peppering Trist with pointed questions about this putative illegality, the wily republican "decline[d] receiving any communications" on this sensitive matter.[150] Like a dodgy litigant, Trist repeatedly refused to receive correspondence on this matter,[151] as if responding would be a diminution of the republic's jealously held sovereignty.

Meanwhile, from 1837 to 1838, the number of U.S.-flagged ships involved in the slave trade to and from Cuba almost doubled. There had been a "large increase in the number of sugar plantations," during this time, as Washington was informed, and this was "chiefly through the investment therein of American capital and American industry"—all of which "enhanced" the "demand for newly imported slaves from Africa."[152] By 1838 the busy Trist had maximized his earning potential by also serving as Portugal's consul in Havana, which allowed him to expand the range of currencies he pocketed—"there were upwards of 100 slave vessels on which Mr. Trist received the consular fees!" claimed a flabbergasted British diplomat.[153]

By 1838, British observer David Turnbull noticed nineteen U.S.-flagged ships "engaged in the Cuba slave trade" in Havana alone—and, quite explicitly, he did not purport to know of all of these vessels. And he too blamed Trist for this sorry state of affairs. Turnbull spoke with Martín Van Buren in Washington who told him that the "Havana consulate was one of the most lucrative offices in the gift of government,"[154] as Trist's lavish lifestyle well exemplified.

U.S. abolitionists ascertained that from the time of Trist's arrival in Havana, the slave trade took a quantum leap. And as Havana became a magnet for this traffic, slave dealers "from all parts of the world" congregated, sparking further leaps. This brought in turn more U.S.-built ships to be sold and U.S. sailors to staff them—all "with regular papers" provided by the "workshop of Consul Trist" in an exercise in "kidnapping and murder. In this way," it was said with immense regret, "the entire slave trade of Cuba, during the last two years," in 1839, "has passed through the hands of the U.S. Consul and under the U.S. flag! That trade amounts to 25,000 souls per annum" landing in Cuba and about the same number "murdered" in the process. Worse, it was thought, Trist was no outlier but instead was connected closely to "gentlemen" with "vast estates" in Cuba—and "some of these gentlemen were personally intimate with Mr. [Daniel] Webster," one of the republic's most important politicians.[155] Trist's warm welcome was symptomatic of Havana's embrace of his role in delivering slaves,[156] which meant foiling London—one and the same, it was thought.

Thus in 1839 the British diplomat R. R. Madden addressed U.S. abolitionists directly, as if he had decided that appeals through established channels were futile, which seemed to be true.[157] He rebuked Trist (who was said to have threatened his British counterparts in Havana with bodily harm), assailed the "scandalous abuse of the flag of your country" and warned ominously that the "Texian [sic] system of conquest, by means of colonization was [not] applicable to Cuba." He denounced the reality that rising U.S. investment in Cuban plantations was undergirding the underlying problem: the spectacular increase in the slave trade. But in extraordinarily scalding terms, he reserved his most intemperate words for Trist, whose elite ties and personal investments in slavery came to symbolize the republic's rapidly growing though corrosive role in Cuba.[158] Interestingly, his condemnation of Trist was mirrored in the republic.[159]

This trend was nothing new: the year of Texas secession, 1836, John Quincy Adams himself reportedly asserted that "if ever you take Texas into the [republican] family, you must also take the island of Cuba."[160] "Some of the Spaniards think our countrymen are emigrating to Cuba with a view to take ultimate possession, à la Texas," said *The Colored American* in concurrence.[161] By 1838, legislators in New York were debating a resolution to recommend the purchase of Cuba from Spain, a call that was to increase its decibel level in coming years.[162]

In a sense, the "Mexican standoff" was resolved when Mexico City's attention was diverted to focus more intently on its rebellious province to the north: Texas. Yet the problem for the grandiose schemes of the two slaveholders' republics—Texas and the United States—was that the Africans had a vote on slavery, and in April 1839 abolitionists were quick to trumpet their rebelliousness, this time in Matanzas.[163] But the republicans in particular had not learned a central lesson of Haiti in 1804: tipping the demographic balance by bringing in so many Africans was inimical to slavery's long-term health. Yet in 1839 a legislative body in Boston found that Africans were arriving in ever greater numbers, not only in Cuba but Texas and Brazil too, which effectively was making the bar against the foreign slave trade "a dead letter."[164]

That same year, Lord John Russell observed that 100,000 enslaved Africans were being delivered in the Americas annually—making a laughingstock of London's efforts to restrain this commerce and emboldening republicans further—with a major trend being Iberian dealers yielding to those from the United States.[165] According to *The Colored American*, by 1840, U.S. slave ships were to be "found in almost every slave haunt on the coast" of Africa.[166]

The handiwork of U.S. slave traders was felt profoundly on the island, and at the same time, London found that "it is but within the last twenty years that the number of Americans holding lands has become at all considerable"; tens of thousands of Africans were arriving annually but overall population growth in this realm was not commensurate—the increase was "very small" due to "ill treatment" and high "mortality among the newly landed" necessitating the need for more Africans.[167]

Finally, in 1840, Alexander Hill Everett arrived in Cuba to investigate the many complaints about Nicholas Trist.[168] There was much to investigate since this spouse of Jefferson's granddaughter, who had studied law under the founder's tutelage, now owned the Flor de Cuba sugar plantations and a hefty holding in a Cuban mining company.[169] However, the politics of the republic were such that whatever the result of this inquiry, the growing republican role in delivering enchained Africans to the island would not cease soon.[170] Lord John Russell was told that the republicans "regard with a covetous eye this magnificent island," possibly a "glorious acquisition" and "at once their strongest outpost in defense of slavery and a mine of wealth for purposes of future aggression and aggrandizement."[171]

So, Trist was hard to contain precisely because his actions dovetailed with those of the ascendant hawks. "If we except Pedro Blanco [slave dealer] and [Captain General] O'Donnell," said Martín Delany, leading U.S. Negro abolitionist, "there is no one who is more our enemy than Mr. Trist." He was "largely into the foreign slave trade. His immediate interest is in the barracoons or slave factories of Cuba."[172] William Lloyd Garrison, another premier mainland abolitionist, provided a letter of introduction for a visiting British subject just arrived from Havana who was "here to show up the character of Consul Trist."[173] For Trist was not just an enthusiast for the slave trade, he embodied the retrograde republican racial attitudes then rising.[174] Likewise, it was evident that the Africans themselves would have something to say about policies attracting unremitting attention from Haiti, Britain—and U.S. abolitionists, particularly Negroes.

CHAPTER 3

Africans Revolt!

JOHN FORSYTH WAS NOT PLEASED.

On 6 September 1839 this slaveholder from Georgia, then serving as U.S. secretary of state, informed the Spanish authorities that weeks earlier within Cuban waters, fifty-three Africans aboard the *Amistad* schooner revolted and slew the captain, the chef, and two crewmen, leaving alive only two of their colleagues who were ordered to guide the vessel to Africa. Instead, the captives—formerly captors—sailed along the U.S. coast before somehow arriving in New London, Connecticut. The U.S. authorities detained the Africans, then sent them to New Haven where a trial ensued to determine their fate. Abolitionists rallied in their behalf—in a major victory that upset an already besieged Havana, straining to cope with an overflow of Africans—before the former slaves were allowed to return home to Africa.[1]

Madrid too was unhappy, irate about the "fanatics"—or U.S. abolitionists—whose influence Forsyth acknowledged he could not wholly ignore and the supposed defamation of Cuban slavery that emerged in Connecticut.[2] Madrid's ire was inflamed further when London intervened, dispatching one of their top operatives in Havana to testify on behalf of the Africans, while reminding one and all that an 1820 treaty—if not earlier iterations—had illegalized the slave trade from Africa, of which the *Amistad* was a part, and like any Africans brought to the island since that date, these captives too should be freed. If followed to the letter, this dictum could throw heavily capitalized plantations into turmoil (and Cuba itself) by freeing Africans en masse.[3] Yet if Madrid's men had been reading the burgeoning press under the aegis of U.S. Negroes, they would have been further upset by the warm encomia for these former captives, now in flight,[4] and the ecstasy with which their freeing was greeted.[5]

Arguing on behalf of the Africans, John Quincy Adams—in a last-ditch attempt to rescue his richly deserved reputation as a collaborator with enslavement—acknowledged Havana's argument that acquiescing to his clients' appeal would endanger Cuba, "where citizens of the United States not only carry on a considerable trade but where they possess territorial properties which they cultivate with the labor of African slaves."[6] Havana could retaliate against these property-holders, or, as *The Liberator* pointed out, refuse to return "fugitive slaves" who made their way to Cuba or comply with extradition requests generally.[7] Still, Madrid was heartened by a resolution from Carolina's John C. Calhoun that sought to bolster the Spanish position if an analogous situation were to arise again[8] and a companion effort in Washington to indemnify Cuban slaveholders for their loss. [9]

This maneuver by Washington was also farsighted because, as an inquisitive U.S. journalist observed contemporaneously, "most of the plantations in Cuba, which have recently [been] brought under cultivation belong to Americans, the number of American slaveholders is increasing"—and as a direct result "importation of human cargoes from Africa finds much of its encouragement from the citizens of our Republic."[10] If present trends continued, bailing out republican slaveholders for *Amistad*-like losses might be necessary.

Havana was unsettled by the avid participation in the *Amistad* case of British nationals, including R. R. Madden who had harassed Trist in Cuba and the seemingly ubiquitous David Turnbull,[11] who announced happily that the case was the "first occasion since the Declaration of American Independence that the efficacy of the writ of habeas corpus has been tried for the protection of an African's freedom."[12] Madrid tailed Turnbull in the region as if he were an elusive prey.[13] Restiveness among the enslaved in Cuba was ascribed to him and those presumably like him, for example, missionaries[14] and not to the worsened slavery regime brought by a tidal wave of Africans borne by U.S. vessels. Turnbull won few friends among the republic's elite when he pointed this out.[15] Madden raised the specter of a like case more directly implicating the republic when he reported the existence of "various American steam boats" that "ply between Havana and Matanzas and Cardenas and on the south side between Batabano and Cienfuegos and Trinidad." Frighteningly—for slavers—he justified the slaying of ships' crews so involved, asserting that it was a rational response to an illegal detention.[16]

Spain was so fearful of a forcible British intervention in the *Amistad* case that she wanted warships dispatched to the waters off Connecticut and insisted that this matter only concerned Madrid and the republic, as she rejected London's increasing freelance role as a protector of Africans.[17] Sternly, Lord Palmerston instructed Madrid that since the Africans at issue hailed from Africa, the attempted enslavement of them was void *ab initio* and that Spain should communicate this to the United States promptly. Her Majesty, all were reminded, "cannot feel indifferent to the fate of these unfortunate persons."[18]

U.S. nationals were transforming Cuba, and the waves of Africans arriving there that inescapably led to *Amistad*-like events were simply the visibly riotous evidence. In 1827, it was said, there were 311,051 Cubans defined as "white"; 106,490 seen as free Negroes and people of color; and 286, 042 enslaved Africans. Just before the *Amistad* set sail there were 400,000 viewed as "white"; 110,000 in the second category; and the number of slaves had mushroomed to 360,000—and was growing.[19] By 1840, Joel Poinsett, the well-placed U.S. agent in the region, thought he had reason to believe that there were "five hundred thousand whites and six hundred and sixty-five thousand blacks & people of color" in Cuba—a matter of potential consequence for the republic.[20]

The energy with which slave dealers had pursued their nefarious trade also contributed to the estimate that by 1840, 43 percent of Florida's population was designated as Negro, this despite an earlier flight when the republicans took over almost two decades earlier.[21] The Innerarity and Forbes families, who had accumulated small fortunes by dint of slave dealing in Florida and along the Gulf Coast, were neighbors in Cuba by 1843:[22] the grinding war on the peninsula with Africans and indigenes had caused others to flee. As in Cuba, deluging so many Africans in Florida was bound to lead to discontent. Maroons from Cuba—a mixture of African and indigenous ancestry—resided at the southern tip of the peninsula. It was in 1840 that they participated in an attack on Indian Key, which confirmed that slaveholders on both sides of the straits had a mutual interest in suppressing Africans.[23]

MONITORED VESSELS WERE TRACKED on their torturous journey from West Africa to Havana and New Orleans and Key West, enslaved Africans aboard.[24] This ugly dragooning of labor—as in Cuba—made for dire results. Africans in Florida were accused of committing murder and robbery to escape to the Bahamas where the British authorities refused to extradite them.[25] Africans in and about St. Augustine—whose martial traditions stretched back centuries—were accused of "plundering the settlers on the coast" with untoward consequences.[26] Key West was affected similarly, leading to anguished cries from the authorities for "proper Maritime Forces," which could mean bruising confrontations with the Royal Navy.[27] As ever, when Negroes were revolting, the Florida authorities chose to wreak vengeance on free Negroes, with spasmodic efforts to bar them altogether from the peninsula, which could serve to push them closer to London.[28] Nearby in the Bahamas, a rich fisheries market was developing in which free Negroes under the Union Jack were participating heavily, to the consternation of the republic. Worse, it was thought, when abolition was enacted in 1834, it released Africans to compete in fisheries and elsewhere and some of these enterprisers that had belonged to "some of our citizens," Washington said, now were their competitors. [29]

With Africans cascading into the territory on both sides of the straits, a continuing conflict in Florida spearheaded by Africans and known to history as the Second Seminole War (1835–1842), and increasing anxiety about the upshot of freeing the enslaved, the resultant fluidity provided apt conditions for "La Escalera" (The Ladder),[30] the name given to what was thought to be a massive conspiracy of thousands of the enslaved in Cuba. This resulted in ever more brutal executions, along with imprisonments and banishments, and binding supposed conspirators to ladders and whipping them mercilessly, as they were interrogated, which gave the plot its name. When the British consul to Cuba, David Turnbull, whose remonstrations against Trist got him expelled from the island near the same time, was convicted in absentia of being the alleged prime mover of this conspiracy, it sent a spine-tingling frisson of apprehension coursing through the slaveholders on the island and the mainland.

Today there are those who question if an actual conspiracy was at play,[31] though at the time, the continuing episodes of unrest in Cuba[32] and Jamaica[33] trumpeted by the U.S. Negro press did little to assuage nervousness on the mainland. The "insurrection among the Negroes, between Matanzas and Cardenas," said *The Liberator* cheerily, meant "the burning of five sugar estates" as "whites fled in every direction and some few were murdered" with fighting "almost as difficult as the Florida war." This journal did not deny that the "insurrection is very generally attributed to the instigations of abolition emissaries from the Bahamas Islands."[34] Nor was warm sympathy extended to U.S. nationals in Cuba who got caught in the crossfire,[35] though severe doubt was expressed about the viability of slavery.[36] Abolitionists flexed their muscles on the mainland when they rescued a slave boy who was put on a ship in New Orleans for Trinidad, Cuba—but somehow wound up in Boston,[37] while these crusaders continued to rail against U.S. slave traders on the island.[38]

Mainland abolitionists continued to instill terror in slaveholders in the region by raising the specter of a "West Indian Army" that "would land in Florida, furnish with arms, ammunition, and provisions the hostile Indians and Negroes there and with the accession of slaves . . . and with fleets" then head to Cuba.[39] Tellingly, the republic's leading emissary in the region—Joel Poinsett—was all too familiar with the unease about the possibility of an invasion of Cuba from Jamaica with the aim of liberating Africans.[40] In Bristol, Rhode Island, in some ways the end of a chain linked to Matanzas, there was the nervous response that all was "tranquil,"[41] a perception that was belied when Mark de Wolfe of that town, one of the island's more substantial slaveholders, chose this moment of unrest to unwind some of his Cuban investments.[42]

But abolitionist attempts to instill terror could only be effective if there was a real threat, which there was, as the visiting physician John Wurdemann discovered when he visited Cardenas in 1843 and found republican residents quaking about the "late insurrection among the slaves near Bemba. . . . They rose to the number of a thousand on six or seven sugar estates."[43] Simultaneously, a mainland carpenter in the vicinity—according to an abolitionist account—was in "a state of insensibility, mutilated [and] wounded," while "several families have been massacred."[44]

That the republicans had a front-row seat as Escalera played out was bound to have maximal impact, given the miasma of fear that had been created. Thomas Rodney of Delaware—like Trist, part of a founding family of the republic[45]—was U.S. consul in Matanzas and experienced firsthand the violence that was detonated. His former cook—Victor—was whipped viciously after being accused of being a conspirator, while his dentist, Andrew Dodge, a free Negro, was fingered as a leader. Ultimately, both were executed. Even some local planters with Wilmington roots had to be bailed out by Rodney, who did not particularly object to the ensuing bloodiness.[46] "I feel keenly for these four young men," said a sad Rodney, "who are now confined in the same prison with 1,200 blacks."[47]

Havana was reacting to the creeping annexationist surge that was enveloping the island in the form of growing U.S. investments in slave-based industries. The engineers overseeing grinding of sugarcane in Cuba were U.S. nationals, with nary a "Spanish engineer in the whole island."[48] John C. Calhoun was told by one of his constituents of vessels heading from Charleston to Havana and Matanzas "every day in the week and the same from Cuba."[49] These newcomers were flocking to Matanzas and Holguin, which were becoming bastions of republican presence.[50]

There was a growing suspicion within the republic that—plot or fantasy—Escalera allowed Spaniards to settle scores with the United States, a nation that had made no secret of its hunger to devour Cuba. Rodney's consulate in Matanzas was stunned when Maurice Hogan, a coffee planter near Cardenas, was jailed; he was from "one of the slaveholding states" and upon arrival in March 1843 "distinguished himself" when "the Negro insurrection at Bemba" erupted "by attacking on horseback, singlehanded and alone [while] holding in check two or three hundred Negroes." Yet, "on Negro testimony, obtained by leading questions under the lash,"[51] he and other republicans were incarcerated. But Havana was unsettled when in 1843 the U.S. consul requested entry into Cuban ports of battleships with imprecisely defined intentions.[52]

Still, a "general slaughter of the whites" was planned, concluded Rodney, but fortunately "we have been preserved from the fangs of infuriated Negroes" and the "retribution will be appalling."[53] This was bound to generate an undertow, sweeping within its ambit those that might not be guilty. According to U.S. abolitionists, "Every free black in the island is said to have been engaged in the plot," along with "several white men," including "two Americans, who will most probably be shot soon." Viewed, perhaps invidiously, as a matter of creativity was the reputed "plans of the Negroes" involving destruction of "the entire garrison of the island (25, 000 men) by putting poison in the bread, which is baked from them daily. The poison was found in the bake house."[54]

Visiting Cuba from Charleston at the time of Escalera, the patriotic Southerner, William Norwood, was sure something dire was afoot. "Placido, a free mulatto of Matanzas, a man of education and a poet is the head of the conspiracy. He was intimate with Turnbull, the former British consul" and, in fact, "visited Turnbull at Jamaica & has kept up an extensive correspondence with other leaders during the past year." He confirmed the poison plot—enough "arsenic" to kill "the whole garrison of 8,000" and the further detail that "another attempt was made" to "poison one of the first families of the city by putting arsenic in their soup." It was "an extensive plot" that "existed mostly over the whole island," involving "2,300 Negroes," adding, almost superfluously, "It is not very pleasant."[55] Subsequently, a U.S. Negro writer was to assert that the erudite Cuban poet Placido was "vaguely suspected of being in sympathy with black conspirators who dreamed of making Cuba a sister republic to black Haiti. . . ."[56]

When Placido was accused of being the instigator of Escalera this propelled him into prominence among mainland Africans as a symbol of principled resistance, and this perception was to last for some time to come.[57] When Placido was linked to Havana's Public Enemy Numero 1—David Turnbull of Britain—the emotional temperature of Havana reached stratospheric levels.[58] It was not long before Havana started espying phantoms of unrest on each arriving vessel.[59]

The U.S. consul in Kingston, Jamaica, Robert Harrison, who was aware "of the almost [constant] intercourse between this place" and Cuba, determined that not only was Turnbull behind this plot but he was "endeavouring to produce the same state of things in America." There was "not the least doubt" about this. He counseled John C. Calhoun that his own Carolina was "greatly exposed" and faced the "worst consequences" unless drastic measures were taken, because a "successful insurrection of the Negroes in Cuba" would ineluctably spread to Dixie. Moreover, "as there are several black regiments in this and other islands, these wretches, might also, in the event of a war with the United States, be turned into one [sledgehammer],"[60] wielded brutally against Dixie.

Caught up in the resultant tidal wave of accusations was Jorge Davison, a Jamaican residing in Cuba whose brother, H. W. Davison of Philadelphia, worked as an abolitionist: this was thought to be not simply a coincidence. Caught up in the bloodletting was Charles Blakely, a Negro dentist from Charleston and his protégé, Andrew Dodge—both men trained in London and were also viewed skeptically: both were executed.[61]

John C. Calhoun, perhaps the most hawkish of pro-slavery spokesmen, was alert to these developments and demanded a "minute and detailed statement of facts" of the "recent insurrectionary movements in Cuba," notably "the parts which foreigners may have taken in these disturbances including our own citizens."[62] Extending U.S. influence in Cuba had a downside, including extending militant abolitionist contagion from the island to the mainland. That U.S. nationals were suspected, then accused, was suggestive of the paranoia about abolitionists and suspicion that the republic still lusted after the island, which, it was thought, they hoped to gain by any means necessary.[63] Yet banishing some of the alleged perpetrators of Escalera to the mainland was the kind of import not relished by republicans. Future president James Buchanan was informed by the U.S. consul in Trinidad, Cuba, that he objected—minimally—because they would "become a charge to our already over-burdened charitable institutions" and they were "entirely destitute, ignorant of our language and unaccustomed to our climate," but Havana was not listening and was "dissatisfied" when Washington balked.[64] Simultaneously, Havana was becoming quite suspicious of U.S. nationals arriving on the island with personally owned slaves in tow,[65] while Madrid upped its surveillance of events within the republic.[66]

In the event, a number of free Negroes from Cuba fled to the mainland in desperation, including at least forty from Matanzas.[67] Though there was a backlash against U.S. nationals by Havana in the wake of Escalera, as the authorities seized the opportunity to downgrade those thought to desire Spain's ouster from the island, there was also a punishment of free Negroes,[68] considered to be behind the plot. Their pulverizing was, however, an ironic reflection of growing U.S. influence in Cuba since republicans held a special and venomous animus toward Africans of this category. Self-styled "patriotic" Cubans warned that if London's abolitionism spread, the "political existence of the United States would be endangered,"[69] further suggestive of the cross-straits influence.

Above all, there was a reign of terror unleashed against free Negro expatriates in Cuba; a British envoy noticed in May 1844 that the "police . . . warn all the male free colored foreigners to leave the island within fifteen days."[70] The Captain General, Leopoldo O'Donnell, sought to soften the blow by averring that "not only all the foreign men of color" should depart "but even those who have come from Spanish colonies."[71]

Attempts to halt the import of enslaved Africans were hapless at best; nonetheless, attempts to halt the circulation of foreign periodicals arriving with foreign Negroes were much more effective.[72] The flow of Africans to Cuba was so formidable that, per usual, the overflow continued to arrive on the mainland.[73] Havana would not have been misguided if it had pointed a finger of accusation northward at the republic, since it was the United States, captaining the slave trade, which fomented all manner of discord.

Visiting the island in 1843, John Wurdemann found that the "free colored have many privileges and are more kindly treated and respected than the same class in our northern free states. The Spaniard has not the same antipathy to color that the Anglo-Saxon has"; and though there was "Spanish cruelty to slaves . . . they offer in their institutions for the relief of the sick Free Negro, an example which might well be followed by many of our Southern States."[74] But with a growing republican presence and Africans arriving regularly at their behest, it appeared that the island was now being remade in Dixie's image with far-reaching consequences for all. This would not be a cakewalk, since Africans of all stripes, and even some Spaniards, objected stringently to the growing republican presence.[75]

Spain's rule in Cuba was not sufficiently strong to afford the alienation of free Negroes as a class, but surely this is what was occurring, driven by republican influence and fear of African restiveness. Cuban elites could hardly avoid noticing trends in their larger neighbor, with some seeing the United States as possessing a slavery model to emulate in which "slavery was abolished" in the North of the republic. It was reported from Havana, "The condition of the Negro is much more worthy of compassion and more unfortunate, than in the Southern States, where slavery is recognized by law."[76]

Madrid's orders to their legations in the republic were swift and certain: no more visas were to be issued to Negroes destined for Cuba—they were to be barred henceforth,[77] and tighter restrictions were to be imposed on visiting Negro seamen, which had severe implications for arriving vessels from the republic.[78] In events more typical of the mainland, reports were emerging about free Negroes being sold into slavery,[79] while free Negroes from other nations residing in Cuba were automatically suspect.[80] Still, African seafarers arriving in Cuba seemed to be viewed most suspiciously.[81] Havana told London that it wanted the restrictive procedures then employed in Charleston, yet another sign of growing republican influence on the island.[82]

In retrospect, 1845 was a pivotal moment in the history of slavery in Florida (as it joined the Union as a state), and, as so often happened, this left a deep imprint across the straits. The influence of republicans and the flux brought by their ministrations in the slave trade engendered a transition from what one scholar has termed the "easy attitudes and practices of the Spanish concerning manumission to the rigidity of those of the Anglo-Americans." "Coartacion," or the right of the enslaved to buy their freedom, began to fade.[83] In an island of ironies, a major one was that in ousting so many free Negroes, the authorities may have created more openings for Euro-Americans—a prime antagonist—as hysteria generated by restiveness among the enslaved continued to resonate on both sides of the straits.

To a degree, this was an unavoidable response, but on the other hand it simply served to intensify insecurity on the island. One result of Escalera—and the tumult that preceded it—was an escalating enhancement of anxiety in Washington and Havana about what to expect from a now firmly abolitionist London, which had cultivated close relations with U.S. Negroes and Haiti alike. Indeed, in 1839 Britain and Haiti inked an important pact to suppress the slave trade, with the latter republic given responsibility for patrolling the waters of Cuba and Puerto Rico—particularly the former since it was "separated from the island of Hayti [*sic*] by a narrow strait."[84] The Mixed Commission that emerged from such abolitionist cooperation had Cuba in the crosshairs and included one of London's top Negro diplomats, Charles Mackenzie—a development that attracted Madrid's attention.[85] By 1841 Madrid was complaining bitterly about supposed Haitian plans to provoke "la revolucion de los Negros" in Cuba.[86] In response there was the initiation of ever more severe measures against the Negro republic, including provocations in Santo Domingo.[87] The prosecution in London of slave dealers with ties to Cuba was unnerving in Havana and Washington alike.[88]

Like a seesaw, as Havana became more fearful of Britain and Haiti and U.S. Negroes, these Africans' ties to London increased. The crisis in Cuba almost effortlessly seemed to deepen seemingly uncontrollable outbursts of hysteria on the part of Havana and Washington, which could serve to compel them further to make wrongheaded decisions. In the prelude to the U.S. Civil War and the concomitant growth in abolitionism it is remarkable how politically wayward and unbalanced slaveholders on both sides of the straits became.

The idea taking Washington by storm in 1843, for example, was that London wanted to create a "black military republic" in Cuba.[89] The idea gained resonance since for hundreds of years Madrid had deployed armed Africans, a notion considered downright bizarre in the republic.

That same year Secretary of State Daniel Webster conceded in a "confidential" message that the thousands upon thousands of Africans pouring into Cuba were actually the handiwork of abolitionist London and not his fellow citizens. London sought to "ruin" Cuba, said Webster, by "offering independence to the Creoles, on condition that they unite with the colored government" in this Negro republic "under British protection," and the increase in Negro population was designed to solidify this plot. A Venezuelan general residing in Jamaica was to "take the command of an invading army," which was to be "seconded" by an "insurrection of the slaves and free men of color," and thus with "600,000 blacks in Cuba and 800,000 in her West India islands, [London] will" then "strike a death blow at the existence of slavery in the United States." Meanwhile in Cuba "wealthy planters"—among these many of Webster's compatriots, which he conspicuously neglected to note—were "blind to the danger" and instead kept "buying Negroes, clamoring for the continuation of the trade." But he had a trump card, he stressed, in that the "whites" of Cuba *"will always prefer the flag of the United States to that of England,"* a governing thought that could serve to further polarize the island racially and extend the shelf life of slavery.[90]

In a sense, what Webster articulated was nothing new, since from the birth of the republic the United States had been hostile to the idea of an independent Cuba; such a nation would not necessarily be another Dixie, but perhaps another Haiti, and thus endanger the Southern states. The island was also the crown jewel of the Spanish Crown, and weakening Madrid's empire, so as to better dominate the hemisphere, was a major republican goal, giving further impetus to taking Cuba. But the steady opposition to this scheme in London and, intermittently, Paris frustrated the republic.[91]

The republic's chief diplomat in Madrid told Webster bluntly that London was pushing aggressively for abolition in Cuba, which unavoidably would have serious implications for the mainland.[92] The U.S. consul in Jamaica, Robert Harrison, concurred, adding that London was "jealous of our rising greatness" and "can never forget that we at one time belonged to them."[93] Unsurprisingly hastened was the gathering consensus that the republic had to take, then remake Cuba, or suffer the consequences of it becoming a Siamese twin of Haiti.[94] Such scary scenarios had the added advantage of allowing Spanish Cuba to edge closer to the republic in order to foil abolitionism, but this was a smothering embrace, for all the hair-raising talk about Cuba becoming another Haiti gave added impetus for the republic to foil this scheme—by taking Cuba for itself.[95]

The republic as a whole was determined to ensure that another Haiti would not arise. As so often happened in the republic, international issues were shaping domestic politics. One need look no further than James G. Wright of Santiago de Cuba. He was a partner in a highly profitable mercantile firm—and formerly a citizen of the republic—but after three decades on the island, he renounced his nationality. He owned numerous Africans and now was lobbying John C. Calhoun, a powerful Carolinian, to be U.S. consul in Santiago. His advocate told Calhoun that "he stands at the head of the anti-British & anti-abolition party in St. Jago de Cuba," was a resolute "Texas annexationist" and "extensive Coffee planter" with formidable clout on both sides of the straits—though Cuba was now drifting into a status as a de facto U.S. state in any case.[96]

Calhoun's son-in-law, Thomas G. Clemson, was involved in a coal-mining venture in Cuba, one of a growing coterie of republicans who were investing heavily in the island.[97] As a result, powerful commercial interests were lobbying intensively—as Wright's case showed—for plum diplomatic posts in Cuba, in maneuvers that carried sectional complications.[98] They had more Cuban assets to protect: by 1846, "an intelligent gentleman," as he was described, estimated that "the value of property in that island owned by Americans" amounted to a hefty "$35,000,000." [99]

A steady stream of republicans, undeterred by fearsome slave uprisings, continued arriving on the island, continuing in their own inimitable and mis-guided way to be astounded by Cuba ("no distinctions made in colours," said William Morton in astonishment in 1846) and added their own unique toxins to an already combustible scene (the "old-fashioned Negro smell" also overwhelmed this visitor),[100] though others found Havana to be "dirty in the extreme." At times these visiting republicans had been chased from revolu-tionary Hispaniola and were in no mood to countenance any rambunctious-ness among Africans.[101] The combustion tended to explode when republican diplomats began paying more attention to—and seeking to take advantage of—growing tensions between Spaniards and those described as "Creoles,"[102] or those born on the island, with whom Washington often sought alliance, particularly after the scalding experience of Escalera, when mainlanders were handled roughly by the authorities. That the Creoles often were literally closer to mainlanders, having attended school in the United States and more likely to be fluent in English, solidified this bond.[103]

The annexation of Texas in 1845 by the republic both increased angst in Havana about a similar fate and gave momentum in Washington to attain this long-desired end;[104] if it was not, Cuba would become more than a figuratively loaded pistol pointing at the republic. This heightened the republican desire to align with Creoles, and also placed Madrid in a prickly dilemma. Should Madrid press independent Texas to abolish the slave trade in order to gain plaudits from London at the expense of what was appearing more and more as a stalking horse for Washington,[105] or acquiesce to the slave trade from Galves-ton on the premise that slavery demanded solidarity?[106] The U.S. republic was an antagonist that desired what they controlled—Cuba—but it was needed to confront abolitionism spreading from Jamaica and Haiti. When abolitionists claimed that Texas annexation actually meant that London "in order to pre-serve the balance of power, will seize upon Cuba,"[107] Madrid's dilemma was neatly illustrated. When during the same decade London appeared to spread a rumor of ceding Jamaica to the republic, to rile up the Africans there and bol-ster Britain's regional role—or so it was portrayed—Madrid's disadvantages were highlighted in the process.[108] When in 1844 unrest began to shake what had been Spanish Hispaniola—which was to eventuate in the founding of the Dominican Republic and the concomitant weakening of Haiti—it was reflec-tive of Madrid's power to shape the region as well as the unsteady future that Cuba continued to face.[109]

In faraway St. Clair County, Illinois, a resolution was passed—unanimously—demanding the "purchase of the island of Cuba with the consent of
the white people thereof,"[110] a resolve that caught the wary eye of the Spanish
legation in the United States.[111] If it was any consolation to Havana, there was
also a cry to annex Canada, too.[112] Abolitionists were complaining about a
different kind of contagion—a Texas fever had become a Cuba fever as even
"patriots of Illinois suddenly in some unaccountable manner fell openly in love
with [Havana]."[113] In response, London's anger with the republic continued
to percolate; pressed by abolitionists, the Crown denounced the annexation of
Texas, followed quickly by the war on and dismemberment of Mexico, which
extended the boundaries of slavery. And now the republicans desired Cuba
for the same purpose. "In Cuba," said U.S. abolitionists, "the American prejudice against color did not exist and colored men were allowed to fill the posts
in the army and elsewhere"—a policy bound not to survive annexation.[114] In
Glasgow, the republicans were excoriated for its policies of "slaveholding,
slave-breeding and slave-trading," which they had sought to extend not just to
Cuba but to the entire hemisphere.[115] With the butchering of Mexico by the
United States, abolitionist attitudes soured accordingly, with some averring
"there is not a more intolerable and wicked despotism in the world than the
existing government of South Carolina. It is not surpassed by . . . Cuba."[116]
Their mood was not improved when Florida began to import bloodhounds
from Cuba to more effectively pursue rebellious Africans and indigenes.[117]

This passionate pursuit of Cuba was intensifying pro-slavery sentiment
within the republic, a fact that Frederick Douglass, the noted Negro abolitionist, discovered when he was sailing from the mainland to Dublin and had to
endure vehement threats from southerners and Cubans alike, who threatened
mayhem because of his mere presence.[118] What Douglass experienced was
an aspect of a larger picture: massive land grabs in Texas and Mexico were
energizing republicans for more—meaning Cuba. "All our strength should
be reserved for Cuba," said the republic's envoy in Prussia in 1848, since it
"belongs to us by nature" and taking it was "becoming more and more necessary to enable the holders of slave property in the U. States to preserve it."[119]

Yet Havana's already parlous position was weakened further when the two
pro-slavery titans—Madrid and Washington—began to weaken their respective positions when quarreling over control of Cuba.[120] Neither of these champions of human bondage had much room for error, given the rising strength
of abolitionism, the growing capacity of Africans in the hemisphere, and the
reality that the planet's leading power in London was sufficiently wily to ally
with Negroes in order to weaken both Havana and Washington. Havana had
to pivot to ferret out the substance of reported plans of a related conspiracy
spearheaded by London, also involving Africans.[121] Even Vera Cruz, miles

away in Mexico, was thought by Havana to harbor conspirators in league with New York[122]—and Madrid thought similarly.[123]

The 1840s were the beginning of tumultuous decades that were to shake the island virtually until slavery was abolished in the 1880s, a process driven by the continuing arrival of manacled Africans, which gave rise to revolt and then created ripples regionally generating abolitionism. These events were then influenced by the turbulence emanating from Europe in the pivotal year of 1848, as St. Croix,[124] then Martínique[125] were among the sites of erupting human volcanoes. That Jamaica was plotting against Cuba in 1848 was an article of faith in Havana.[126] At the same time, U.S. nationals could not seem to refrain from enslaving more Africans and dumping them in the region,[127] which provided more kindling for now leaping flames and prompted London to insist upon the right of search of suspect vessels, even those flying the Stars and Stripes.[128] So many Africans were arriving on the island that plans emerged to send some of them to the huge hemispheric neighbor that was Brazil.[129]

This process continued post-Escalera, as if this major scare did not occur.[130] Even some elite Cubans were starting to complain that the surge of Africans was generating fears of "frequent insurrections"; these men saw Dixie as a model where—supposedly—the slave trade had ceased, but this was as unrealistic as their dream of maintaining enslavement.[131] Indicative of the impact of Escalera was the rather dry comment made by a British official at Sierra Leone in late 1844, who remarked that the number of "Spanish vessels" involved in the slave trade would have "been even larger than it is, but for the temporary repressing effect which the recent disturbances amongst the slave population has had in creating a want of confidence." Still, this trade was increasing nonetheless and was being "conducted perhaps more systematically than it has ever been hitherto." How? Why? The United States, as had been the pattern, filled the breach with an almost nonchalant disregard of the possible catastrophic consequences for island stability.[132]

In May 1844 London's legation in Madrid warned that in the last year there had been "three insurrections of Negroes" in Cuba "besides several minor outbreaks. And in most cases the ringleaders of these insurrections were found to be Negroes who had recently been torn from their families in Africa"—by U.S. slavers, it could have been added. Suicide among Africans was rising, along with torture of them, as they were "cut to pieces and butchered wholesale"— yet they kept arriving.[133] In 1821, the year the republic seized Florida, there were, according to one account, 265,000 enslaved Africans on the island; by 1827 this figure was said to have crept to 286,942—and by 1841, it had leapt to 496,495. London, however, considered this figure "much under the reality"; it actually might be twice as high, an "unnatural and alarming increase" with probable alarming consequences.[134]

The continuing influx into the island of enslaved Africans continued to spur rising alarm in London with potentially dire consequences for Cuba and the republic alike, as the awful commerce was attracting an ever more diverse range of entrepreneurs,[135] suggesting that this commerce's durability was not eroding. Madrid agreed with Washington about slavery but was nervous about reputed plans to support the island's independence on the grounds that slavery would be preserved.[136] The problem for the pro-slavery caucus, spearheaded by the United States, Spain, and Brazil, was that they were relatively disunited compared to abolitionist forces led by Britain, Haiti, U.S. Negroes, and Africans generally in the hemisphere. As a general rule, ultimately the united prevail over those who are not. Thus a Spanish-language publication in 1845 lamented the growth of coffee production in Brazil, driven by U.S. consumption, which had decimated Cuban production. Free Negroes were abandoning Texas and the United States for Haiti and Canada, strengthening the latter two against their adversaries, while enslaved Africans kept arriving in Cuba, raising the prospect of another Escalera that could convert the island into another Haiti, or at least another Jamaica. With the annexation of Texas and the savaging of Mexico, the republic seemed to be riding high, but even a cursory look at underlying forces suggested it had much to be concerned about.[137]

The republic had clamored for Cuba not least since it stood astride important shipping lanes.[138] That abolitionist London ruled the seas made this acquisition all the more important when slaveholding interests sought to ship their most important capital from one port to another, only to find the Royal Navy intervening, not just in halting massive slave shipments but obstructing more quotidian commerce.[139] Buoyed by British abolitionism, U.S. abolitionists continued to generate sleepless nights in Madrid and Havana alike.[140] And in Washington John C. Calhoun conferred with Madrid's delegate about a supposed "war of the races" then unwinding with the aim of maintaining the "superiority" of the "white race." Reporting to Madrid, the Spanish representative took note of his interlocutor's role in a coming split of the republic on the axis of slavery—but did not seem overly concerned. In their tour of the horizon, they expressed joint apprehension about Venezuela, but most worrisome was London and its alleged plans for domination of Cuba and the republic in league with Africans.[141] London's attempt to suppress the slave trade was viewed by its opponents as hypocritical cant, a way to cut down to size rivals and accomplish abolition indirectly.[142]

But, again, the unity of pro-slavery advocates was a mile wide—and an inch deep: not only because republicans longed to control the island but also because despite the apparent racial unity, many republicans harbored searching doubts about the racial bona fides of the Cuban elite. As a visiting invalid put it upon arrival in Trinidad, Cuba, Spaniards "are dark complexioned," which was not the best advertisement in the color-obsessed republic,[143] although the constant and beating sunshine may have been a factor in coloring visages.[144] Madrid was seen as too feudal, too anti-modern to take advantage of the possibilities provided by slavery. Visiting the island in the 1840s, the New Englander Daniel Nason was struck by the reality that the "American dispatch business—horse and cart—are unknown here. The Negroes carry most of the burdens upon their heads."[145]

Madrid was viewed—conveniently—as not being up to the task of controlling Cuba in a way that would insure the security of the republic. In 1848 future president James Buchanan spoke in favor of the island's acquisition, though he must have known it is not easy to buy what is not for sale. Still, he sent an emissary to Barcelona to tell Spanish republicans not to emancipate the enslaved of Cuba if their party secured control of Spain.[146]

Though they may not have realized it at the time, time was expiring for Madrid and Washington alike when it came to maintaining slavery in Cuba. Both powers had a justifiable concern that Faustin Soulouque, Haiti's leader, had a burning desire to extirpate slavery from the hemisphere—and, as the powers saw it, unite all Africans in a sort of "Black *Mare Nostrum*." or African Empire. The massacre of the melanin-deficient in Haiti in 1848 did little to dissuade these powers from this viewpoint. So prompted, an eminent son of Dixie concluded that Soulouque was "inciting the blacks of Cuba and Puerto Rico to rise and join him. . . . He or his successors may cause serious trouble not only in Cuba and Puerto Rico but in our own Southern States."[147]

So moved, the republic, perhaps due to enlightened self-interest, adopted a decided concern for the fate of Hispaniola, particularly the eastern half of the island, which was to secede on barely camouflaged racial grounds. Ben Green, scion of a prominent republican family, thought that his nation should "promote the immigration and settlement" in Hispaniola "of a white population friendly to the United States, rather than to permit one under the control of G. Britain."[148]

Splitting Haiti and obstructing Britain was something on which Madrid and Washington could concur, though who was to control the Bay of Samana was another matter altogether. The oft-feuding powers would either hang together—or hang separately—and it appeared that destiny was delivering the latter. Even Frederick Douglass knew of this, noting in his journal in 1849 that the republic had "probably several thousand citizens scattered throughout Cuba" and "as high as forty millions of dollars" invested there. Of late a new proviso had been promulgated that "after a residence of five years, all foreigners must either quit the island or else forswear allegiance to their own country"—which was "aimed" at republicans.[149]

Martín Delany, who may have excelled the dedicated Douglass in his throbbing interest in Cuba, assayed that of the "whites" in Cuba there were "probably fifty thousand either belonging to or formerly residents of the United States" and they were the "source and origin of all dissatisfaction that has risen against Spain." What this meant was that the Havana regime was "dependent upon the colored subjects, and the military, the mainstay of the law—the protector and defender of the Captain General and his authority, is composed of this class, both bond and free." Thus "the slave of Cuba has a right unknown to the American slave. He has a right to purchase himself whenever he so desires." Fortunately, some Spaniards "would rather see the island fall into the hands of the blacks than annexed," which provided tremendous leverage for those like Delany. Madrid, he emphasized, to obviate annexation would see that *the slaves shall be armed in and the island laid in destruction and blood.*"[150]

Douglass also noticed that "more than half of the island" had not "been reduced to tillage" and with the mounting push for annexation, there would come along with it a push to bring Africans "in large numbers from the United States," providing a further boost to enslavement,[151] though annually there were "more than fifty thousand slaves" arriving in Cuba, which led inescapably to a boost for republican slavery. "In this high-handed manner," said his abolitionist comrade Martín Delany, "the provisions prohibiting the importation of slaves into the United States after the year 1808" were a dead letter. Adding his own twist to census calculations, he estimated there were 600,000 enslaved Africans in Cuba as of 1849—and 450,000 in 1830. Thus, U.S. Negroes were in the vanguard of warning against the republicans' "perfidious wicked design" on the island. There were "more Americans directly interested in possessions in the isle of Cuba than in any other foreign territory." All the major financial interests within the republic had holdings in Cuba—but it was slavery that was "the deep and abiding interest" that glued them together.

Hence there was "but one party more interested than all others" capable of barring annexation—and that was the "colored people themselves." Turning slavery advocates' fear on its head, Douglass's periodical trumpeted that if Cuba ceased to be Spanish, it would become another Haiti and a boon to the beleaguered Africans in the hemisphere. Africans—most notably within the republic—should speak in "one united voice of solemn indignation" against annexation: this was "our heaven-required duty." And if the republicans dared to annex the island, at that "instant" should be emitted "the signal for simultaneous rebellion of all the slaves in Southern States and throughout the island."[152]

But republicans were not standing still in the face of this verbal onslaught. David Levy Yulee, soon to be elected to the U.S. Senate representing Florida, demanded annexation precisely to forestall what Delany envisioned—abolition. Worryingly, he was joined by Jamaican planters who spoke bluntly of breaking with London and aligning with the republic.[153]

But verbiage, no matter how provocative or militant, would not have the final say in Cuba: action would. By mid-1848, *The North Star* was rapturous about yet another "insurrection" on the island, led by "one Valdez, a mulatto poet" and, like Placido, said to have been collaborating with David Turnbull. Carolinians were among those frightened by these events in Matanzas: "In short, the position of Cuba, in this respect, is very critical and she may soon witness tragedies not less bloody than those which resulted in the ascendancy of the blacks in St. Domingo."[154]

CHAPTER 4

The United States to Seize Cuba
to Prevent "Africanization"?

FREDERICK DOUGLASS WAS STRUCK by what he had heard. In the spring of 1850 his journal reported with astonishment that the "number of American travelers" in Cuba "on the 20th of March was so great that the hotels could hardly contain them." Why? "Rumors are rife," the article said portentously, "of plots to revolutionize Cuba."[1] Months earlier an "armed invasion" of Cuba was nigh,[2] since "agents of the disaffected slave-owners of Cuba" were "cooperating with some of our citizens in arranging an expedition [to spur] civil war in Cuba."[3] Douglass found it curious that "hundreds and perhaps thousands of American citizens have now landed on that island and that many more are on their way," which reminded him of Texas "just prior to" the 1836 secession from Mexico. "Then as now" a steady stream of "freebooters, pirates and plunderers" were arriving on the island and, just as with Texas "great meetings" were being held in "almost all southern cities and many northern ones" with a clamor for Cuba.[4] In fact, the newly minted Lone Star State did more than just cheer for filibustering, for on 12 July 1850 250 heavily armed Texans left the ports of Corpus Christi and Galveston with the aim of aiding the freebooter and desperado Narciso Lopez in conquering Cuban.[5]

Douglass, in sum, was on to something—a revelation that would have been confirmed if he had been able to read the correspondence of the influential republican military leader George Cadwalader. The latter had been told in a "confidential" message that a provisional Cuban state already had been formed with a "president," a development for which he purportedly professed "deep sympathy." Leading this soon-to-be failed effort was Narciso Lopez, a Cuban, and unnamed "Havana planters," along with a "secret Cuban council."[6] Douglass was among those who denounced this escapade,[7] but he was not alone in sensing something sinister in it.[8] The 1850s were a decade of freebooting and filibustering, republican adventurers ranging far and wide, including attempts to snatch Nicaragua by adventurers with ties to Cuba.[9] William Walker, the leader of that effort, was accused by abolitionists of seeking to establish a base in Central America so as to better seize Cuba—"the great prize they are after."[10]

Havana should have recognized that Cuba was targeted when in 1852 William Rufus King, then resting in Guamacaro, took his oath of office as vice president of the republic there.[11] "Cuba will be ours within seven years," boasted one republican in 1853. "I met a Southerner," he said, "a Florida slaveholder, the other day . . . who told me that the plan was all cut and dried both for the acquisition of Cuba and the whole Mosquito Coast."[12]

Louisiana's powerful Pierre Soule was a driving force behind the Ostend Manifesto, which fundamentally demanded that Spain turn over Cuba or risk war, a desperate gambit deemed necessary in order to foil what was seen as the island's "Africanization," viewed as inimical to the republic's security.[13] The manifesto was not just an idle threat. After the failure of the Lopez-led venture, a few years later Douglass still found a potentially hazardous scene: "Men are nightly drilled at or near New Orleans, where a powerful secret expedition is said to be preparing against Cuba."[14] The manifesto had been prompted in part by the case of the *Black Warrior*, a U.S. vessel that arrived in Cuba in 1854 but was detained by the authorities due to paperwork defects, leading to a hefty fine. Congressman Giddings thought this case was a feint, designed to merge in the public mind the Kansas-Nebraska controversy over slavery with a presumably more popular conflict over the same issue involving Cuba, which would provide needed momentum for the former. But this would backfire since defenders of Cuba could "bring the war into this American Africa and rear the standard of freedom on our own soil, while our army shall be fighting for slavery in Cuba." In paralyzing words, he concluded, "I can easily imagine that this war which the President invokes may prove the overthrow of slavery in Cuba as well as in our own land."[15] Douglass too paid attention when a Georgia congressman demanded that Madrid relinquish Cuba, and if not, "then we should go for undisguised, open war with Cuba by force."[16] But Douglass also knew that the "flesh-mongers of the South" chose to "hesitate to swallow Cuba" since in case of war, Spain would be backed by London and Paris which would then back "emancipation." Even with a Dixie victory, Washington would then have to contend with the difficult digestion of so many free Negroes.[17] Just in case, Douglass counseled sedition in Cuba to keep the republic at bay,[18] which was already in motion with grave implications for republicans.[19]

It was such bellicose machinations that impelled his fellow abolitionist Martín Delany to capture the ideas of numerous Negroes, saying of Cuba,

"The cause is ours . . . every colored man should make common cause of it, uniting in mind, heart, sentiment and action"—that is, to rebuff the filibusters and free the island.[20]

Intoxicated by the stupefying success of the swallowing of Texas and the devastation inflicted on Mexico, the republic now turned with alacrity to Cuba. Even the irascible Carolinian William D. Valentine confided that "the invasion of Cuba by lawless [forces] from this country" was "the consequence of our success in the Mexican war"; it was a "lawless, piratical act" when the "invaders pretended to believe that the islanders were ripe for revolution."[21] A problem, however, was the staunch opposition of London to an outright seizure. However, Her Majesty had her own problems by then: containing unrest in India, digesting Hong Kong, jousting with the republic in the area surrounding what is now British Columbia, squabbling with Russia in the Crimea, which was to explode in war not long after Douglass noticed what was going on in Cuba. London's problems emboldened the republicans.[22] (Naturally, Dixie backed Russia.)[23]

The republicans had helped to create the problem they were now seeking to resolve via invasion. The tsunami of Africans arriving on the island had exacerbated an already unstable polity, creating the distinct possibility of a twin for Haiti, which an invasion could thwart. Besides, snatching Cuba was seen as necessary to bar London from doing the same; the prominent politician, statesman, and orator Edward Everett objected when Lord John Russell reportedly said that his nation had as much claim to the island as the republicans, given the proximity of Jamaica.[24]

One of the prime Cuban plotters, Ambrosio Jose Gonzales, who was close to those who were to foment secession about a decade later, addressed a U.S. audience directly (in English, in which he was fluent) as to why it was in the republic's interest to see that Madrid was ousted from the island. Cuba had "550,000 whites and 600, 000 blacks," due to a slave trade that was "carried on for the special benefit of the Queen Mother, the Captain-General, and a powerful Spanish clique at Havana" (and not republicans). This was "horrid," he cried, referring to "over half a million of human beings" brought to the island since 1826. Cuba, he advised mainlanders, was a base to "insidiously undermine American influence and prejudice American interests as is the case in Mexico at this very day." All the while, he complained, "white colonization" of Cuba was "discountenanced" so "that the threat of a colored population may be held to the Cubans." Thus, he said balefully, "we have against us not only Spain" but, as well, "France and England and the menace of the blacks."[25]

The Cuban conspirators exposed their political leanings when they offered Jefferson Davis, soon to lead Dixie into war, the command of the expeditionary forces to overthrow the regime in Cuba (he declined and recommended

Robert E. Lee,[26] turning down a reputed $100,000).[27] The offer to Davis was not a matter of happenstance, for he had long worried about alleged British designs on Cuba and what that might mean for his most cherished institution: slavery.[28] Nor was he the only prominent son of Dixie who had deemed the seizure of Cuba to be a sacred cause.[29] The U.S. envoy Thomas M. Rodney was told that the governor of Georgia and a leading republican general were "at the head" of the expedition.[30]

Subsequently, well-placed sources in Savannah reported that 250 men, mainly Kentuckians—many veterans of the war with Mexico—"sailed from a port near New Orleans" destined for Cuba. This Georgia town, like Dixie generally, was said to have "fairly quivered with excitement" at the prospect of their victory, for Lopez "had become a hero of the South."[31]

Lucy Holcombe Pickens, the spouse of South Carolina's secessionist governor, Francis W. Pickens, and one of the most renowned republican women—the only woman featured on currency of Davis's Confederacy—wrote a gung-ho novel hailing Narciso Lopez, Gonzales's comrade. Her roots were in Texas, and she too saw the island as ripe for annexation. In her roman à clef, she condemned Madrid for supposedly foisting "'the undying stain of African equality'" upon Cuba and was aghast that the Spaniards were considering "arm[ing] the dark race against their own."[32] Such fervor emanating from Dixie was a function of the fact that even without Lopez and Gonzales, these quixotic expeditions would probably have occurred anyway, so worked up were Southern elites about Cuba.[33]

As in Texas and Florida, the invasion of Cardenas had been preceded by the curious arrival on the scene of numerous mainlanders. "The town contains from 5,000 to 6,000 inhabitants, mostly Spaniards," said one of this group, "but many Americans. There are in the bay 17 Yankee brigs and boats"; a "first-rate railroad running through the principal street to the Havanna [*sic*] which is distant 126 miles" was deemed of relevance. Also noteworthy was the preexisting Negro population: "They are thick as blackbirds here," said the visiting U.S. national, Dickie Galt, with a curious combination of disgust—and satisfaction, that is, their presence was an emblem of the all-important cheap labor. He noticed that non-slave men had "either his holsters or a saber," since "they still seem to dread Lopez as more troops are daily expected here."[34]

Republicans had been casing Havana suspiciously as the date for toppling the colonial regime in Havana was arriving.[35] The expedition to Cardenas had only five Cubans aboard and among the nearly 500 involved in the Bahia Honda expedition, perhaps 10 percent were of Cuban or Spanish origin.[36]

Lopez and Gonzales were not exactly ciphers in this venture. The latter had roots in Matanzas, widely regarded as a citadel of mainland influence, and was well connected with ties extending to President James Polk, which came in handy when the time arrived to recruit veterans of the war in Mexico—brigands who were to play such a large role in the invasion of Cuba. Despite this republican participation, Gonzales was the first man ashore at Matanzas—and the first Cuban wounded. Lopez, of Venezuelan origin, knew all too well about the threat posed to slavery by his homeland and Caracas's Haitian allies. He felt that annexation would bollix the prospects for Cuban abolition and somehow bar slave revolts. When Gonzales named his son after him, it solidified further their already close tie.[37]

Gonzales, a Creole, was emblematic of those Cubans who sought to collaborate with the most retrograde of republicans. Born in Cuba in 1818, he was schooled in New York and, as suggested by his remarks above, was as anxious about "Africanization" of the island as any mainlander. Of course, he became a leading general in the so-called Confederate States of America, upon secession.[38] It was in 1855 that the swashbuckling Cuban married fifteen-year-old Harriett Elliott, herself part of a founding—and slaveowning—family in South Carolina.[39]

These failed expeditions worsened further the deteriorating bilateral Madrid-Washington relationship. Spain's legation in Washington heard of an invasion of Cuba from the mainland in the summer of 1849,[40] and in 1850 Secretary of State Daniel Webster took the extraordinary step of contacting various marshals, district attorneys, and officials of the republic warning about an upcoming invasion of Cuba to be launched from New York and New Orleans and requesting their vigilance.[41]

But alerting republican officialdom to a plot that Washington itself would have embraced if it had succeeded was hardly the way to improve relations with Madrid. By July 1850 the U.S. consul in Trinidad, Cuba, was bemoaning the reality that "a positive hatred" was the most accurate descriptor of the feeling then prevailing "amongst the Spanish part of the population here towards our Government and countrymen."[42] This opprobrium was hardly unique to Trinidad, for in Santiago de Cuba, Webster was told that "the Spanish part of the population" was now "greatly exasperated . . . against everything American. . . . There can be no doubt that attempts will be made to retaliate upon the persons and property of American resident in the island." The remedy requested—"some part of our naval force . . . being ordered to this port for our protection"—may have worsened the malady.[43] As time passed, the situation worsened with the U.S. consul complaining about how both church and state in this growing city were heaping "the most sweeping abuse" upon him, which was "widening the breach already existing between the two nations" and "exciting the hatred of the populace against us"; this did "tend to render our residence here unsafe, if not altogether impossible" since the "people" were "essentially superstitious & bigoted."[44]

In the event, the invasion failed miserably and the perpetrators were banished to a harsh imprisonment,[45] some on an island off the coast of the Yucatan,[46] signaling a Spanish-Mexican rapprochement, which was not good news in Washington—ditto for the 5,000 fresh Spanish troops ordered to Cuba. Other republicans were sent to dank prisons in Spain[47] and still others, in the ultimate indignity, were jailed in a Spanish colony in Africa. [48] Ironically, among those imprisoned at Cadiz was a man described as a "mulatto" and the "body servant of Narciso Lopez," who even the U.S. delegate in Spain admitted "can scarcely be regarded as having been a free agent in connection with the invasion of Cuba."[49] Perhaps worse for the republicans was the mainland Negro press reporting happily that in response to these incursions Madrid was to add "three thousand Negro troops" to augment those already there.[50]

One of the republicans captured with Lopez was astounded by the prominent presence of Africans on the island, particularly within the military,[51] as if their inability to detain and chain him was an outlandish reversal of fortune that had to be overturned at any cost. This hair-raising perception was confirmed when Lopez himself was executed by an African, who garroted him expertly.[52] "As the Negro executioner quickly turned the screw the victim's head fell forward," said a still stunned Dixie journalist, decades later.[53]

The presence of armed Africans in Cuba was both an outrageously dangerous provocation as far as republicans (and their Creole allies) were concerned,[54] and, as U.S. Negroes saw it, a guarantee that invasions from the mainland would flop ignominiously.[55] Unbelievably, huffed a visiting republican, "in point of civil privileges" in Cuba, "the free blacks are the equals of the whites."[56] Consequently, rumored and attempted invasions of Cuba by freebooters proliferated in the 1850s,[57] particularly after the Captain General in Havana—under British pressure—signaled emancipation for enslaved Africans who had arrived before 1835: this would create a "Negro or mongrel Empire on our borders," complained Mississippi's John Quitman.[58]

Eventually, U.S. inability to capture Cuba fed secession, in that Dixie felt that a harder core of slave states would be more forthright in challenging Madrid and London without having to take into account pesky abolitionist sentiment, such as that represented by Frederick Douglass. Yet what was curious about the still Dixie-driven republican policy was that as it pointed to the danger to white supremacy from the growing African population in Cuba, massive slave trading continued unabated, often with the ample assistance of New Orleans, in some ways Dixie's commercial capital. Since the slave trade was capitalized so heavily in Manhattan and so many of the vessels were built in Maine, and since Virginia particularly was profiting so handsomely from "breeding" Africans and the South was concerned about competition from slave-engendered produce from Cuba and Brazil, David Turnbull held out the vain hope that Dixie would unite with London to quash the slave trade. He was to be disappointed, since Dixie's overriding concern was to control Cuba as a slave state and, he said, that control was hard to obtain.[59]

It was received wisdom that Louisiana was nervous about Cuba joining the republic for fear of what it would mean for sugar planters generally.[60] Carolinian James Hammond, a celebrated hawk, while acknowledging that "if we had Cuba we could not make more than two or three slave states there," also asserted that with London hampering the slave trade, the island "besides crushing [our] whole sugar culture by her competition" could also become an outlet "for all the slaves in Missouri, Kentucky and Maryland." Eventually, this could mean "every slave in America might be exterminated in Cuba, as were the Indians"—but given the investment in enslavement, what would that mean for slaveholders?[61]

Part of the reason why the republicans were unable to snatch Cuba (island resistance and great power opposition set aside) was that the United States was hardly united in pursuing this risky proposition. Turnbull may have been better advised to play on the tensions between Spaniard and Creole, with the latter—symbolized by Gonzales—prone to collaborate with the republicans, who in turn held Madrid in contempt, a fact that Douglass well recognized.[62] Douglass underlined that "the colored population" in Cuba "has always been a source of fear to the native whites and they have endeavored by every means in their power to put an end to fresh importation of Negroes." Apparent tension between Creoles and republicans was also worthy of exploitation and at least would have tested the notion that the former were actually using their "power to put an end" to the slave trade.[63] By the same token, free Negroes in Cuba had good reason to oppose the continuing republican encroachment in Cuba, for upon arrival they sought to impose their unique folkways, particularly a rigid racial segregation.[64]

Gradually an abolitionist bloc was developing that did not include republican allies, that is, Creoles,[65] but could—or at least so thought Douglass and the influential senator, Charles Sumner[66]—include Spaniards. The Lopez-Gonzales invasion was designed to forestall this, and in the aftermath, Douglass believed that Spain—"rather than yield to the invaders"—should "free Negroes, who will fight to the death sooner than submit to American planters" and "once this slave war is commenced, *who is to guarantee that it will not spread? . . .* May not the flame of revolt," he asked, "extend to the mainland, and a slave rebellion arise in the heart of the Southern States themselves?"[67] The remarkably farsighted Congressman J. R. Giddings of Ohio agreed.[68]

Ironically, Douglass's view of Madrid's intentions was shared by Washington. Just before he issued his stunning declamation, Horatio J. Perry of the U.S. legation in Madrid stressed to President Franklin Pierce that "*Spain is* resolved, *in the last resort—if all the ordinary resources of War should fail her—to emancipate the black population of Cuba and give them arms.*" This was not just idle gossip, he emphasized: "I have been for more than three years in immediate contact with the men who rule this country," and he knew they intended "to organize & equip regiments of the blacks in Cuba under Spanish officers, and turn their arms against the Creole whites." This doomsday scenario would worsen further "should a war with the United States break out" simultaneously, which would guarantee "*this great blow of Negro emancipation may be looked upon as certain in the circumstances referred to.*"[69] Actually, London had raised an aspect of this dilemma earlier with Madrid, which the republic may have suspected and which could only increase mainland alarm.[70] As ever, a U.S. diplomat in Havana fretted about the free Negro militia—a stumbling block earlier to the taking of Florida—and had spoken with "some old Spaniards" who wondered if the United States might intervene militarily in Cuba in order to "check any atrocities" contemplated against Washington's Creole allies.[71]

At times it seemed that the republic's nervousness about the fate of their Creole allies was just a proxy for apprehension about Washington's own destiny. Charles Davis, a U.S. emissary in Havana, worried that all these Africans arriving on the island eventually "would attack the whites they hate" in league with a still feared Haiti, the "Black Empire whose example they would feel proud to imitate and whose asylum they could fly to in case they were conquered" allowing them to fight another day. The "black regiments" in Cuba were seen as not just a local problem.[72]

This was part of the paradox of U.S. policy toward Cuba in the 1850s: those seeking their own 1776 in Havana were uncomfortably close to Dixie for abolitionist tastes whereas viewing Madrid as an abolitionist force—given its history[73]—was suggestive of the abject weaknesses of mainland abolitionism, which was banking on war against slavery in Cuba to spark a revolt in the republic. Creoles supposedly were fearful about the arrival of so many Africans, yet they were allied with those very same slave dealers who were responsible for this outrage.[74] Like so many others, Secretary of State William Marcy howled about "Africanization" of the island—even blaming Spain for this—while turning a blind eye to his compatriots who were the actual perpetrators.[75] One blinkered Virginian blamed London for "Africanizing" Cuba, "rendering her . . . a dangerous neighbor but an unenviable possession," which Lord Howden deemed to be "laughable" and "strange" though "wicked."[76] Even Spain's legation in London termed this notion as no more than a pretext to rationalize filibustering.[77] Nonplussed, republicans continued to insist that the arrival of so many Africans was designed to keep Creoles in line.[78]

Frederick Douglass, furthering the paradox, cited a New Orleans journal for the proposition that acquiring Cuba without legalizing the African Slave

Trade "would result in the utter annihilation of the institution on this continent, within the brief space of twenty years or less," which would have vitiated the rationale of the much bruited republican acquisition.[79] The paradox stemmed ultimately from the reality that republicans were heightening enslavement in Cuba and though Madrid did not necessarily object to slavery in principle, they did object to the growing U.S. influence this process delivered—while seeking to keep on side the major power that was London, which happened to be abolitionist.

The awkward dance between Madrid and Washington was at the heart of the paradox with even the First Secretary in Madrid realizing that it was driven by his nation—and its island colony—being trapped between an annexationist republic and an abolitionist monarchy.[80] Douglass emphasized that Cuba beyond the grasp of Madrid or Washington "would peril the security of slavery" in the republic itself.[81] Repeatedly, republicans were coaxed into fixating obsessively on Cuba because of the fear that, if they did not, emancipation would ensue and the free Negro class in Cuba would be enlarged, providing even more danger for the mainland.[82] On the island itself, Spaniards—or *peninsulares*—and Creoles buried their conflict long enough to be mutually "hostile" to the Captain General because of his "apparent energy" in "suppressing the slave trade"—or so thought a U.S. diplomat: "The trade affects the interests of the Spaniards, as the traffic is almost exclusively confined to that race, although with the annexation of the island to the United States his occupation would cease."[83] Spaniard cooperation with republicans in enslavement, while retaining opposition to annexation, generated paradoxical ructions. Like a pendulum, when it seemed a crackdown on the slave trade was in the offing, some *peninsulares* and Creoles alike became more favorable toward annexation.[84]

Both Madrid and Washington were in favor of weakening Haiti, though the republic was nervous about Madrid's growing influence in what became the Dominican Republic.[85] Both were under enormous pressure from abolitionist forces, and the republicans desired the island that His Catholic Majesty possessed: this created taut tension that led some to conclude that Madrid was somehow a secret abolitionist and others to assert that it was the major purveyor of enslavement. In 1855, the U.S. minister in Spain, Augustus C. Dodge, demanded a Canada-type status for Cuba under U.S. suzerainty that Juan de Zavala, minister of foreign affairs, thought to be ridiculous. Dodge made it clear that his proposal was driven by fear of London and abolitionism, which were seeking to undermine republican slavery that "involved more than $1,500,000, 000 worth of property"—the heart of the economy. Zavala regretted that Cuba did not have even more slaves than it did, contravening the idea in some circles that his nation was covertly abolitionist, which seemed to be an invitation to even more smuggling of Africans by republicans as a concession to Washington's ire.[86] These tensions too generated paradox.

Unfortunately for the republic, Madrid seemed to worry even more about inflaming London's ire and was pleased when Her Majesty agreed to cooperate with His Catholic Majesty in blocking filibustering expeditions,[87] though the tradeoff—cooperation in halting importation of enslaved Africans—was a steep price to pay.[88] London pressured Havana to emancipate those Africans who had arrived illicitly, particularly after 1820, but was to be continuously disappointed.[89] London pressured Havana to move toward gradual abolition[90] and to be more aggressive in suppressing the illegal slave trade to the island— and was even more disappointed.[91] London veritably deluged Madrid during this pivotal decade with various laws and edicts from Argentina, Venezuela, and elsewhere concerning abolition and suppressing the slave trade.[92] Instead, Madrid was so upset with the abolitionist persistence of London's man in Havana, Joseph Crawford, that it demanded his removal.[93]

Crawford in turn expressed "indignation" about the "discourteous" attitude of the Captain General and his "many insults."[94] What prevented a total rupture in this tenuous tie was mutual concern about how the republic would benefit if this were to occur,[95] notably how it would inspire the always eager filibusters.[96]

John Backhouse, posted by London to Havana to monitor the slave trade, was among those who sensed the tensions at play. Havana, he said in 1853, "seems very much afraid of another Yankee invasion, or perhaps is endeavouring to raise the price of the island [should] the Yankee Govt. offer to purchase it"—but because of the former fear, there was an "actual presence in harbour here of 11 Spanish ships of war including some steamers." Yet, he wondered, "why don't some of these ships of war intercept some of the slavers that have been coming so thick lately? If they can't do that, how can they prevent a Yankee invasion?"[97] Spain had a ready—though sly—reply, arguing that it was under so much pressure from filibusters and republicans that it could hardly focus on mere slave dealers.[98]

Backhouse had raised a telling question nonetheless, suggestive that neither the pocketbook[99] nor the patience of London was inexhaustible, a point that even Madrid recognized when the abolitionist writer Harriet Beecher Stowe received a rhapsodic welcome upon arriving in Britain in 1853.[100] Madrid did not ignore the blistering accounts of their rule in Cuba emanating from the London press, replete with stories of high-level corruption and complicity in slaving and how Her Majesty was being treated like a chump: paying to keep slaves out of Cuba and paying to block a republican takeover of Cuba.[101] It "seems indeed strange," said a British representative in Havana, "that the Slave Trade can be carried on as it is, almost openly and with impunity"; thus the Captain General was complicit, given the ordinary "vigilance of the Police and Coast Guard."[102]

Still, mainland abolitionists were not wholly oblivious, for the dynamics in the 1850s were pushing toward abolition of some sort; it just so happened that it occurred first within the republic. As abolitionists saw things, the taking of Cuba was "only part of one vast scheme for the universal spread of slavery over all tropical regions."[103] Senator Sumner thought that if abolition were to occur in Cuba "the slave trade would cease & slavery itself would receive its death blow. The Slave-Power of the U.S. must then prepare to die."[104] Yet, if abolition did not occur in Cuba, he thought that it would empower Dixie "fire-eaters," inspiring them to secede while fueling "new schemes of Slavery-extension" and reopening of the slave trade—legally.[105]

By the time Sumner spoke, there were those in Florida who thought that the slave trade had opened already, so busy were slavers in peninsular waters.[106] Nearby Cuba was viewed as so essential to republican dreams that one British official thought the republicans would take the island then begin deporting part of their own enslaved population there.[107] Cuba was at the heart of the expansionist wave that earlier had swept Texas within the ambit of the republic.[108] Cuba was the fulcrum upon which the destiny of slavery rested—or so it was thought.

The stakes were sky-high, and increasingly, so was the decibel level. A fierce debate erupted in the halls of Congress in the 1850s about the fate of Cuba, though ultimately what was at issue was the fate of slavery. This debate was freighted by the weight of public opinion; thus David Campbell spoke for many when he denounced the attempt to annex Cuba since he did not "want any more mongrels in our Congress"; "we are bad enough already," he said with disgust. Soon "Central America" would be added and then "we will soon have another St. Domingo."[109] Frederick Douglass thought the United States wanted to take Cuba, convert it into two separate slave states, then take Haiti and Puerto Rico to add to this toxic mix.[110]

John Thrasher, a notorious filibuster,[111] took an opposing tack, warning that the republic had to intervene to prevent a "war of the races in Cuba," the "result" being "the utter annihilation of the black race in Cuba."[112] Increasingly macabre scenarios for Cuba were becoming par for the course among republicans, suggesting the high stakes.[113]

Just before ascending to the White House, James Buchanan was conspiring in Paris in order to acquire Cuba, arguing that it "belongs naturally" to the republic and had "become to us an unceasing danger, and a permanent cause of anxiety and alarm."[114] Contrarily, Senator Anthony Kennedy of Maryland was pro-slavery and hailed from a state notorious for its brand of bondage, yet he worried that if the United States could wage war to take Cuba and preserve slavery, why couldn't London wage war to free the slaves in the republic? Would not taking Cuba induce the same kind of turmoil that at that moment— 1859—had Kansas on bloody tenterhooks?[115] Congressman William Boyce of South Carolina objected to taking Cuba, warning about the peril of absorbing "two hundred thousand" free Negroes. There was the "startling fact" of "this army of Free Negroes" and their "special and exclusive advantages of schools" while "marriages between the two classes have been encouraged," meaning miscegenation with Spaniards. But again and again republicans like Boyce returned angrily to military matters: "What is more striking," he added disbelievingly, was that "free Negroes have been enrolled in the military, taught the use of arms and instructed in military tactics, while the Creoles have been regularly excluded from the army." This was "most dangerous" and was "not auguring well for the institution of slavery." There was a "volcano" on the island since "the slave who can change his master when he pleases is hardly a slave, he is almost free"—and that's what he detected in Cuba. Spaniards were playing a dangerous game, he thought, establishing a most peculiar institution of slavery that hung "like a portentous cloud" over the hemisphere, which had frightening long-term repercussions. He wondered if under pressure from London, Havana would free all enslaved Africans brought to the island since 1820—the majority, he said—which would maximize the peril for the republic. Besides, the vaunted Creoles were unreliable: "Slavery is never secure," he maintained, "where the masters are an inferior white race." There was too much "ultraism [*sic*]" on the island among Creoles and Spaniards alike that tended toward the "extreme of anarchy" and even "socialistic revolution," he contended with horror. Besides, Dixie was on the verge of a "great struggle with the hostile majority of the North and we will need all our resources" and should not divert same to Cuba. Instead of fighting Spain, it should become a collaborator against the mutual foe in London—and with the addition of Russia, still smarting over their tiff in the Crimea, Her Majesty could be neutralized, if not defeated.[116]

Again, Congressman Giddings warned that waging war to take Cuba would cause London—and Paris too—to bring war to the mainland itself.[117] Subsequently, General Lewis M. Ayer of the republic also objected to taking Cuba since it would bring U.S. borders closer to Haiti and Jamaica, a potential disaster: "The bitterest enemy of the South could not concoct a more infernal contrivance to delude and ruin her."[118]

On the other hand, his colleague Senator Stephen Mallory of Florida was miffed at opposition to taking Cuba and the characterization of it as a "sectional issue" pushed by Dixie. Cuba as a U.S. state had been a priority since earlier in the century, he said, a "necessary consequence" of the Louisiana Purchase. He too worried that Cuba was a target for British abolitionists, bringing these energetic forces dangerously close to the mainland—another "St. Domingo," that is, "a free black colony under [London's] protection at the doors of the Southern States," which was not unlikely since "she has twice attempted to get Cuba secretly" in an attempt to create a "Gibraltar" under the republic's nose.[119] Congressman Volney Howard of Texas was fuming at alleged attempts to convert Cuba into a "Second St. Domingo" by the "great European powers" since "Cuba is far more necessary to us than Gibraltar or Malta is to England."[120] Congressman Lawrence Keitt of South Carolina dismissed the notion that seizing an island with such a large number of Free Negroes was "dangerous" since if they proved to be not "tractable," their "residence in the island" would be "terminated."[121]

Congressman M. S. Latham of the recently admitted state of California hedged, conceding the need for a takeover of Cuba but worrying that if Spain managed to effectuate abolition beforehand, a "considerable" republican military force would be needed to "protect the lives of the white inhabitants" and, in any case, annexation could spur messy "sectional struggles."[122]

Senator John Slidell of Louisiana argued that like falling dominoes, Cuba logically should follow Florida and Texas into the republic. He dismissed sectional concerns about "mixture of races" there since "the feeling of caste or race is as marked in Cuba as in the United States. The white Creole," he assured, "is as free from all taint of African blood as the descendant of the Goth on the plains of Castile"; besides, "hundreds of their youths" were "in our schools and colleges," and though they may have objected to the reputed 30,000 Africans arriving annually via the slave trade, this was due to their opposition to the Spaniards, who supposedly were the prime beneficiary. This trade "would cease to exist the moment we acquire possession of the Island of Cuba,"[123] a strange conception that was ironically endorsed by certain abolitionists.[124]

When Senator Jacob Collamer of Vermont took the floor on 21 February 1859 as sectional conflicts raged that would shortly explode in civil war, he was interrupted repeatedly—at times angrily—as the matter of seizing Cuba was debated. He worried that bringing more Africans to Cuba—10,000 annually was his figure for recent years—would mean more free Negroes and more problems for the republic: but Senator Judah Benjamin interjected to say the figure was "twenty-five thousand." Undeterred, the Vermonter then asserted that the price of enslaved Africans—now $500 per head, he opined—could be impacted by taking Cuba but Senator Slidell said the figure was "$850." Undaunted, Senator Collamer wondered if snatching the island would mean Africans costing "$2000"? Plus, he added, the so-called breeding states, Maryland and Virginia, did not want Cuban competition that could incite conflicts in Dixie itself. Besides, what about adding a mostly Catholic island to the republic? And would taking Cuba lead to a kind of domino theory whereby the United States would feel compelled to take the Bahamas, then Haiti and Venezuela?[125]

Actually, it was as if some Dixie politicos were bolstering their region in contemplation of secession, when they advocated taking Cuba,[126] a perception gleaned from the heavy push for the island generated from the slave states.[127] This prospect had occurred to Frederick Douglass, who warned against Russia joining the republic in a war against Britain and France with the aim of wrangling Cuba in the process, since "in the event of a dissolution of the Union," this "would enable them [Dixie] to become a *naval* power [and] would give them the command of the coasting and Gulf trade."[128] At a disunion meeting in Worcester in 1857, the talk was that "another Union shall be formed with the Spanish slaveholders of Cuba"—and ousting non-slave states.[129]

John Quitman, a comrade of Lopez and Gonzales, was thinking along parallel lines. He was so "deeply agitated" about the "perilous" condition of the republic, as suggested by the perceived pusillanimity over Cuba, that he was "fully satisfied that no Southern statesman can honestly and consciously discharge his duties to his country, without subjecting his name, his character and his reputation to obloquy and abuse."[130] By 1856 he was on his way to Kansas with 2,000 men, determined to make it a slave state and driven by the failure to accomplish the same in Cuba.[131]

Alexander Stephens, who was to become Jefferson Davis's vice president, was unequivocal: "As for myself," he said in mid-1854, "I am for Cuba and I think if our citizens see fit to go and rescue the island from Spanish misrule and English abolition policy they ought not to be *punished* by us for so doing" and "if the people then resist I am for aiding them." As he sized up the situation, this was necessary to prevent "another St. Domingo struggle and any American in my opinion should feel a sympathy for his own race. I am against Cuba becoming a *Negro state*."[132]

Davis himself, speaking in his home state of Mississippi, echoed these words, arguing that in taking the island there should be deployed a "force so large as to admit of simultaneous debarkation at every port, that resistance should be crushed by a single blow and the fiendish threat to renew in Cuba the scenes of San [*sic*] Domingo be put to rest before its execution should be attempted."[133]

All the while, the powerful slave-trading faction was busily dumping Africans in Cuba—with some making their way to the mainland—which was raising fears about another Haiti. But incorporating a Haiti into the republic seemed to be a recipe for disaster, though that was precisely what some were advocating. This set the stage for the decadal debate of "Africanization," the Ostend Manifesto, and the diplomatic mission of Pierre Soule[134] and other matters implicating the island, which had converted Cuba into a trigger of civil war on the mainland.[135]

But driving all items on the agenda was the continuing participation of U.S. nationals in delivering enslaved Africans to Cuba, for this had even captured the attention of ordinarily somnolent Washington journalists,[136] The Manhattan press, and British diplomats alike.[137] Yet elected officials in Louisiana had the temerity to debate a resolution reproving the "intention of Spain to 'Africanize' the island of Cuba by the emancipation of their slaves" and expressing "our disapprobation of the tolerance shown by the present Federal Administration by its non-interference."[138] Unsurprisingly, mainland Negroes were infuriated.[139]

British abolitionists concluded that from 1841 to 1855 "not less than 10,000" Africans annually were arriving in Cuba and "not less than 150,000" all told. Like others, they too saw that this could prove to be a catastrophic triumph for slaveholders, as it laid the basis for a "servile war," a prospect that in turn alarmed Dixie.[140] At no other period have so many slaves been introduced as in the "first six months of the present year," said Don Mariano Torrente in 1853.[141] This horrific commerce to Cuba, said London's delegation in Spain in late 1855, was now "carried on with more boldness than has ever been known hitherto in that island."[142] There was "more than its customary activity" when it came to the slave trade, said the British legation in Madrid in early 1856.[143] British diplomats found that republican slave traders had become so incautious that they were trading shares openly on the Havana stock exchange.[144]

Yet when efforts finally were made to prosecute this illegality, for example, in Baltimore in 1857, defendants were acquitted, leading London's consul to lament "how difficult it is to ensure conviction in such cases in this community."[145] Instead in that same year of 1857, a naturalized U.S. national of Portuguese origin—Joao Alberto Machado—was reported by authoritative sources to be smuggling hundreds of Africans regularly from Angola to Cuba.[146]

Republicans had seized upon the outbreak of the war in the Crimea and the diversion of the British fleet to escalate slaving and their dream of annexation.[147] Republican boldness toward Cuba was also incited by the instability that gripped Hispaniola and the unsteady emergence of the Dominican Republic: that Spain sought to reclaim Santo Domingo was upsetting in Washington, though viewed by many in the republic as a great leap forward from rule by Port-au-Prince. After all, the republic had no quarrel with Madrid's conclusion that it was unacceptable that those defined as "white" faced handicaps in Haiti they did not encounter in what was to become the Dominican Republic.[148]

The problem was that the republic considered itself better placed to rule in Hispaniola than His Catholic Majesty. By way of sharp contrast, Senator Albert Gallatin Brown asserted that "with Cuba and St. Domingo, we could control the production of the tropics and with them, the commerce of the world."[149]

Meanwhile, British representatives in Havana continued to carp about slavers departing from "New York . . . Charleston and New Orleans" under the guise of propriety, then taking on an otherwise reviled "Spaniard" who upon arrival in Africa "superintends the getting on board [the] slave equipments and cargo, together with a slave crew"—and all head to Cuba.[150] The numbers of Africans arriving in Cuba on U.S.-flagged vessels were so staggering that the chief British diplomat in Havana hastened to assure in 1853 that he was "exceedingly careful" in detailing this commerce.[151] Even the top U.S. envoy in Trinidad, Cuba, seemed stunned to report in mid-1854 that "three cargoes of slaves amounting to upwards of fifteen hundred have been landed within a few days near the port."[152]

"The slave trade still goes on profitably," said one visiting republican to Cuba at the same time, "and for the most part in American bottoms, sailing under the American flag." The "frequent advertisement in the Havana journals," he added knowingly, "of 'a new handsome and swift American barque, entirely ready for sea' has a meaning easy to be mastered." He pointed to one region of the island as "the promised land of the small planters of Kentucky and Virginia" since "many of these properties yield princely revenues and are worked by 'gangs' of slaves, much larger than are common in the American States."[153]

London had more than a passing interest in this matter of bonded labor since republicans were increasingly seizing British subjects by dint of means most deviously foul and enslaving them.[154] Meanwhile, republican diplomats in Trinidad, Cuba, were reporting gleefully that "British cruisers" were "perfect nullities as far as capturing slaves is concerned" and their "zeal" had "wonderfully subsided of late."[155]

By 1856 it was reported that the slave trade to Cuba perpetrated disproportionately by U.S. citizens "was never prosecuted with greater energy than at present";[156] this was repeated in 1857 with the addendum that "the great haunt of these vessels [is] the River Congo."[157] London complained bitterly about the lethargy of the U.S. squadrons in African waters,[158] supposedly slated to arrest this commerce, which would have been difficult in any case, for in the 1850s U.S. slavers more than ever began rounding the Cape of Good Hope and heading to Mozambique, Madagascar, and their environs.[159] There Africans cost a mere $28, making for stupendously ballooning profits in Cuba[160]—not to mention the mainland. "The profit on victims who can be sold in Cuba," said one republican, was "at from six hundred to seventeen hundred per cent profit," which, he added with gross understatement, "amply repays the great expenses of these horrible speculations."[161]

Even pro-bondage Senator Stephen Mallory of Florida conceded that U.S. ships as late as 1859 were sailing for Angola, buying Africans for as little as $70, then selling same for almost $1,200 in Cuba.[162]

This in turn was fueling trade between the island and the mainland [163] and growth in the newer Cotton Belt in Texas, since slave prices in Cuba were still cheaper than on the mainland.[164] Aiding this process was the leading U.S. diplomat, Thomas M. Rodney, who arranged to send prime tobacco seeds from Matanzas to the mainland.[165] Across the straits in Florida, sugar was failing to become the equal of cotton as a profit center due in part to competition from Cuba and Louisiana.[166] But with the slavery-fueled growth on the island, Florida filled the breach by boosting its cattle industry, which exported beef to Cuba. This began in 1858 and by 1860 four hundred head a month arrived in Havana butcher shops. In turn Key West competed with Cuba as a transit point to the California goldfields, which brought attention to its then tiny tourist market.[167]

Things seemed to be going so swimmingly for the republicans in Cuba that the affluent Pennsylvanian Sidney George Fisher claimed in 1857 that "investments in sugar planting" were so "immensely profitable" and "American capital & enterprise" were so "rapidly going to the island" that "in twenty years it will be completely Americanized without annexation."[168] The popular writer Richard Henry Dana noted approvingly that "Cuba contains more good harbors than does any part of the United States south of Norfolk,"[169] which augured well for future commerce.

Perversely, the more some republicans nattered on about "Africanization," the more some republicans carted Africans away from their home continent to Cuba. This neologism was a reflection of this reality and, as well, a demographic trap slavery encountered due to "breeding" of Africans: this praxis honed on the mainland resulted in high birth rates that tended to dwarf those of non-slaves.[170] In Manchester abolitionists worried that the "breeding states" of the mainland—Virginia, for example—would ship Africans to Cuba, which "would be essentially identical with a foreign slave trade" and would "seriously menace the peace, security and freedom of the free colored communities of the whole of the West India islands."[171]

Moreover, as the attack on Fort Sumter approached, British diplomats claimed that the slave trade was executed "to an extent hardly exceeded in the most flourishing period of that inhumane and detestable traffic,"[172] while "scandalous abuse" of the "American flag" continued, notably in "the great slave mart" that was the "River Congo" basin.[173] Some republicans were in high dudgeon when confronting British vessels seeking to halt their illicit activity.[174] President Buchanan blamed Cuba for "the late serious difficulties" with London, which "could never have arisen had Cuba not afforded a market for slaves," which compelled Britain to demand "the right of search" of U.S.-flagged vessels.[175] In response London was outraged when it was revealed that their possessions—for example, the Caymans—were being used as a staging ground by U.S. slavers to deliver Africans to Cuba.[176]

Predictably, some of these Africans wound up landing in Charleston,[177] though Cuba was the preferred destination of these ships. Frederick Douglass, whose passion for Cuba has been noted,[178] asserted that the "impunity" accorded this commerce caused it to expand and included indigenes from the Yucatan.[179] As the Civil War was slithering closer, it seemed that it would be preempted by an attack on the republic by an exasperated London, which became more aggressive in combating U.S. slavers.[180] London only blocked a small percentage of the enslaved Africans crossing the Atlantic to Cuba, which suggested that the republic was merely fattening the island for eventual plucking—which could then become a base to launch attacks against Jamaica and other British holdings.[181] To that end, by the spring of 1859, Douglass offered the opinion that "it is easier to land a cargo of Negroes from Africa on that island than a barrel of flour."[182]

Africans in Cuba did not require advice in rebelling against slavery, with the resultant ripples being so far-reaching that they ensnared a visiting British diplomat, sent to Havana to monitor the slave trade.[183] A mainland visitor found the "whip too zealously applied" on the enslaved, then detected the result: "Yesterday morning a Negro was to be garroted for killing his master."[184] Another visitor to Cuba in 1856 was stunned to observe that the Africans had such a "deep-rooted hatred for this American production," that is, sugarcane, that "they will not sweeten the least drop of water with cane sugar."[185]

Rosa Phinney, daughter of a Rhode Island governor, lived on a Cuban sugar plantation during this time and noted ruefully that "they make nothing of killing people and throwing them into the cane fields or stripping them. . . . Which would not be so pleasant, you know. Theodore [spouse] never goes out without a pistol in his hand and ready to fire. . . . What would you think of sleeping with a pistol at the head of your bed every night?" and "It is always worse around Christmastime." "Just think, Theodore and Elizabeth are the only white persons I have spoke to since I got here."[186]

Things were so horrid for Africans on the island that one visitor noticed the use of the aphorism "miserable as a Negro."[187] But Africans were also making life miserable for their opponents, which had not escaped the attention of arriving republicans. Expert poisonings were rampant, for example, a skill that could easily survive a journey across the straits.[188] These Africans in Cuba in turn were simply emulating their brethren in Africa who were resisting enslavement with a growing ferocity. This was complicating demented Dixie dreams,[189] while torturously regenerating the idea of the island as a seat of African restiveness that had to be subjugated, lest it subvert the republic itself.

CHAPTER 5

Slavery Ends in the United States—and Cuba?

M ARY CHESTNUT WAS BEAMING.
This spouse of a former U.S. senator was a grand dame of elite
South Carolina society that was then in the throes of prosecuting a
bloody rebellion against Washington in order to preserve slavery (she and her
husband owned hundreds of Africans). Yet in August 1861 she was ecstatic to
be in the company of Ambrosio Gonzales: "a handsome Spaniard—Cuban—
leader of rebellion there too" was her generous description. He was a "fine
person" and "has a fine voice. He sings divinely" and was well-connected too
within the so-called Confederate States of America, the slaving entity to which
they both had sworn allegiance. Gonzales, who was on intimate terms with
Robert E. Lee, the bloodthirsty commander of CSA military forces, administered the all-important Tredegar Iron Works in Richmond—cradle of the Confederacy—which manufactured the cannon that sent many a U.S. soldier to his
death. Gonzales was a general in the military as well and chief of artillery in the
Palmetto State and in that capacity was responsible for numerous casualties.[1]

The Civil War on the mainland was of similar consequence for the island,
providing a boost to abolition, which was one reason why a number of Cubans
threw in their lot with the rebels. Actually, an undetermined number of Cubans
participated on both sides of this painful conflict.[2] In any case, secession was
a shock only to those who were not paying sufficient attention, for as early as
1856 one premature Dixie patriot warned that his region was seeking to "ally
herself with Russia, with Cuba and Brazil" as an alternative to the Union.[3]
Unsurprisingly, a Dixie journal said cheerily in 1862 that Spain "is the natural
ally of the South. If the South has had a friend from the beginning of her troubles, it has been Spain."[4] Madrid was the final European nation to withdraw
belligerent status from the CSA,[5] though Havana did not envision contraven-
tion of this when it pledged neutrality between the contending parties.[6]

Madrid was in a bind. Though it would not mind the splitting of a major rival, it was nervous about the North's and South's respective intentions, while Washington considered Spain as possibly its most dangerous enemy excepting Dixie itself.[7] Madrid was not unsympathetic to either balkanization of their republican rival or survival of slavery but was concerned that a fortified Dixie could resume its seemingly inexorable quest for Cuba.[8] The mainland too was in a quandary, for even the most fervent sons and daughters of Dixie suspected that if Cuba were to be ruled from Washington, or even Richmond, enslaved Africans could more readily be diverted to the island, converting even a stalwart like Virginia into a de facto free soil area, perversely strengthening the Union.[9]

Still, though Havana was as generous to Dixie as could be expected, after all, there had to be anxiety about retaliation from Washington. The CSA military leader Raphael Semmes was among those displeased with Cuba's stance, which only hardened Madrid's skepticism toward secession. "I planned a very pretty little quarrel between the Confederate States and Spain in case the former should be successful in establishing their independence," he confessed later. "Cuba, I thought, would make us a couple of very respectable States, with her staples of sugar and tobacco and with her similar system of labor."[10] His feelings were congruent with those of a New Yorker whom a republican visitor encountered in Cuba during the war. Like others of his ilk, he visited home "for two months every summer" where his wife and children continued to reside. "He says he was a great abolitionist several years ago when he first came here," said Mary Davis, but now in the redolent Cuban atmosphere, he changed his mind about slavery: "No man with two eyes could help seeing they were the happiest class of working poor people in the world." She spoke to a Cuban who insisted he "was not a Spaniard!" then insisted further that the island "was a place for 'niggers' but not for gentlemen. To all of which I agree," she proclaimed intensely.[11] A fellow republican, C. H. Rogers, did not disagree when he said around the same time that "the laws of Cuba in regard to slavery are so stringent and rigidly enforced that the slaves on this island are exempt from many of the abuses they receive in the Southern States."[12]

For various reasons Ms. Davis and Mr. Rogers were not unique in choosing to visit Cuba at this fraught moment—with uncertainty as to the course of the war, dreams of more slave-induced wealth, etc., republicans were crossing the straits steadily. This struck John Abbott, who as the war approached was aboard a ship to Cuba along with a "Cuban planter" and "his brother, a Mississippi planter." He encountered yet another seeker of slave-induced wealth who "said that for a respectable plantation in Cuba, one needed two thousand acres of land and two hundred Negroes"—neither of which was that difficult to obtain. An "able-bodied slave would readily bring 1,500 dollars and the planter generally preferred those freshly imported from Africa to those who were natives of Cuba," which was a clarion call for mainland slave dealers and builders of slave ships.[13] This also proved to be a boon to certain Manhattan businesses, for example, Brown Brothers, which by 1862 engaged in booming business in Havana.[14]

Equally unsurprising was that after the Civil War concluded, Cuba was wracked with a similarly devastating conflict that stretched from 1868 to 1878.[15] Once the flow of enslaved Africans on U.S. vessels to Cuba was curtailed, Havana's model of development was cramped, which ineluctably forced capital into labor-saving machinery—and, to a degree, bonded Chinese labor—which upset the apple cart of class relations instigating revolt.[16]

After the U.S. Civil War, Creoles contended that it was they—unlike Madrid and their island allies—who backed Washington, maintaining that it was "El Siglo, a Havana paper that represented the liberals of the Cuban party" that "used to applaud with enthusiasm the triumphs of the Federal army." It was they who after the war pushed a reluctant Madrid toward emancipation: "Accordingly, one of the first acts of Carlos Manuel Cespedes in October 1868 was to proclaim the abolition of slavery."[17]

"Overthrow slavery here," said a mainland abolitionist in 1864, "and you overthrow it everywhere—in Cuba, Brazil and wherever a slave clanks his chain"[18]—which proved to be prescient. It was not long after slavery was abolished in the United States that Madrid began receiving tips on how to accomplish the same in Cuba from both London and Washington.[19]

In other words, the U.S. Civil War split the island, just as it divided the mainland, a result that greeted the U.S. diplomat Albert G. Riddle when he arrived in Matanzas as the bloodbath plodded on. He well knew that pro-bondage Cubans were busily engaged in "blockade running," assisting their slaveholding colleagues in evading Washington's embargo. He did not avoid the CSA envoy there but dined with him "daily"—though he was not universally popular: "My position made me sought by all the Cubans and avoided by all the Spaniards, whom every Cuban hated with an ardor and consecration which gave me a new conception of hatred," he underscored. "This was more than fully reciprocated by their masters" and "apparently they hated us with the same ardor which they cherished for the Cubans who had a boundless love and devotion for us."[20]

These dueling hatreds fueled what was already a horrific conflagration. Dixie received a foretaste of what happens when the deck is reshuffled. Louisiana lost sugar markets in the North to Cuba after secession. Could the North rule out wholly the prospect of a merger between Dixie and Cuba on the platform of slavery (or even a kind of antislavery) in order to corner Washington?[21] Things had changed so dramatically that by October 1861 U.S. abolitionists were speculating as to whether Spain and the CSA would "proclaim emanci-pation" in *"self defense."*[22] Still, President Abraham Lincoln had surmised in January 1861 that his nation "will have to take Cuba as a condition upon which they [Dixie] will stay in the Union"[23]—suggestive of the unrestrained lust for slavery expansion to Cuba that was to cloud thinking in the CSA. It was the failure of the republic to take Cuba, said a concurring Jefferson Davis before launching secession, that convinced him that the United States was no longer safe for slaveholders. When he addressed a state convention in Mississippi in 1859, he spent more time grousing about Cuba than on the presumably more pressing matter of expanding enslavement into the territories of the mainland.[24]

In 1860, for example, meeting in Charleston, the Democratic Party dis-cussed at length its long-standing desire to effectuate the "acquisition" of Cuba.[25] In that vein, Madrid increased the number of its troops in Cuba from 19,000 in 1853 to 30,000 by 1859.[26] Cuba exported to the United States about five times the dollar amount of goods she imported, as the war was about to begin, which induced a remarkable consensus across sectional lines that it should no longer be controlled from Madrid.[27]

Nonetheless, Havana officialdom allowed CSA vessels to land in local ports, which was seen as de facto recognition of secession.[28] Reportedly, 100 CSA ships docked in Cuba in 1862 alone.[29] Cuban ports, especially Havana, provided repairs and safe harbors for CSA vessels.[30] CSA activity in Cuba was so industrious that by 1864 the U.S. emissary in Bermuda thought that vessels from Dixie were about to abandon this British possession altogether for the more favorable environment that was Havana.[31] The role of Cuba was so pivotal during the war that contestation with London over the role of the island almost led Washington into a potentially game-changing conflict[32] that could have bailed out the CSA.[33] Ultimately, Washington felt compelled to warn Madrid bluntly that what it deemed to be too warm an embrace of the CSA was forcing the Union to more actively intervene in the internal affairs of the island, which imperiled both slavery and colonialism,[34] the dangers to which materialized dramatically after 1865. So warned, the Spanish consul in Charleston by May 1865 was debating the fate of Francis Montaner y Morey, a resident of that city who commuted regularly to Cuba, conducting business for a Spanish firm with facilities on the mainland and island, They advised that "he has never directly or intentionally committed any acts hostile to the United States Government," though their careful wording suggested a differ-ent interpretation.[35]

Madrid did not remove its diplomats from Dixie once the war commenced and, instead, these men monitored the bloodiness closely,[36] paying careful attention to the blockade, ship journeys, troop movements, trends in Florida and the like.[37] There was much to monitor since New York's trade with Cuba and the region doubled during wartime with weapons of all kinds, ammunition, railroad iron, telegraphic equipment, shoes, blankets, provisions, medicines, and even ships, purchased for blockade running, entered the Confederacy as a direct result.[38] Blockade runners were buying rum for seventeen cents per gallon in Cuba and selling it for $25 per gallon in Florida.[39]

Major General Leonidas Polk, writing from Kentucky, reported contentedly in late 1861 that arms from Cuba had reached CSA forces.[40] One Charleston druggist evaded the blockade and obtained a large supply of leeches from Cuba, one of many merchants who made a small fortune by way of trade with the island.[41] J. A. Diaz in Montgomery, Alabama, offered the finest Cuban cigars from his shop at 38 Market Street.[42] In 1861 an impressed visiting Londoner commented enthusiastically that Cuba was "probably enjoying a larger extent of prosperity than any country in the world," which suggested that it was "vain to expect the African slave trade can be extinguished."[43]

This boom was due to figures like James Roberts, a British subject sailing out of New Orleans on a hefty 102-ton New Jersey-built vessel with a crew that included Spaniards. The latter came aboard in Havana on a journey that was to end at Matamoros, Mexico—then possibly on to Texas. The ship's cargo included 108 bags of coffee, numerous cases of cigars, and fifty sacks of salt, sulphuric acid, nails, and gunpowder among other items. Roberts had been involved in such blockade running for some time, generally between New Orleans and Havana, before he was captured within hailing distance of Louisiana after a great gale stretching over forty-eight hours blew them off course. A Spanish crew member actually resided in Charleston with his family and confessed that he thought he was on his way to Brazil. Intriguingly, found on board were numerous Spanish military documents.[44]

This case, which would end up in a U.S. court, was one of many during the war, with others involving vessels bound for Matanzas from North Carolina containing items ranging from rice to molasses. Another vessel seized was running between Mobile and Havana carrying quicksilver, printing paper, cigarettes, whiskey, and coffee. "I was born in the state of Kentucky," said crew member Theodore Lewis, and "I am a citizen of that portion of the United States now called the Southern Confederacy."[45] Another vessel from London to Cardenas, Cuba, was said to contain "Long Enfield Guns," along with "British rifled muskets with triangular bayonets," "16 cases [of] Brunswick rifles," and "15 cases of cavalry sabers."[46]

Yet another detained vessel had a rich haul, including "four tons of powder and also 1,008 loaded shells," along with "some 600,000 ball cartridges" and countless "bales of gray army cloth"—the cloth of CSA uniforms. This ship was captured twenty-five miles from Key West and had aboard various flags; it elicited the apt comment from Earl Russell in London that "every cargo which runs the blockade and enters Charleston is worth a million of dollars and that the profit on these transactions is immense." Apparently it had embarked from Cardenas, a key port for this kind of business.[47] The record tends to reveal commerce between Dixie and Cuba that was intercepted, though it is apparent that such was a small percentage of the overall trade.[48]

Given recent history, Madrid could also not afford to be indifferent to the steady stream of visitors from the mainland, who continued to arrive in Cuba even as the war approached—and continued. Matanzas continued to be a favored site for these visitors, particularly at the appropriately named hotel, the "Carolina House."[49] Some of these erstwhile tourists seemed to be scrutinizing the area as a potential site of exile, depending on how the war ended. Some Northern visitors, now writhing in disgust at what the tolerance of slavery had delivered, questioned if Africans in Cuba would be better or worse off under the Stars and Stripes.

Julia Ward Howe, like others, compared U.S. slavery invidiously to that of Cuba, though she acknowledged that the "sugar smells of the blood of the slaves." "Some of the wealthiest and most important families," she said with shock, "are of mixed blood" while "the Public Executioner of Havana" was a "Negro" and did away with those who could be deemed "white"—unimaginable on the mainland. Like others, she thought that Havana tended "to favor the Negroes and allow them definite existence as a third class, which would be likely to [support] the Government in case of civil war," that is, to set "loose the slaves throughout the island, at the first symptom of rebellion, that they may turn all their old rancor against their late masters."[50]

Among the mainland analysts of Cuba who were becoming ever more concerned with how the island would impact the trajectory of slavery were U.S. Negroes. Foremost among these was Martín Delany, who adopted Cuba as a special cause; as the war crept closer, he published his novel *Blake*, probably the most important work of fiction by an African during this era, which implicitly suggested that it was the island that would lead to the downfall of slavery on the mainland. In blistering terms, he denounced the racially rancid attitudes of the United States that increasingly had polluted Cuba, with a particular focus on "the planters near Matanzas," who "generally being Americans" were a "restless, dissatisfied class, ever plotting schemes to keep up excitement in the island." Looking back nostalgically at Placido, the hero of La Escalera, Delany's hero was made to say to him, "Cousin, don't you know me?"—he had returned to Cuba after a sojourn on the mainland and now had arrived to "help to free my race." He was among those who were bent on establishing a "Negro government" in Cuba while ousting colonialism and freeing slaves on both sides of the straits.[51] Sounding a theme that was to resonate throughout coming decades, Delany posited that racism in Cuba had been exacerbated with the arrival of more mainlanders.[52] His fictional Placido was made to assert that "as bad as things were before, since the advent of these Americans in the colony, our people have scarcely an hour of peaceful existence."[53]

Delany's creation could have added that the trend that had begun decades earlier—mainlanders shipping Africans en masse to Cuba—had shown no surcease with the roaring of the guns at Fort Sumter. Just before this armed assault, the British emissary in Havana observed that the "slave trade" continued on a "most extensive scale" with "more persons even of capital and influence engaged in it than ever"; the vessels were "mostly ... American built" and departed from the United States; the "number of Spanish ships has consequently become quite small," he said.[54]

According to one contested account, perhaps 750,000 enslaved Africans had been dragged to Cuba from the time that the republicans had taken Florida into the Civil War, overwhelmingly because of the ministrations of U.S. nationals, with even some free Negroes on the island being forced to retreat to servitude as an outgrowth of this brutal process.[55] Official British estimates were that 30,000 Africans had arrived in Cuba in 1859 alone,[56] while London abolitionists argued that "forty thousand Negroes were imported into Cuba in 1860–61" alone. "It costs the taxpayer of Great Britain one million sterling annually in efforts to extinguish this traffic in human beings," and the war-torn republic knew that neither the treasury nor the patience of the Crown was inexhaustible.[57] One scholar estimated that one million Africans were brought to Cuba over the centuries, with a whopping 450,000 alone between 1820 and 1864.[58] Yet despite this massive population movement, by one account there were only 370,000 enslaved Africans in Cuba (including only 60,000 females) in 1865, suggestive of the high mortality rate that accompanied this bloodily distorted process.[59]

As late as 1868, a slaver was caught on the River Congo by British authorities "with 96 slaves on board" and with 700 more Africans reportedly poised for a similar embarkation. "Slave dealers have not yet given up the idea of introducing slaves into Cuba," it was said with disconsolation.[60] Even the U.S. Navy noticed in 1870 that this iniquitous commerce continued "on the southeast coast" of Africa where "no less than 40,000 slaves are carried off annually."[61]

A U.S. naval officer, Robert Wilson Schufeldt, speaking of Cuba, reported in 1861 that "it is a notorious fact that more Negroes have been landed since January 1860 than the aggregate of the previous five years," and a "moderate estimate places the number at 50,000" in a year. It was no less "humiliating" a "confession" to acknowledge—it was "beyond question," he insisted—"that nine-tenths of the vessels engaged in the slave trade are American." Equally problematic was the direct participation of U.S. diplomats—continuing the handiwork of Nicholas Trist—in this illicit commerce. No left-winger he, Schufeldt worried about the island becoming "Africanized" and wrung his hands about "the eternal Law of Compensation" being fulfilled, whereby the "Master & the Tyrant of tomorrow will surely become the slave or the victim of tomorrow" with Cuba headed heedlessly toward "rapine & destruction—& finally in the barbarism of another San Domingo."[62]

Less gloomily, Frederick Douglass too concluded in 1861 that Cuba "is fast becoming Africanized and must ultimately pass into the hands of a free colored race."[63] Douglass would not have been surprised by the 1861 report from Spain's Vice Consul in Sierra Leone that a U.S.-built vessel had just been detained by a British cruiser as it was prepared to traffic in slaves.[64] Nor would he have been surprised by a report from Cadiz late in the same year about U.S. vessels engaged in slaving.[65]

By late 1862, Frederick Douglass estimated that 40,000 Africans were pouring into Cuba annually.[66] So many Africans were arriving that, typically, mainlanders were both enjoying the immense profits and worrying about the consequences in terms of revolts.[67] In its latter stages—most vividly—this inhuman commerce was decidedly in the best interests of Dixie, providing more free labor, and it took a while for Washington to realize that its well-worn policy of tolerating this now was virtually suicidal.

In an astonishing spurt, Florida's enslaved population increased by an eye-popping 298.2 percent between 1830 and the onset of the Civil War, and it was difficult to separate this dramatic increase from trends just across the straits.[68] By the 1860s Florida's population was estimated to be about 47 percent African, and given this group's penchant for allying with invaders against slaveholders, this held dangerous potential for national security.[69]

Delany had, in a sense, anticipated this trend, noting in his novel that "the American steamers plying between Havana and New Orleans, as a profitable part of their enterprise, are actively engaged in the slave trade between the two places," amounting to a "legal traffic of masters removing their slaves,"[70] confirming his earlier supposition that the island was the "great key-of-entry to the United States."[71]

The slave trade to Cuba had become big business; in 1861 Douglass detected what others had pointed to earlier, that there was a well-capitalized firm based in Havana with close ties to Manhattan whose sole purpose was bringing even more Africans to Cuba.[72] A glut of U.S.-built vessels—and customarily avid slaving expeditions—had incited the trade further.[73] Then, adroitly hedging and uncertain as to who would prevail in the war, island planters began buying extra Africans, though others cautioned that steps toward abolition should be taken forthwith, lest a victorious Union be provided with further reason to try to seize Cuba, causing something of a retreat by 1864.[74] Hedging also meant engaging in talks in London concerning the introduction to the island of work-ers who were free Negroes.[75]

With hesitation the Lincoln administration moved reluctantly to cur-tail Dixie's lifeblood, which had meant the arrival of enchained Africans in Cuba, with countless numbers seeping into Florida. This critical departure in Washington doubtlessly curbed a further influx of Africans to Cuba, pro-pelled by the needs of local planters and Dixie alike.[76] As to the latter, in the prelude to war, and in a taste of what had been going on for decades, manacled Africans began arriving steadily in Key West.[77] During the spring and summer of 1860 this small town became the new home of 1,432 African refugees, brought there after slavers bound for Cuba were captured.[78] By 1861 London's consul in the region had found a remarkable increase in commerce of various sorts between Dixie and Cuba, which opened the door for slav-ing.[79] A Spanish envoy in England noticed that with the war, Washington had generally removed its fleet from Africa—which was ineffectual in the best of times—and this had given a boost to all manner of illegality by U.S. nationals feasting on the beset continent.[80]

As had been the case for some years now, enslaved Africans were increas-ingly arriving from Mozambique, as U.S. slavers sought to elude the Royal Navy along the west coast of the beleaguered continent.[81] Still, the Congo River basin was favored too by U.S. slavers [82] and the area farther south reach-ing into Angola.[83] The stultifying scent of profit was too strong to ignore, since by 1861 it was reported that an African could be had for $50 on the continent and then sold for $1,000 in Cuba.[84]

But before the critical juncture of abolition was reached, slavers were work-ing overtime in their effort to deluge the island with Africans. Edmund Ruffin, an exemplar of the coterie of wildly militant "fire-eaters" that dominated Dixie, had threatened "war" on London because of the Royal Navy seeking to halt slavers "on the coast of Cuba," while his comrade, James Hammond, pre-dicted a like result if somehow Cuba was wrested away from Spain into the hands of London or Paris.[85] "By far," said a British envoy in Havana in the fall of 1860, "the greater portion of the vessels to be employed in the Slave Trade are fitted out in the United States,"[86] with Mobile joining the usual points of embarkation—New York, New Orleans, and Charleston. [87] In August 1861 London uncovered a plan "intended to be carried into operation in the ports of the Southern States of America" that involved "procuring slaves from the coast of Africa to be imported into Cuba."[88]

It was as if Dixie had decided to offload some of its slave production to a war-free Cuba in order to bolster the war-torn CSA. In early 1862, Lon-don's emissary in Havana asserted that "owing to the state of affairs in the U.S. trade" Cuba had "become stagnant" and thus there had been a "revival of interest in expeditions to the slave coast of Africa" destined for the island.[89] Yet remarkably, despite the Civil War being, inter alia, a detonation of sectional tensions, Northern cities continued to be essential to the financing and operation of the illicit slave trade. In November 1861 a British officer noticed a vessel from Boston—"under American colours"—landing a "cargo of Negroes on the South Coast" of Cuba in the "district of Manzanillo."[90] As late as November 1862, Lord Lyons was told that "vessels under American colours are in the habit of shipping slaves from the west coast of the island of Madagascar."[91]

Months after the Civil War had begun, Consul Joseph Crawford in Cuba announced with sadness that the "Slave Trade was never so flourishing as it is now almost everywhere on the coast of Cuba."[92] Just before that, Appleton Oaksmith, an infamous slave trader, managed to escape from jail on the mainland and was suspected of being determined to resume slaving expeditions to Cuba.[93] By early 1863 F. P. Drain, a CSA national with ties to Mobile had cleared Bordeaux with a cargo of wine supposedly destined for Mexico but instead of going there the vessel landed at Cuba where it was found to contain slaving equipment: weeks earlier the same vessel had landed 1,200 Africans on Cuba's north side.[94]

At any rate, by 1862 under the sledgehammer blows of the CSA and pressure from London alike, Washington capitulated and agreed to crack down on slavers. When Madrid realized that the United States would no longer lend tacit—or explicit—support to the slave trade to the island, Spain made a more determined effort to suppress this unclean business by appointing a captain general with more enthusiasm for obeying the letter of international law and bilateral accords.[95] By early 1862 a debate had erupted at the highest level in Madrid with one well-placed source warning that the "tempest," meaning the Civil War, "will not blow away with slavery in that country; and will it not cross the headlands of Florida, on the narrow arm of sea which divides it from Cuba? And, lastly, slavery will disappear in Cuba." Still, with stubbornness one Spanish leader warned that though Madrid was opposed to the slave trade, Spain was "fully resolved to maintain slavery in Cuba and Puerto Rico."[96]

That Madrid—and Havana—would have to retreat from this rigidity was indicated when Washington, despite a relevant treaty, extradited a Spanish officer to Cuba after machinations involving the slave trade. Secretary of State William Seward declaimed portentously, "A nation is never bound to furnish asylum to dangerous criminals who are offenders against the human race."[97] A great hue and cry ensued, indicating that the path to abolition would not be smooth.[98]

But once embarked on this road, Washington proceeded, which was not good news for the slaveholding class in Cuba either, as it was their suppliers who were most in jeopardy. Erastus H. Booth found himself in a Manhattan courtroom in 1862, charged with "forcibly confining and detaining" about "five hundred Negroes" with the intent of converting them into slaves.[99] Likewise, Mary J. Watson found herself indicted for seeking to bring enslaved Africans to Cuba.[100]

Yet as the death knell sounded for slavery in Dixie and slaveholders realized that their once valuable property could become a nullity, CSA supporters recognized that they could continue to earn a nice return due south. Thus, in late 1864, U.S. abolitionists reported that "Cuba has been made a depot for [the] kidnapped from whence they were brought into the United States."[101] Shockingly, a number of Spanish-surnamed individuals residing in the republic were accused of trying to transport to Cuba "one thousand Negroes, one thousand mulattoes and one thousand persons of color."[102] Interestingly, when Mary Davis was in Cuba during the war, she visited a plantation near Matanzas where she found "the slaves on this estate all speak English."[103]

A regnant fear that emerged among U.S. Negroes as the Civil War was winding down was that their tenure as slaves would be extended—or initiated—via an unwanted sojourn in Cuba. During the war there were a number of recorded instances of arrivals in Cuba of persons of color from the republic,[104] though, previously, they were not necessarily welcome there.

But when the Union stiffened its spine and finally chose to crack down on those involved in the most odious of commerce, it was the equivalent of an injunction being slapped on slaving expeditions. Or so thought Joseph Crawford, London's man in Havana, who remarked in 1862 on the "conviction and sentence of death which has been passed at New York upon Captain [Nathaniel] Gordon" for snatching Africans from the Congo River basin and trying to smuggle them into Cuba. His execution, said Crawford with reserve, "will doubtless have its effect in deterring Americans," though he predicted it would drive "the Spaniards" into a more direct role in the slave trade.[105]

Crawford was correct: a fork in the road had been reached in an utterly oppressive trade that had endured for centuries. But now with what had been its most energetic practitioners—U.S. nationals—being forced to the sidelines, it was evident that this would have monumental consequences for what had been a prime target: Cuba. The impact of this profound change was felt early on. In September 1865, months after the formal surrender of the CSA, a British diplomat reported that in 1860 alone over 30,000 Africans had been brought against their will to Cuba with 596 captured by the local authorities, but during the previous eighteen months, he noted with seeming surprise, "143 only are known to have been imported into that island."[106] But U.S. slavers continued to trickle into Cuba even after the Civil War had ended.[107]

Madrid did not appear to be enthusiastic about Lincoln's Emancipation Proclamation in 1863. Close attention was paid to the dearth of compensation to slaveholders and the related suppositions that the usually besieged Negro had "amigos" that were "muy numerosos" and that this edict dovetailed with the wishes of the all-important "público inglés," or English public. The concatenation of these events unavoidably would mean more "agitacion" targeting Madrid.[108] London's stated intention to "cruise off the coast of Cuba in order to intercept slave traders" was not embraced happily in Madrid.[109]

Thus, during the war Cuba was portrayed as a negative example, an exemplar of why Washington was willing to suppress a sectional rebellion. Cuba was the bogeyman used to frighten mainland Africans into toeing the line for fear they would be shipped to the island Hades. Union soldiers went into battle chanting ditties hammering Cuba as a bastion of slavery where the "4 largest own the island . . . may Spain free her Cuba of the slavery dominion. And all others likewise have Freedom and Union."[110]

With the slave market in Cuba quickly receding, the capital in Africans rapidly disintegrating, and the prospect of being tried for treason not unlikely, nationals of the once doughty CSA were scattering to the four corners of the planet, though Cuba seemed to be a close and favored place to alight. Records of the Spanish consulate in Charleston register a dramatic uptick in vessels heading from there to Cuba in 1866.[111] As early as 1856, a visitor from Charleston found that Havana was "crowded with 'Americanos,'" which then accelerated in the spring of 1865.[112]

During the war, Albert G. Riddle, U.S. consul in Matanzas, saw a crucial role for mainlanders in Cuba since "the Creole fails in skilled labor," and rushing to fill the gap after the collapse of the CSA were sons of Dixie. Riddle had noted that "the eight hundred miles of railroad are built by American engineers. The machinery that grinds the cane was made in the United States"; in fact, "all" of the engineers he saw were mainlanders.[113] Cuba had become a colony in exile for those who held slavery dear and harbored deep resentment of Washington.[114]

SHORTLY AFTER SURRENDER WAS being formalized the once mighty Mary Cadwalader Jones set out from a once powerful, now prostrate Charleston headed southward to Cuba. "Entering the harbor of Havana is like going into the neck of a demi-john," she observed; "as it widened we saw for the first time the Confederate flag flying on ex-blockade runners openly exultant over the murder of Lincoln." This was heartening to her but providing a premonition of disappointment to come, the new migrant seemed disappointed to note that "one heard nothing but Spanish."[115]

She was not alone, neither in her migration nor in her disappointment. Still, they kept coming, arriving even before the war ended—but as living embodiments of how it would conclude. "I find the weather here very pleasant," said Oskar Aichel after arriving in Havana in 1863; "no sickness is prevailing"—unlike the Carolina he departed hastily. Best of all, he told his "dear wife," "I have found numerous friends here."[116] Edmund Kirby Smith, a former CSA general, may have made similar remarks upon his July 1865 arrival for in his hotel were such secessionist luminaries as Judah Benjamin, a former Louisianan. He was in Matanzas where he—and other accused traitors—were entertained royally.[117] Unlike others, his fluency in Spanish eased his abrupt transition.[118]

It was in Cuba that Jefferson Davis checked on funds that had been deposited there for him by the mercantile-minded.[119] In May 1865 Davis, leader of a collapsing regime, was told that the better part of wisdom would be for him to retreat to Cuba forthwith.[120] That he did, and as late as 1869 he remained at the Hotel Cubano in Havana, holing up with relatives. He had also visited there in December 1867, communing with former comrades then resident in the city. A few months later he was in Cuba again, warmly received by Ambrosio Gonzales and his family, some of whom wound up becoming pillars of South Carolina society. Birkett D. Fry, a former CSA general who had lived in Cuba since 1865, and Gonzales's cousins entertained Davis in Matanzas as if he were a touring potentate. Being a supporter of Narciso Lopez, Cuba was not unfamiliar territory for him; he had visited the island as early as the winter of 1835. But this latest trip seemed to be most inspiring, as he was surrounded by the like-minded; his hotel was a haven for accused traitors, one of many said to be operated by mainlanders.[121]

Various entrepreneurs were among a number who descended on Cuba, fleeing a vaporized ruin of a once proud nation for better climes. From Jacksonville, the Spanish consul in Savannah was informed in 1866 of the desire of a "foreigner, a Pole by birth and machinist also" to migrate to Cuba.[122] The lengthening list included James Alexander McHatton who fled his sugar plantation near Baton Rouge in favor of another in Cuba.[123] The former CSA Secretary of War, John Breckenridge, fled incognito in July 1865 across the straits of Florida to Cuba, with an enslaved African in tow.[124] The journey of the latter—possibly unwilling—sojourner was not unusual. A year later Senator Charles Sumner of Massachusetts was irate about reports of a ship from Pensacola delivering Florida Africans to Cuban planters.[125]

The rebel Trusten Polk arrived in Havana—"a magnificent panorama," he thought; he had been there two decades earlier and had arrived from Mexico, another redoubt for traitors. Having dodged prosecution he now was inebriated with the sight of Cuba, finding it "most beautiful" and "enchanting" and a "fairy-like scene." Quickly he found a former Louisiana governor, Thomas Overton Moore, ensconced comfortably on a plantation near Havana, and CSA "General E. Kirby Smith was also with a friend on his plantation not far from

Matanzas." Polk was no nonentity either, having graduated from Yale in 1831 and serving in the U.S. Senate representing Missouri before being expelled for disloyalty in 1862 and going on to become a hanging judge in Mississippi.[126]

After Appomattox, said the traitorous writer Eliza McHatton-Ripley, "scarcely a day passed" without a fleeing rebel making it to Cuba, including a flock of high-ranking generals. There they were subjected to such indignities, she recalled with lingering bitterness, of compelled "baptism for infants" where the toddlers had to consort with "little darky babies," which filled her with anxiety. Though she "soon settled down" there, somehow she never grew accustomed to the presence of "stupid Negroes" who were like "dumb driven cattle." Apparently, this disgust did not encompass Zell, the African she brought with her from the mainland. She despised the "war taxes" imposed to fight what came to be called the "Ten Years' War" of 1868–78. "Uniformed men lighted down upon us almost daily," she grumbled, "armed with orders we could not understand"—like most of the émigrés, her Spanish was primitive at best—"and which they could not explain." When she resisted, she was curtly told that "they had the power to seize Negroes or sugar to the amount demanded." But where could she flee? Her options were limited since she reveled in the island reality that "servants" were "everywhere." Then "gradual emancipation" commenced and, she groaned, in "an inevitable sequence, an untold number of valuable estates were abandoned by their impoverished owners, thereby revolutionizing the entire financial and domestic status of the island"—ending her cherished way of life.[127]

For Ambrosio Gonzales and his wife, a national of a now despised mainland republic, the return to Cuba was bittersweet, though it was a relief to get away from Tampa where the "Yankee" presence was disappointingly "very numerous."[128] But Cuba was not easy for them either, since their children's Spanish-language skills were rudimentary at best,[129] though a rapidly adjusting daughter "never imagined anything more beautiful" than Havana.[130] They may have been hunted criminals on the mainland, but in Cuba these rebels were often greeted as heartwarming heroes. Clothes, food, and rousing welcomes from thousands in Cardenas was not an atypical response during this time.[131]

The arrival of mainlanders was not necessarily humanizing attitudes on the island toward the enslaved African, for they not only brought slaves with them but mossback sentiments too: at least, this was the considered opinion of Martín Delany. Strikingly, Madrid retained this abolitionist's words asserting that "in its worst form," slavery in the "Antilles" was a "blessing almost compared with the miserable degradation of the slaves" on the mainland. But now these "assumed superiors" from the North had "intruded themselves into Cuba, contaminating society wherever they located." Previously, "black and colored gentlemen and ladies of rank mingled indiscriminately in society. But since the advent of the Negro haters, the colored people of Cuba have been reduced nearly, if not quite, to the level of the miserable degraded position of the colored people of the United States."[132]

Henry Latham, a Londoner, visited a "large plantation" in 1867 in Cuba and found that "resident overseers are despotic over the slaves," and not coincidentally, the "sugar master and the engineer were Americans." Still, he found that the "condition of the Negro population" in Havana was "better, as far as material comfort goes, than in any city of the United States" and in comments that would have been disheartening to Dixie exiles, he ascertained an "acknowledged fact in Cuba that as a result of the abolition of slavery in the States and in consequence of the pressure of public opinion from without, the institution will not last many years longer in this island."[133] The second city of Santiago resembled Havana to a degree.[134]

As so often happened—for example, veterans of the U.S.-Mexican War joining filibustering expeditions to Cuba and Nicaragua—disgruntled and unemployed veterans with expert skill in killing began migrating to Cuba just in time for the 1868–78 war against Spanish rule, which also allowed these adventurers to exact revenge against a Madrid they had long hated. They did so too because, at least in the early stages, it was unclear on the mainland what direction this conflict was heading. A correspondent of Secretary of State Seward, writing from Matanzas, found a diversity of opinions on slavery. The "more intelligent," even some slaveholders, wanted abolition and realized that a cessation of the wicked African slave trade would only occur effectively with abolition. Still, there were "a few Cuban and many Spanish proprietors" who disagreed and wanted this iniquitous commerce revived.[135] Symptomatic of a brief period of mainland progressivism, brought by the temporary setback to Dixie, Washington encouraged abolitionism and provided translations of abolitionist doctrines. Thereby it was assured in 1869 by its envoy in Madrid that "a decree would soon be issued initiating the gradual abolition of slavery, by giving freedom to all Negroes born after" a said date.[136]

Attention was paid in Madrid to the point that the "estimated value of slaves before the war" on the mainland was a considerable $2 billion, and "no compensation" was made to the former masters. Though it was with probable relief that it was ascertained that cotton, tobacco, and other slave-driven crops were now "produced with as much free [labor] as was produced with slave labor."[137] In the midst of the 1868–78 conflict, on 25 March 1873, the U.S. Senate "received with joy the intelligence that the republican government of Spain has abolished slavery" in Puerto Rico, a huge step that presaged full abolitiion in Cuba thereafter.[138]

Secretary of State Hamilton Fish was explicit in his instructions to his envoy in Madrid: "Make the abolition of slavery a *sine qua non*. . . . Do all in your power to secure complete emancipation not only in Cuba but also in Porto Rico. . . . This contest cannot terminate," he stressed, "without the abolition of slavery." Washington was well aware of the vise in which Madrid was placed as a result, which could redound to the benefit of the republic.[139] Taking the hint, Spain slowly realized that for slavery the jig was up in 1865, and that unless abolition ensued, civil war surely would.[140] Reputedly, the leader of the Cortes in 1866 conceded that "conditions are different. . . . This is due to the result of the Civil War in the United States."[141] He had anticipated—if not responded to—a contemporaneous abolitionist view in Massachusetts that scorned the continuation of enslavement in Cuba.[142] Upping the ante (and anticipating the twenty-first-century push for "universal jurisdiction"[143]), abolitionist Gerrit Smith, a former congressman, argued that the world was one unit, and just as in 1861 there was serious discussion of Britain intervening forcefully to halt U.S. slavery, the United States should now think seriously of intervening to halt Cuban slavery.[144] Unfortunately, by the time abolition ultimately arrived with full force in Cuba in the 1880s, the mainland's temporary infatuation with justice for the African had dissipated.

Actually, this mainland attitude was in full force as early as 1861, when George Fitzhugh warned that a free Cuba would make that "rising nation" an "irreconcilable enemy," given the inexorable abolition that would follow in the wake of anti-colonialism. Cuba was full to the brim with "Free Negroes, Mulattoes and Coolies," he complained—"how should we dispose of them?" Thus "to defend Cuba we must annex the West Indies," which was more than a notion. He concluded, "Let us guarantee Cuba to Spain, so long as she preserves Negro slavery intact and strike a blow for Cuban independence the moment that institution is interfered with."[145] By late 1873 his dour opinion was replicated when William Cullen Bryant told the secretary of state that "we do not want Cuba, with her ignorant population of Negroes, Mulattoes. . . . alien to our own population."[146]

In the antebellum era Congressman Joshua Giddings had rebutted such thinking when he peremptorily dismissed a Carolina view that possession of Cuba was more important than controlling Nebraska—loss of the latter "would be but a slight restriction to slavery"—and the related view that the "island in the hands of emancipated blacks . . . would be a total loss to the commerce of the world and a death-blow to the extension of slavery." He was aghast at the increasingly popular idea that "the security of this Republic depends on the continuance of human servitude in Cuba."[147] This view was confirmed by ever more anxious reports from the Spanish consul in Galveston warning about an active and permanent conspiracy against Cuba based in that frontier town.[148]

The changing view on the mainland of tumult in Cuba was not just a matter of politics. For island unrest was compromising the capital that had arrived with the challenge to slavery on the mainland and the defeat of the CSA. "Our sugar market has again fallen into great inactivity," moaned a major New England firm in 1868, as "declining prices" were now besetting the major markets that were the mainland and Europe.[149] Subsequently, some of their estates had been put to the torch by infuriated slaves; the bad news continued in December 1869 with the acknowledgment that "our sugar market has been very dull," as "discouraging news" proliferated.[150] Then, in addition to "immolation," there was a "storm" making "cooperage materials, lumber & provisions" for economic expansion "exceedingly scarce,"[151] all of which was hitting at a time when mainland opinion was gradually turning against full freedom for Africans and what that was said to represent, not least turmoil, as Cuba now seemed to suggest. On the other hand, one prominent mainland sugar baron felt that abolishing slavery in Cuba would provide an advantage to Louisiana.[152]

The vast U.S. investment in Cuba meant that Washington was hardly a disinterested spectator of events unfolding on what was seen as its doorstep. Inocencio Casanova had become a naturalized U.S. citizen in 1859 and accumulated sizable holdings in Cuba and, according to his defenders, a decade later had sought to "hasten the abolition of slavery" there, "although he was the master of many slaves, whose joint value did not come short of half a million of dollars." But, it was said with regret, this led to a clash with fellow slaveholders and he was forced to migrate—at a great loss. Worse, the Captain General had issued a warrant for his arrest.[153] By way of contrast, Ramon Cespedes, identified as leader of the Foreign Diplomatic Commission of the Republic of Cuba, assured that the "slaves of American citizens, who have been embargoed or confiscated by the Spanish on account of the real or supposed connection with the revolutionists of Cuba, must certainly receive the powerful protection of the United States,"[154] a message that miraculously leaned toward abolition and slaveholding, independence and even annexation simultaneously.

Responding in kind, a U.S. envoy in Cuba in 1874 found that the "insurgents" had "considerable force," though "they have abstained from inflicting any loss upon the Creoles but have greatly injured if not ruined several plantations belonging to Spaniards. The animosity existing between the Creoles & Spaniards, seems to be irreconcilable."[155] Earlier, General Ulysses S. Grant was told that "strange to say the natives who own the land & *slaves* would favor abolition whilst the Spaniards favor slavery, because slaves produce the sugar, which makes Cuba so valuable to Old Spain." Thus, said General William T. Sherman, washing his hands of the problem, "it is for them to solve. We have enough problems of our own."[156]

Nonetheless, to the extent that the forward-looking spirit of Reconstruction had impact across the straits, it was a boon to the anti-colonial crusade in Cuba, which unlike the founding of the United States, was not at loggerheads with abolition.[157] The massive bloodletting that was the handmaiden of the U.S. Civil War was clarifying and for many unveiling the high costs that accompanied slavery, which led to more scrutiny of that lingering phenomenon just next door in Cuba. A mainland teacher, identified as "Miss Holt," found herself there in 1865 when the embers of war on the mainland were still aflame and remained until 1869. One evening a "poor boy with naked, swollen and bleeding back, came to implore protection from the overseer. This was the dark side of Slavery," she implored, "which I now saw for the first time. . . . Here the slaves were locked up every night in a long brick building closely resembling a jail"—a "contrast," that was "striking," she insisted, "to the same institution" as it had stood in her homeland.[158]

Moreover, even non-African Cubans in communicating with mainlanders spoke in the newly enhanced language of abolitionism.[159] Described as "Commissioners of the Republic of Cuba," Francisco V. Aguilera and Ramon Cespedes told a U.S. audience that those they represented were "convinced" of the "intimate connection between abolition of slavery and the independence and welfare of the country," a point they had been "taught by the history of the United States": they knew as a result that failure to address bondage "might imperil the very existence" of the island. They did not seem displeased when Washington proposed that U.S. nationals be barred from "possessing directly or indirectly slave property abroad." They were pleased that the United States had adopted the "Holy Mission" with "regard to slavery that England played with regard to the slave trade."[160]

Bolstering the anticolonial front was a beehive of activity in Manhattan by Cuban exiles. Spain well knew of the activism of Cubans and Puerto Ricans in New York, particularly their promising abolition of slavery,[161] and their agents retaliated by terming Cespedes a dictator.[162]

Aware of the new dynamics unleashed by Reconstruction, Cubans on the mainland condemned Spain in blunt terms, particularly concerning slavery and the slave trade—"under the name of *counter-balancing of races*, in order to overawe the Creoles with the increasing number of Negroes, when in reality the only object of the Spaniards was to enrich themselves with the large profits arising from the inhuman traffic." Left tactfully unsaid was the responsibility of their Manhattan hosts, who associated themselves with the losers in the U.S. Civil War: "The Cubans distinguished themselves from the Spanish residents of the island by their open sympathies with the cause of the Union."[163]

Some of the insurgents spoke so warmly about the republic that the leading U.S. diplomat in Santiago was convinced in 1869 that "it is the general wish that this island be annexed to the United States."[164] This view was complemented by the growing view in Washington, expressed by Congressman Jacob Ambler in 1870, that Cuba had a right to revolt against Spain.[165]

But—perhaps not coincidentally—as Reconstruction was snuffed out, the revolt in Cuba came to an end absent an unequivocal victory for either anticolonialism or antislavery. Tellingly, the leading twentieth-century African American attorney from Chicago, Earl Dickerson, thought that this Cuban conflagration marked the point when the United States chose to "turn from being a standard maxim for free society to being a supporter of oppressors." Thus "when the Cuban people revolted from Spanish rule, abolished slavery, established equality under the law and ended the privilege of a favored few . . . they appealed for help from the United States government [and] our government did not give the Cubans help. Instead our government accommodated itself to plutocratic Spain."[166]

The Spaniards were insufficiently agile and unable to pivot and embrace abolition fervently to checkmate the Creoles and avoid being ousted altogether, an eventuality that the 1868–78 war foreshadowed. Surely Madrid won few friends among newly enfranchised U.S. Negroes when the prime minister was reputed to have asserted that the suppression of the "mulatto" revolt would be a "major victory for European civilization," a view in agreement with his supporters who saw the conflict as one between "the white Spanish and the racially mixed lower classes."[167]

Instead, Madrid seemed incapable of mounting a ready response to, for example, Miguel de Aldama, a Cuban based in New York in 1869, who conceded that "I was the owner before October 1868 of about 2,000 slaves" but "I now regard these slaves as all free and as my equals," a viewpoint that would gain fewer and fewer adherents on the mainland with every passing day. As a leader of the rebellion against Madrid, he concurred with the junta's "emancipation of all slaves" which "has met with the universal approval of all adherents of the republic" proclaimed in Cuba.[168] Such sentiments placed the rebels in sync with certain currents on the mainland, which gave the revolt increased momentum. Before mainlanders in Cuba seemed to be wholly in accord with slavery but now William C. Tinker, a native of New York but a resident on the island since 1852, was enthusiastic in praising abolitionists in his new home and observed that the formerly enslaved Africans he had spoken with "understood that their freedom had resulted in some way from the emancipation of slaves in the United States. They had pictures of Abraham Lincoln and spoke of him familiarly as *emancipador* or emancipator." But unlike other analysts, Tinker admitted that he had "conversed freely with all classes of persons" and "almost unanimously they looked to the [United States]" not just for "recognition" but for "annexation"[169]—a troublesome sign that was to manifest dramatically in the wake of the 1898 war.

Hence, in Richmond there was "recruiting" and advertising for mercenaries in Cuba, as H. H. Harrison was told: "excitement" was promised for the "dare devil fellows" willing to accept an offer and willing to traverse the at times difficult "climate."[170] "I would like to know if it is possible to get some kind of position?" was the query of W. L. Hamilton of Charlottesville, adding with emphasis that his colleague "Pollard who was a fine soldier in the CSA will join if he can get a position."[171] H. H. Kay of Baltimore offered to organize a "command (say a Company or cavalry) for a Cuban expedition," though— unlike others—he raised the idea of "avoiding neutrality laws," which seemed to preclude such foreign junkets. Though he was "an officer" in "the late war"—"Lieut. Col. was my rank"—he was willing to "accept a subordinate position" and volunteered to recruit others "connected with the CSA army."[172]

Fighting in Cuba was described as enlisting in the "Patriots Cause" and, according to Don C. Vosnea formerly of the U.S. Army and based in West Virginia, "there are a great many in this vicinity that would enlist had they the opportunity"—depending on "terms of services, the wages paid," etc.[173] It is unclear how many from the mainland went to fight in Cuba—but certainly enthusiasm was high.[174]

It incited 163 mainland men to launch yet another militaristic expedition to Cuba—leading to what the now elderly abolitionist William Lloyd Garrison termed the "summary execution of thirty-seven of her filibustering crew." Garrison was critical but nonetheless acknowledged that "bedlam" had erupted throughout the republic, for the "Cuban adventurers and their sympathizers" were able to "present the struggle as in the interest of Negro emancipation as well as of Cuban independence" which appealed particularly to "our colored citizens and their [leading] advocates." In some instances "the bait has been swallowed," which almost led the United States "to precipitate us into an unjustifiable war with Spain"—though Garrison had "great confidence that a decree of emancipation will speedily be made" by the Havana authorities.[175]

Others were not so sure, which gave momentum to those aboard the *Virginius*—though since this same vessel had been suspected of smuggling Africans from the mainland to Cuba, this cast doubt in the eyes of some on its then stated mission of smuggling guns to Cuban revolutionaries.[176] Nor was it reassuring that the ship had formerly been deployed as a blockade runner for the CSA.[177] That some mainlanders in Cuba were expressing anxious concern at the same time about events in Cuba—"Three Negroes today attempted to assassinate an officer of the volunteer artillery"—gave this mission a pointed poignancy.[178] That the most prominent man aboard this vessel was a former leader of the CSA navy—Joseph Fry—was hardly reassuring to those like Garrison; the same could be said of the support rendered to this adventure by former CSA general James Longstreet.[179] Thus, when the well-known Fry—in particular—was executed, great upset ensued in Dixie.[180]

Madrid was not necessarily surprised by this venture since as early as 1866 the Spanish legation in Washington advised about the existence of New York–based conspiracies targeting Cuba.[181] That same year Havana was warned about secret agents from the mainland engaged in revolutionary machinations in league with Cuban émigrés.[182]

By 1869 the U.S. consul in Santiago reported that a "cargo of men and munitions of war" had landed near Guantánamo, led by "naturalized citizens of the U.S. who were brought to this city and publicly shot," adding that "Americans are in bad repute and to be called American here is considered a gross insult."[183]

Washington's man spoke harshly of the "bloodthirsty desire of the Catalan volunteers" who "being an ignorant and sanguinary people are only satisfied when some unfortunate prisoners are executed (who are all considered as American citizens) and have no delicacy shouting fresh Yankee Beef Steak tomorrow for breakfast."[184] This consul, A. E. Phillips, was under fire, taken by the idea that "intrigues are the order of the day." He confided that the "Governor and the principal local authorities visit me in an unofficial manner and disclose too often the secrets of the Palace" while often conveying a combination of gossip and veiled threats. "It is hoped [by them] that our Government will not forget that in this vicinity there is a large number of American planters, native-born citizens whose estates have been plundered, whose Negroes have been forced into the rebel ranks and have been obliged to seek refuge in this city," suffering and "penniless." Still, he asserted, the "hope of annexation to the U.S. is so apparent that it has become a fixed principal [sic] in the minds of everyone."[185]

Thus continued the idea buoyed by mainlanders that during the 1868–78 war, Creoles desired U.S. support while Spaniards heightened their dearth of appreciation for Washington. One mainland visitor was "painfully aware of the dislike and bitterness entertained against Americans by the Spaniards here." But that was not his only worry: "The Negroes are manifesting a restless spirit," he noted with nervousness. "They require to be governed with the greatest severity and it is often necessary to shoot a refractory slave" since "Cuban planters are continually in dread of a general uprising." Thus, in 1874, this mainland visitor to the island found it "inevitable" that annexation would occur.[186]

The points were linked: numerous mainlanders continued to be haunted with the specter of uncontrollable Africans who often pursued their own interests, which were inimical to the reigning white supremacy.[187] Detaching Cuba from Spain and attaching it to Washington was one way to forestall the nightmare scenario. It was during this time that a U.S. emissary on the island roared against the "dangerous Negro capable of anything." He wondered if unrest had reached a danger point: "Have the Negroes on the estates the authority to seize a white man?"[188] If so, could not there be a contagion spreading across the straits that could rock an already storm-tossed mainland, reeling from the effects of Reconstruction?

By 1870, Washington got hold of a report to the Captain General that found Guantánamo and Baracoa were "free from insurgents"—"with the exception of . . . runaway Negroes and criminals."[189] There had been a long-standing fear on the mainland that abolition in Cuba would somehow "poison" the United States.[190] After abolition that anxiety had been transmuted into something else: Could Africans in the United States be exploited so shamelessly if Africans in Cuba were empowered?

The bloodcurdling events on both sides of the straits were reinforcing each other, creating an exponential leap in intensity in both conflicts. While Washington was groaning about Cuba, Spanish envoys on the mainland were mortified by the racial violence then unwinding in New Orleans. Madrid was told of pitched battles over Negro suffrage in 1866 with supposed incitement to kill all "whites," as scores perished and hundreds were wounded.[191] That Havana continued to monitor the arrival from New Orleans of persons of color from New Orleans during the Civil War did not abate the concern.[192] There was a "guerra" of "razas"—or war of the races, between blacks and whites, in New Orleans in 1874.[193] That some of these free Negroes arriving from the mainland had high-level relations with foreign powers—including Russia—hardly reduced the rising unease.[194] In Havana there was a generalized fear in late 1865 about an insurrection of Negroes in Dixie with untold ramifications for Cuba.[195] When Secretary of State William Seward and his son chose to visit Cuba in late 1865 the hysteria in Havana seemed to link his journey to this generalized fear.[196]

This may illuminate why by 1866 the Spanish legation in Washington increased their communication with Havana in a now indecipherable code.[197] Madrid could hardly be reassured by a report received from New York in 1872 about how those plotting against Havana tended to favor Africans in Cuba and, at the same time, sought to involve the United States in a war with Spain.[198] Given the historic ties between New Orleans and Havana, how long would it take for this kind of disturbance to reach the island? Throughout the tumultuous era stretching from 1868 to 1898, there was reluctance in certain precincts in Dixie to intervene in Cuba due to uncertainty as to how that would influence racial dynamics on the mainland.[199]

This apprehension echoed the considered opinion of war hero Congressman Benjamin F. Butler of Massachusetts. He warmly endorsed Cuban "independence" from Spain—then "annexation" to the United States. "I sympathized with Lopez and Crittenden and was a warm personal friend of Quitman," their comrade, he added.[200] In some ways, 1868–78 adumbrated

1898–1902 in that bloody war was followed by full-throated cries for "independence" then "annexation." In both cases dissenting voices in Cuba were ignored or downplayed. Butler was a Union man but it seemed that a bipartisan consensus on Cuba had emerged. Madrid had reason to think so—which is why the Foreign Ministry clipped a mainland news item dated March 1869 noting the arrival in Cuba "of the men who once wore the blue with those who wore the gray" too. This would have meaning for the 1868–78 war signaling a change from "defense and guerilla operations to an open and aggressive campaign."[201]

Why this might be so was revealed when yet another mainlander provided the ultimate endorsement of this 1868–78 conflict, assaying that "Creole ladies are lighter in color" than "the Spanish." Still, there was disconcertment at the perception that "everywhere the Negro blood is so intermixed that it is impossible to make a distinct separation between any of the races; a fact of difficult management in the event of self-government or any step toward it"—a point that also bolstered annexation. For Cuba seemed too much like Haiti in that in the former island there were "not fifty families" that were "untainted by African blood."[202]

CHAPTER 6

Toward De Facto Annexation of Cuba

A S THE U.S. CIVIL WAR UNWOUND, Spain was trapped. For decades it had engaged deftly in a delicate game of political arbitrage, manipulating the interstices between abolitionist London and slaving Washington, managing to hold on to Cuba because neither of these major powers wanted the other to prevail. But when the United States moved toward abolition of slavery, mimicking Britain, Spain's room for maneuver was reduced correspondingly.

However, there was another party in this multifaceted relationship that both complicated Spain's position and, it was thought, allowed an opportunity for further maneuvering: Haiti. The United States felt compelled—finally—to recognize the black republic during the Civil War. At the same time, a terrible bout of discontent hit Hispaniola like a thunderclap during this period, which allowed Madrid to make revanchist gains and establish a toehold on the island; earlier this had led to the establishment of the nation now known as the Dominican Republic. At that juncture some in Washington were thinking that if slavery were the cause of the Civil War, then why not get rid of the slaves, perhaps send them to Hispaniola, a prospect Madrid found profoundly distasteful in that these erstwhile U.S. Negroes could either become a stalking horse for Washington or, perhaps worse, an ally of Africans in the region. That plan expired in utero, but then as Cuba became unsettled by the 1868–78 war, Washington, now liberated from slavery and beginning to flex its global muscles, began to eye Hispaniola ravenously as a site for a base of operations, at Samana.[1]

Spain was convinced that in seeking to hold Cuba it was not simply engaged in typical colonial brigandage but holding down the fort against the kind of racial rapine and revenge-seeking that was said to characterize Haiti, which was now thought to be aided by a mainland republic that had become wobbly on this crucial front. As a result, the colonialists unleashed a wave of terror of their own in Cuba, leading to a whopping 170,000 civilian deaths in the 1890s, which led one contemporary scholar to assert that this was a "large enough catastrophe . . . to qualify the event as genocide."[2] Even before that tumultuous decade, it was in 1875 that the affluent New Yorker Moses Taylor received word from Havana that Spain was pursuing a policy of extermination in Cuba. Prisoners were to "be shot as fast as made"—including "every Cuban or Negro or coolie."[3]

As early as 1873, few would have disagreed with abolitionist Gerrit Smith when he described "poor Cuba" as a "land of horrors—the land of slavery and slaughter."[4] Cuba, both softened up and battered, thus became easier prey for a de facto annexation, particularly when the collapse of Reconstruction on the mainland served to unleash even more retrograde racist attitudes. Thus was the region kept on edge as the march toward the hinge year of 1898 proceeded apace.

HAVANA'S CONCERN ABOUT TURBULENCE in Hispaniola increased in the 1840s, when, as was the case during Haiti's formative years in the transformative 1791–1804 era, refugees began fleeing, arriving in Santiago or, perhaps more worrisome, Jamaica, where the eternal foe that was Britain could possibly be strengthened.[5] Forwarded to Madrid were newspaper articles from Jamaica about Haitian anniversaries being marked replete with a "forest of bayonets," as "cannons roared and filled the air with detonations . . . 10,000 men at one moment impressed a certain feverish agitation upon the spectators present."[6] An apparently nerve-wracked Spaniard, who had just departed Haiti, reported with fury about the hurried departure from the island of French and U.S. merchants, abandoning their enterprises. Although one might have thought that Madrid would be gleeful about setbacks to rivals, evidently racial solidarity prevailed.[7]

But during this period Madrid—and Havana—were perpetually concerned that London would steal a march by allying with what was perceived as black nationalism, even converting Haiti into a protectorate to that end.[8] What was occurring was that the turmoil in Haiti facilitated this island joining New York, New Orleans, and Savannah as bases for subversion by Cuban exiles[9]—except that those operating from Hispaniola were thought to have racial agendas not necessarily present in these mainland ports.[10] Likewise, Haitian turmoil facilitated the ability of the United States to gain influence in Samana, which had begun to occur as early as 1855.[11]

Both were perceived ultimately as threats to Cuba; and after the mainland moved to abolition, Haiti was deemed now to be joined by Washington as threats to the racial order. As early as 1855, the Spanish envoy in Hispaniola convinced himself that he was treated well in Santo Domingo, but

Port-au-Prince was overflowing with anti-white sentiment that could easily spill over to Cuba.[12] It may have been worse than that, it was thought, since even darker subjects from Puerto Rico were said to be harassed routinely in Haiti.[13] At the same time, Spain kept a wary eye on migrants of color from New Orleans who were arriving in Hispaniola in ever greater numbers, whose presence was perceived as threatening for multiple reasons.[14]

The problem for Spain was that its adamant inflexibility toward Haiti made colonial Cuba even more vulnerable to U.S. annexation. The overflow of Spanish racism directed at Hispaniola washed up on the banks of Cuba, undermining Madrid, particularly after the mainland moved toward abolition. Moreover, Washington's adamant desire to seize Samana combined with its lust to annex the Dominican Republic itself, both of which were a stepping-stone toward taking Cuba: Spain's inured colonial racism was ill-equipped to resist the grand ambitions of the now renewed republic. But just as France thought it could establish a stronghold in Mexico while the United States was wracked with sectional tension and violence, Spain thought similarly that it could perform a similar operation in Hispaniola.[15] There were some in Dixie who cheered Spain on in the Dominican Republic, feeling that it was not only protecting its interests in Cuba by taking on Haiti but performing a larger racial service.[16] So prompted, by the onset of the Civil War Spain effectively annexed the Dominican Republic.[17]

Animus toward Haiti may explain why some mainlanders aided Spain in this venture, including arranging for the migration there of those deemed to be "white."[18]

"I declare to you," journalist and lobbyist Jane Cazneau emphasized, speaking from Santo Domingo in 1862, "that I believe this to be the best if not the only place in the world for the happy solution of the great problem of races. Those who think that the Antilles will be given up exclusively to the blacks are utterly mistaken," she stressed, not least since Haiti was now under unremitting pressure on the island it now shared with Spain. As she saw it, it was the United States that was about to "shock the world" by the "ferocity" of "war of the races," whereas in eastern Hispaniola "the social equality of races" meant there was "no danger of war."[19] By 1865 she was so sanguine about things that she had linked Cuba with Hispaniola and was seeking to "emancipate the Cubans of all colors." She had confidence, because "I handled the preliminary of the Texas annexation movement" and now—once more—"would like to do the same."[20]

Cazneau had capacious and ambitious plans for what she called the "Antilles," but so did some U.S. Negroes, now envisioning a radically different status. Strikingly, the Foreign Ministry in Madrid, no doubt ever cognizant of repercussions for Cuba, retained reports and composed files concerning the planning of Martín Delany and his comrades for "South America" and "the Antilles" and particularly "Cuba" as a site for emigration,[21] all filed tellingly with Haitian materials. That same year of 1862 Madrid was seized with concern about emigration plans of these U.S. Negroes to neighboring Haiti, particularly since the plan was backed (for a while) by Washington. A U.S. envoy, Benjamin Whidden of New Hampshire, was conferring regularly with the leadership in Port-au-Prince about a venture that could potentially upend the entire region, including Cuba[22]—a migration of thousands of U.S. Negroes accompanied by Haiti becoming a U.S. protectorate,[23] all of which came a step closer when a direct shipping line was established between New York and Port-au-Prince.[24]

By 1864—at least as Madrid saw things—serious negotiations were under way between a direct agent of President Lincoln himself to send thousands of U.S. Negroes to Haiti, with a British firm roped in to provide aid.[25] This could spell ill not only for the recent Spanish encroachment in Hispaniola but Cuba, too.[26] Madrid thought Washington had become intoxicated with abolitionist fervor and was not thinking clearly—though their aim was to get rid of thousands of Negroes—and that Spain had not lost grasp of the long-term racial consequences; it was thought that these new emigrants would bond with Haitians on the basis of anti-whiteness, which could jeopardize colonial Cuba[27] and bring back the 1791–1804 horrors.[28] Proposals to ship U.S. Negroes west of Cuba to Central America were viewed with similar alarm.[29]

Once Spain helped to split Hispaniola on racial grounds, Madrid was forced to become the race police in the region, which became a handicap when Washington moved to abolition and the republic considered deporting the U.S. Negroes. Thus, when Jamaica, as was its tradition, erupted in revolt in 1865, Havana was hardly positioned to take advantage.[30] As things turned out, Havana could breathe a sigh of relief when thousands of U.S. Negroes balked at departing the mainland: "Why is it that we hear no schemes for getting rid of the free colored people in Cuba or the free colored people of Brazil?" asked Frederick Douglass querulously—which was a fair point.[31]

Also in 1865 the British envoy in Havana was remarking about the "uncertainty of the coloured race in Cuba"; with the end of the U.S. Civil War there was a disinclination to invest in the slave trade, which suggested that slavery itself was withering.[32] "Apprehensions exist throughout the island," said Robert Bunch, "that the late emancipation of the Negroes in the United States, coupled with the evacuation of Santo Domingo by the Spanish forces, might induce the coloured population to try their strength against their oppressors"— which was all too true. Besides, "[Cuban] Negroes showed much concern at the assassination of Mr. Lincoln."[33] Spain had overreached by stepping into Hispaniola, forced to suppress a rolling insurrection in the process,[34] when it should have recognized that events on the mainland mandated Cuban consolidation. And now Havana had to scurry to suppress an island-wide revolt that prefigured Madrid's dual nightmare: anti-colonial independence accompanied by abolition. Madrid's overreaching had generated an inflamed counter-reaction among abolitionists. The noted journalist James Redpath, known to have close ties to Haiti, called for a filibustering expedition against Cuba that would enlist U.S. Negroes in order to facilitate the ouster of Spain altogether from eastern Hispaniola.[35]

The unraveling of the status quo in Cuba driven by the twin imperatives of independence and abolition was manifested on the mainland, most notably in the realm of black politics in Florida—which was to be affected to varying degrees to the present day. Key West, then a major statewide population node—and once the site of shipwrecked Africans fresh from the continent—was now the home of newly minted "African Americans" eager to exert political power. An influx of Bahamians and particularly Cubans fleeing an island torn by war helped to keep the Republican Party—then the vessel of enfranchised black men—in power in Monroe County at a time when it was being routed throughout the region. These Cuban migrants leaned toward abolition, which drove this bilateral alliance. In February 1874 F. V. Aguilera, leader of republican forces then fighting Spain in Cuba, arrived in Key West and noticed a trend that was to bedevil emigrants from the island for decades to come as they scrambled to adapt to a different environment. Those of African descent had withdrawn from Cuban efforts to organize the community to which Aguilera objected and called an urgent meeting to that end. But it was an uphill climb for as the opposition Democratic Party gradually gained influence—which was to be the case for decades to come—patterns of segregation were asserted, even among Cuban emigrants.[36]

The steady growth of this pattern did not deter U.S. Negroes, intoxicated by the heady brew of escaping enslavement, from rushing to identify with a free Cuba. In 1872, the famed abolitionist Henry Highland Garnet joined with numerous others at Cooper Institute in Manhattan to ally with the "Cuban Anti-Slavery Committee." Their resolve on behalf of "the Colored People of the United States, who have so recently been so invested with the rights of citizens" and well aware of the "evil effects of slavery" could not ignore "the condition of five hundred thousand of our brethren, now held as slaves in the island of Cuba." They were repaying the debt owed to "other men" who held "conventions" and the like on their recent slave status. They were pleased that in Cuba "the colored inhabitants battle side by side with the white, holding the rank of officers and in numerous instances, colored officers commanding white troops"—which seemed otherworldly on the mainland. Speaking personally, Garnet said, "I have twice visited Cuba and have witnessed the horrors of slavery as it exists there and allow me to state that the slavery recently abolished in our country was mild when compared with the crime that Spain today upholds in Cuba."[37] This meeting was followed by a similar one in Boston with a similar resolve, all of which was monitored by the Spanish consular authorities.[38] The wider point was that U.S. abolition combined with Madrid's missteps in Hispaniola to jeopardize further Spanish Cuba.

The Manhattan gathering in particular received extensive press coverage with the *New York Herald* finding that "agents and supporters here of the Spanish authorities were quick to take the alarm from this movement of our colored citizens" and went so far as to make sure that a "printed circular was scattered around the hall" of the confab, "warning them of the folly of supporting the Cuban rebels." Choosing his words carefully, the journalist who witnessed these events wrote that "it does not appear that these colored men entertain any filibustering designs," though "these black citizens call for the intervention of their government for the extinction of the evil in Cuba and by such action as they hold to be within the law of nations."[39]

A few weeks later Secretary of State Hamilton Fish was visited by what he described as a "delegation of prominent colored men, representing in part the Cuban Anti-Slavery Society of New York"; they delivered a petition demanding belligerent rights—de facto recognition—of the Cuban rebels.[40] Other U.S. Negroes demanded belligerent rights of a sort for themselves, informing President U.S. Grant that "we the Taylor Guards Colored of Williamsport offer you our services for Cuba. . . . we can furnish one hundred men."[41] The militant cleric, Henry Turner of Georgia, informed the White House that "at an enthusiastic mass meeting of the colored citizens. . . . indignation [was expressed] at the butchery of our fellow citizens in Cuba." Thus "five thousand . . . colored citizens are ready to enlist for Cuba to teach the Spanish authorities respect for the American flag."[42]

Secretary Fish was well acquainted with Negroes; his chief messenger, Eddie Savoy, was described as a "short, squat colored man" with "hair slightly tinged with gray." It was Savoy in 1869 who was deputized to deliver ever sterner messages to Madrid's envoy in Washington concerning the ever bloodier war in Cuba. Savoy had delivered so many messages to the legation that he had come to know personally and admire the chief minister who presided at the imposing building on Massachusetts Avenue and felt badly when on one occasion he outwitted this diplomat who was determined to avoid receipt of Washington's message.[43]

All this was occurring at a time when Reconstruction seemed to be on course, along with a new birth of freedom for the U.S. Negro. In late 1871 President Grant reproved "the apparent abolition of slavery in Cuba and Porto Rico" because it left "most of the laborers in bondage, with no hope of release until their lives become a burden to their employers"; since citizens of the United States were "large holders in foreign lands of this species of property," Washington could not stand by idly. He demanded "stringent legislation" from Congress "against the holding, owning or dealing in slaves or being interested in slave property in foreign lands, either as owners, hirers or mortgagers."[44]

In a similar vein, Congressman Clinton L. Cobb of North Carolina hailed the coming "independence" of Cuba and poured cold water on "annexation," though "such an event may happen and doubtless will. The history of Texas may be repeated," but the immediate concern was slavery and the failure to abolish it, which "would detract materially from the glory of our recent achievement. Our recent work is but half done while a slave groans under his burdens in the Western Hemisphere." U.S. Negroes above all, though "rejoicing over their own liberation," still chose to "stretch out yearning hearts to their kindred in bonds within a few days sail of our shores." He felt it would be wise to secure their Republican Party adherence by aggressively backing abolition in Cuba. "This bears upon the safety, welfare and perpetuity of the Union," he said beseechingly.[45]

Reference was made to President Grant at the above noted Boston meeting, who had taken a decided interest in these matters. He had told Congress: "All that is produced in Cuba could be produced [in] Santo Domingo," thus circumventing the riotousness of the former for the presumably relative placidity of the latter.[46] This remark was preceded by his accurate conclusion that "the property of our citizens in Cuba is large"[47]—and was now in jeopardy. The White House was pressed by abolitionists to slap stiff tariffs on imports from Cuba as long as slavery persisted; this "would powerfully operate in favor of emancipation in Cuba and Porto Rico" and Brazil as well, and coincidentally "would stimulate the production of sugar in our own country."[48] Of course, that some of those sugar plantations in Cuba were controlled by U.S. nationals would handcuff Washington's ability to act as abolitionists suggested.

Nevertheless, Henry Sanford, a budding diplomat, also recommended that President Grant consider the "expediency of a discriminatory duty on Slave-grown products not only for its political effect at home but for the advantage of the South and its influence abroad" since the "expenses of the war in Cuba are paid by the Slave owners there who, in fact," he stressed, *collect them from us* in return for their sugars." This could be "a fair and effectual blow to the war and to Slavery in Cuba" too, and it would "greatly stimulate" the "culture of sugar in Louisiana, Texas and Florida." There would be a sheen added to the U.S. escutcheon: "The world would generally look with favor upon such course, as the natural completion of the Great Act of Emancipation at home, that we should protect our Freemen from the unpaid labor of foreign slaves"—and "protect our lately emancipated slaves from the competition of those owned [by] the armed opponents of Cuba Libre!"[49] Such a boycott of slave-produced products from Cuba, said Madrid, "would completely ruin Cuba, as the United States buys over half her products."[50]

Those with interest in Cuba on the mainland were not all pacifists. There was, for example, James Thomson of Blackville, South Carolina, who, in light of the "probability of a war" with Spain, was "desirous of organizing a light battery of Artillery."[51] It was unclear if he agreed with abolitionist Amos Briggs of Philadelphia, who told President Grant that the "geographical position of Cuba must ever render it a source of anxiety to our Government, as in time of war it would be the ugliest military depot against us." Besides, "with Slavery abolished in the U.S. there can be no peace with Slavery in Cuba and without peace there, there can be no permanent security here, in view of the liability of our people becoming involved in their struggle in one way or the other."[52] Briggs could have added what a group of Boston Africans charged—that U.S. Negroes were being shanghaied from the mainland and dragged to Cuba: "There were colored men kept there in slavery who were once citizens of this country," it was stated with sadness.[53]

The pounding on the White House seemed to be having an effect when the London press reported in 1870 that "there appears to be no doubt that the American government intends to dispatch a fleet of four or five vessels to Havana" with assistance to the rebels on the agenda.[54] But Cuban exiles in Manhattan alleged that the United States—or at least the "Remington's Arms Manufactory"—was supplying Madrid with arms to crush the revolt: "They have also allowed the Spaniards to contract and fit out here thirty gunboats," allowing for the capture of prominent rebels who were then "executed." Cubans "are pursued on the seas by American ships," it was charged, and "those who fall to the struggle are wounded by American weapons"; those who favored abolition, the "admirers" of the republic, were "persecuted, arrested and punished" as official Washington apparently chose to "look with contempt upon the abolition of slavery declared by the Cuban Republic." Was it merely rumor that "Madrid and Washington had formed a secret alliance to crush the insurrection"?[55]

Jose de Armas y Cespedes, a Cuban exile in New York, reproached the United States, reminding that "in their gigantic struggle with the slave owners of the South, no one more admired their efforts than myself," but now his comrades were being arrested on the mainland. Havana was a "headquarters for the Confederacy" from whence "were constantly dispatched vessels laden with munitions of war" for the CSA, yet now Madrid was allowed to kidnap dissidents in the United States "who had sought refuge here" and "illegally send them back to Cuba." The cause he represented was "essentially abolitionist"—so why back Madrid, which was "strengthening the institution of slavery for an indefinite length of time by encouraging fresh importation of Negroes from Africa"? This was in 1869 and as he wrote Cespedes charged that "two cargoes" of the enslaved had just arrived in Cuba at the behest of the "notorious slave trader, Julian Zulueta."[56]

Yet Madrid too was displeased with what it perceived to be external inter-ference into an internal matter—the administration of Cuba. With haughti-ness Washington was told by Spain that the "movement for secession"—asso-ciating island rebels with mainland traitors—"carried away a part, certainly the greater . . . or the most important part, of the white population of the island, especially the unreflecting and rash youth, who, misled by their own inexperi-ence, imagined that it was possible to establish an independent and republican government in which the African race formed by far the major portion of the population and was still in a state of slavery." These Africans—these "bands of fugitive Negroes"—"are able to live in the jungles and deserts of the islands and thence fall upon estates and other property." Again, Madrid sought sym-pathy by analogizing the recently concluded traitorous revolt in neighboring Florida to the ongoing uprising in Cuba, but the U.S. emissary in Madrid replied with equal hauteur, remarking that since in Cuba "the governors and the governed" were "all the same in race, and with defects aggravated in the latter by tropical life and by association with slaves, [they] are at least equally to blame for the calamities in Cuba."[57]

Not to be undone, a London editorialist piled on, lecturing Washington for having the gall to "lecture Spain 'on the interests of humanity,' the treat-ment of her colonies and slavery. [Washington] seems to forget that probably America would to this day be exhibiting herself as of old the inhumanity of slavery but for the accident of the revolt of the Southern provinces," making this nation "hardly the country to lecture another on the subject of slavery." Washington was a self-interested party, having desired Cuba for decades—it was the "friendship of the wolf to the lamb," but "luckily the wolf has got no teeth; America has neither army nor navy worth mentioning and she cannot even deal with her Red Indians" and was armed with little more than "her pet-tifogging selfishness."[58]

What neither London nor Madrid nor insurgents may have realized was that Washington was not necessarily in favor of either Spain or its island oppo-nents and could just as well favor seeing them all drained in a bloody conflict, and thus facilitating a de facto annexation. Madrid should have considered this point when it began meddling in the internal affairs of Hispaniola, drain-ing resources that could have been better deployed to shore up Havana.

In that seething context, in early 1876 U.S. emissary Caleb Cushing met in Madrid with his Spanish counterpart who announced he was in favor of "emancipation of the slaves," but his hand was stayed by the "predatory bands of runaway blacks, headed by foreigners from [the] Dominica[n Republic] and Venezuela, engaged in the work of incendiarism and devastation," and consequently "if the slaves were now emancipated at once many of them would betake themselves to the mountains as maroons and become additional agents of disorder and bloodshed." Despite the sympathy for abolitionism in Washington, Madrid knew that there was staunch opposition there to "acts of naval or military hostility on the side of those incendiary bands." Hitting notes that would resonate on the mainland, Madrid emphasized the "robber character" of the "insurrection in Cuba," driven by "scattered parties of Negroes and mulattoes."[59]

Madrid argued that it was the militant revolt in Cuba that was delaying abolition. But for this uprising, said Fernando Calderon y Collantes, "there would not now have been for some time a single slave in the island of Cuba." Knowing Washington was in the throes of a debate about the destiny of the recently emancipated Africans, he stressed that the "Negroes and mulattoes" were the "principal elements of the insurrection," meaning immediate freedom for the enslaved would be a "very grave peril, not only for Spanish rule, and for all the Spaniards and Cubans faithful to the metropolis, but also for the whole white race of the island."[60]

This racial rhetoric was rising as the prospects for Reconstruction were diminishing, thus complicating the struggle for abolition and independence in Cuba. Senator Charles Sumner of Massachusetts was asked pointedly "what kind of men" were in rebel ranks: "Would they not be Negroes recruited from the plantations? Then what is this but a Negro insurrection?" And what did that mean for always unsteady race relations on the mainland? "The Negro males are far superior, both numerically and physically to the white males," it was said, and if the former prevailed it could "lead to the total extinction of the power of the whites and the establishment of another black republic," another Haiti in other words.

"History has demonstrated that the two races, white and black, cannot live together upon a footing of equality. One must be subject to the other. . . . Which race will rule upon the island of Cuba, in case the Spanish authority is overthrown, need require no oracle to determine"—and what would that mean for the mainland? "Horrors" were predicted, "similar to those perpetrated by the Negroes of San Domingo and Hayti [sic]," when Africans "gained the ascendancy." "Is there any reason to believe the island of Cuba would escape a like fate?" In Haiti "we have seen the blacks and mulattoes banded together for the destruction of the whites" and now Cuba was similarly beset. Why, asked writer Francis Norton, "place arms in the hands of its mixed population, that they may wage a similar war of extermination against each other—to recognize a government which has no actual existence and which is upheld in the field by a few robber bands of Negroes and mulattoes? . . . What is this but a Negro insurrection?" he cried.

"Will it not lead to the total extinction of the power of the whites and the establishment of another Black Republic?" Like the "savage black hordes of Toussaint" who "brutally massacred" the "whites of both sexes, young and old," Cuba was now undergoing a replay of history. Keeping slavery was a must, insisted Norton. "Are we not carrying our love and admiration for the Negro too far? Have we not done enough for him for one generation," he asked as he conflated race relations on both sides of the straits. "To give the Negroes their freedom in this country, we have sacrificed nearly a million of precious lives and expended more than $3,000,000,000" and now here comes Cuba requesting intervention, though "nine-tenths of the able-bodied men (those called white) ran from the country like sheep" and "weeping more like school-girls than men"—and now they wanted a bailout from mainlanders. [61]

The changing climate on the mainland was seemingly influencing the usual stream of visitors to Cuba. Yes, there was the older sentiment: "To be sure," said W. M. L. Jay in 1871, "the civil law of Cuba is kinder to the slave than ever our own was."[62] But by early 1878 this group included J. B. Russell who on his "first Sunday" there was disappointed that "there are no Protestant churches" and "few Catholic ones" either "in this place," a sign of moral turpitude: there was a "total ignorance of the people of the existence of such a being as God." He scoffed that "this whole place is strange beyond description" and "different from anything I ever saw," particularly since "all of the architecture here is Moorish," a possible sign of suspect racial origins. "The people," including "natives, Negroes and coolies are hideous, even the best of them." His revulsion was regurgitating, which meant he had "lost . . . many a good meal on this island. . . . I feel now as tho' I should not care to eat any more sugar as long as I live."[63]

Another mainlander was even more leery, though too immersed in a racial dynamic. He pointed to the prominent role in the struggle of Antonio Maceo, "the right hand of Máximo Gómez"—the latter's roots in Hispaniola made him similarly suspect. But it was Maceo who was defined by this self-proclaimed "American" as "an illiterate mulatto"—plus "the men whom he has drawn into this unhappy conflict are colored men." It was Maceo "who exercises, notwithstanding his low origin, considerable influence over the Negroes of Guantánamo." It was Maceo who "has a passion for war"—besides, "the whites of the party regard him with disfavor." Then there was "Carlos Roloff," a comrade of Maceo who "was born in Poland" and was "a Jew, and by his acts proves to be a nihilist and a dynamiter." But he was unique since a preponderance of the "guerilla leaders are Negroes," yet, concluded this mainlander, "we are told . . . that we should be their accomplices in robbery."[64]

By way of contrast, Congressman Josiah Walls of Florida—a Negro—urged the recognition of the belligerent rights of Cuba.[65] As early as 1873, he introduced a resolution in support of the Cuban belligerency. In no uncertain terms he castigated Madrid for its laggard approach to abolition despite tentative steps in that direction in 1870.[66]

Congressman Walls may have been aware of mainland press accounts asserting that official Havana "detects or fancies" that he sees "in every native the taint of Negro and of slave blood"; what U.S. Negroes were taunted with—"a touch of the tar brush"—was hurled at the island's anti-colonial forces. More than this, islanders were said to have "Moorish blood" flowing in their veins, which was disqualifying. And even if not, these suspect Cubans "ha[d] been for many generations nursed by Negro women" and thus "evince strong sympathies with the Negro race." This evident sympathy toward the "Negro race" was "the cause of the Cuban insurrection" and at the root of the struggle over emancipation. This particular account was retained by Moses Taylor, one of New York's most affluent who also had significant holdings in Cuba.[67]

Taylor also had reason to believe that as of 1873 the price of enslaved Africans had increased fivefold over the past four decades and that possibly imports continued. Slavery was still endorsed by many planters, whose "estates" were "deeply mortgaged" to some bankers in Taylor's Manhattan. If Cuba were to "undergo the fate of Jamaica," it was said, "the consequences of the catastrophe would be felt in the counting houses of . . . American citizens."[68] There may have been 1,500 slaveholders in Cuba in 1873, it was reported, but only 150 were not crushed by debt, in hock to those like Taylor—and this smaller number were heavily not Creoles. This suggested that some Creole support of war was also a wise financial strategy designed to foil mortgage holders—though "annexation" was generally consistent with Washington's long-term aims.[69] In gauging his strategy, Taylor also was informed that London's long-standing antipathy to annexation had dissipated since "the Americans now have no slaves" and there were "too many coloured people always coming into collision with white people at home to look for more abroad."[70]

But when Maceo visited New York in 1878 to raise funds with which to continue the war against Spain, he was besieged by reporters eager to meet and confer with the famed Cuban leader. U.S. Negroes assembled to pay him solemn honor. Later a leading guesthouse in New York's Negro community was named "Hotel Maceo," the beginning of a growing legacy whereby infants too received his name, a trend that continues to this very day on the mainland. On the other hand, some on the mainland, stunned by his military prowess and popularity which sent such a troubling message (in their minds), denied that he was an African and claimed that his dark visage was a product of too much exposure to sunlight.[71] As the 1868–1878 war bled effortlessly into the decisive 1890s conflict, the mainland response increasingly was shaped by the declining popularity of the U.S. Negro.

One scholar argues that "the brilliant Cuban general, Antonio Maceo . . . a mulatto [*sic*] indirectly redounded to the credit of American Negroes"[72]— which provided impetus on both sides of the straits for reactionaries to abort both Reconstruction and the anticolonial and abolitionist war in Cuba. Even the former U.S. senator from Kansas, John Ingalls, conceded that Maceo exhibited "flashes of military genius," terming him the "Toussaint L'Ouverture of the insurrection," and "the noted Negro commander Flor Crombet" was "its Dessalines," not exactly reassuring in the circles in which this reputed solon routinely circulated.

To counter the appeal of Maceo, Spain was seeking to recruit Africans of its own—"the lieutenant-colonel of the royal body-guard of Captain-General Weyler was a Spanish-French Negro, born in New Orleans, and once a servant of ex-Senator P. B. S. Pinchback" of Louisiana—the latter also defined as a Negro on the mainland. Weyler's aide had fled the state in the midst of racist terror and had become a "distinguished chiropodist in Havana" and now sported "a dazzling array of diamonds and decorations. He is Vice-Chairman of the Weyler Junta" and "chief of the colored fire brigade. He also owns a tri-weekly newspaper, which invariably reprints from the American press all the accounts of lynchings of Negroes in the Southern States. In his editorial columns he alludes to them as an argument against annexation to the United States." Senator Ingalls also opined that the "Negro has been such a creation of implicit obedience" that "he obeys on the [military] field as he would in the cotton row"[73]—which may have been good news for Washington's forces, but not so much when it came to confronting Cubans on the battlefield. The larger question was how could the United States maintain its swaggering white supremacy while living next door to a neighbor not only willing to allow Africans to climb to the highest level but, perhaps worse, allow fleeing refugees from the mainland with apparent revenge-seeking in mind to do the same?

The broader point was how could Washington back forcefully either the insurgents or Madrid when both were seemingly willing to cooperate with Africans—a group that was rapidly losing clout on the mainland?

Nevertheless, it was this same General Weyler who repeatedly fomented racist fears, not only denouncing Maceo as a "mulatto" but raised a furor about the women who were said to be fighting alongside the insurgent leader by declaring that, yes, "many of them are mulattoes." Maceo's comrades denied fervently what Madrid charged—that this was no more than an "uprising of Negroes." Vainly appealing to the more constructive sentiments of mainlanders Salvador Cisneros-Betancourt replied, "But even if it were a Negro rebellion, would the people of the United States frown upon it?" These were "insults [to] the memory of the grand army of the dead" during the Civil War. "We are proud to have our colored brothers with us in this glorious struggle for freedom," it was said huffily.[74] But the Civil War had been over for decades by then; Reconstruction had been quashed; and a new more racist worldview was coming to prevail among many mainlanders, which apparently was not well understood in Cuba.

As the light of Reconstruction began to flicker, also dimming was any residual mainland sentiment for those in Cuba who resembled those at issue in Washington—the besieged African.[75] Retrenchment on one front fed retreat on the other—and vice versa—in a seemingly endless feedback loop. As Reconstruction petered out in 1877, what came to be called the Ten Years' War lurched to a fitful conclusion by 1878. A signal in this direction was emitted as early as January 1876 when the ill-famed Ambrosio Gonzales told President Grant of his leading role with the traitorous Confederates, while adding familiarly, "When you were in Charleston after the War, on a tour of inspection, I was one of a deputation of merchants and planters who called on you to request the removal of colored troops"—a request that was granted to the detriment of U.S. Negroes and their solidarity with a free Cuba too. For his part, Gonzales confided that he was "ruined by the war" and had "been to Cuba four times since its close," though his exact duties there remained mysterious.[76]

What was clear was that his fortunes quickly revived while those of many Cubans and U.S. Negroes declined. By early 1878, the U.S. legation in Cuba received word that "hostilities" had been "suspended,"[77] though in April of that pivotal year, the Spanish consul in New Orleans forwarded news items concerning a "patriotic Cuban club" that viewed with "indignation" the "conditions of peace agreed between the Spanish government" and "some members of the Cuban House of Representatives."[78]

Yet as Spanish envoys nervously monitored New Orleans, Cuban exiles on the mainland—who proclaimed their antislavery—discussed convening a "convention of the colored people of this country," which was deemed to be "most important."[79] Racists could understandably see the prospect of this envisioned "international convention to be held at New Orleans" as a dangerous provocation of the Cuban Anti-Slavery Society; indeed, it was announced happily in mid-1873, "delegates from the state of Texas have already been appointed," while these activists were "in correspondence with Hayti, St. Domingo, England, France and other states," in addition to "all of the states on this continent north and south."[80] With good reason, Dixie could see Cuban abolitionists as being an enemy in the same league with mainland Africans.

It was this conflicted context that seeded the rise of the Gonzales family in the violence-prone politics of the Palmetto State. The offspring of Ambrosio became early followers of those who succeeded in toppling Reconstruction and bringing to an abrupt close a brief era subsequently dismissed furiously as a reign of "Negro misrule." Such racist characterizations were bound to redound to the detriment of the Gonzales family—for, as one analyst put it, "in South Carolina a dark, rather Latin-looking young man with a Cuban name would have a handicap in politics." Still, Narciso Gonzales avidly backed measures to minimize the impact of the Negro vote: he despised the symbol of Negro political power, Robert Smalls—as did other Jim Crow advocates—and denounced him repeatedly in colorful terms. In 1881 the younger Gonzales, as he put it, "plugged him in the eye," then, he said, Smalls—who had a "heavy stick," then "cuffed me, bear fashion, on the side of the face twice." Then an enraged Gonzales "doubled him up with a kick in the expansive region below the belt. A friend of his took his arm and led him away and I remained in possession of the field," he said boastfully, solidifying his manliness and his whiteness simultaneously. "If I had had a pistol," he noted contemptuously, "I would certainly have shot him and wanted to go for him afterwards." Thereafter, Gonzales was introduced proudly as the "Man who knocked [expletive deleted] out of a Nigger Congressman." Press across the land blared this story to a wider audience, giving the impression that those constituted as "white" had a lengthening list of allies. It also made Gonzales into a celebrity—though his Cuban ancestry marked him as a "mongrel" who had descended from a people who had been bested by mere Moors for centuries.

Undeterred, Gonzales tripled down on bigotry, promoting exclusion from the mainland of Chinese migrants, as he felt compelled time and time again to reassert his firm belief in white supremacy when critics accused him of being sympathetic to the Negro, particularly since his own racial bona fides were questionable. He was a classic man in the middle and, as so often happens, those whose racial loyalties are questioned are often the most passionate in their defense of the racial elite. This marginal status helps to explain his prickliness, his quickness to feel insult and defend his challenged honor, his exaggerated defense of the (alleged) virtue of Southern white womanhood—an emblem of Dixie masculinity. All were symptoms of his insecurity in a racially polarized society, for his olive complexion and coal black hair made him stand out in Charleston.[81]

Whether he knew it or not, Gonzales was walking a narrowing tightrope in postbellum Dixie. For a while, support from his likes was needed desperately by former Confederates, at sword's point with the likes of Robert Smalls. In 1874 the Spanish consul in Charleston expressed "surprise" at the difficulty of his nation's flagged vessels gaining access to the key port for supplies needed in the midst of an insurgency.[82] At this point, even aromatic cigars were considered suspect contraband.[83] Nevertheless, anticolonial Cubans could not be pleased that in 1876 as they were fighting against increasingly adverse odds, three to four Spanish ships were clearing monthly from Brunswick, Georgia, alone carrying cargo valued in the thousands of dollars.[84] In New York trade was so brisk in 1876 with Spanish flagged-vessels that a request was made to increase consular staff there in response.[85] By 1878, as the intra-island conflict was winding down, the Spanish consul in Charleston was being invited to intimate social gatherings with former Confederates as guests of honor.[86]

Still, it would have been instructive for him if he had been able to skim reports from Madrid's man in New Orleans. This emissary had noticed an increase in cotton exports, but with the abolition of slavery and the seeming inability to attract more European migrants—and the hostility toward Chinese—there were labor constraints.[87] The political situation was skidding toward instability with racial clashes becoming normalized to the point where a number of Cuban emigrants were pleading to return to the island.[88] As so often happened, events on this side of the Gulf Coast were emanating outward, and soon there were reports of arms flowing from New Orleans to Havana for purposes Madrid deemed to be suspect. In 1877 the envoy in New Orleans, Miguel Suarez, objected sternly when he found that "Cuban insurgents here intend to have a . . . demonstration."[89]

As Africans in Cuba strained against the shackles of slavery, Suarez watched with concern as U.S. Negroes, all of whom were involved with the Republican Party, were holding raucous meetings, replete with their very own elected officials. This was in the midst of a tangled controversy as to who was actually elected as governor of Louisiana. Adding to the conflict was the presence of 10,000 armed troops, who seemed to be hostile to the party to which Negroes were loyal.[90] Those troops proved to be essential in squelching Reconstruction and though the "insurgents" in Cuba did not oust the colonialists from Havana, they were able to make progress in eroding slavery—a reality that the Negroes in LaFourche parish in Louisiana saluted, as their representative tendered "thanks of the colored people" to "the Spanish nation" for the "liberation of the colored brethren in the island of Cuba," in "destroying the last vestige of that debasing institution."[91] Once again, the destinies of Africans on both sides of the straits appeared to be conjoined.

Gonzales, in sum, was simply adjusting to the mainland zeitgeist, which was turning against the ambitions of Africans wherever they might reside. This was a spirit embodied by David Croly, the prominent New York writer and editor who argued that not only Cuba but Jamaica and Haiti too should be annexed by Washington since "universal suffrage is a farce when exercised by savages." Neither of these nations—and Africa—could "ever be redeemed, except in two ways: either the natives must be forced to work, or they must be killed off to give place for the races who will work."[92] Soon even more mainland investors were pouring into Cuba, particularly eyeing sugar holdings,[93] perhaps not animated by the spirit of genocide but its close relative: shameless exploitation.

Yet, as white mainlanders were arriving in ever greater number on the island, eager to take advantage of a land that in some critical sites resembled a smoldering ruin, U.S. Negroes were being ousted. In 1879 the U.S. consul in Cienfuegos reported that the authorities were seeking to limit the arrival of "American citizens of color," in a replay of the "old law of 1844"; this would "entail great loss and delay to the American vessels arriving with colored crews" and would probably lead to their sacking in order to facilitate commerce. These Negroes were to "be sent to jail" or forced "to remain on board their vessels." Recalling the days of yore, he asked London's envoy for aid since British subjects were also to be penalized. However, times had changed: the envoy was a "large slaveholder and a violent pro-slavery man and looks with favor" on such measures. The consul, no abolitionist enthusiast, was also concerned that "slaves" from the recent "insurrection" only recently "made free" were "allowed to visit their old homes and recount to their companions in slavery the deeds of blood and fire by which they gained their freedom and inciting them to do the same."[94] Still, the victim the consul reported on shortly thereafter was "George Dickson, colored," who "died in the hospital" in Cienfuegos "in consequence of injuries inflicted on his person" at the hands of a fellow sailor after tensions exploded on board the vessel when he was not allowed to disembark.[95]

Among the mainland visitors allowed to disembark were John Dean Caton, a former chief justice of the high court in Illinois, who was keen to note the presence of the "American fleet now in the bay of Havana" just after hostilities ceased, as Washington did not necessarily embrace either victory for the rebels or continuation of colonial rule. As to slavery, Caton, well aware of the convulsions this institution had inspired in his homeland, reported with noncommittal brio that the "abolitionist movement is embarrassed and retarded by the Civil War, because any encouragement now given to it appears like a concession to the rebels, who have made abolition one of their cardinal principles."[96] This provided untold leverage for mainlanders, now formally committed to abolition, as Madrid clung anxiously to the past. This also provided impetus for more filibustering expeditions, as Madrid's consul in Savannah was informed in 1887.[97]

One has to include the qualifier "formally" for as explicit abolition approached in Cuba in 1886, U.S. envoys on the island were not cheery. One of their number cautioned that the experience with antislavery on the mainland should not compel enthusiasm about the same prospect on the island. It was a "step in the right direction," it was said grudgingly, but "will hold out no such incentive to personal worth and patriotism" and, worst of all, was apt to make the African "become a very unreliable and indifferent tiller of the soil." Fortunately, their numbers were decreasing, not least in the aftermath of a devastating war—"seventy-five years ago, it was put at 1,500,000, last year [1882] it was put at 1, 344,409."[98]

These envoys may have received a warm reception from some islanders, for one mainlander reported enthusiastically that Cienfuegos, "like Cardenas," was "called an American capital. It has some twenty-five thousand inhabitants, a large proportion of whom speak English"; true, there were "comparatively few slaves to be found on the plantations or elsewhere" in the neighborhood as the peculiar institution was "rapidly disappearing," but that hardly precluded opportunities for exploitation.[99] For part of the battering and softening up of Cuba that led to the de facto U.S. annexation post-1898 was the reality that the Ten Years' War contributed to Cuban planters becoming indebted to mainland shippers and consequently compelled to relinquish their estates to their creditors to settle unpaid debts when sugar prices fell in 1884.[100]

In 1884 President Chester A. Arthur inked an agreement with Madrid increasing imports from Cuba and Puerto Rico.[101] Simultaneously, the number of vessels travelling between Wilmington, North Carolina—not exactly a prime mainland port—and Cuba continued to rise, reflecting increasing ties.[102]

One of the most affluent mainlanders in Cuba—Edwin Atkins—reluctantly acceded to emancipation. It was "unavoidable, "but "free labor is almost as cheap now." Still, he had to endure "a good deal of trouble" from these newly christened proletarians. "One or two Negroes I would like to send off," he groused, "but you can't do it now as it would only induce others to behave badly."[103] Afterward, he prayed that the insurgency would be defeated, a hope in which he was joined by John Burgess, noted historian, whose racial theories provided sustenance both to imperial expansion abroad and suppression of the Negro at home. Resuscitating the antebellum, but continuously relevant, fashion of twisting the lion's tail, he blamed London for stories about Spanish atrocities in Cuba.[104]

By this point there were other interlopers in the region, causing Washington to seek to fasten an even tighter grip on the island. By 1886, the U.S. consul in Santiago was fretting about the "chances of German annexation of this island," which would not occur since "the people as expressed privately" were supposedly "in favor of annexation by the United States."[105] The larger point was that as the world was changing, the mainland had more worries beyond Madrid as to the fate of Cuba.

The Cuban people were unfortunately reeling from the "possibility of a smallpox epidemic" with some concern that it would spread to the mainland, though relief was expressed that the "full force" would be blunted since "in all probability" it would be "confine[d] . . . to the Negro population" few of

whom were "vaccinated"—though the U.S. envoy was "notifying health officers along the U.S. Atlantic coast" to be on the safe side.[106]

The racial retrenchment on both sides of the straits was rippling outward.
Thus, in 1888, Key West's James Dean became the first black judge in the
South after Reconstruction with substantial support from those of Cuban
origin. Born in 1858 in Ocala, he was educated at Cookman Institute in Jacksonville, before graduating at the top of his class at Howard Law School. His
support from those with Cuban heritage was timely since others defined as
"white" resented him on racist grounds, with some traveling to other cities
to get their marriage licenses because they did not want one issued by him.
Tellingly, he was removed reportedly after issuing a marriage license to a so-
called mixed race Cuban man who wanted to marry a black woman, as the
post-Reconstruction ethos asserted itself more forcefully. The case involved
a Cuban pattern that fit awkwardly on the mainland. Antonio Gonzales, who
described himself as "part black"—but was not viewed thusly by many mainlanders—wanted to marry a "Cuban black woman."[107] Judge Dean was further
charged with being overzealous in compelling Cubans described as "white" on
the mainland to leave simple cohabitation for marriage[108] in unions curiously
akin to that of Gonzales.

A mass meeting of 800 Floridians to protest his ouster was chaired by a man
of Cuban ancestry, Jose De C. Palmino. After his ouster, Negro judges in Dixie
were few and far between before the 1950s.[109] But Key West's reputation as an
outlier was reflected when the now defrocked former chief executive, Ulysses
S. Grant, chose to visit there and spent time addressing "colored citizens."[110]

Despite the fall of Judge Dean, Key West continued to be an anomaly—
the farthest point south in Dixie, yet harboring politics unlike the benighted
region because of the presence in great numbers of Cubans. "The Cubans
run the island to a very great extent," said one Negro journalist in 1888 with
seeming relief. There was a "conglomeration of American colored and white
folks" and "white Cubans and colored Cubans" but those from the island were
in ascendancy: "They not only control the cigar business, which is the leading
and almost only industry here. but they seem to own a majority of the smaller
shops and stores"; hence "when you go on the streets you hear nothing but
Spanish." Their influence was refracted politically in the Republican Party,
where they allied with U.S. Negroes; at their rallies "there is generally one
speech in Spanish" and "one in English." A new kind of social relations arrived
with them too, for now, "if you want to court a Cuban girl you must make up
your mind to court the mother too, or the father as the case may be."[111]

Though Reconstruction generally had been terminated elsewhere in
Dixie in 1877, by 1888 U.S. Negroes continued to hang on to office in Key
West because of the substantial Cuban presence. There was "no attempt at

bulldozing and intimidation during campaigns and at elections here," said an astonished visiting Negro journalist from New York. "No Negroes are murdered here in cold blood," which had become the norm elsewhere, even in Florida. "There is a liberal sentiment here due to the presence of foreigners for any ex-slave holding foreigner is better than an ex-slaveholder. The Cubans probably have the same reason for being prejudiced as the Southern whites." Yet he said, seemingly puzzled, "Not withstanding slavery has been only recently abolished there, they are not equally so [prejudiced] by any means." These Cubans may have had "prejudices" but "they are not so foolish as to let the bugbear of social equality frighten them into denying a man his natural rights because he happens to be colored." Painting Key West as Paradise Found, not least because of the Cuban presence, he said with wonder, "Colored men here speak and act their sentiments, with none to molest or make them afraid and there is nothing cowardly and servile about them."[112]

There were so many regarded as "colored" that combined with the civilizing presence of the Cubans, Key West stood out even more. At this juncture, Key West had a population of about 13,500 with Cubans as the second-largest population group at 33 percent of the total and Bahamians at 24 percent.[113]

But even as visiting Negro journalists were dazzled by Key West, things were slowly changing. How could Key West remain an outpost of progressivism in a state moving oppositely? True, the instinct among mainland Cubans was to oppose the Democrats, perceived as reactionary and comprised of defenders of enslavement. But as the GOP capitulated and surrendered Reconstruction, which was accompanied by a reluctance to support the insurrection against colonial Cuba, incensed mainland Cubans slowly began to withdraw support from this now compromised party.[114]

But another process was unfolding at the same time, which was of equal moment for the mainland: Cubans in Key West of African descent were being redefined as U.S. Negroes.[115] Perversely, this process whetted the appetite and contributed more culturally distinct targets to bludgeon into accepting an unfamiliar racial status quo, for between 1882 and 1930, the Sunshine State had the highest per capita lynching rate in the United States.[116] "Florida," says one contemporary analyst, "since becoming a U.S. territory in 1821, has been especially dangerous for black people," which was all too perceptive. This violence had a sociopolitical purpose in that by 1814 colonial figures revealed that 57 percent of the total population of then Spanish Florida was of African origin— and driving that figure downward to a level consistent with mainland norms was an outcome and purpose of racist mobs running amok.[117]

As Africans of Cuban origin were pounded, those of European origin also found it difficult to escape punishment, as Narciso Gonzales would find later. In 1884 a company in Mississippi hired Spaniards and Portuguese for various difficult jobs, but soon they were complaining that they were treated worse than slaves in Cuba and it was recommended that they depart posthaste. They wished to return to Iberia, were unable—and wound up distraught in Cuba.[118]

Tampa too was being transformed by an influx of Cubans, many of whom were fleeing unrest. Peter Claver was a Jesuit priest who dedicated himself to the plight of enslaved Africans, and was sainted after his passing in 1654, which made appropriate the naming of a parochial school for him in Tampa that schooled generations of Negro and Cuban children, including the famed actor Butterfly McQueen. The perception among whites was that this school was flouting Jim Crow norms.[119] One nun subsequently recalled how the St. Peter Claver School was burned to the ground in February 1894. "It was almost like if you were Cubans," said her interlocutor, "you were just a little better than bein' a 'nigger,' you know, just one step beyond, you know." Still, this influx opened an escape hatch for U.S. Negroes to flee bigotry, for "if your hair was curled, and you were brown you could pretend to be Cuban and then you would be a little better off."[120]

The problem was that when Negroes and melanin-deficient Cubans were thrust together in small schools, Jim Crow advocates objected violently. The Jesuits had been warned about continuing this school before it was torched— then it was moved from its location near a white neighborhood and closer to the Negro part of town. Even then, nuns were arrested for violating a law barring white teachers from instructing Negroes.[121]

With the brief promise of Reconstruction destroyed and Cuba reeling from war, smallpox and maladies of biblical proportion, a consensus was growing among mainland elites that the time had now arrived to accomplish a goal that had been maddeningly elusive since the founding of the republic. A Detroit newspaper thought Cuba would "make one of the finest states in the Union," which was propelled by the presence of a "strong party growing up in the island in favor of reciprocity with and annexation to the United States. We should act at once and make this possible."[122]

Also propelling this rapidly accelerating movement was a souring attitude on the mainland toward Africans—and not just post-Reconstruction asperity. A Chicago writer in 1891 captured these dour sentiments while visiting the island. After comparing emancipation there and in Dixie, he observed with surprise that now in Cuba "everything is different. Wages have to be paid the blacks for their work, and as they are a thriftless lot . . . wages are high." Perhaps worse was the reality that "the lines between the whites and blacks do not appear to be so closely drawn in Cuba as in the States and the prejudice against the Negro not so great."[123]

"That hatred of the Negro because he *is* a Negro, so common among very good people in the United States," said another sojourner from the mainland was not as prevalent on the island. "I have never heard here," said James W. Steele, "the equivalent of that frequent expression of the old times among my high-toned ancestors, 'a miserable free nigger,' except from an American or Englishman." The level of miscegenation he espied made him predict that "in a hundred years the probabilities are that Cuba will be a black country." There was a "peculiarity" of "the Latins in their association with the Negro," that he found confounding.[124] Yet another analyst did not seem pleased to ascertain that when slavery was banned in Cuba, "the slaves were more active than with us, in the use of arms to secure their freedom."[125]

But how could the mainland head pell-mell toward the "nadir" in an evolving racism, "the betrayal of the Negro" as one eminent scholar termed it,[126] if Cuba presented a different example ninety miles away? Possibly, swallowing Cuba and forcing conformity with mainland norms would erase this opportunity for the Negro to engage in adept political arbitrage.

A U.S. representative in Santiago, Cuba, thought that the process leading to a mainland "nadir" was compromising mainland interests on the island. He was irked by "misinformed" newspaper accounts detailing a "war of races" in Cuba, which were "simply absurd." It would be a "great pity," he intoned, if these "false rumors" served to "deter our capitalists from making profitable investments" in Cuba.[127] He was objecting to journalistic accounts in 1890 that detailed "outrages and murders committed by a band of colored desperadoes" in the "eastern part of Cuba"; they were "well armed and mounted, under the command of Calixto Maceo [sic] one of the black chiefs in the past insurrection." These men had "attacked and plundered" and their "number is said to be increasing." Troubling was that "the commencement of a war of races" had been "initiated by the Cuban Negroes,"[128] and the question was how could the mainland continue safely with their own vast array of depredations perpetrated against Negroes when just across the straits it appeared a radically different scenario was unfolding: armed Africans fighting back with the prospect of taking power in league with allies? At this point, even officialdom in Cuba sought to discredit such accounts, dismissing them with "profound astonishment."[129]

But many mainlanders not only objected to Africans but seemed to think that Spaniards were undeserving of Cuba too; actually, the two seemed to merge seamlessly as the 1890s dawned. In 1890 the Spanish consul in Manhattan criticized what he saw as a commercial war—"la guerra commercial"—that Washington had launched against his nation's interests with the aim, possibly, of detaching Cuba.[130] At that point, there seemed—in a historical pattern—to be a convergence of interests between Washington and the "Creoles" or, more precisely, the Cuban exile community on the mainland: both sought the hasty departure of the Spanish colonialists from Havana, though many of the exiles did not seem to comprehend that Washington's goal was not true independence for the island. By 1890 some of these exiles were making the inflammatory allegation that abolition of slavery—actualized, it was thought, in 1886—was a sham. Supposedly, said Fidel Pierra, in April 1869, "all the slaves were declared absolutely free," yet "the partial abolition was not declared by Spain until 1880, while during the years intervening between this date and 1878, hundreds of Negroes [were] . . . again enslaved by the Spaniards with the connivance and assistance of officials, high and low." So why should the 1886 abolition proclamation be trusted?[131]

This was bound to strike a chord with U.S. Negroes who were descending precipitously and rapidly on the mainland after the failed promise of Reconstruction and the inconclusive results of the Ten Years' War. Even a now elderly Frederick Douglass confessed in the late 1880s that he had long rejected mass emigration of U.S. Negroes, but given the "wretched condition" he now saw spreading, his new view was " 'Godspeed' in your emigration scheme."[132] As more mainland attention was drawn to Cuba as the 1890s war of insurgents sought to fulfill what had not been attained by 1878, more U.S. Negroes began to look longingly to Cuba as a site of exile, particularly since the perception had persisted for years that racism was not as intense there.[133] The arrival of Negro soldiers with the 1898 war was to speed up this process.

In a morally askew manner, the example of mainland Cubans like Narciso Gonzales, still basking in the glory brought by his fracas with Robert Smalls, may have increased—for a while—the attraction of the island among U.S. Negroes. After all, given those to whom he was compared, Gonzales may have seemed like a liberal: he objected to mass deportation of Negroes from South Carolina, timidly accused lynchers, and did not embrace measures like literacy tests to bar Negroes from the polls. He even backed a measure that would impose a fine on any county in which a lynching occurred, which led to his being burned in effigy in 1892 after he denounced the lynching of a Negro. Actually, he was identified with the dwindling political faction that believed the Negro vote should be courted, not abolished.

Paradoxically, as the struggle in Cuba intensified in the 1890s, Gonzales changed his tune as he sought support for the insurgents among the preponderance of mainlanders not renowned for their enlightened view of U.S. Negroes. "Our dearest wish," he announced unctuously in February 1896, "has been that the Negroes in South Carolina could be reduced to a minority so that whites might not suffer." Scrambling to avoid association with heralded figures like Maceo, he hastened to assure local elites that the color line was drawn in Cuba "as strictly as in the American South"—a gross overstatement that would have discredited him if the actual reality had been exposed. With fervor he began to preach a most vile gospel of white supremacy.[134]

The intensified conflict in Cuba in the 1890s engendered similar political gymnastics in others. There were those who hungered to annex Cuba, realizing a decades-long dream and fulfilling the mainland's nascent imperial ambitions. But, as with the "Africanization" scare of the 1850s, there were those who were reluctant to swallow Cuba, fearing the indigestion (and armed Africans) it was thought to bring: they rued the idea that the "nadir" for U.S. Negroes, which seemed to be proceeding right along, could be knocked off course with the addition of yet more noisome Negroes. The eruption of the insurgency in Cuba—once more—in the 1890s forced an anguished reconsideration of these troublesome issues. "Africanization" continued to be more than a recurring ghost: it was invoked in 1896 by all sides in the U.S. Senate, with one lawmaker reduced to quoting the portentous 1859 words of the former leading Confederate Judah P. Benjamin, who warned that "we shall be ever insecure against hostile attack until this important geographical and military position"—Cuba—"is placed under our protection and control."[135] Why? One reason was the presence of so many armed Africans with so much perceived power meant they would seek powerful allies globally to counter a white supremacist mainland.

Slowly but surely official U.S. observers began to report what were deemed to be troubling details about a growing insurgency in Cuba. In late 1893 the consul in Santiago, Pulaski Hyatt, reported that "two Cubans, William Moncada, colored, a Brigadier General in the Cuban forces during the late revolution here and Garzon by name were arrested."[136] Then, in early 1895 Hyatt told of U.S. nationals blown off course to Hispaniola, where they "wanted to remain but the natives (blacks who are commonly known to hate the sight of a white) would not permit them to remain longer," so they scrammed to Cuba and were promptly jailed.[137] Could white supremacy really thrive in such a neighborhood?

Hyatt may well have posed that disturbing query in August 1895 when he informed his superiors that "five thousand insurrectionists under command of Antonio Maceo" were "encamped within one and a half miles" of Santiago "and have been nearby for the last five days."[138]

Actual reports from the battlefield in Cuba were hardly enhancing mainland composure either. From the U.S. consulate in Havana in 1896 came a striking report, detailing that this "struggle is unique—a guerrilla warfare" with "no large armies," simple "skirmishing," it was stressed, with untold ramifications for a "large" mainland army.[139]

George Bronson Rea, like some other mainlanders, had gone to join the war on the island and found himself with Maceo's troops, where he witnessed chilling episodes of Africans blithely wielding finely sharpened machetes against their opponents. "The Negroes afterwards laughingly told me that the man [slain] fell with his head split clear down to the shoulders and that they rolled the body down the hill so his friends would find him in the morning." Rea was pro-Madrid in this conflict; thus he was outraged when he met with the insurgent leader, Máximo Gómez, who with temerity proceeded in "extolling the virtues and merits of [Benito] Juarez" of Mexico, then went further to refer to "some Negro of Santo Domingo or Hayti as the next highest type of an American soldier. His egoism was sublime," he said with disgust, for "as he proceeded in his discourse, he studiously ignored all reference to Washington or Grant. It is hardly necessary to add that I was virtually indignant at what I considered an insult and slur on the Americans."[140]

Hyatt was beginning to think the unthinkable: Would an "independent" Cuba be "capable of self-government," particularly since the part of the island where he was posted "contains the largest proportion of Negro population and is known as the 'hotbed of rebellion'"?[141] Even when the authorities made headway, the signs could be perturbing. For example, in late 1895 Hyatt found that "large numbers of Cubans are being arrested and sent to Ceuta, Africa," for various offenses,[142] a reminder of what befell mainland miscreants decades earlier.

The ground was being prepared for a direct U.S. military intervention in Cuba and the presence of numerous armed Africans was an ostensible reason. But this 1898 intervention was to bear bitter fruit when U.S.-style Jim Crow was exported to the island, a cumbersome fit at best that eventuated in revolution in 1959.

The author Murat Halstead confronted this irritating dilemma in 1896 when he advocated annexation of the island. He pooh-poohed how Havana tended to "make much of the conspicuity of the Maceos"—Antonio and his brother—"in the effort to persuade people that the insurrection is an affair of black men chiefly and means the conversion of Cuba into a larger San Domingo," which was precisely the apprehension of some of his fellow citizens. Well, he conceded, "the Maceos are said to be, and doubt truly [are] very ambitious to advance the black race," but given the immense stakes at play this was hardly a reason to block annexation: others were not as certain.

From a certain mainland viewpoint, Havana was needlessly complicating things by responding to this insult to Jim Crow by "giving black men in the Spanish army" discrete concessions, which would serve to guarantee that no matter who prevailed, Africans would be empowered, a mainland nightmare that cried out for intervention. Officialdom in Havana magnified the indignity by portraying Washington in caricatures offensively with a "tremendous mouth with ample digestion, a bulbous, disreputable nose, broken teeth and bad manners towards colored people of both sexes." This was dirty pool, it was thought, violating the basic norms of racial rule. Washington was portrayed as either "conducting himself with familiarity toward a black woman or handing a torch to a black man, bidding him to go and burn canefields or houses, and he is doing this with a diabolical leer. This style of art is also seen in personifying insurrection in a brutal black man whose lips are excessive, imposing his attention upon a slender, graceful figure—a young white woman who represents Cuba, and regards him with horror. A black man is always equipped with a knife with which he is assassinating a Cuban woman, or a big blacking brush with which he is supposed to be blotting Cuba from the map." In short, Cuba was becoming another Haiti.

"Representations of blacks as the rebels-in-chief and cane-burning demons with forked toe-nails" was the norm. Yet even Halstead knew that General Valeriano Weyler, Spain's chief military figure on the island, was "treating black men with consideration" in his own forces, with potential long-term negative consequences for the mainland. "Negro soldiers are often on guard at the government palace," he conceded. Shockingly, when General Weyler "was asked what his policy towards the Negroes was, he said, 'Just the same as to others.'" It was recalled that during the Ten Years' War that his "cavalry escort was of black men." Antonio Maceo aside, Halstead felt "the anticipation was that the Free Blacks would prefer the Spaniards to the Creoles"—perhaps because of the perception that the latter were much too close to the despised mainlanders. General Weyler had cultivated this sentiment, he reported, by seeking to "invite the friendliness of the black people"—no small matter since "the black rebels are among the bravest of the fighters for freedom." This was causing cracks in Madrid's coalition since now the "disappointed and angry Spaniards speak of the 'Negro Insurrection.'" Playing a dangerous game, the Spaniards made "artful use of the prominence of colored insurgents in the war"—the Maceo brothers, for example—"to excite race issues." Pursuing a scorched earth policy in the ideological and material senses, Madrid seemed poised to immolate Cuba in order to save it. Halstead, who hailed from a nation where playing upon racial fears was well-honed, thought Madrid's race-baiting would play into the hands of Washington, both eroding Havana's base among the "white majority" of Cuba and erasing the apprehensions of those in Dixie about a massive U.S. intervention, perhaps among some anti-imperialists too. Highlighting the "Black Scare" while relying on the equivalent of the "sable arm" (black troops in the Union Army) that had devastated Dixie was a dangerous game for Spain to play.

Halstead reminded his mainland audience that "in each of the six provinces" on the island "the blacks can no more rule Cuba, politically and socially, than they can make themselves, as blacks, the masters of Kentucky." Yet he warned that the Africans in Cuba had displayed "high capacity" and were "in a better position than in any of the American states" to exercise real power[143]—but what would that mean for the developing "nadir" in Dixie?

Madrid was allying with some Africans while chanting incantations to the monstrous "Black Scare." Those Euro-Americans who were not frightened out of their wits by the former were likely to be heading for the (Cuban) hills at the prospect of the latter: Spain seemingly was demanding a U.S. military intervention in Cuba. The U.S. Senate observed in 1896 that "the Spaniards charge, in order to belittle the insurrection, that it is a movement of Negroes."[144] The problem was that those who dismissed this scare tactic were prone to be terrified by the sight of armed Africans on both sides of this battle.

Official Washington was echoing the dread of Halstead. Madrid had "spies in New York," the State Department was informed, and given the thousands of discontented Africans there this was not an easy allegation to dismiss peremptorily.[145] Insurgents were burning property and estates of U.S. nationals in Matanzas, which was kindling a roaring anxiety in elevated mainland circles.[146] At one point a furious U.S. diplomat in Sagua La Grande, Cuba, reported that a "gang of insurgents" who were "under the command of a mulatto" had "put fire to the cane" with untold damages inflicted.[147] Then this emissary was informed that "an insurgent band led by a colored man" had "set fire to the cane fields," which belonged to "an American company" now seeking compensation from "the Spanish Government."[148] Washington was told that the U.S. citizens in Sagua La Grande "with rare exceptions" were "all . . . owners, lessees of, or employed on plantations" and there was a "strong prejudice" against them, cultivated by the authorities—although it seemed the insurgents who were making off with their horses and mules were the actual malefactors.[149]

Washington received an earful from a self-described "American citizen," owner of a sugar estate twenty miles south of Sagua La Grande, "comprising 3,000 acres of land . . . planted with cane" and containing "40 houses." His sprawling estate was stocked amply with "oxen...horses [and] cattle," along with "4 buildings forming the factory with 8 steam boilers" and "tools necessary for making 30, 000 bags of guar (of 350 lbs.) per crop." But now he was caught in a crossfire between insurgents and officials, which left him no option beyond making an "appeal to you" to save his estate "worth $400,000."[150] At this juncture there were about 166 U.S. nationals in Santiago alone, and envoys left the impression that the sangfroid of all was under siege.[151]

Their numbers were not great but their significance in the economy was. One mainland visitor spoke glowingly in 1897 of "two of the most prominent American land-owners in Cuba"—"Mr. O.B. Stillman and Mr. [Edwin] Atkins of Boston, owners of the states Trinidad and Soledad, the former situated in the valley of that name, and the other near Cienfuegos. During my last trip . . . I met a young rebel lieutenant in the hills near Trinidad who gleefully explained to me how he had placed a dynamite bomb under the furnace of the factory managed by Mr. Stillman."[152] This visitor was hardly amused, and as a consequence was joining a growing chorus demanding a muscle-bound intervention by Washington. Unfortunately for Washington, in Cuba a similar growing chorus was developing curdling views of their northern neighbor, represented most pointedly by the symbol of the 1890s revolt, Jose Martí.[153] "As a result of his radical ideas," says Ivan Cesar Martínez about the patron saint of revolutionary Cuba, "Martí stood out among the white [sic] leaders, politicians and thinkers of the America[s] of both the nineteenth and twentieth and even in this new century."[154]

By 1896 the mainland delegate in Santiago reported to Washington what should have been good news. "General Jose Maceo" was killed, yet the envoy found this to be "rather advantageous to the Cuban cause" since he was a "Negro, and unlike his brother Antonio, he possessed in a marked degree some of the objectionable characteristics peculiar to his race." He was "brutal" and a "poor disciplinarian"; he "lacked tact" and had "shown prejudice against the white race. Consequently, the probable selection of a fearless and capable white to command the insurgent army of this province, promises to improve the standing and effectiveness of the Cuban cause."[155]

As had been the case—and would increase as 1959 loomed—Washington had misjudged Cuba. The blinkered racism that was au courant on the mainland was one reason; more precisely, for centuries the approaches to the Africans of the island and the mainland were not always congruent. But as the United States marched steadily toward imperialism after dispensing with the last gasp of armed Native American resistance, this incongruity appeared to be even more important than previously thought. Yet clubbing Cuba into a naked acceptance of mainland norms would prove to be an important way station in the race to revolution.

CHAPTER 7

War! And Jim Crow Enforced in Cuba

B Y THE END OF 1898, marriages between U.S. Negro men and Cuban women were no longer deemed to be overly unusual.

The declaration of war upon Spain earlier that year—which led to a de facto annexation of Cuba and the ouster of Madrid after hundreds of years of colonial rule—led to the dispatching to the island of three full regiments of African-American men, mostly to the province of Santiago which also had a full complement of Negroes; these included detachments from Kansas, Louisiana, Mississippi, Texas, and Illinois among other states, all of which had their own unique version of torturous racism. The deployment from Illinois was composed of about 1,200 men with 76 officers—entirely Negroes. This was the first time in the state's history—and, it was reported, any state's history—that a regiment wholly of Negroes was sent to war abroad. Most were from Chicago and thus not necessarily acclimated to the peculiar folkways of rural Dixie, which tended to define racism nationally.

It did not take long for a goodly number of these men to enter connubial bliss with Cuban women. At least a few of the latter, according to one observer, were "two beautiful senoritas of the pale face and long-haired variety"—which would likely have been a lynch-ready offense in Dixie. "Neither of the grooms could speak or understand a complete sentence in the language of the brides, who in turn could hardly speak a word in English," but this did not snip the blooming of love, nor did it signal a halt in what was to amount to a quantum leap in the ties of singular intimacy between U.S. Negroes and Cubans, which was to become normative in the run-up to 1959. "I know several more who are preparing for the same important step" toward marriage, "strange as it may seem," said Corporal W. T. Goode. These "colored soldiers," he asserted, were "in Cuba to stay," with some "making investments" including two officers who "have closed a deal for a coffee farm." Trumpeting a call that was to define

the new century, he blared that "colored carpenters, blacksmiths, bricklay-
ers, in fact all mechanics can find employment" in Cuba—and without, it was
thought, the festering racist pestilence that was the hallmark of the mainland.[1]

This also meant that Washington had a real problem when the insurgency
in Cuba gained traction, with its racial heterogeneity juxtaposed to the image of
"white" Spain. Did not the reinvigoration of white supremacy on the mainland
demand support for the latter? Yet it was Madrid that the United States sought
to oust, which mandated that the insurgents had to be quickly swept aside,
lest Washington be accused of racial treason or its complement: the creation of
another Haiti. On the other hand, armed Africans fighting their way to power
on the island was not the kind of message that Jim Crow advocates desired.

A Santiago writer was cited for the proposition that the United States
sought to deport Negroes as a whole to Cuba, a perception not allayed when
Negro troops landed on the island,[2] which was hardly comforting to those who
wondered about the mainland stumbling into creating another Haiti. Moreover, Florida was split by the possibility of war, with many fearing that a freed
island would become part of the United States and challenge the peninsula's
nascent tourism industry. When the *Maine* was detonated in Havana in February 1898, the nation erupted—Florida to a lesser degree; but then it was
decided that Cuba would not be annexed—at least formally: and jingoism on
the peninsula grew accordingly.[3] So prompted, reporters like Grover Flint,
who by his own admission was "marching with Gomez," a top insurgent, was
reassured that there was a "steadily decreasing percentage of [Cuban] Negroes
since 1841, when it was 58.4 [percent]." When he spoke with another rebel
leader—a "New York Cuban"—and "asked if he feared a race war when Cuba
had gained her independence, his answer was absolutely borne out by my own
experience of the Cuban Negro. 'No, decidedly no!' he said. 'Our Negroes
are far superior to the colored race of the United States" since " 'they desire to
be white, and like the whites. . . .'" Though when this Cuban added brightly
that "General Maceo has Negro blood in him and is the pride of us all," this
islander may have vitiated his attempt to allay racial concerns.[4]

When a U.S. Negro trooper visited the family of the then deceased Maceo
and spoke movingly of his discussions with his "mother and two sisters,"
mainland elites may have pondered what forces they may have unleashed
unwittingly.[5] When the first Negro to be nominated for U.S. president—
George Edwin Taylor—referred to "'General Maceo [as] the greatest Negro
soldier and general of modern times," Washington may have wondered about
the fuller implications of closer engagement with Cuba.[6]

With U.S. adventurers arriving steadily in Cuba in the 1890s, landing with
them was their anxiety about another Haiti rising in the region. J. H. Peck
was typical of this breed, lamenting that the "nigga here knows [that here] it

is estimated over 500 white men, women and children perished in one week," and, yes, it was not trivial in this context that Haiti was a mere "55 miles away from the eastern end of Cuba" and relations "between the slaves had been maintained secretly through the medium of small sailing vessels for several years." Thus, the victory in Haiti in 1804 "was followed by that of the runaway slaves living in the mountains of Cuba in 1809."[7] Would not the triumph of Maceo's forces allow history to repeat?

And was not this a real prospect given ongoing trends? For as they came into closer contact—not just on the island but on the mainland too—Cuban men also began marrying U.S. Negro women. By the early 1880s Rafael Serra, a Cuban revolutionary leader with African roots had migrated to New York where he was involved in founding La Liga Antillana, a night school for migrant laborers. When they left behind the cigar factories and immigrant social clubs that bound them to each other as Cubans and cigar makers, these men lived in a city divided by a color line that seemed impermeable. Thus they had frequent and at times close contact with people of color of varied backgrounds and rarely lived among Cubans identified as "white." One scholar has found that a number of these migrant men of color married English-speaking women—U.S. Negroes. To a degree, for many of these men it was more common to wed a U.S. Negro than a Cuban woman, which was unsurprising since these men often resided cheek by jowl in rooming houses, apartment buildings, and city blocks inhabited by U.S. Negroes. In some ways, life on the mainland split Cubans along color lines, as it integrated a portion of this émigré community into a wider, already diverse U.S. Negro community. To an extent this weakened the lobbying strength on the mainland of a unified Cuban community—which may have been countervailed by a corresponding strengthening of the mainland Negro community, which was reflected as these émigrés turned to a U.S. Negro entity to form a social lodge for men of color: arising was a distinct Cuban branch of the Prince Hall Masons (which also reflected the reality that such fraternal groupings were not totally integrated among U.S. Negroes either). Arturo Schomburg—a Puerto Rican of African descent who was a comrade of Jose Martí[8] and whose bibliophilic bent led to the creation of a premier library and archive in his name in Harlem—joined a lodge where men of color gathered to socialize in Spanish before repairing to abodes in Negro neighborhoods, where the lingua franca was English, which often was the language of their wives and children. Schomburg's first wife was a Negro from Virginia and they resided with their three sons in a black neighborhood on West 62nd Street. His two subsequent wives were also U.S. Negroes and like many from Spain's former colonies, this brought him to commune with his spouses' culture—music, dance, social networks, etc. Similar points can be made about the exile experience in New Orleans, where Maceo spent considerable time.[9]

The El Sol de Cuba Lodge had a majority of U.S. Negro and British West Indian members in 1911 when Schomburg was elected to leadership, though it was founded by Cubans and Puerto Ricans in 1881, suggesting the fluidity and concord between and among those "of color."[10] Understandably, when Spanish agents on the mainland began searching for Cubans believed to be seditious, they gravitated effortlessly to predominantly Negro neighborhoods—a process that well preceded 1898.[11]

Still, just as U.S. Negroes at times sought to "pass" as Cuban, not only because of the latter's heroic profile but also as a way to escape the most repellent forms of bigotry, Cubans arriving on the mainland at times sought to avoid being "mistaken" as U.S. Negroes in a similar attempt to evade the strictly enforced color line. This could complicate relations between the two groups who could be seen as "colored." In short, Schomburg, who sailed in an opposing direction, was not necessarily the norm, though his life reflected a growing view. That is, as the "nadir" was reached on the mainland, then exported to Cuba, concomitantly arising in the United States was the ideology of Pan-Africanism, which sought to unite the victims of Negrophobia across geographic lines, which also reached into Cuba. Rafael Serra was among those who compared the plights of Cubans of African descent and U.S. Negroes. His journal *El Nuevo Criollo* often published articles on U.S. Negro uplift.[12]

The instrumental presence of Maceo, leading a fierce struggle so close to mainland shores, brought unusual attention to him and served as a bridge between mainlanders and islanders of color. One Manhattan correspondent conferred with him before he was killed, though they "did not converse in English. He greeted me very kindly." He informed his readers that "the party of General Maceo was spoken of as the black party. It was composed almost exclusively of the darker-complexioned Cubans, although there were many white officers. It was a very uncommon thing to see white men in the ranks of General Maceo's army," while "in the army of General Gomez which was designated the white party, there were not half a dozen colored men."[13]

Yet even after Maceo departed the scene, the 1898 intervention in Cuba seemed to heighten interest of Negroes in him and his legacy. He was the "greatest hero of the nineteenth century," according to one U.S. Negro journal.[14] At a public gathering in New York where his picture was exhibited, the audience went wild with applause, vigorously waving handkerchiefs amidst rowdy hurrahs. Naturally, he was seen as the reincarnation of Haiti's heralded Toussaint, yet another reason for the United States to intervene militarily.[15] Non-Negroes were also paying attention to Maceo, including the historian Trumbull White, who in 1898 termed him a "man of acute intellect and a general of great military skill" with the "rare gift of personal magnetism." He was "about five feet ten inches in height and unusually broad shouldered," but unlike Negroes he failed to mention his African ancestry.[16]

This fascination with Cuba also included an admiration of Jose Martí—slain in the midst of battle—who had warned that the United States would seek to seize Cuba and would whip up racial hatred against the Negro in order to do so. [17] In 1895 Martí bumped into Schomburg on 60th Street and Broadway in Manhattan, just after a frustrated attempt to land arms from Key West on the island. Despite this setback, the Cuban was calm and convincing though, as the Puerto Rican recalled, "This was the last time I saw this great man." They had been conferring regularly in that neighborhood prior to this chance encounter. Schomburg was part of the security detail tasked with ensuring that no harm befell this hero.[18]

Other Negroes were penning elated words from Cuba describing with wonder the opportunities for farmers, dentists, physicians, merchants and shopkeepers. One proposal from a Cuban of African descent who belonged to the Odd Fellows, a fraternal organization of Negroes composed mostly of mainlanders, called for a movement to bring 10,000 African Americans to the island to grow tobacco, sugar, and other crops.[19] This was a version of what occurred in Jacksonville earlier, when the leading Negro physician—Dr. A. H. Darnes—joined the Cuban physician Dr. D. M. Echemendia in leading the charge against a yellow fever epidemic on the peninsula.[20] In short, the ties between U.S. Negroes and Cuba soared beyond the conjugal.

Likewise, U.S. Negroes had been heavily involved since the early 1800s in the cattle trade to Cuba, which expanded after the Ten Years' War drove more islanders to the mainland.[21] U.S. Negroes long had been attracted to Hispaniola and this included John Stephens Durham who learned sugarcane production in the 1890s by managing a plantation in Santo Domingo. This attorney—who was quite light-skinned but in the distorted process of the mainland was defined as "colored" because of a hint of the "tar brush"—was able to maneuver more effectively in the Caribbean. Certainly his marriage to a woman defined as "white" would have been illegal—possibly an ignition for violence—on a good deal of the mainland but was less of a problem in Cuba, where he wound up prospering.[22] He was akin to Dana Dorsey, who arrived in Miami from Georgia in 1896 and parlayed a $25 parcel of land into a business empire that included substantial holdings in Cuba.[23]

However, it was missionary work rather than commerce that seemed to animate the labor of the U.S. Negro in Cuba during this new era. By the early 1890s the African Methodist Episcopal Zion church of Key West had begun to proselytize among Cubans, particularly in Tampa. Corporal W.T. Goode reported that "we are proud to say that the first Protestant church planted in Santiago and possibly on the island, was established by a colored man, in the personage of Rev. H.C.C. Astwood," who "boarded the Yale at New York City, when we did" with a "special commission" from the "President and War Department," who seemingly thought that his presence would be useful in disrupting the monopoly of the Vatican on the island. Since this Louisianan previously had been a "consul to the Dominican Republic" and while there "established an AME [African Methodist Episcopal] church," he was no neophyte.[24] Also searching for souls was Mother Francis of the Oblate Sisters, an order of nuns composed of women of African descent, who arrived in Havana from the mainland in 1899 and stayed on for ten years while starting a school.[25]

What was also occurring on the peninsula was that Africans of varying heritages, Cuban and Bahamian particularly, were merging with a larger U.S. Negro populace, not least because of the machinations of Jim Crow, which acted as an adhesive.[26] Even before the 1898 war, a Negro from Jacksonville—James Floyd—made repeated trips to Cuba bringing arms to the insurgents, which led Havana to honor him in 1927.[27] When he was honored, it was revealed that the Cuban insurgents had mainland branches replete with U.S. Negro members, particularly in Florida and New York. It was claimed that Floyd operated the "chief means of furnishing the Cuban revolutionists with arms and ammunition" and confirmatory evidence was presented when Havana in 1927 asserted that he was "as much of a Cuban patriot as those who, with the arms he took in his tug, fought the Spaniards in our country."[28] Even before the 1898 war there were credible reports that a mainland company founded by mainland Negroes was running guns to Cuban insurgents.[29]

There was no singularity to this appeal and example, in other words: still, the 1898 war led a number of U.S. Negroes to deepen their engagement with the island, which included ongoing political alliance, which did not exclude emigration—symbolized by the forming in 1899 of the "Afro-American Cuban Emigration Society."[30] John Waller, a Negro from Kansas, was so impressed with the more forgiving racial environment he encountered in Cuba that he poured his energy into the AACES and urged other Africans to go to Cuba where they could "prosper and enjoy the ballot." The "coming of our race to this island," he enthused, "would result in the foundation and establishment of one of the greatest settlements in the West Indies." It was in Cuba that he announced his abandonment of the GOP in favor of any party that would back the island's independence, again leaving Washington to contemplate the dire need to control this troublesome island, which seemed to provide refuge to mainland dissidents not in accord with the prevailing ethos.[31]

Whether merchant or missionary, U.S. Negroes had begun looking to an independent Cuba as a haven, redolent with opportunity and relief from racism. The bedazzled included the military, as it was estimated half of Negroes from Kansas deployed there chose to remain permanently. Reverend W. L. Grant of

Kansas, convinced that Negroes could "never get justice in the United States" petitioned Congress to back a hefty grant to assist the settling of his group in Cuba and other territories including Africa. John T. Vaney, a Negro Baptist clergyman of Topeka, proposed the forming of a colony of thirty U.S. Negro families near Santiago.[32]

His outlook was not inconsistent with that of Mary Burkett of Maryland who announced in the midst of the war, "Let others fight for Cuba, I am fighting for the Negro in the United States."[33] Lewis Douglass, son of the exalted Frederick, thought it would be folly to fight for a nation that would not protect you from mob violence.[34] The Negro intellectual William Calvin Chase declared, "There is no inducement for the Negro to fight" since "'his own brothers, fathers, mothers, and indeed his children are shot down as if they were dogs and cattle."[35] A Negro leader argued passionately that those of his ancestry could not become the allies of a rising imperialism without re-enslaving those like himself.[36] Daniel Middleton of South Carolina declared this was a "white man's war and let the white man carry it"—though with a like militancy, other Negroes there thought they should fight for what they deemed to be freedom of a "Negro Republic."[37] The well-known Georgia Negro cleric Henry Turner reflected a gnawing sentiment when he proclaimed, "Negroes who are not disloyal to the United States deserve to be lynched."[38] Even Booker T. Washington, who with his customary slipperiness, could often be found on both sides of many controversies, seemed to have shared some of this militancy at one point[39] although he eventually backed U.S. intervention.[40] (At one point, Washington found it "inexplicable" why "the whites of the Southern States espoused the cause of the Cubans" since by his calculation "of the total Cuban population of 1, 631,687" about "528,998 are classed as Negroes and mulattoes."[41]) Still, whether supportive or opposed to the 1898 war, virtually all U.S. Negroes thought Cuba should be independent.

Interestingly, at least two-thirds of Negroes enlisted after it became evident they would not fight in Cuba but instead would be confined to a less dangerous garrison duty.[42] More interesting still is that Congressman George White—a Negro who managed for a while to survive the purge of his group from the halls of power—abstained from voting on a bill that granted the president the power to use the military to intervene in Cuba as war was launched in April 1898.[43]

John Mitchell, Jr.,[44] a talented mainland Negro journalist and activist, led a burgeoning list of those who challenged the fundamental assumptions of an expansionist foreign policy.[45] The war in Cuba, he charged, was a "war of conquest," as he speculated that "Colored Cubans" would be no better off under a U.S. administration than under Spanish rule. If, as was contended, this was a humanitarian intervention, then there should be a like intervention

in Mississippi or Louisiana or Texas. Surely, he said, things there were "as barbarous" as "that which is alleged to exist in Cuba." His antiwar editorials circulated freely among Negro soldiers, which hardly improved their disposition
to join the fray. His antiwar credo was deepened when Virginia Negro soldiers
suffered their first casualties, not on the island, but in Georgia at the hands
of racists. Conflicts on mass transit featuring armed Negroes was becoming
habitual by this point. Rather than battlefield glory, Mitchell's Virginia unit
won the nickname "The Mutinous Sixth" because of their unwillingness
to submit to Jim Crow. His view was that shedding blood in order to attain
rights—the position of many Negro centrists—was balderdash, a stance that
was vindicated when the commonwealth's disgusted governor banned Negro
militia units.[46] Mitchell was not unique nationally nor in the Old Dominion.
"The colored people are by no means of the same mind" about the war against
Spain, said one opinion journal accurately. In Norfolk there was outright inso-
lence at the notion of enlisting in a Jim Crow army and, in a familiar theme,
a prominent Negro in Richmond doubted if the plight of "colored people in
Cuba" would improve if mainlanders prevailed.[47]

Other U.S. Negroes were so swept up in the romance of Cuban insurgency and independence that the *Baltimore Afro-American* recommended
that "Jackson McHenry, the ranking colored officer of the Georgia militia"
should be considered to "succeed Maceo," slain only recently.[48] It did not
take long for U.S. Negroes in 1898 to counsel abandoning the mainland for
a more forgiving clime. "Will Cuba be a Negro republic?" pondered W. C.
Payne. "Decidedly so," was his prompt answer, "because the greater portion
of the insurgents are Negroes and they are politically ambitious." Moreover,
he said with amazement, "in Cuba the colored man may engage in business
and make a great success" or even become "shippers and commission merchants. . . . There isn't the slightest doubt of it."[49] A concurring U.S. Negro
added, "There is room for thousands of Negro families in Porto Rico," and "if
we get Cuba either outright or under a protectorate, a million Negroes could
make a living there," as "the history of the Kansas exodus shows," referring to
a mass migration from Dixie northward.[50] One reason why was captured by an
acute observer of the era who said of the island, "One finds dusky Othellos in
every walk of life"; often there were "Creole belles" found "promenading with
Negro officers in gorgeous uniforms"—or alternatively, these men could be
found alongside "octoroon beauties."[51]

Payne may have noticed the most important Cuban newspaper targeting
Negro readers. *La Fraternidad* in early 1899 carried a front-page picture salut-
ing the sainted and then deceased Frederick Douglass, days after his recognized birthday,[52] a reminder of his status as a champion of the insurgency.[53]
Perhaps Payne encountered an African with the bruised anti-Washington

sentiments of Esteban Montejo who argued angrily during this time that "the Americans didn't like the Negroes much. They used to shout 'Nigger, Nigger' and burst out laughing"; brimming with rage, he confessed openly, "I couldn't stomach them and that's a fact."[54] Apparently, he was not unique in his view. The influential Briton James Bryce confirmed that Cubans with African ancestry were "averse to union with the United States, because tales of lynchings of Negroes in the South" were widespread on the island.[55]

Yet with all of the scintillating impact these U.S. Negroes had on the island, their raw force may have been even more significant on their homeland, particularly the peninsula whose destiny had been linked to that of Cuba since the days of Ponce de Leon.[56] Perhaps not coincidentally, in 1886, the year slavery was effectively banned, the first cigar factory was built in Tampa, accompanied by the arrival of about a million workers from Cuba and other lands touched by Spain. The problem, as noted, was the intercourse between and among Cubans across the racial divide, which mainlanders thought was much too easy and friendly, and created enormous complications. Irrespective of color—figuratively throwing up their hands—Euro-Americans began referring to all islanders as "Cuban niggers," which provided an incentive for those so insulted to seek refuge beyond this besieged Negro community, introducing a veritably impassable divide. Still, in cigar factories, Cubans of various colors sat together rolling and receiving the same wages—though this was an unsustainable pattern. Of course, Cubans of African ancestry often attended school, received medical care, and engaged in leisurely activity among others who were "colored."[57]

What was in store for mainland Negroes in light of the war in Cuba was most readily glimpsed in Tampa. There was a tricky political course to navigate by these soldiers upon arriving there. By 1890 the city contained 5,532 residents, of whom 41 percent were native-born "whites"; 26 percent were foreign-born, mostly in Italy and Spain, though some Cubans too were counted in this amorphous category. And about 26 percent were considered to be Cubans of African descent and native-born Negroes—who emerged from differing cultures that Jim Crow sought to elide.[58] By one count, 1,632 Negroes were in the city in 1890 and 2,926 a decade later, with this group said to comprise 20 percent of the population.[59]

The arrival of Cubans, many of whom could be defined as "white" in a Jim Crow society, brought strains to the peninsula, particularly since some of these émigrés harbored opinions about bedrock matters like unions and racism that were inconsistent with the prevailing consensus.[60] Like a curious anthropologist, one New Yorker observed that the Cubans were "a mixed race" in that "some are as black as ink, others are yellowish brown and some are white," yet—astonishingly—"in their social intercourse there is no race distinction among them."[61]

Obviously, they had to be induced to accept a different mainland reality, particularly since, as one commentator put it decades earlier, "All the customs of this country [Cuba] ally it much more closely to Europe than to America."[62]

The Cuban insurgents themselves were in an army that was said to be about half African, which helped to shape the more forgiving émigré attitudes on racism. The Spaniards had amassed 200,000 troops, though it was no secret that Madrid had been compelled by Maceo's prominence to make their own overtures to Africans. Sending U.S. Negroes to combat in Cuba must be considered in light of the makeup of the regiments of the rebels and Madrid. To prepare for their island venture, these U.S. Negro troops had been sent to a city—Tampa—that contained an enclave, Ybor City, where Cubans of various colors resided in a kind of harmony that was as anomalous as the persistence of the GOP in Key West. On the other hand, when the battleship *Maine* was blown up in Cuba in early 1898—the ostensible casus belli[63]—almost two-dozen Negro sailors perished, which could not help but strike an emotional chord with U.S. Negro troops. Also tugging at the heartstrings was the intense propagandizing of the real suffering endured by ordinary Cubans at the hands of Spaniards[64]—though one mainland Negro journal felt constrained to ask boldly, "IS AMERICA ANY BETTER THAN SPAIN?"[65]

On the other hand, Ybor City, like Key West, could hardly be an island of sanity in a sea of Jim Crow for as Cubans entered this settlement they were sorted into racially segregated enclaves within an enclave.[66] By October 1892, C. D. Valdez, president of the Cuban Democratic Club in Ybor City, said that he was assaulted by several Cubans of African descent because of his opposition to the GOP. They also were said to have threatened a boycott of any cigar factory that gave him employment.[67]

Cubans of various colors shared a local bar for a while, but otherwise, they too had to follow and adhere to Jim Crow strictures. As in New York, Cubans of color were frog-marched into an overall Negro community and thus attended Jim Crow colleges. One of the sons of this community—who identified himself as "Black Cuban" and "Black American"—recalled "but one black Cuban hero, Antonio Maceo" while in Florida; whereas, he said, "my heart and mind belonged to Nat Turner, Frederick Douglass, Harriet Tubman, Sojourner Truth, Paul Laurence Dunbar, John Brown" et al.[68]

Still, there is some question as to whether or not the 1898 war worsened race relations in Tampa. Reportedly, prior to 1900, an individual's location along the racial color line, at least for a lighter-skinned Cuban, was negotiable. The question was whether this latter group had as much flexibility after 1900 as a result of the deepening of Jim Crow. As late as 1894 darker-skinned Cubans in Tampa had organized a baseball club that faced U.S. Negro squads and Italian and other "white" teams, but this became quite rare in the new century.[69]

Yet the rudimentary sign of the meaning of the increased Cuban presence in Florida and elsewhere arrived when baseball teams comprised of U.S. Negroes began calling themselves "Cubans," a recognition of islanders' enhanced reputation, the importance of Maceo, and, similarly, a possible way for these mainlanders to hide under another identity on the premise that persecution would not be as severe.[70] In 1885 Negro waiters at the Argyle Hotel in Brooklyn formed the Cuban Giants team and began chattering in gibberish on the field to "pass" as islanders; by 1900 the five major professional teams among Negroes on the mainland included the Cuban Giants and the Cuban X Giants.[71] The Cuban Stars were the first island team to tour the mainland and then joined the Negro National League in a merger that symbolized the resonance between the two groupings represented.[72]

Mainland racism served to fuel antiwar sentiment among U.S. Negroes at a time when it was thought that maximum unity was required. Ultimately, as Spain was substituted by Japan and the Soviet Union, among other foes, a dynamic was created whereby the consensus developed that imperial obligations and attempted world leadership were inconsistent with radically antediluvian racial patterns. That was in the future. But even in 1898 those contemplating an enhancement of Washington's global role may have had second thoughts when confronted with the reactions of the darker citizenry.

This was a national concern that had a peculiar impact in Florida, the strategic point of embarkation for the mission to seize Cuba and in the key urban node that was Tampa, all was not sweetness and light. When the press spoke of the arriving Negro regiments as being "immune" to a yellow fever that had devastated the island, this perception underscored their presumed strangeness.[73] Confederate royalty Fitzhugh Lee, then serving in Cuba, thought that Negroes were best poised to deploy in Cuba, though he did not indicate if this was an inherent virtue.[74] Other Negroes, eager to display their mettle and demonstrate, contrary to widespread opinion, that they were not innately subversive, argued that the "white soldiers cannot stand the rainy and sickly season in Cuba; the black soldiers can," and if the authorities were to "turn them loose on Cuban soil, they will shell the woods and free Cuba before the rainy season is over and before the white soldiers can get there."[75]

Such bold talk may have been deemed to be mere blather when a few months after their arrival, over fifty of these armed Negro men reacted violently when the authorities arrested one of their comrades—wrongly they thought—and responded by threatening to set loose all those behind bars.[76] This was just one of a number of tormenting incidents that many of these Negroes found highly displeasing.[77] The flip side of these angry confrontations was that the impression was left—as one furious Georgia Negro put it—that his "white" compatriots seemed to be more respectful of those with weapons, becoming "cowardly" in their presence: "I have not heard of one soldier being insulted" when armed, he said, a stark contrast to the unarmed norm[78]—and a dangerous message to transmit besides.

Samuel Swain, a Negro from Tampa, who, by his admission, was a "grown man, I was about thirty years old" during World War I, also recalled the soldiers departing from his hometown to Cuba in 1898. During both conflicts, distress was aroused for "if they armed the Negro, who was going to disarm them?" Since the Negroes "fought too good in Cuba" this distress metastasized. Then the U.S. Negroes began to consort closely with mainland Cubans—"Oh yeah, they was all right," said Swain: "Cubans and blacks were always together . . ." This was so particularly so since "the Florida people"—meaning whites— "wouldn't let the Italians [or] the Cubans go to the white . . . schools."[79]

As the drumbeat of war began to sound, Tampa was disrupted. Mayor M. E. Gillett noted that "we have among us a large number of Spaniards, I may say a number of our most influential citizens" and it is "only natural that they should feel some alarm for their personal safety and business interests" and are "feeling very uneasy"; they were "too important a factor in the commercial development of our city to allow them to feel at all uneasy." There had yet to be a "clash between our Cuban and Spanish citizens," though he seemed unaware of how the color line his regime enforced was disrupting the Cuban community.[80]

By May 1898 Negro troopers by the thousands began streaming into Tampa, where their demand to be allowed to drink in bars and partake of prostitution like those constructed as "white" stirred a cauldron of resentment. That Joseph Walker, a U.S. Negro and member of the Knights of Labor— viewed by certain elites as innately seditious—was elected to the city council in 1887[81] suggested that the flood of armed Africans combined with preexisting anxiety.[82] By June 1898 these troopers were enmeshed in what was termed a "riot," no minor matter since many of these men were well armed and trained in the use of weapons. Troopers objected vividly when white soldiers from Ohio began shooting at a Negro youth; they took issue with signs proclaiming "'No Dogs, Niggers or Latins Allowed" and were not pleased when told that a public execution of a Negro had brought a cheering crowd of 5,000.[83] Seemingly, Washington did not realize that it was utterly hazardous in a Jim Crow society to place weapons in the hands of men of various colors in such close proximity. Racial clashes between these men became customary. In a fierce battle in neighboring Alabama one black soldier was killed, one white soldier seriously wounded, and several soldiers and civilians left wounded.[84] The mood of these Negro soldiers was not assuaged when the press heaped malicious abuse upon them.[85]

A wily Spain did not help Washington by continuing to attack the mainland as a cesspool of racial hatred, particularly as it pertained to Africans and indigenes, [86] a cry that was echoed, tellingly, in Berlin.[87] Similarly, in contrast to mainland journalists who tended to tiptoe around roiling racial controversies—for example, unrest in Tampa—British correspondents found this topic to be of great interest. British journalists, hailing from a nation that had crossed swords with mainlanders more than once, took careful note of the martial abilities of Negro soldiers, particularly their expert horse-riding ability, a skill that had engendered terror since the heyday of the Mongols.[88] Despite protestations to the contrary from those who accused them of cowardice—it may have been a simple reluctance to commit wholly to a Jim Crow military—U.S. Negroes' martial competence was well known, as suggested by the presence in Cuba of David Fagen, who deserted and wound up in the Philippines fighting fearlessly against U.S. forces alongside combative insurgents.[89] Strikingly, in 1899 a British envoy forwarded a "confidential" report on "the Question of Negroes in the Southern States" noting that they "form the majority" in a number of states in Dixie, while referring to events in Cuba.[90]

Florida was disturbed profoundly by the arrival of armed Negroes in a Jim Crow society, with some having to be diverted to Lakeland to relieve the pressures. The *Tampa Tribune* found it "very humiliating" to "the people of Tampa" to "be compelled to submit to the insults and mendacity perpetrated by the colored troops." These Negroes' ire may have been induced, the writer suggested, since it was known that an "alleged [Spanish] spy was arrested in St. Petersburg attempting to poison the water supply."[91] Already, Tampa's "sizeable Spanish community" was "viewed with suspicion as potential spies"[92] while it was reported authoritatively that Spanish agents had continually visited Manhattan, Washington, Jacksonville, Key West, and Tampa,[93] all thickly populated with discontented Negroes.

There was no unanimity of opinion among U.S. Negroes as it pertained to this war, and this was not wholly due to the energetic ministrations of spies from Madrid: true, there was support for the heralded Maceo, and yes, there was a feeling that shedding blood for the mainland might improve citizenship status. But it was not a secret that over the centuries Spain had not fastened upon Cuba a system as odious as the now commonplace Jim Crow and a nagging question persisted as to whether the war was about changing that island reality.[94] On the other side of the coin, the sight of armed Negroes guarding Spanish prisoners on the mainland was wildly at odds with prevailing racial realities and was bound to generate a fierce reaction from those who cherished white supremacy.[95] Even when Negro troopers did their jobs and shot and killed Spaniards—for example, the epochal Battle of Las Guasimas—it could prove unsettling.[96] Washington sanctioning the murder of "whites"—that is, Spaniards—by armed Negroes was bound to create friction.[97] "We hate the Spanish more and more every day," said one Negro trooper with disgust, a comment that may very well have been easily transferable to the adversary's entire racial group.[98]

These armed Negroes were necessary since only in retrospect can it be said that Washington's triumph over Spain was inevitable. Jackson Cox of Athens, Tennessee was in neighboring Mexico on the day in early 1898 when the battleship *Maine* was sunk in Havana's harbor. The "general opinion" among those with whom he spoke was that "the United States would be given a thorough whipping by Spain" if war ensued. A "Frenchman was positive that one Spanish soldier was well able to whip ten Americans," and even after he was proven wrong, this son of Gaul contended that Washington had "bought the admirals and generals" of their adversary to guarantee victory. And yes, a "very large percentage of the Mexican people sympathized with Spain," which could have advantaged Madrid if the war had lasted longer.[99] Washington was in the anomalous position of recruiting Negro soldiers to enforce a Jim Crow regime in Cuba.

Theodore Roosevelt, who was catapulted into further prominence after his wartime experience in Cuba—alongside Negro troops—acknowledged that the latter "lost a greater proportion of its officers than any other regiment in the battle"; however, he caused controversy when he alleged that "under the strain the colored infantrymen . . . began to get a little uneasy" in the heat of battle and "drift[ed] to the rear"; the bumptious patrician promptly "drew my revolver, halted the retreating soldiers and called out to them that I . . . would be sorry to hurt them but that I should shoot the first man who, on any pretence whatever, went to the rear." This, he boasted, "was the end of the trouble for the 'Smoked Yankees,'" who then "flashed their white teeth at one another, as they broke into broad grins and I had no more trouble with them." Roosevelt did not consider if antiwar sentiments or ill treatment may have motivated these men, nor did he rebut effectively the fierce contestation of his words by angry Negroes.[100] Most U.S. Negroes thought Roosevelt had uttered a slur against them and subsequently the mere mention of his name brought forth protests and hisses at several major gatherings of Negroes.[101]

Years later at a New York meeting marking the 121st anniversary of the Haitian Revolution, Reverdy Ransom reminded TR that "there are millions in our race who still possess the same fighting spirit and courage that saved his ungrateful life when he was a soldier in Cuba."[102] The man with whom TR shared a repast in the White House some time later—Booker T. Washington—to the outraged consternation of Dixie (and possibly to tamp down Negro anger at him), reflected the sentiments of many of his fellow Negroes when he reported the words of a Negro soldier that during the war their Spanish adversaries "say there is no use shooting at us, for steel and powder will not stop us."[103]

Roosevelt was a true comrade of the leading U.S. military men on the island. Fred Funston became a household name overnight after his celebrated military service,[104] being wounded in Cuba as early as 1895,[105] and—typically—was fixated on the racial makeup of the insurgents. When he first encountered Máximo Gómez, one of his men insisted on greeting him Cuban-style with an *"abrazo"* or hug. "I took my medicine," said Funston with asperity toward being in such intimate contact with one of uncertain racial origins, "but not with noticeable enthusiasm."[106] The racial heterogeneity of the insurgents was a prime mainland concern since otherwise the United States could be accused of racial perfidy in aiding Negroes fighting "white" Spain. This is "not a Negro Movement" insisted Congress, speaking of the insurgents, since "less than one-third of the army are of the colored race."[107]

"Much to my surprise," Funston claimed, "fully nine-tenths of them" were "white men, which was accounted for by the fact that these troops were raised in Camaguey, which has a smaller percentage of Negroes than any other province in Cuba." But in "the southern part of Santiago province," the insurgents were "almost entirely [composed] of Negroes"—but be assured, he continued, "there were many more whites than blacks in the insurgent forces." Though some of these Negroes were "quite capable in guerilla warfare," others were "mere blusterers and blunderers." Nevertheless, "white men of the best families" in Cuba, he recalled with surprise, "did not hesitate to serve under Negro officers."[108]

Funston, whose service in Cuba preceded the April 1898 declaration of war, had a servant in Cuba who had been brought from Africa in the final stage of the illicit slave trade in the 1870s and still spoke what was described as a "Congolese tongue." This relationship did not shake Funston's ingrained racism, which riled insurgents who found it destabilizing their efforts.[109] Funston, who served in Cuba for two years, made an even deeper impression on mainland audiences because of his celebrity, which led to his being compared by one star-struck observer as "Daniel Boone or Captain John Smith"—"We do not need to read Defoe or Scott or Kingsley or . . . or Dumas or any of the other romancers," just consider "Fighting Fred."[110]

Leonard Wilson, a top aide to a former CSA commander—General Joseph Wilson, now playing a leading role in Cuba—carefully measured the military forces the United States confronted (the "Insurgent Army" had 35,000 troops while those of Spain were 190,000 men) and concluded that the latter would not be hard to beat and it turns out he was not altogether inaccurate.[111] Perhaps he should have consulted with the numerous filibusters, who in continuing a decades-long trend, had been pouring into Cuba in the prelude to the 1898 war, a point that Madrid well knew.[112]

Reputedly, between 1895 and 1898 there were seventy-one filibustering expeditions departing from the mainland to Cuba.[113] It was in 1897 that the famed writer Stephen Crane—who had earned notoriety with his blood-drenched writing about the Civil War—was bound for the island with the backing of Manhattan newssheets seeking stories about insurgency and revolution.[114] Among those running guns and providing aid to Cubans were such luminaries as Napoleon Bonaparte Broward, "Dynamite" Johnny O'Brien, and Senator Wilkinson Call.[115] Also with the insurgents, according to one observer, were "many adventurers in the ranks from the United States, Jamaica and other neighboring islands" and "several officers who had served in the armies of Central and South American republics." Referring to an earlier stage of the conflict, he found it "remarkable" that in Gibara the "consular agent" of the U.S., Jose Beola, was a "naturalized citizen of the United States"—and "captain of a company of Spanish soldiers."[116]

In effect, Madrid and Cuban insurgents engaged in a thirty-year slugfest that decimated the latter and wounded the former, and as this death match was lurching to a close, the United States stepped in, knocked out Spain, and declared itself the rightful inheritor of its bounty: a weakened insurgency was not in the most advantageous position to resist effectively. Washington had kept the pot boiling by continuing to wink at filibustering expeditions, which grew in the 1890s as the conflict weakened both sides.[117]

Remarkably, Dixie, routinely the most hawkish section of the mainland, was split on this war, with some worrying, à la the "Africanization" scare, about the impact of absorbing an island with so many of the darker-skinned. Many whites in Dixie refused to volunteer for the armed forces, which made it all the more necessary to enlist Negroes. Many in Dixie were nervous about U.S. Negro men being left behind as white men departed for Cuba, as this would leave "their" women to confront the alleged "black beast." This led some in Dixie to advocate sending Negro men abroad to serve to forestall such a nightmare scenario. Still others were apprehensive about providing training in warfare to Negroes for fear how such skills would be allocated. Complicating matters were rumors circulating that Dixie, still smarting from the Civil War, might consider seceding once more and joining Spain in crushing Washington. Congressman Henry Clayton of Alabama's toxic opinion—"I would not give one white faced, straight haired, blue-eyed boy in Alabama for all the half-breeds in Cuba"— was not a notably unique view. On the other hand, the xenophobic "Pitchfork" Ben Tillman of South Carolina argued passionately that the Cubans of the 1890s were the equivalent of the Confederates of the 1860s[118]—which was intended as a compliment.

Tillman denounced the prospect of a "Reconstruction or Carpet Bag Government" in Cuba.[119] His Carolina comrade, Matthew C. Butler—who served variously as Confederate commander, U.S. senator, and U.S. major general in Cuba—thought the "problem" on the island was "much more racial and social than political and should be dealt with accordingly." Spain was a nation he dismissed as "corrupt and merciless" without the moxie nor will to resist "annexation" of Cuba.[120]

His fellow racist, John Tyler Morgan—former Confederate general and U.S. senator—envisioned Cuba becoming part of Dixie, not unlike Florida. In 1898 he told President McKinley that the island was fated to "become as thoroughly American as California," as he compared Cuba to Gibraltar,[121] and "as indispensable to the United States as Ireland is to England."[122] Yet the senator became queasy at the means by which this goal should be attained— deploying "members of the dependent race" by "putting guns in the hands of Negroes as soldiers and making them the peers of white men." Some Negroes may have thought that volunteering to kill—and be killed—would solidify their fraying citizenship status, but it did not turn out that way and in fact may have boomeranged in the sense that the thrust abroad reminded the retrograde of the "colored" Achilles' heel, hastening the process of disenfranchisement, which had been entrenched by 1901.[123]

When William D. Smith testified before the Senate about Cuba, legislators pressed him about the racial composition of the insurgency, as if they did not want to stumble in assisting it to become another Haiti. "What is the proportion of the Negroes" he was asked. A "little over three quarters white" was the response. "Are the Negroes good soldiers?" "Yes sir," replied Smith, "if they have white men with them," as "in our army."[124]

Others in Congress recalled that the United States had no stomach to intervene in the 1868 war in Cuba, feeling that the "Negro Question" was unsettled on the mainland, so why should they compound the matter by injecting Washington more forcefully into Cuba? This was seen as a striking contrast to Madrid's recognition of CSA belligerency—calling for a like response in 1898.[125]

Nonetheless, there was tremulous timidity in Darien, Georgia—where the Negroes enjoyed a 10–1 majority: when whites were deployed to Cuba strife ensued.[126] Nearby Macon had a parallel fear: it was a staging ground for Negro troops and city burghers worried ceaselessly about their presence, particularly when they chopped down a tree where a lynching had occurred and tore down signs reading "'No Dogs and Niggers allowed in here"—then throttled those that sought to intervene. When they proceeded to march into saloons and restaurants in flagrant dismissal of the color line, some feared the apocalypse was nigh.[127]

Was this war worth it, given the social costs? This timidity was reflected in the impassioned words of Congressman St. George Tucker of Virginia— descended from a leading republican family—who wondered why his nation should become the "'wet nurse" for Cuban liberation from Spain: "I speak for 20,000 brave Confederate soldiers," he maintained.[128]

A New Haven–based historian expressed a "great desire to see the West India islands free from the control of the influences of European governments." But there was a problem: "The Cubans are to a large extent Negroes, Chinese and a mixed breed of Creoles," he said dejectedly: "Can these people govern themselves?" Probably not, he concluded, but, fortunately, embedded in "insurgent forces" were "our countrymen"—"There are many Americans in their ranks"—and these rebels had "learned much" from "intercourse" with their presumed betters.[129]

"Why should we tolerate Spanish savages," asked one noted mainland writer vituperatively, "merely because they call themselves 'the Most Catholic' but who in reality are [little] better than this naked Negro?" "What difference is there between the King of Benin," he asked waspishly, "who crucifies a woman because he wants rain, and General Weyler who outrages a woman for his own pleasure and throws her to his bodyguard of blacks?"[130]

The youngish observer Winston Churchill, who was obsessed with perpetuating colonialism to a similar degree as his mainland counterparts were obsessed with white supremacy, observed that "two-thirds of the insurgents in the field are Negroes. These men," he warned, "with Antonio Maceo as their head would, in the event of success, demand a predominant share in the government"[131]—and what would that mean for white supremacy on the mainland?

Similarly, a group of Confederate veterans from Florida declared their sympathy for the anti-Madrid struggle, signaling that there was no unanimity among Jim Crow advocates about the 1898 war.[132] One self-described "old Confederate veteran" thought that there were more like him who felt "burning shame" about the "atrocities perpetrated by brutal Spain" in Cuba. This "inhuman butchering" and "suffering" had to be halted by any means necessary.[133]

It was during the apex of the Ten Years' War that a knowing journalist observed that the "strongest partisans of Spain in the island have no other tie to the Mother Country than gratitude for her long protection of their slave-holding interests." With abolition, the "immigrant Spanish population," it was said in 1873, would flee and Cubans "would soon find themselves at the mercy of the Negroes," à la Haiti, jeopardizing the 75 percent of island sugar said to be heading to the mainland. To some this predicted nightmare had arrived by 1898, leaving no alternative to intervention.[134] Harsh measures in Cuba may have appealed to some mainlanders, since in the United States a bloody sword had been unsheathed to subdue Africans quite recently during the death throes of Reconstruction.

At this juncture the mainland seemed overstretched with one soldier in 1898 wondering what would happen in the event of an "outbreak on the part of the noble (?) Redskins," who were "scattered all around us," where he was training in Kansas.[135] The regiment of John Mason, he told his "dear mother," was "the only one that was in every skirmish and battle of the Santiago campaign"—and was now tasked to "watch the Indians," from his unsteady perch in Fort Riley, a base for murderous operations against indigenes.[136]

Nonetheless, Mason made it to Cuba where "we were in the thick of the fighting from start to finish." "964 of us whipped 4,000," he boasted, "and sent them helter skelter into Santiago." He was sufficiently generous to note the role of the "colored" troops in this process. They were needed since the top brass were "absolutely incompetent and is not entitled to any credit"; he was fortunate to have "escaped with a bullet hole through my hat and a slight attack of malaria"; and this may have been even more catastrophic but for the presence of the "colored." As it was, "we left many sick in Cuba," said Mason, even as the embers of war still simmered.[137]

As Mason portrayed it, the fighting was fast and furious; "the firing was hottest ever heard." Teddy Roosevelt, the future president, was "in command of our brigade," which included the "colored" who later were to be accused of a dearth of enthusiasm in battle. But Mason called them the "fighting brigade" and reserved his critique for his commanders—and the Cubans, whom he thought were "no good." Said Mason in a view that had become the Washington consensus: "I pity Cuba if Uncle Sam is fool enough to turn this island over to the natives."[138]

And why should Washington do so? Mason's fellow mainlander Harry S. Bowman, like others, was pleased by the comforts of home he found on the island, for example, being able to purchase "nigger wool tobacco" at reasonable prices.[139]

George Kennan—who influenced his great-nephew of the same name, an architect of the Cold War—arrived in Cuba from Texas as the flames of war leapt on 25 June 1898, disembarking at "the little village of Siboney, twelve miles east of Santiago," just in time, he recalled, "to see the Cuban army of General Garcia" depart. It was about 1,500 men, "the most dirty, ragged assemblage of armed [men] that I had ever witnessed. In the [first] place," he huffed, "at least four-fifths of the common soldiers were colored or black and one-fifth of them were boys," all resembling scarecrows, which contributed to his rapid "disillusion & disenchantment." Then he bumped into a fellow mainlander who did not seem to have enjoyed his breakfast, and when asked why, he spat out furiously, "That's the first time I ever sat down to breakfast with a nigger!" This intensified Kennan's peevishness about Cuba, which was worsened when he saw Cubans socialize—"They certainly cannot dance," he claimed, comparing them invidiously to U.S. Negroes: the islanders displayed "neither grace nor dignity" and exposed what he saw as a prime debility, "the influence that the Negro in Cuba has had over the Spaniard." The music he heard was even less appealing to him, being as "unmistakably African as anything to be heard on the Upper Nile or a jungle on the banks of the Congo. Why the danzon should be preferred to the waltz—as it is everywhere in Cuba—I don't know, unless it be for the reason that the music is more wild and passionate and the dance itself more in harmony with the ardent, sensual nature of the half-Spanish, half-Negro population." He loathed the dearth of religiosity he perceived and was baffled by what he deemed to be an inordinate consumption of alcohol with no seeming drunkenness. His conclusion was that of others who sought to impose a mainland diktat on the island—"Never trust a Cuban."[140]

One resident of Tupelo, Mississippi, who was coming into contact with Cuba for the first time in 1898, echoed Kennan in his contempt for the Spanish language and his perception that islanders might have difficulty picking up English because to speak the latter "a man" must "have all his teeth" to do it well, and this dental requirement was apparently lacking en masse in Florida's southern neighbor.[141]

This rabid hostility was reciprocated in the considered opinion of Esteban Montejo—a Cuban of African origin who was formerly enslaved—whose view of the U.S. arrival was acerbic. "Any fool here knew that the Americans blew up the *Maine* themselves so as to get into the war," he asserted. Their arrival made the Spanish presence seem benign by comparison: "Frankly," he averred, "I prefer the Spaniards to the Americans, the Spanish in Spain, that is. Everyone should stay in their own country, though the fact is I don't like the Americans even in their own country . . . the whole pack of degenerates who ruined this country!" was his bitter evaluation.[142] Even a Tampa Bay journalist admitted in January 1899 that the Cubans did not care much for the Spaniards, and avidly distrusted the mainlanders.[143]

U.S. Negroes as well were not sanguine about the handover from Madrid and this lengthening roster included the famed journalist T. Thomas Fortune. Having been born in Florida, this intellectual had few illusions about U.S. rule and thus recognized more quickly than most that the more forgiving racial policies on the island were now slated for a severe rollback.[144] It did not take long for U.S. Negroes seeking to establish a grubstake in Cuba to be subjected to immediate deportation.[145] Insurgent leaders like Máximo Gómez were accused by mainlanders of favoring Africans and disfavoring others,[146] which primed the pump for Washington-style racist conflict and the tragic slaughter of Cubans by 1912.[147] As with the mainland, the virulent racism introduced by Washington in Cuba helped to inspire ever more militant responses by Africans, which in turn were greeted with ever more virulent racism.[148]

It took a shorter time still for certain Cubans to petition Washington to effectuate the prompt removal of all U.S. Negro troops from Santiago.[149] What Fortune and other U.S. Negroes may not have grasped was how the mainland takeover in Cuba would have impact on the Florida peninsula itself. For it was not long before Cubans in Tampa who could be defined as "white" sought to exclude darker Cubans from various entities.[150]

There were quickly shifting sentiments among U.S. Negroes. Months after the last Spanish flag had been removed and stored, Dr. C. T. Walker of Augusta, Georgia, mounted the pulpit at the Central Baptist Church to address the already sensitive matter of "Cuba and Negro Soldiers." "'Nearly one-half of Cuba's population are black. All are Cubans. There has not been, nor will [there] be any caste, prejudice and color trouble unless Americans carry them there"—and this had already begun, he said, as the audience cheered his insight lustily. Similarly, despite the heroism of U.S. Negroes in fighting in Cuba—notably at San Juan Hill where "it was a Negro who devised the scheme of cutting the barbed wire, breaking up the hill," etc.—the pace of lynching had not ceased and may have increased.[151]

Dr. Walker did not mention that which had captivated so many of his fellow Negroes—one of the first casualties of the war was a Negro cook who in Cardenas, Cuba, had both of his legs blown off by adversarial fire.[152] Among those hunkered down at San Juan Hill was A. C. Goggins, born in South Carolina and who formerly spied for the CSA, then served as leader of an ex-slave club. He was wounded and lost a middle finger before repairing to Miami where his flowing beard and bushy hair was a familiar sight on the streets there.[153]

What was not sufficiently understood by U.S. Negroes of that era was as well the instrumentality of Cuba as a tool to forge a sectional unity. This was the point made by David Starr Jordan, the eminent educator, before the then infant Stanford University which he helped to found and headed. "The war has united at last the North and the South," he said. Fitzhugh Lee—nephew of the top Confederate general, Robert E. Lee—who served Washington in Cuba, was now "called a Yankee and all the haughty Lees seem proud of the designation," which meant that "the old lines of division exist no longer." The problem for Negroes on one side of the straits and Cubans on the other was that this "victory" was at their expense. "Whenever we have inferior and dependent races within our borders today," he continued, "we have a political problem—'the Negro problem,'" the "Chinese problem," the "Indian problem" were all of a piece. In places like Cuba these "problems are perennial and insoluble," he said, though he left unclear precisely as to what was to befall these "problems" on both sides of the straits.[154]

The war with Spain lasted a mere 114 days (roughly April to August), costing mainlanders a hefty $150 million, though emerging with such prizes as the Philippines, Puerto Rico, and Cuba made it seem worthwhile to some.[155] Though soundly beaten, Madrid did not help its cause when it—per usual—sent some prisoners of war to their African colony, Ceuta. Howls and peals of outrage were emitted as a result of this indignity and, what one complainer described as "a most terrible story of the sufferings inflicted by Spain" in "her African Siberia."[156] The famed writer Richard Harding Davis informed his many readers that those who fought Spain faced "a lingering life in an African penal settlement."[157] Similarly, one of Davis' contemporaries was outraged that "American citizens have been sent to the penal colonies, the property of some have been confiscated and others have been murdered in cold blood."[158]

Arthur Kennickel, a Euro-American, was among those celebrating the taking of Cuba. He was in Havana and witnessed the unfurling for the last time of the Spanish flag, terming it "the most exciting day that I have ever witnessed," as the "streets, windows, housetops and all vacant spots" were "crowded with excited Cubans shouting 'Viva Americana,' 'Hurrah for the American flag'"—and "Viva Cuba Libre," a more telling indicator of sentiments. "At noon the Spanish flag was lowered from old Morro Castle never to be raised again."[159] Caroline Wallace, whose work was well received on the mainland, was similarly enthusiastic as she rhapsodized about the mines of Cuba, "perhaps the richest in the world." As for the residents, she was not as enthusiastic, finding the "color" of the women not "desirable," though they gained artificially "an additional whiteness" by a "free use of cascarilla, a cosmetic prepared from white shells, ground up into an impalpable powder." She seemed to admire, however, a Cuban system whereby "white" girls on the island were accorded a "playmate among the colored children, chosen from the servants or slaves [sic] of her own age, who grows up with her in the double capacity of companion and servant." These "servants," she added with a haughty sniff, were "of every shade, from darkest mahogany to palest yellow."[160]

It did not take long for Washington to seek to bring Cuba into line, eroding the differing course of race relations that had characterized the island—and which had incited U.S. Negroes rapturously—by straining to impose a rigid Jim Crow. Mainland iconographers contributed to this skewed mentality, portraying "Mr. Cuba Libre" contemptuously in a stereotyped grass dress, black skin, white lips, and top hat with stars and the insignia: "U.S. protection." President McKinley was depicted kicking a Negro-representing Cuba—in the posterior with the inscription: "There! Take your independence!" Cuba was portrayed with small dark-skinned children standing behind Uncle Sam, as walking toward them is a similar stereotyped child labeled "Jamaica," carrying a sign inscribed: "I want to be annexed."[161] "Alternatively, in Spanish Cuba, the United States was represented as a hog, with the U.S. flag used for trousers, whereas Spain was depicted as a noble and valiant lion.[162] The sharpness of the battling images was a reflection of the sharpness on the battlefield that eventuated in Madrid's disastrous loss—and what was to become Havana's too as a form of Jim Crow arrived with an intensified U.S. presence.

In November 1898 a hotel in Santiago owned by a white mainlander was prevented from drawing the color line against a Negro trooper.[163] Weeks later, as Cuba began to resemble Dixie, a crowd of Negroes entered a café late one evening and ordered drinks but, it was said, refused to pay, leading to a dispute wherein the proprietor and his assistant were stabbed. U.S. troops arrived—which seemed to inflame rather than calm—and they were fired upon. The enraged troops then chased the Cubans of African origin down the street, arresting four, killing one, and wounding six.[164]

The attempted implantation of Jim Crow in Cuba, an inevitable hand-maiden accompanying the arrival of U.S. forces en masse, was neither simple nor easy and culminated catastrophically for Washington on 1 January 1959. As early as 1899 signs proclaiming "We Cater to White People Only" were posted in Havana at the insistence of U.S. leaders, while the air was filled with alarm by candid remarks of what many considered to be the favorite main-land pastime: "Nigger Lynching."[165] Weeks after the last Spanish flag came down in Cuba, Juan Ducasse—viewed as a Negro by mainlanders and as a hero by most Cubans—entered a bar bent on refreshing his palate. But the U.S. barman refused to serve him, which led to a spirited protest. In response the café was closed for a week—but kept intact the "For Whites Only" sign designed to exclude those like him. The Cuban intellectual Rafael Lopez Valdez argued persuasively in 1971 that this abrupt change from Spanish rule helped to spawn "democratic, anti-imperialist, anti-discrimination"—and ultimately—"revolutionary" ideals and thus became a crucial signpost on the road to 1959.[166]

Seemingly befuddled, U.S. generals conferred about the increasing racial conflicts, which enforcing Jim Crow was bringing. "The American café keep-ers refuse to serve colored visitors," said one account, "and trouble is bound to occur if some agreement is not reached on the subject." It was "[Mr.] Mora, the Civil Governor of Cuba," who was "desirous of satisfying the colored Cuban officers" who were hotly opposed to Jim Crow. Yet, amid the morose-ness, there was good news: "The celebrated Cuban Negro general, Quintin Banderas, arrived [from] Santiago. He says that the Cuban army in that prov-ince is being rapidly disbanded."[167]

One analyst argued that since "racism and racial discrimination were never as deep or widespread" in Cuba as the mainland, "segregation came to Cuba in 1898 with the occupying (and segregated) armed forces of the United States," a Jim Crow that was exacerbated by the fact that a major reason for military inter-vention was the decades-long fear of another Haiti arising in the Caribbean.[168]

Still, from the inception of the U.S. occupation, islanders seemed to attain more success, with more rapidity, in combating Jim Crow than their main-land counterparts. Late in 1899 the *Baltimore Afro-American* reported with seeming disbelief that there is "no color line" in Cuba and, as a result, "three Americans . . . have each been sentenced to two months' imprisonment and to pay a fine of $65 and two-thirds of the cost of the proceedings for placing over their saloon a sign reading: 'We cater to white people only'"—referring to the Ducasse case.[169]

The mainlanders seemed oblivious to the forces they were unleashing or, more to the point, sought to remake Cuba in light of their experiences with U.S. Negroes—and perceptions of Haiti. It did not take long after the handover for a "confidential" message to be delivered to Secretary of State Elihu Root, advising that "in dealing with Latin races it is not advisable to yield under pressure, unless one is prepared to give up to everything and submit to be ruled"; thus "universal suffrage"—notably allowing Africans to vote, generally forbidden on the mainland—"would be fatal to the interests of Cuba" since "giving the ballot to this element means a second edition of Haiti and Santo Domingo in the near future."[170] As for Cuban independence, that was out of the question: "To go now," Root was informed, "would be to betray the cause of civilization and to turn this country within three months into a republic, not unlike those of Haiti or Santo Domingo."[171]

Leonard Wood, who as military governor of the island was to oversee mandates inimical to both independence and antiracism, warned against the mainland "having at our doors a demoralized, poverty-stricken island, such as Santo Domingo or Hayti."[172] Fortunately from his viewpoint the 1900 census was to show the "number of Negroes" in Cuba was "only 32 percent of [the] total."[173] Actually, the repeated dismissive references to Hispaniola by mainlanders reflected the point that the defeat of Madrid contributed mightily to the long-standing wish of Washington to gain an even firmer foothold at Samana. Nonetheless, in a sign of which way the racial winds were blowing, Negro rights activist Archibald Grimké who, had followed Frederick Douglass as an envoy to this heavily African island, was ousted as the mass arrival of U.S. nationals in the region signaled that the presumed racial sinecure the two men had occupied was eroding.[174] Indeed, it was Douglass's inability as a diplomat in Haiti to acquire a key site there for the United States that incited the mainland to lust after Guantánamo.[175]

U.S. officialdom in Guantánamo rued the fact that they had to negotiate not just with Negroes but enfranchised Negroes. Their activism rankled; besides that their example provided a suggestive—subversive in some ways—example to U.S. sailors of all colors, not to mention mainlanders generally. U.S. Negro sailors were marrying Cuban women, too, which increased the personal ties and illuminated further the example provided by militant Cubans.[176]

The long-standing lust for Cuba, its racial ratios, and strategic location serve to inform the considered opinion of one scholar that after 1898, "the

independent [*sic*] nation of Cuba enjoyed less political and economic autonomy and sovereignty in its imperial relationship with the United States than
the annexed territory of Hawai'i did."[177] "Autonomy" for Cuba, said one influential mainlander in 1898, "never can succeed."[178] This abortive sovereignty
also paved the way to 1959, inter alia, which was a revolt against not just foreign domination but foreign Jim Crow domination.[179]

Since Cuba was so much closer to the mainland than the Pacific archipelago and contained many more Africans, it was perceived by some as potentially more of a threat to U.S. national security. Moreover, the U.S.-style Jim
Crow that arrived with U.S. forces also had the added "advantage" of circumscribing opportunities on the island for U.S. Negroes and limited their ability
to establish in Cuba a base for subversion against the mainland.[180] By limiting competitors, Jim Crow also widened opportunities for those who identified as "white," thereby creating a renewed foundation for rule in the midst of
the wreckage created by the ouster of Madrid after centuries of hegemony.[181]
Louisiana's sugar barons could breathe a sigh of relief when their competitor
in Cuba came under virtual U.S. rule.[182]

The establishment of what amounted to Euro-American colonial enclaves
in Cuba—with 13,000 U.S. nationals having title to land in Cuba by 1905 at a
value of $50 million—was an essential element of this renewed foundation.[183]
The United States had one of the largest, if not the largest, populations in the
world of those who could be viewed as "white" and with more of them moving
to the island, this quickened a process already in motion. According to the
historian Alejandro de la Fuente the proportion of those not defined as white
in Cuba's population declined throughout the second half of the nineteenth
century from 55 or 60 percent to about 33 percent by 1899.[184] This lessened
the possibility of the island becoming yet another Haiti or becoming a racial
ally of Negro mainlanders, a noticeable fear in South Carolina where Senator
Tillman repeatedly inveighed against the Negro majority in his state (and in
Mississippi) and demanded more "white immigration."[185]

Hence the U.S. Negro Reverend Astwood radiated the feeling then growing among Negroes that Cuba was a "paradise for the colored man." But as
time passed he counseled that "the color line is being fastly [*sic*] drawn by the
whites here and the Cubans abused as Negroes," for the "majority of Cubans
are Negroes and now that this fact has dawned upon the white brother, there
is no longer a desire to have Cuban independence."[186] Even Booker T. Washington came to recognize that in Cuba a "race problem similar to what we have
in the United States is likely to rise there."[187]

CHAPTER 8

Race/War in Cuba?

J AMES TILLMAN WAS PREPARED TO KILL.
This nephew of South Carolina's premier politician, "Pitchfork" Ben, had been pummeled in the press by Narciso G. Gonzales and then finished a poor third place in the 1902 gubernatorial primary. On 15 January 1903 he spotted the scribe of illustrious Cuban origin on a major thoroughfare in Columbia and promptly pulled his German Lugar pistol and shot him in the abdomen. Gonzales crumpled to the ground and died four days later. But it was as though he had killed a Negro or slaughtered a hog, for Tillman was acquitted.[1]

In addition to eviscerating Tillman regularly, Gonzales, now prominent in the Palmetto State as one of its leading columnists, had devoted numerous articles to the unfolding drama in Cuba, exceeding the sustained attention of probably any other mainland journal. By 1898 he sought to put his body on the line by heading to Tampa with the intention of joining the insurgents, fulfilling the ambition of his celebrated father. But by 1903 his funeral attracted thousands of mourners, perhaps the largest crowd to attend such a ceremony in that state in a half century, excepting that of his in-law Wade Hampton, the state's governor when Reconstruction was drowned in blood. Not only was his slaying—and Tillman's acquittal—a setback for the rights of the population of Cubans on the mainland, which had been growing since the outbreak of unrest in 1868, then jumped in the 1890s, it was inseparable from the ongoing growth of bigotry symbolized by the brutalization of the Negro.[2]

The murder was a mainland sign that Cubans, irrespective of phenotype, would not easily enter the hallowed halls of "whiteness" but would be forced into a subordinate status, consistent with that of Cuba's as a protectorate: the "Creole" alliance with Washington came to an ignominious conclusion, a signpost on the road to revolution. Cuba's "sin," to an extent, was its incongruence racially with its new mainland master. Gonzales was not as racially demented as the Tillmans, though he had traveled far down that road and should have realized that attacking this eminent Dixie family on any grounds would open the door to closer scrutiny of himself, a test he would find hard to pass. After the war a mainland resident of Havana declaimed that "the Cuba Libre of the Blacks would be a veritable hell upon earth, a blot upon Christian civilization." Others believed that real independence for Cuba would result in a mass exodus of those deemed to be "white," creating another Haiti with untold repercussions for the mainland. Naturally, it was after the war that the United States strived to "whiten" the population further by attracting more migrants from the Canary Islands. Ironically, some of these had maternal ties to the family of Fidel Castro, yet another backfiring step in the race to revolution.[3]

The 1898 war not only marked the transition of Spain to becoming a minor power after centuries of major power status but the rise of the United States as an imperial nation; but the demotion of Spain also suggested (at least in U.S. eyes) a demotion of those with historic ties to Spain, for example, Gonzales.[4] Quite infamously, it was "Pitchfork" Ben who had proclaimed, "Down with the niggers, but if we must tolerate them, give us those of mixed blood,"[5] which seemed to provide an opening for an entente with Cubans. However, the vicious slaying of Gonzales seemed to put paid to this darkening Havana spring.

After slavery ended in Cuba, an arriving mainlander in 1898 argued that "Spain had the ability of reducing to real slavery the whole native population, both white and black"—and the 1890s revolt was in part resistance to this diabolical scheme. But as the departing Spaniard Marquis de Apezteguia also said in 1898, a constrained Madrid was compelled to pursue "two lines of conduct: satisfy the whites as far as possible and you must content the black so that he will not lend his brute force to the discontent of the white." The post-1898 regime then accelerated revolt by seeking to impose a rigid Jim Crow on the island.

A mainland planter in Cuba cautioned that same year that even though "the Canary Islander is the best laborer," they tended to be "rather difficult" to deal with, unlike the Africans, who had survived the degradation of war better than most. A fellow planter, Evaristo Montalvo, was wary of alienating African labor altogether since there were "about 80,000 people in the province of Santa Clara" who were illiterate, while "more Negroes know how to write than whites." Yet another member of the managerial class in Cuba, Walter Beal of Boston, argued that "one Negro in cutting cane can do as much as two of any other class," and there was little hope of this force being replaced by the incoming "American Negro" since they would be unable to "put up with hardships here and a style of eating and living" that was alien. There was a delicate balance of labor and race in Cuba that did not fit altogether U.S. preconceptions, yet when the rollicking mainlanders arrived, this applecart was upset, throwing the island into a frenzy.[6]

Symptomatic of this ham-fisted approach was the analysis of the Washington-based journalist Charles Pepper. In 1899 he was astonished to find that "the Negro or the mulatto may call himself 'Don' and ask that . . . you [use][,] the [respectful and deferential] prefix [,] in addressing him. This is more than the simple 'Mister' of American familiarity," which was certainly not accorded to the beleaguered U.S. Negro. "However distasteful it may be to American prejudices," he conceded reluctantly, "the code will be enforced nor will there ever be discrimination on account of color in the privileges of railroad travel." More astonishingly, "The American military authorities from the outset showed a scrupulous regard for the civil rights of the blacks," not least since they were concerned about the "nightmare" of a "Black West India republic" which would make the Antilles a "menace, at least a bar to civilization of the continent." Unfortunately, Weyler's policies had a more devastating impact on "black victims," rather "than the whites"—hence the need for population rebalancing by bringing in more Canary Islanders. There had been "free movement of the blacks throughout the West Indies" and a "sprinkling of all these classes of blacks was found among the insurgents—the Bahamas and Santo Domingo furnishing the greater number of them," but was this past policy consistent with Washington's ethos? If Negro labor were needed, he much preferred that it come from the mainland, but this policy too had its problems since "the Cuban Negro is on a higher plane than is his brother in the United States" in terms of "industrial life" and synchronizing the two could be difficult.

Then there was the nettlesome issue that the "blood of the Latin races does not repel the African blood so violently as that which runs in the veins of their fellow Caucasians of the Saxon stock," which virtually mandated an "overwhelming wave of Americanism with race prejudice on the crest." This was already occurring with "Americans urging their own ideas of inferiority and telling the white Cubans that the only hope for them is ignoring the African race," but this was fomenting even more difficulties, as 1912 was to show. Thus when the "color line" was drawn sharply by the new occupiers, "then the solidarity of the race of color [sic] began to show itself," since "there are sections in which the blacks are numerically preponderant," this could bruit the fearsome idea of the "Black West India republic." The "white element in Santiago," he presciently warned, "is today fearful of the experiment of independence." They had been encouraged, he said, when Maceo fell in battle, which was said to dissipate the fear of "Negro supremacy," but it could arise again.[7]

"Under Spanish rule," complained the *Afro-American*, "every man had the same rights and privileges" but "under American rule race prejudice holds sway until in almost every section of the island the black Cuban has almost as hard a time as he has in this country."[8] One possible remedy was to redefine race: the arriving occupiers in 1898 mused that it had "been customary to reckon among Negroes having one-fourth, one-half or three-fourths white blood" and though this was the norm on the mainland, in Cuba it was seemingly "philosophically unjust and makes the Negro element appear larger than it really is," which was even more unfortunate since "for thirty or forty years the Negro element has been both relatively and absolutely decreasing."[9] General Leonard Wood thought the proper approach was to bar the immigration to Cuba of any persons of African descent.[10]

Although the so-called Platt Amendment had for all intents and purposes suffocated the Cuban sovereignty that so many "Creoles" had crusaded for over the decades,[11] the 1898 war had ignited a trend possibly as potent—U.S. Negroes setting up shop on the island. W. C. Warmsley, a Negro trooper, painted a rhapsodic picture of the island for readers of the Negro press in Washington, D.C., "surrounded with palm and banana trees and beautiful landscape scenes" near San Luis, twenty miles from Santiago. He was in the latter metropolis where the "population is about 50,000 the majority of whom"—he added with anthropological acuity—"are colored from a Cuban point of view." Importantly, "there is not a colored doctor here at present. In fact, I am the only colored physician on this end of the island"; also of importance was that "the towns near and around Havana are too near America but on this end"—nearer Haiti—"the professional colored man would be idolized. I know from simple experience," he said with confidence. "One could get rich in Santiago teaching English."[12]

Warmsley's Negro comrade John E. Lewis was equally intrigued with the prospects presented by Cuba, stunned that there "you find the colored man in all kinds of business and trade; all colors working together in the greatest harmony." Imbued with optimism, he claimed that "there have been Americans who came to this island and tried" to "draw the color line but the Cubans would not submit to such treatment and cleaned up the place"—which provided an object lesson for his homeland: "It is only a question of time," he counseled, referring to dark days ahead for the mainland, "if the South is not more just to the American blacks." Hence, it was with "regret," bordering on gloom, that he was "about to return to the States and to the South."[13]

But others remained. Booker T. Washington was told by one that the "presence of so many Americans (colored) whom the Cubans, i.e. the darker ones, know are their friends seems to have stimulated them"; the Cubans he knew were "kind and gentle," which augured a flourishing relationship.[14] Another Washington correspondent told him that the "soil in Cuba is ready for the seeds from Tuskegee & Hampton to be planted," referring to two of the more important Negro universities. To fertilize the ground, some of Washington's work was to be published in Spanish and by 1903 about "one thousand copies" of his affecting autobiography had been sold.[15] Washington was proud of his ties to the island having debated as a student "whether or not the United States should own Cuba. I took the view that we should."[16] Tuskegee was not unique in that its competitor, Washington's Howard University, had enrolled fifteen students from Cuba and Puerto Rico by 1910.[17] Their competitor, Hampton Institute, proudly claimed as an alumnus Alexander Santa Cruz, born in Cienfuegos in 1870 (and who wound up teaching at the Virginia campus, this after arriving on the mainland in 1888).[18] Nonetheless, despite his prominence, Booker T. Washington incurred the wrath of the Alabama authorities when he admitted to Tuskegee what Governor Joseph F. Johnston referred to as "five white boys" from Cuba.[19]

It was also in 1910 that the British journalist William Archer arrived in Cuba to investigate and instantly found it "obvious" that the "colour line" was relatively absent compared to Dixie. "I see a good many black policemen; and there are black motor-men and conductors on the street cars. Among the passengers in the cars there is no distinction of colour"—a stark contrast with the "Southern States." Even the cemeteries were integrated racially, he noted with wonderment. Yet in interviewing mainland whites he was cautioned by those who feared a replay of Reconstruction or a Negro surge politically. "Well, sir," said one of these troglodytes, "I'm a Southern man myself and all I can say is that the nigger here don't seem to me the same as he is at home." This was because during slavery "Cuban planters" were supposedly more selective in dragooning Africans than those in "Charleston or New Orleans," as "they knew precisely the qualities of the different breeds"; thus, the island "got the pick of the basket and only the lower class—the mere brawny animals—got to the United States." These expatriates also blamed wily island Africans for the ouster of President Tomas Estrada Palma in 1906; "ninety-five percent of those who took active part in the Revolution of 1906 were Negroes," Archer was told.[20]

And Archer could have added that U.S. Negroes were drawing inspiration from Cubans fighting the installation of Jim Crow. It was in 1902 that the *Baltimore Afro-American* monitored a "meeting of the colored inhabitants" in Havana, where "participants voted to petition the Cuban Congress to annul the existing military orders which make distinctions against the blacks. They denied any intention of [a] rising,"[21] which was said to come in 1912. Among the journal's contributors was I. W. Jenkins, a graduate of Howard University, who "never missed the opportunity to bring before the public in an unbiased manner the Cuban Negro, the backbone of the republic."[22]

If journeying to Cuba via New Orleans, Negroes might have been aboard a crowded vessel. In the war's aftermath, it was not just this group who were being attracted to the island. Travel between Havana and this Louisiana port became so heavy that one travel guide found it "impossible to provide accommodations for all those [who] desired to take this . . . 610-mile journey."[23] In 1901 a U.S. official announced proudly to Secretary of State Elihu Root, after having visited the "interior of Cuba, comprising the provinces of Pinar del Rio, Matanzas and Havana," that "I met several American farmers who were doing well. More are expected to settle in that productive country."[24] Leonard Wood, the leading mainland official in Cuba, reflected his class's unfavorable view of Negroes on both sides of the straits; he termed those in Cuba as "illiterate mass of people . . . unable to become responsible citizens."[25] Soon Negroes were to find that the kinds of retrogressive attitudes they had sought to escape were descending upon the island with the onset of de facto U.S. rule.

This should not have been surprising. For example, as North Carolina was gearing up for the invasion of Cuba in 1898, it was embroiled in a searing racist conflict that amounted to a coup d'état in Wilmington.[26] State leaders were debating the efficacy of deploying "colored" troops there as a result; the "genuine case of war fever" expressed by one eminence in the Tarheel State could well be considered a proxy for the internal war then raging.[27] Attorney Frank Carter of Asheville found it to be an "unspeakable disappointment" when some white forces were not sent to Cuba (his correspondent Marion Butler was prominent in the revealingly named journal *The Caucasian*), perhaps because they would be unable to gain the military experience that could prove valuable at home.[28] As Washington was circumscribing voting rights at home, there was an attempt to do the same in Cuba.[29]

Another Carolinian, Henry Bagley, writing from Havana, found the city to be "decent" considering the damaging "reports" he had heard; there were numerous taxis, for example, and the "whole city" was "as noisy at night" as "Fayetteville Street in Raleigh," which he thought was tremendous—and they were the "politest people I ever saw." But, alas, hardly anyone he encountered spoke English, not to mention other unique habits—for example, "If when smoking I ask a man for a light he will hand me his cigarette with the lighted end toward me and when I hand it back I must stick at him the part that has been in his mouth." These were among the "thousand things" he found "peculiar."[30]

But it was not just tobacco that captured Bagley's attention, since by March 1899 he was vexed about a potential "uprising among the Cubans," particularly if the U.S. military force were reduced: "There are shooting affairs in town nearly every night," which was terribly upsetting.[31]

Octavius Coke, then serving militarily in Cuba, found "the natives" to be "an odd set of human beings," which made him "feel very lonesome" for the "people & language is entirely foreign to us." A residence in Cuba, as for many mainlanders, led to comparisons detrimental to islanders. "There is no place like America," he said, speaking of his homeland. "We are the greatest nationality on the top side of the globe." Fortunately, "the Spanish soldiers have vacated now" and the mainlanders could now see themselves as masters of all they surveyed.[32]

As a result, the U.S. forces—as the sailor William P. Upshur put it— became rapidly "engaged in the interesting operation of collecting the rebels' arms," which, fortunately, were "of the most miserable character" and "in horrible condition." He had to endure the indignity of having to "shake hands with the nigger generals," but there were compensations since his mates seemed to "like [Cuba] so much," they didn't "want to leave at all, at least they don't want to go back to the ships."[33] Yes, he said with satisfaction, Cuba "doesn't seem at all out of the way," nor "strange" with the only "great impediment" in Guantánamo being "the thorns" that were "very strong and sharp"[34]—as the impending revolt against U.S. domination was to be seen.

This revolt occurred not least because the rancid attitudes brought by the 1898 war rubbed many Cubans the wrong way, particularly after so many had shed blood for sovereignty only to find a new "master," and one with racial attitudes that made the departing Spaniards seem thoroughly modern. "A dead Indian is not nearly so valuable as a dead 'nigger,'" said Upshur, tellingly writing after target practice and summing up mainstream mainland attitudes in the wake of the conquering of a continent.[35]

Mainlanders brought their culture with them in sum, including racially offensive minstrel shows,[36] which became a staple for U.S. forces. One in Pinar del Rio, said Upshur contentedly, featured a "Georgia plantation scene, a minstrel troupe, a troop of Eastern dancing girls"—and, to top it all off, "the Confederate cruiser *Alabama*."[37] After two especially boisterous shows, he found that "everybody seemed to have a good time."[38] He didn't speak Spanish, like most of his companions—the "heathen sounds" escaped him. Adjusting to the region was not easy for Upshur and his fellow sailors; thus when they traveled to Trinidad, the British colony, they seemed surprised to find that "the police are Negroes" with some being "mounted." More striking was that the "Negroes here speak very much better English than ours do."[39] Predictably, the "vile liquor" they imbibed "coupled with the hot climate" tended to "arouse the fighting spirit" and "indignation" of his mates, notably when a "big black, white-coated policeman" sought to enforce the law. All ended well, however, since the colonialists "have the darkies in a splendid state of discipline and they jump like a flash when an officer speaks."[40]

With such odoriferous attitudes invading Cuba, it was unavoidable that racist tensions in Cuba would rise.[41] By 1904 a mere baseball game between U.S. sailors near Guantánamo and what officialdom in Cuba called "persons of colored race" resulted in a "great tumult and free fight" that was quite "violent" with such "alarming proportions" that the "police force there was insufficient"—"two sailors of the Naval Station were badly hurt."[42]

In some ways the new century that brought a new "master" in Cuba was a race between two contrasting trends: official Washington, whose regime facilitated the arrival of U.S. capital, and the strict enforcement of Jim Crow and U.S. Negroes who—at least—were not supportive of the latter, which their nation saw as essential to its rule. James Weldon Johnson was an exemplar of these trends: he served as both a U.S. diplomat in Latin America and as an early leader of the new organization that had arisen to confront Jim Crow, the National Association for the Advancement of Colored People (NAACP), while penning what came to be called the "Negro National Anthem," "Lift Every Voice and Sing." His maternal great-grandmother had been placed by a French army officer in Hispaniola aboard a steamer bound for Cuba, just before the final collapse of Parisian rule in 1804; the vessel was captured by the British navy and was taken to Nassau and from there the family made it to Florida, where Johnson was born in 1871. His father was a prominent pastor in Jacksonville where he became friendly with Ricardo Ponce of Havana, whom Johnson described as possessing an "elegance and courtliness such as I had never seen before," a description subsequently applied to Johnson himself.

It was the custom then for certain Cuban families to find mainland homes in which their sons could reside and become effectively bilingual, which is how Ricardo Rodriguez became his boyhood friend. Symptomatic of the great hopes for Cuba held by U.S. Negroes, Reverend Johnson "made a great effort" to ensure that his son learned "the Spanish language. We used to sit for an hour at a time when he drilled us." Jacksonville then had a population of "several thousand" Cubans, but it seemed to be growing daily. Rodriguez's arrival allowed Johnson's fluency to leap: "There had grown between us," recalled Johnson, "a strong bond of companionship; and what was, perhaps, more binding, the bond of language"; eventually, they only addressed each other in Spanish.

Like so many others, Rodriguez wound up attending a Negro college—in his case he followed Johnson to Atlanta University. On the train there, an episode unfolded emblematic of Cuba's role as an escape hatch for U.S. Negroes. When the conductor heard them conversing in Spanish, he became more friendly: "He punched our tickets and gave them back, and treated us just as he did the other passengers in the car." They were to reside in the same dormitory room, chattering away in Spanish, which prepared him well for service in Nicaragua and Venezuela.[43] It was Johnson, also one of the brightest stars in literati's constellation, who weaved Cuban themes into his celebrated novel.[44] It was Johnson who became an early analyst of what he called "Aframerican poets of the Latin languages" with a focus on the heralded Cuban, Placido.

Comparing Cuban writers to U.S. Negro writers, he felt the former aspired to "greater universality" since the latter "is always on the defensive or the offensive," laboring under "suffocations" hardly imaginable south of the border: "The colored poets of Latin American," he opined sagaciously, "can voice the national spirit" with fewer "reservations" than their mainland counterparts, providing added sinew to their work.[45]

Given such close contact it is not surprising that many Cubans followed the progress of U.S. Negroes carefully. This trend was facilitated when more Cubans followed Rodriguez into mainland schools that catered to Negroes, as when, for example, Pedro Santos from Guantánamo studied dentistry at Meharry Medical School in Nashville.[46] A society in the name of Booker T. Washington was formed on the island in 1915,[47] and in Havana there was a Booker T. Washington Institute of Popular Education.[48] The Tampa-based Cuban grouping, which adopted the names of both Jose Martí and Antonio Maceo in its name, warmly embraced Washington as an emblem of their embrace of the U.S. Negroes the Tuskegee leader purported to represent.[49] Likewise U.S. Negroes welcomed enthusiastically a "native Cuban" from Matanzas, slated to lecture on "Cuba, Africa and [the] Holy Land." Thoughtfully in the land of Jim Crow, there were "reserved seats for our White Friends."[50]

The back-and-forth between the island and the mainland, which stretched back to the days of slaves as commodities being traded, continued to percolate. When Rose Sonnivell of Chicago, billed as the city's "oldest local citizen," passed away at the age of 116, after being born in Cuba in 1805, the local Negro journal said: "She was never a slave, and that is thought to have aided her longevity somewhat."[51] A Chicago analyst felt that Negroes could learn a thing or two from Cubans, not about longevity but militancy[52]—a tendency that could have been handy when George Thompson, who had fought in Cuba in 1898, was jailed on the mainland for the offense of marrying a woman defined as "white."[53]

As a U.S. Negro writing from Mexico in the NAACP journal put it, U.S. Negroes should consider emigrating not just to Cuba but to "Central and South America and the islands" too, since there were "no prejudices in these countries"; their presence was desperately needed since "the white men who come here use every opportunity to give us a black eye."[54] P. W. Mallet, corresponding from Argentina, agreed.[55] "Afro-Americans," said a Philadelphia Negro, "have not only the United States, and . . . Canada as fields for their living and striving, but they have all of Latin America [including] Cuba."[56] Writing from Cuba's neighbor, Puerto Rico, Hallie Queen told of "at least two colored Americans, whom I know personally, are making excellent records on the island—one in law, the other in dentistry," while even the Euro-Americans she met "seem to have forgotten Colorphobia." This strained credulity, though easier to accept was the contention that on this island "never a murderous rope has been coiled, nor a Jim Crow sign hung, nor a door of opportunity closed to a man because his face was black."[57] Booker T. Washington did not necessarily disagree, speaking of the "letters" he had received from "Cuba and South America, all asking that the American Negro be induced to go to these places as laborers."[58]

Seeking to foil the historic flight of Negroes from Dixie northward, the Negro press trumpeted the ominous words of the racial theorist Madison Grant, who warned that "the West Indies, the coast region of our Gulf states, and perhaps the black belt of the lower Mississippi Valley"—and Cuba—"must be abandoned to the Negroes."[59] But worry persisted, as one Negro journalist put it, that "at the present time the color line stops at the Rio Grande"—but with the growth in influence of the United States, how long would that last? And did not that provide an incentive for Negroes in the hemisphere to resist U.S. expansion, providing a material basis for a nascent Pan-Africanism, if not anti-imperialism?[60]

R. M. R. Nelson arrived in Cuba in 1898 with mining in mind and a plan to bring "10,000 Negro farmers" to the island. "Prejudiced Americans who have come to Cuba," said the *Pittsburgh Courier*, whose readership was overwhelmingly composed of Negroes, "to make their fortunes naturally do not want to see American Negroes here for obvious reasons," though his plan was "feasible and practical" for this "beautiful isle."[61] By 1916 he was still at it, conferring with Cubans about purchasing sugar mills.[62] "Every paper in Cuba," said the *Afro-American*, "is now discussing his plan." Nelson with panache called Cuba "this Edenland" and the paper asserted that "prejudiced Americans" were hotly opposed to his plans.[63] "Are colored men in the United States asleep?" wondered Nelson, since there were fortunes to be had in Cuba.[64] No, they were not, as John Edward Bruce could have told him; as early as 1912 he was offered space in a Spanish-language journal on the island to write a column supporting mainland Negro investments in Cuba.[65]

After that comment about somnolence, inquiries increased with one Negro from Alabama arriving to study law at the prestigious University of Havana. He also spoke Spanish and, it was said, "deposited $15,000" in the bank, this after having "purchased eighty-three acres as the nucleus for other landholdings for the accommodations of fifteen families from his former home in Bessemer."[66] This Alabamian, George Davis, raised hogs, watermelons, chickens, vegetables and fruit. One of his visitors marveled that in Cuba "a black man was just as good as a white man. There were colored motormen and conductors on the streetcars." Since Key West was "only five hours" away, this guest envisioned "50,000 colored farmers from the South" repatriating there.[67] Even

Ben Davis, Sr.—prominent Negro Republican from Atlanta and father of the man who was to become the leading Negro Communist on the mainland—found time to sample Cuba.[68] Not accidentally, these Havana dreams were arising as the Panama Canal was opening since Cuba was a gateway to it and, it was reported, this "will cause land values to advance" on the island.[69]

Davis had been preceded by the fabulously wealthy Negro entrepreneur Madame C. J. Walker, who sailed to Cuba with dreams of expanding her hair care empire—converting the woolly locks of Africans into something that resembled the strands of those seen as white.[70] She was followed by William Dammond, formerly of Detroit, who had taught at Paul Quinn College, a school for Negroes in Texas, and was the first African-American graduate of the University of Pittsburgh. He had designed buildings across the United States and Britain and then opted to design a sugar factory in Cuba.[71] Subsequently the eminent Philadelphia lawyer of African descent, Raymond Pace Alexander, advised mainland Negroes to travel as much as possible—if only to be reassured that the vicious Jim Crow they encountered daily was not necessarily normative globally—but travel to Cuba, first of all.[72]

Apparently Negroes did not need to be urged in this direction since according to one contested analysis, roughly a century ago there were about 5,000 U.S. Negroes residing in London and a like number in Paris and in Buenos Aires. But for all that, a consensus was developing that even with Washington busily seeking to install Jim Crow, Cuba was the preferred site of exile for U.S. Negroes.[73]

The coming and passing of the First World War, when thousands of mainland Negroes were enticed to fight, supposedly for a democracy they did not enjoy, led to numerous expressions akin to Alexander's considered sentiments. Claude McKay, paragon of the literary explosion denoted as the Harlem Renaissance, was an example. As U.S. influence spread, he said, U.S. Negroes should follow by pushing for the "world propagation of their grievances" and force their cause forward "as a prime international issue."[74]

It did not take long for such counsel to be heeded entrepreneurially, as a Negro was dispatched to Cuba to represent a major Chicago firm in managing a sprawling labor force that included Cubans, Belgians, Hungarians, Greeks[75]—a virtually unheard-of occurrence on the mainland. Pullman porters, most of whom were Negroes, had developed their own business ties with Cuba, as they were accused of smuggling bootleg liquor from the island via New Orleans, then on to Chicago hidden in compartments in the dining and sleeping cars of trains.[76]

The U.S. Negro chanteuse Azalia Hackley—the "Queen of Song," as she was termed—compared the mainland to Cuba, with the mainland coming off the worse.[77] This was a gathering opinion, for it was also in 1912 that affluent

Negroes—including Robert S. Abbott of Chicago, the rare Negro with capital—began to consider significant investments in Cuba.[78] Cuba, said the Negro academic Charles Alexander, was "really the future hope of those ambitious men and women who really are seeking a home where there is no color line." He had his eye on Los Pinos Farms, which comprised "ten thousand acres" of land "as rich and fertile as any land in the island of Cuba."[79] By 1917, Abbott, who controlled the *Chicago Defender*, opened a bureau in Havana where his journal immodestly noted that the "English reading Cubans have gone wild over it"[80] and was to develop an avid readership there.[81] By 1920 his paper was reporting that "W. M. Weaver, a well-known citizen of St. Louis" was "about to join the small army of Americans who are seeking liberty and freedom in a free country-Cuba."[82] Cuba's consul in Chicago—according to this periodical—"probably did not wish white Americans to know that in his home country the people of darker [hue] can 'go as far as they like.'" The island was portrayed as an ideal to which the U.S. should aspire: Cuba "sets [for] this country a splendid example."[83]

Since they had shed blood in Cuba, U.S. Negroes felt this had enhanced their right to full citizenship; what they did not seem to realize was that by assisting the imposition of Jim Crow in Cuba, they had created momentum for their own demise. After being barred from a Dixie restaurant, a Negro postal worker complained that "we did not want to go to Cuba but Uncle Sam made us go, so now we feel that we are citizens and will go into every public place under the Stars and Stripes, even in the South."[84] The problem was this: Uncle Sam begged to differ. U.S. Negroes did not seem to understand that their blood sacrifice was not seen by Washington as something worthy of honor but, instead, just another mandate for chumps—they were to have an autonomy as limited as Cuba's. Not quite grasped by most was what one scholar has called "the Transnational 'Negro Question,'" the attempts by white elites to impose interlinked regimes of political and economic control over African Americans and Africans"—and this included a Cuba that "became fundamental to the renewed colonial civilizing mission" so sanctimoniously and hypocritically pursued.[85]

Implanting a Jim Crow regime in Cuba created enormous strain. One prominent Havana hotel caused a furor when a bartender refused to serve drinks to two leading politicians who were perceived as Negro. An enormous crowd gathered that included war veterans but the result was minor penalty on the segregationists. Afterward a procession of 400 Cubans led by the two politicians marched to the hotel chanting, "Viva Maceo, Viva La Patria." They barged into the hotel, demanded drinks and were served with no further protest. According to a mainland press account, "Many Cubans are sympathizing with the attitude of the American hotel management," suggesting that Jim Crow had a base of support on the island, which could serve to generate even more dissidence. The *Baltimore Sun* took note when "*El Triunfo*, a government organ, publishe[d] a bitter editorial declaring that all blacks and whites in Cuba are on a plane of absolute equality," and that the "Americans must be taught [by] the strong arm of the law that they shall not be permitted to introduce into Cuba the anti-Negro sentiments prevailing in the United States."[86]

Apparently the celebrated James Weldon Johnson and Rodriguez did not bond on the baseball diamond or in the boxing ring, but for many other U.S. Negroes and Cubans that was to be the case (particularly in the realm of music, where jazz was one of their many innovations).[87] Reportedly, between the turn of the twentieth century and the triumph of the Cuban Revolution, over 150 U.S. Negroes who were professional baseball players had a sojourn on the island. And many Cubans played in the U.S. Negro professional leagues, with Martín Dihigo one of the most talented to ever grace mainland diamonds.[88] U.S. Negro players and mainlanders who were perceived as "white" found it easier to compete against each other in Cuba—and Latin America generally— where they too could eat in the same restaurants, stay at the same sumptuous hotel, and bask in a comparable hero's glory and build more easily truly human relationships that were next to impossible to make in the United States.[89] With excessive optimism, one mainland Negro felt that "with the admission of Cubans of a darker hue in the two big leagues it would be easy for colored players who are citizens of this country to get into fast company."[90]

This was a variation of the then widespread view in Manhattan that Spanish-speaking Negroes escaped much of the racial segregation visited upon monolingual English speaking Negroes with roots on the mainland.[91] Weldon Johnson may not have played baseball alongside Rodriguez, but he learned to play the game as a youth at the knee of the Cuban Giants, a team of mostly U.S. Negro players who were employed by the Ponce de Leon Hotel in St. Augustine.[92]

When the New York Giants and Cincinnati Reds visited Cuba, one condition was that no U.S. Negroes would be allowed to play on Cuba teams with whom they competed (presumably, Cubans of African descent were acceptable).[93] The mainland star Judy Johnson loved the island while his fellow Negro league competitor, Oscar Charleston, learned Spanish.[94] Coincidentally, Jim Crow on the mainland began to disintegrate as revolutionaries in Cuba began to rise—and vice versa. The U.S. appeal to Cuba and to other territories viewed as up for grabs in the Cold War facilitated a steady retreat from Jim Crow on the mainland, which in turn created a liberalized opening for revolutionaries, forcing agonizing reappraisals in Washington, and so on.

Of course, this process was neither smooth nor felicitous, as exemplified by the massacre of Cubans of African ancestry in 1912, which could be seen as an organic response to the forcible insertion of Jim Crow into an island whose racial patterns had diverged from those on the mainland for quite some time. On 25 May 1912 the *Chicago Defender*, whose readership was mostly Negro, reported breathlessly that the island was "in throes of revolt. Spaniards and Negroes in rebellion in eastern province [and] may hold out for months . . . especially in Oriente, where an immense majority of the population is blacks." Supposedly, the "better class of blacks" were not involved.[95] Their editorial charged that "the Negroes in Cuba demand recognition politically on the ground that they compose 85 per cent of the revolutionary armies"—but pushing these militants into a cul de sac, their conclusion was: "they are wasting time demanding. Why not do some taking?"[96]

It was a "Negro Conspiracy," charged a mainland observer accusingly; "the uprising," which meant "about 3,000 Negroes were killed," said Leland H. Jenks, "was effective only in Oriente Province," the site of many Africans but also "where large American corporations were the principal property-holders." The "suppression cost Cuba some $150,000 for Krag-Jorgensen rifles purchased from the United States" and "about $200,000 for damages to American property," Yet, he averred by way of indictment, "this brief record does scant justice to the terror to which American corporations in Oriente surrendered themselves or the horrible calamities" they supposedly endured, as "Washington and New York" faced once more their worst "nightmare"—"a Black Republic!" If Cuba had not acted aggressively, then mainlanders would have sought a more muscular "intervention" for fear of the outward ripples across the straits. "Senator Knute Nelson of Minnesota charged that the rebellion had been incited by American or corporate interests with the object of bringing about American intervention or annexation" in order to quash incipient Negro militancy on the island.[97]

It was left to Arturo Schomburg, the Puerto Rican of African descent who had become an intellectual leader in New York City, to explain the meaning of these difficult events to U.S. Negroes. The Independent Party of Color (PIC) had "sprung up like mushrooms all over the island. In a year there was a club for every city and the party had a membership of over 60,000 voters" and was "a success." He too condemned the Morua Law, which "in effect forbade the formation of any political party along racial lines"; that this proviso was devised by a Cuban of African origin meant "he was afterward looked down upon by the Negroes of Cuba as a Judas to his race." When he died, it was "of a broken heart" for this law was as "despicable as the American Dred Scott decision"—which was an apt analogy. Thus Negro objectors were now "hunted by spies, threatened with imprisonment and misrepresented in the press." Citing "my friend, the late Jose Martí, the apostle of Cuban freedom," he lamented this turn of events, adding portentously that "during the colonial days of Spain the Negroes were better treated, enjoyed a greater measure of freedom, and happiness than they do today. Negroes were esteemed for their talents and respected for their industry and integrity" but now "many Negroes curse the dawn of the Republic. . . . The Negro has done much for Cuba; Cuba has done nothing for the Negro. The black men of Cuba have taken to the woods because conditions are intolerable."[98]

A writer for the NAACP concluded that the United States was "the last government on earth capable of interfering for good in such a dispute" as now raged in Cuba for Washington could only act "on behalf of the whites and can only aggravate and make permanent racial division."[99] This organization, which had been called into being in 1909 as the "nadir" hit a new bottom, seized upon the conflict in Cuba as representative of what Washington's rule meant. Though their investigator found "the prisons of Santiago filled to their capacity," their count still showed that "of the eighty members of the Cuban House of Representatives, some twelve are professedly of Negro blood"; unlike the mainland, in Cuba "the Emancipation Proclamation has brought real freedom and opportunity" to the African. Readers were reminded that Theodore Roosevelt had said, "If we were in control in Cuba the Negroes would be kept within bounds, socially and politically"—which was chilling in light of the buckets of blood already shed. The NAACP writer was flabbergasted by an idea then propounded by certain Cubans that American intervention would "advance the status of the Negro more rapidly, " and "fortunately for Cuba," it was said with relief, "the majority of the colored people, and a large number even of the Independents were entirely opposed" to such poppycock.[100]

U.S. Negroes were trapped in an abusive relationship with TR's GOP and were constrained. TR, contrary to the island's direction, had cautioned against Cuba becoming a "protectorate," though his endorsement of "some of our troops" remaining to "steady things" undermined this sentiment.[101]

The indiscriminate killing of Africans was both a fierce response by the U.S.-backed regime to real and imagined opponents to Jim Crow and a defining event that undermined whatever shreds of confidence remained in a dominant Washington. The victims were trapped in a violent wind shear featuring on the one hand the aspirant and old Cuba whereby racism was not as intense—even during the days of slavery—as on the mainland, and on the other the new regime of Jim Crow where sharp lines were drawn between the "whites" and the "colored." Unfortunately, some Cubans seemed unaware that their island was undergoing this jolting transition wherein the implantation of Jim Crow by a malignant external force unavoidably caused its victims to band together; instead, these victims were charged with engaging in a kind of racism contrary to Cuban traditions.

The contemporary Cuban intellectual Fernando Martínez Heredia has underlined the turning point that triggered the founding of the Independent

Party of Color in 1908, which was spearheaded by a number of war veterans disappointed with the fruits of their struggle—a struggle that had been hijacked by Washington. As on the mainland, the victims were accused of racism when they sought to shield themselves collectively from the blows of racism and in 1910 the so-called Morua Amendment to the Election Law was passed in order to strangle groupings like the PIC. Events skidded out of control from there, leading to the murder of "3,000 defenceless non-whites." Martínez Heredia points the finger of accusation quite properly at "pressure of the United States and the reality of its impositions."[102] (Another observer, a Cuban with African roots, Bernard Ruiz Suarez, claimed that "five thousand" died.)[103]

Enrique Manuel Lopez, a contemporary student of Cuba, argues that the massacre was precipitated when the United States heightened discriminatory policies, the seeds of which had been sown by Spain, all of which was "welcomed by the racist Cuban elite." Cuban racism was "hidden among false beliefs of equality" and when overt mainland racism was implanted, murderously irresolvable tensions were created.[104] Another contemporary student, Renee Caridad-Delphin, argues that influential Africans in Cuba opposed the Platt Amendment, which effectively deprived the island of sovereignty, since they were concerned that mainland racism would impinge upon their hard-won rights. Then the United States proved them prescient when Washington discriminated against them in appointing officers for the newly created rural guard and artillery corps,[105] contributing inexorably to the 1912 crisis.

Thus, concludes the scholar Jules Robert Benjamin, the "possibility" exists that the revolt of 1912 was "manipulated by Cuban annexationists to precipitate a new U.S. occupation." And, I would add, further bring Cuba in line with mainland Jim Crow. Consequently, Benjamin continues, "except within the Cuban Communist Party, no significant black leader was to emerge before 1959."[106]

With such a background, racial catastrophe loomed menacingly. Even before the massacre, a leader of Cuban armed forces was expressing *"mi satisfaccion"* for the intelligence provided by the U.S.[107] In 1910 the *Baltimore Afro-American* reported that the "appointment of two Negroes as Cabinet members" in Havana "has not reconciled the colored men of Cuba to the [José Miguel] Gomez administration." This was in the dangerous context of "agitation in favor of annexation." Plus there was the "curious" charge of the rise of the PIC being "parallel" to the "carpetbaggism in our Southern States" since a key leader of the Africans was a "Jamaica Negro" who had a "personal following of Haitians." Also the "tradition of Maceo's mighty deeds, the absolute terrorizing of the Spanish workers by Negroes under a Negro leader, never will be forgotten. To a race of former slaves they mean more than most white men can understand"—though events two years later would call this supposition into question.[108]

In February 1912, Madrid's man in Havana reported at length about the dangerous situation emerging on the island, detailing the number of Africans in Oriente and the *"agitacion"* among the *"gente* [people] *de color"* and the fear it was generating.[109] In March the *Afro-American* spoke of these Cubans' grievances being taken to the highest level in Washington and regretted that the PIC "has been prevented from holding a meeting." "While conditions are not as prejudiced here" in Cuba "as in the United States, colored men have had to contend for every bit of recognition they have received."[110]

Also in March the Spanish delegate contended that the Morua Law contradicted constitutional guarantees but ever angrier protests continued with rumors emerging of U.S. intervention.[111] In April he said that the PIC had a concentration of forces in Havana with the role of the United States becoming murkier.[112] As emotions were strained, in May 1912 the Spanish envoy, on the outside looking in after centuries of rule, reported that the PIC had launched armed struggle and the authorities had responded in kind.[113] By late May he said that the United States had sent "500 hombres" to Guantánamo, and it was clear they did not intend to intervene to protect the vulnerable PIC.[114] By early June, 3,000 more of these forces were landed as the *"insurreccion"* grew.[115] As constitutional guarantees were suspended, he faulted the new occupiers and doubted Washington's explanation that it was sending troops in order to protect various commercial enterprises—as opposed to crushing the PIC.[116] At the same time, he was said to have been aware of Africans burning houses, robbing proprietors, and violating women, with the authorities apparently whimpering helplessly.[117] An irate Washington said that it had even received requests from protection from Spanish enterprises,[118] needling Madrid's debility. Madrid had reason to believe that the Cuban president was relying mostly on its own forces to suffocate the Africans, though it was also reported that a number of Cubans who were "Negros" were killed by U.S. forces.[119]

Madrid's envoy was deeply skeptical of Washington's role in this outrage, believing that it was caught up in the reelection campaign of William Taft, who was to be defeated by the Democrat Woodrow Wilson, returning this party of Dixie to the White House after a lengthy absence. Taft's party, the GOP, had the misfortune of being associated with the now wildly unpopular Negro community, and like so many presidents since, felt constrained to demonstrate that the portly Ohioan and his party were not beholden to the Negro, nor unwilling to be seen as shedding her blood.[120] Taft—who considered Charles Magoon, "formerly provisional governor of Cuba" as a "personal friend of mine"[121]— also had a personal concern in Cuba and its evolution.

One in a position to know said that Secretary of State Philander Knox "at first took no vigorous steps to head off a Negro revolution"[122]—but was persuaded to reverse field. Subsequently, Fernando Ortiz contended that there was a "threat" made to Havana "that American troops would be landed in the Province of Oriente if [they] did not very speedily put down a Negro uprising which broke out at that time."[123] Apparently, part of the indictment against the PIC was that they had received a pledge of technical and financial aid from U.S. Negroes, which Washington would not view with equanimity.[124]

Thus by June 1912 Madrid's emissary reported that the war of the races, *la guerra de razas*, was in motion in Cuba.[125] Retained for the ages by this envoy was a report alleging that Haitians were conspiring with Africans in Cuba and arming them with dynamite. These Haitians were said to have been arrested; then their guards supposedly received secret orders to free them, which was done. Then, it was said, the entire episode was enveloped in silence.[126] The hysteria was such that even an otherwise respectable U.S. Negro newspaper also pointed to the presence of "Haitian Negroes" as igniting the flames of perturbation—though it stated that the unrest was the "yield of the harvest from the seed of race prejudice, which has been sown in the United States."[127]

With seeming sarcasm this same organ told of a "little white girl" in Philadelphia who was told that it "took a mob of 2,000 white men to kill one bad colored man," which made her wonder "how many it will take to kill [all] those bad colored people in Cuba. I guess we will have to send all of our warships and soldiers."[128] Revealingly, U.S. Negroes tended to blame Washington for this racist outbreak in Cuba:[129] "Where a white American lands, one of the first things he attempts to do is to draw the 'color line' "—and then "there is trouble."[130] The *Pittsburgh Courier* seemed dazed to ascertain that "Negroes are bound in chains" in Cuba "and ordered shot for alleged assaults upon women and the photographs of such Negroes have been made and distributed throughout the United States"[131]—as if terror on the island would now be used to intimidate mainland Negroes. A leader in Havana denied such stories, adding casually, "I have learned that the American mining companies have armed their . . . laborers."[132]

The 1912 massacre was the ineluctable result, according to the *Afro-American*. "As the colored Cubans say, they form over eighty percent of the island's population,"[133] and a system anticipating apartheid would only generate friction—even revolution.

The U.S. authorities in Havana long had paid close attention to the island press and its messages, [134] suspecting correctly that even some local elites might not be altogether in accord with the Washington consensus of Jim Crow and imperialism. The *Havana Post*, an English-language periodical, was one response—readership was heavily composed of mainlanders—and it predictably clanged alarms repeatedly about the threat said to be posed by an African presence. The lesson of 1912 had not been absorbed, it reported, for in 1913 "Negroes" were "reported to be planning [an] uprising. Many in

Havana said to be contributing 25 cents each weekly to [the] cause."[135] A "Negro Congressman" in Havana was flayed for having the temerity to raise the matter of the "color line."[136] These editors seemed to be battling racial apparitions, as their readers were then told about "Negroes . . . celebrating Hideous African Rites,"[137] as grave concern about "voodoo" rose along with what amounted to neurasthenia generated by Haiti.[138] The headline "Negroes hold big race meeting" in Philadelphia also denoted concern.[139] This apprehension bled into foreign policy with musings—e.g. "would Cuba aid United States" in war with Japan?—of note to Cuba since the mainland's "principal coaling station" was in Guantánamo.[140] Weeks after the massacre U.S. authorities were "organizing and instructing the Rural Guard of Cuba," with the island's president spending "the whole day in the sun," being "warm and enthusiastic in his appreciation," perhaps gearing up for yet another racist confrontation.[141]

One Cuban took "great pleasure" in thanking Frank Parker of the U.S. military for those armed forces "so wisely trained by you" during "the revolution of the Negroes," since "crushing the revolt" displayed "efficiency" that he well appreciated.[142] Another Cuban also thanked Captain Parker effusively for his aid in perpetrating racist massacres.[143] Cushman Albert Rice, a prosperous Euro-American residing in Cuba, observed gleefully that the Cuban dissidents "went off into the woods to run a government of their own [and] we had to go out and shoot them."[144] U.S. missionaries in eastern Cuba, concerned about their life and limb (and property), urgently requested the presence of Marines in 1912, which allowed Cuban forces to attack Africans; when their prayer was answered, Africans were decapitated, hung from trees, and subjected to firing squads. Reportedly, these missionaries were more outspoken about reported atrocities in the 1890s than those of 1912.[145]

"We call upon Congress to prevent the sending of United States warships to Cuba," demanded the National Negro Independent Political League, conferring in Philadelphia—but by then it was too late.[146] Yet even as the blood was flowing, the *Afro-American*, vainly seeking to hold on to the faith, argued that "the Negro does not encounter the same prejudices in Cuba as he does in the United States."[147] A disbelieving R. M. R. Nelson counseled that the "trouble" was unwinding "500 miles from Havana," seeking to delimit the damage.[148]

There was a built-in lobby in Cuba for a more active presence for a growing colony of mainlanders residing in what was called the Isle of Pines; they seemed to object to what the *Havana Post* called the "mulatto mayor." Sympathetic to colonizing interests, this periodical acknowledged that "a mayor with Negro blood in his veins is the real [objection] of the attitude of the Americans . . . who want to be free from Cuba and a part of the United States."[149]

The African in Cuba was to find that being grouped with the despised U.S. Negro betokened a forbidding fate, as those nervous about being so designated often scurried to escape such an embrace for fear of being pulverized, whereas organizing among the racial victims was seen as a dangerous invocation of what mainlanders came to call the "race card" and thus had to be squelched by any means necessary. On the other hand a few decades later those with African roots were leaders of the Communist Party in Cuba, as the blocking of Negro qua Negro organizing simply pushed them into another channel, which proved to mark a designated path in the race to revolution. Mainland policies, according to the scholar Louis A. Perez, "revived and reinforced many of the most deleterious aspects of race relations in the colonial regime."[150] More than this, the United States worsened many of Madrid's past policies, converting informal forms of bias into rigidified forms. Though Cuba was under the U.S. thumb, the *Chicago Defender* continued to advise that if the island was wise then "it will shun annexation."[151]

The intersection of Jim Crow, U.S. Negroes, and Cuba came to a head when the Galveston-born boxing champion Jack Johnson traveled in 1915 to Havana to fight the Euro-American giant Jess Willard. This was something of a surprise since in early 1912 the *Havana Post* noted ecstatically that "mixed fighting is over"—"white and black men not [to] meet in ring." As so often happened, segregation was a means whereby loyalty to a regime could be consolidated on the basis of constructing a racist job trust, limiting opportunities to those defined as "white."[152]

The *Post*, which frequently targeted Johnson, said that his previous Euro-American punching bag, Tommy Burns, should not have fought him and did so "only because the newspapers forced him to do so." [153] Cuba, like other jittery nations, had sought to ban the film of the ebony pugilist's victory over yet another Euro-American combatant, Jim Jeffries. The "black-white" spectacle undulated globally but, in particular, on both sides of the Straits, as Johnson—no unskilled amateur politically[154]—was accused of seeking a return to the racial tumult of 1912.[155] Actually, Johnson was an unwitting participant in a micro-replay of 1912, because it was freely admitted that at stake was whether Willard could "return the pugilistic scepter to the Caucasian race." If so, "the Caucasian race throughout the domain of Uncle Sam," which now included Cuba, "would celebrate."[156]

After his defeat Havana became a refuge for Johnson: "When all other places refused the Johnson-Willard fight," said the *Defender*, "Havana accepted it," though "boxing was not well known there at the time."[157] Though the gigantic Willard prevailed, a spooked Washington still sought to destroy the films of the fight.[158] The young Frank Grillo—a Cuban of African descent who attained fame musically and percussively as "Machito"—was present at the

controversial fisticuffs where Willard triumphed. "There was so much commotion," he recalled, "it was in the daytime, it was so hot, you know" during
this "long fight." Like others, he believed Johnson intentionally lost[159] in a
futile attempt to gain the good graces of Washington. One positive result was
to invigorate further the sweet science, to the point where the Cuban known
as "Kid Chocolate" was to be compared to the esteemed Johnson himself,[160]
which led to the NAACP investigating the Kid's deportation.[161] The rise of the
Kid helped to erode the bad taste left by Johnson,[162] as boxing established a
bastion on the island that it would not relinquish after 1959.[163]

Still, staging this bout in a racially straitened Cuba was not a recipe for
concord. Yet the racial contest seemed to be the preoccupation of mainlanders
more than islanders; the latter, for example, did not seem to appreciate similar spectacles from Hollywood—e.g. *Birth of a Nation*—with Cuban critics
continuing to unload on this movie and *Gone with the Wind* as late as the
1950s, though both were revered to a degree on the mainland.[164] The mainland Negro woman known to posterity as "Mrs. John Blair" led the successful
fight against the former movie, taking on this herculean task after arriving with
Negro troops in 1898.[165]

The problem for Cuba was that as a noxious Jim Crow was being introduced, U.S. investments were soaring, and not just in the infrastructure of
pugilism and cinema. Elisha Atkins, born in Cape Cod in 1813, made huge
investments in sugar in Cuba and during the 1868–78 war, many debtors
became heavily indebted to U.S. interests, e.g. Atkins himself. Even before
the 1898 war, he was controlling an estimated 10 percent of production.[166]

Between 1898 and the late 1920s sugar consumption increased dramatically on the mainland, with Cuba essential to this process. Per usual, there was
resistance by domestic producers with Congressman Charles Timberlake of
Colorado, a firm defender of beet sugar, complaining about competition from
"cheap black labor" in Cuba, while a commenter in the *New York Times* complained that Cuba was the "would-be sugar dictator of the world." This was a
misnomer, however, since by 1920 nearly 50 percent of the sugar produced in
Cuba was made in mills owned by mainlanders. High prices of this commodity
in 1919 led many Cuban planters and refiners to invest heavily, accruing debt
that far outpaced their ability to repay loans once prices returned to normal.
When the bubble burst, many Cuban-owned mills, farms, and banks failed,
leaving their enterprises to be masticated and swallowed by mainlanders. As
for "cheap black labor," it was ironic that this "white gold," the key to the
island's prosperity, depended heavily on ebony arms. Moreover, during this
time laborers from Haiti and Jamaica swelled the island's workforce[167]—complicating an already entangled racial context—while the growth in commercial
relations between the island and mainland led to closer ties between Cuba and

Dixie. For example, Savannah-Havana ties grew accordingly, which tended to fortify Jim Crow.[168] But when members of the Cuban Congress got into angry confrontations there due to rigid Jim Crow regulations, it did little to quell revolutionary fervor.[169]

Yet, in seeking to dominate Cuba, the United States continued to face stiff competition from both London and Berlin in terms of the crucially important sectors of travel by ship and sugar machinery. "I have bumped up against obstacles in the export business," complained Pennsylvanian W. C. Olds in 1908, that "Secretary [of War William Howard] Taft never knew existed and my experience ought to be worth more to manufacturers than his political blarney." Such pressure generates miscues and blunders making 1912-style massacres more likely, along with revolutionary upsurges.[170]

Historically, the U.S. elite had tended to group Africans collectively, be they on the mainland, Cuba, or the bête noire, Haiti. The massacre in Cuba was followed swiftly by the Wilson restoration in Washington—which hardened Jim Crow—then the occupation of Haiti, as if clockwork were operative. William Upshur was part of the occupation force in Hispaniola, and not atypically he was a repetitive fount of complaint about the "hundred-year prejudice of the black man for the white"; Haitians' "parents and grandparents told them of the passing of the English and the French—and explained it as due to the superiority of the black man," but now since "the pale faces are among them again" and "their prowess has come to nought—they find the white man can outmarch and outfight them" too, "that he is cunning and resourceful beyond his understanding—and so he has taken up his duties in the proper plain like his brother in America, though he doesn't altogether realize it." Patrolling Haitian cities, he said, was little different than patrolling analogous districts in Richmond, Virginia.[171]

Upshur expanded the ambit by comparing Haitian rebels to those harassing his colleagues in the Philippines, though he was pleased by the growth of the "American colony" which was "quite large now."[172] When the time came to depart Port au Prince, he was sad, "even though they [Haitians] have black blood in their veins and would be looked down on and classed to themselves at home."[173] Yet the mainland rift was no better exemplified when James Weldon Johnson—he of the Caribbean ties—led the NAACP crusade against the U.S. occupation of Haiti.[174]

The rough insertion of mainland-style Jim Crow into the island, followed by racist massacres, then the migration to Cuba of Jamaicans—and Haitians fleeing U.S. occupation—led to the inevitable: the virulently Negro-phobic policies installed in Cuba caused the victims to organize based upon their common victimization, the murderous crackdown on the PIC notwithstanding. The Pan-African movement led by the Jamaican Marcus Garvey

flourished in Cuba. A disciple of sorts of Booker T. Washington, he had
arrived on the mainland just as the Tuskegee sage was expiring and the First
World War was inspiring a new global correlation of forces that would lead
to the Bolshevik Revolution and the rise of Communists, who established a
beachhead on the island too. Jamaica's close ties over the centuries to Cuba
should not be discounted in assessing Garvey's popularity. His spouse—Amy
Jacques Garvey—had a father who spent his early years in Cuba and spoke
Spanish fluently.[175]

Ongoing interest by mainland Negroes in Cuba prepared the ground for
Garvey. U.S. Negroes paid close attention when in 1925 one of their journals reported "a long series of unwarranted assaults, murders, and exploitation" of Jamaicans in Cuba, with Havana seemingly unable to respond to the
"unspeakable conditions" they faced. In addition the crude application of the
Monroe Doctrine hampered the ability of London to speak up on behalf of
those they had colonized, all of which created an opening for Garvey.[176]

Garvey was building on an increasingly cosmopolitan mainland Negro
community; for example, Alonzo Holly, a Negro religious leader in Florida,
was educated in Haiti and matriculated in Barbados, the latter being part of
the circuit traveled by Garvey's organizers.[177] The Reverend John S. Simmons, once one of Miami's outstanding Negroes, was born in St. Croix in
the recently U.S.-acquired (from the Danes) Virgin Islands.[178] George Vaze, a
linguist toiling in 1920s Berlin, was described as a Negro, being "very dark";
he was fluent in German, French, Italian, Portuguese—and Spanish, as his
mother was Cuban. Yet he was described as a U.S. Negro.[179] A chief agent for
Garvey in Cuba was Louis La Mothe, born in 1893 in Haiti.[180] One of Garvey's
leading disciples, Carlos Cooks, was born in Santo Domingo in 1913, though
his parents were from the nearby island of St. Martín.[181] The transnational
movement that was Garveyism thrived by appealing to an African community
that was cosmopolitan and which leaned toward Pan-Africanism as a direct
response to the collective demonizing of Africans generally, as Washington's
hemispheric influence expanded.

For a while it seemed that Garvey was the wave of the future in Cuba, for
by 1920 he was supposedly considering moving his headquarters from Harlem
to Havana,[182] as the latter was more advanced ideologically. "People here are
just crazy about the organization," said a Garvey lieutenant in 1919 speaking
from Sagua La Grande.[183] When Garveyites met in a packed Harlem hall in
1920, a prime speaker was the great-grandson of Frederick Douglass, but it
was Arthur Schomburg who told the assembled that he was connected with the
Cuban Revolutionary Party, which "had brought Cuba its independence."[184]
By 1921, Garvey had established a freight service from Hampton Roads to
Cuba featuring an all-Negro crew.[185]

By the mid-1920s at least fifty branches of his movement were in place in Cuba, forming an organization that became difficult to ignore or subvert successfully. Not amazingly, this was more than in any other nation except the United States, with some continuing on the island until the 1950s (there were Garvey branches throughout the Caribbean, Central America, and Africa).[186] Garvey's group was so influential in Cuba that London reportedly considered extending quasi-diplomatic recognition to it in order to represent the Crown's subjects, for example, Jamaicans. Their mutual aid society was extensive.[187] One of the ships launched by Garvey's group was named after Maceo and a precursor of his Pan-Africanism—Daniel William Alexander, who fought alongside the British in the so-called Boer War in South Africa in the early twentieth century—was the son of a Cuban father.[188]

At least initially anti-Garvey hostility was not due to staunch opposition from the authorities. "The major part of the Cuban army consists of Negroes," said Garvey's journal with astonishment in 1920, "and when they saw Negroes with the uniform of a steamship line," speaking of his vessel, "they thought they would go wild with enthusiasm." Garvey's organizers in Cuba were said to repeatedly address audiences in venues "crammed to full capacity."[189] The president of Cuba was among those who expressed support for Garvey's movement in 1920, and pledged to do everything in his power to aid their growth and development.[190]

Garvey's operatives conferred in 1920 with the chief executive and his cabinet. President Mario García Menocal told Garvey's man, "You are welcome here and as long as I am President of this Republic, see me for anything you want." From Havana, the delegation from Manhattan traveled to Santiago, where they carved the initials of Garvey's Universal Negro Improvement Association (UNIA) into a tree for presumed perpetuity.[191] When Garvey himself visited Cuba, President Menocal rolled out the red carpet for him, and large and enthusiastic assemblages were organized to greet him. He journeyed by train through the island, speaking in towns large and small.[192]

Hugh Mulzac, a native of St. Vincent, was part of the delegation and recalled a "party nearly every night" in Cuba in a rousing welcome. He was struck by the "banquet at the Presidential Palace" and the promise of "support from the Cuban government"—and, most of all, that "many other Cuban businessmen and landowners also pledged their cooperation" and others "bought stock in the Black Star line," the Garveyite shipping operation designed to knit together the Pan-African world.[193] The Garvey movement helped to solidify ties between Havana and the north Manhattan neighborhood known as Harlem, a trend that Schomburg had adumbrated.[194]

The rise of the Communist Party in Cuba with its tight focus on racism and day-to-day socioeconomic issues drew militants that otherwise might have

been drawn to Garvey, and, at the same time, curbed the kind of racial antago-
nism that the mainland, with its sizable majority defined as "white," was not
as energetic in combating. Simultaneously, Garvey's forces were being routed.
In 1924 one of his organizers complained of the "quarantine system": "There
is discrimination shown against our colored men and women after landing in
Cuba, the whites being allowed to go free while our people are detained and
are made to suffer untold hardships while in quarantine." This was occurring even though ostensibly the "Cuban Government is in sympathy with the
movement."[195] Pressure from Washington may have been responsible.

   Thus, in succeeding years, Garveyism did decline in Cuba. Havana municipal authorities detained a Garvey ship because of claims by creditors in 1925.[196]
In 1928 Havana banned his journal, the *Negro World*.[197] By 1930 Cuba joined
the United States and Canada in barring him[198] on grounds that resembled the
Morua Law.[199] That is, he was allegedly inciting racial animus. By 1931, General
Manuel Delgado, secretary of the interior, denounced Garvey and shut down
his branches, including Havana's.[200] On the other hand, there was a discernible
strain in Cuba which feared that if the island were to lean toward Garvey, then
it would come to resemble even more the horrific mainland. [201]

SURELY, THE RISE OF GARVEYISM in the hemisphere was a response to
the lengthening shadow of the mainland colossus. Bernardo Ruiz Suarez was
a Cuban of African origin—and a lawyer and poet besides—who chose to
address this touchy matter from his perch in Manhattan. He found it curious
that "in the Spanish American countries," it "is a common thing to hear" the
frantically rendered comment, "I am not an American Negro," so as to escape
the sharpest clawing of the mighty eagle. He too objected to the Morua Law
and knew that the PIC was a response to heightened Jim Crow. What seemed
to rankle him was that "the black people of the United States have far more
ground for complaint than had the leaders of the Cuban revolution of 1912,"
yet it was the latter who were massacred. What he should have noted was that
U.S. Negroes with centuries of bloody experience with maniacal mainland
racists had grown more circumspect, whereas Cubans just experiencing this
brutal maltreatment were not sufficiently steeped in mainland culture to realize
what they were up against. He did not understand why "there is no political party composed of members of the race" in Harlem, though he critiqued
Garveyism and anticipated the Communist debate in Cuba and the mainland
about "A Black Nation within a White Nation," a remedy then contemplated
since the United States had "fallen far short of the ideal of Lincoln"—and,
like the *Chicago Defender*, he thought the mainland should learn from Cuba
and Latin America, rather than what was occurring: the mainland imposing its
reactionary racist policies in the hemisphere.[202]

The problem for all those concerned about the rising tide of racism was that though the main wave was crashing ashore from the mainland, there were powerful eddies from elsewhere. Understandably, Spanish influence on the island was still potent and continuing the cockeyed policies that led to it being ousted from its possession, Madrid began to echo Washington's racism, perhaps more strongly, which gave added force to this poison. Even U.S. officialdom seemed to be taken aback when Madrid newspapers began arguing that the influx of Haitians and Jamaicans to Cuba was harming the interests of Spaniards, as they sought to revive the nineteenth-century argument about "Africanization."[203] Presumably Madrid was heartened by reports of hundreds of Jamaicans and Haitians being massacred in Cuba.[204] Some U.S. Negroes viewed with alarm this growing clamor that Cuba was "being Africanized" though the claim at play was a conflict between mainlanders who demanded cheap labor and Cubans of European extraction who felt unable to compete.[205]

These Spaniards did not seem to realize that Jamaicans and Haitians were arriving in Cuba not because the authorities had a soft spot in their hearts for Africans but because their cheap labor was desirable. When a Harlem Negro sought to lure Jamaicans from Cuba to New York, the mainland authorities sought to hamper his activity.[206] Still, even the *Afro-American* had reported that the PIC "had more ignorant Jamaicans and Haitians among [their] followers in the recent uprising than Cubans."[207]

If Madrid had been alert, it would have noticed that—just as in 1898—the U.S. authorities found it necessary to repress Negroes more than usual, after wooing them to make the ultimate sacrifice in World War I when their selfless service generated dreams of equality. A prelude to this alarming trend on the island was a recrudescence of the terrorist and racist Ku Klux Klan in Key West. This influenced in particular darker-skinned Cubans, such as Eduardo Suarez from Matanzas, who fell in love and married a woman of African descent in Florida, which caused him to lose his job as a baseball player there. Since increasingly Cubans were wedding such women, his ouster was notably destabilizing.[208]

In a community that dated to territorial days on the peninsula, Africans of Bahamian, Cuban, and mainland descent resided in a twelve-block area of beauty in Key West—but as color-phobia's tempo increased, this area could hardly be termed idyllic.[209] Key West, where Republicans had persevered while being routed elsewhere in Dixie, was an anomaly that Jim Crow could hardly tolerate since for the longest time it contained schools where Cubans of African and European descent matriculated side-by-side (though public schools were rudely segregated racially).[210] The essence of the matter was one that continues to bedevil those who engage in cross-straits relations: those who are "white" on the island may not be deemed as such on the mainland, though Cuba was not as taken with color difference as the obsessively crazed United States.

The changing climate in the Sunshine State was discovered rudely by Manuel Cabeza, born on 17 June 1897. On Christmas Day 1921 he was beaten, shot, and hanged—this, after having fought in the U.S. military during the war. Actually, two days before his lynching he had made history as the last man—officially—to be tarred and feathered in Key West. In the sections of this small town where he socialized, which was mostly Negro and Cuban or both, he was known as "El Isleno," the islander, in recognition of his roots in the Canary Islands. He was described as handsome, muscular—and "white," while others described him as being "mixed." After returning from the war, he cultivated a Robin Hood reputation for taking care of poor Negro families by breaking up card games and stealing from the affluent. He owned a small bar and sporting club called the Red Rooster at the foot of Thomas Street. But then a woman known as Angela, described as small, attractive and "mulatto"—and also of Cuban descent—began to cohabit with him, which was a gross violation of prevailing racial norms.

Promptly five or six hooded KKK members sought to crash through his door and grab both. He was beaten with baseball bats but he fought back valiantly and managed to unmask four of the assailants. Bound with a strong fishing line, he was then carried to Petronia Street where he was tarred and feathered and told to leave town—forever. Undaunted, Cabeza cursed them. The very next day he sought one of his attackers who toiled at the railroad terminal at Trumbo Point, but it was the man's day off. The following day Cabeza jumped in a taxi and hunted for William Decker, manager of the local cigar factory and brought along a Colt revolver in his belt as an equalizer. As he drew near a local club, he spotted Decker in his own car headed in the opposite direction. The cabbie would say later that Cabeza yelled: "Turn around fast. He's going to stop by the trolley." Cabeza leaned out the window of the cab as they pulled alongside and reputedly asserted with emphasis: "Decker, this is how a *man* kills a man," and shot him dead on the spot. The bullet shattered Decker's jaw as his car slammed into a utility pole, a dressed Christmas turkey on the backseat. Within minutes armed members of the KKK began a two-hour shootout with Cabeza, who said he would only surrender to the U.S. Marines—but then agreed to surrender to two constables and was marched to the local jail. At about midnight, the sheriff told the Marines that all was quiet and they could go home for the holiday. But early in the morning of Christmas Day, five cars with their lights dimmed—with fifteen hooded men inside—exited the autos near the jail, then strolled silently to Cabeza's cell. They dragged him by the heels down the stone steps of the jail and tied him to the back of a car, then dragged him to the hanging site, where he was hanged as each man emptied his revolver in his dangling body. The grand jury's ruling was that he "brought it on himself because he was 'living with a Negro woman.'"[211]

A sad result of the U.S. occupation of Cuba was that some islanders came to be treated in a fashion thought to be limited to mainland Negroes. Even U.S. missionaries, then arriving in Cuba in search of congregants, believed that there were points in common between and among Cubans, Puerto Ricans, and U.S. Negroes. Many of these missionaries, especially Methodists and Baptists, came from Dixie, and when they arrived in eastern Cuba, they felt compelled to address the concerns of Cubans defined as "white" who were apprehensive about the presence of so many Africans and the proximity to Haiti. Many of their boarding schools excluded Cubans of African origin and Jamaicans alike as segregated schools migrated across the straits.[212]

Apparently oblivious to what was being revealed on both sides of the straits, Ambrose Gonzales, scion of an illustrious Cuban family in the Palmetto State, continued to mouth the most foul imprecations about U.S. Negroes. "The Southern white man knows what he is doing" in excluding Negroes, he maintained. "To give an inch to Negro makes him itch for an ell," and yes, "familiarity breeds contempt." There was an "infamy" in "giving the Negro the ballot and backing with Federal bayonets the Negro's pillage of the South"—this was all "without a parallel in history."[213] Such racist thinking lubricated the path for the further insertion of Jim Crow on the island—and thus, ironically, accelerated the race to revolution.

CHAPTER 9

The Rise of the Reds—on the Mainland and the Island

D R. RAMON COSTELLO HAD GOOD reason to be furious.
He was Cuban, but the U.S. nationals in Hungary in 1931 perceived
him as a Negro: therefore they sought to bar him from a hotel swim-
ming pool.[1] Formerly of New York City, he was no stranger to Jim Crow but
may have thought his sojourn in Budapest and then Paris would have exempted
him from the long arm of Uncle Sam. This was occurring in a nation where
the proto-fascist Miklos Horthy ruled. When the mayor promptly issued an
order mandating his use of the contested waters it suggested that—in some
respects—the United States might be to Horthy's right. A distraught Costello
sorrowfully noted that "the idea of a black man being [in] the same pool with
their wives and daughters was too much for them." The affair excited passionate interest in Budapest where a leading theater featured it in a skit and an offer
was made to him to play the leading role, but the dignified Cuban objected. He
did deign, however, to appear in a theater box where he was applauded loudly.
The mayor gave him a medal making him an "honorable citizen of Budapest."
Born in Santiago and a student for years at Columbia University in Manhattan, he was also an amateur boxer, but chose not to display his skills on the
noggins of his mainland adversaries.[2]

Dr. Costello should not have been overly surprised at the prospect of being
bitten by Jim Crow. In 1926 the famed Cuban painter Ramon Loy, who happened to have roots in Africa, was en route from France, where he had been
working, to the island when storms forced his vessel into Newport News, Virginia. "I had no desire to risk being insulted in the South," said the proud
islander, "so I remained on board the entire time."[3]

With every passing day it was apparent that the U.S. occupation of Cuba
was engendering raw fury. Yet as the case of Dr. Costello exemplified, escaping the island brought no surcease, for as long as the island was denied true

sovereignty, Cubans were doomed to be treated like abused step-children wherever the United States wielded authority. However, a new force was arising on both sides of the straits in the form of the Communist Party, which attacked Washington energetically at its Achilles' heel—Jim Crow—and, at least on the island, this racism ironically hastened the race to revolution. For the Communists were not just a cross-straits force, they were a global force, and this is what was needed to confront a growing mainland power that thought its remit reached into eastern Europe.

U.S. Negroes too were in a bind. Over the years they had adopted the posture that—though imperfect—Cuba was a haven for those fleeing Jim Crow. But now with the deepening of the island's role as a protectorate, this supposition was being challenged bluntly. Ultimately, the confluence of these tensile strains was to explode in the 1930s with the transformative Scottsboro case in Alabama,[4] which was to internationalize the anti-Jim Crow movement and thereby sketch a special role for Cuba in its demise. This decade also witnessed regime change in Havana, which led to the rise of Fulgencio Batista and also quickened the race to revolution on the island.

Those who were paying attention in the run-up to Dr. Costello's uncomfortable confrontation would not have been surprised. Even during the First World War, when one would have thought concessions would be made in the face of a stiff challenge from Berlin, there was a fierce debate in Washington about immigration wherein one legislator conceded that slated for exclusion were Cubans who "were not of the white race."[5] Negro entrepreneur R. M. R. Nelson was still plugging away in Havana, seeking to build viable business enterprises but even his infectious optimism was chilled when a preacher from Georgia arrived to provide "lectures for whites only"—not to mention "separate sermons for [the] West Indian." A disgusted Nelson wondered how the "world is being made safe for democracy" by such odious maneuvers.[6]

On the other hand, U.S. Negroes continued to look hopefully to Cuba as not just a site of exile but an exemplar, and here the news was hopeful. They were pleased with the organizing by "colored people" in Havana of an "Abraham Lincoln Club," featuring "handsome quarters with a large audience room, palm garden on the roof with a clear sweep for the breezes from the Gulf of Mexico," and, most desirably, a "fine dancing floor." There was a "physical culture department and classes for instruction in Spanish and English"—an indicator of cross-straits ambitions—and President Menocal himself was chairman of the board of trustees.[7] Despite the strenuous activities of Washington, when the *Baltimore Afro-American* determined that there were "more colored nations than white," Cuba was listed with the former.[8]

The journal also noticed when it was a Negro who managed a major "presidential campaign" in Cuba, which was out of the question for the mainland.

When Dr. Alfredo Zayas y Alfonso was elected president in the 1920s, the *Afro-American* was quick to say that this showed his "black manager knew how to campaign" and a vindication of this man who "was constantly made fun of by whites in the campaign." Also hailed was a congressman with a daughter at Howard University, yet "another black man who holds positions of honor and trust here."[9] It could hardly be believed when Cubans of obvious African origin were seen casting ballots in the election,[10] just as it was predictable when it was reported that Dr. Zayas had "trouble" being seated because of the "advent of color prejudice": was "filtering in [through] the efforts of Southerners from the United States since the Spanish War." [11]

U.S. Negroes were flocking more and more to the island, with a number choosing to spend their winters there, while others were choosing to invest,[12] and their often brusque encounters with Jim Crow helped to prepare the battlefield for the internationalizing of the crusade against U.S.-style racism. Since 1898 the U.S. authorities had been concerned with racial ratios, hence the anxiety about the arrival of Jamaicans and Haitians. But the arrival of U.S. Negroes was a separate category, for their residence in the belly of the beast of Jim Crow gave them added leverage, particularly when they could ally with islanders of like mind. Arturo Schomburg, whose close ties to Martí automatically made him a trusted interpreter of Cuba, concurred, as he stressed the island's racially desegregated schools, as he urged U.S. Negroes to make a "trip to Cuba" to gain "inspiration and a revelation that might astound."[13]

The most publicized episode of this exchange began innocently enough with a journey to Cuba by the prominent Negro educator Mary McLeod Bethune, whose college in Daytona Beach, Florida , still bears her name and distinguished legacy. Accompanied by her grandson, she contemplated a frictionless visit—but would be disappointed. She and R. P. Sims, the leader of a fellow predominantly Negro college, Bluefield Institute in West Virginia, were detained on disembarking by Cuban officials, who claimed they were acting pursuant to the wishes of U.S. officials. Actually, President Sims and his family, being lighter-skinned than the quite dark Bethune, had passed muster but were detained when they spoke up on her behalf. William Pickens of the NAACP,[14] who also had a full complement of melanin, escaped reproach since he was escorted by leaders of the Club Atenas, composed heavily of Cubans of African descent (but varying hues).[15]

Hardly amused, an irate Pickens accused Havana of "imitating the great nation to the north—the 'white' element in Cuba is belly-aching to make the island a 'white man's country,'" though "the "population seems to be eighty or ninety percent colored, as 'color' goes in the United States."[16]

Just before then, the noteworthy bard of Harlem, Langston Hughes, was not allowed to buy a ticket on a ship heading from New York to Havana, further confirming for U.S. Negroes that in motion was a devious plan to convert Cuba into yet another version of Dixie,[17] a suspicion not allayed when it emerged that the transporter not Havana was to blame.[18] These interlinked cases created a huge splash among U.S. Negroes, helping to bring Cuba even further into the spotlight.

Yet it was Pickens who took the most umbrage at racist offense. "American money dominates Cuba," he said with little satisfaction, "The everlasting 'National City Bank of New York' can be found in every city. . . . The Cuban makes no paper dollars at all; the American paper dollar is the currency of Cuba." Inevitably, "some blessed Americans" had "started some all-white schools here."[19] Like most U.S. Negroes, he blamed the United States, which he saw as being in mortal combat with a contrasting tendency. The Africans in Cuba "gave no hint of an inferiority complex" and relished the renaissance of "African music and instruments" that "are becoming the rage in Cuba." Imagine "in Harlem—Negroes doing their uttermost to be as Negroid as possible, and white folks taking it all as a matter of course," which is how he experienced Cuba and saw as impossible on the mainland. His organizational affiliation allowed him to confer with the powerful secretary of the interior, Jose Manuel Delgado, at his home and also with Juan Gualberto, "the Frederick Douglass of the island." They all agreed, he said, that Africans in the hemisphere "should be in close touch" for reasons of "defense," and comforting to General Delgado was the subsidiary idea that "on all sides there is repudiation of any 'Garveyism' or back to Africa ideas."[20] Pickens was incensed upon finding that Euro-Americans had commenced "discrimination which [has] grown worse in Havana, where Americans frequent, than in other parts of the republic."[21]

Still, Pickens, like many of his mainland compatriots, had difficulty adjusting to the Cuban reality. The NAACP leader charged that the son of the celebrated Maceo "passes for white," which was influenced by his going to school in America where he "married a white girl from Syracuse." But since his analysis taught him that "darker Cubans" tended to "suffer from [the] U.S. color line," he was able to adjust his view of Cuba to his overarching perspective.[22]

But it was the case of a woman—Ms. Bethune—that seemed to be most stirring, perhaps because of her wider influence. "I am at a complete loss," she told NAACP members, "to understand the discrimination and unjust treatment that was given me on my arrival in Havana recently." She was infuriated when the melanin deficiency of Sims and his entourage allowed them to enter unmolested and "during the time we were being held up, scores of white men and were passed in." Who did this? "Both the Cuban and American governments are responsible," she thundered. Still, undiscouraged, she added, "I shall again visit Havana" since "there is much to be gained from visits there."[23] This was so because like many she was fascinated by the differences in treatment of the African on the mainland versus the island: repeatedly, she insisted that "color prejudice" was more acute than "race prejudice" in Cuba in that lighter-skinned islanders of African origin did not face as much discrimination as those of darker hue.[24]

The Cuban intellectual Gustavo Urrutia told the NAACP—and an island audience as well—that it was not "absurd to think that the government in Washington maneuvers to discourage Negro travel in these countries which are under the influence" of the mainland. This was noticeably relevant in the case of Cuba since on the island, he reminded, "there are no laws that prohibit or hinder the admission of Negro tourists." Also, unlike the United States, on the island the "Cuban knows he can prosecute in the courts any immigration official who is delinquent, as in these cases, and cause him to be punished."[25]

Still, Cuba had changed for the worse since the U.S. occupation, because "formerly the man of color functioned, equally, as a Cuban and as a Negro. And now he functions as a Cuban and refrains from functioning as a Negro"— which could only be of detriment to mainlanders who proudly (or not) identified as Negro.[26] Arturo Schomburg agreed that the Cuba of the 1930s had changed: Maceo, he reminded, "was a colored man and in Cuba today the government is entrenched in the hands of whites."[27]

Bethune and Pickens joined with Urrutia in raising a furor about racist travel restrictions, protesting directly to Secretary of State Henry Stimson. The NAACP asserted that "leading colored citizens of Cuba are eager to join hands with leading colored citizens of the United States, in work for advancement of the race."[28] Pickens took the lead on this important initiative and it was he who "found much interest among Cuban leaders in the idea of a closer relations and better acquaintanceship between the leaders of their race in the United States and those in Cuba."[29] Jose Garcia Ynerarity, writing from Cuba, said it would be "very necessary to have [a] branch of [the] NAACP in Havana" for that "will be the beginning of the understanding of the American Colored people and the Latin Colored people and also will open the eyes of the Negro that there are other countries where Negro[es] have many opportunit[ies] for all kind[s] of business." As he saw it, "The American white people are here doing big business, even the Jews, why the colored people don't come here and do the same [since] we have many colored people. . . . I just want to help my race in every way."[30]

Ynerarity was well positioned to assist, being a respected agricultural engineer in Havana and grandson of a war hero. When he visited the mainland, he was hosted by a prominent Negro cleric, and the *Afro-American* gushed that "nine of the twenty members in the Havana City Council and political and civil officers everywhere" were African. The honored guest was planning "the establishment of an insurance company in Cuba, modeled after the

Afro-American Insurance Company of Florida."[31] Responding, a NAACP leader urged him to stay "in touch with the Negro in America" so that "race prejudice may not be permitted to grow in Cuba."[32]

Ynerarity, who had attended Hampton Institute, confessed, "I know well the colored condition," having been the "first man that brought to Cuba the Colored Medical Association from Florida in 1926." He also took the lead in the protest over Bethune's mistreatment. He was seeking to forge interracial accord: he "sent today a picture of colored students that gave 500 grams [sic] of his blood to white students of Havana University that got shot [during a] riot between the students and the policemen."[33] Like others, he too had a census estimate—"1,200,000 colored population" out of 4 million: this led him to tell the affluent entrepreneur from Black Chicago, Claude Barnett, that "here are many good opportunit[ies] for American colored m[e]n to do business," since Cuba was "not prejudice[d] in business" like the United States.[34]

When donations from the island began flowing into NAACP coffers[35] and Cubans of African descent began attending mainland meetings of Negro fraternal groupings,[36] the alliance was solidified. "I think we could get 25 or 30 members out of the Club Atenas to start with," said Pickens, speaking of NAACP members. "A branch of the Association in Havana would not only be helpful to American Negroes coming to Havana, but would also be very useful to the colored people of Cuba by bringing them into helpful cooperation with the colored people of the United States."[37] When Urrutia offered to write for the NAACP periodical, the alliance was enhanced further.[38] When Urrutia castigated the United States after the spouse of President Hoover was assailed for simply inviting the spouse of a Negro congressman to the White House, mainland Negroes felt they had gained a real ally.[39]

This was simply the continuation of a long-term trend, for in 1908 the association's soon-to-be paramount leader, W. E. B. Du Bois, asked rhetorically, "Who freed Cuba?"—then answered, "Black Men."[40] Stunningly, it was Du Bois who urged unity of the "Negro and Filipino, Indian and Puerto Rican, Cuban and Hawaiian," underlining the danger for the United States of intervening aggressively abroad.[41] Once again, it was Du Bois who during the 1930s turmoil in Cuba took a direct role in pressuring Washington and the Havana regime.[42]

Despite her ruffled arrival, Bethune went on to foment even more interest in Cuba by U.S. Negroes. "I visited for the first time beautiful Cuba," said this woman who would soon develop close ties with the spouse of President Franklin D. Roosevelt, and found it "most attractive," despite the "poor classes" and the "homeless" she saw, living "wretchedly." The "wealthy classes," by way of contrast, "live in luxury and indolence." Being a U.S. Negro, she could not help but notice that "the servant class, except for a few

Jamaicans, is almost exclusively composed of Spanish peasants. Every colored family able to hire a servant, employs these White [sic] Spanish peasants. And these peasants, like the Jews, serve faithfully and loyally." This captured her attention not least since such a racial cum class reversal was hardly the norm on the mainland. These employers were liable to be part of the "Club Atenas (most exclusive Colored Social Club)," which was composed of "the topmost social strata of business men, professional men and government officials." Yet because the "Cubans are very indolent," it was "strange to discover" that the "resources of Cuba are being monopolized by Spaniards, Americans and Chinese. All business is run by them." As she surveyed the landscape, she found that "racial classification is not based upon blood but upon color." Worse, "the Cuban woman is practically a chattel." Not least since it presented a different view of matters racial than what obtained on the mainland, she insisted that a "trip to Havana, Cuba, should be contemplated by as many American Negroes as possible" for awaiting was "thrill after thrill, information, inspiration and enjoyment."[43]

Bethune was featured in the Cuban press as a "certain dark woman, North American" with a "dominating manner and figure" whom her Havana interlocutor encountered at the Club Atenas. He then met her at the home of a U.S. Negro couple, the Martins, who had become prominent in Havana, "occupying positions of social distinction" as the reporter put it. When they sat down for the interview, she was holding a pen and paper, which he thought was for himself, but, as it turned out, Bethune was interviewing him. As they talked, Robert Sims of Bluefield sat to his left and she on his right, in a kind of "crossfire." He asked her about the persistence of lynching and she asked him about the "Cuban Negro," observing in passing, "We need to know the special condition of the Negro of each country, to have a general idea so that we may study in behalf of the unified progress of our race." They spoke for an engaging ninety minutes.[44]

The prominent Cuban intellectual Gustavo Urrutia told her that he publicized her case widely in the Havana press, including a lengthy interview. He also translated into Spanish various Pickens' plaints and published those too. "This matter of the admission of colored tourists to Cuba," he told her, "is a very important one in my opinion" so he planned to highlight it in the Diario de la Marina in what he called "my Negro page." He confessed that the "abnormal conditions" of "Cuban politics" was a hindrance in this regard but promised to continue blaring near and far "this matter."[45]

Thereupon, Urrutia firmed an alliance with the U.S. Negro press, translating articles into Spanish and highlighting the crusade against lynching.[46] Urrutia was to become the major Cuban liaison with the NAACP, with the latter's leader—Walter White—once telling him that "Langston [Hughes] and

I often speak of you."[47] The busy Urrutia was in frequent touch with Schomburg—who in turn was in contact with the esteemed poet Nicolás Guillén. When another part of this charmed circle—Fernando Ortiz of Cuba—visited the mainland in 1930 he signaled solidarity by terming Harlem the capital of the Pan-African world.[48]

Margaret Ross Martin, a U.S. Negro then living well in Cuba and who had hosted Bethune, also found the island abnormal—but she was not complaining. Like other mainlanders accustomed to "one-drop-of-Negro-blood-makes-a-Negro" regime she found the "Negro Question in Cuba" simultaneously "enlightening and amusing." With a U.S. definition, Cuba was "seventy percent colored and thirty percent white"—"but Cubans say precisely the opposite." Nevertheless, "it thrills the soul of the American Negro to witness the honor and glory heaped unstintingly upon the memory of that colored man," meaning Maceo, since Africans on the island "are ungrudgingly accorded the respect and recognition to which their rank and position entitle them." But like the United States, in Cuba "we find the black man confining his amours to black or almost black women. It is more rare to see colored men associating with white women here." But, like Urrutia and Bethune and legions of others, she too accused the United States: "The blame for the rapidly spreading prejudice and segregation in Cuba can be traced indirectly to the American Tourists" who oriented themselves racially upon arriving on the island by exclaiming, "They're all niggers anyway"—"the tourist's favorite exclamation on noting the presence of Negroes almost everywhere." As a result, she said with sorrow, "race prejudice is spreading in Cuba" since "the ever-growing American colony has imperceptibly, yet definitely set the standard and white and near-white Cubans anxious to ingratiate themselves with the lordly 'Americanos' do not hesitate to follow their example."[49]

Although Martín found that some of the "wealthiest men" in Cuba were "colored," she worried since "whenever a voice is raised" in protest of seeping Jim Crow, "the [Cuban] Negro is quickly lulled to sleep again with that soothing refrain: 'There is no difference in Cubans, we are all Cubans.' In fact that very phrase has proved the Cuban Negro's undoing. Some time ago a colored Senator succeeded in having a law passed prohibiting forever the segregation of either group for any purpose. Sounds good at first but it has so tied the hands of the colored people that they can never organize for any purpose whatsoever pertaining solely to the colored people."[50]

Other observers were not as nuanced, with one reporter from the *Chicago Defender* marveling that in Cuba, unlike the mainland, there "are no signs reading: 'for white only.' There are no trains carrying Jim Crow coaches" and "no problem created by a black officer being put in command of white Cubans."[51] The danger for the mainland was this question: if this could happen in Cuba, why not the United States—and, more so, why was this madness occurring on the mainland?

Still, what were Africans in Cuba to do once the unruly racism of the mainland arrived? It did not take long for the "Kaballeros Ku Klux Klan de Kuba" to launch its devilment on the island.[52] The "lynching spirit [has] spread to Cuba" mourned the *Afro-American*,[53] as the *New York Amsterdam News* took up the cudgels against the KKK.[54] Like their mainland counterpart, these racists zeroed in on miscegenation and elected officials who happened to be African.[55] The "lynching spirit" was of concern to Bernard Ruiz Suarez among other Cubans since "a nation that deprives its own citizens of their rights is not likely to have much genuine respect for the rights of other nations."[56]

Across the straits, the writer, Zora Neale Hurston had begun organizing NAACP branches across Florida,[57] but it was unclear what impact she—and they—could have if the KKKK was allowed to fester in Cuba. A partial answer came in 1934 when the Florida Negro Claude Neal was lynched with primordial viciousness in one of the signature episodes of the decade.[58] E. P. Sanchez, an NAACP leader in the state, who was thought to be of Cuban ancestry, termed it "prehistoric savagery,"[59] which was the general island view of such bestiality.[60] Another answer came when the KKK in Florida emulated their island neighbor by attacking Ybor City and chasing Cubans away from neighboring Sunset Beach.[61]

Still, said William Pickens, in Cuba the president once served under a Negro general—unfathomable on the mainland: "Just imagine Pershing," he said with wonder, speaking of the famed U.S. general, "having become President of the United States and then appointing Colonel Charles Young," a Negro, "as Secretary of War! If you can imagine," he concluded with embellishment, "you are a genius and ought to go writing poetry or something right away."[62] Though there were racial problems in Cuba, to harassed U.S. Negroes it seemed like paradise recovered, a perception bolstered when Nancy Cunard, the notorious heiress to a major fortune and her Negro companion Ansell Colebrook, in seeking "a country where we will be less bothered than in the United States, which we left with a deplorable impression,'" headed straight to Cuban shores.[63]

Carter G. Woodson, an intellectual lodestar among U.S. Negroes, was among those who saw intentionality in the besmirching of Cuba on the mainland. He bewailed how "historians of the United States" have "exaggerated the evils of Spanish rule not only on this island [Cuba] but throughout Latin America." Still, "the Negroes in Cuba, however, have begun to realize that instead of being better off in Cuba as a protectorate of the United States, they find themselves daily approaching the status of their sable brethren along the Atlantic, since race hate and segregation follow the United States flag."[64]

Yet of all those who brought Cuba to the doorstep of U.S. Negroes, it was Langston Hughes who stood out. A fluent Spanish speaker who had spent considerable time in Mexico, Hughes translated the works of Latin American writers and brought Cuban writers, e.g. Regino Pedroso[65] and Nicolás Guillén,[66] to a U.S. audience. He first traveled to Cuba in 1927 while working on a freighter. It was not a pleasant encounter, given the racism he experienced—which at least had the benefit of preparing him for future journeys there. By 1928 the Cuban journalist Jose Antonio Fernandez de Castro had translated some of his poems into Spanish. Then Hughes sought a Cuban collaborator for a proposed opera. His comrade, Guillén, who also happened to have roots in Africa, observed that "Hughes is very concerned about blacks in Cuba. Wherever he goes he asks about blacks. 'Do blacks come to this café? Do they let blacks play in this orchestra? Aren't there black artists here? Boy, I'd like to go a black dance hall.'"[67]

"I have a deep interest in Cuban poetry," Hughes informed a comrade in Cienfuegos,[68] an interest assuaged when he finally made it to the island in 1930 and conferred with Juan M. Leiseca of the Association of Cuban Poets.[69] Hughes helped to introduce the "syncopated tittering and stuttering of Cuban orchestras" to U.S. Negroes.[70] Hughes introduced Ramos Blanco to an admiring mainland public, finding it meaningful that "the first great figure by this dark Cuban sculptor is that of a Negro heroine" since "we . . . have so few memorials to our own racial heroes in this country," meaning the United States.[71] Returning the favor, his fiction was translated into stylish Spanish in Cuba.[72] This bicultural transaction benefited both sides: Guillén penned affecting poems about lynching and the Ku Klux Klan that were of moment on both sides of the straits.[73] When the first exhibit of Cuban art went on display at Harlem's main library branch, Hughes could claim credit justifiably.[74]

This yeoman service was all the more remarkable in light of the immense difficulties he faced—similar to what befell Bethune and Pickens—in simply crossing the straits. Hughes had just turned in a finely wrought novel and planned to head to Havana to celebrate. He trooped down Fifth Avenue in Manhattan to the steamship line to reserve passage but was told that a new law barred selling a ticket to "Chinese, Negroes and Russians." The next day, he ambled over to the consulate of Cuba where officials contradicted what he had been told. He then repaired to the NAACP offices and conferred with the leadership who promptly sent cables of protest to Washington and the Havana embassy. He then bought a ticket on the Cunard line.[75]

Urrutia's journal provided coverage to this contretemps, though Havana denied complicity.[76] Though the steamship company was blamed, their agent dissented: "We have never refused transportation to members of your race," said William Campbell after being pestered by Hughes and his allies. Instead, he insisted, they were "forced because of the attitude of the immigration authorities of Cuba to announce that we would not continue that practice." "I personally made a trip to Cuba last October," he said in March 1930, "to interview the Commissioner of Immigration and he most emphatically stated that Negroes, American citizens or otherwise, would not be allowed in Cuba." Campbell said he was flabbergasted and refused to "broadcast such information" since it "was discrimination" and "had no legal standing whatsoever." On the other hand, "Dr. Sanchez del Portal, Commissioner of Immigration," said that "members of the colored race of the prominent class, of reputable standing coming to Cuba as tourists, would be admitted, but would be excluded the same as members of other races if they attempted to enter Cuba because of contract to perform labor." After laying out his confused fact pattern, Campbell apologized to Hughes.[77]

Finally Hughes made it to Cuba, where he engaged in a round-robin of meetings and activism with the assistance of Urrutia. The activism was driven when he visited a dance hall that he called a "white mulatto place" and was "refused" admission on the claim that it was a "private club," leading to a fierce back-and-forth.[78] Undaunted, Hughes was arrested when he sought admittance to a bathing beach and was turned away, though he wound up claiming front-page headlines in Havana.[79] "There is a color line in Cuba," said Hughes, "but it is a subtle thing except when the influence of American money and prejudice [is exercised]. And this menacing influence is spreading. It was because of this that we had trouble at the Havana beach," he continued, "which is controlled by American capital for American tourists."[80]

Even though the island was dominated by the United States, it was a separate jurisdiction with a separate culture and Washington had to consider if Cuba could become a kind of rear base for subversion against the mainland, a role played in the previous century by the Bahamas, Bermuda, and Canada.[81] Bootleggers had long since found Cuba useful in this manner, as the noted case of Pullman porters smuggling rotgut from the island exemplified. The nephew of pugilist Jack Johnson had called Cuba a "great country," and more fellow Negroes were agreeing,[82] even if smuggling was not part of their repertoire. When in 1929 a bill was debated in Havana that would bar newspapers from designating the "race" of persons mentioned in news items, U.S. Negroes interpreted this as a turn away from the mainland practice of typically identifying criminal defendants who were Negroes as such—and not "whites."[83]

Cuba was receiving an increasing amount of column inches in the press of the U.S. Negro, an important shaper and reflector of opinion. This was particularly true for the *Chicago Defender*, sited in the second most populous mainland metropolis. Like other commentators, this journal underscored the importance of Africans playing a leading role in anticolonial struggles—symbolized by

Maceo—as a critical factor in the inability of mainlanders (thus far) to degrade Negroes to the extent the United States had. "It thrills the soul of the American Negro to witness the honor and glory heaped unstintingly upon the memory of that colored man." This led the way for Africans to sit in the Cabinet and Congress and as "judges, chiefs of police, army officials (though none in the navy)." Readers were no doubt stunned by the interracial fraternity—"Here white mothers and colored mothers fondle one another's babies; white children and colored children play to school together, go to school together"—all unimaginable on the mainland.

But there was a serpent in the Eden, in the form of white mainlanders, blamed for a changing environment. There was a lesson even here as U.S. Negroes learned that their xenophobic compatriots, who said they were inflexible in the rarified realm of racism, at times bent to the prevailing winds of the island. Thus when Dixie cotton-growers arrived in Havana, they conferred amicably with "colored" Cubans, even shaking their hands, which was inconceivable back home.[84] The very existence of Cuba, even under mainland domination, was undermining Jim Crow's sturdiest rationales, while sharpening the ability of U.S. Negroes to analyze this despicable system.

Bridging the gap between U.S. Negroes and Cubans in Tampa was the aptly named Martí-Maceo grouping, which earned considerable revenue by renting their facilities to African-Americans, who did not have many options in this sphere. Well-known entertainers such as Chick Webb and Cab Calloway performed there, becoming better known among Cubans as a result.[85] Jim Crow drove a stake through the heart of the Cuban community, but the upside was that those of African descent were driven into the arms of U.S. Negroes, along with Bahamians and others from the Caribbean, helping to fortify forces overall,[86] since Cubans of color tended to enjoy advantages not allowed to the descendants of Dixie slaves.[87]

Enrique A. Corderop of Tampa, brought to the mainland from Cuba at the age of seven, recalled that in the 1920s there were U.S. Negroes in clubs supposedly targeting Cubans. He contends that this existed as late as the 1980s since if one spoke Spanish, one was considered a Negro and there was little socializing between Cubans of African descent and "white" mainlanders.[88] Jose Rivero Muniz, writing from Havana in 1961, argued that when he was residing in Tampa in the 1930s, "the relations between Cuban whites and Negroes were most cordial and there was no racial discrimination," which arose later—though "Cuban Negroes and whites did live in different neighborhoods"; as he saw things, "Cuban emigration" was the "decisive factor" in the "development of Tampa."[89] The major festival in Tampa—which marked the historic exploits of Captain José "Gasparilla," a pirate, who had Negro sailors on his marauding voyages—laid the basis for bridging the gap between the two communities.[90]

The rift was exemplified in the early twenty-first century when Belinda Casellas-Allen and Paul Dosal, both of Cuban origin, discovered they were cousins: she is darker, he lighter, and the split in the family that led to their estrangement was most likely over "racial issues." She served as the leader of Martí-Maceo, heavily Negro, and he the leader of "Circulo Cuban," which was not. The two clubs started as one but split because of Jim Crow in the early twentieth century, which effectively split the family too.[91]

In Ybor City and West Tampa various Cubans and U.S. Negroes in the 1930s often lived side-by-side. The grandfather of Lydia Lopez had married a "mulatta" and then felt compelled to move to Ybor City where it was thought they could reside without being harassed.[92] Robert W. Saunders, who succeeded the heroic Harry T. Moore as state leader of the NAACP, after he had been murdered by racists in the early 1950s, recalled that in his Tampa neighborhood in the 1930s, "my family had neighbors from a variety of ethnic groups, including Cuban and Italian, as well as Black and Caucasian families," quite unusual for Dixie.[93] There was a steamship that regularly plied the waters between Tampa and Key West and Cuba, and that, said Saunders, facilitated a "lot of marriages." The "youngest sister of my grandmother," he said, "married Felix Marrera from Cuba who couldn't speak English, but he was a cigar maker and he was dark-skinned" like Saunders' grandfather who also became a cigar maker.[94]

The investigator, Arthur Raper, found that in the cigar factories—often owned by Spaniards and Cubans—"the Negro artisans work under exactly the same conditions as the white cigar makers, most of whom are Spanish, Cuban or Italian." The "best-paid worker in one of the factories," he scrutinized, "making the highest-price cigars" was a "Cuban Negro" and "at another factory, home of a lower priced cigar, an American Negro earns the highest wage."[95]

"One family of Negroes lived right next door to a friendly family of Cubans," it was said by a curious researcher. "The Negro Cuban attends the Negro schools" while those "of the fairer type" did not. The close interaction meant that many U.S. Negroes were bilingual in Spanish and many Cubans spoke English, of course.[96] The "St. Peter Claver Catholic Church and School for Negroes and Cubans" in Tampa had been rebuilt after being burned to the ground and by the 1930s consisted of four sizable buildings and a continuing "mixed membership."[97] Such institutions helped to ease at times frazzled relations between U.S. Negroes and Cubans.

Catholicism was not the only religion that served as an adhesive bonding U.S. Negroes and Cubans. In the 1930s the island-based religion popular among many Africans known as Santería migrated northward in more substantial numbers. The scholar Raul Canizares has written of "Mercedes, an African-American woman" who "told me that her great-grandparents who moved from Cuba to Ybor City in 1876" and were affiliated with this faith with penetrating African roots. The "first documented case of a non-Hispanic being initiated" in this faith was that of Walter King, another U.S. Negro, who later became a "well known figure in the Black Power movement" on the mainland.[98]

Another point of unity between mainland Negroes and Cubans was gambling. A form of the Cuban lottery named *bolita* took hold to the point where "Bolita Alley" was the name given to an iconic Negro community in St. Petersburg.[99] Tampa was similar; a Negro man there actually controlled part of this illicit form of gambling.[100]

Yet bolita was not peculiar to Tampa; it also existed in Jacksonville, which suggests the cultural impact of the island on the peninsula. In the latter city during the 1930s, one analyst finds "almost universal addiction" to it, with an intake of almost $15,000 per week, making it a major employer; since the reward for a winner could amount to $1,500, which made it a major stimulus during a time of economic anguish. From Florida the lottery spread nationally to mainland Negro communities and from there spread to other neighborhoods. One estimate was that by 1936 the money gambled on bolita totaled $500 million annually. This game that arrived in Tampa in the late nineteenth century borne by seafarers and railway employees with Cuban experience had arrived in crude form in Jacksonville by 1911. Like any lottery, one bet on whether a certain number—be it the last few digits of stock exchange activity for the day or receipts at the race track—would be selected: or, classically, 100 small numbered balls were mixed thoroughly with bets taken on which would be selected. Volume—gross numbers of bettors was critical since the bet could be a few pennies—provided a mass base for bolita. It also fed the flourishing of gangsters on the island and the peninsula, as well as corruption, with police officers being bribed and pastors who were avid players too. It fed racial tension in Florida as "white" gangsters felt compelled to seize this profitable enterprise, which might have been the most lucrative business in 1930s Jacksonville.[101]

Such a conflict led to the murder of the affluent Negro in Tampa known as "Charlie Moon," who ran afoul of "Italians, Cubans and a cracker gangster named Charlie Wall," according to Robert Saunders.[102] Moon had been a close colleague of the Lopez family, a leading family in Tampa.[103]

Then there were those in 1930s Florida who were natural bridges—for example, Thomas Moreno, born in Pensacola in 1841—a former slave who claimed "Spanish descent" and spent a considerable amount of time in Cuba over the years.[104] Julia La Congo, who died in Key West in 1930, was captured by Spanish slavers in about 1860 and sold into slavery in Cuba, before migrating to Florida.[105] Of course, there were chasms to be bridged, for example. in

St. Augustine where one of the more brutal plantations was administered by a Spanish-surnamed man, who happened to be Catholic. Protestant missionaries were beaten after emancipation, as suspicions lingered that they had been abolitionists.[106] That enslaved African labor was deployed in St. Augustine as early as the sixteenth century meant the roots of racism ran deeply.[107] At times the relations between Minorcans—viewed as Spaniards and perhaps Cubans—and Negroes in Florida was not ideal. [108] Fortunately, the rise of the nonsectarian left helped to salve these wounds.

Another profoundly significant factor that altered radically the racial calculus on both sides of the straits was the Russian Revolution of 1917, which led directly to the formation of Communist parties in Cuba and the United States, both of which were hostile to the U.S. occupation of the island and the Jim Crow that marked both nations, This pestiferous plague gave the Reds quite a bit of raw material with which to work. By 1938 the Cuban Communists were said to have a membership that was 25 percent African,[109] while on the mainland, there was a similar percentage. The 1930s were the decade when a potent anti–Jim Crow trend was manifest, particularly given the rise of Communist parties, escalating radicalization. The Scottsboro case—which arose in the early 1930s and involved nine Negro youths in Alabama being falsely accused of sexual molestation of two white women—was the vehicle that drove this trend and its complement, the internationalization of the struggle against racism. This factor was to spell doom for Jim Crow. It not only marked the beginning of the end of this precursor of apartheid, it also tended to weaken the grip on the island by the most retrogressive mainland forces, thereby materializing the race to revolution. In the short term, however, the 1930s witnessed the rise to power in Cuba of Fulgencio Batista, who, at least among mainland Negro liberals and centrists, was seen as an exemplar of the heights to which the "colored" could soar, which complicated solidarity with those opposed to his rule in the 1950s.

Ironically, though mainland Negro liberals and centrists, among others, repeatedly sought to distinguish Cuba from the United States when it came to the question of racism, when it came to analyzing Batista over the years this perspective was lost and they reverted to simply seeing a leader of color as progressive with hardly a searching glance at his actual politics.

Nonetheless, it was Hughes who set the pace in radicalism, collaborating with the Havana writer Manuel Marsal in producing the latter's "splendid book." "So far as I know," said the Harlemite, "yours is the first book to deal with the Scottsborough [sic] case."[110] Hughes, like other activists, also linked the two struggles, wondering at one point why "with all the marines and warships and Marines and officers and Secretary of the Navy going to Cuba, can't they send even one sergeant [to] Alabama?"[111] William Patterson, the Negro

Communist who led the campaign on the mainland, observed not without reason that the Scottsboro case linked the "Cuban workers of Tampa" and the "oppressed Negro masses inseparably together."[112] The case allowed the much ballyhooed alliance between and among Africans in the hemisphere to emerge, which did not escape the attention of the U.S. State Department. From Haiti the secretary of state was told that "Communist activities" there had "revealed close connections with radicals in the United States, notably New York," with Patterson fingered as the chief culprit.[113]

Patterson arrived in Havana in 1934 and was monitored there by the local press and the State Department. His International Labor Defense (ILD) had a Cuban affiliate, "Defensa Obrera Internacional," a "radical organization along Communist lines" said the U.S. envoy in Cuba. Patterson saluted his affiliate—and Moscow—while the press spoke of him fondly as a distinguished attorney.[114] The affiliate had been organized illegally in 1930 but then had become legalized, an emblem of the strengthening of island radicalism.[115] By 1935 the *Baltimore Afro-American* was impressed with the "wide agitation on the Scottsboro case" in Cuba "with three pages of the latest issue of Cuba's ILD organization devoted" to the important matter.[116]

Patterson was knocking on an open door for in light of the island's astringent taste of the KKK, tales of horror from Alabama rang all too true. Candido Suarez of the island was quoted in the *Defender* as being "full of indignation" about Scottsboro, to the point that it had made him "want to be an American Negro"—"because I will satisfy myself to be sacrificed for a cause that I consider sacred. . . . I will kill 10 to one," he threatened angrily, "before they finish me." Pleased, the *Defender* found his fury "encouraging" and indicative of "the reactions of foreign countries against lynchings" that was creating a "powerful force."[117] When the Tobacco Workers Union of Santiago protested Scottsboro,[118] further evidence was presented that a new zenith in cross-straits antiracist cooperation had been reached.

When Cuban soldiers mutinied rather than attack a meeting of the Communist-led ILD, a loud signal should have been sent that the island was racing further along the road to revolution than had been imagined.[119] When even the *Afro-American* found it newsworthy that a "black lieutenant" in Cuba administered the "first Soviet in Cuban hills," a community of "15,000," alarm bells should have been clattering.[120] Sumner Welles, then spearheading the White House's so-called Good Neighbor policy, was understandably concerned by "Negro officers" in Cuba and how their actions could "aggravate the situation."[121]

"Communists in Cuban appeal to Negroes," said another U.S. Negro journal.[122] Even the *New York Herald Tribune* seemed taken aback when a "Cuban Red" emerged to predict "revolution and Soviet rule at an early date." There

were almost 5,000 "members of the Communist Party in Cuba," it was stated
in late 1934, "an increase of about 500 percent" since mid-1933, with "about
30 percent of the members" being "Negroes"—though, per usual, this elusive
term was not defined.[123] The NAACP retained a *Washington Post* article of
similar reportage with the words scribbled with emphasis on it that were to
bring the planet to the brink of nuclear destruction a few decades later: "Would
you like a Soviet stronghold 90 miles from your shores—what are *you* going
to do about it?"[124]

It is difficult to separate general Cuban revulsion at the reality of the
mainland stranglehold over the island, which included the attempted forcible insertion of Jim Crow, from solidarity with Scottsboro, a ready vehicle for
expressing this disgust. Cubans took to the Scottsboro campaign like fledg-
ling birds to flight, attacking U.S. entities on the island with inflamed gusto.
Numerous arrests and injuries—even a death or two ensued—which provided
a rationale for martial law.[125] Nominated for the exalted status of martyrdom
was Domingo Ferrer, who fell victim to machine-gun fire during a Scottsboro
demonstration in Havana.[126]

This solidarity was not wholly altruistic. For as the decade unwound there
were more complaints coming from Cuba about the arrival of "race haters"
from Dixie. "American white men," spat the *Defender*, were "seeking to disturb the harmonious and peaceful relationship that has existed between the
white and black Cubans for centuries"—and like Scottsboro, it "starts with the
propaganda that white women are being insulted by black Cubans."[127]

In short, Patterson's journey was part of a larger project: His ILD had
helped to form the Cuban affiliate, which was seen as part of outreach to workers of Cuban and Puerto Rican descent on the mainland. Targeted in Cuba
were "agricultural" workers who "are mostly Negroes and are virtually slaves
living on the plantations of the landlords in barracks, constantly in debt for
food, clothing, etc." Mass meetings were planned "in which the terror in Cuba
is linked up with the . . . Scottsboro case" and events in Tampa.[128] On cue, the
ILD affiliate in Cuba was said to have devoted numerous pages in its organ
to Scottsboro.[129] This was followed by repeated trips to the island by James
Ford, the mainland's leading Negro Communist, who in 1938 addressed an
uproarious crowd of 50,000; this, after a 1934 visit to the confab of the National
Confederation of Labor. At the former rally, he was quick to say, "I greet the
Negro masses of Cuba."[130]

This greeting from Ford, which may have sounded anodyne to mainland
ears, conflicted in a sense with the developing Cuban philosophy stressing
the "Cubanidad" of all. Taken alone, it could be dismissed but in succeeding years mainlanders—including U.S. Negroes—often not only viewed the
island through a mainland lens but often sought to force Cuba in that direction.

Much has been made of the post-1959 relationship of Havana to Moscow, with the latter supposedly unduly influencing the former but if there has been any distorting factor on the island, it has been the influence of the United States. Thus the U.S. Communists who wielded significant influence on their Cuban counterpart, not least because of easier communication between Manhattan and Havana, as opposed to Moscow and Cuba, sought to apply doctrines on the island that emerged from the mainland (and, arguably, were of questionable relevance there). For example, Ford—like other U.S. Communists—was "fighting for self-determination for the Negroes in the Province of Oriente where one half of the population is Negro."[131] Now this slogan, self-determination for Negroes in the "Black Belt" of Dixie, up to and including self-determination or even secession, was arguably not consistent with the developing "Cubanidad."

Minimally, mainlanders—particularly U.S. Negroes—found it hard to accept that "race" and racism evolved in a different manner on the island. According to the scholar Darien Davis, "For many Cubans racial affirmation did not mean that blacks should be proud of being of African descent"—the mainland pattern—"but rather that they should not feel ashamed of it." This was more than a subtle distinction.[132]

Still, as in the United States, this slogan of "self-determination" up to and including secession seemed more rhetorically hortatory than actionable, with the stress placed on day-to-day socioeconomic and political struggles. In those same remarks before 2,000 cheering trade union delegates, Ford placed greater emphasis on forming a "workers' and farmers' government to replace the rule of landlords and capitalists" in Cuba, stressing how the island was a "brilliant example" for "the Negro toilers in the West Indies to study and emulate."[133] Even the erudite Cuban intellectual, Bernardo Ruiz Suarez, gave ballast to the idea of a "Black Nation within a White Nation," a concept that "has long been recognized in the white man's International Law," referring to "European settlements in Chinese cities, in Turkey and elsewhere in Asia," not to mention the Canal Zone in Panama.[134]

Following up, Ford addressed the Cluba Atenas where he was greeted with warm toasts, though he modestly—and correctly—observed that the warmth was "not solely a personal tribute." Speaking bluntly in the racial terms that were au courant on the mainland—not so much on the island—he declaimed, "For us . . . Negroes, there is a bond of culture, fraternity and liberal aspirations running down through the ages" since "we have never been exploiters" and "we have rather been liberators and strugglers for freedom." He praised the "kind hospitality" he had been shown: "During the last several days I have travelled from Havana across your country to Santiago" and "met with colored societies at Santa Clara, Camaguey and Santiago."[135]

The Communist Party central headquarters in Manhattan was lending aid to one and all, authorizing island Reds to send students to the mainland for study of revolutionary theory and authorizing a Cuban comrade to work on their daily newspaper so as to become better acquainted with editing and managing an enterprise. The U.S. party provided a subsidy to its island counterpart of $200 per month and provided a gift of $1,000 for launching a journal of their own. The U.S. party also started a campaign among the Spanish-speaking population of the mainland on behalf of the Cuban party. The latter began to provide a weekly bulletin to the U.S. Reds about island activities while dispatched from Manhattan to Guantánamo was—what was described as—"anti-militarist literature."[136] The U.S. party for various reasons was the conduit through which Moscow communicated with the Cuban counterpart, including funneling funds to Havana for various purposes.[137]

It was also Moscow's understanding that anti-Negro racism was the debilitating weakness of its staunchest island and mainland foes, which gave buoyancy to island and mainland radicals.[138] Since the nineteenth century Negro sailors, artists, entertainers, and athletes had been visiting Russia and returning with stories about the dearth of racism they faced, compared to the mainland.[139] Increasingly, the Communists were recruiting the "best and the brightest," a lengthening list that included Dr. Jose Lanauze Rolon of Puerto Rico, who had graduated from Howard University.[140]

The impact of Moscow on the new correlation of forces in the hemisphere was exposed when Emmet J. Marshall of Akron spent several months in Havana in 1934, "this deservedly famed City of Charms." In Santiago he met Dr. R. M. R. Nelson, an alumnus of the Dental School at Howard University, who arrived there in 1898 and was now the "confidential agent and limited partner of a coal black genius, . . . Mauricio Rebollar y Plancht, one of the world's great inventors." Dr. Nelson said that "big business" had "stopped him from making [his] goal in Havana," and thus he was next considering heading to "Lynchland," meaning the mainland, for successful completion of his venture but, he said, "if invitations are not forthcoming, he will give the inventions to the Russian Soviet Government."[141]

Not to be outdone, Urrutia reported that "one of the biggest Havana dailies" had "published a long special message from New York" on the Scottsboro case—though, in a sign of the times, the more left-leaning Cuba reported that the NAACP was lagging behind the Communists in rising to the defense of the youth.[142] Urrutia, who had become a major liaison with U.S. Negroes and wrote about Scottsboro himself, was quite concerned,[143] and entered the ideological fray by defending the NAACP against the ILD attack that it "never took part in the Scottsboro cases."[144]

This was occurring as the *Chicago Defender* told of how the case "stirs Cubans" with the "Havana office of an American steamship line" attacked, as "windows and doors were smashed."[145] This was part of an erupting working-class militancy on the island, with the *New York Sun* being among the journals that warned direly of "race trouble" targeting "American residents of Cardenas in Matanzas."[146] Soldiers with guns were sent to the Hershey sugar plantations just across the border from Matanzas in order to protect management from strikers. "Racial outbreaks were threatened in the district" said the *Sun*. "Most of the sugar interests are Americans."[147] When the talented mainland writer Josephine Herbst visited the island in the 1930s the scenes of racism she witnessed were heartbreaking,[148] for despite Cuba's manifest problems, it continued to attract migrant labor from surrounding islands.[149]

Cross-straits trends were driving the movement. As early as 1922 Bishop John Hurst of the African Methodist Episcopal Church was boasting to the NAACP about the "well-organized community; large and wealthy" in Tampa. "The colored people there represent a great deal of strength, intellectual and financial,"[150] and this affluence was hard to separate from commercial and related ties to the island. As had been the case at least since 1898, U.S. Negro missionaries continued to descend in droves on the island.[151] But this relative wealth and the churches supported by same could hardly survive the deprivations delivered by an economic downturn. Driven in part by the unforgiving misery of the Great Depression, the Communists were flexing their muscles, not just in Havana but also in Tampa, with the commonality in both sites being the militant prominence of Cuban workers.[152]

The growth of cross-straits radicalism combined with growing economic desolation proved to be combustible, most notably in Cuba. It was precisely the shredding of the social and political fabric of Cuba that captured the attention of so many U.S. Negroes in the early 1930s. In 1930 an NAACP resolution pointed to the "domestic tyranny and oppression" emerging in Cuba and the "special responsibility" of mainlanders given "the intimate treaty relations between the two governments" and the "preponderant power of American interest in Cuba"; such U.S. influence, it was said, historically "has operated invariably against the interests of the colored populations."[153] The NAACP journal adopted Juan Gualberto as their symbol for a beset Cuba. "Born of slave parents," he had been jailed by the authorities and sent into exile in Europe and Africa. When he died in March 1933 as the cauldron of protest was burbling, NAACP members and supporters were told his dying words were, "Better death than American intervention."[154]

Langston Hughes spoke breathlessly in the summer of 1931 that "the situation in Cuba is tense. Soldiers parade the streets, newspapers and telegrams are censured [*sic*]. There is a spirit of unrest" since "the American sugar tariff [a strand of the punitive Smoot-Hawley tariffs enacted in 1930] has created an economic crisis."[155] As for the Cuban president, Gerardo Machado y Morales, Pickens dismissed him as an "abominable tyrant"—"it is not surprising that the people of Cuba are in rebellion."[156] He was a "more disreputable gangster than Al Capone," said the NAACP leader; he scorned "the dirty attempt of the Machado regime to limit the right of colored Americans to visit Cuba. We predicted Machado's end," he said grimly, and, thus "the sympathy of colored Americans should be with the present rebels."[157]

Also descending on Cuba was a mainland delegation that included the ILD delegate—and Negro—Frank Griffen and the left-wing playwright Clifford Odets. Griffen seemed to be singled out for imprecations most foul by menacing soldiers.[158] "A fat, fierce Cuban suddenly jerked one of our Negro delegates up from a chair," said the bewildered Odets, "and in one second would have hurled him across the room had not several others intervened. These boys understood a black skin with no questions asked!"[159]

As the situation deteriorated, the *Amsterdam News*, the Harlem weekly, warned against U.S. intervention. "Cuba is in hock to Wall Street," while "many of her peasants are working for 10 cents a day. Thousands are jobless" and, it counseled in 1933, "if Cuba wants to turn to Communism" that "should be the concern of the Cubans." And if "Mr. Roosevelt," the recently installed president, "thinks his leathernecks need some practice, he could have them polish up on a few lynchers in our own dear Dixie. We hear that mobs down there are actually killing Americans"[160]—as opposed to the reports trickling in from the island. "If the United States could mobilize its entire fleet to protect the interests of Wall Street in Cuba," charged one furious New Yorker, "I don't see why it could not have done something to prevent that lynching which took place in Marianna, Florida, the other day."[161]

The late hero Gualberto was not hallucinating, for already Guantánamo had morphed into an important U.S. base and a thorn in the flesh of Cuba. In 1927 mainland sailor William O. Spears spoke cryptically of "100 young Cuban girls from the surrounding country" that "officers" were now eyeing.[162] A mimeographed newsletter on his vessel provided insight with revealing humor: "An inconsistent guy," it said, "is one who stops kissing the maid in order to slap his wife for saying good-morning to the delivery boy."[163]

By late 1933 Spears was informing "my darling" about a different kind of excitement: he had "been rather busy" since in Havana harbor "we were awakened by an air attack on the city. Firing from anti-aircraft batteries took place in all directions. The attacking forces flew directly over us. Shots were falling all around us. From then on for about 36 hours there was constant firing. The rebels first took nearly all the city but were driven out by government forces," while "our destroyer was in the line of fire." Scores were killed and wounded ashore. "All for what!" he decried, since "the government represents about ¼ or less of the population. The army maintains the government in power by force of arms"—though he warned about "anti-American and Communistic" tendencies. All of which was "not for publication."[164]

Cuba was a "powder keg," he advised, with the U.S. ambassador headed to Warm Springs, Georgia, "to confer with the president." Harshly, he found the mess to be "80% our fault."[165] Since he was dining with the "ex-Minister of War and Navy," in Havana, a "graduate of West Point, Class of '13," he was well informed. He expected "another revolution at any minute." He also had "dinner with a U.S. Secret Service agent" who despite his lowly status resided in a "very luxurious house." Through him Spears "met dozens of ... agents." He thought his "job must pay well" but hinted that corruption might be providing his golden eggs because he heard a dizzying array of stories about "smugglers of dope, narcotics and aliens. I felt like I was living through a detective novel."[166]

Spears continued his marathon Bacchanalian revel with "the high society of Havana," even as he reported, "the situation grows worse." He also found time for "dinner with Mr. and Mrs. Hedges. He is the son of a very wealthy manufacturer here" and was worried. Nothing much here but "bolos y balas"—rumors and bullets—with the accent on the latter.[167] The passage of time did not assuage his apprehension. "The country has gone haywire," he said glumly—though he still found time for "cocktails at the Steinhardts . . . rich Jews who own everything in Havana."[168]

"Our Navy will have to expand considerably," advised Spears as he witnessed a disintegrating Cuba and scanned "the news of the world," not to mention the imminent arrival of a "French cruiser."[169] After having "dined with the Italian Minister and wife and played bridge afterwards," he leaped to the opinion that "the future of the Navy looks brighter now than it did 2 years ago with all the pacifist talk."[170] Yet nothing could deter him from sampling yet another "excellent" dinner with "no end of champagne and fine wines," this one with Greek royalty. But even this reverie was interrupted when a reputed Communist barged in "and started to draw his gun." Spears "went into action and disarmed the man, threw his cartridges overboard," though apparently the assailant did not go splashing with his projectiles. "Something doing every minute now. Night before last an armed car passed the house" of the "American ambassador and riddled it with machine-gun fire. The soldier guard assigned replied to the fire and a regular battle took place." With withering understatement, he concluded, "This does not look like a very healthy place for Americans on shore right now." Even the dentist he visited was evidently untrustworthy and may have "purposely pulled [his] tooth for the gold value and that the one next to it is the real one that was discussed." It "aches night and day," he moaned, and something similar could be said about the decaying mainland role in Cuba.[171]

Still, the ambassador had a "marvelous mansion for which he pays $150 per month furnished—that indicates how cheaply you can rent houses"—which apparently made risking death in Cuba worthwhile. Spears, on the other hand, could only afford $50 per month, not counting "José for chauffeur and servant" and a "cook and washwoman;" "[I] live very cheaply," he noted with satisfaction but perpetually peering over his shoulder, Spears found there was "always something about to upset the applecart."[172] The latest was an "account of revoking the treaty with Cuba and doing away with the Platt Amendment," which was potentially jeopardizing his repasts.[173]

For the time being, there was more of the same—"a nice picnic in the country at the estate of a Cuban banker, it was very nice"—but Spears might have gathered that the jig might be up sooner rather than later.[174] For soon things were "very busy" with "two large bombing attacks. They almost got the President. The attack on the parade took place right in front of the American club where it was witnessed by most Americans," then "the shooting started."[175]

This seditious ferment combined with an already blossoming interest of U.S. Negroes in the island and led to the journey there of the noted historian from Howard University, Rayford Logan.[176] The multilingual Logan, who felt that "the Spanish language should be taught in every public school instead of French or German," was well placed for this assignment.[177] Nevertheless, Logan, a specialist on Hispaniola, was more optimistic about Haiti than Cuba since in the former republic, "capital has not penetrated into this country with the intensity and rapidity that upset the whole social life of Cuba. American capital ruined the Cuban peasants," who were akin to "Dixie sharecroppers."[178]

His detailed reports were so fine-grained and persuasive that the the *Afro-American*, the paper that published his reporting, said more U.S. Negroes should move to Cuba.[179] Week after week in 1933 as tumultuous events rocked the island, Logan was on the scene reporting regularly to avid readers of the *Afro-American*. As in 1898, he was taken by the reality that Africans were to be found "on both sides [of the] bloody Cuban revolution"—"instead of being used as strikebreakers," a distressing mainland trend: "Colored workers here helped to overthrow the president." Unlike on the mainland, Cuban Negroes were prominent in the major labor federation, as James Ford could have told him. "The final blow against Machado was delivered by troops, many of whom are colored"[180]—though "Major Ortiz, black army officer who is said to have committed 40 murders for President Machado, is safe in Europe."

"Communism has taken firm root in Cuba" was the message delivered, not hysterically but as a factual matter. In the pivotal shipping industry, "most of the workers are colored"—along with their "leaders"—while the port workers union was led by Reds. Despite this, he said with disbelief, "no newspaper has attempted to inject the race issue" while "unconfirmed reports from Santiago de Cuba indicated likewise a trend toward Communism." As had other perceptive observers, he thought this was somehow related to the rise of the left in Spain. Logan was in the midst of the action, once being forced to leap "on the curb along the Prado opposite of the Capitol just in time to get out of the way of an automobile that swung around the corner at full speed with a young Cuban in civilian clothes on the running board brandishing a revolver."[181] "They have stopped playing the rhumba in Cuba," cracked one mainland Negro journalist, "the popular tune is rumble."[182] "There is a decided anti-American feeling in Cuba," he warned apprehensively.[183]

Fortunately, Logan's jaunts around Havana were not always so hair-raising, as he had time to ferret out the disproportionate number of "interpreters" who were "from the British West Indies," signaling their key role, particularly since "Americans are more likely to employ colored guides to show their wives and daughters around since the white guides are more inclined to be flirtatious." The "colored Cuban," he concluded, "is a long way from extinction."[184] Peering intently from the balcony of his hotel room at the Hotel Venus in Santiago he could see one of "Machado's henchmen" being stalked by a deadly assailant. "It is news for colored men to lynch a white man" on the mainland, he mused, but par for the course in Cuba. He had a hard time comprehending that "under Machado white and colored men oppressed white and colored men"—then "white and colored men killed the white and colored oppressors."[185] Still, he opined, "many of the most distinguished colored Cubans were opposed to Machado."[186] It was "significant," said Logan, "that many colored people detest the colored supporters of Machado."[187]

Although they commented at length about the difference between the island and the mainland when it came to the bedrock matter of race and racism, U.S. Negro observers—Logan not necessarily excepted—seemed incapable of examining Cuba without a U.S. lens. The *Norfolk Journal & Guide* found it "puzzling" when a "delegation of Cuban Negroes" sought "protection . . . inasmuch as the present government of Cuba is the first in more than a generation in which an American-imposed color line has not been dominant." On the other hand, this lens could prove useful, for this same journalist found it mentionable that "the participation of all color elements in the Cuban population in Cuba's new government is responsible for American hostility toward it and the ambition of certain interests to force American financial interests which have passed the word down that the black leaders who helped Cuba's war for independence were not to receive any reward."[188] "Thousands of Negroes" in Havana, said this periodical, "staged a demonstration around the presidential palace to emphasize their support" of a "law that requires that at least 50 percent of the employees of all foreign firms in Cuba to be native Cubans. . . ." Colonel Batista addressed the crowd of 30,000.[189]

The *Atlanta Daily World*, which appealed to Negro readers in Dixie's keystone city, also found the "Negro issue" to be "dominant in Cuba" since they "constitute the majority of the republic's population" and "represent the so-called leftist elements," and were facing off against "pro-American white Cubans and white American business interests."[190] "The threat of black labor" was "making Cuba definitely Socialist," said the *Courier*, and thus "Americans and Cuban capitalists saw their tremendous investments passing" and sought feverishly to have the "threat of black worker control . . . removed."[191]

It was even more significant, Logan declaimed, that "all classes of Negroes feel that Cuba is their own country. Any American Negro who is frank with himself will understand what I mean." Like the "Jews in Germany," then facing unbelievable horror, "we are still," he said of U.S. Negroes, "in many respects, 12,000,000 men [*sic*] without a country. We enjoy more rights abroad than we do at home," while in Cuba, "I repeat, the situation is totally different." Not least because of the prominent role played by Maceo, "colored Cubans look upon Cuba as their country in a much fuller sense than American Negroes look upon the United States as their country."[192]

This dynamic was animating the turbulence, Logan felt. In Havana Matthew Molamphy—"white American manager of the United Fruit Steamship Line"—barely escaped kidnappers after he had been accused of causing the death of "Margarito Igelsias, colored leader of the port workers," a massive crowd of 100,000 mourning his passing. Also forced into hiding were "white American officials of the Chapana Mill in Oriente" where "most of the workers are colored" because of labor unrest. As Logan saw it, radical change in Cuba was "hopeless"—"unless in some manner this stranglehold of U.S. ownership is thrown off altogether," a realization that came to fruition in 1959.[193] Allegedly, Molamphy paid "$5000 cash" for this death,[194] underscoring the danger of U.S. ownership.

Even the White House was alerted when Shepherd Morgan of the Chase National Bank branch in Cuba got wind of a plot to "kill" a number of "prominent Americans," though the conspirators apparently were not left-wing radicals since "they felt that that was the only way they could bring about foreign intervention that would result in a change of government in Cuba."[195] At the beginning of Herbert Hoover's presidential term, his secretary of state was warned about an impending "revolution" which was "sure to follow,"[196] a prediction that proved to be enormously prescient. And even before then, as the First World War was still raging, the future secretary of state—and then powerful lawyer—John Foster Dulles was engaged in urgent consultations with Washington about the "serious" situation in Cuba that bordered on "revolution."[197] In short, as 1959 approached, there were numerous signs pointing to an upending of the status quo.

In Santiago Logan conferred with Juan B. Mancebo—a graduate of mainland Negro colleges—and concluded that "Oriente has solved the race problem with more fairness than any other region of which I know except possibly Brazil"; he was astounded to see "the walls of the buildings in Santiago . . . covered with posters showing the photographs of colored candidates for municipal council," a veritable impossibility in a comparable U.S. metropolis, and "attractive, efficient, courteous [colored] girls" serving at a local hotel "a white man and his colored wife." Santiago represented "one of the most interesting experiments in race relations anywhere in the world."[198] This was so in large part because the "colored women of Cuba are thoroughly modern" and were "generally more alert than our American colored girls" to "economic theory" and Marxism. "The most surprising thing to the American observer," he said with amazement, "is the fine camaraderie, the absence of restraint, the naturalness of the relations between white and colored girls. There is none of the inevitable coalescing in separate groups as in most of our interracial gatherings. There is none of the deliberate missionary enterprise of some 'radical' white girl seeking to make an agitated colored girl feel at home."[199]

Yet Logan found it curious that it was precisely in Santiago that a disproportionate share of "thirty [U.S.] warships in Cuban waters" were stationed just off Oriente, a province that also happened to contain "the largest number of sugar mills and plantations run by white Americans. Here the Cuban population is the thickest and bad blood exists between the whites, many from the southern part of the U.S., and the black Cubans. Laborers have been treated worse here than in any spot in Cuba and hunger and poverty have been worse"; of the thousands of these expatriates in Cuba, a larger share were in Havana but the most reactionary seemed to be in Santiago.[200] An echo came from the NAACP, which in protesting "foreign intervention" in Cuba denounced the "injection of race prejudice by Americans" there.[201] Repeatedly during this conflictive era the association rose to the defense of islanders, a process facilitated by mainland Cubans who kept the leadership informed,[202] though suggestive of wider mainland interest; even the elite Council on Foreign Relations in Manhattan felt compelled by the Cuban chaos to organize a "study group" to scrutinize more carefully "the situation in Cuba."[203]

Unfortunately, the usually perceptive Logan lost his composure when it came to analyzing a major winner of the 1933 tumult—Fulgencio Batista. Though not unaware of the difference between how the mainland and the island viewed "race," he seemed incapable of being unimpressed with the fact that the newest leader of the military "is what is known as a Negro in the United States." Readers were told that "a white Cuban, Alfredo Francisco,"

made a point to instruct visiting mainland Negro journalists that he and Colonel Batista "played together as children. His mother is a dark colored Cuban
and his father if of the lighter or white type." Logan was suspicious when the
Chicago Tribune deleted such details "to keep white readers from knowing that
there are Negroes, or mulattoes in Cuba in positions of leadership."[204] "One
would not know from reading these newspapers," said the *Pittsburgh Courier*,
about the "Negro Revolution in Cuba," that "most Cubans are what Americans would call Negroes; that the leaders of the present revolution are chiefly
Negroes and mulattoes; that most of the Communists who are seizing and
operating sugar mills in Cuba are black men led by black men and the Chief of
Staff of the Cuban Army is today a dark mulatto." It was "capitalist America"
that did not "want the American people and the world to know that the eco-
nomic-political troubles at the bottom of the Cuban revolution are essentially
racial: a subjected black and mixed race being ruthlessly exploited by white
men represented by Wall Street."[205] The U.S. sailor William O. Spears was
among those itching for a "showdown regarding this army. It is inconceivable," he grumbled, "that the country will stand for being ruled and regulated
by a mutinous army most of whom are black."[206]

    Like Logan, the mainland Negro press seemed to be heartened by the fact that
this "Negro soldier" was the "power behind the throne" in Havana.[207] "Batista
says Negroes played a big part in Cuba Revolution," according to the *Pittsburgh
Courier*, since "the colored races in Cuba cooperated to the end of bringing stability to the republic."[208] The "hope of [the] Negro rests with Batista," said the
Courier, finding that this was congruent with the wishes of the "so-called leftist elements" too—though some "Negro mulatto elements" disagreed. [209] This
"new dictator" of Cuba, said yet another Negro mainlander, was "one of the
most popular figures in Cuba" and "held in high favor by rich and poor alike."[210]

    And, intermittently in the prelude to 1959, Communists on the island and
mainland were far from hostile to Batista. In 1938 James Ford praised the "full
collaboration" between the Cuban leader and the White House, suggesting
that Logan's enthusiasm was not his alone. [211] Ford may have been bamboozled
by Batista's apparent friendliness to the organized left, to the point that in 1934
the *Philadelphia Tribune* called him "an avowed Communist and may attempt
to make Cuba the first Soviet state in the Western Hemisphere."[212] No, said its
cross-state competitor in Pittsburgh, Batista was a "Socialist"[213] and "popular"
besides.[214] It just so happened that in 1938, Batista spent 2.5 hours holed up
in the Cuban embassy in Washington with leading U.S. officials where—the
record showed—he "expressed the emphatic opinion that Communists would
never make any formidable showing in Cuba."[215]

    J. A. Rogers, another premier intellectual among mainland Negroes, took
up the challenge presented by Logan, and encouraged African Americans to

become more involved in "washing of one's dirty linen" abroad so as to pressure Washington, a practice spearheaded by Communists in the Scottsboro case. He reminded that "in all that region south of the Rio Grande, the population is predominantly colored," and "these Latin Americans"—particularly Cubans— "have no love for the big white brother in the north."[216] Concurring, Idelfonso M. Contreras, described by the *Defender* as "one of Cuba's most progressive young leaders," was praised by this journal for his "theory of racial betterment" which "includes a united black front in the Western Hemisphere."[217]

As ever, it was difficult to rationalize the degraded condition of the U.S. Negro when ninety miles from the mainland, as the *Defender* exulted, Africans were "members of the faculty of the University of Havana," whereas "nowhere in the United States do black people enjoy the luxurious comforts and facilities as evidenced by the Club Atenas." This club has "persistently striven to inter-est black peoples of North and South America to join hands with Cuba in the pressing forward of united black front in the Western Hemisphere." Miscege-nation could give rise to murder in the United States while in Cuba "intermar-riage is as common as the sale of bananas." As a consequence, the journal was flooded with "numerous requests for information as to the status and accommo-dations in the islands." Naturally, there was praise for "Colonel Batista, a black man [who] holds in the palm of his hand the political destiny of the island."[218]

The Associated Negro Press (ANP), which provided articles to mainland periodicals, chimed in, requesting cooperation with Atenas "to present the case of Negro Cubans" to "the 70 most important papers of the country."[219] But it was Colonel Batista who responded most swiftly, speaking on behalf of the "la raza de color."[220] The ANP in turn was concerned about reports that "described racial friction" said to be "due to racial animosities engen-dered by mistreatment of white women in Havana by colored men, due to the license developed during the unrest," though it seemed similarly engaged with answering with another inquiry: "Is Col. Batista a mulatto?"[221]

"The American military occupation deliberately fostered race hatred," according to two U.S. leftists, "destroying Negro organizations" and estab-lishing a "Jim Crow system." This "met with the approval of the white Cuban overlords" but ignited mass protests, and when Colonel Batista—a presumed "mulatto"—emerged as the power behind the throne, many U.S. Negroes concluded that this was a step forward.[222]

Cubans eager for mainland solidarity were not in a position to challenge forcefully this presupposition; as one Cuban proclaimed in Havana, "The common enemy of one Negro is the common enemy of all Negroes. The Cuban Negro cannot and must not ignore the welfare and the struggles of his brothers in the United States."[223]

CHAPTER 10

War! And Progress?

L ANGSTON HUGHES AND HIS CUBAN COMRADE, Nicolás Guillén, were under fire.

In 1937 both were in Barcelona—headed south to Valencia—where they, along with many others, had come to show solidarity with the valiant Spanish republic, now being bombarded by the descendants of those responsible for foisting distress upon countless Africans over the centuries—the precursors of fascism, in other words. Paul Robeson, the famed artist and activist, was there too along with, as Hughes indicated, "ordinary Negroes like those I met in the Cuban club in Barcelona."[1]

Hughes and Guillén had arrived in Barcelona at a time when there were no lights and pitch darkness greeted them as they decamped from their train. They managed to flag a bus to their large hotel and snared rooms on an upper floor. The next day Hughes and his comrade were sitting in a sidewalk café on a tree-lined boulevard when they encountered a Puerto Rican friend who knew Hughes from New York and who invited him to visit the "Mella Club" where Cubans and "West Indians" gathered. It occupied the second floor of a large building near the center of town and featured a beautiful courtyard for games and dancing and a little bar where (mostly) Cuban drinks were mixed. There they encountered other Cubans—both "black and white," Hughes was keen to say. But pleasantness soon departed, for after returning to their hotel, suddenly all of the lights were dashed, as a siren blared louder and louder. The lobby was jammed with men, women, and children chattering nervously in Spanish, English, and French, as they awaited what well could have been a death sentence.[2]

Hence the escape to Valencia, and from there Hughes emerged to say that his experience in Spain was "one of the greatest" of his life: "It is itself a heroic poem, a living poem," but he and his comrades were not able to stave off defeat.[3] Later Hughes in a poem would link "Spain, Alabama, Cuba" to the flamenco and the blues and the son of Cuba,[4] as a further expression of anti-fascist solidarity meant to shred the shards of fascism and racism that tormented all three sites. By way of unlikeness, Hughes compared Dixie invidiously to what he had experienced in Soviet Central Asia.[5] It was no secret that Hughes and Guillén and many of their compatriots who arrived in Spain were close to Communists, as exemplified by their joint reverence for Julio Antonio Mella, founder of the party of Cuban Communists, who had spent time in Moscow before being murdered in Mexico in 1929.[6]

The rise of fascism can readily be seen as an ineluctable outgrowth of the racism to which Africans had been subjected for centuries. The European fascists most notably believed that slavery and relentless persecution should not be limited to Africans alone but should be extended across "racial" lines. Those with the most acute sensitivity to this onrushing trend often were those of the left—like Hughes and Guillén—not least since they were lined up to be double victims of this process: on both political and racial grounds. "The forces that seek to enslave Spain," warned Hughes, "are the same forces that oppress the people of color throughout the world" and thus "Negroes have come to fight on the Spanish front in the international brigade" that rallied to the republican side—"American Negroes, Cubans, Porto Ricans, Africans."[7] According to Robeson, "100 colored men" were with the "loyalists," "mostly" from the United States but including Cuba and Puerto Rico.[8]

But this may have been a gross undercount, since the *Chicago Defender* found that "700 Cubans fight for Spanish Red Loyalists" and "among them are at least 200 black Cubans"—amazingly, none had "asked for money" for their service.[9] There may have been even more volunteers, but a crisis was brewing in Ethiopia and a corps of sixty trained Cuban nurses awaited deployment: reportedly it was "the largest of its kind to volunteer" and among the nurses were the "first black women in the Western Hemisphere" to do so.[10] There was a "monster mass meeting" in Havana, said the *Defender* decrying the Italian invasion, as cries arose to form an armed legion to intervene there.[11]

As on the mainland, the invasion of East Africa by fascist Italy stirred Cuba, with Havana's leadership going as far as monitoring Atlanta opinion for guidance,[12] which was an outgrowth of a plan to train young Cubans militarily in Georgia.[13] Islanders were also participating in the formation of the National Negro Congress, the left-led formation, which also saw saving Ethiopia as a sacred cause.[14]

The anti-fascist alliance tended to undercut anticommunism, which had been the weapon of choice for discrediting the left—the NAACP, for example, grew from a membership of 40,000 in 1940 to 400,000 in 1944.[15] In the process the racism that inhered in fascism was discredited to a degree, which created an opening for U.S. Negroes to push for a fuller palette of rights, which in turn gave them more say about other matters, including Cuba. This same era witnessed the emergence of a number of powerful Communists in Cuba of African descent, but the continued rule of Batista, who became increasingly authoritarian, was to have a dramatic impact on the island's left wing.

Thus, sensing their fate could be determined on the battlefields of Spain, Africans from the mainland and the island flocked to Madrid in the late 1930s.[16] But others came too, particularly from Europe and Euro-America where they were able to practice the kind of egalitarianism that was not present in the mainland's Jim Crow army.[17] Walter Garland, a twenty-four-year-old U.S. Negro, was in charge of training a number of English-speaking recruits, an impossible feat in his homeland. Hughes was struck to see "American, Cuban, Mexican, English, Irish, Nordics, Negroes, Jews," all "standing in formation before the young Negro officer."[18]

Hughes was also struck by the presence in Spain of Basilio Cueria, a "well-known Cuban baseball player and resident of Harlem" who was the "captain of a machine-gun company." Hughes spoke frequently with this "tall, fine-looking young Negro captain" who, while residing in Manhattan, started the "Julio Antonio Mella Baseball Club of the Latin American section of Harlem." Cueria had a well-justified reputation for courage, having survived "the most terrific artillery and air bombardments known in history." But he was not alone in this bravery, as there were a "large number of Cubans fighting in Spain on the government side, many of them colored Cubans," though they had to fend off questions from Spaniards who considered them "Moorish," and too heavily represented on the other side of the battlefront. Hughes found that "colored Cubans" fleeing into exile often had chosen Spain over the United States since in the latter nation "they might run into difficulties on the basis of complexion," but now they were all in jeopardy from fascists.[19]

It was in Spain that Hughes's personal relationship with Guillén deepened. He was the "Carl Sandburg of Spain," said the admiring Harlemite. Introducing him to his vast U.S. Negro audience, Hughes elicited the comment from Guillén that "most Cubans feel we are the most 'Americanized' of all the Latin Americans. The Cubans, of course, follow with pride the achievements of the colored people of the United States," as this "brown-skin man from Havana, the son of a famous Cuban Senator and newspaper owner" expressed fervent interest in "visiting the great colored universities and learning about our brothers there at first hand. And of course I would like to live in Harlem for a while" and "translate some of the fine things American colored writers have done into Spanish."[20]

Guillén confessed openly his admiration for the bard of Harlem—but stressed that Hughes and himself "are fundamentally different. I am first a Cuban poet" and Garcia Lorca, the poet of Spanish progressivism, had influenced him most. Even their common African ancestry was an insufficient explanation for their bond since, said Guillén, "the Cuban Negro has retained more of his ancestral African cultural heritage than the Negro in America. The cultural amputation was less complete than in the United States" and, besides, "the Negro in Cuba is much more an organic part of the nation's life than is the Negro in the United States. The Cuban people are in a more advanced stage of transculturation," he emphasized. Moreover, Africans in Cuba were "a larger national minority—one fourth of the total population."[21]

Although Hughes downplayed the frequent comparisons that were made between the two this tendency did not dissuade the mainland Negro Mercer Cook, who was chairman of the French Department at Atlanta University.[22] They were "almost identical in age and complexion," he said ruminatively, "they even resemble each other"—all of which was true. Just as Hughes was raised in the middle of the continent, far from cosmopolitan climes, Guillén was "born in Camaguey, capital of Cuba's most prejudiced and backward province," and also a regional headquarters for U.S. influence. They both were hounded by Washington because of their politics: in 1941 Guillén was "refused a visa" to "attend the Congress of American Writers in New York, probably because he is a radical," said Cook.[23]

It was also in Spain that Guillén's personal relationship with Robeson deepened. The Cuban poet went to see the burly artist at his hotel, where he found him "blockaded by a group of people hanging on his most insignificant gestures." He managed to ask him if he knew Cuban music, and said Robeson, "Yes, I know it and I like it enormously. In fact, I am also thinking of going to Cuba to study its musical folklore."[24]

The ever closer ties among Hughes and Guillén and Robeson were indicative of ever closer ties between U.S. Negroes and Cubans. The tumultuous changes on the island in 1933–34, interpreted on the mainland as leading to a rise in Negro power was a factor, as well as the continuing complaints by Cubans against Jim Crow—not least when visited upon African-American tourists. This trend became clear when Congressman Arthur Mitchell of Chicago arrived in Cuba and was refused service in a Havana hotel because he was a Negro, a slight that was greeted with raucous and massive protests on the island,[25] which was duly noted in the U.S. Negro press.[26] Celebrated by U.S. Negroes was Dionisio Borrayo y Paula, described as a "brown-skinned giant" and the "only admittedly colored policeman in Havana who has been assigned to work with tourists." He could converse "fluently" in English, which allowed him to be Garvey's interpreter at the height of his popularity in Cuba. When he discovered that a Havana hotel had barred Congressman Mitchell on racist grounds, this 6'3" 235-pound behemoth said threateningly to the manager, "If I had been here, you wouldn't have got away with this."[27]

He was mirroring the sentiments of Serapio Paez Zamos of Havana, who upon starting a new magazine referred to "our racial comrades of North America"[28] in seeking a tie with the Associated Negro Press, which in turn sought "closer contact with our brothers in Cuba."[29]

A professor of U.S. history at the University of Havana—Herminio Portell Vila—captured an island consensus when he expressed doubt about the viability of Washington's so-called Good Neighbor policy given the odious persistence of Jim Crow. Ultimately, being a good neighbor was considered to be inconsistent with savaging one's own citizenry, which teed up the tectonic changes in the landscape that were to rock the mainland as 1959 approached.[30]

Yet, due to the informal sanctioning of Jim Crow tourism, Professor T. A. Daley of Dillard University in New Orleans continued to charge in 1939 the "colored man is persona non grata" in Cuba [31] and Havana continued to charge that such allegations were "absolutely without foundation."[32] Havana instead pointed at the airlines as the culprits.[33] Yet when Pablo Suarez, son of Cuba's Consul General in Manhattan, was quoted as saying that the Cuban flag was removed from the island's site at the New York World's Fair because the Cuban "dances" offered there were "more African than Cuban,"[34] it was evident that the momentum for Jim Crow had arisen on the mainland and radiated outward.

Still, a similar disjuncture in U.S. Negro views of Cuba was barely recognized. Langston Hughes called the regime embodied by Fulgencio Bastista a worrisome and proliferating example of "semi-fascistic types of dictatorships,"[35] but his was hardly a consensus view in Harlem. As one astute analyst put it, "The Negro press has particularly taken Cubans to its bosom, largely because of Colonel Fulgencio Batista," who "is of Negro ancestry and hence of interest to the Negro public."[36] Jim Crow on the mainland was so asphyxiating that it cut off oxygen to the brain, veritably forbidding U.S. Negroes to see the island on its own terms but through the mainland prism where the rule of the melanin-rich on the island was seen as a victory. Although Batista is "dark in complexion," the *Defender* reminded, "his color has not interfered with his progress"—his "wife, who is white" was an example of a reality that could not then exist on the mainland.[37] Cuba, it was reported enthusiastically, was one of "only four countries in the world" where "can be found official monuments honoring black citizens."[38]

Hence, more typical of mainland Negro views was the gushing interview conducted by two leading academics—Ben Carruthers of Howard and William Allen of Fisk University—who met with the "Strong Man of Cuba" for two hours. "We were bowed into the antechamber in which the high ranking officers of the staff were seated at a long table," they told their no doubt impressed readers in the *Afro-American*. They were led down a "long corridor" to Batista's inner sanctum and as they stepped into the "beautifully furnished but thoroughly military study" their eyes were drawn from the massive desk, "the throne-like chair, the coat-of-arms," to the steely eyes of the Colonel, Batista. He "is one of the most handsome men in an island of handsome men"; his "skin is a deep olive" and in that era when such things mattered deeply to U.S. Negroes, his "hair is jet black and very deep." His pearly-white teeth were equally "beautiful" and though Batista "speaks excellent English," the conversation, such as it was,was conducted in Spanish.[39] The interviewers were seemingly floored when Batista endorsed a "student and teacher exchange" with their campuses.[40]

Yet the drooling correspondents—and their readers—were to be disappointed shortly thereafter when their colonel visited the mainland with an itinerary that was described disappointedly by the *Afro-American* as wholly "lily-white," though there was a last-minute phone call to Howard University by way of compensation. Batista did deign to visit Fort Myer in neighboring Virginia where he inspected the all-Negro Tenth Cavalry. "His reaction was both of approval and disapproval," it was reported, "for in Cuba colored soldiers would have been distributed throughout the regiment, never closely segregated."[41]

This guileless reporter was also impressed that Batista remembered Professor Carruthers when their paths crossed, just as he was bowled over when "the cream of Washington's white society paid tribute to a sepia [leader]" at the Cuban embassy.[42] Yes, it was noted with satisfaction in 1938, "Cuba is probably the nearest thing to perfect equality between whites and blacks in the world today."[43] Even the Communist writer Mike Gold got swept up in the euphoria when he observed that "Cubans live almost free of prejudice" in a nation where "at least half are colored."[44] Yet some of these correspondents failed to examine the obvious chinks in Batista's tarnished armor.[45]

Still, there was a basis for this acquiescence, for when Batista visited Harlem he received a hero's welcome; his arrival, said the *Amsterdam News*, "stirred Harlem's 100,000 Latin Americans, most of whom are Negroes." The visit to this Negro capital was made in the face of opposition from his advisors. Batista, said this Harlem periodical, was "the greatest living statesman in the Caribbean and ranks with" Martí, Maceo, and Toussaint. He was "the strongest individual ruler in Latin America, if not in the New World."[46] "The colonel has always drawn his supporters from the Negro population of Cuba," readers were assured.[47]

On subsequent visits to Washington, Batista was interviewed at Blair House, where he told one and all "there no racial differences in Cuba," a view not challenged.[48] This view was parroted by the Communist leader James Ford, who after returning from the island claimed that "discrimination against

the Negro in the Cuban republic is gradually becoming a thing of the past"
and that the Colonel could be applauded as a result—though it was "true he
played a reactionary role after the overthrow of the Machado government."[49]
The canny colonel was keen to have his closest aides greet visiting mainland
Negro "bigwigs" from the AME church when they docked in Havana,[50] while
in Harlem his close friend Pablo Rodriguez y Mora told all who would lend
an ear of Batista's "socialist program" and the "advanced position of the Negro
in Cuba."[51] Carruthers termed Batista a "man of great vigor and intellect" and
stressed how the Colonel had "a marble bust of the late President [Lincoln]
enshrined in the presidential palace of Havana."[52]

Hence, when a coup was foiled in early 1941, the *Amsterdam News* seemed
as elated as the Colonel himself. It was no more than a conspiracy of the
"American dollar and white diplomacy," and "believers in white supremacy"
were determined to "displace" this "Man of the people," huffed the journal
about those miffed that "the Negro was no longer the disinherited of Cuba."
Still, the periodical was sensitive to the "Black Scare" and "Red Scare," con-
cluding, "It is not known whether Batista's Negro ancestry is more abhorrent
to the American ruling class than the support that has been given him by" the
"Communist Party of Cuba."[53] On the other hand, these interlocutors were
understandably swayed when Batista called on U.S. Negroes to join the war
effort,[54] at a time when this persecuted group had its doubts in light of highly
persuasive propaganda from Tokyo.

Yet some were so taken by the color of Cuba's leaders they often lost sight
of Washington's (and Batista's) policies; even the U.S. ambassador to Cuba,
George Messersmith, contended that the island was treated "shabbily." When
the mainland produced enough sugar, he said, imports from Cuba were suppressed, which had "corresponding depressing effects" on the island. Cuba
was treated like an unkempt doll, though "sugar can probably be produced
more cheaply in Cuba than in any other country."[55] Unlike the Negro press,
the U.S. ambassador was struck by the casual corruption in Cuba, for example,
the shady dealings engaged in by Joseph Davies, the notorious U.S. envoy in
Moscow, during a whirlwind visit.[56] Batista himself was no slouch: he was
"already a rich man," said Messersmith. "I know of considerable properties
which he owned, principally in the way of real estate in Florida."[57] When
Messersmith tentatively raised his concerns with Batista, the cunning leader
flashed his dazzling smile and reminded him coyly and threateningly that
"there were some people" on the island who were not friendly toward this
mainlander and "I ought to take some precautions," like those adopted for
example, his predecessor, who "when he went out usually had one automobile
precede his [and] another follow it." Batista smilingly told Messersmith that
"some thugs" were itching to "beat me up" and for some reason they thought

"they were doing him, Batista, a favor." It was unclear if the Colonel could—
or would—restrain these "thugs."[58]

Still, like a typical mainlander, Messersmith was fixated by the visage of
Batista—his "natural complexion is very dark"—though meeting him one
night, he seemed "almost white"; perhaps it was then that he termed the dictator a "very decent man" who was "in many ways misrepresented."[59] Although
insightful about Cubans, Messersmith had little to say about his compatriots, for example, Albert Cannon, then serving at Guantánamo, and who with
barely concealed rage remarked about his posting, "The only thing I don't like
is the way the niggers act."[60]

Amid the jubilation that depicted Cuba as the site of endless racial exhil-
aration, the NAACP reported more sobering news. Just a few years before
the Carruthers-Allen interview, the association, speaking of the over 13,000
U.S. nationals said to be residing in Cuba (many of them Negro), cautioned
about overreaching in Havana. That is, over the years the racial makeup of the
island had fluctuated—the "colored population exceeded in number the white
population" for a good deal of the nineteenth century—and, yes, the "Negro
population of Cuba has been assimilated to a much greater degree than that
in the United States." But as of the 1930s there was "no national organization
of colored persons" and now "following the downfall of Machado," a "fear of
Negro uprising again took hold." There was also dismay when "Negroes were
among the leaders of seizing sugar properties and making exorbitant demands
on mill managers." Moreover, following the "revolt of the sergeants"—which
propelled Batista—"the percentage of Negro officers and enlisted men in
the Cuban army greatly increased." This has "alarmed many conservative
Cubans" and was bound to generate a backlash that could easily envelope
credulous U.S. Negroes. That the Communists were playing an increasingly
conspicuous role on both sides of the straits, with those on the island going so
far as broaching "the idea of an autonomous state in Oriente," would kindle
passions and create unpredictable ramifications.[61] Unsurprisingly, as Urrutia
saw it, there was room for another opening. "What Cuba needs," he insisted,
"is something like the NAACP."[62]

In other words, if non-Negro mainlanders, such as the usually perceptive
Communist writer Mike Gold, were seduced by Cuba's version of race, it suggests there was more to it than wishful thinking. Though Batista was referred
to routinely as a "virtual dictator," he was lauded by a U.S. Negro analyst as
"one of the most popular figures in Cuba today,"[63] while his opponents were
portrayed as having "fear" of the "power of [the] Negro army chief."[64]

Another in Gold's category was the Communist writer Joseph North, who
acclaimed Justus Salas of Santiago as "Cuba's First Negro Mayor," victorious though "Bacardi Rum threw thousands of dollars into reaction's war chest

to defeat" him. All of which presented a bracing "lesson for America" with national "reverberations." For, as on the mainland, the "Chamber of Commerce couldn't sleep nights thinking of the possibility of the Negroes winning out," since they were "70 percent of the city." Salas, "the candidate of the Communist Party and the Liberal Party," overcame the right wing's slogan: "Keep the Negro Out" by dint of a "White Front." Though U.S. Negroes were applauding Cuba as a racial Shangri-la, North saw importance in Salas's victory since "dark-skinned Santiagans were not permitted in the park as recently as a year ago. Even today Negroes cannot find work in the city's stores or in the restaurants. Discrimination," he cautioned, "is quieter, more subtle, than it is in the United States."[65]

North was echoing the concern of the visiting U.S. Negro scholar Mercer Cook, who saw in Cuba the "world's queerest color line," the most "zig-zag-giest" of all. He found the Cuban Catholic Church to be segregated: "There is not a single colored priest on the entire island," which provided an obvious opening for U.S. Negro missionaries.[66] Yet Cook was in Cuba long enough to see the "first colored priest" appointed in Havana, a breakthrough he attributed to "the war, public criticism and the Communist threat."[67] Cook was suitably impressed when on the first anniversary of the bombing at Pearl Harbor, "radio stations were silent throughout the day," and Havana was enveloped in silent stillness to honor Maceo's death, a "strange coincidence" that brought home at once the difference between the island and the mainland and how the compulsion of war was altering the landscape of the latter.[68]

Driven by the pressure of war, even the U.S. ambassador, J. Spruill Braden, came to pay his respects to the Club Atenas where he quoted Maceo admirably. The influential Miguel Angel Céspedes quoted Du Bois with equal favor, pressing his point that to win the war, Jim Crow had to go. "The one sour note in the program was that the Municipal Band of Havana had to play the inevitable 'Dixie' "—yet Cook was heartened by this official reproving of an encrusted system of bias.[69] Cook spotted the irony of the July Fourth holiday being celebrated in Havana by a group of "lily-white" mainlanders.[70]

Cook did not realize that his attention to the centenary of the Negro major general, Guillermo Moncada, so essential to emancipation in Cuba during the 1868–1878 war, would take on a new and different meaning after 26 July 1953 with the attack on the barracks that carried his name. Mayor Salas of Santiago had pushed to make his birthday a public holiday,[71] which was reawakening in the most fevered imaginations long-standing anxieties about the "Africanization" of the island. Cook also introduced his audience to Miguel Angel Céspedes—"tall, well-built and looking considerably younger, looking younger than his fifty-six years"—a man of color who was in charge of radio in Cuba and "exercises considerable authority over railroad, postal and telephonic

communications." Cook was "impressed by the large number of Negroes
to whom he has given employment." U.S. Negroes frequently lamented the
absence of monuments to their heroes and thus Cook found it worth noting
that Céspedes "in 1927 sponsored the erection of the monument to [an African woman], who sacrificed all her sons on the altar of Cuban liberation." On
the walls of Club Atenas were further signs of what could be called Africanization—"photographs of eminent black Cubans and of people like Booker
T. Washington, Frederick Douglass and Toussaint L'Overture, Dr. Du Bois,
Mme. Evanti, William Pickens and other distinguished American visitors to
Havana" that had been "entertained there." Since the Atenas building was
designed by a Cuban who attended Tuskegee, further evidence emerged of a
solidarity that did not decelerate during the war.[72]

Unlike the mainland, U.S. Negro readers were informed, "on streetcars
and buses white men offer their seats to colored women. It is by no means rare
to see a colored girl strolling along the Prado on the arm of a white boy." It
was this different racial environment combined with the liberalizing impact of
antifascism that caused Cook to conclude that "if ever the employment problem is solved, the lot of the colored Cuban girl will be happier than that of her
North American sister."[73] Cook was enlivened to find in Havana "open flirt-
ing between white men and colored women," as opposed to the subterranean
romances of a similar kind on the mainland.[74]

Cook drew a distinction between Havana and Santiago, finding the latter
"less prejudiced" than the former, perhaps because there were "three colored
persons to two whites," and Santiago's proximity to Haiti rather than Miami.
Likewise in Santiago there were "many prosperous colored people," including
a broad array of those in the professions, ranging from physicians to attorneys.
Here he got the impression that "many whites were afraid of blacks."[75]

The growth of anti-fascism as propagated by Hughes and Robeson and
Guillén began to eat away at this racism, inducing heightened expectations of
what was just, which may help to account for why it seemed that mainland
analyses of racism in Cuba were becoming less celebratory and more measured.
"Negroes represent around 40 percent of the population" on the island, said an
analyst from the National Urban League, yet they "are conspicuously absent in
hotels as bellboys and waiters, in stores, as sales people, in office as bookkeep-
ers and clerks." When a "colored woman" from Manhattan arrived in Havana,
she was "advised by the management that since there were a large number of
Floridians in the hotel," she should take her meals in her room. "If the Negroes
of Cuba are not alert and 'on their toes,'" they were advised, "in twenty-five
years from now it will be difficult to distinguish the racial pattern of Havana,
Cuba, from that which now prevails in Miami, Florida; and the Negro Cubans
will for all their noble history be permanently established in an inferior status."[76]

Miguel Angel Céspedes, leader of the Club Atenas, also outraged by proliferating Jim Crow, found it abominable that students of African descent were excluded from some of the better private schools.[77] "I have not yet seen one colored waiter in any of the Havana hotels or restaurants," agreed Cook.[78]

Though an Urban League analyst in early 1942 "expected in the Cuban Negro an ascendancy unparalleled in the Western Hemisphere," he was buffaloed when seeing that "the majority of the surprisingly large hordes of prostitutes" were "Negro women," suggesting that like the mainland, "the Negro is the despised, downtrodden element," both "underprivileged and impoverished." There was, for example, a dearth of "Negro businessmen." Yes, the Club Atenas was formidable, housed in an imposing building of bluish-gray stone with marble-floored verandas, featuring a large enclosed basketball court and a wide marble staircase; magnificent Persian rugs covered the floors, which lent a palatial air. U.S. Negroes were moved to find that in the library were books by their eminent writers. But this fine display of erudition and exquisite taste could not obscure the racial ugliness of Havana. Yet, as had been the case at least since 1898, this analyst too pointed northward since bashing the African was "the wisest way of currying favor" with Washington, and "in this matter of race," Cuba "must bow to the preachments from above of her cruel task-master." And though the "Cuban Negro gazes upon his colored American fellow of the United States with wistful, envying eyes," this brightened gaze was darkened by the powerfully looming presence of Uncle Sam.[79]

With the coming of the Second World War to Washington, the United States was faced with its usual wartime problem: how to convince Negroes that their polecat status would erode if not end if only they would make a blood sacrifice for the nation. After being fooled in 1898 and 1918, Negroes were loath to be fooled again, which meant they had to be induced by more concessions—or offers of same. Cuba, on the other hand, had to be wooed away from competing powers[80] at a time when anti-communism was not as effective in destabilizing local Communists because of the U.S. alliance with Moscow. A similar dynamic also made it more difficult to halt Communist progress in the Harlems on the mainland.[81] Washington had been maneuvered into a position where it had to rely on Reds while under siege and in the bargain being forced into the ultimate indignity: easing the suffering of mere Negroes.

Thus Washington was becoming more skeptical of Batista, seeing him as much too close to the Communists, which was curious since the U.S. president was then conferring regularly with Stalin himself. Still, when the federal police chief, J. Edgar Hoover, scrutinized Batista during the war, he was singularly unimpressed, finding this man "believed to have been born in 1901" and "reported to be part Negro and part Chinese" as a danger. Why? He has "openly courted the favor of the Communist Party in Cuba and in April 1943

Batista appointed to a cabinet position the Cuban Communist leader, Juan Marinello." Hoover was told "in the strictest confidence" that "President Batista hates Americans." In the same file was a report on Communist leaders seen as "Negro," which was quite a few.[82]

Hoover's inflammatory words were forwarded to Sumner Welles, Roosevelt's chief advisor on Latin America, and he was not only hearing from the FBI about growing Communist strength on the island. Welles had been told anxiously by an informed Cuban that the "Negroes are showing more aggressiveness, which is backed and encouraged by the Communist Party. The Federation of Colored Societies is a demonstration of those activities." But, as was said of Batista, "the ideals maintained by the Negroes" also involved "hatred of the Americans" as they "openly express their sympathies to Russia"[83]—the soon-to-be ally of Washington itself.

Actually, it was more like "hatred" of the policies brought by the "Americans," something the visiting Negro scholar Mercer Cook noticed in Havana when watching the Hollywood film *Kitty Foyle* in English with "translations in Spanish." He found it striking when the translator "simply omitted the word 'white' when used by a character," changing it to "we are all human beings."[84] Du Bois's colleague Irene Diggs was dumbfounded when watching a movie in Havana with the translated title *The Negro that Had a White Lover*, which not only involved an African man kissing a European woman but a white bootblack who shined his shoes. There was no riot, no controversy, unlike the United States.[85] Telling for Cook was the invasion of the Spanish language itself, by mainland terms, for example, "linchamiento" or lynching.[86]

Willfully, Washington misinterpreted revulsion at the sight of its policies with "hatred" of U.S. nationals, a distortion revealed when U.S. Negroes (particularly) continued to wed Cubans,[87] and Cubans, for example, Dr. Louis Martín (who had matriculated at the University of California and Meharry Medical School, overwhelmingly comprised of Negroes), continued to send offspring to the mainland. His son of the same name became a power broker and journalist among African-Americans and a top aide to President Jimmy Carter.[88]

As was typical, Cuba found it necessary to react to mainland political disputes that implicated racism and anti-communism, bringing these twins into sharper focus on the island: in the same year as Hoover's report, a bundle of newspapers from Gary, Indiana—whose population was becoming more and more Negro—was refused entry in Havana because of a flaming editorial blasting right-wing U.S. Congressman Martín Dies after he had launched a tirade against Pickens and Bethune.[89]

Higher education continued to be the venue where Africans on both sides of the straits encountered one another, which meant for the most part universities like Howard, where the Cuban ambassador appeared in 1941 to present a bust of Maceo, which complemented the fact that it was not so long ago that his portrait hung in many a home of U.S. Negroes.[90] Cuban agricultural experts routinely repaired to Hampton Institute to sharpen their skills.[91] Their path was eased in that Cubans had been matriculating on this Virginia campus at least since 1907,[92] just as they had been attending the Palmer Memorial Institute in North Carolina, which catered to elite U.S. Negroes.[93] Then there were the Cubans who served on the faculties of mainland Negro campuses, for example, Amando O. Bustamante at Clark University in Atlanta[94] and Dr. Angel Suarez who taught history at Howard.[95] When a mental health clinic in Harlem in the shadow of City College was named after Paul Lafargue, a Cuban with familial ties to Karl Marx, this tie was solidified further.[96]

When the heralded Dr. George Washington Carver of Tuskegee passed away his Cuban colleagues told his school's leader about the "agricultural radio meeting" that was organized in Santa Clara to highlight "what he signified in life for the agricultural world," which was a mutuality in that an Alabama delegation had visited the island and, said their leader, William Levi Dawson, they relished the "courtesies" shown, including "smoking the cigars very much!"[97]

Mercer Cook spent the summer before the onset of war at the University of Havana, where he was joined by Benjamin Mays of Morehouse College, who was to serve as mentor of Dr. Martín Luther King, Jr.[98] and countless other U.S. Negroes.[99] Cook, said a mainland Negro journalist, was able to arrange a birthday party for Mays's spouse "in one of the exclusive cafes" in Havana—an impossibility in Atlanta.[100] Among this growing group was Irene Diggs—who was to serve as a chief aide to Dr. Du Bois—who studied at the University of Havana. Born in Monmouth, Illinois, she had studied at the University of Minnesota and Atlanta University before becoming the first U.S. Negro woman to get a doctorate from the University of Havana, writing a dissertation on the leading scholar, Fernando Ortiz.[101] "Were it not for her clothes and English language," said a fellow Negro, "she would seldom be taken for an American. The Cubans fail completely to recognize colored Americans" primarily "because they have gained their conception from American movies and magazines."[102]

Like other visiting Negroes, generally Diggs escaped the Jim Crow that had come to characterize her existence. Cook was transfixed by one "white girl from South Carolina" who was upset after being reprimanded by a librarian—not because of the words uttered but because, she said, "I had never before in my life been bawled out by a colored man,"[103] suggesting the island's corrosive influence on Jim Crow.

The University of Havana, one of the oldest and most prestigious schools in the hemisphere, was routinely adding U.S. Negroes to its faculty and student body and, thereby, challenging mainland counterparts.[104] There was a reverence for learning that drew the two together, which led to a rapturous welcome for the visit to the island of Dr. W. E. B. Du Bois, no longer with the NAACP in 1941 but still an intellectual force to the reckoned with. As he stepped onto Cuban soil, cameras whirred as the leading dailies captured his arrival and dignitaries greeted him. "Cuba is an ideal place to study relations," said the diminutive and aging intellectual.[105] Like many U.S. Negroes he viewed Cuba as part of a wider Pan-African community.[106] Speaking at Atlanta University after his whirlwind tour, Du Bois urged students to study and visit the region, though he cautioned that visas were difficult to obtain since "there is a definite effort to keep Negroes out of Mexico and Cuba."[107] The difficulty in securing visas was a repetitive complaint of U.S. Negroes seeking entry to Cuba.[108]

Du Bois, a seasoned traveler, spent a week motoring between Havana and Santiago, 1,200 miles all told. "There are white people, yellow people, brown people and blacks," he remarked of a tour that featured an audience with "the Governor of Oriente" who supplied him with "a very delicious cocktail." Though Du Bois was often persona non grata on the mainland, in Cuba "the Governor sent his own car, his chauffeur and an interpreter" to accompany him.[109] While on the island he engaged in a series of erudite conversations among intellectuals covering the present state of the world—it was "an excellent idea, imperfectly carried out," he said. The problem may have inhered in the process since words were flowing not only in Spanish and English but also French, Portuguese, Italian, and German. He compared the gathering nonetheless to the better known "Races Congress in 1911 in London."[110]

Cook rubbed shoulders frequently at the university with the head of the English department, Dr. Consuelo Serra G. Veranes, "one of the most prominent colored women in Cuba today," he said of this "stately, dark brown-skinned" intellectual who had an "amazing fluency in English" that was honed in the public schools of Manhattan, Hunter College, and Columbia University. This daughter of "the great black Cuban patriot" Rafael Serra was "Cuba's Mary McLeod Bethune" and a boon companion of U.S. Negroes.[111]

Another island analyst prowling the streets of Havana was Jesse Thomas, a comrade of Mays and a confidant of the Urban League. He and Mays spent 45 minutes conferring with the then aging "ex-president of Cuba, General Mario G. Menocal," a "graduate of Cornell" and a "gracious gentleman, politician and statesman." He in turn was on good terms with Dr. Marion Watson Rudd, a "colored chiropodist, born and educated in the United States" but a resident of Cuba for twenty-five years. Among her patients were "75 of the 100 most prominent citizens" of the island, a practice virtually unthinkable in her homeland. Like others, Thomas warned that "unless the Negroes and their friends stay on the alert in a quarter of a century it will be difficult to distinguish Havana, Cuba, from Tampa, Florida"; not lost on him was that he—and those like him—had access at the highest levels in Cuba, which provided leverage on the mainland.[112] This thought may have occurred to Daddy Grace, the widely acclaimed Negro cleric—or charlatan, depending on one's predilections—when he fled the mainland for Cuba with tax agents hot on his trail, amid claims that he was a victim of prosecutorial discretion run amok.[113] Years later he was still to be found basking in the sunshine of Cuba.[114]

But after a while, Cook's rosy view of Cuba began to alter perceptibly. When Negro journalists began to organize, Cook was surprised to find that some prominent Cubans objected.[115] Then there was the irritation of Jim Crow beaches: "There were no printed signs" saying as much, "merely a fence and a rope separated the two races on the beach and in the water." Even here he spotted a difference with the mainland, for on this privately owned beach "for the first time in my segregated life" Cook "saw separate accommodations that were absolutely equal."[116] Like others, Cook placed the weight of Jim Crow on the shoulders of mainlanders finding that when "Havana hotels sometimes break Cuba's anti-discrimination law and refuse to admit colored guests, they do so because of their white American patrons." Yet, when "white Cubans" engaged in such practices, more than likely they had "lived in the States. They bring back with them all the worst features of American relations. And their daughters bring back large supplies of peroxide so as to bleach their hair and appear whiter than ever."[117]

With the accrual of time, it seemed Cook tired of blaming mainlanders, a trend that became clear when his view of Batista began to change. He found it irksome in late 1942 when the Colonel sought to "fire his colored minister" Ramon Vasconcelos, which was indicative of "estrangement between Batista and colored Cubans."[118] Cook went to see the deposed leader "at his luxurious new home in Miramar" where Vasconcelos derided Batista's views denying the existence of racism in Cuba. "Vasconcelos remarked caustically that this was true only insofar as Batista himself was concerned," as he accused the Colonel of "color prejudice."[119]

Cook responded by deeming the Colonel a "tragic figure" who "denies his own color" and "does little to help [the] race." His record was one of "ruthlessness and opportunism." Sure, the Communists backed him but it was merely "lukewarm support which will cease as soon as he steps out of line or as soon as they become the majority." Vasconcelos then told Cook that Batista was "the most prejudiced president Cuba has ever had," not least since he was "sensitive about his complexion." The Colonel, he said, "cultivated no social ties with Negro Cubans" and under his reign, "promotions for colored officers [have] become increasingly rare" and Africans were "kept out of the Air Force" altogether—though he conceded that "since Cuban planes are manufactured and most Cuban pilots are trained in the States," this "exclusion of Negro pilots may have been dictated by Washington." Even the heralded 1940 Constitution, so advanced on antiracism and guaranteeing economic rights that FDR sought to mimic in 1944, was described as "the work of Communists and that none of the credit belonged to Batista." Sure, there was "less race prejudice in Cuba" than "Dixie"—but if the latter was the benchmark, the island was doomed to retrogression in any case. Batista, Cook was told, was a "discredited leader, a man without a party, almost without a public."[120]

When Cook witnessed "colored" veterans of the 1898 war camped in Havana before the capitol, demanding a steep increase in their meager pensions, his thinking was transformed. Poking around, he found that by 1913 many of them had been purged from the military, thanks to Washington; hope arose when Batista seemed to be bent on reversing this trend but now disappointment had set in. Yet even here Cook was startled to find that the "Afro-Cuban sailor encounters fewer obstacles than in the U.S. Navy," for "sailors of both races fraternize" to a "much larger degree than in the States."[121]

The growing influence of Communists, the continuing deterioration of Cuban lives as a result of misrule, and the progressive climate brought by antifascism were combining not only to erode Batista's regime but, as well, belief in it by usually credulous U.S. Negroes too often misled by his color, neon smile, and soothing anti-racist words. Cook praised the Cuban painter Ramon Loy extravagantly since he had "labored constantly for the advancement of the colored Cuban. In this he has differed from some of his compatriots, who have become less and less colored as they have waxed more and more prosperous," like a certain Cuban colonel.[122]

In assessing the agonized retreat of the mainland from Jim Crow, what needs to be factored into the equation is the unremitting pressure placed on the United States by untamed Cubans, who in doing so also impaired the normalized U.S. rule over the island, preparing the battlefield for revolution. During the midst of the war, one Cuban—speaking for others—wondered why there were "no colored American soldiers stationed in Cuba," and more than this, "why are colored Cubans so rigidly excluded from the tangible benefits of our Good Neighbor policy?" And "why is the censor so difficult about permitting colored newspapers to enter Latin America," for example, the *Afro-American*, which frequently failed to reach its intended destination. "Could this cover-up of the news be prompted by a desire to conceal from colored Latin Americans the injustices to which their North American brothers are subjected?" And why did U.S. airlines give instructions to its agents to denote passengers by color and do so by invoking the malevolent "North American yardstick: 'one drop of African blood'" makes a Negro. And why did so many U.S. envoys in Cuba speak no Spanish? In Cuba newsreels often showed action in East Africa featuring armed indigenes, though "white distributors in America must think this film diet not good for Americans" since such was not screened there reportedly.[123]

Mercer Cook was encouraged by the revulsion felt by popular opinion in Havana when the racist "hate" strikes against Negro workers took place in Philadelphia. "The undemocratic attitude of the strikers is almost incomprehensible here," since "politically the colored Cuban is far in advance of his North American brother. . . . Two of the four most important political parties here—the Liberals and the Socialists [which would become the Cuban Communist Party]—are headed" by Negroes, while "to be legal every ticket must sponsor candidates of both races." Yes, "the lighter [the] skin, the better the chances of finding . . . employment," but here Blas Roca was determined to "put teeth in Article 74" of the 1940 Constitution, toughening anti-racism provisos,[124] enactments that had aroused U.S. Negroes.[125]

U.S. Negroes also began to focus their benevolent attention on Salvador Garcia Aguero, "Cuba's Fighting Red Congressman," as he was described, a comrade of Blas Roca, the latter termed a "mulatto" and the former depicted as "champion of the colored Cuban's cause." With suitable awe, it was noted that "every Communist ticket in Cuba has an equal number of white and colored candidates," even though "colored Cubans constitute less than 25 per cent [of] party membership." Aguero was the "father" of the island's "Civil Rights Law with teeth," which put to shame tepid mainland efforts. Married and a father of two, Aguero was vice president of Club Atenas and a "member of the Society of Afro-Cuban Studies and one of the directors of the National Federation of Colored Cuban Clubs." Aguero won plaudits from U.S. Negroes when in 1938 he travelled by bus from New York to Florida and saw "horrible things" and "almost started a riot in Daytona Beach trying to get something to eat"; he departed hurriedly with disgust and then "had to wait five days in Miami for the boat that would [bring him] back to civilization."[126] Aguero, the president of the Cuban Senate and a former high school teacher, was praised in the mainland Negro press as "the most competent orator of all Spanish-speaking countries."[127]

THE ANTI-FASCIST CLIMATE created fertile conditions for cross-straits progressivism and African solidarity—which often was the same thing, though this was hardly comforting to those who long had raised a hue and cry about "Africanization," a racist appeal that barely shrouded class and ideological interests. In short, Cuba in the 1940s, spurred in part by the response to Spain and Ethiopia in the previous decade, tended to conflate the two major frights of Washington: the "Red Scare" and the "Black Scare." The powerful New Yorker Ogden Reid was foremost in this apprehension when in late 1941 he witnessed Batista addressing a crowd of 70,000 workers, alongside Lázaro

Peña, an African described as "Communist Party representative in the Chamber of Deputies." Mention of Moscow, it was reported, "drew prolonged applause from the workers, among whom are many Communists."[128]

Peña, visiting Manhattan in 1946, explicitly urged mainland Negroes to aid the island's growth.[129] In 1947 Cuba was—perversely—described as the "nerve center of both Fascist and Communist propaganda in the Western Hemisphere." The latter trend was dominant and embodied by Peña, "a big handsome loud-voiced Negro" whose hegemonic presence caused one analyst to ask plaintively—and presciently: "Will Cuba be the first Communist republic in the new world?"[130] When Peña was arrested in July 1952,[131] it was thought that a deathblow had been dealt to Cuban radicalism, but as things turned out, this was simply a slight detour in the race to revolution.

Peña—a Communist, senator, president of the Cuban Federation of Trade Unions, and African—led the charge against Washington when the war ended. The embassy in Havana was a nest of spies targeting not just Cuba but all of Latin America, he charged. He assailed the mainland labor movement for bowing to Jim Crow and denied there was "no discrimination against black-skinned citizens of Cuba"; in fact, Cubans had been protesting racism, particularly as it impacted "the mistreatment of Negro Americans," at least since "the Scottsboro case."[132]

When Lázaro Peña arrived in New York, the hatred he exhibited toward Jim Crow was hardly suppressed. Described as a possible future president and the "strongest man in Cuban politics," this African was also said to be "revered and loved by the lowly workingman, reviled and hated by wealthy business interests."[133] Thus this Communist trade union leader denounced the "great number of American secret police" in Cuba who inevitably fortified a racist status quo and made a point to condemn the "vicious Jim Crowism practiced in the U.S."[134]—all of which was reported at length in the U.S. Negro press.

The fabled mainland Negro conservative George Schuyler was not alone in finding it quite curious, if not frightening, that the "Four Bigs" of the Communists in Cuba were "all Negroes" and more important, all "voluble opponents of Yankee imperialism."[135] But even with the focus on the "Four Bigs," Juan Marinello was regarded as the first Communist ever named to a cabinet post in a Latin American nation, signaling that even before 1959, Communist influence in Cuba was far from minor.[136] Esther Cooper—who was wed to one of the top mainland Negro Communists, James Jackson—encountered this influence directly in 1945 when she attended an international congress of the left in London and met Raul Castro, Cuba's future president. Jack O'Dell, who was then with the National Maritime Union but was to emerge as a key aide to Dr. Martín Luther King, Jr., parlayed with Cuban Communists in Camaguey during this same time.[137]

Another Negro journalist "never averse to a dig in the ribs of our pink (white) fellow countrymen" reasoned that the "high incidence of communism in Cuba" was due to factors that these "countrymen" would find unsettling. They were "demanding higher living standards, social security, division of big sugar estates, half of which are owned by wealthy people of the United States and," boldly pronounced, "AN END TO RACIAL DISCRIMINATION. It is this last point which makes the Communists popular, for a high percentage of all Cubans are colored."[138]

Cuba was drifting steadily to the left, motivated by an influential Communist Party considered by mainlanders to be led by Africans, and was to be victimized by a fierce anticommunist reaction and draconian crackdown led by Batista. But this served to create an opening for the 26 July Movement that triumphed on 1 January 1959. In the meantime during the war, Washington could only look on with apprehension as a left-leaning Cuba driven by Africans, as it was thought, continued to serve as a role model for U.S. Negroes; being ninety miles from the mainland simplified the journey to Havana of Willard Townsend, a leading Negro trade unionist, when he spoke to 1,300 of his Cuban counterparts in late 1944.[139]

U.S. Negroes were not taken aback when Cuba was listed as one of "9 colored nations" invited to a left-leaning "world parley,"[140] nor was it surprising when in 1947 the island was listed with other "dark nations"—for example, Liberia and India—on the vote at the United Nations on Palestine.[141] During the war, Du Bois spoke explicitly of "Colored Cuba" joining Haiti and the Caribbean in "united effort with Black Africa and Negro USA and eventually with India, S.E. Asia and China," in a bloc that would transform the planet.[142]

Objecting strenuously to this turn of events, were those that eventually chased Hughes and Guillén from Spain. The Falange—described by the mainland Negro press as "Francisco Franco's Ku Klux Klan"—was prominent in Cuba and was displeased with the perceived leftward tilt of the island, thought to be driven by African Communists. It was reported that the Falange was collaborating with Dixie leaders, for example, Senator Tom Connolly of Texas and even William Green, president of the American Federation of Labor, who was concerned about Cuban labor's perceived radicalism. Dixie thought that the Cubans were overly concerned with Jim Crow, while the Negro press thought the Falange wanted to convert Cuba "into a second Mississippi." But the Falange was not destined to prevail on the island, a reality that was evident as early as 1946 when their leaders called for shutting down the U.S. base at Guantánamo since if Africans revolted on the island, "American Negro soldiers and sailors . . . could not be depended on to crush it."[143]

Cuba, shaped like a weapon, was used by U.S. Negroes to pistol-whip Washington on the altar of Jim Crow. Even before the war, the NAACP's

Pickens hammered his homeland after seeing a photo of the U.S. secretary of state, Cordell Hull, a Tennessean, in a "close tete-a-tete" with Batista: "It shows up the hypocrisy and uncivilization [*sic*] of these Southerners," as—unlike at home—the New Dealer ignored the "interesting fact" that Batista could be defined as a Negro. Typically, Hull and his entourage in Havana "lost track of their anthropology and forgot his origin," an example of "our idiotic American race prejudice!"[144]

The *Afro-American* sensed this mainland queasiness about "race" in Cuba when it asserted that President Ramon Grau San Martín "is colored but that no daily paper or magazine has yet identified him as such."[145] In a comment that continues to sound, Claude Barnett, noted Negro entrepreneur, complained in 1944 that "practically every picture of Cuba and South America which appears in the daily press or even the magazines of North America carefully exclude the pictures of peoples of color. The result is that most Americans think of Cuba as a land of whites and mulattoes alone."[146] Thus, to counter this, Barnett demanded that his colleagues in Havana provide more material for the mainland Negro press concerning "those Cuban people who have a pronounced amount of African blood in their veins."[147] This would not be too difficult, for one correspondent from Havana had just encountered a "Cuban senator" who was "dark as Marshall Davis,"[148] the latter a reference to the Negro journalist soon to relocate to Honolulu where he became a mentor of a future United States president.[149]

How could New Dealers rationalize embracing Negroes in Cuba while bowing to Dixie in shunning them at home? This query was being posed as Washington found it had to compete more and more for the affection of Negroes in competition with Moscow and Tokyo, with inability to prevail presenting a potentially mortal challenge to national security. The neat solution devised on the mainland was to grant civil rights concessions while squashing the left represented by Robeson and Du Bois. When the latter tactic was imposed on the island, it served to create an opening for the 26 July Movement of Castro—in part because the tactic deployed in Cuba was more murderous, quite literally, as when Jesus Mendendez, a Communist legislator, trade union leader and described by the *Afro-American* as "colored," was slain.[150]

The mainland-induced swerve to the right in Cuba took a particularly perilous turn. Later that year, even the U.S. State Department was reporting anxiously that "an anti-Semitic campaign" had erupted in Havana.[151] Apparently taken by surprise, Robeson indicated in 1949 that mere political repression could not halt him: "They can't stop me from earning dough," he said. "I'm going down to Cuba now and get a pile."[152] But this was a misjudgment for soon that avenue too was blocked. The wise journalist Roi Ottley declared that the "fact is, the [Communist] Party did more than any other agency in

American life toward breaking down the rigid color barriers" on the mainland, notably the "ruthless manner in which the party fought . . . white chauvinism" made a "deep impression on Negroes."[153] But with the war's end and Washington's decision to make an agonizing retreat from the excesses of Jim Crow, as tensions with Moscow escalated, the Communists—and allies like Du Bois and Robeson—were slated for marginalizing at best, with a similar fate designated for their island counterparts.

Still, as Menendez's slaying suggested, regressive forces did not retreat easily. As a prelude to fierce battles on the mainland in the 1950s, fiercer struggles erupted on the island. Conventioneers from the National Negro Business League of the United States upon arriving in Havana in 1947[154] threatened mass civil disobedience, including marches and sleeping in the street, against Jim Crow practices imposed in hotels after—according to their litigious counsel, Harold Flowers of Arkansas—"certain tourists from America" objected to their presence. The mainland delegation included A. G. Gaston, the illustrious Alabama entrepreneur soon to gain notoriety from his involvement in demonstrations spearheaded by Dr. Martín Luther King, Jr., and their cause was argued avidly by numerous Cubans, including Mario A. Suarez, a young Cuban attorney and friend of Flowers.[155] After this pressure, the Hotel Sevilla-Biltmore capitulated and granted full and equal hotel accommodations to Negro visitors.[156]

Indicative of the pincers launched by the "colored" on both sides of the straits was a delegation of 100 led by Pedro Portuonda Cala, which landed in Florida then traveled by train from there to Washington to get the full flavor of Jim Crow. In turn they invited the NAACP to journey to Cuba in order to compare notes on bias.[157] "Growing race hate in Cuba blamed on white tourists," was the summary of the remarks by this Cuban intellectual, then conferring with leading NAACP attorney Charles Hamilton Houston. "Many of the first-class hotels, restaurants and business establishments are barring colored Cubans because of demands made by American tourists,"[158] but their hysteria about Jim Crow helped to create even more mass discontent, preparing the ground for revolution. Similarly, the Cuban visitor told his hosts that though the "Cuban Negro" was "losing the control he had once" of "all the principal crafts in the country," this seriousness was "not the same as that brutal discrimination that our Negro brothers from the South in the country has to put up with."[159] Houston's sagacious initiative seemed to be vindicated when after a brutal lynching of Negroes in Georgia, vitriolic protests were lodged against the "gangsters" involved by the National Federation of Cuban Negro Organizations.[160]

This kind of protest was even more evident in the realm of sports, ostensibly frivolous but actually a contest that helped to define the all-important sphere that was masculinity, where Negroes were thought to be deficient but where boxing and baseball proved otherwise. Moreover, even under heinous Jim Crow, it remained possible for mainland Negroes to earn incomes a cut above the mass of the downtrodden and/or travel in the hemisphere to gain more income and notoriety that could then be deployed for righteous purposes. Such was the case of Canada Lee—who was to become an eminent actor—but it was as a boxer that he began to gain applause and insight that led him to a deeper understanding of exploitation. In this journey as a pugilist, his manager was a Cuban.[161] U.S. Negro Bill Sawyer claims that as the sport soared in popularity, "I used to play baseball on the streets here in Miami with Fidel Castro."[162] It was certainly true that on the peninsula, baseball helped to bind Negroes and Cubans of various stripes.[163]

Of course, there was another side to this formula: when the United States allowed Cubans defined as "white"—for example, Adolph Luque—to play baseball at the most lucrative levels and barred those seen as "Negro," the island was further split along a bitter racial divide, as suggested by Luis Tiant, Sr., the Cuban father of a noted hurler for the Boston Red Sox. Fortunately, ebony athletes had an opportunity to ply their trade because of the acumen of Cubans like Alejandro Pompez, who would be defined as "black" on the mainland and was a major force in the Negro baseball leagues.[164] And as had been the case for years, this led to even more U.S. Negroes marrying Cuban women, as occurred when the slugging Hank Thompson exchanged vows with Maria Quesada.[165]

Yet after becoming enmeshed in a horrific war with fascism that mandated the deployment of tens of thousands of Negro soldiers and being forced to denounce racism in uncompromising terms in the process, the United States was under enormous pressure to change its bigoted baseball ways. This led to the Brooklyn Dodgers baseball team signing Jackie Robinson. Sent to Havana for training, the star Negro athlete found the racism there less intense, thus easing his transition to the so-called major leagues.[166] Cubans celebrated his arrival in a nation where baseball had become a "religion,"[167] according to the veteran mainland Negro journalist, Sam Lacy. Lacy found "great hero worship for Jackie" in Cuba, as he was "built up to the skies."[168]

But when Havana gained a minor league baseball team authorized by mainland teams, mainland rules sought to bar the Cubans from hiring athletes that could be defined as "Negro."[169] A few years later, those in this category were barred from these Florida teams—Cubans and mainlanders alike—which angered island executives and pleased their Miami and Tampa peers.[170] Still, when the Dodgers considered a training site for the mainland, the peninsula was rejected because of such Jim Crow rules.[171]

An awkward disjuncture had arisen in cross-straits relations, with the island being guided to a degree by battle-hardened Communists of African descent while Florida was moving in an opposing direction. The peninsula state had the largest Ku Klux Klan membership in the nation in the 1940s, which was fueled by such undistinguished factors as the state—along with its neighbor, Alabama—being the last to relinquish the totalitarian convict-lease system. And for the first few decades of the twentieth century, Florida had the highest per capita rate of lynching on the mainland.[172] The police force of Miami was dominated for years by the Klan.[173]

At the same time Florida was undergoing spectacular population growth that was to make it one of the nation's largest states, which was creating strain by its very nature. Between 1830 and 1945 the state's population had increased from 34,730 to 2,250,061—then to 4,951,560 by 1960.[174] Surely this spectacular population growth (and racist trends then emerging concomitantly), was not a plus for Africans on both sides of the straits.

As Jim Crow retreated, motivated in part by elite calculations about the position of the United States in the international community and the discredit delivered by officially sanctioned racism, it was not only the Communist-oriented left that was battered. In Miami in 1948 radio station WWPB sacked Clarence McDaniels after he dared to introduce a news item telling of a KKK cross-burning in a Negro neighborhood.[175] By late 1949 NAACP membership in the state had "fallen off tremendously," according to their attorney, Franklin Williams,[176] a trend that was punctuated shortly thereafter by the assassination of the state chapter's leader, Harry T. Moore, and his spouse.[177] This was a prelude to and continuation of the crackdown on Cuba's Communists, also thought to be led by Negroes.

As had been the case since 1898, Cubans continued to unload a fusillade of angry fire against the importation of Jim Crow, which fit uneasily with island norms. The Cuban intellectual Mirta Aguirre told the *Amsterdam News* that "the press, the movies and the radio are to a large extent imported commodities," and waiting in the wings was television slated to emulate the three. "The motion picture industry does not exist in Cuba," she said, "because powerful foreign interests already disturbed [by] the success of cinematography in Mexico and Argentina and to a certain extent in Brazil, have not permitted its development in Cuba"—and she could have added that sports and entertainment had evolved in a similar direction.[178]

The postwar scene with its rhetorical barrage against racism motivated an intensified aggressiveness against Jim Crow—on both sides of the straits. As for the press, Irene West of the *Afro-American* came to Havana to confront directly the *Havana Post*, an English-language journal, on this score, informing its editor bluntly, "You frighten me." She told her readers to avoid Havana in favor of Mexico City since even in 1946, "when a black Cuban wants accommodations in the best Havana hotels, he takes with him to the desk a white

Cuban of importance" for "if he applies alone, he is told there is no vacancy."[179] There was a downside to this imposition of Jim Crow, however, for in Mexico she found "none of the suppressed hatred" of the United States she detected on the island[180]—hatred that would hasten the race to revolution.

By way of contrast, Charles Hamilton Houston of the NAACP found that Mexicans—more than Cubans—were more willing to confront U.S.-style Jim Crow. "To me," he said with a scoff, "Cuba is a colored country with a white overlay"—particularly "at the top"—since U.S. nationals were "more in evidence in Cuba than in Mexico" and "wherever white Americans go in large numbers they take their race prejudice with them and try to infect the local population." Throwing down the gauntlet, he charged that "Mexico has forced the United States to treat her as an equal," unlike Cuba[181]—but events in the coming decade were to challenge this easy assumption. Houston was pleased to find that Cubans were becoming even more interested in the plight of U.S. Negroes, as evidenced by the numerous delegations trekking northward. This was part of "the gradual awakening of the colored people of the world to a sense of their common destiny," which mainland Negroes were reciprocating, indicating that "all the colored peoples of the Western Hemisphere have a date with destiny," indicating further that "we can be the decisive force for freedom."[182]

Because of the more flexible racial regime, more mainland Negroes were opting to reside on the island. Daddy Grace, the evangelist, was among them; he had fled there years earlier and by the 1950s he was settled comfortably in Havana's suburbs in a stately mansion on a winding country road nestled in the soft shadows of towering palm trees. The entrance to his handsome abode featured ornate ironwork marked by riotously colorful tropical flowers, which kept the uninvited a safe distance from the finely manicured gardens surrounded by a massive cement fence that extended for several city blocks. His was an example that attracted ever more mainland Negroes seeking a sanctuary from Jim Crow.[183]

When the Negro composer William Levi Dawson traveled to Cuba in 1946, he informed his cousin, the Negro congressman of the same name, that "it was wonderful to be able to taste a little genuine Freedom!"[184] A reason why was revealed by the Negro journalist Lu Harper, who upon arriving in Cuba in 1949 was ebullient, feeling he was finally "in a spot where for once I can forget I'm a Negro with all the labels attached to him," which made him realize that "prejudice and discrimination can be wiped out completely."[185] Perhaps it was the contrast between the island and the mainland—notably the supposed dearth of bias—that shocked visiting Negroes, who were so extravagant in their praise of Cuba. Honeymooning in Cuba, Dr. Edward Welters of Illinois (though born in Key West), the rare Negro who served in a state legislature, asserted stoutly that the island contained "no discrimination whatsoever."[186] But Sam Lacy of the *Afro-American* may have disputed this thinking, for upon recognizing that "you're sunk if you let 'em know you're an American" on arriving in Cuba, he thus went to great lengths to "pass" as an islander, including abandoning his fedora, hiding his handkerchief, and dressing like a Cuban.[187]

Then there were the numerous Negro musicians and singers who found appreciative audiences on the island, a salve for often not being able to do so at home. This included Dorothy Maynor, whose arias were greeted enthusiastically in 1946 by an audience that included the island's First Lady.[188] Sarah Vaughan, another charming chanteuse, was among those who vacationed there.[189]

Cab Calloway, the premature hipster and Negro bandleader, said of Havana in 1949 that it was "one of the craziest places I've ever been around," which was both a compliment and a reflection of the Sin City reputation the metropolis had garnered.[190] Sam Lacy was stunned by the "freak shows where for a price one sees disgraceful performances by dark-charactered men and women in which everything goes," not to mention "brazen love-making in plain view."[191]

This debauchery was a companion of gangster-driven entertainment that allowed Havana to anticipate Las Vegas, and this decadent process was a complement of the bludgeoning of the Cuban Communists, as manifested in the assassination of Menendez. At these booze-soaked sites in Havana, mainland Negro entertainers like Calloway were a major draw: "I'm going back as soon as I can," he said early 1950. "I can stand Havana in large doses."[192] Thus, in 1955 the *Defender* told of the "socko welcome" accorded to the silken-haired crooner, with "sellouts for every place he was slated to appear"[193]—but within a few years these opportunities were to shrivel to nothingness.

Robinson and Calloway were not the only high-profile eminences who made their way to the island. Jesse Owens, who took the world by storm at the 1936 Berlin Olympics, was reduced to racing a horse in Havana subsequently.[194] Joe Louis, the heavyweight boxing champion, was invited to Cuba at the behest of Batista himself.[195] Thousands came from the island to watch their own Kid Gavilan fight the glorious Sugar Ray Robinson in Philadelphia.[196]

Nonetheless, the growth of Havana as an entertainment mecca and the concomitant rise of Miami brought island and mainland artists closer together. Quite famously, Jelly Roll Morton spoke of the "Spanish tinge" of the music called jazz,[197] which—not coincidentally—came into being at the same time roughly as the 1898 war familiarized more U.S. Negroes with Cuba. Morton asserts that jazz came from New Orleans, and had a distinct Cuban influence. "I heard a lot of Spanish tunes," he says, "and I tried to play them in correct tempo. . . . In fact, if you can't manage to put tinges of Spanish in your tunes, you will never be able to get the right seasoning, I call it, for jazz."[198]

This music brought to the fore those with roots on both sides of the straits, for example, the sweet-sounding trumpeter, Fats Navarro, whose distinctive sound was shaped by Cuban radio, as he was born in 1923 in Key West: his parents were born in the Bahamas, and his grandfather arrived on the mainland from Cuba in 1895.[199] He gained fame with bands led by mainland Negroes, for example, Billy Eckstine, where he replaced Dizzy Gillespie. Perhaps the turning point in the fecund and new direction in the music blazed by Charlie "Yardbird" Parker occurred when Navarro was replaced in his band by Miles Davis.[200] Navarro was the counterpoint to Davis on the horn, with the Illinoisan replacing him in Eckstine's band and succeeding him in Tadd Dameron's combo. But even Davis—and Clifford Brown and Gillespie and Freddie Hubbard, even Wynton Marsalis—were influenced in some ways by Navarro.[201] Davis, viewed as being at the apex of artistry, says that Navarro was "one of the greatest trumpet players I ever heard. He could also play saxophone like [John] Coltrane. He didn't imitate anybody—he had his own style, he created it."[202]

Yet Navarro too had to endure the quotidian bigotry that was the mainland's landmark and succumbed to heroin, perishing in 1950, but leaving behind a style of playing that influences trumpeters to this very day.[203] Navarro didn't copy Gillespie or Parker directly, as so many others have over the years, but he wove their musical insights into his own, more lyrical voice. He was also politicized and provided a model for up-and-coming musicians like Charles Mingus to emulate.[204] It was Navarro who railed against the role of the "underworld" in the business, which already had become a reality in Havana. "You breaking into whitey's private vault when you start telling Negroes to wake up and move in . . . where they belong," for "when the time comes when the black man says I want mine, then hide your family and get yourself some guns. 'Cause there ain't no better business for whitey to be in than Jim Crow business." So, he told the bassist, "get yourself some heat, guns, cannon, and be willing to die like *they* was. That's all I learned when I was a kid, how bad they was and [be] not afraid to die—to arms, to arms," he cried.[205]

Francisco Perez Grillo, otherwise known as "Machito," was born in 1908 in Cuba but like many of his fellow islanders found himself in Manhattan where he organized a band—Machito and the Afro-Cubans—which held its first rehearsal at the headquarters of the evangelist, Father Divine, at 122nd Street and 7th Avenue in Harlem. He was baffled that his band was able to evade the strictures of Jim Crow in Miami Beach though members were "black and white." The exemption existed because they were Cuban and not the descendants of mainland slaves—the club even provided them with a bodyguard to smooth their way. "I used to live in a white hotel," ate in "white restaurants," he recalled. The sole U.S. Negro in the band was encouraged not to speak and betray his regional accent and that "made the difference." Why the difference? "They consider the Cubans [are] not black," he said. At the same time, U.S. Negroes were dazzled by his music: "It was a black music," said Machito, "you didn't have to make no explanation to a black person." Thus, he recorded with Parker and called the leading mainland Negro horn player, Sonny Stitt, "a good teacher." Machito considered Batista to be "an outstanding guy," which he did not perceive as being in conflict with his reverence for his African roots, having recorded "Kenya" with the peninsula Negro horn player Julian "Cannonball" Adderley in 1958 at a moment when this East African nation was in the throes of a liberation struggle.[206] This was a revealing marriage since Adderley had roots in Key West and the Bahamas.[207]

This was a reflection of the fact that when Machito named his band the "Afro-Cubans" in the early 1940s, he was miles ahead of many U.S. Negroes who had been compelled to abjure the slightest association with the beleaguered continent.[208]

Then there was Mario Bauza, born in Havana in 1911, who played with Calloway and influenced Gillespie and the trailblazing saxophonist, Charlie "Yardbird" Parker.[209]

He arrived in Manhattan for good in 1930, and may have had more influence on music associated with U.S. Negroes than any other Cuban. He had come to New York in 1926, heard the music called jazz and headed back to Cuba where he mastered the saxophone. He joined Noble Sissle's band in 1930 and as a trumpeter he played with the outstanding drummer Chick Webb. It was Webb who told him, "If you can get the American Negro accent in your music, you're going to be great, because you've got the other side of the coin—the finesse, the technique." The "accent" quickly came, which led him to Calloway's band.[210] But it was Bauza's stint with Webb that catapulted him into music history, not least because he was responsible for the discovery of the enchanting U.S. Negro singer Ella Fitzgerald—and that feat was only exceeded by persuading Calloway to hire Gillespie.[211] But what makes Bauza more than a music legend—more than his influence on giants like Art Blakey and Horace Silver—was his crusade in the musicians' union against racism. He was outraged when he was invited to their "mostly white" meeting at 110th Street and 5th Avenue on the edge of Harlem. "I never saw a black musician work in a Latin orchestra in midtown," he carped, though he exempted Xavier Cugat—viewed as "white" on the mainland (he was raised in Cuba)—as he "hired dark and mulatto musicians."[212] Bauza felt betrayed by the racism he experienced among fellow Cubans in New York who had adjusted all too well to the mainland.[213] Bauza, who was of a darker hue, had left Cuba partly due to racism only to wind up in the headquarters of same. He was driven to stand and fight in Harlem as a result, recalling a revealing moment when he bumped into the mainland bandleader, Jimmy Dorsey, who told him bluntly, "Mario, it's a shame that you're black, because you're such a good musician."[214]

Bauza notwithstanding, his fellow Cuban—Chano Pozo—may have done more to bring the African roots of island music to the mainland. Still, it was Bauza who introduced him to Gillespie, with whom he made his mark, which was quite remarkable since Pozo's English-language skills were elemental at best. But as Pozo reputedly put it, in words that resonate through centuries of struggle and interaction, "Dezzy no speaky Spanish, me no English . . . we speak African!" Yet it was the English-speaking mainland that may have led to Pozo's premature death. A tour through Dixie and its Jim Crow regime made him distinctly ill at ease, so he returned to Manhattan where on 22 December 1948 he was murdered in a Harlem bar.[215] He left behind an indelible mark on music, for as Gillespie assayed, "He knew rhythm—rhythm from Africa. . . . [He] taught us all multi-rhythm; we learned from the master."[216] Cuba's Africans had retained more of their culture from their continent of origin than their mainland counterparts and it was through figures like Pozo that U.S. Negro musicians were brought closer to African music.[217]

Being perceptive, U.S. Negroes observed how certain Cubans were seemingly exempt from harsher aspects of the Jim Crow regime and some chose to "pass" as islanders. Born Lee Brown in Newark, after a stint with Lionel Hampton's band (where Navarro once played) he renamed himself "Babs Gonzales." At times donning a turban, he claims he received better treatment generally from this point forward. His elementary knowledge of Spanish helped, particularly when in 1960 he played in Tampa in a "nice club owned by 'Cuban' people catering to colored."[218]

But as the century passed its midpoint, the forces that drove Lee Brown to become Babs Gonzales were beating a hasty retreat. Jim Crow was on the run and unavoidably this was to have an impact in Cuba, as those backing this evil were now unmasked as being simple defenders of mainland heresy. This was occurring as the "Bigs" of the Communist Party were also being bludgeoned, which did little to improve the deteriorating living standards of ordinary Cubans and, instead, opened the door for the rise of the 26 July Movement—and revolution.

CHAPTER 11

Race to Revolution

DIGNA CASTAÑEDA FUERTES was taken aback. Ambling down a Havana street in the 1950s, this young Cuban woman suddenly spotted a group of U.S. Marines. "It was scary enough for a young black Cuban woman to see this foreign force," she recalled years later but what startled her was the stunning reality that these men were "totally racially divided, black troops marched on one side and whites on the other. I had never seen Cuban people so starkly separated like that."[1]

Like the lunar tides, the mainland had exerted a determined pull on the island for centuries in a process that only accelerated with the occupation of 1898. The forcible installation of Jim Crow had not been "successful" in that it contributed to a "race war" of 1912 and no doubt facilitated the rise of one of the strongest Communist parties in the hemisphere, which—from Washington's viewpoint even worse—was exerting a similar pull on the U.S. Negro population. But with the onset of the 1950s, a tidal wave of anticommunism was unleashed that washed away a good deal of the strength of U.S. Negro Communists and wounded those in Cuba. On the island this took place in the context of deteriorating socioeconomic conditions and enhanced terror that helped to erode whatever support the Cuban puppeteer (then U.S. puppet), Colonel Batista, once held. Moreover, as the United States was forced to retreat from the more egregious aspects of an odious Jim Crow, those that had upheld this moth-eaten banner in Cuba were discredited further, contributing to the taut unease felt by Digna Castañeda Fuertes.

When a regime is compelled to move away from what had been deemed theretofore to be holy writ—Jim Crow—it erodes its legitimacy. On the mainland this gave momentum to liberal reform in what has been termed the Civil Rights Movement, which on the peninsula had as one of its key tribunes, a skilled attorney of African descent and Cuban roots, Francisco Rodriguez. On the island an opening was created for Fidel and Raul Castro and the 26 July Movement whose mission was congruent with that of Cuban Communists,[2] as the young Esther Cooper had discovered in London in 1945 and as other U.S. Negro Communists discovered when forced to flee to the Cuban "underground" in the 1950s. This too hurried the race to revolution.

For Cuba, 1952 was also a turning point, for it was then that "swarthy Fulgencio Batista," as the Negro press tabbed him, popped from behind the throne and chose to occupy it for himself, releasing in the long run an orgy of violence. The *Amsterdam News* did not seem overly perturbed by this turn of events reminding cheerfully that "Harlemites will find Havana a less costly and more cordial place to vacation than many places in the United States." By way of encouragement, readers were told that their hero—Jackie Robinson—was a "minor god" in Havana and that Cubans "have the same sense of humor or better than we have."[3] Readers were meant to be reassured when another organ reported that Batista "has [a] colored mother"; he "is what would be known as a colored person in the United States." On the mainland, this was typically a signal of one predisposed to challenge white supremacy, but Batista—in a sign of dissonance—made "his first legal action . . . against the unions" led by stalwarts such as Peña and supplanted a "republic" with "dictatorship."[4]

This messiness was not sorted out, perhaps because U.S. Negroes were already confounded with their own rapidly changing status from third to second-class citizenship. Meanwhile, Roger Baldwin of the ACLU found in 1957 that he could not get a visa for the musician Felix Guerrero to come to the mainland, since "many years ago [he] took out a card in the Cuban Communist Party."[5]

This messiness was also not sorted out because Batista's ascension was presented as a blow against the enemy du jour: Communists. Days before his coup, even the *Norfolk Journal & Guide* felt constrained to reprint the overheated remarks of syndicated columnist Bob Considine, who warned darkly that "if Cuba went ag'in and took up with the Russkies we'd have the Soviet A-bomb . . . smoldering within 30 minutes of Miami. . . . Cuba is our largest customer per capita in the world"—yet not only Communists but ebony Communists, no less, were rising.[6] The inveterate anticommunist bloodhound Howard Rushmore told his wide audience—before Batista's coup—that the island had been "long" a "center of Red activity," and the former Red, Benjamin Gitlow, said correspondingly, that "Cuban Communists would meet with us in New York and our delegates would travel to Cuba" for reasons that remained mysterious.[7]

In this febrile climate, Batista's past ties to Communists, real and imagined, made him suspect in the eyes of some in Washington. The influential columnist Drew Pearson was told by an informant in 1952 of the Colonel's closeness to Communists.[8] Also suspicious, as Pearson was told, were "the ties between the Cuba of Batista and the Guatemala of Arevalo," referring to a reformist regime thought to be not unfriendly to Communists. Such suspicions may have driven Havana to be "holier than thou" in their administration of anticommunism, particularly given Cuban Communists' proximity to the mainland and their well-publicized African leadership, thus driving the island to an extreme at a time when Cuba was already under stress given that its patron in Washington was retreating anxiously from Jim Crow. Thus when Batista was linked with Arevalo in the same message was the note that the despised Lázaro Peña was then in Moscow receiving "indoctrination."[9]

Washington knew all too well that recently the potent mainland Negro publication *Ebony* had praised Peña as "the most powerful Negro labor leader of his time"; it was known that U.S. Negroes considered him to be a dear friend because of his withering criticisms of U.S. racism, notably in the labor movement.[10] The increasingly important voice in the echo chamber of Cuban policy—the *Miami Herald*—added that the ebony Communist was "ordered to Moscow" for "fresh instruction."[11] Carlos Hevia, who billed himself as "former president and former Minister of State of Cuba," reminded Pearson—whose columns were pored over in Washington's corridors of power—that Batista had been allied with Peña; he went on to detail alleged Comintern activity and other supposed Moscow-directed activity in Havana at a time when, it was thought, the Reds may have been on the verge of seizing power.[12] Hevia, like many of Batista's conservative detractors, could easily be defined as "white" on the mainland, which the Colonel could not; and given the flux brought by simplistic racial thinking, primitive anticommunism and high-level ebony Communists, Batista's room for maneuver was quite limited.

Actually, as had been the case for some time, beleaguered Communists on the island and mainland did huddle as both came under unremitting fire. Howard "Stretch" Johnson, a pillar of the Harlem Communist Party, confessed subsequently while he was "underground"— seeking to elude the long arm of the law by making himself scarce in his usual haunts—he "was given the mission by the National Committee of the Party to take a trip to Cuba to make arrangements there for the transport of some of our people in the United States to some of the socialist countries."[13]

In 1950 while he still held a valid passport and the right to travel abroad, the veteran Negro Communist William Patterson crossed paths with Cuban Communists at a critically important London gathering.[14] After the attack on the Moncada barracks in 1953 by Fidel Castro and his comrades, the Civil Rights Congress—led by Patterson, who had traveled to Havana for political purposes decades earlier—dispatched delegations to Cuban consulates in Manhattan and Detroit and staged a picket-line at the United Nations in pro-test.[15] Still, Washington may have been wrong-footed by Patterson who in the immediate aftermath of the epochal events of 26 July 1953 referred not only to the "brutal suppression of democracy and reign of terror in Cuba unleashed by the U.S.-backed regime of General Fulgencio Batista" but the "unsuccessful uprising of some misled adventurers" that had provided a "pretext" for this bloodshed.[16] In short, Washington may have been misled as to the ultimate socialist intentions of many within the leadership of Castro's forces, since it seemed that mainland comrades were critical of them—and this may have given these forces the breathing space they needed to attain success.

Aboveground, Cuban Communists openly attended the 1957 national con-vention in Manhattan of their U.S. peers, along with scores of journalists from the mainland, Rome, Warsaw, Moscow, and elsewhere.[17] Also in 1957 Patter-son, who concentrated substantially on solidarity with an island under siege, coordinated with Roger Baldwin of the American Civil Liberties Union, to promote press coverage of "the Batista terror."[18]

The U.S. authorities scrutinized Cuba through the lens of surveillance of domestic Communists, which meant that they were focused on Cuban Com-munists at a time when the Castro forces were surging. In 1958 J. Edgar Hoover was informed confidentially that monitoring of mainland Reds revealed still close contact with their Cuban peers and, it was said, criticisms of Castro's forces. Cuban Communists were said to "have a positive attitude toward the Castro movement, even if it is, at the same time, critical of this movement." Yet, as with Patterson, the overall tenor of U.S. Communists was to lend support to the "Cuban revolt," and one way to do this, according to an FBI surveil-lance report, was to "find the link to the Negro people" of the United States since "the population of Cuba is made up of 30% Negro, 30% white and 30% mixed Negro and white. The most suppressed people in Cuba are Negroes. . . . The American Negro would see this, so there are possibilities of reaching the Negro leaders in this connection."[19] Hence hysteria reigned in Washington—which is not a recipe for clear thinking—about Red encroachment when an island revolt with murky ties to Communists was said to be linking up with U.S. Negroes then in the midst of long-term unrest.

As the pivotal decade of the 1950s unfolded, past trends seemed stunningly intact. Marta Terry, a Cuban of African origin, wrote a University of Havana dissertation on "The Impact of Slavery on White Society in the South up to 1860" and thus had to travel to the mainland. Like others who walked in her footsteps, she was no stranger to bias of the Cuban variety, but the U.S. con-figuration puzzled her. She went with another young woman—who happened to be French—to a restaurant in Maryland. At first because of her darker hue,

Terry was refused service but when the proprietor found out she was a for-eigner, she was quickly served.[20]

In the Cold War competition with Moscow, Washington had made a bet that the world's majority, not sufficiently endowed to be admitted into the hal-lowed halls of "whiteness," would be no less pleased if given a kind of "honor-ary white" status. The problem was that this was a chancy wager, the exposure of which created propulsion for the erosion of Jim Crow altogether. For the intellectual curiosity that brought Terry to the mainland was no asset of hers alone: in the 1950s there was a noticeable trend of Cubans—particularly of African descent—matriculating at historically black colleges and universities in Dixie,[21] just as Cuban professors continued to be hired as professors at these same institutions.[22] Professor Benjamin Carruthers conceded in 1952 that "my contacts with Batista have grown cold," but this U.S. Negro scholar continued to maintain contact with Suarez Rocabruna who "taught for a year" at Howard and his "very good friend, Professor Teodoro Ramos Blanco, one of Cuba's most famous sculptors and the donor of the Maceo bust to Howard Univer-sity,"[23] the leading institution of higher learning for Negroes, sited strategically in Washington, D.C.

Despite the strenuous efforts of Washington, Jim Crow had not sunk deep roots on the island, which continuously impressed visiting U.S. Negroes and undermined the presupposition that this racist framework was both unavoid-able and mandated by the heavens. Instead, U.S. Negroes were impressed with the reality that as their homeland struggled to maintain—or erode Jim Crow—Cuba continued to pass anti-discrimination laws, even under the Batista dic-tatorship.[24] The profound words of Robert Abbott, publisher of the *Chicago Defender*, who years earlier had urged his fellow Negroes to learn Spanish as a tool of education and weapon of liberation, continued to be cited.[25]

The University of Havana's soccer team was competing with Howard, at times "baffling" the mainland Negroes with a "swift moving attack," as the 26 July Movement would exhibit in another field.[26] This was followed by a delegation of forty Cubans arriving at their Washington campus on a hill to present a bust of Martí to complement the earlier donated one of Maceo. The browsing room of the library was festooned with Cuban flags; thus, appropri-ately, a collection of Martí's work was also donated, as the Howard president saluted the Cuban hero as one who engaged in mighty "resistance against all forms of human enslavement."[27]

Still, all encounters with mainland Negro students and alumni were not so becalmed for it was in mid-1958 that the 26 July forces captured the former Vir-ginia Union University student Hannibal Holmes, Jr., then serving with U.S. forces in Guantánamo, who provided a firsthand account of the transformation that was soon to come.[28] The twenty-two-year-old bespectacled young man said he was "treated royally, had lots of beer and good cigars" and was sure to note that he "saw only two girls with the rebels, secretaries to Raul Castro" and "other officers" and was otherwise unscathed.[29] He was a mite more lucky than the nineteen-year-old Negro Marine Joseph J. Anderson of Queens who lost twenty-one pounds after being detained for three weeks by the rebels in the vicinity of Guantánamo.[30] But the dominant trend remained—ties of singular intimacy between mainland Negroes and Cubans, as demonstrated in late 1958, when Jeanine Henry, described by an admiring journalist as "dimpled and pretty," married Pedro Zambrana of Havana.[31]

At the same time, mainland Negroes continued to flock to Cuba, including a group from Norfolk residing at the eastern end of the island, which was seething with revolutionary ferment.[32] U.S. Negro professionals continued to see Cuba as a resort destination, with the National Medical Association planning a "mid-winter cruise to Havana" in 1958 as the revolutionaries were poised to take power.[33]

Jim Crow was slowly being dismembered on the mainland, but its replacement, though surging, was unclear: anti-racist activists and Africans simply trying to live their lives were caught in the maelstrom and at times shaped it. As Jim Crow cracked, more opportunities arose for its victims, allowing more opportunity for tourism, particularly to an island ninety miles from the mainland.[34] A travel correspondent found Havana to be "more Americanized" than ever, which did not bode well for ebony visitors.[35] This led Florencio D. Baro of Havana—self-described as a "colored Cuban citizen"—to warn mainland Negroes in 1952 about the "constant flow of white tourists from your country" and the perils they presented.[36] At the same time, U.S. Negroes were informed that "it is not only unlawful but downright unhealthy in present-day Cuba to show prejudice against anyone because of his complexion," as there were "stiff fines and even imprisonment for anyone convicted of racial discrimination." Yet the contradictions continued to flow ceaselessly since "the swanky tourist hotels," for example, the "Nacional in Havana and the Internacional in beautiful Varadero Beach, still make it pretty clear that 'gente de [people of] color' are not welcome"—though these were "U.S.-run hotels" filled with U.S. tourists taking advantage of the "seven airlines" that "fly daily to Havana," said a Harlem journalist.[37]

Josephine Baker, who had fled Jim Crow St. Louis for Paris and international stardom, travelled in the 1950s to Havana where she encountered what she thought she had left behind.[38] The U.S. embassy in Havana planted a story that she "might use the Cuban press, particularly its Communistic elements [to] spread tales of the abuse of black Americans."[39] She was handled roughly and interrogated by military intelligence in Havana, who also seized a large number of books and pamphlets from her, thought to indicate "Communist leanings."[40]

But even the stalwart mainland republic had to bend to the winds of change: "For the first time in history," crowed the *Pittsburgh Courier* in 1952, "a U.S. Ambassador here has entertained an American Negro at the ambassadorial mansion in the fashionable Country Club residential district of Havana." To be sure, the guest was melanin-deficient and celebrated—the talented pianist and biracial daughter of the conservative Negro columnist George Schuyler, who had sounded the alarm about the rise of Communists of color on the island.[41] Still, for the mossback mainland, this was progress. The same could be said of shocking events in May 1954—hours before the U.S. Supreme Court was to rule that Jim Crow was unconstitutional—when a minor league baseball team in New Iberia, Louisiana, deigned to allow Negro and "white" baseball players to compete against each other, and when darker-skinned Cubans were also allowed to ascend to this lofty status, it was apparent that a new day was arriving.[42]

But like a new day itself, it did not arrive all at once but slowly and gradually. Claude Barnett, a leader in Black Chicago, in 1952 contacted hoteliers in Richmond, Virginia, on behalf of "Cuban tourists" who were heading northward from Miami by bus and wanted to "stop at a good hotel," that is, those that were not marinated in the indignity that was Jim Crow.[43] This was at the behest of Pedro Portuondo Cala of Havana, who worried that a delegation of "Cuba colored tourists (lawyers, physicians, teachers, etc.)" might encounter "racial discrimination" in Dixie and thus wanted a listing of "any place, restaurant or hotel of Negro people."[44] Between 1940 and 1960 the number of Cubans in New York alone increased by 84 percent,[45] which meant more back and forth between the island and the mainland as air travel was upgraded— and the opportunities to be subjected to alienating racial harassment.

On the one hand, such bigotry drove islanders and Negro mainlanders closer together and solidified their joint interest in destroying a humiliating Jim Crow and base of support for the U.S. right wing; on the other, it was folly to expect Cuba—as the gateway to the Caribbean and Latin America— to stand easily alongside Washington in its twilight struggle with Moscow when islanders were maltreated so appallingly. For as the mainland made its wrenching transition away from Jim Crow, paroxysmal violence mushroomed, which was not the best advertisement for Washington's way of life. Nicolás Guillén wrote poetically about cases in which the dwindling U.S. left led the way—for example, the Martínsville 7—and others, e.g. desegregation in Little Rock,[46] and the butchering of the Negro youth Emmett Till in Mississippi.[47] Dr. DuBois, though he was to be deprived of his passport and his wings were clipped, continued to be in close touch with Fernando Ortiz and other Cuban intellectuals who continued to view the mainland skeptically.[48]

Cuban visitors had reason to believe that what they were seeking to avoid on the mainland had sunk its claws into the island. The problem for

Washington—and Batista—was that it was difficult to repress a rather sturdy Cuban left wing while upholding an island right wing that was not sturdily anti–Jim Crow. The former goal was more important in a Cold War atmosphere, which made it difficult to accomplish the latter. Thus, in 1955 Serapio Paez Zamora, a longtime friend of Claude Barnett and an affiliate of the Instituto Interamericano de Lucha Contra la Discriminacion Racial—or the Inter-American Institute Opposed to Racial Discrimination—answered emphatically "Yes!" when asked "Is prejudice growing in Havana?" It was "alarming," he confessed, since it was not just this metropolis but "all the national territory" that was impacted. "In the great business and industrial concerns the discrimination against the Negro is 100%," while Batista "seems indifferent to our problem and grief." He lamented that "we have no access to the diplomatic careers . . . nor the Naval Carriers" and "in his Cabinet there's but one Negro." The "President does nothing on behalf of the extermination of the racial discrimination."[49] He did not have to add that this only fueled insurgency.

Yet despite this coruscating denunciation, Barnett, whose news service was a mainstay of mainland Negro opinion, continued to court Batista, consoling him in 1957 with the idea that press coverage of his misrule was "slanted and bordering on the unfair," but reminding him that "there is one section of the population which always stands for you. These are the Negro Americans"—"our hearts are with you," he exhorted.[50] Batista expressed his "gratitude" for "the kind sentiments."[51]

Surely, Barnett was not speaking on behalf of a monolithic Negro community—those of the left, e.g. Langston Hughes, refused to be charmed by Batista. Still, the 6'4" Barnett was no outlier, as there were 350 Negro newspapers who utilized his Associated Negro Press. Interestingly, he earned his political spurs working for the 1920 GOP presidential nomination of Leonard Wood, who had sought to foist Jim Crow upon the island decades earlier.[52] Thus Barnett's words do betray a nagging and persistent trend that stretched back years, that is, though mainland Negroes continued to marvel—and revel—over how the island's racial patterns differed from those of the mainland, it seemed that when it came to Batista, he was viewed by those like Barnett, through the prism of the mainland Negro experience, whereby a "Negro" leader was bound to be besieged and destabilized by hardened racists. Thus it was in 1958 that Barnett told the Cuban consul in Chicago—Jose Valera—that "ever since the Castro disturbances . . . people of color would naturally feel inclined to cast their sympathies with President Batista" with one major reason being that "some of our American newspapers" were so "hostile" to the dictator and "we thought the ogre of race may have had some influence."[53]

Jim Crow habits die hard, which handicapped Washington's ability to influence Cuba positively. Neill Macaulay of South Carolina, a graduate of the

Citadel, served in the U.S. military before decamping to 1950s Cuba. There he spoke with an islander who "admired the South; 'There you have the correct attitude' toward the Negroes,'" he said. The problem was that Washington was busily seeking to jettison this "correct attitude" so as to better engage in Cold War competition but doing so was bound to confuse, if not undermine, Macaulay's amenable interlocutor.[54]

There had been a consonance between Cuba and Florida for centuries, and this was no less true as zero hour approached in January 1959. For on the peninsula, a state that had been a lodestar of Jim Crow was now awkwardly seeking a retrenchment from this detritus of slavery. Ironically—if not poetically—a critical player in this process was a Cuban of African descent, Francisco Rodriguez, Jr. His father, Francisco Rodriguez, Sr., was born in Cuba in 1888 and arrived in Tampa in 1909, mostly bereft of English language skills, which hardly changed during his long life. He recalled in 1978 that work was scarce then and, thus, Negro workers were the first to lose their jobs; Spaniards often owned the cigar-making enterprises that were a staple for the working class and they often employed Cubans. Ebony Cubans were not deemed equal to those who were "white"—but were considered better than U.S. Negroes. Actually, the latter fared better in Spanish-owned firms than those controlled by Euro-Americans, he said, for they worked in all of the former but were barred from "Hav-a-Tampa," which was owned by the latter. Unions, he said, at times went on strike to maintain the status quo.[55]

Still, there was a merger between ebony mainlanders and islanders in Tampa that was reflected in the cuisine. Otis Anthony, one of the former grouping, today points to a "Cuban-African-American way" of cooking various dishes. His mother at an early age worked in a cigar factory: "She knew how to roll cigars," and "this talent was passed down by the old cigar makers from Cuba, the Afro-Cubans, and then they taught the African-Americans" and something similar happened with cuisine.[56]

The Rodriguez family was a natural bridge between these two cultures: U.S. Negro and Cuban of African origin. Rodriguez Jr. says he "lived in two cultures at the same time. Latin—maybe three—Latin, black and American" in Ybor City, which was like a "Cuban colony," since the "signs in the stores were Spanish." Unsurprisingly, his father "made me read and write Spanish" and Rodriguez added French.[57]

Rodriguez Sr. was from Pinar del Rio and his wife hailed from Havana. Rodriguez Jr. recalled in 1983 that she was of "Afro-Latin-Oriental stock"—i.e. and his mother was "simply Afro-Cuban." The latter's grandmother had been a slave and his Tampa-based father part of the Martí-Maceo formation and, besides, was considered an expert on Cuban politics. Rodriguez grew up in a community where some of his closest relatives "never learned to speak a word of English" though they had been in Florida for decades, which unavoidably led to his own immersion in Cuban realities. Indeed, "I remember my first day of school—can't ever forget it, because I couldn't speak English"—and this was at an "all black school," of course. Back then he was asked if he saw himself as "black or as Cuban." "Neither," he responded. "I guess I saw myself as black" since "you can't get around that," for "we were ridiculed so much in public schools" because of "speech, dress, and the like" which meant "we shied away from the idea of being Latin." Thus there was a perception that "black Cubans weren't quite so black"—just as he could have added that "white Cubans" were often thought to be "not quite white." Still, the gambling game of bolita—a fixture among U.S. Negroes—was a bonding agent: "It was a way of life," says Rodriguez, "my dear mother was a walking encyclopedia of all the numbers."

Rodriguez Jr. was born in 1916 and grew up in Ybor City in a neighborhood that he said was heavily Negro—though he lived right next door to an Italian family and we had very good relations." As for Spaniards there, "we had a beautiful relationship" though "they thought they were better than Cubans." He recalled that "there was no racial tension between white and black Cubans—never, never. That never came up. But they tended to isolate themselves, you know," speaking of the melanin-deficient Cubans, "with the others—the whites—and of course they had an excellent excuse because it was following the law of the land." There was a kind of interracial dating, "even in the days of the toughest segregation, there was some goin' on," he concedes. "Usually," the norm in interracialism was a "black Cuban man marrying an American," meaning "white" woman "and usually she was perceptive enough to accept all Latin ways and usually in a matter of six to seven months or a year she was speaking Spanish." But, he amended, "among Cubans . . . in [many]cases it involved a white man married to a black woman." There was a flexibility within the rigor of Jim Crow in that "we would not look upon it with any degree of bitterness if a white Cuban would not let us come into his establishment or restaurant"—it was the law.

His mother was a "devout Catholic" as was his sister and brother. But "I'm one of the rare exceptions" in not being Catholic. "Black Cubans," he opined, "have a very strange approach to religion. They have two sets of saints," one Catholic and the other "the African equivalent." At the famed Peter Claver Catholic school, there were "black Cubans and black Americans," which brought the two together. Though he became a leader of the U.S. Negro community, he was not enthralled with what was thought to be their shelter from the storm, the "black Protestant church." It was a "liability" in that folks there "feel if they can just pray, everything will straighten out" and some were even "anti-education."

Nevertheless, Cubans and U.S. Negroes came into contact—appropriately enough—via Martí-Maceo since, inter alia, it had a social welfare component, like "Medicare, Medicaid. All those things before America ever thought about it." Plus, "you could always go there on Sundays and see a comedy and see concerts," but in Florida, "we were always taught that though we were blacks, we weren't black Americans." Instead, Rodriguez Jr. observes, "I was always taught that the sun rose in Cuba"; thus "my mother thought that a doctor who didn't have a Spanish name couldn't possibly be a good doctor," and on Cuban holidays the household would be deluged by island visitors. His father was the same, being "very prejudiced against anything American"—if it was "not Latin," then it was "no good," since he felt that "Cuban people were the most moral, the most intelligent and were the most organized" and that "Americans were the most backward and the most immoral people in the world."

Yet when the time came to attend college, Rodriguez headed straight to Florida A&M University, a Jim Crow institution for Negroes. During the war he detoured to study in China before getting his law degree from Howard University. As a Marine, he was in Asia "right after they had dropped the bomb" and toiled as a librarian and teacher—instructing in English and Spanish, while studying Chinese. There, his feistiness intruded when he came close to being court-martialed for protesting Jim Crow. But Rodriguez by his own admission emerged "from a family of rebels. We were never reconciled to [Jim Crow]." His father was a labor leader and a tremendous orator. It was in college that he learned that "there was a tremendous advantage in being bilingual." Later as an attorney he was conscripted as an interpreter in court and the baffled judge wondered where he learned the language, and he said his parents were Cuban. Replied the judge, "You mean after all of those years you been coming here. . . . I thought you were a nigger."

Arguably, his Cuban origin allowed him to navigate on behalf of U.S. Negroes, whereas members of that group might face obstacles he did not. He recalled once being in Fort Pierce, Florida, and contrasted it with Ybor City. "Being a Latin, I would see white people in my house and what have you," which was nothing to be concerned about, but in "Fort Pierce . . . where Negroes just stay in the corner," they "were not accustomed to a black person who even looked directly [at] a white person." This gave him an advantage in being the tribune of the dispossessed, though it made him a kind of "misfit" there. This "misfit" wound up filing "sixty different types of civil [rights] suits" on behalf of the NAACP, then toiled in the 1970s for its running mate, the National Urban League.[58]

"I filed practically every lawsuit that was filed against the state of Florida," to dismantle Jim Crow, he recalled in 1978. "I exposed my life to multiple dangers" as chairman of the Legal Redress Committee of the NAACP for "the entire Southeast region." Despite this yeoman labor, "I was barely paid," he says ruefully, but without apparent regret. He had lived through the 1930s economic downturn exacerbated by the introduction of machinery in factories that "destroyed the Latin colony" and had developed a sense of injustice that transcended mere mercantile concerns.[59]

Intriguingly, as the Castro forces were surging to power in the 1950s on the peninsula investigators were wringing their hands about "Communism and the NAACP,"[60] with the organization's most prominent figure a Cuban. It was "guilty by association," the NAACP leadership—known to be skittish about Reds—was told in 1957: investigators planned to "gun" for Rodriguez and the tack was to "quiz" him and others "on their association with whites," since that was viewed as marker of Communism and Rodriguez's Tampa upbringing made him exceedingly vulnerable on this score. The plan was "to break the back" of the organization in Dixie and "weaken it throughout the nation."[61] Rodriguez was grilled before a state legislative committee,[62] just as he was gearing up to charge into court against Jim Crow.[63]

For Rodriguez was a critically important figure in the anti–Jim Crow movement in Tallahassee, the locus of the investigation and site of a bus boycott that rivaled the better known equivalent in Montgomery;[64] there was also a hotly contested voter registration campaign in a nearby peninsula town, Bristol.[65] Rodriguez cooperated with future Supreme Court Justice Thurgood Marshall in an investigation of questionable police shootings of Negroes in greater Miami.[66] Rodriguez advised Negro "shop workers" on their multi-faceted disputes.[67] When Ezekiel Daniel was dismissed because of his job as a railway porter because of his NAACP activism as a result of lobbying by the White Citizens Council, and his union, the Brotherhood of Railway and Steamship Clerks, refused to represent him, it was Rodriguez who was asked to intervene.[68] It was Rodriguez who the NAACP turned to in mid-1956 to make a recommendation to the FBI about contesting civil rights violations in Quincy.[69] It was Rodriguez who in 1958 won a crucial case mandating the admission of Negroes to the University of Florida.[70]

Befitting its history of widespread lynching and KKK infiltration of police departments, the unwinding of Jim Crow in the Sunshine State was noticeably violent, with the bombing of synagogues and Negro schools and with ire vented at not only Negroes but also a growing Jewish population.[71]

Not coincidentally, across the straits, a similar reign of terror was launched at Batista's behest. "Pressures are stemming from the increased activity of the Ku Klux Klan," Wilkins was told in 1956. "They are holding meetings all over the state and are recruiting members at their rallies," featuring "cross burnings" and "fanatics" on the march.[72] Nelson Wardell Pinder, of Bahamian origin, fought in Korea, and graduated from Bethune-Cookman in 1956, but this little prepared him for visiting Miami Beach shortly thereafter: "That's when I really got struck with what segregation was. We had to have an identification tag," as in "the Union of South Africa." Then there was the segregation of Miami—"Jamaicans had a neighborhood, the Cubans had a neighborhood," as did "Black Cubans, Puerto Ricans had their neighborhoods."[73]

The KKK, on the other hand, thought they had reason to revolt when the *Fort Lauderdale Daily News* asked on 9 March 1957, "Is Florida to become a fertile propaganda field for the Kremlin?" In nearby Dade County reputed Communists, some of Cuban origin, were subpoenaed and jailed for contempt after their responses were deemed to be inadequate.[74]

Understandably, there had been a confluence of interests in Florida of Cubans and mainland Negroes, for example, when Aurelio Fernandez chaired an Urban League investigation on "the need for Negro public school teachers" in the state,[75] and when the NAACP held membership meetings in the "Cuban Hall Patio" in Tampa.[76] But since the political climate on the island was to the left of that on the mainland, this was bound to foment convulsions as the Red Scare deepened in the Sunshine State.

Given the xenophobia of the Red Scare, which assumed that radicalism was a foreign import, Rodriguez's leading role was even more conspicuous. In 1957 a Spanish-language journal in Tampa warned that "Communist will be a key word" in Tallahassee, in hearings designed to ensure that "we pro-integration forces will lose ground in Florida."[77] In such an inflamed context, those of Cuban origin like Rodriguez became easy targets. He was the state NAACP's leading litigator[78] and a frequent speaker at their many fundraisers.[79]

Thus, by 1958 as revolution crept closer in Cuba, a state legislative committee in Florida asked the state bar association to take action against NAACP lawyers, particularly Rodriguez.[80] Just before this remarkable maneuver, Helen Williams, a mainland Negro, considered herself "quite lucky" when her hotel—within shooting distance, one half block from the presidential palace in Havana—came under fire. A clerk at a record store in Pittsburgh, she was unaccustomed to such excitement and wholly unprepared when about forty people were killed in an attack on Batista's home; a tourist at her hotel—which was riddled with bullet holes—was also killed.[81]

It is rarely easy for a regime to retreat from principles thought to be inviolable—for example, Jim Crow—without giving rise to forces that can become difficult to contain. When an all-consuming anticommunist overlay is added to the mix, various forms of destabilization become well-nigh inevitable. This ended in Florida with the agonizing retreat of Jim Crow—and in Cuba with regime change.

From Havana, the U.S. State Department sought to monitor this complexity. Thus, in early 1955 there was extensive reporting on a new decree establishing "Penalties for discrimination on the ground of 'sex, race, color or class'"; it was conceded that racism on the island was real, "albeit more subtly and successfully disguised and adjusted to" than the mainland. It was thought that Batista found "a large percentage of his political support among the Negro part of the Cuban population," which was boosted by the "progress that is being made in the United States toward a solution of the color question"; this was "having some influence on Cuba thinking regarding treatment of the Negroes and the country's own color problems."[82] Naturally, the Havana embassy circulated propaganda in Cuba about the retreat of Jim Crow, but this could serve to make some islanders wonder about their own status.[83]

Moreover, in the 1950s there were thousands of U.S. nationals residing in Cuba, and it was unclear if they had chosen to adapt to the prevailing anti–Jim Crow line.[84] What was also not said was that passing anti-discrimination laws while socioeconomic conditions were allowed to deteriorate was a surefire way to at once raise unrealistic expectations that are then diverted into radicalized channels.

Besides a maniacal focus on the fortunes of Cuban Communists as the key to keeping the island in Washington's sphere, the United States, quite typically, had engaged in a kind of affirmative action for a small elite circle over the years as a way to staff the Havana embassy, which was not the best way to monitor a rapidly changing environment. There had been an "unwritten rule," Secretary of State John Foster Dulles was told, "of a resident of Florida" leading the legation.[85] Previous occupants of this Havana sinecure seemed to spend an inordinate amount of time flitting among rich Cubans who would be described as "white" in Washington.[86] Though Cubans were suffering from unemployment, in 1956 the embassy was moaning about how it was "practically impossible for a U.S. national to obtain employment" on the island. It was thought amazing that "in isolated cases where Americans do find jobs, they are required to be bilingual."[87] Yet this same embassy was instrumental when "free entry" by Cubans to the United States was revoked, which exacerbated unemployment; this was seen as a measure to "control subversives," given the island's justified reputation for radicals, but it closed off a safety valve whereby unrest could be released by dint of migration, which left the option of unrest festering on the island.[88]

For the unrest was proliferating in mid-1958 when the powerful Congressman Mendel Rivers of South Carolina fumed that "so far as Cuba is concerned I would favor turning the Marines over and just clearing out Castro and all his kidnapping thugs."[89] But he was opposed by Harlem's Congressman Adam Clayton Powell, Jr., who in the same year demanded, "We should get out and get out at once" of Cuba: "There should be immediate stoppage of the flow of arms and ammunition from this country."[90] In rebuttal, in mid-December 1958 the segregationist Senator Allen Ellender of Louisiana, speaking from Havana, called Castro and his comrades "a bunch of bandits" and asserted that those predicting imminent upheaval in Cuba were mistaken though he hedged by adding, "I might be wrong."[91]

Ellender had the gift of prophecy: he was wrong. On 1 January 1959 the "bunch" he derided came to power. On that day in Ybor City, Jose Alvarez—who had recalled being called a "Cuban Nigger" and had been a Communist, was among those who "went wild. Big parties" ensued "and there was song."[92] Nicolás Guillén, Langston Hughes's companion in Spain, was similarly ecstatic, but he quickly resumed his berating of the mainland because of its Jim Crow policies, denouncing a litany of horrors and denying that the United States could even be called a *"democracia"* in light of the chamber of horrors routinely visited upon the Negro.[93]

This was emblematic of a deteriorating relationship that was punctuated by the attempted overthrow of the regime in 1961 and the world brought to the brink of nuclear disaster in October 1962 with Cuba in the crosshairs. Yet even the assistant to the chief of protocol for President John F. Kennedy, Pedro Sanjuan, was appalled by race relations in the nation he represented. He was born in Cuba in 1931 to Spanish parents. His father, a well-known composer whose music drew on African traditions embedded in Cuba, was friendly with Africans. Thus the young Sanjuan was horrified by South Carolina, which differed so sharply from what he had known in Cuba. He found it hard to fathom how and why "decent" folk of European ancestry treated those of African origin as less than human. Once, while a young man, he insisted his companions let him out of the car in which they were riding when they began shooting into "Nigger Town for sport."[94]

With the triumph of the revolution and Cuba becoming closer to the Soviet Union, it became even more imperative for Washington to erode its apartheid system, for now Jim Crow was becoming an ever more insistent stumbling block in the execution of U.S. foreign policy. As Guillén's reproachful words were published in Cuba, J. Edgar Hoover informed the White House in a "top secret" report that "Fidel Castro is very interested in the Negro problem in the United States," and "would like to see United States Negroes visit Cuba so that they could get a picture of how Cuba fights discrimination." U.S. Communists were "expected to assist in this Cuban project."[95] Hoover also had the gift of prophecy, for in coming years, Havana did reach out repeatedly to U.S. Negroes—even as they evolved into "African-Americans"—which became even more useful as they inched away from their previous skunk-at-the-party status.

The NAACP remained under pressure from the right wing and, having purged many from its ranks thought to be Communists, found it advantageous to put distance between itself and Havana,[96] though on the formal level the organization was agnostic toward the revolutionary government.[97] The NAACP had to tread carefully for, as their comrades in the Urban League in Miami pointed out in 1961, there were "racial implications" in "this Cuban refugee problem" that was now increasing. It seemed that in Jim Crow Florida, "the Cuban refugees who are colored" were "finding it harder to find jobs, places to live and schools to which to send their children" with apparent implications "from their treatment" for "lessons on the treatment of Negro Americans" in the state.[98]

Ben Davis, the leading black Communist on the mainland, was wildly enthusiastic about the new Cuba—though he was surprised when in July 1960 he greeted his sister, who had just returned from Havana and a convention of Negro doctors. Though she was no radical, she praised both Cuba and Castro. He told his sister that if he knew she was going there he would have given her a letter of introduction to Cuban Communist leaders, and—as the FBI listened intently via illicit means, probably most carefully when she called it astounding that power could be seized in a nation of millions by a few thousands—he expressed his own interest in a visit.[99] Soon—again by illegitimate means—the FBI captured Davis telling his spouse that he felt "good" since "last night was a big revelation to me. Castro's move to Harlem in the Theresa Hotel," during his 1960 visit, "has really got the pot boiling. All Harlem is excited about it & it has really united the Negroes, Cubans & Puerto Ricans together for the first time."[100] William Patterson, the Negro Communist who had first visited Cuba in the 1930s, was equally enthusiastic, particularly when in 1961 his youngest daughter continued a lengthy trend by marrying a Cuban, Roberto Camacho.[101]

But as the decades unwound, other African-Americans were not as sanguine about the regime, causing some in 2009 to enter a fray with a long historical pedigree—relations between islanders and mainlanders of African descent—with little apparent knowledge of same. Leading intellectuals, including Cornel West and Maya Angelou, accused the Havana government of being racist. In response Nancy Morejon and other Cubans disputed their accusation: "More than 350, 000 Cuban volunteers fought alongside their African brothers against colonialism. More than 2,000 combatants from the island died" in Africa doing so. "More than 350,000 young African students" were "trained in our schools over the last 40 years" and then there were "Cubans of African descent who were among the most afflicted victims of the colonial model" then prevailing, who had been uplifted since 1959. Recalled were the personal ties between Guillén and Hughes and Robeson. Acknowledged was an "objective discrimination, a phenomenon associated with poverty" that still existed.[102] Not mentioned was that "African-American" analyses of Cuba stretched back at least to Frederick Douglass and Martín Delany, continued with the 1898 war and the tragic events of 1912, accelerated in the 1930s, then reached an ignominious plateau with the curious sympathy in the 1950s for Colonel Batista. It would have been helpful—minimally—if contemporary critics of Cuba had nodded at least perfunctorily to this uneven history.

Still, this exchange demonstrated that a centuries-long relationship between islanders and mainlanders continued to resonate, even as the situation of Africans on both sides of the straits improved during this lengthy era. During this epoch, the exportation of slavery, then Jim Crow, declined, then disappeared. Yet, ironically, today there may be less contact between Africans on both sides of the straits than in the nineteenth century, when thousands of the enslaved were bought and sold in Havana and Pensacola and Galveston.

Notes

INTRODUCTION

1.   Throughout this book I use various designations to characterize those of African descent in the United States, including Negro, colored, black, and—when appropriate—African-American. Since a major theme of this book is Africans as commodities during the slavery era, whereby one could be a resident of the United States one day, Cuba the next, and perhaps Brazil after that, "African" may be the only signifier that can travel with these individuals as they cross boundaries. As for those of African descent residing in Cuba, see below. See also Horace Randall Williams, *No Man's Yoke on My Shoulders: Personal Accounts of Slavery in Florida*. Winston-Salem, NC: Blair, 2006.

2.   Edward Pierce to Salmon P. Chase, 8 March 1862, in John Niven, ed., *The Salmon P. Chase Papers*, vol. 2, *Correspondence, 1823–1857*. Kent, OH: Kent State University Press, 1994, 145–46.

3.   D. C. Corbitt, "Shipments of Slaves from the United States to Cuba, 1789–1807," *Journal of Southern History* 7/4 (November 1941): 540–49; Frances J. Stafford, "Illegal Importations: Enforcement of the Slave Trade Laws Along the Florida Coast, 1810–1828," *Florida Historical Quarterly* 46/2 (October 1967): 124–33; Daniel E. Meaders, "South Carolina Fugitives as Viewed Through Local Colonial Newspapers with Emphasis on Runaway Notices, 1732–1801," *Journal of Negro History* 60/2 (April 1975): 288–319, 304. Note presence in Carolina of a fugitive "born in Havana" who "speaks Spanish and French" and others "strongly suspected that they are going southward on their way to Havana." See also *The Liberator* [U.S.], 20 July 1860: "Slaves are regularly imported into Florida from Cuba. . . . This traffic is one of the streams that help to feed the slave trade between Africa and Cuba."

4.   Report, June–July 1854, Legajo Estado 8047, Archivo Historico Nacional–Madrid (hereinafter AHN-Madrid): "Juan Criollo, slave in Havana, alleged that he was born in Charleston, South Carolina, but as a child was sold improperly into slavery in Cuba." (All translations are by author unless indicated otherwise.) See also *The Liberator*, 11 August 1848 and 1 September 1848: "James Lytle," born in the United States, enslaved improperly in Cuba for the last decade or more. See also *The North Star*, 11 August 1848, where he is denoted as John Lytle. *The Liberator*, 7 June 1834: "A planter in Louisiana of forty years standing assured me that there are a set of miscreants in the city of New Orleans, who are connected with the slave traders of Cuba"—and trade Africans back and forth.

5.   *The Liberator*, 16 October 1863. See also *The Liberator*, 5 December 1862: "Southerners are beginning to run off their slaves and sell them to Cuba." *Richmond Enquirer*, 12 June 1863: "Selling Negroes in Cuba seen as alternative to colonizing them elsewhere as way to reduce their overall number in North America"; "Secret History of the Slave Trade to Cuba Written by an American Naval Officer, Robert

Wilson Schufeldt, 1861," *Journal of Negro History* 55/3 3, (July 1970): 218–35. See also "Registro de Pasaportes, 1861–1867," Box 21, Papers of Spanish Consulate, Charleston, Duke University. By 1865 a flood of U.S. Southerners were heading to Havana and Matanzas, with some heading to Barcelona.

6. Grant Thomas et al. to Hon. Charles Packer, 24 February 1863, Minutes of Assembly, 1862–1863, Barbados Department of Archives.

7. U.S. Congress, House of Representatives, 20th Congress, 1st Session, Rep. No. 270, 14 January 1828, American Antiquarian Society–Worcester, Massachusetts: "Anna Dubord of New Orleans took 13 slaves with her to Cuba on a journey to Cuba and now wants to return home and concerned about running afoul of laws concerning slave importation."

8. *The Liberator*, 3 November 1837. For a parallel account of this episode, see *The Colored American*, 21 October 1837.

9. Letter from E. Stephens, 23 April 1841, Roll 2, Despatches from U.S. Consuls in Santiago de Cuba, National Archives and Records Administration–College Park, Maryland. (Hereinafter denoted as NARA-CP.)

10. *The North Star*, 27 April 1849.

11. "Message of the President of the United States Communicating in Compliance with a Resolution of the Senate of the 5th Instant, a Report from the Secretary of State Upon the Subject of the Supposed Kidnapping of Colored Persons in the Southern States for the Purpose of Selling them as Slaves in Cuba," 15 March 1866, University of North Carolina–Chapel Hill. See also Report by Philip Sheridan, 14 March 1866 in John Y. Simon, ed., *The Papers of Ulysses S. Grant*, vol. 16:, 1866. Carbondale: Southern Illinois University Press, 1988, 192. "Concerning rumors of kidnapping of Negroes in Florida for sale as slaves." See also Edith M. Dabbs, *Sea Island History: A History of St. Helena's Island*, Spartansburg: repr., 1983, 120–21, 124, 146–47. During the war—and as federal troops approached the Carolina shore—some slaveholders warned the enslaved that the invaders would herd them into boats and ship them all to Cuba to a worse form of slavery. The press reported that one besieged slaveholder was actually assembling a cargo of Africans for transportation and sale in Cuba. See also Report from Spanish Legation in Washington, D.C., 11 May 1866, Box 5, Papers of Spanish Consulate, Charleston, Duke University: "Boat from Pensacola, Florida, with a cargo of Africans headed for Cuba." Anxiety by some U.S. Negroes about being sold into slavery in Cuba after the Civil War was so formidable that one U.S. diplomat in 1866 averred emphatically that "Mary Roberts, a free colored woman" from the mainland then residing in Santiago was *"not sane* on the subject of her fears of being sold into slavery." She was then earning "800 per month" as "an interpreter" but was not assuaged. Consul to Assistant Secretary of State, 27 May 1866, Roll 6, T55, *Despatches from U.S. Consuls in Santiago de Cuba*, National Archives and Archives Administration, College Park, MD. On post-1865 exporting of "slaves" from the United States to Cuba see James W. Cortada, "Florida's Relations with Cuba During the Civil War," *Florida Historical Quarterly* 59 (July 1980): 42–52, 49–50.

12. Margaret Ray to President Grant, 20 April 1872, in Simon, *The Papers of Ulysses S. Grant*, vol. 23: *February 1–December 31, 1872*, 75–76.

13. As noted below, the definition of what was "white" in the United States and Cuba often differed, so I will seek to be careful in deploying this freighted term; at times I will use the term "Euro-Americans" to designate those defined as "white" in the United States, though aware that our hemispheric neighbors often blanch understandably at the term "Americans" when arrogated by those in the mainland republic.

14. Caitlin A. Fitz, "Our Sister Republics: The United States in an Age of American Revolution," Ph.D. diss. Yale University, 2010, 288–89.

15. Peter M. Voelz, *Slave and Soldier: The Military Impact of Blacks in the Colonial Americas*. New York: Garland, 1993, 24.

16. Kathleen Deegan and Darcie MacMahon, *Fort Mose: Colonial America's Black Fortress of Freedom*, Gainesville: University Press of Florida, 1995.

17. Gerald Horne, *Negro Comrades of the Crown: African-Americans and the British Empire Fight the U.S. Before Emancipation*. New York: New York University Press, 2012, 35–36.

18. Hubert Aimes, *A History of Slavery in Cuba, 1511 to 1868*. New York: Putnam's, 1907, 249–50.

19. Jay Coughtry, *The Notorious Triangle: Rhode Island and the African Slave Trade, 1700–1807*. Philadelphia: Temple University Press, 1981, 174, 175. "By 1794, Rhode Island slave sales at Havana alone, superseded sales at all other ports combined. . . . Only Charleston offered any real competition to the Cuban market throughout the quarter-century ending with abolition of the slave trade in 1807, and that challenge was brief, lasting only from 1804 to 1807." See also Herbert Klein, "North American Competition and Characteristics of the African Slave Trade to Cuba, 1790 to 1794," *William and Mary Quarterly* 28 (January 1971): 86–102, 91. By 1794 the United States had the "lion's share" of the slave trade to Cuba. Likewise, by the early 1790s Cuba had begun to emerge as the major source of supply for the New Orleans slave trade, which in turn helped to supply the entire region. See Jean Pierre Leglaunec, "Slave Migration in Spanish and Early American Louisiana: New Sources and New Estimates," *Louisiana History* 46 (Spring 2005): 185–209, 188.

20. Louis A. Perez, Jr., *Cuba and the United States: Ties of Singular Intimacy*. Athens: University of Georgia Press, 2003, 8. Between 1512 and 1763, 60,000 Africans were enslaved in Cuba—in the next thirty-five years, almost 100,000. See also *Letters from the Havana During the Year 1820 Containing an Account of the Present State of the Island of Cuba and Observations on the Slave Trade*. London: Miller, 1821, 21, 26. After the Missouri Compromise and the augmenting of slavery it portended, the idea arose that Cuba could be a transit point for an influx of Africans into the republic. This was already occurring, for "in the past thirty years more than 900,000 Negroes have been brought from Africa to this island. . . . 60,000 more have perished in the transit." Florida-based slave traders, e.g. John and James Innerarity, had extensive holdings in Cuba. See C. L. Ogden to Amory, Callender and Co., 9 March 1815, Reel 1, *The Papers of Panton and Leslie and Company*, University of Alabama–Tuscaloosa.

21. Robert V. Haynes, "The Southwest and the War of 1812," *Louisiana History* 5/1 (Winter 1964): 41–51, 50. See also Jared W. Bradley, "W. C. C. Claiborne and Spain: Foreign Affairs Under Jefferson and Madison, 1801–1811," *Louisiana History* 12/4 (Autumn 1971): 297–314.

22. Isaac Joselin Cox, "The American Intervention in West Florida," *American Historical Review* 17/2 (January 1912): 290–311, 296. See also Wanjohi Waciuma, *Intervention in Spanish Floridas: A Study in Jeffersonian Foreign Policy*. Boston: Branden, 1976.

23. U.S. Consul to Naval Committee, 25 July 1806, Roll 1, T191, *Despatches from U.S. Consuls in Cape Town*, NARA-CP.

24. Report from Captain Brunswick Popham, HMS *Pelican*, 24 December 1838, in *British Parliamentary Papers, Correspondence with British Commissioners and with Foreign Powers Relative to the Slave Trade [Class A and Class B]*, vol. 17. Shannon: Irish University Press, 1968, 33.

25. *The Colored American*, 1 June 1839.

26. Report from Havana to Lord John Russell, 4 August 1840, CO318/149, National Archives of United Kingdom, London (hereinafter designated as NAUK).

27. Statement on Cuba, 1840, Joel Robert Poinsett Papers, Historical Society of Pennsylvania, Philadelphia.

28. *The Colored American*, 4 December 1841.

29. Report, 1 January 1841, in *British Parliamentary Paper:. Correspondence with British Commissioners and with Foreign Powers Relative to the Slave Trade [Class A and Class B], Volume 21*, Shannon: Irish University Press, 1969, 166–71.

30. Report by Lord Palmerston, 19 March 1849, in *British Parliamentary Papers: First and Second Reports from the Select Committee of the Slave Trade with Minutes of Evidence*, Appendix and Index, vol. 5. Shannon: Irish University Press, 1968, 16.

31. James W. Cortada, *Two Nations Over Time: Spain and the United States, 1776–1977*. Westport, CT: Greenwood, 1978, 60. By 1859 there were an estimated 2,500 U.S. nationals in Cuba. See Louis A. Perez, Jr., ed., *Impressions of Cuba in the Nineteenth Century: The Travel Diary of Joseph J. Dimock*, Wilmington, DE: Scholarly Resources, 1998, 40.

32. Sam McLean to William L. Marcy, 22 May 1854, *Despatches from U.S,. Consuls in Trinidad, Cuba*, Roll 1, T699, NARA-CP.

33. *The Liberator*, 15 March 1850.

34. *New York Times*, 27 February 1858. See also W. E. B. Du Bois, *The Suppression of the African Slave Trade to the United States of America, 1638–1870*. Baton Rouge: Louisiana State University Press, 1969, 161. Trade between New Orleans and Mobile, suggests the author, was actually a cover for the slave trade to Cuba.

35. Report, 1 June 1858, in *British Parliamentary Papers. Correspondence with British Commissioners and other Representatives Abroad and with Foreign Ministers Relative to the Slave Trade in Cuba [Class A and Class B]*,vol. 45. Shannon: Irish University Press, 1969, 166.

36. Sir Edward Thornton to Earl of Derby, 5 June 1876, in ibid., vol. 55, 171. U.S. ships sailing from New York to Rio de Janeiro were mostly involved in transporting enslaved Africans "from one Brazilian port to another."

37. Horne, *Negro Comrades of the Crown*, passim.

38. Speech of Mr. Joshua Giddings of Ohio, in the House of Representatives, March 16, 1854, American Antiquarian Society–Worcester, MA (hereafter designated as AAS).

39. Speech of Hon. William W. Boyce of South Carolina Delivered in the House of Representatives, January 15, 1855, Massachusetts Historical Society–Boston.

40. Dean B. Mahin, *Olive Branch and Sword: The United States and Mexico, 1845–1848*, Jefferson, NC: McFarland, 1997, 5–6, 11. Trist had varying ties with James Monroe, James Madison, Martín Van Buren and James Buchanan.

41. Report by J. Kennedy and C. J. Dalrymple, 27 October 1839, *British Parliamentary Papers. Correspondence with British Commissioners and with Foreign Powers Relative to the Slave Trade [Class A and Class B]*, vol. 18. Shannon: Irish University Press, 1968, 148–150. See also the astringent assailing of Trist in the *New York Commercial Advertiser*, 9 September 1839.

42. Reverend James Rawson, *Cuba*. New York: Lane & Tipper, 1847, AAS. The "celebrated bloodhounds" of Cuba "are very fierce and dangerous . . . generally kept for the purpose of hunting runaway slaves. When nearly grown, the dog is chained up, and a Negro is sent to worry him by whipping him and other means. After a long training, and when the dog has acquired a perfect hatred of his tormentor, the Negro whips him severely and then runs to a great distance and climbs a tree. The dog is now set loose, and follows his track, nor will he leave the tree until he is taken away, or the Negro descends." See also *The Liberator*, 9 April 1841: Florida "taxed to pay for the importation of Cuba bloodhounds to trail runaway slaves." And in the same periodical, 10 July 1840 edition: "Floridians journey to Cuba to buy bloodhounds." See also James W. Covington, "Cuban Bloodhounds and the Seminoles," *Florida Historical Quarterly* 33/2 (October 1954): 111–19. See also Cornelia B. Jenks, *The*

Land of the Sun, or, What Kate and Willie Saw There. Boston: Crosby, Nichols, Lee, 1860, 57. In Matanzas, "the bloodhound named Harold, was indeed a faithful watchdog; he would not allow any strange Negro to enter the doors unnoticed." These Cuban beasts were also discerning: see Mary G. Davis Journal Typescript, 1861–1863, Massachusetts Historical Society–Boston: "The bloodhound never attacks a white man for a Negro on the darkest night." Gary W. McDonogh, ed., *The Florida Negro: A Federal Writers' Project Legacy*, Jackson: University Press of Mississippi, 1993, 25: In 1837, bloodhounds were brought from Cuba "and loosened in [the] St. Johns River area to regain a number of Indians who had escaped into the country occupied jointly by Seminole Indians and Free Negroes."

43. Charles Stearns, *Facts in the Life of General Taylor; The Cuba Blood-Hound Importer, the Extensive Slave Holder and the Hero of the Mexican War!!* Boston: CS, 1848, Historical Society of Pennsylvania–Philadelphia.

44. Samuel B. Smith, *Rosamond: Or a Narrative of the Captivity and Sufferings of an American Female Under the Popish Priests in the Island of Cuba*. New York: Leavitt, Lord, 1836, 188: "Those who eat bought and eat them, said they were the best they ever eat. They called them French sausages."

45. Clipping, n.d., and Henry E. Palmer, "The Proctors—A True Story of Antebellum Days and Since," 13 April 1933. "Proctor," Vertical File, St. Augustine Historical Society–Florida. See also Lee H. Warner, *Free Men in an Age of Servitude: Three Generations of a Black Family*. Lexington: University Press of Kentucky, 1992, 18; and Kathleen Deegan and Darcie MacMahon, 37: After the United States seized Florida, "all of the [African] inhabitants of the Spanish colony left their homes and sailed to Cuba. . . . Some of the [Africans] settled in the Matanzas province." See also Ruth B. Barr and Modeste Hargis, "The Voluntary Exile of Free Negroes of Pensacola," *Florida Historical Quarterly* 17 (July 1938): 3–14.

46. Howard Jones, *Mutiny on the* Amistad*: The Saga of a Slave Revolt and its Impact on American Abolition, Law and Diplomacy*. New York: Oxford University Press, 1988. See also Marcus Rediker, *The Amistad Rebellion: An Atlantic Odyssey of Slavery and Freedom*, New York: Viking, 2012.

47. *The Liberator*, 9 August 1861. For another account of this incident, see *Frederick Douglass Monthly*, September 1861.

48. Daniel L. Schaffer, "'A Class of People Neither Freemen nor Slaves': From Spanish to American Race Relations in Florida, 1821–1861," *Journal of Social History* 26/3 (Spring 1993): 587–609, 387.

49. Report on the insubordination of some Negroes in Charleston, 14 July 1849, Asutnos Politicos, Legajo 215, Numero de Orden 15, Archivo Nacional–Havana (hereafter ANC). At a detention center a Negro fellow had been sentenced to be hung for an assault on two police officers but he became unruly and was joined by about thirty others, who used hammers in an attempt to escape.

50. Report, 7 March 1823, Asuntos Politicos, Legajo 113, Numero de Orden 58, ANC.

51. Report, 5 April 1836, Asuntos Politicos, Legajo 36, Numero de Orden, 35, ANC.

52. Report, 3 May 1844, Asuntos Politicos, Legajo 140, Numero de Orden 140, ANC.

53. Report, 9 May 1844, Asuntos Politicos, Legajo 140, Numero de Orden 34, ANC.

54. William E. Farrison, "William Wells Brown in Buffalo," *Journal of Negro History* 39/4 (October 1954): 298–314, 305. In 1840, the Negro activist and intellectual William Wells Brown visited Cuba and Haiti. During the same period, the noted Negro abolitionist Henry Highland Garnet made two journeys to Cuba: See W. M. Brewer, "Henry Highland Garnet," *Journal of Negro History* 113/1 (January 1928): 36–52, 40.

55. John C. Calhoun to Franklin Gage, 25 April 1844, in Clyde Wilson et al., eds., *The Papers of John C. Calhoun*, vol. 28. Columbia: University of South Carolina Press, 328.

56. John C. Calhoun to Thomas M. Rodney, 4 May 1844, in ibid., 436.

57. Roger W. Hite, "'Stand Still and See the Salvation': The Rhetorical Design of Martín Delany's 'Blake,'" *Journal of Black Studies* 5/2 (December 1976): 192–202, 200–201.

58. Lisa Brock, "Back to the Future: African-Americans and Cuba in the Time(s) of Race," *Contributions in Black Studies: A Journal of African and Afro-American Studies* 12/1 (1994): 9–32, 16.

59. Martín Delany, *Blake or the Huts of America*. Boston: Beacon Press, 1970. Originally published in 1861.

60. David Luis Brown, "An 1848 for the Americas: The Black Atlantic, 'El Negro Martír' and Cuban Exile Anticolonialism in New York City," *American Literary History* 21/3 (Fall 2009): 431–63, 438.

61. *Provincial Freeman*, 13 October 1855.

62. *The Liberator*, 24 December 1836.

63. David Turnbull, *Travels in the West. Cuba; with Notices of Porto Rico and the Slave Trade*, London: Longman, Orne, Brown, Green and Longmans, 1840, 92.

64. *The Liberator*, 15 October 1841. See also Kenneth F. Kiple, *Blacks in Colonial Cuba, 1774–1899*. Gainesville: University Press of Florida, 1976, 51.

65. Theodore G. Vincent, *The Legacy of Vicente Guerrero: Mexico's First Black President*. Gainesville: University Press of Florida, 2001.

66. Report from London, 25 May 1853, Legajo Estado 8048, AHN-Madrid.

67. "Report from Santiago for the Captain General on emissaries of Desalines who are seeking to organize a slave revolt," 25 March 1807, Asuntos Politicos, Legajo 138, Numero de Orden, 138, ANC. See also Proclamation, 15 April 1811, Asuntos Politicos, Legajo 213, Numero de Orden 29, ANC: "On the proclamation of the Negro Cristobal as King of Haiti with the name Henry I." See also Captain General to Santiago, 15 October 1811, Asuntos Politicos, Legajo 213, Numero de Orden 156, ANC: "Guidelines on the conduct that should be observed by boats with Mulatos and Negros from Haiti visiting Cuba"; Report, 27 August 1830, Asuntos Politicos, Legajo 121, Numero de Orden 12, ANC: "Concerning the hostilities of the Africans of Santo Domingo toward Cuba."

68. Report, 13 September 1802, Asuntos Politicos, Legajo 8, Numero de Orden 50, ANC: "Barring the disembarking of los Negro insurrectos . . ."

69. Report to San Puerto Principe, 23 February 1812, Asuntos Politicos, Legajo 214, Numero de Orden 46, ANC: "Concerning the uprising of the Africans and the participation of Hilario Herrera, alias el Ingles." See also Report on the Aponte Revolt, 5 April 1812, Legajo 12, Numero de Orden 23; and also on the Aponte revolt, Report, 25 March 1812, Asuntos Politicos, Legajo 12, Numero de Orden 18, ANC.

70. John E. Baur, "Faustin Soulouque, Emperor of Haiti, His Character and His Reign," *The Americas* 6/2 (October 1949): 131–66, 147.

71. "Dedicated to the Press and People of the United States by the Editors of 'La Verdad,'" ca. 1849, Phillips Library–Salem, MA.

72. Report, 8 July 1862, Despatches from Haiti, Ministerio de Asuntos Exteriores–Madrid (hereafter designated as MAE–Madrid): Bar Haiti from "enviar una expedicion al mando de una Garibaldi Negro a sublevar las plantaciones de nuestras prosperas colonias." Madrid's fear of U.S. Negroes moving to Hispaniola was substantial. See Memorandum, 23 October 1860, Box 5, Papers of Spanish Consulate in Charleston, Duke University.

73. Horne, *Negro Comrades of the Crown*, passim.

74. *Frederick Douglass Monthly*, February 1863.

75. See contract between State Bank of Charleston and I.M. Morales and Company of Havana, 4 February 1861, Box 5, Papers of Spanish Consulate in Charleston, Duke University.

76. John S .C. Abbott, *South and North; Or Impressions Received During a Trip to Cuba and the South*, New York: Abbey & Abbot, 1860, 52.

77. Letter, 24 November 1869, Folder 4, Records of Churchill, Brown & Manson Company, G.W. Blunt White Library, Mystic, CT. This firm, whose main office was sited in Portland, Maine, engaged in substantial trade with Cuba involving sugar and molasses and the exportation of lumber, hogsheads, and the like. In 1869 a number of their estates were torched in Cuba in the midst of a "slave conspiracy" in Sagua La Grande.

78. Canter Brown, Jr., *Florida's Black Public Officials, 1867–1924*. Tuscaloosa: University of Alabama Press, 1998, 69–70, 75, 88, 97, 116, Jose Juan Figueroa, born in 1855 in Cuba was a councilman in Key West in 1875–1876. Heraldo Hernandez, born in 1838, was a councilman in Pensacola in 1869 and a county commissioner in 1873–74. Salvador T. Pons, born in 1835 in Mexico, served in the state legislature representing Escambia in 1868 and on the city council of Pensacola in 1868–69.

79. Paul Ortiz, *Emancipation Betrayed: The Hidden History of Black Organizing and White Violence in Florida from Reconstruction to the Bloody Elections of 1920*. Berkeley: University of California Press, 2005, 39–40.

80. Emetetrio S. Sanovenia, *Lincoln in Martí: A Cuban View of Abraham Lincoln*. Chapel Hill: University of North Carolina Press, 1953, 41. Martí "considered Lincoln inclined to view ignorance and justice in light of what would be beneficial to his country even though detrimental to another country. The basis for this belief was the President's plan to remove the newly freed colored people from the United States."

81. Henry Turner et al. to President Grant, 25 November 1873, in John Y. Simon, ed., *The Papers of Ulysses S. Grant*, vol. 24: *1873*. Carbondale: Southern Illinois University Press, 2000, 247. In the same volume, see the excerpt from the diary of Hamilton Fish, 19 February 1873, 209–10: "A delegation of prominent colored men, representing in part in the Cuban Anti-Slavery Society of New York" presents a petition demanding belligerent rights for Cuban rebels. See also *St. Louis Democrat*, 20 February 1873.

82. John White to President Grant, 17 November 1873, in Simon, *The Papers of Ulysses S. Grant*, vol. 24: *1873*, 247.

83. Antonio Gallenga, *The Pearl of Antilles*. London: Chapman and Hall, 1873, 158.

84. Francis L. Norton, "Cuban Question," New York, 1873, New York Historical Society–Manhattan.

85. Fernando Calderon y Collantes to Hamilton Fish, 3 February 1876, in U.S. Congress, Senate, 54th Congress, Senate Document no. 213, Message from the President of the United States, Brown University, Providence, RI.

86. Joe M. Richardson, *The Negro in the Reconstruction of Florida, 1865–1877*. Tallahassee: Florida State University Press, 1965, 181, 183.

87. Bess Beatty, "John Willis Menard: A Progressive Black in Post–Civil War Florida" *Florida Historical Quarterly* 59/2 (October 1980): 123–43, 123.

88. Lawrence E. Prescott, "Journeying Through Jim Crow: Spanish American Travelers in the United States during the Age of Segregation," *Latin American Research Review* 42/1 (2007): 3–28, 8.

89. *New York Age*, 1 December 1888.

90. *New York Evening Post*, 7 June 1898.

91. Willard B. Gatewood, Jr., *Black Americans and the White Man's Burden, 1898–1903*. Urbana: University of Illinois Press, 1975, 17, 18.

92. *New York Amsterdam News*, 14 February 1953.

93. *Norfolk Journal and Guide*, 30 October 1926.

94. Mark A. Sanders, *A Black Soldier's Story: The Narrative of Ricardo Batrell and the Cuban War of Independence*. Minneapolis: University of Minnesota Press, 2010, xxiii.

95. Philip S. Foner, *The Spanish–Cuban–American War and the Birth of American Imperialism*, vol. 1: *1895–1898*. New York: Monthly Review Press, 1972, 417.

96. Paula J. Giddings, *Ida: A Sword Among Lions*. New York: Amistad, 2008, 378.

97. Walter Barker to U.S. State Department, 9 May 1896, Roll 4, T583, NARA–CP.

98. Interrogation of Reverend A. J. Diaz, ca. 1896 in U.S. Senate, 55th Congress, 2nd Session, Report no. 885, "Report of the Committee on Foreign Relations . . . Relative to Affairs in Cuba," 1898, Kansas Historical Society–Topeka.

99. *Baltimore Afro-American*, 8 April 1899. In Cuba "one can see colored men in all professions and trades. As an artisan, such as tailors, masons, carpenters, cigar makers and in other branches where skilled labor is required he can be found in any part of Havana. It seems though that he excels best as a musician. . . . I find him in every orchestra of prominence in the city." In Havana "one can see some prejudice, but not the uncalled for prejudice as in the States. There are no separate cars and such. . . . That practice has not been dreamed of in this country."

100. *Baltimore Afro-American*, 2 July 1898. The sight of armed Negroes guarding Spanish prisoners of war was upsetting to some: "In times of war, in times of national peril, provincial prejudices and easy-going conservatism of all sorts are suddenly and rudely shaken in the storm."

101. Michael C. Robinson and Frank N. Shubert, "David Fagen: An Afro-American Rebel in the Philippines, 1899–1901," *Pacific Historical Review* 44/1 (February 1975): 68–83, 70.

102. Leonardo Acosta, *Cubano Be, Cubano Bop: One Hundred Years of Jazz in Cuba*. Washington, D.C.: Smithsonian, 2003, 3, 5, 6, 103. "Santiago Smood, a black American musician . . . arrived in 1898 and lived in Santiago, Cuba. . . . [He] sang the blues and played the banjo and in Oriente he learned to play the *tres* (a guitar with double–strings) and to sing in Spanish. He moved to Cuba" where he became an exemplar of a growing phenomenon—a "Cubanized African American"; he died in Havana in 1929. Jelly Roll Morton, a founder of this new music, also acknowledged the Cuban influence. W. C. Handy brought a band to Cuba in 1900. See Eileen Southern, "Letters from W.C. Handy to William Grant Still," *Black Perspective in Music*, 7 (Fall 1979): 199–234.

103. Peter C. Bjarkman, *A History of Cuban Baseball, 1864–2006*. Jefferson, NC: McFarland, 2007, 27, 29, 85.

104. Adrian Burgos, "Playing Ball in a Black and White 'Field of Dreams': Afro-Caribbean Ballplayers in the Negro Leagues, 1910–1950," *Journal of Negro History* 82/1 (Winter 1997): 67–104, 85. "Ray Dandridge learned Spanish well enough to manage teams comprised mostly of Latinos." Also fluent in the language were Brooklyn Dodgers stars Roy Campanella and Joe Black, U.S. Negroes who in turn translated for Sandy Amoros when he joined the squad. *Pittsburgh Courier*, 30 August 1952.

105. Corporal W.T. Goode, *The Eighth Illinois*. Chicago: Blakely, 1899, 239, 283.

106. Charles E. Wynes, "John Stephens Durham, Black Philadelphian: At Home and Abroad," *Pennsylvania Magazine of History and Biography* 106/4 (October 1982): 527–37, 535.

107. Clipping, 27 December 1898, Scrapbook, ca. 1898–99, Box 1, Elmer Roberts Papers, University of North Carolina–Chapel Hill: "Riotous Negroes fired on" and "loot a Spanish restaurant and stab its owner." In the same collection, see clipping, ca. 15 February 1899: "Color line in Havana café. American proprietor refuses to serve drinks to the Cuban General Ducasse. . . . Holman's Washington café in Central Park has been ordered closed by Senor Federico Mora, Civil Service Governor of Havana, because of the refusal of the proprietor to serve drinks to a mulatto, the Cuban General Ducasse. . . . As the existing Spanish laws prohibit race discrimination," this

was protested vigorously. "Mr. Holman, who is an American, says he will reopen, asserting that he is sustained by the American authorities."

108. See Lewis Pinckney Jones, "Carolinians and Cubans," Ph.D. diss., University of North Carolina–Chapel Hill, 1952; Stephen Kantrowitz, *Ben Tillman and the Reconstruction of White Supremacy*, Chapel Hill: University of North Carolina Press, 2000.

109. Report, 30 July 1912, Despatches from Cuba, MAE–Madrid.

110. See Louis A. Perez, Jr., "Politics, Peasants and People of Color: The 1912 'Race War' in Cuba Reconsidered," *Hispanic American Historical Review* 66/3 (August 1986): 509–39; Aline Helg, *Our Rightful Share: The Afro–Cuban Struggle for Equality, 1886–1912*. Chapel Hill: University of North Carolina Press, 1995.

111. *Pittsburgh Courier*, 14 June 1912.

112. *Baltimore Afro-American*, 5 October 1912. Strikingly, the U.S.-controlled Cuba Company demanded that the recently organized political party that spoke to the concerns of Cubans of color be squashed. See Manager of "Igenio Jatibonico" to George Whigham, 25 May 1912, Box 15, Cuba Company Papers, University of Maryland–College Park.

113. *Baltimore Afro-American*, 15 June 1912: "The dark cloud of race hate is spreading and our hope is the good sense of the world will destroy it like it did slavery."

114. William Upshur to "Dear Mother," 12 January 1916, Box 2, Folder 16, William Upshur Papers, University of North Carolina–Chapel Hill. Writing from Haiti, he wrote: "We are living very comfortably . . . everything has been great here." As for the "dark republic," he noted, "many of our little foraging parties reminded me of Dixon's 'Leopard Spots' and the Ku Klux Clan [*sic*]—we have a number of bad men, badly wanted by the authorities.... The white man is on the job day and night."

115. Biography File: Manuel Cabeza, Clipping, 28 May 2000, Monroe County Public Library–Key West.

116. Robert Robinson, *Black on Red: My 44 Years Inside the Soviet Union*. Washington, D.C.: Acropolis, 1988, 29, 31. His mother hailed from Hispaniola and his father was Jamaican and grew up in Cuba and thus spoke Spanish. His encounter was not unusual in that U.S. Negroes often reported that they could escape the highest form of persecution by masquerading as Cubans or Spanish-speakers generally. See Kenneth W. Mack, *Representing the Race: The Creation of the Civil Rights Lawyer*, Cambridge, MA: Harvard University Press, 2012, 33–34. During the same era, the eminent Raymond Pace Alexander, a Negro attorney, was able to escape the strictures of Jim Crow in Philadelphia by speaking Spanish. See also Babs Gonzalez, *I Paid My Dues: Good Times . . . No Bread*, New York: Lancer, 1967. This leading musician, born Lee Brown in Newark, altered his name to Gonzalez in order to escape the quotidian oppression heaped upon U.S. Negroes.

117. Adrian Burgos, *Cuban Star: How One Negro League Owner Changed the Face of Baseball*. New York: Hill and Wang, 2011, 200.

118. Marvin Dunn, "The Illusion of Moderation: A Recounting and Reassessing of Florida's Racial Past," in Irvin D. S. Winnsboro, ed., *Old South, New South or Down South? Florida and the Modern Civil Rights Movement*. Morgantown: West Virginia University Press, 2009, 22–46, 26. On the frankly terrorist means used to oust Spain from Florida, see Frank Marotti, *The Cana Sanctuary: History, Diplomacy and Black Catholic Marriage in Antebellum St. Augustine, Florida*. Tuscaloosa: University of Alabama Press, 2012.

119. James Weldon Johnson, *Along this Way: An Autobiography*. New York: Viking, 1933, 3, 58, 59.

120. See Gerald Horne, *Powell v. Alabama: The Scottsboro Boys and American Justice*. New York: Watts, 1997; Gerald Horne, *Black Revolutionary: William Patterson and*

the Globalization of the African American Freedom Struggle, Urbana: University of Illinois Press, 2013. .

121. *Chicago Defender*, 30 April 1932: "32 Cuban writers and journalists cable the Alabama governor protesting Scottsboro." *Chicago Defender*, 20 February 1934: "Cubans demonstrate militantly at the Havana office of a U.S. steamship company, protesting Scottsboro: windows and doors smashed."

122. Minutes of the Central Committee of the Communist Party of the United States, 8 December 1934, Reel 268, Records of the Communist Party–USA, Library of Congress, Washington, D.C.

123. Gerald Horne, *Red Seas: Ferdinand Smith and Radical Black Sailors in the United States and Jamaica*. New York: New York University Press, 2005. See also Harry Haywood, *Black Bolshevik: Autobiography of an Afro-American Communist*. Chicago: Liberator, 1978. The author, a sailor, arrived in Havana in March 1946 and visited Red headquarters "located in what appeared to be an old mansion" where he conferred with leader Blas Roca, a "light brown mulatto . . . short and stocky build" who asked about a U.S. comrade "James Ford, whom he knew. Ford had attended a congress of the Cuban party as a fraternal delegate several years before. . . . We had talked for about an hour," then he "stopped to look at the statue of Antonio Maceo on horseback."

124. John J. Munro, "The Anticolonial Front: Cold War Imperialism and the Struggle Against Global White Supremacy, 1945–1960," Ph.D. diss., University of California–Santa Barbara, 2009, 102. This point was confirmed by Ms. Jackson in a conversation with the author on 13 October 2011 at the Tamiment Institute at New York University.

125. *Pittsburgh Courier*, 19 July 1947.

126. *Pittsburgh Courier*, 25 January 1947: "Blas Roca, General Secretary of the Communist Party; Jesus Menendez, leader of 500,000 sugar plantation workers; Lázaro Peña , General Secretary of the Confederation of Cuban Workers and Garcia Aguero, Communist Senator. All are voluble opponents of Yankee imperialism."

127. *Pittsburgh Courier*, 1 November 1947.

128. *Atlanta Daily World*, 12 July 1947.

129. Juan Pastor Diaz y Diaz to Harry S. Truman and Members of Congress, 25 July 1948, OF (Official File), Box 769, Harry S. Truman Presidential Library–Independence, Missouri.

130. Text of Resolution and Letter, 9 December 1947, Reel 9, #751, Confidential U.S. State Departments Central Files, Cuba: Internal Affairs and Foreign Affairs, 1945–1948. University of North Carolina–Chapel Hill.

131. "Protests of the incident involving Congressman Arthur Mitchell at the Hotel Saratoga in Havana, 2 December 1937–13 January 1938," Legajo 39, Numero de Orden 14, Secretariat of the Presidency, ANC. See also *Diario de la Marina*, 1 January 1938. See also Frank Andre Guidry, *Forging Diaspora: Afro–Cubans and African–Americans in a World of Empire and Jim Crow*, Chapel Hill: University of North Carolina Press, 2010.

132. Francisco Rodriguez, Oral History, 18 June 1983, University of South Florida–Tampa; Reverend C. K. Steele to Roy Wilkins, 26 September 1956, Group III, A276, NAACP Papers, Library of Congress: "Our fight here in Tallahassee against segregation continues. . . . The trials for the eleven of us . . . put off. . . . Attorney Rodriguez from Tampa was here last week and conferenced [*sic*] with our attorney." The bus boycott in Tallahassee in some ways outstripped the one occurring in neighboring Montgomery that catapulted Dr. Martín Luther King Jr. into prominence. The absence of Spanish surnames at times has masked the presence

among U.S. Negroes of Cubans of African ancestry; for example, the leading novelist Paule Marshall, whose father was Cuban. Lawrence P. Jackson, *The Indignant Generation: A Narrative History of African American Writers and Critics, 1934–1960*. Princeton: Princeton University Press, 2011, 494.

133. *Atlanta Daily World*, 18 August 1948.

134. *Atlanta Daily World*, 11 September 1951.

135. *Atlanta Daily World*, 16 June 1949.

136. Quoted in Adrian Burgos, Jr., "An Uneven Playing Field: Afro-Latinos in Major League Baseball," in Miriam Jiminez Roman and Juan Flores, eds., *The Afro-Latin@ Reader: History and Culture in the United States*. Durham, NC: Duke University Press, 2010, 127–41, 135–36.

137. Howard Johnson, 6 June 1988, Oral History of the American Left, New York University.

138. *New York Amsterdam News*, 29 March 1958.

139. C. D. Jackson to "Dear Harry," 16 February 1962, Box 69, *C.D.* Jackson Papers, Dwight D. Eisenhower Presidential Library–Abilene, Kansas.

140. *Charleston News and Courier*, 3 August 1957.

141. *Charleston News and Courier*, 16 January 1958.

142. Gerald Horne, *Black and Red: W. E .B. Du Bois and the Afro-American Response to the Cold War, 1944–1963*. Albany: State University of New York Press, 1986.

143. Jose Felipe Carneado, "La Discriminacion Racial en Cuba no Volvera Jamas," *Cuba Socialista* 2 (January 1962): 168–82. See also Louis A. Perez, Jr., *The War of 1898: The United States and Cuba in History and Historiography*. Chapel Hill: University of North Carolina Press, 1998, 127.

144. Eliseo Riera–Gomez, "Batista and Communism," n.d., Drew Pearson Papers, University of Texas–Austin.

145. Blas Roca, *The Cuban Revolution: Report to the Eighth National Congress of the Popular Socialist Party of Cuba*. New York: New Century, 1961, 71.

146. Thomas Sumter to "Sir," 13 May 1815, Box 1, William Crawford Papers–Duke University. See also David Luis Brown, "An 1848 for the Americas," 438: "Anglo North Americans often viewed light-skinned Cuban Creoles not as whites, as they conceived of themselves but instead as members of a third, Iberian race."

147. Ray Allen Billington, *The Protestant Crusade, 1800–1860: A Study of the Origins of American Nativism*. Chicago: Quadrangle, 1964. See also By a Citizen of Cambridgeport, *A Journal of a Tour From Boston to Savannah Thence to Havana*. Cambridge, NA: Author, 1849, 45, Western Reserve Historical Society: "The only religion tolerated here is Roman Catholic."

148. Philip Wayne Powell, *Tree of Hate: Propaganda and Prejudices Affecting United States Relations with the Hispanic World* Albuquerque: University of New Mexico Press, 2008; Margaret R. Greer et al., eds., *Rereading the Black Legend: The Discourses of Religious and Racial Difference in the Renaissance Empires*. Chicago: University of Chicago Press, 2007. See also Margaret C. Florence, *The Life, Career and Awful Death by the Garote* [sic] *of Margaret C. Waldegrave*. New Orleans: Orton, 1853. A lurid tale that presents Cuba in a highly unflattering light—they even execute white women!

149. Letter from Nicholas Trist, 4 December 1834, Box 3, Nicholas Trist Papers, University of North Carolina–Chapel Hill.

150. To "Dear Cousin," 10 May 1809, Carter–Danforth Papers, Rhode Island Historical Society–Providence.

151. Citizen of Cambridgeport, *A Journal of a Tour from Boston to Savannah*, 60.

152. Demoticus Philaethes, *Yankee Travels Through the Islands of Cuba, or the Men and Government, the Laws and Customs of Cuba, as Seen by American Eyes*. New

York: Appleton, 1856, 319 314. "It very seldom happens that I pass before a cluster of Spaniards, especially soldiers, seamen or storekeepers, without hearing insulting words addressed to me . . . trusting that I would not understand them."

153.   Alexander Humboldt, *Island of Cuba*, New York: Derby & Jackson, 1856, 43.

154.   Joseph J. Dimock, "Impressions of Cuba," in John Jenkins, ed., *Travelers' Tales of Old Cuba*, Melbourne: Ocean Press, 2010, 64–78, 71, 67.

155.   "Mary G. Davis Journal Typescript," 15 February 1861, Massachusetts Historical Society–Boston.

156.   Martín Delany, *Blake or the Huts of America*, 63, 237: "These mongrel Creoles are incapable of self-government and should be compelled to submit to the United States. . . . One of the hateful customs of the place is that you must exchange civilities with whomever solicits it, consequently, the most stupid and ugly Negro you meet in the street may ask for a 'light' from your cigar. . . . I invariably comply but as invariably throw away my cigar! If this were all, it would not be so bad, but then the idea of meeting Negroes and mulattoes at the levees of the Captain General is intolerable! It will never do to permit this state of things so near our own shores." Delany added, "Were Cubans classified according to their complexion or race, three out of five of the inhabitants called white would decidedly be claimed by the colored people, though there is a larger number much fairer than those classified and known in the register as colored."

157.   Maturin M. Ballou, *Due South or Cuba Past and Present*. Boston: Houghton Mifflin, 1888, 62; Herbert Klein, *Slavery in the Americas: A Comparative Study of Virginia and Cuba*. Chicago: University of Chicago Press, 1967, 226. In Cuba, says Klein, "the fundamental criteria for ranking an individual were not his racial attributes [*sic*] but his cultural and economic background."

158.   Carleton Beals, *The Crime of Cuba*. Philadelphia: Lippincott, 1933, 56. This fundamental definitional difference is a major reason why it is so difficult to formulate a descriptor that covers adequately large groups of individuals in Cuba, e.g. "Afro-Cuban." Given the tenor of this book, which mostly involves examining U.S.-Cuban relations from the viewpoint of "African-Americans," I will lean toward the latter's definitions, though cautiously. See Michelle A. Hay, *"I've Been Black in Two Countries": Black Cuban Views on Race in the U.S.*. El Paso, TX: LFB Scholarly Publishing, 2009.

159.   Oliver C. Cox, "Race Relations," *Journal of Negro Education* 12/2 (Spring 1941): 144–53, 144.

160.   Fernando Ortiz, "On the Relations between Blacks and Whites." Washington, D.C.: Division of Intellectual Cooperation, Pan American Union, Number 7, October 1943, Biblioteca Jose Martí–Havana.

161.   Bernardo Ruiz Suarez, *The Color Question in the Two Americas*. New York: Hunt, 1922, 22. See also Darien J. Davis, "Nationalism and Civil Rights in Cuba: A Comparative Analysis, 1930–1960," *Journal of Negro History* 83/ 1 (Winter 1998): 35–51, 40. "For many Cubans racial affirmation did not mean that blacks should be proud of being of African descent, but rather that they should not feel ashamed of it."

1. SPANISH FLORIDA FALLS, CUBA NEXT?

1.   Daniel Horsmanden, ed., *The New York Conspiracy or a History of the Negro Plot with the Journal of the Proceedings Against the Conspirators at New York in the Years 1741–1742*. New York: Southwick & Pelsue, 1810, 28. For useful photocopies of eighteenth-century documents from the archive at Seville, see Box 1, William W. Pierson Papers, University of North Carolina–Chapel Hill.

2. Samuel McKee, *Labor in Colonial New York, 1664–1776*. New York: Columbia University Press, 1935, 136. "The freedom or slavery of captured Spanish Negroes, Indians and mulattoes was a constant problem in New York City . . . during the trial of Negroes for the so–called plot of 1741, the freedom of some accused Spanish Negroes was of utmost importance because, if they were free, the testimony of slaves could not be admitted against them."

3. Matthew Restall, "Black Conquistadors: Armed Africans in Early Spanish America," *The Americas* 57/2 (October 2000): 171–205, 172. See also Jack D. Forbes, "Black Pioneers: The Spanish-Speaking Afroamericans of the Southwest," *Phylon* 27/3 (1966): 233–46; and "Military Manpower in Florida, 1670–1703," *El Escribano* 8/2 (April 1971): 55–56.

4 See *Council Journal, Upper House*, 2 February 1739, South Carolina Department of Archives and History–Columbia. "Dangers we are exposed to by the Spaniards giving open protection & encouragement to the Negroes who desert from this province." See also Gerald Horne, *The Counter-Revolution of 1776: Slave Resistance and the Origins of the U.S.A.*, New York: New York University Press, 2014; Peter Wood, *Black Majority: Negroes in Colonial South Carolina from 1670 Through the Stono Rebellion*. New York: Knopf, 1974.

5. See "Ex Parte Seventeen Indians, Molattos [sic] & Negroes," 23 September 1746, in Charles Merrill Hough, ed., *Reports of Cases in the Vice Admiralty of the Province of New York and in the Court of Admiralty of the State of New York, 1711–1788*. New Haven: Yale University Press, 1925, 29–31. A vessel "belonging to the King of Spain" was seized and those aboard were brought to Manhattan, "& seven of them adjudged to be slaves by this Court." In response, "sundry letters" from Cuba arrived "certifying that Seventeen of the said Twenty" are not slaves, leading to controversy. See also *Council Journal*, 25 July 1734, South Carolina Department of Archives and History–Columbia, for more conflict involving ships from Cuba.

6. See *The Capture of Havana in 1762 by the Forces of George III*, 1898 Massachusetts Historical Society–Boston. A version of this document, originally published in 1762, is also at Tulane University. Also see *A Correct Journal of the Landing of His Majesty's Forces on the Island of Cuba and of the Siege and Surrender of the Havannah* [sic], *August 13, 1762*. London: Green and Russell, 1762. See also *The Two Putnams, Israel and Rufus in the Havana Expedition, 1762*; Hartford: Connecticut Historical Society, 1762; and Bruce Campbell MacGunnigle, ed., *Red Coat and Yellow Fever: Rhode Island Troops in the Siege of Havana, 1762*, Providence, RI: Webster Press, 1991; Nelson Vance Russell, "The Reaction in England and America to the Capture of Havana, 1762," *Hispanic American Historical Review* 9/3 (August 1929): 303–16.

7. Thomas N. Ingersoll, "The Slave Trade and the Ethnic Diversity of Louisiana's Slave Community," *Louisiana History* 37/2 (Spring 1996): 133–61, 141: "The British poured thousands of slaves into Cuba, for example, while it remained in their possession." See also Hubert H. S. Aimes, *A History of Slavery in Cuba*. New York: Putnam's, 1907, 27; Gregory E. O'Malley, "Beyond Middle Passage: Slave Migration from the Caribbean to North America, 1619–1807," *William and Mary Quarterly* 66/1 (January 2009): 125–72, 155, 156. There was a spectacular jump in imports to Florida from 1766 to 1770, during London's reign.

8. See David Eltis, "The Nineteenth-Century Trans-Atlantic Slave Trade: An Annual Time Series of Imports into the Americas Broke Down by Region," *Hispanic American Historical Review* 67/1 (February 1987): 109–38; Herbert S. Klein, "North American Competition and the Characteristics of the African Slave Trade to Cuba, 1790 to 1794," *William and Mary Quarterly* 28 (1971): 93–110.

9.   Jane Landers, "Traditions of African American Freedom and Community in Spanish
     Colonial Florida," in David R. Colburn et al., eds., *The African American Heritage of
     Florida*. Gainesville: University Press of Florida, 1995, 17–41, 25.

10. Herbert S. Klein, *Slavery in the Americas: A Comparative Study of Virginia and Cuba*,
     Chicago: University of Chicago Press, 1967, 215.

11. Light Townsend Cummins, "Spanish Agents in North America During the
     Revolution, 1775–1779," Ph.D. diss., Tulane University, 1977. See also Winston
     de Ville, "Louisiana Soldiers in the American Revolution," Ville Platte, Louisiana:
     Smith, 1991, Tulane University.

12. See Report, Circa 1785, Oliver Wolcott, Jr. Papers, Connecticut Historical Society–
     Hartford: "The following is the present state of the military & naval forces upon the
     island of Cuba. . . . At the Havana and environs 100,000 men which be brought under
     three equal descriptions . . . one third *nearly* [sic] white and one third of colour and
     another 100,000 souls of like proportion in colours." The "Havana Militia consists of
     four separate corps . . . a regiment of white infantry, a battalion of horse, one regiment
     of coloured and another regiment of Black infantry, each of 1,377 men. They are all well
     disciplined. . . . Inhabitants of the whole island of Cuba may without any exception
     be pronounced universally dissatisfied with the heavy yoke imposed by their despotic
     system . . . will at some future period eagerly embrace the earliest favorable opportunity
     to shake off the galling chain. . . . The slightest view of the soil and attention to the happy
     climate of the fertile island must force conviction that were the inhabitants permitted to
     purchase slaves proportioned to their abilities to pay for their, their exports in the several
     articles of produce would be increased manyfold, for no industry is to be expected from
     the exertions of the white inhabitants of that region of sloth."

13. David R. Murray, *Odious Commerce: Britain, Spain and the Abolition of the Cuban
     Slave Trade*, London: Cambridge University Press, 1980, 15; Laird W. Bergad, *The
     Cuban Slave Market, 1790–1880*, New York: Cambridge University Press, 1995. See
     Paul Finkelman, "Suppressing American Slave Traders in the 1790s," *OAH Magazine
     of History* 18/3 (April 2004): 51–55; Aileen Moore Topping, "Alexander Gillon in
     Havana, 'This Very Friendly Port,'" *South Carolina Historical Magazine* 83/1 (January
     1982): 34–49. See also Contract for Providing Negroes to the Cuba and Caracas, 27
     May 1786, Legajo 22, Numero de Orden 7, Reales Cedulas y Ordenas, ANC. At the
     same site, see also Letter Granting to Vassals [*Vasallos*] of America the Introduction
     of Negroes from the French Colonies During the War, Legajo 16, Numero de Orden,
     74, Reales Cedulas y Ordenas and Letter broadening the right of neutrals to buy
     Negroes, 16 March 1781, Legajo 17, Numero de Orden 40, Reales Cedulas y Ordenas.

14. Louis A. Perez, Jr., *Cuba and the United States*, 5.

15. Ibid. Caitlin A. Fitz, "Our Sister Republics: The United States in an Age of American
     Revolution," Ph.d., diss., Yale University, 2010, 25: "Half of the 22 U.S. ships that
     arrived in Montevideo in 1805 carried slaves from Africa; in 1807 the number grew to
     20 of 30."

16. Daniel Rasmussen, *American Uprising: The Untold Story of America's Largest Slave
     Revolt*, New York: HarperCollins, 2011, 89.

17. Aimes, *A History of Slavery in Cuba*, 40. See also Jean-Pierre Leglaunec, "A Directory
     of Ships with Slave Cargoes, Louisiana, 1772–1808," *Louisiana History* 46/2 (Spring
     2005): 211–30.

18. Jean-Pierre Leglaunec, "Slave Migration in Spanish and Early American Louisiana:
     New Sources and New Estimates," *Louisiana History* 46 (Spring 2005): 185–209,
     188. Before 1796, arrivals "originated primarily from the island of Jamaica" but "in the
     early 1790s, Cuba began to emerge as the major source of supply for the New Orleans
     slave trade."

19. Captain General Conde de Santa Clara to Governor of Santiago, 30 December 1796, Legajo 30–A, Numero de Orden 1, Correspondencia de Los Capitanes Generales, ANC.

20. James W. Cortada, *Two Nations Over Time: Spain and the United States, 1776–1977*, Westport, CT: Greenwood, 1978, 55.

21. Convention between Spain and the U.S. for the Restitution of Negroes and Fugitive Slaves, December 1797, Legajo de Estado 3890, AHN–Madrid.

22. See *Documents Pertaining to the Floridas which are Kept in Different Archives of Cuba*, Appendix Number 1, Havana, 1945, Tulane University.

23. See correspondence from Don Enrique White, 9 August 1797; 16 June 1798, 1 July 1798, Box 1, Papers of Spanish Consulate in Charleston, Duke University. At the same source, in Box 2, see White's correspondence, 15 June 1799.

24. Proclamation by Alejandro O'Reilly, New Orleans, 24 August 1769, in Lawrence Kinnaird, ed., *Annual Report of the American Historical Association for the Year 1945*, vol. 2: *Spain in the Mississippi Valley, 1765–1794, Transactions of Materials from the Spanish Archives in the Bancroft Library*. Washington, D.C.: Government Printing Office, 1949, 89–90: "Individuals. . . . using no restraint about selling goods to slaves of both sexes . . . continuing to buy from the said Negro slaves everything which they bring to market or elsewhere . . . so contrary to good order."

25. Report, 1767, Legajo 21, Numero de Orden 28, Correspondence of the Captains General, ANC–Havana.

26. Letter from George Washington and Thomas Jefferson, 18 March 1792, Legajo de Estado 3890. Reportedly, both Jefferson and Benjamin Franklin claimed they could read and speak Spanish with some facility and encouraged others to emulate their example. See James W. Cortada, *Two Nations Over Time: Spain and the United States, 1776–1977*, Westport, CT: Greenwood, 1978, 131. The leading U.S. military figure in 1890s Cuba said, "I had a fair reading but not a speaking acquaintance with that language." See Frederick Funston, *Memories of Two Wars*. New York: Scribner's, 1911, 5.

27. William Carmichael to Principal Minister, 1791, Legajo de Estado 3890.

28. William Carmichael to Minister of Finance, 1 October 1793, Legajo de Estado 3890.

29. Message from the President of the United States, Transmitting a Report from the Secretary of State, and Sundry Documents Relative to Certain Spoilations and other Proceedings Referred to, in a Resolution of the House of the 8th of January Last, 20 April 1802, American Antiquarian Society–Worcester. Documents conflicts over Spain seizing U.S. vessels in the Mediterranean.

30. William Carmichael to Minister of Finance, 26 May 1793, Legajo de Estado 3890.

31. Letter from Baron de Carondelet, 30 July 1795, Legajo de Estado 3890: "La emigracion de los muchos refugiados Franceses, Holandeses, Flamencos, Alamanes. . . ."

32. Message from the President of the United States, 20 April 1802, American Antiquarian Society–Worcester.

33. James W. Cortada, *Two Nations Over Time: Spain and the United States, 1776–1977*. Westport, CT: Greenwood, 1978, 55. See also Lester D. Langley, "Slavery, Reform and American Policy in Cuba, 1823–1878," *Revista de Historia de America* 65/66 (January–December 1968): 71–84, 72.

34. Agreement concerning formation of a company for brining slaves from Africa, 1803, Legajo 106, Numero de Orden 9, Asuntos Politicos, ANC. See Receipts for sales of Angolans in Havana, 27 November 1803, Felix Bonnet Papers, Rhode Island Historical Society–Providence. For more on slave sales to Cuba by U.S. nationals in the early nineteenth century, see Correspondence, 1806, Folder 7, Christian Miltenberger Papers, University of North Carolina–Chapel Hill.

35. Marcus Christian, "The Battle of New Orleans: Negro Soldiers in the Battle of New Orleans," 150th Anniversary Committee of Louisiana, 1965, 6, 7, 41, American Antiquarian Society–Worcester. See also R. Thomas, *The Glory of America: Comprising Memoirs of the Lives and Glorious Exploits of Some of the Most Distinguished Officers Engaged in the Late War with Great Britain.* New York: Ezra Strong, 1834, Georgia Historical Society–Savannah.

36. Report, 15 May 1808, Legajo de Estado 5549, AHN–Madrid.

37. General Commandant of the Provinces of New Spain to Madrid, 1809, Legajo de Estado 5550, AHN.

38. Report, 12 June 1804, Legajo de Estado 5541, AHN. Spain took a similar approach to arriving Frenchmen, see Spanish official in Aranjuez to Captain General in Louisiana, 22 April 1799, Estado 86B, V 104, 2, Archivo General de Indias–Sevilla.

39. Letter from the "Gobernador de Santiago de Cuba," 31 March 1792, Legajo 30–A, Numero de Orden 58, Correspondence of the Captains General, ANC.

40. Albert G. Robinson, *Cuba Old and New.* New York: Longmans Green, 1915, 90.

41. Horne, *Negro Comrades of the Crown.*

42. Report, 22 December 1804, Legajo de Estado 5543, 5545, AHN–Madrid. This occurred near the shores of Peru when the Africans turned the tables, seized weapons, and killed 18 of 33 captors. They kept the captain alive to assist them in their attempt to return home to Senegal. See also Greg Grandin, *The Empire of Necessity: Slavery, Freedom and Deception in the New World,* New York: Metropolitan, 2014.

43. Gabriel H. Lovett, *Napoleon and the Birth of Modern Spain.* New York: New York University Press, 1965; Charles J. Esdaile, *Fighting Napoleon: Guerrillas, Bandits and Adventurers in Spain, 1808–1814.* New Haven: Yale University Press, 2004.

44. Jose de Limonta, Cadiz, to Colonel Pedro Suarez, 28 August 1811, Legajo 213, Numero de Orden 130, Asuntos Politicos, ANC.

45. Governor to Captain General, 26 October 1809, Legajo 210, Numero de Orden 61, Asuntos Politicos, ANC.

46. Report from Maurice Rogers, 22 April 1808, Legajo de Estado 5549, ANC. See also Timothy Pickering, U.S. State Department to "Sir," 5 October 1799, Box 1, Papers of Spanish Consulate–Charleston.

47. John E. Baur, "International Repercussions of the Haitian Revolution," *The Americas* 26/4(April 1970): 394–418, 402.

48. Donald E. Everett, "Emigres and Militiamen: Free Persons of Color in New Orleans, 1803–1815," *Journal of Negro History* 38/4 (October 1953): 377–402, 386: "The loyalty of these colored men to the American government was tenuous. . . . Of greater concern was the certainty on the part of large numbers of white citizens that once the colored militia was armed it had only to give the signal for the inevitable slave insurrection. . . . More plausible that the free colored population might cast its support with the Spanish . . . should an invasion occur." See also J.C.A. Stagg, "Soldiers in Peace and War: Comparative Perspectives on the Recruitment of the United States Army, 1802–1845," *William and Mary Quarterly* 57/1 (2000): 79–120, 94: "Of the 27 men with 'black' complexions in the systematic sample of the men enlisted between 1812 and 1815, two (7.4%) were born in Ireland . . . another two (7.4%) were born in Cuba and Italy, respectively."

49. Maurice Rogers to Robert Smith, 22 April 1809, Roll 1, T55, *Despatches from U.S. Consuls in Santiago de Cuba, 1799–1806,* NARA–CP.

50. To "Dear Cousin," 10 May 1809, Carter–Danforth Papers, Rhode Island Historical Society. "I am delighted with this climate" in Cuba, said this Rhode Islander, for "there cannot be a better" one.

51. Letter, 26 July 1809, Stephen Arnold Papers, Rhode Island Historical Society.

52. Coughtry, *The Notorious Triangle*, 233.

53. Letter to Jacob Babbitt in Bristol, Rhode Island, 13 November 1823; and Letter to Edward Spalding in Bristol, 12 January 1824, Edward Spalding Letters, Emory University.

54. Matt D. Childs, *The 1812 Aponte Rebellion in Cuba and the Struggle Against Atlantic Slavery*. Chapel Hill: University of North Carolina Press, 2006, 54, 131.

55. Intendente Hacienda to Captain General, 16 January 1811, Legajo 212, Numero de Orden 259, Asuntos Politicos, ANC.

56. Horne, *Negro Comrades of the Crown*; James G. Cusick, *The Other War of 1812: The Patriot War and the American Invasion of Spanish East Florida*. Gainesville: University Press of Florida, 2005.

57. Jane Landers, "Black Community and Culture in the Southeastern Borderlands," *Journal of the Early Republic* 18/1 (Spring 1998): 117–34, 130.

58. Captain General to Intendente Hacienda, 5 January 1810, Legajo 211, Numero de Orden 2, Asuntos Politicos, ANC, on the urgent necessity of supplying St. Augustine.

59. Report, 1816, Legajo 126, Numero de Orden 120, Asuntos Politicos, ANC.

60. Instructions, 22 September 1809, Legajo 210, Numero de Orden 50, ANC. See also Captain General to Governor of Santiago, 14 September 1811, Legajo 213, Numero de Orden 143, Asuntos Politicos, ANC, on the disembarking of a dozen Euro–Americans; Captain General to Governor of Santiago, 26 October 1811, Legajo 213, Numero de Orden 165, Asuntos Politicos, ANC, on more vigilance needed in scrutinizing visiting foreigners.

61. Captain General to the Governor of Santiago, 13 January 1810, Legajo 18, Numero de Orden 27, Asuntos Politicos, ANC, andCaptain General to Governor, 31 January 1810, Legajo 211, Numero de Orden 27, ANC.

62. Captain General to Intendente Hacienda, 25 January 1812, Legajo 214, Numero de Orden 28, Asuntos Politicos, ANC, on arrival of Negro emigrants from "Santo Domingo."

63. Report, 9 May 1809, Legajo 210, Numero de Orden 20, ANC: Spain designated a consul for Carolinas and Georgia, who resided in Charleston. See also David Eltis, "Slave Departures from Africa, 1811–1867: An Annual Time Series," *African Economic History* 15 (1986): 143–71.

64. Jane Landers, "Black Community and Culture in the Southeastern Borderlands," 130.

65. Captain General to Governor, 28 March 1810, Legajo 211, Numero de Orden 70, Asuntos Politicos, ANC. See also Jane Landers, *Atlantic Creoles in the Age of Revolutions*. Cambridge, MA: Harvard University Press, 2010, 83: The author argues that during this era Spain "sought to create a two-caste racial system like that of the United States." The question is, to what extent did growing U.S. influence bend Madrid—and Havana—in this direction?

66. Francisco Venegas to the Governor of Santiago, 20 April 1811, Legajo 213, Numero de Orden 30, ANC. See also Ignacio de la Pezuela to Governor of Santiago, 22 September 1811, Legajo 213, Numero de Orden 146, Asuntos Politicos, ANC: Manuel Martínez of Spain has made a presentation indicating discontent in "America."

67. Joe G. Taylor, "The Foreign Slave Trade in Louisiana After 1808," *Louisiana History* 1/1 (Winter 1960): 36–43, 38. For example, on 14 April 1808, 2 U.S. ships cleared Havana for New Orleans carrying 98 enslaved Africans, 43 of whom had just arrived in Cuba from Africa. Michael E. Stevens, "'To Get as Many Slaves as You Can:' An 1807 Slaving Voyage," *South Carolina Historical Magazine* 87/3 (July 1986): 187–92. Charleston was "teeming with the slaving business." In 1807 at least 43 vessels set out for Africa with a much of the resultant cargo ending up in Cuba.

68.   "The Letters of Charles Caleb Cotton, 1798–1802," *South Carolina Historical and Genealogical Magazine* 51/3 (July 1950): 132–44.

69.   J. Ogden to "Dear Father," 20 February 1812, Ogden Family Papers, Duke University.

70.   Robert Franklin Crider, "The Borderlands Florida, 1815–1821: Spanish Sovereignty Under Siege," Ph.D. diss., Florida State University, 1979, 78, 208. John Forbes of East Florida moved "his sugar plantation" in 1817 to Matanzas. Forbes, a slave dealer, also joined another investor in this realm with an ever deeper involvement in the Cuban market.

71.   James Innerarity to John Forbes, 12 August 1815, in "The Panton Leslie Papers," *Florida Historical Quarterly* 12/2 (January 1934): 123–34, 123. See also Leora M. Sutton, *Success Beyond Expectations: Panton Leslie Co. at Pensacola*. Pensacola: Vowel, 1991, 40, 57, 75.

72.   Letter to John Forbes, 24 October 1816, Reel 20, Panton Leslie Papers, University of Alabama-Tuscaloosa..

73.   John Innerarity to John Forbes, 24 May 1817, Reel 21, ibid.

74.   James Innerarity to John Innerarity, 9 August 1817, Reel 21, ibid.

75.   William S. Coker, "The Papers and History of Panton, Leslie and Company and John Forbes and Company," *Florida Historical Quarterly* 73/3 (January 1995): 353–58, 354.

76.   See William Fales to Lydia Fales French, 7 November 1818, Fales Family Letters, Brown University. From his estate in Madruga, Cuba, this resident of Bristol, Rhode Island, wrote, "Thomas can talk very plain [in] a little Spanish and he is all the time playing with the little Negroes."

77.   Wilbur H. Siebert, *The Legacy of the American Revolution to the British West Indies and Bahamas: A Chapter out of the History of the American Loyalists*. Boston: Gregg Press, 1972, vii.

78.   C. S. Monaco, *Moses Levy of Florida: Jewish Utopian and Antebellum Reformer*. Baton Rouge: Louisiana State University Press, 2005, 65. See also "Petition of the Executor of David Nagle, Deceased & Antonio de Frias, Subjects of Spain . . ." 24th Congress, Referred to Committee on Foreign Relations, 4 January 1836, Attorney for Above, John Nicholson, St. Augustine Historical Society. Nagle and de Frias were the owners of 84 Africans shipped to the United States in 1818 via Havana and intended for Pensacola. "Voyage of the vessel was from Havana to New Orleans," then on to Florida. But on arrival it was seized by U.S. forces "under the guns of Fort Barancas" and the men were charged with violation of slave trade laws and their property was condemned. They appealed and in 1824 won and applied to a judge in Florida for "restitution of the slaves" but only "fifty-four of the eighty-four" were returned; the 54 were sold for $19,920—the rest had died or dispersed to Mobile. Of course, Cuban slave dealers—Fernando de la Maza Arrendondo—had branch operations on the mainland. See Landers, *Atlantic Creoles*, 150.

79.   William S. Coker and Thomas D. Watson, *Indian Traders of the Southeastern Spanish Borderlands: Panton, Leslie & Company and John Forbes & Company, 1783–1847*. Pensacola: University of West Florida Press, 1986, 326.

80.   "Real Cedula de 21 de Octubre de 1817 sobre aumenta la poblacion Blanca de la isla de Cuba." Records of the Spanish Consulate, Norfolk–Virginia Historical Society–Richmond.

81.   "Real Orden . . . sobre el aumento de la poblacion Blanca de estrangeros . . ." 12 March 1822, Records of the Spanish Consulate, Norfolk. Also see also Clipping, 1 June 1818, for details for those wishing to migrate.

82.   Aimes, *A History of Slavery in Cuba*, 59.

83.   John Quincy Adams to John Forsyth, 16 March 1819, in William Manning, ed., *Diplomatic Correspondence of the United States Concerning the Independence of the*

Latin American Nations, vol. 1 New York: Oxford University Press, 1925, 96–97.

84. Ministry–Madrid to Captain General, 6 August 1818, Legajo 110, Numero de Orden 107, Asuntos Politicos, ANC. For more on what Spain's Minister in Washington described as the danger of permitting entrance of North Americans into Cuba see his letter to the Captain General, 26 August 1818, Legajo 110, Numero de Orden 107, Asuntos Politicos, ANC. For an earlier iteration of this anti-foreigner policy, see Report, 15 April 1812, Legajo 214, Numero de Orden 101, Asuntos Politicos, ANC.

85. William Earl Weeks, *John Quincy Adams and American Global Empire*. Lexington: University Press of Kentucky, 1992, 89.

86. Report, 19 October 1818, Legajo 125, Numero de Orden 9, Asuntos Politicos, ANC. For more on this point, see Report from Spanish Minister in Washington, 19 October 1818, Legajo 125, Numero de Orden 9, Asuntos Politicos, ANC

87. Captain General to Governor of Santiago, 4 December 1817, Legajo 110, Numero de Orden 27, Asuntos Politicos, ANC. Also see Mr. Garay to Intendente of the Army in Havana, 26 August 1817, Legajo 123, Numero de Orden 16, Asuntos Politicos, ANC. Impeding the entrance to Cuba of French, English and Americans and foiling the propagation of seditious and alarming ideas was the suggestion made here.

88. Governor of Santiago to Captain General, 30 April 1811, Legajo 213, Numero de Orden 41, Asuntos Politicos, ANC. Also Captain General to Governor of Santiago, 12 August 1811, Legajo 213, Numero de Orden 125, Asuntos Politicos, ANC, on developments in Santo Domingo.

89. Captain General to Governor of Santiago, 31 May 1811, Legajo 213, Numero de Orden 67, Asuntos Politicos, ANC: also Documents referring to Cortes Plan for Abolition of Slavery, 25 June 1811, Legajo 213, Numero de Orden 81, Asuntos Politicos, ANC.

90. Jane Landers, "Gracia Real de Santa Teresa de Mose: A Free Black Town in Spanish Florida," *American Historical Review* 95/1 (February 1990): 9–30, 28.

91. "Speech of the Hon. William Hunter in Secret Session of the Senate of the United States, February 2nd 1813. On the Proposition for Seizing and Occupying the Province of East Florida, by the Troops of the United States." Newport, RI: Rousmaniere & Barber, 1813, Rhode Island Historical Society.

92. Sir John Beresford to Viscount Melville, December 1813, Viscount Melville Papers, Huntington Library–San Marino, California: "What renders their conduct more reprehensible is that Spain has done them no injury & is at present engaged in a contest for her existence as a nation. And the American government is vilely taking advantage of her distress."

93. Alexander Cochrane to Chief of Indian Nation, 1 July 1814, Reel 19, Panton Leslie Papers. On the same point and in the same collection see Sebastian Kindelan to George Woodbine, 30 December 1814, Reel 20; Sebastian Kindelan to George Cockburn, 31 January 1815, Reel 20; Sebastian Kindelan to George Cockburn, 18 February 1815, Reel 20; Alexander Cochrane to Mateo Gonzalez Manrique, 10 February 1815, Reel 20.

94. Interim Political Chief to Governor of Puerto Principe, 23 February 1812, Legajo 214, Numero de Orden 46, Asuntos Politicos, ANC;also Report, 24 December 1810, Legajo 212, Numero de Orden 147, Asuntos Politicos, ANC, on meetings of enslaved and free Negroes in Havana at the home of a mulatto who apparently speaks English.

95. Report by Governor of Santiago, 29 February 1812, Legajo 214, Numero de Orden 54, Asuntos Politicos, ANC.

96. Letter to Governor of Puerto Principe, 3 March 1812, Legajo 214, Numero de Orden 61, Asuntos Polticos, ANC.

97. *Boston Weekly Messenger*, 14 January 1815, Legajo 297, Numero de Orden 297, Asuntos Politicos, ANC.

98. Andrew Jackson to Governor of Pensacola, 23 April 1816, Reel 20, Panton Leslie Papers.

99. *Boston Weekly Messenger*, 24 December 1815, Legajo 297, Numero de Orden 297, ANC.

100. Captain General to Governor of Santiago, 16 June 1816, Legajo 124, Numero de Orden 47, Asuntos Politicos, ANC; also Captain General to Governor of Santiago, 13 March 1817, Legajo 109, Numero de Orden 86, Asuntos Politicos, ANC, on the arrival in Honduras of a British frigate carrying accomplices of the unrest in Barbados.

101. Letter from James Buchanan, 24 July 1818, FO5/135/37, NAUK. For more on this point, see James Buchanan to Foreign Office, 4 March 1819, FO5/144/60; and James Buchanan to Under Secretary of State, 8 March 1819, FO5/144/60.

102. T. S. Smith to Joel Roberts Poinsett, 27 August 1810, Joel Roberts Poinsett Papers– University of Texas.

103. Minister of Spain in U.S. to Intendente Hacienda, 26 August 1815, Legajo 124, Numero de Orden 25, Asuntos Politicos, ANC.

104. Report, 24 November 1816, Legajo 124, Numero de Orden 83, Asuntos Politicos, ANC. For more on Bolivar, see Governor of Santiago to Chief General of the Army, 28 February 1816, Legajo 123, Numero de Orden 5, Asuntos Politicos, ANC.

105. Governor of Santiago to Minister of State, 7 June 1816, Legajo 124, Numero de Orden 150, Asuntos Politicos, ANC. Havana had long viewed Jamaica with suspicion and circulated the racist maunderings of the planter Edward Long, who had major interests there. See Notes on Long's history of Jamaica, 20 April 1782, Legajo 3, Numero de Orden 42, Asuntos Politicos, ANC.

106. Captain General to Governor of Santiago, 28 February 1816, Legajo 123, Numero de Orden 5, Asuntos Politicos, ANC

107. Report from Spanish Consul in Norfolk, 18 January 1820, Legajo 18, Numero de Orden 42, Asuntos Politicos, ANC.

108. Letter from Governor, 7 August 1819, Legajo 125, Numero de Orden 13, Asuntos Politicos, ANC See also R.C. Dallas, *The History of the Maroons, From their Origin to the Establishment of their Chief Tribe at Sierra Leone, Including the Expedition to Cuba for the Purpose of Procuring Spanish Chasseurs.* London: Cass, 1968 (originally published 1803).

109. Captain General to Governor of Santiago, 29 May 1815, Legajo 109, Numero de Orden 10, Asuntos Politicos, ANC.

110. Thomas Sumter to "Sir," 13 May 1815, Box 1, William Crawford Papers–Duke University: "Their Peninsular situation and their occupations out of Europe have separated them from much in everything from Europe and its changes. . . . their local & political circumstances saved them from the purification of the reformation." See also Miguel Gonzalez-Gerth, "The Image of Spain American Literature, 1815–1865," *Journal of Inter-American Studies* 42 (April 1962): 257–72.

111. Prosecutions for Slave Trading, 1816, Box 9, RG 21, Records of the United States District Court for the Eastern District of Pennsylvania, National Archives and Records Administration–Philadelphia.

112. *U.S. v. Henry Kennedy*, October 1820, Box 5, RG 21, Records of the U.S. Circuit Court for the Eastern District of Pennsylvania, Criminal Case Files, 1791–1883, National Archives and Records Administration–Philadelphia.

113. Report, 6 May 1817, Legajo 109, Numero de Orden 104, Asuntos Politicos, ANC. For more Spanish views of plots devised in Galveston and Amelia Island near the Florida-Georgia border, see Spanish Consul in Norfolk, Virginia, to Intendente General, 24 March 1818, Legajo 110, Numero de Orden 58, Asuntos Politicos, ANC.

114. Minister of Spain in U.S. to Intendente General, 25 October 1817, Legajo 110, Numero de Orden 16, Asuntos Politicos, ANC. On a Spanish soldier taken prisoner in Galveston by pirates who infested this port, see Captain General to Intendente de Hacienda, 9 December 1818, Legajo 110, Numero de Orden 128, Asuntos Politicos, ANC. See also Captain General to Intendente General, 12 June 1819, Legajo 111, Numero de Orden 9, Asuntos Politicos, ANC, on suspicious movements of U.S. troops in the vicinity of New Orleans.

115. Vicente Sebastian Pintado to Jose de Soto, 29 April 1815, Reel 20, Panton Leslie Papers.

116. Letter from Juan Jose de Estrade, 22 December 1815, Reel 20.

117. Report from the Intendente of the Army in Havana, 3 July 1818, Legajo 99, Numero de Orden 102, Asuntos Politicos, ANC.

118. Letter from Intendente de Hacienda, 27 June 1819, Legajo 125, Numero de Orden 10, Asuntos Politicos, ANC.

119. Captain General to Intendente General, 6 September 1819, Legajo 111, Numero de Orden 18, Asuntos Politicos, ANC.

120. Captain General to Intendente General, 17 September 1819, Legajo 111, Numero de Orden 21, Asuntos Politicos, ANC.

121. Intendente of the Army in Havana, 15 November 1819, Legajo 17, Numero de Orden 17, Asuntos Politicos, ANC.

122. *Southern Patriot*, 4 March 1817, Legajo 298, Numero de Orden 4, Asuntos Politicos, ANC. The importance of Pensacola was recognized during the era of British Florida, when it was linked to Jamaica, just as during the era of Spanish rule it was linked to Cuba. See Correspondence, 4 April 1781, Reel 1, Panton Leslie Papers.

123. C. L. R. James, *The Black Jacobins: Toussaint Louverture and the San Domingo Revolution*. New York: Dial, 1938, 103–6, 123–24. Jorge Biassour [Georges Biassou], Vertical File, St. Augustine Historical Society; also see Vertical File on Blacks, *St. Augustine Record*, 14 April 2002. Felipe Edinboro, born in West Africa, received 100 acres near St. Augustine, ca. 1794, and served as a sergeant in the Spanish militia. See also Jane Landers, "Jorge Biassou, Black Chieftan," *El Escribano* 25 (1988): 85–100.

124. Frank Marotti, "Negotiating Freedom in St. John's County, Florida, 1812–1862," Ph.D. diss., University of Hawaii, 2003, 47.

125. Susan Parker, "African Americans in Florida and the Caribbean, 1763–Today," St. Augustine Historical Society; alsosee file on "Military: Second Spanish Period, Wars." See Cusick, *The Other War of 1812*, 183. From Havana there arrived the "Cuban Disciplined Black Militia [*sic*] who had volunteered for service in Florida." On the official Spanish view of this conflict, see Luis de Onis to Intendente Hacienda, 1 April 1812, Legajo 214, Numero de Orden 90, ANC.

126. Rogers C. Harlan, "A Military History of East Florida During the Governorship of Enrique White, 1796–1811," M.A. thesis, Florida State University, 1971.

127. Kevin Mulroy, *Freedom on the Border: The Seminole Maroons in Florida, the Indian Territory, Coahuila and Texas*. Lubbock: Texas Technical University Press, 68–69. On the invasion of St. Augustine, see Captain General to Intendente Hacienda, 26 March 1812, Legajo 214, Numero de Orden 88, Asuntos Politicos, ANC.

128. Letter from Havana to Intendente General, 20 October 1820, Legajo 111, Numero de Orden 64, Asuntos Politicos, ANC.

129. *National Intelligencer*, 8 December 1819, Legajo 298, Numero de Orden 15, Asuntos Politicos, ANC.

130. Thomas Sidney Jessup to "Sir," 5 September 1816, Thomas Sidney Jessup Papers, Duke University.

131. Ibid., 21 August 1816..

132. Andrew Jackson to Thomas Sidney Jessup, 6 September 1816, Andrew Jackson Collection, Duke University. For official Cuban views of what was described as the maneuvers of General Jackson, see Governor of Santiago to Captain General, 30 May 1818, Legajo 110, Numero de Orden 81, Asuntos Politicos, ANC.

133. Thomas Sidney Jessup to "Sir," 11 September 1816, Thomas Sidney Jessup Papers.

134. Correspondence, 26 September 1816, Thomas Sidney Jessup Papers.

135. *Niles Weekly Register*, 15 November 1817.

136. Ibid.; Sir John Beresford to Viscount Melville, December 1813, Viscount Melville Papers..

137. Unnamed British subject to Lord Castlereagh, 20 May 1818, FO5/135/265, NAUK. The writer added that "from the North Pole to the extremity of Cape Horn may one day extend a continuous chain of Republican and federative systems" menacing London and Europe as a whole. Florida was seen as the "spot upon which to fix the Archimedan lever of policy" since it was the "most important division of North America." See also William S. Coker et al., eds., *Anglo–Spanish Confrontation on the Gulf Coast During the American Revolution*. Pensacola: Gulf Coast History and Humanities Conference, 1982.

138. Horne, *Negro Comrades of the Crown*, 36.

139. J. Freeman Rattenbury, *Remarks on the Cession of the Floridas to the United States of America and on the Necessity of Acquiring the Island of Cuba by Great Britain.* London, 1819, University of West Florida–Pensacola. See also Dorothy Dodd, "The Schooner Emperor: An Incident of the Illegal Slave Trade in Florida," *Florida Historical Quarterly* 13/3 (January 1935): 117–28.

140. See Real Orden, 8 December 1819, Legajo 18, Numero de Orden 33, Asuntos Politicos, ANC, on the execution of a treaty demanding abolition of the slave trade. On a similar point see the "Additional Convention and Treaty of 22 January 1815 between the U.K. and Portugal on the Slave Trade" [translated from Portuguese], Legajo Estado 8033, AHN–Madrid.

141. John Forbes to Pedro Antonio de Ayala, 1 January 1818, Reel 21, Panton Leslie Papers.

142. Letter to Andrew Jackson, 26 May 1818, Reel 21, ibid.

143. Andrew Jackson to Jose Mascot, 23 May 1818, Reel 21, ibid.

144. John Quincy Adams to G. W. Erving, 28 November 1818, Reel 21, ibid.

145. Correspondence, 6 May 1818, Legajo Estado 5560, AHN–Madrid. This Spanish diplomat had a tough assignment, however. In the 1819 treaty ceding Florida and giving the United States claim to what is now the Great Plains and the Pacific Northwest, he received a shallow promise—the United States would abandon all claims to Texas.

146. Letter from James Buchanan, 12 April 1818, FO5/135/25, NAUK. On Havana's response to the Scottish adventurer Gregor MacGregor, who had particular plans for Spanish colonies then straining toward independence, see Minister of Spain to Intendente Hacienda, 15 January 1818, Legajo 110, Numero de Orden 41, Asuntos Politicos, ANC.

147. Alexander Humboldt, *The Island of Cuba with Notes and a Preliminary Essay by J. S. Thrasher.* New York: Derby and Jackson, 1856, 11, 12.

148. James Buchanan to Under Secretary of State, 8 March 1819, FO5/144/60, NAUK.

149. Minister of Spain in U.S. to Intendente General, 5 February 1818, Legajo 10, Numero de Orden 45, Asuntos Politicos, ANC.

150. James Monroe to Andrew Jackson, 19 July 1818 in *Correspondence Between General Andrew Jackson and John C. Calhoun, President and Vice-President of the U. States, on the Subject of the Course of the Latter, in the Deliberations of the Cabinet of Mr. Monroe, on the Occurrences in the Seminole War.* Washington, D.C.: Duff Green,

1831, South Carolina Historical Society–Charleston.

151. Report, 12 May 1814, James DeWolf Papers, Redwood Library–Newport, RI.

152. Antonio Rafael de la Cova, "Ambrosio Jose Gonzalez: A Cuban Confederate General," Ph.D. diss., West Virginia University, 1994, 22.

153. Diary of John Quincy Adams, 20 June 1822 (citing Calhoun), in W. Edwin Hemphill, ed., *The Papers of John C. Calhoun*, vol. 7. Columbia: University of South Carolina Press, 1983, xxxvi.

154. See Susan L'Engle, *Notes of My Family and Recollections of My Early Life*. New York: Knickerbocker Press, 1888, 28–29. In 1812 indigenes "came down in force upon the plantations along the St. John's River and commenced the work of massacre and devastation. . . . they never killed Negroes."

155. Landers, "Black Community and Culture in the Southeastern Borderlands," 134.

156. Frank Marotti, *The Cana Sanctuary: History, Diplomacy and Black Catholic Marriage in Antebellum St. Augustine, Florida*. Tuscaloosa: University of Alabama Press, 2012, 92, 104. See also Daniel L. Schafer, *Anna Madgigine Jai Kingsley: African Princess, Florida Slave, Plantation Slaveowner*. Gainesville: University Press of Florida, 2003. See also file on Zephaniah Kingsley for Kathy Tilford, "Anna Kingsley: A Free Woman," *OAH Magazine of History* 12 (Fall 1997), St. Augustine Historical Society.

157. George Klos, "Blacks and the Seminole Removal Debate, 1821–1835," *Florida Historical Quarterly* 68 (July 1989): 55–78, 60.

158. Landers, *Atlantic Creoles*, 143.

159. Article from *El Escribano*, July 1971, Box 1, Geoffrey Mohlman Papers, St. Augustine Historical Society.

160. Frank Marotti, "Negotiating Freedom in St. John's County, Florida, 1812–1862," 104, 108, 129, 137. See also Peter James Lampros, "Merchant–Planter Cooperation and Conflict: The Havana Consulado, 1794–1832," Ph.D. diss., Tulane University, 1980.

161. Daniel L. Schafer, "A Class of People Neither Freemen nor Slaves: From Spanish to American Race Relations in Florida, 1821–1861," *Journal of Social History* 26/3 (Spring 1993): 587–609, 587. See also Alejandro de la Fuente, "Slave Law and Claims-Making in Cuba: The Tannenbaum Debate Revisited," *Law and History Review* 22/2 (Summer 2004): 339–69.

162. William Ryan, "Based on the Book 'Osceola, His Capture and Seminole Legends,'" 2010, Vertical File on "Blacks," St. Augustine Historical Society. See also Lawrence Kinnard, "International Rivalry in the Creek Country: Part I. The Ascendancy of Alexander McGillivray," *Florida Historical Quarterly* 10/2 (October 1931): 59–85.

163. *Florida Times-Union*, 11 November 2007. On U.S.–U.K. relations in the antebellum era. see Horne, *Negro Comrades of the Crown*.

2. TEXAS, CUBA, AND THE AFRICAN SLAVE TRADE

1. Alexander Hill Everett to U.S. President, 30 November 1825, in *The Everett Letters on Cuba*. Boston: Ellis, 1897, 12. See also U.S. Congress, 18th Congress, 2nd Session, Extract of a Letter from Francis Adams, Commercial Agent of the United States at Matanzas to the Secretary of State, 30 December 1824. Washington, D.C.: Gales & Seaton, American Antiquarian Society–Worcester (hereafter AAS).

2. Alexander Hill Everett to Secretary of State, 12 December 1827, in 32nd Congress, 1st Session, House of Representatives, Ex. Doc. No. 121; "Island of Cuba: Message from the President of the United States in Reference to the Island of Cuba," 31 August 1852, Massachusetts Historical Society.

3. Military Commander to Governor of Santiago, 30 June 1823, Legajo 113, Numero de Orden 104, Asuntos Politicos, ANC.

4. Lieutenant Governor to the Governor of the Province of Holguin, 22 March 1824, Legajo 125, Numero de Orden 24, Asuntos Politicos, ANC.

5. Gilbert Robertson to Stratford Canning, 21 April 1823, FO352/8/7, NAUK.

6. Occie Clubb, "Stephen Russell Mallory, Part III," *Florida Historical Quarterly* 26/1 (July 1947): 56–76, 59.

7. James Morton Callahan, "Cuba and Anglo-American Relations," *Annual Report of the American Historical Association for the Year 1897*. Washington, D.C.: Government Printing Office, 1898, 195–215, 201, 213.

8. Commanding General to Governor, 19 December 1830, Legajo 215, Numero de Orden 90, Asuntos Politicos, ANC; also see Report to Commanding General, Bayamo, 23 December 1830, Legajo 121, Numero de Orden 213, Asuntos Politicos, on how Haiti to send spies to Cuba and Puerto Rico; and Report, 15 October 1830, Legajo 121, Numero de Orden 213, Asuntos Politicos, on fear of an invasion by Haiti.

9. Vernon Lane Wharton, "The Movement in the United States for the Annexation of Cuba, 1789–1861," M.A. thesis, University of North Carolina–Chapel Hill, 1931, 6.

10. *The Liberator*, 23 June 1837: Translation of speech of the Deputy Sancho in the Cortes of Spain: "If, gentlemen, the island of Cuba, should cease to be Spanish, it must belong to the Negro. . . . If left to itself, it must become a *Negro* [emphasis–original] government. The effeminate and enervated whites would not be able to oppose the Negro population in that burning climate." Message: retain slavery, colonialism, and Madrid—or risk another Haiti.

11. Ralph E. Weber and Joel R. Poinsett, "Joel R. Poinsett's Secret Mexican Dispatch Twenty," *South Carolina Historical Magazine* 75/2 (April 1974): 67–76, 69, 72. See also Edward H. Tatum, "To Forestall Britain's Designs on Cuba and New World Markets," in Armin Rappaport, ed., *The Monroe Doctrine*. New York: Holt, Rinehart and Winston, 1964, 22–33. Checkmating London in Cuba is viewed here as a prime motivating force of the Monroe Doctrine.

12. Joel Roberts Poinsett to "Dear Sir," 10 August 1825, Joel Roberts Poinsett Papers, University of Texas-Austin.

13. Message from U.S. President, 5 February 1826, Legajo 130, Numero de Orden 1, Asuntos Politicos, ANC.

14. Ben R. Milam to "Sir," 28 August 1825, Joel Roberts Poinsett Papers.

15. Joel Roberts Poinsett to "My Dear Sir," 28 January 1826, Joel Roberts Poinsett Papers. See also Ralph Sanders, "Congressional Reaction in the United States to the Panama Congress of 1826," *The Americas* 11/2 (October 1954): 141–54; N. Andrew Cleven, "The First Panama Mission and the Congress of the United States," *Journal of Negro History* 13/3 (July 1928): 225–54.

16. Joel Roberts Poinsett to U.S. President, 26 April 1827, Joel Roberts Poinsett Papers.

17. Dr. Thomas Cooper to "Dear Sir," 16 March 1926, in "Letters of Dr. Thomas Cooper, 1825–1832," *American Historical Review* 6/4 (July 1901): 725–36, 728–29.

18. Charles R. Vaughn to George Canning, 21 December 1825. in C. K. Webster, ed., *Britain and the Independence of Latin America, 1812–1830: Select Documents from the Foreign Office Archives*, vol. 2: *Communications with European States and the United States*. New York: Octagon, 1970, 536–37. Years later, the abolitionist Frederick Douglass was still denouncing Clay. *Frederick Douglass's Paper*, 29 January 1852: "Should Cuba be conquered, its inhabitants would acquire their freedom and freedom in Cuba would be dangerous to despotism on the southern shores of the United States. The Cabinet at Washington was no less alarmed at the prospect of such near contiguity to enfranchised people, than was the Russian Czar at the Hungarian insurrection. Mr. Clay instructed our Ministers at the Panama Congress, to make known that in view of the probable results of the contemplated struggle in

Cuba," Washington would intervene and "go to war" to insure the status quo.

19. Henry Clay to Daniel P. Cook, 12 March 1827, in William Manning, ed., *Diplomatic Correspondence of the United States Concerning the Independence of the Latin American Nations*, vol. 1, 282–83.

20. Memorandum, 24 September 1828, Legajo 33, Numero de Orden 16, Asuntos Politicos, ANC. "Daniel Cook" has come to investigate Cuba; special vigilance required.

21. Correspondence between Henry Clay and Spanish diplomats, 12 May 1827, Legajo de Estado 6369, AHN–Madrid.

22. Military Commander, Baracoa to Military Governor, Santiago, 6 March 1823, Legajo 113, Numero de Orden 56, Asuntos Politicos, ANC: news of expeditions from the United States and the necessity to mount a defense. Military Governor of Santiago to Intendente of the Province, 16 March 1823, Legajo 113, Numero de Orden 60, Asuntos Politicos, ANC: possible attack by an expedition proceeding from the United States. Spanish Consul in Philadelphia and Baltimore to Captain General, 20 June 1823, Legajo 123, Numero de Orden 58, Asuntos Politicos, ANC: conspiratorial plans published in the gazettes of the mainland. Royal Decree, 13 April 1820, Legajo 111, Numero de Orden 72, Asuntos Politicos, ANC: more suspicions of nefarious activities of U.S. nationals.

23. Antonio Rafael de la Cova, "Ambrosio Jose Gonzalez," 22: "The pear, when ripe, falls by the law of gravity into the lap of the husbandman, so will Cuba eventually drop into the lap of the Union."

24. Cited in Prefatory comments in W. Edwin Hemphill., ed., *The Papers of John C. Calhoun, 1823–1824*, vol. 8. Columbia: University of South Carolina Press, 1975, xxxii.

25. F. M. Diamond, Vice Commercial Agent of U.S. in Havana to His Excellency, 8 October 1825, Roll 3, Despatches from U.S. Consuls in Havana, 1783–1906, Monroe County Public Library: U.S. vessel just arrived from Gibraltar and mate "forcibly taken from his vessel by a party of soldiers and confined among criminals in the . . . jail of this city at the instigation of a Black man named John Robinson, who was steward of the ship and has deserted since . . . arrival here."

26. John Warner, Havana, to "Sir," 2 March 1823, Roll 3, Despatches from U.S. Consuls in Havana–Monroe County Public Library.

27. Message from John Quincy Adams, 5 December 1826, Legajo 118, Numero de Orden 122, Asuntos Politicos, ANC.

28. Ibid. Upon the demise of Czar Alexander, Adams referred to him as a "tried, true, steady and faithful friend."

29. *New York Herald Tribune*, 23 August 1937, citing John Quincy Adams to Reverend William Channing, and Speech in House of Representatives, 25 May 1836 and 1822 letter, Folder 2, John Quincy Adams Papers–New York Public Library.

30. Letter, Havana, 6 March 1830, William Lander Letter Book, Phillips Library.

31. Wayne H. Bowen, *Spain and the American Civil War*. Columbia: University of Missouri Press, 2011, 21.

32. Linda K. Salvucci, "Trade and the Origin of American Interest in Cuba: Philadelphia and Havana, 1780–1830," 25 December 1989, Paper Presented to the Philadelphia Center for Early American Studies, Historical Society of Pennsylvania–Philadelphia. See also Linda K. Salvucci, "Merchants and Diplomats: Philadelphia's Early Trade with Cuba," *Pennsylvania Legacies* 3/2 (November 2003): 6–10. See also Spanish Consul in Philadelphia to Captain General, 23 October 1839, Legajo 40, Numero de Orden 27, Asuntos Politicos, ANC: Plans by pirates to engage in slave trade. See also 18th U.S. Congress, 2nd Session, U.S. Senate, 30 December 1824, AAS: Seaman

George Brown says that near Matanzas, his vessel was boarded by 12 men "armed with muskets, cutlasses, pistols and knives"—"about 40 men" all told—who then beat the crew and set afire the ship. See also 18th Congress, 1st Session, 19 May 1824, "Report of the Committee on Foreign Affairs. . . . piracies committed on the commerce of the United States in the neighborhood of the islands of Cuba and Porto Rico."

33.   *The Liberator*, 13 November 1840. At this point, a journey by vessel from New York to Cuba was said to take 7 days and from Charleston to the island took 4 days: *The Liberator*, 1 May 1840.

34.   *U.S. v. Robert Allen*, November term 1840, "Records of the U.S. Circuit Court for the District of Maryland, Criminal Case Files, April Sessions 1837–November 1840," Box 6, HM 03/2009. RG 21, NARA–Philadelphia: Vessel from Baltimore involved in slave trade to Cuba. Defendant charged with "intent to employ the said vessel in procuring Negroes from a foreign country." (Roger Taney has involvement in this case.) See also correspondence between the Captain General of Cuba and the First Secretary of State on the Introduction of Slaves, 1817–1873, 12 December 1829 and 16 June 1830, Legajo de Estado 8022, AHN–Madrid, on slave ships built in Baltimore and bearing the U.S. flag sailing to Guinea and returning to Havana.

35.   Martín Van Buren to Mr. Van Ness, 2 October 1829, in 32nd Congress, 1st Session, "Message from the President of the Untied States." See also John Blake, *Ramon: The Rover of Cuba, the Personal Narrative of that Celebrated Slave.* Boston: Richardson and Holbrooke, 1829.

36.   J. Carlyle Sitterson, "Antebellum Sugar Culture in the South Atlantic States," *Journal of Southern History* 3/2 (May 1937): 175–87, 181.

37.   Captain General to Intendente General, 25 October 1828, Legajo 120, Numero de Orden 60, Asuntos Politicos, ANC: U.S. still seeking land concessions from Spaniards in the Keys.

38.   Thomas Norman DeWolf, *Inheriting the Trade: A Northern Family Confronts Its Legacy as the Largest Slave-Trading Dynasty in U.S. History.* Boston: Beacon, 2008, 186. See also *Ensayo Politico Sobre La Isla de Cuba, Por El Baron A. De Humboldt, Con un Mapa.* Paris: En Casa De Jules Renouard, 1827, Boston Public Library.

39.   *The Liberator*, 28 July 1837. See also Claire M. Badaracco, "Sophia Peabody Hawthorne's Cuba Journal: Volume Three, 31 October 1834–15 March 1835," *Essex Institute Historical Collections* 118 (1982): 280–315. This invalid governess resided in San Marcos, 100 miles west of Havana, where she was caretaker for children of Dr. Robert and Laurette de Toussard Morell, who owned slave plantations.

40.   William Goddard to "Dear Sir," 26 April 1830, Goddard Family Collection, G. W. Blunt Library, Mystic,CT.

41.   Karen Robert, ed., *New Year in Cuba: Mary Gardner Lowell's Travel Diary, 1831– 1832.* Boston: Northeastern University Press, 2003, 6–7, 9, 14, 16, 71, 88. See also *An Invalid, a Winter in the West Indies and Florida.* New York: Wiley and Putnam, 1839, 97. This U.S. visitor said "slavery appeared here [Cuba] rather more severe than at St. Croix, for some of the slaves had chains around their necks."

42.   Badaracco, "Sophia Peabody Hawthorne's Cuba Journal," 280.

43.   Thomas Fales to Lydia Fales French, 13 April 1833, Fales Family Letters, Brown University. See also letter "To My Dear Grandmother," 21 December 1834, Tidd– Lord–Henchman–Carret Family Papers, Massachusetts Historical Society: "The cholera has left us. . . ."

44.   *An Invalid, a Winter in the West Indies and Florida*, 104.

45.   David Turnbull, *Travels in the West, Cuba; with Notices of Porto Rico and the Slave Trade.* London: Longman, Orne, Brown, Green and Longman, 1840, 91.

46. Robert L. Paquette, *Sugar Is Made with Blood: The Conspiracy of La Escalera and the Conflict Between Empires Over Slavery in Cuba*. Middletown, CT: Wesleyan University Press, 1988, 72.
47. *The Liberator*, 13 November 1839.
48. Manuel Barcia, *The Great African Slave Revolt of 1825: Cuba and the Fight for Freedom in Matanzas*. Baton Rouge: Louisiana State University Press, 2012, 78, 90, 144, 183. See also G. D. Davis to W. D. Davis, 1 May 1840, Davis Family Papers, Rhode Island Historical Society–Providence. Described here is the execution of a "Negro" in Matanzas for "killing his wife and the overseer on the estate of his master."
49. John P. Story to Dear Eliza, 24 June 1829, Box 1, Story Family Correspondence, Phillips Library–Salem, Massachusetts; also here "Cuban Sugar Trade Documents, 1811–1845." See also *The Liberator*, 29 October 1836: "There are slaveholders now living in this town," i.e. Bristol, Rhode Island, and "several kidnappers, slave drivers and *cowskin* heroes, fresh from Cuba and the South are now tarrying here for a season."
50. Nicholas Trist to "My Own Dearest," 9 February 1836, Box 3, Nicholas Trist Papers. See also Alberto Perret Ballester, *El Azucar en Matanzas y Sus Duenos en La Habana: Apuntes e Iconografia*. Havana: Ciencias Sociales, 2007
51. W. S. MacLeay to Viscount Palmerston, 24 June 1831 in *British Parliamentary Papers. Correspondence with British Commissioners and With Foreign Powers Relative to the Slave Trade [Class A and Class B]*, vol. 13. Shannon: Irish University Press, 1968, 101–3. Isidro Powell is a supercargo, born in Havana of U.S. parents, educated in the U.S. and formerly a clerk in a mercantile house, but now deeply involved in the slave trade to Matanzas. "His skill in the slave trade is so considerable that his capture will affect the various factories in the Rio Pongo much." See also Alexa Findlay and William Smith to Earl of Aberdeen, 31 August 1830 in *British Parliamentary Papers*, vol. 12, 33: Spanish slave schooner condemned for illicit slave trade "commanded by Francisco de Paula Golget, formerly an American subject [*sic*], born in the Floridas."
52. *The Liberator*, 15 November 1839.
53. Report from the Commanding General of the Eastern Department, 18 December 1830, Legajo 215, Numero de Orden 89, Asuntos Politicos, ANC. See also Maria Dolores Gonzales-Ripoll, Consuelo Naranjo, Ada Ferrer, Gloria Garcia and Josef Opatrny, eds., *El Rumor de Haiti en Cuba: Temor, Raza y Rebeldia*. Madrid: CSIC, 2004.
54. Murray, *Odious Commerce*, 78, 129.
55. Abiel Abbot, *Letters Written in the Interior of Cuba, Between the Mountains of Africana, to the East, and of Cusco, to the West in the Months of February, March, April, and May 1828*. Boston: Bowles and Dearborn, 1829, 96, 97.
56. Report by U.S. Consul, 6 July 1821, Roll 1, T55, Despatches from U.S. Consuls in Santiago de Cuba.
57. Thomas Yoseloff, ed., *Voyage to America: The Journals of Thomas Cather*. New York: T.Y., 1961. Cather asserted that there were 260,000 slaves in Cuba and 1.665 million in the United States. From 1790 to 1820, he said, 372,449 slaves were brought to Cuba. U.S. abolitionists also paid close attention to the free Negro population of Cuba, envisioning them as essential players in the hemispheric antislavery struggle. See also *The Abolitionist*, 9 February 1833.
58. Frank Marotti, "Negotiating Freedom in St. John's County, Florida, 1813–1862," 41.
59. British Minister to Madrid to the Duke of Infantado, 2 July 1826, Legajo de Estado 8022, AHN–Madrid.
60. Henry Kilbee et al., to George Canning, 22 February 1826, Legajo de Estado 8022, reports Spanish ship confronted by the Royal Navy off the coast of Africa; most of

the crew escape—but the scores of Africans left on board were all severely wounded, with about 23 dead bodies floating in the water.

61.   Ibid. Hundreds of Africans found aboard a Spanish vessel in deplorable conditions.

62.   Ibid. See also David Eltis, "The Export of Slaves from Africa, 1821–1843," *Journal of Economic History* 37/2 (June 1977): 409–33.

63.   John Reffell and William Smith to Earl of Dudley, 14 February 1828, in *British Parliamentary Papers. Correspondence with British Commissioners and with Foreign Powers Relative to the Slave Trade [Class A and Class B]*, vol. 12, Shannon: Irish University Press, 1968, 20. From Sierra Leone it was reported that a Spanish schooner "having on board 155 slaves" was detained; the vessel was bought in Havana "from one James Francis, an American for 5,000 dollars. . . . Slaves on board were to have been delivered on the Coast of Havannah." In the same volume, 96–98, see Henry Kilbee and W. S. Macleavy to Earl of Dudley, 3 January 1828, on a Spanish slave ship chased by the Royal Navy ran aground in Florida: "Some American wreckers came to their assistance. . . . found to have a cargo of between 500 and 600 Negroes on board." Two wreckers take the Africans to Havana and Matanzas—about 400 all told—and a third wrecker takes the remaining Africans to Key West: it is unclear if families were split in the process with one evolving as "African-American" and another as "Afro-Cuban." See also Black History File #1, Africans at Key West, John Quincy Adams to Senate and House, 20 April 1828, Message from the President of the United States Relative to the Disposition of the Africans Landed at Key West from a Stranded Spanish Vessel, April 30, 1828. Washington: Gales & Seaton, 1828, Monroe County Public Library–Key West. This authoritative 1828 document was blunt: "In the month of December last, one hundred and twenty-one African Negroes were landed at Key West from a Spanish slave-trading vessel, stranded within the jurisdiction of the United States, while pursued by an armed schooner in his Brittanic Majesty's service. The Collector of the Customs at Key West took possession of these persons, who were afterwards brought over to the Marshal of the Territory of East Florida, by whom they were conveyed to St. Augustine, where they still remain." In the same document, see Waters Smith, Marshall, Eastern District of Florida to Richard Rush, Secretary of Treasury, 2 April 1828: "121 African Negroes. . . .While they were at Key West, attempts were made to take them from the possession of my deputy, by force and by bribery; and the night before I removed them from the island, an attempt was made to carry off a part of them. . . . Absolutely necessary to remove the Negroes from Key West: they were not safe there. . . . They were placed in my custody perfectly naked, many of them sick and extremely weak and feeble." Also see Black History File #1, Gail Swanson, "The Africans of the Slave Ship 'Guerrero.'. . . The story of the wrecking of their en route to Cuba at the Florida Keys, their Subsequent Slavery in North Florida." October 1998: The ship crashes in Florida on 19 December 1827 with 561 Africans aboard who had just traveled 4,000 miles in an attempt to reach Cuba. Also see at the same site, Lt. Edward Holland to Rt. Hon. Charles R. Vaughan, 1 January 1828; and Case of Spanish ship *Guerrero*, 1827, wrecked off Key Largo with 121 Africans aboard, brought to Key West.

64.   Captain General to Governor of Santiago, 18 August 1826, Legajo 124, Numero de Orden 116, Asuntos Politicos, ANC.

65.   "Abstract from a Proclamation Issued by the Governor of Cuba," 10 March 1822, Roll 3, Despatches from U.S. Consuls in Havana—Monroe County Public Library: "The many complaints made to this Government of the depredations and piracies committed on the coasts of this island by the crew of armed launches and small crafts who rob vessels." See also Aaron Smith, *The Atrocities of the Pirates, or a Faithful Narrative of the Unparalleled Sufferings Endured by the Author, During his Captivity*

Among the Pirates of the Island of Cuba with an Account of the Excesses and the Barbarities of those Inhuman Freebooters. New York: Lowry, 1824; and Daniel Collins, *Narrative of the Shipwreck of the Brig Betsey, of Wincasset (Maine), and Murder of Five of Her Crew, By Pirates, on the Coast of Cuba, December 1824.* Wincassett: John Dore, 1825. See also 18th U.S. Congress, 1st Session, 19 May 1824. "Report of the Committee on Foreign Affairs. . . . Piracies Committed on the Commerce of the United States in the Neighborhood of the Islands of Cuba and Porto Rico," American Antiquarian Society–Worcester; and Congress, 2nd Session, extract of a Letter from Francis Adams, Commercial Agent of the United States at Matanzas to the Secretary of State, 30 December 1824. Washington, D.C.: Gales & Seaton, 1825; and 18th Congress, 2nd Session, U.S. Senate, 30 December 1824. Appearing before John Mountain, Vice Commercial Agent of U.S. at Havana, seaman George Brown asserts that near Matanzas, his vessel was boarded by 12 men "armed with muskets, cutlasses, pistols and knives"—about "40 men" altogether—who then terrorize the crew and set afire the vessel. For a Cuban view of U.S. pirates, Juan Gualberto de Ortega, Vice Consul–Charleston to Intendente de Hacienda, 3 January 1822, Legajo 112, Numero de Orden 131, Asuntos Politicos, ANC. On piracy near Puerto Rico, see Report, 20 July 1824, Legajo 6376, Correspondence with the Captain General, AHN–Madrid.

66. Military Commander, Baracoa to Santiago, 2 April 1823, Legajo 113, Numero de Orden 68, Asuntos Politicos, ANC.

67. J. Pulling, Havana, to W. S. MacLeay, 19 November 1829, in *British Parliamentary Papers*, vol. 12, 75–76. See also *Correspondence with the British Commissioners of Sierra Leone, the Havana, Rio de Janeiro and Surinam, Relative to the Slave Trade.* London: Clowes and Sons, 1835.

68. David Turnbull, *Travels in the West. Cuba: With Notices of Porto Rico and the Slave Trade.* London: Longman, Orne, Brown, Green and Longman, 1840, 443.

69. Miguel Tacon, Captain General to British Commissioner, 22 July 1836 in *British Parliamentary Papers. Correspondence with British Commissioners and with Foreign Powers Relative to the Slave Trade [Class A and Class B]*, vol. 15. Shannon: Irish University Press, 1968, 172.

70. W. S. MacLeay to Earl of Aberdeen, 30 December 1829 in ibid., 81.

71. H .T. Kilbee to Secretary Canning, 4 September 1824; and Letter from J.P. Clarke, British Consul in Santiago, ca. 1824, in ibid., 12:104–5, 12:217.

72. W. S. MacLeay and Edward W.H. Schenley to Viscount Palmerston, 27 February 1836 in ibid., 15:16–17.

73. C. D. Tolme to Captain General, 16 December 1839, in *British Parliamentary Papers. Correspondence with Foreign Powers Relative to the Slave Trade [Class B, C and D]*, vol. 19. Shannon: Irish University Press, 1969, 30.

74. Earl Granville to the Duke of Wellington, 2 January 1835, in *Correspondence with Foreign Powers Relating to the Slave Trade* London: Clowes, 1836.

75. Letter from James Baker, 1 March 1830, FO5/262/69, NAUK. See also 19th U.S. Congress, 1st Session, House of Representatives, Document Number 126, State Department, Letter from the Secretary of State in Reply to a Resolution of the House of Representatives of the 2nd Instant, in Relation to Certain African Captives Seized in the Harbor of Pensacola, 10 March 1826. Washington, D.C.: Gales & Seaton, 1826, University of Virginia. See also *The Liberator*, 28 January 1832: "About thirty thousand slaves are annually landed from Africa" in Cuba—with many then "smuggled into the U. States at Key West."

76. Dorothy Dodd, "The Schooner Emperor: An Incident of the Illegal Slave Trade in Florida," *Florida Historical Quarterly* 13/3 (January 1935): 117–28. See also *The*

Liberator, 9 June 1837, on pursuit of slave dealers along the Apalachicola River—formerly the site of the "Negro Fort"—"for bringing African Negroes from Cuba."

77.   *The Liberator*, 14 July 1832: "Clandestine introduction of slaves from Africa, via Cuba."

78.   *The Liberator*, 3 September 1831. See Treaties for the Abolition of the Traffic in Negroes involving Britain and France in *Le Moniteur Universel*, 1 September 1833, Legajo de Estado 8033, AHN–Madrid.

79.   *New York Herald*, 15 June 1839: "The American slave trade, carried on by American vessels, American sailors and American papers, is a disgrace to the nation. It is a most serious injury to the South, who are in no way participators in it. The Southern States are abused for the misconduct of some few scoundrels in the North."

80.   Black Seminoles History, Folder 158, George Klos, "Blacks and the Seminole Removal Debate, 1821–1835," *Florida Historical Quarterly* 68/1 (July 1989): 55–78, 60, Florida Collection, Jacksonville Public Library.

81.   *Niles Register*, 15 November 1823: U.S. vessels bring to Key West a slave ship captured near Havana.

82.   Edward Livingston to William Shaler, 25 July 1832, Arthur Bining Collection, Historical Society of Pennsylvania.

83.   Captain General to Intendente General, 5 March 1820, Legajo 111, Numero de Orden 48, Asuntos Politicos, ANC, on more rigor needed in admission of foreigners.

84.   Royal Order, 24 February 1828, Legajo 32, Numero de Orden 25, Asuntos Politicos, ANC; see also Captain General to Governor, 14 May 1828, Legajo 120, Numero de Orden 4, Asuntos Politicos, ANC. For more on this point, see Decree, 21 December 1828, in Luis Marino Perez, ed., *Guide to the Materials for American History in Cuban Archives*. Washington, D.C.: Carnegie, 1907, 78.

85.   Memorandum, 3 January 1825, Legajo 117, Numero de Orden 86, Asuntos Politicos, ANC.

86.   Royal Order, 29 April 1825, Legajo 29, Numero de Orden 43, Asuntos Politicos, ANC. Also on Varela, see "Papeles de Padre Felix Varela,." 10 December 1825, Legajo 129, Numero de Orden 1, Asuntos Politicos and Royal Order, 20 July 1824, Legajo 24, Numero de Orden 19, Asuntos Politicos: more on Varela. Report, 13 December 1824, Legajo 29, Numero de Orden 14, Asuntos Politicos, ANC; and Report from Spanish legation in Washington, 14 May 1839, Legajo 135, Numero de Orden 14, Asuntos Politicos, ANC. See also Juan Navia, *An Apostle for the Immigrants: The Exile Years of Father Felix Varela y Morales (1823–1853)*. Salisbury, MD: Factor Press, 2002.

87.   See Circular on Foreign Negroes and Mulattoes arriving in Cuba, 1835, Legajo 1641, Numero de Orden 82521, Gobierno Superior Civil, ANC.

88.   *The Liberator*, 15 December 1837.

89.   *The Colored American*, 21 October 1837, and 16 June 1838. George Davison—member of a family of abolitionists—was "arrested and thrown in prison in Havana," as "copy of 'Lundy's War in Texas' was found in his trunk" and only the interference of British diplomats saved him. See U.S. Consul R.R. Stewart to Captain General, 6 February 1835, Roll 1, T699, *Despatches from U.S. Consuls in Trinidad, Cuba*, NARA–CP. "Adams, a coloured . . . seaman [from] Baltimore which vessel came to an anchor in the Port of Casilda" and said to have "murdered the captain . . . and being now secure in the prison of of this city by the order of your Excellency." See also "Case of Abraham Wendell, Jr. of the Brig Kremlin of New York Arising from an Outrage Perpetrated by Him Upon William Bell, First Officer of Said Brig, in the Port of Havana, July 1838 (Being an Extract from a Document Recently Printed by Order of the House of Representatives)," Massachusetts Historical Society. For reasons

apparently involving corruption, the chief U.S. diplomat in Cuba, Nicholas Trist, was said to have been "guilty of secretly inciting Spanish authorities to the unlawful condemnation and imprisonment of American captains and seamen for alleged and *unfounded offences* preferred by him against them. . . . *One hundred and fifty-five* respectable ship masters and citizens of Havana comprising nearly all that reside here [concur]." (Emphasis–original.) There was a "petition for Mr. Trist's removal, signed by every American resident in the island of Cuba, as well as by captains and traders at the several ports, has, we understand, been forwarded to the President." See "Reply of N. P. Trist, Consul at Havana, to the Preamble and Resolutions Adopted by the Meeting of Ship Masters and Ship Owners, Convened at the City of New York, on the 8th and 14th of August 1839; and Transmitted to the President of the United States on the Ground of their Demand for the Instant Recall of Said Consul," G.W. Blunt Library–Mystic, CT.

90. Count of Ofalia to Sir George Villiers, 5 January 1838, in *British Parliamentary Papers*, 15:3. See also Murray, *Odious Commerce*, 118. Madrid protests against U.S. abolitionists targeting Cuba: 1838.

91. Report from Angel Calderon de la Barca, Spain's Minister in Washington, 8 December 1836, Legajo de Estado 8036, AHN–Madrid: There was an extraordinary growth of numerous abolitionist societies especially in the northeast. There was literature on mixing of blood between black and white. This was leading to strains within the Union and could provide a tremendous danger. See also Report, 21 October 1835, Legajo de Estado 8036, AHN–Madrid: the purpose of abolitionism was to sponsor slave revolts; also see Reports of 31 August 1837 and 31 August 1835 on growth of abolitionism and notably the role of Methodists; also in same file reams of translations of English-language abolitionist literature. See also Memorandum from Madrid, 23 October 1837, Legajo 39, Numero de Orden 36, Asuntos Politicos, ANC.

92. Miguel Tacon to Governor, 14 July 1837, Legajo 39, Numero de Orden 18, Asuntos Politicos, ANC.

93. Vice Consul of Spain to Captain General, 1 April 1839, Legajo 40, Numero de Orden 1, Asuntos Politicos, ANC. See also Report by Minister of Spain in Washington, 1836, Legajo 841, Numero de Orden 28253, Gobierno Superior Civil, ANC, on the activities of abolitionists and Maroons of the Caribbean.

94. Naturally, Havana was riveted by the idea of Jamaicans visiting the island after 1834: See Report, 1837, Legajo 841, Numero de Orden 28258, Gobierno Superior Civil, ANC.

95. Report by U.S. Consul, 26 February 1838, Roll 2, T55, *Despatches from U.S. Consuls in Santiago de Cuba*.

96. Letter from R. R. Madden, February 1839, CO318/146, NAUK: Seeking "permission for the black troops on board HM's ship Romney to land occasionally." In the same file, see R.R. Madden to Secretary of State for the Colonies, 29 May 1839. See also Memorandum from British legation, Madrid, 26 February 1839, Legajo de Estado 8036, AHN–Madrid: Reprimand of "the treatment to which British subjects being free Negroes and men of color are exposed on arriving as part of the crew of British vessels trading to Cuba. . . . Liable to be seized and thrown into prison on account of their colour, unless the Captain or owner. . . . shall enter into a Bond of one thousand hard dollars" ensuring that "none of the individuals in question shall come ashore during the time the vessel remains in a Port of the island."

97. Philip M. Hamer, "Great Britain, the United States and the Negro Seamen Acts, 1822–1848," *Journal of Southern History* 1/1 (February 1935): 3–28, 21.

98. *The Liberator*, 14 May 1831.

99. *The Liberator*, 9 July 1831. Emphasis in original.

100. *The Liberator,* 1 October 1831.
101. *The Liberator,* 27 June 1835.
102. *The Liberator,* 13 February 1836.
103. *The Liberator,* 26 January 1849. Africans were brought via Cuba to Texas in significant numbers in 1835. In the 24 March 1836 edition of this periodical it is reported: The "great number of these poor wretches," i.e. the enslaved of Brazoria, Texas, "have been imported within the last six months from Cuba." The conflict between Mexico and Texas was seen basically as a rift over slavery. In 16 April 1836 edition, more on slave trade between Cuba and Texas. Edition of 17 September 1836: "Importation into Texas of slaves from Cuba had taken place." Edition of 24 March 1837: "Corroboration of the fact that a covert traffic in slaves is carried on briskly between that island," i.e. Cuba and the United States; edition of 31 March 1837: ditto. Edition of 21 July 1837: Africans imported into Texas from Cuba. 21 September 1838: ditto. Edition of 31 May 1839: "Project of some unprincipled speculators to smuggle slaves from Cuba into the new republic," i.e. Texas. *The Colored American,* 15 June 1839: Plans afoot to import slaves to Texas from Cuba with ships from New Orleans: story embroidered in the 1 June 1839 edition.
104. Viscount Palmerston to H.M. Commissioners, 15 December 1836 in *British Parliamentary Papers. Correspondence with British Commissioners and with Foreign Powers Relative to the Slave Trade [Class A and Class B],*vol. 15. Shannon: Irish University Press, 1968, 202–3: "Contracts to supply the province of Texas with Bozal Negroes. . . . attempted by the Havana slave dealers."
105. David Turnbull, *Travels in the West. Cuba; With Notices of Porto Rico and the Slave Trade,* London: Longman, Orne, Brown, Green and Longmans, 1840, 148. The price of "Bozal Negroes" in the 1830s was about "$320 per head" in Havana and "three times" as much in Richmond (45). Subsequently, Turnbull was cited for the proposition that in 1838–9 23,000 Africans were arriving annually in Cuba from various sources. Alexander Jones, "Cuba in 1851: A Survey of the Island, its Resources, Statistics, Etc., from Official Documents in Connection with the Present Revolt." New York: Stringer & Townsend, 1851, Historical Society of Pennsylvania. See also *The Liberator,* 11 October 1839: Britain's Joseph Sturge "will vouch—showing from an eye-witness that in the present year there were imported into Texas from Cuba, no less than between 250 and 300 slaves in a single cargo and that this was not a solitary importation in the present year." W. E. B. Du Bois, "Suppression of the African Slave Trade," ca. 1936, Monroe County Public Library–Key West: "The Consul at Havana reported in 1836 that whole cargoes of slaves fresh from Africa were being daily shipped to Texas in American vessels, that 1,000 had been sent within a few months, that the rate was increasing." *The Liberator,* 24 August 1838: "Foreign importation of slaves into the United States by way of Cuba, was 13,000 annually." *The Liberator,* 21 March 1835: "As many as 11,000 were imported annually" from Cuba to the republic. Note: the estimated number increases with every passing year. Madrid well knew of this commerce. See Reports, 5 February and 4 April 1837, Legajo de Estado 8036, AHN–Madrid: A cargo of slaves from Cuba to Texas; also see Report, 28 October 1836. At times, U.S. officials objected when Negroes in the republic found their way onto U.S. ships in U.S. ports. Memorandum of Minister of Spain in U.S., 1832, Legajo 840, Numero de Orden 28241, Asuntos Politicos, ANC: Spanish ship detained in New Orleans after bringing Negro aboard; Also see Report on cargo of Africans destined for Texas, 27 June 1837, Legajo 105, Numero de Orden 220, Reales Cedulas y Ordenas, ANC; and Correspondence on New Orleans slave who escaped, 1836, Legajo 938, Numero de Orden 33090, Gobierno Superior Civil.
106. *Sketch of the Seminole War and Sketches during a Campaign by a Lieutenant of the*

Left Wing, Charleston: Dowling, 12, 19. 21, 22. See also Turnbull, *Travels in the West*: While in Washington, Turnbull wandered over to Congress and heard a Carolinian declaim on taking Cuba, annexing Texas, then attacking Canada—all of which was "received with the most rapturous applause. . . . It was not easy to restrain a smile at the vehement tone of his oration, and the extravagant gestures with which it was enforced; but both would have strangely damped, had any one whispered the word 'Seminoles' in his ear, and recalled to his recollection that, for several years, within a few hours' sail of Cuba, the whole military force of the Union has been fruitlessly employed in the attempt to subdue a mere handful of [indigenes]."

107. For more on these matters, see Horne, *Negro Comrades of the Crown*.

108. Report, 8 August 1831, Legajo de Estado, Correspondence of the Captain General, AHN–Madrid; andalso Report, 26 August 1832, Legajo de Estado 6374: Uprising in Jamaica with implications for Cuba (there is quite a bit on this revolt, signifying its impact). See Correspondence on Uprising of Negroes and Mulattoes in Jamaica, said to be against the white population, 27 April 1832, Legajo 25, Numero de Orden 25, Asuntos Politicos, ANC. See also Correspondence on arrival in Trinidad, Cuba of 5 abolitionists from Jamaica, 8 May 1839, Legajo 40, Numero de Orden 7, Asuntos Politicos, ANC; and Correspondence on Measures to Disrupt Clandestine Associations of Negroes, 29 November 1839, Legajo 40, Numero de Orden 27, Asuntos Politicos, ANC.

109. See plans involving 800 armed men from Haiti and Venezuela with the aim of abolishing slavery in Cuba: Report, 14 July 1837, Legajo 39, Numero de Orden 17, Asuntos Politicos, ANC.

110. Thomas Yoseloff, ed., *Voyage to America: The Journals of Thomas Cather*, New York: TY, 1961, 68.

111. Consul to State Department, 20 October 1833, Roll 1, T567, *Despatches from U.S. Consuls in Puerto Principe and Xibara*, NARA–CP. See also Memorandum from British legation, Madrid, 2 May 1839, Legajo de Estado, AHN–Madrid. Reference is made to the anti-slaving treaty of 1817, then the treaty of 1835 to plug the latter's loopholes.

112. Grace Gebelin, "Lopez's Filibustering Expedition to Cuba," M.A. thesis, Tulane University, 1929, 3.

113. Earl of Aberdeen to H. U. Addington, 17 February 1830 in C. K. Webster, ed., *Britain and the Independence of Latin America*, 472–75.

114. *The Liberator*, 4 June 1831.

115. *The Liberator*, 13 February 1836.

116. *The Colored American*, 22 March 1838.

117. Letter to "My Dear Brother," 20 January 1838, Tidd–Lord–Henchman–Carret Family Papers, Massachusetts Historical Society–Boston. "These Maroon[s]" that "live in the woods and mountains hold intercourse with the plantation slaves, make the attack and some will join them. . . . Easy for the Negroes to make their assaults and retreats."

118. Report by W. S.MacLeay and Wdeard W. H. Schenley, 1 January 1836, in *British Parliamentary Papers. Correspondence with British Commissioners and with Foreign Powers to the Slave Trade [Class A and Class B]*, vol. 14. Shannon: Irish University Press, 1968, 206–07,

119. Among the many stern rebukes of Madrid by London, see British legation to First Secretary of State, Don Francisco Martínez de la Rosa, 13 February 1835, Legajo de Estado 8034, AHN–Madrid. He is warned "seriously" that failure to act on the slave trade will "endanger the amicable relations" between the two monarchies. The "nefarious traffic" to Cuba "is carried on without disguise and without punishment."

120. U.S. legation to Secretary of State for Foreign Affairs, 10 March 1838, Legajo de Estado 8036, AHN–Madrid: U.S. Negroes were not "unkindly treated." London was blamed for U.S. slavery. Abolitionists were deemed "disturbers of the rights of others." He found it "commendable & praiseworthy" that Madrid "earnestly desires a general exemption of slavery from the world." Emancipation was condemned: "Will they be able to associate with the white population & to intermarry with it? . . . Impressions are sought to be made that the U. States desire to possess Cuba. No idea can be more ridiculous!" The U.S. "desire [*sic*] nothing more than for the island of Cuba to remain as it is." A version of this lengthy mission can be found in William Manning, ed., *Diplomatic Correspondence of the United States Concerning the Independence of the Latin-American Nations,* vol. 1, 310–13. See also Correspondence on Emancipation in Cuba and Abolition of the Slave Trade, 1836, Legajo 132, Numero de Orden 17, ANC.

121. Edward W. H. Schenley and R. R. Madden to Viscount Palmerston, 2 January 1837 in *British Parliamentary Papers,* 15: 216–18.

122. Viscount Palmerston to H. S. Fox, 20 January 1837 in ibid.15:142–43.

123. Edward W. H. Schenley et al., to "Sir," 16 March 1838, in *British Parliamentary Papers, Correspondence with British Commissioners and with Foreign Powers Relative to the Slave Trade [Class A and Class B],* vol. 17. Shannon: Irish University Press, 1968, 90.

124. C. D. Tolme to Viscount Palmerston, 5 January 1839, in ibid.,17:97–98: "One Spanish schooner, the 'General Espartero' proceeded to Key West and returned as the 'Thomas of Havana.' " See *The Liberator,* 22 October 1836: In Matanzas, "many ships of the United States are sold . . . for the purpose of being made slavers . . . now buying leaky, unsuspicious ships."

125. Edward W. H. Schenley and R. R. Madden, 25 October 1836 in *British Parliamentary Papers,* 15:191–92:.

126. James A. Fawley, "Joseph John Gurney's Mission to America, 1837–1840," *Mississippi Valley Historical Review* 49/4 (March 1963): 653–74, 670, 671. See also Murray, *Odious Commerce,* 104, on many slave ships built in Baltimore. On this latter point, see *The Liberator,* 13 December 1839. See also *An Invalid, a Winter in the West Indies and Florida.* New York: Wiley and Putnam, 1839, 75: In Trinidad harbor, "there is a good harbor and many vessels, principally American. . . . In the year 1838, about one hundred American vessels cleared from that port—a larger number than those of all other nations together."

127. James Pinckney Henderson to Colonel Morgan, 25 May 1838, James Morgan Papers, Rosenberg Library–Galveston: London "still delays the recognition of Texas. . . . there are too many circumstances which operate against that measure in England. I had hoped before I left London that I would find the French Government more disposed to favour my views than the English were, but in that I soon learned that I was destined to be disappointed. . . . Our friends here believe that France will not recognize Texas although they may virtually be at war with Mexico and I fear there is too much correctness in that belief. They say there will be even stronger objection to our recognition here than in England on the ground of slavery. . . . The French are a queer people & I believe now that Texas has more to expect from England than France."

128. Nicholas Trist, letter, 19 March 1834, Box 3, Nicholas Trist Papers: "bound to Havana. . . . "

129. Turnbull, *Travels in the West: Cuba,* 436.

130. Nicholas Trist to spouse, 27 March 1834, Box 3, Nicholas Trist Papers: "I am assured by one who knows that my office is now worth twice as much as it was. Don't talk of

this, however, even in the family: for it would leak out, and be sure to excite envy & cupidity."

131. Nicholas Trist letter, 4 December 1834, ibid.

132. M. A. Holley, Lexington, Kentucky, to Nicholas Trist, 5 April 1836, ibid.

133. Nicholas Trist letter, January 1835, ibid. See also W.S. MacLeay and Edward W.H. Schenley to Viscount Palmerston, 6 November 1835 in *British Parliamentary Papers*,vol. 14: "We have seen an article copied from the American papers, which imputes an insurrection in the Havana on the 12th July last, to the Africans emancipated by this Mixed Commission [led by London]. . . . This riot, which took place in the suburbs of the city, has been grossly exaggerated into an insurrection; and secondly, that the emancipated Negroes had not the least concern with it whatever. . . . A tissue of misrepresentation and evidently penned under the influence of that fear which too often produces in these slave colonies first exaggeration, and then cruelty."

134. Nicholas Trist to "My Own Dearest," 10 June 1835, Box 3, Nicholas Trist Papers.

135. Nicholas Trist letter, 27 June 1835, ibid.

136. Nicholas Trist to "My Own Dearest," 5 January 1835, ibid.

137. Ibid., Nicholas Trist letter, 13 April 1835, ibid.

138. Nicholas Trist letter, 18 June 1836, ibid.

139. Nicholas Trist letter, 27 June 1835, ibid.

140. Letter, 6 January 1837, ibid.: "to sell or not to sell the Cuba property will now be the question with you. No doubt Cuba has many advantages over Louisiana in regard to the cultivation of sugar. . . . at least double the capital in land & Negroes is required here to make the same quantity of sugar—Negro men are now selling from $1000 to $2000 cash" in New Orleans.

141. Letter to Nicholas Trist, 7 January 1837, ibid.

142. Letter, 3 April 1832, Legajo de Estado 5580. AHN–Madrid. On the numerous U.S. ships sailing from Havana to New Orleans and Charleston, see *El Noticioso. . . . Diario Mercantil, Politico y Literario*, Havana, 17 December 1834, Legajo de Estado 8034, AHN–Madrid. New Orleans ranked with Cadiz as a destination for ships from Havana.

143. Letter to Nicholas Trist, 8 June 1838, Box 3.

144. *The Liberator*, 5 July 1839. Cf. *The Liberator*, 13 February 1836: "Slaving from the port of New York" to Cuba meant Africans "brought $800 each" on the island.

145. Nicholas Trist to "My Own Dearest," 14 March 1835, Box 3: ". . . we shall be as safe here as in Washington, war or no war . . ."

146. Letter to Nicholas Trist, 31 January 1836, Box 3, Nicholas Trist Papers.

147. Nicholas Trist letter, 11 July 1835, ibid.

148. Marianna Gardner to Nicholas Trist, 22 September 1838, ibid.: "Your slave . . . came to me this morning to get me to beg for her. . . . She promises to be good hereafter if you please to pardon her. I am no friend to bad Negroes."

149. W. S. MacLeay and Edward W. H. Schenley, 27 February 1836 in *British Parliamentary Papers*, 17:139.

150. Edward W. H. Schenley and R. R . Madden to Viscount Palmerston, 30 November 1836 in ibid., 15: 211–12.

151. Viscount Palmerston, 21 January 1837, in ibid., 15:143.

152. H.S. Fox to John Forsyth, 29 October 1839, in ibid., 19:164–177.

153. J. Kennedy to Alexander Everett, 28 May 1840, in *British Parliamentary Papers. Correspondence with British Commissioners and with Foreign Powers Relative to the Slave Trade [Class A, B, C and D]*,vol. 20. Shannon: Irish University Press, 1969, 272.

154. Turnbull, *Travels in the West: Cuba*, 448, 35.

155. *The Liberator*, 13 December 1839. See also *The Liberator*, 27 December 1839, on: "abuse of the flag of the United States in the island of Cuba by Consul Trist." See also

The Colored American, 13 July 1839: "The way these American clippers are engaged in the business is this: the vessels are built and fitted out either in New York, Baltimore or Philadelphia, take in a cargo for the West Indies, Havana in particular, and sail with American papers and crews." Then arrive in Cuba where "the vessels are sold, the American crews discharged and a mixed crew of Spanish, Portuguese and Americans shipped and a Spanish Captain goes out as passengers. . . . The Hispano–American owners of these redoubtable clippers get American cut registers in some way or manner, from the American Consulate at Havana and we have heard it openly asserted that the Consulate is well acquainted with the trade and its ramifications and gives out these registers notwithstanding."

156. See U.S. Consul to John Forsyth, 9 November 1836, Roll 1, T699, *Despatches from U.S. Consuls in Trinidad, Cuba*: "There is no no part of the world where Consular establishments are more required or are of more utility to our commerce than upon this side of the island of Cuba. . . . I am happy to say that I am personally treated here by all classes with distinguished respect, by authorities and citizens."

157. Henry Addington to First Secretary of State, 28 November 1831, Legajo de Estado 8033, AHN: Slave trade to Cuba "continues with unrepressed vigor."

158. R. R. Madden, *A Letter to W.E. Channing, D.D., on the Subject of the Abuse of the Flag of the United States in the Island of Cuba, and the Advantage Taken of its Protection in Promoting the Slave Trade*. Boston: Ticknor, 1839: "The entire slave trade of the island of Cuba was then passing through [Trist's] hands. . . . *An incapable, intractable, injudicious, overbearing person*," he stressed, with "rude demeanor, a supercilious carriage, an insolent tone" along with "prolix pedantry." This document can be found at both the Historical Society of Pennsylvania and the Massachusetts Historical Society. At the latter, see "Reply of Nicholas P. Trist, Consul at Havana to the Resolutions at a Meeting in Boston on the Subject of the Cases of Abraham Wendell, Jr. and the Crew of the Ship William Engs," Washington, D.C.: 1840.

159. *New York Morning Herald*, 15 June 1839: "The conduct of Mr. Trist . . . has been of so extraordinary and (as we think) improper a character, as to call for the immediate interference of the Executive of this country and the instant removal of Mr. Trist from the station he at present occupies. . . . There is a strong suspicion that the various slavers detected with American papers have been furnished with them in some underhanded way or contrivance connected with the American consul at Havana."

160. *The Republic*, 4 June 1836. See also D. R. Clarke to Lord John Russell, 5 November 1839, CO318/146, NAUK: "That the American people generally and perhaps the government, do wish and would rejoice to see this rich and invaluable island a dependency or a member of the Union, there is not a doubt"—and only apprehension about London's reaction stays the republican hand.

161. *The Colored American*, 18 April 1840.

162. *The Colored American*, 19 April 1838.

163. *The Liberator*, 5 April 1839.

164. *The Liberator*, 15 March 1839, reports that 54,000 Africans had been brought to Brazil and 40,000 to Cuba and "not a few" to Texas; given the relatively small size of the island compared to its two peers, the influx to the island was remarkably stunning. All of these Africans were brought "for the most part" by ships of "American construction" and "employed on account of American citizens."

165. "The Third Annual Report of the British and Foreign Anti-Slavery Society for the Abolition of Slavery and the Slave Trade Throughout the World. Presented to the General Meeting Held in Exeter Hall. On Friday May 13, 1842." London: Thomas Ward, 1842, Johns Hopkins University. See also R. R. Madden to "Sir," 21 August 1839, CO318/146, NAUK: "The general use of the Portuguese flag and of late to

a considerable extent the American flag has prevented the Spanish treaty from producing those effects in this part of the world that might have been expected from it." See also *The Liberator*, 13 March 1840: "List of American vessels engaged in the slave trade on the West Coast of Africa during the Spring and Summer of 1839."

166. *The Colored American*, 13 March 1841.

167. D. R. Clarke to Lord John Russell, 4 August 1840, CO318/149, NAUK.

168. Her Majesty's Judge to Viscount Palmerston, 15 June 1840 in *British Parliamentary Papers*, 20:271–72. See also Correspondence on Trist, 4 December 1841, Legajo 41, Numero de Orden 24, ANC; U.S. Senate Resolution "in regard to the granting of papers to vessels engaged in the slave trade" by Trist, 20 July 1840, in Clyde N. Wilson, et al., eds., *The Papers of John C. Calhoun, 1839–1841*, vol. 15. Columbia: University of South Carolina Press, 1983, 315.

169. Antonio Rafael de la Cova, *Cuban Confederate Colonel: The Life of Ambrosio Jose Gonzalez*, Columbia: University of South Carolina Press, 2003, 5.

170. Trist had his defenders. See *A Letter to William E. Channing, D.D. in Reply to one Addressed to him by R.R. Madden, on the Abuse of the Flag of the United States in the Island of Cuba, for Promoting the Slave Trade by a Calm Observer*. Boston: Ticknor, 1840, Tulane University.

171. D. R. Clarke to Lord John Russell, 20 November 1840, CO318/149, NAUK.

172. *North Star*, 3 March 1848; Robert S. Levine, ed., *Martin R. Delany: A Documentary Reader*. Chapel Hill: University of North Carolina Press, 2003, 84–85.

173. William Lloyd Garrison to "Dear Sir," 1 November 1839, Roll 1, American Missionary Association Manuscripts, Tulane University.

174. *The American Captives in Havana, Being Ferdinand Clark's Reply to Nicholas P. Trist, Consul at that Place* Boston: Howe, 1841, AAS: Trist "proceeds to note an assault upon his dignity, inflicted by my sending a Negro boy to his office on an errand. . . . The sensitive functionary, it seems, sat choking with wrath at the outrage. . . . Whose white teeth and wooly pate put the Consul into such a paroxysm of rage. . . . [This occurs though Trist] also carries on trade in a small way through a buxom servant girl, who hawks dulces [sweets] for him through the streets." See also *Remarks Upon a Letter Written by Mr. Luis C. Vanuxem of Matanzas to Substantiate a Certain Allegation Circulated at That Place in Regard to the Conduct of N.P. Trist, American Consul at Havana, Towards Nathaniel Cross, Esq.* Boston: Ticknor, 1841, AAS.

3. AFRICANS REVOLT!

1. U.S. Secretary of State to Spanish authorities, 6 September 1839, Legajo de Estado 5584, AHN-Madrid. See also Howard Jones, *Mutiny on the* Amistad*: The Saga of a Slave Revolt and its Impact on American Abolition, Law and Diplomacy*. New York: Oxford University Press, 1987. See also "The African Captives. Trial of the Prisoners of the *Amistad* on the Writ of Habeas Corpus, Before the Circuit Court of the United States for the District of Connecticut, at Hartford," Judges Thompson and Judson, September term, 1839. New York: "Published for sale at 143 Nassau Street, 1839." Massachusetts Historical Society.

2. Memorandum from Pedro Argaiz, 30 October 1839 and Spanish Minister to U.S. Secretary of State, 7 December 1839, in Legajo de Estado 5584. See also Correspondence on the *Amistad*, 1839–1842, Legajo 1293, Numero de Orden 50402, Gobierno Superior Civil, ANC; also see on the *Amistad*: Report by Governor of Matanzas, 1840, Legajo 843, Numero de Orden 28295, Gobierno Superior Civil, ANC.

3. British legation in Madrid to Evaristo Perez de Castro, 5 January 1840, Legajo de Estado 5584. See also "26ᵗʰ U.S. Congress, 1ˢᵗ Session, Doc. No. 185, House

of Representatives, "Africans Taken in the Amistad. Congressional Document Containing the Correspondence in Relation to the Captured Africans." New York: Anti–Slavery Depository, 1840, Massachusetts Historical Society.

4. *The Colored American*, 2 January 1841 and 12 December 1839.

5. *The Colored American*, 13 March 1841.

6. "Argument of John Adams Before the Supreme Court of the United States in the Case of the United States Appellants v. Cinque and others, Africans captured in the Schooner 'Amistad' by Lieutenant Gedney." New York: Benedict, 1841, University of Kansas.

7. *The Liberator*, 25 February 1841.

8. Resolution, 1840, Legajo de Estado 5584.

9. Legislation, 10 April 1844, ibid.

10. *The Liberator*, 21 January 1841.

11. Entry, 17–18 January 1841, Alexander Hill Diary, Massachusetts Historical Society: "Soon after breakfast Mr. Turnbull called. . . . He left me with an extra 'Anti–Slavery Reporter' containing the report of the proceedings in the 'Amistad' case." Turnbull's imprint on the region was ratified when in the 1930s, a former enslaved African in perpetually militant St. Augustine, said they were termed derisively "Turnbull's darkies." See interview with Christine Mitchell, 10 November 1936, in George Rawick, ed., *The American Slave: A Composite Autobiography*, vol. 17. Westport, CT: Greenwood, 1972, 226. This interview can also be found in Box 4, Florida Negro Papers, University of South Florida. See also Reports monitoring Turnbull, 1841–1843, Legajo de Estado 8054, AHN–Madrid. See also Report on Turnbull, 1 February 1841, Legajo 40, Numero de Orden 57, Asuntos Politicos, ANC. Also see Report on Turnbull, 8 February 1841, Legajo 40, Numero de Orden 60 and Minister of State–Spain to Captain General, 30 June 1841, Legajo 41, Numero de Orden 10, ANC.

12. Turnbull, *Travels in the West*, 269.

13. Pedro Argaiz to Secretary of State–Madrid, 21 January 1840, Legajo de Estado 5584, AHN–Madrid. See also Report, 1842, Legajo 941, Numero de Orden 33191, Gobierno Superior Civil, ANC, for protest against Turnbull. For various documents on Turnbull, 1840–1847, Legajo 40, Numero de Orden 46, Asuntos Politicos, ANC.

14. George Villiers, British legation to Count Ofalia, 10 April 1838, Legajo de Estado 8036, AHN–Madrid: Villiers denies that London's agents are seeking to "create disturbances among the slave population in Cuba" or "encouragement and protection" to those who seek to do so; if a slave revolt occurs, it is due to "cruelty on the part of the owners of the revolted slaves." Also, Reports, 4 October 1839–29 November 1844, Legajo de Estado 8038, for Baptist publications from Jamaica that include material on a war on Cuba in order to free the enslaved. See also Daniel Nason, *A Journal of a Tour from Boston to Savannah Thence to Havana*, 1849, Georgia Historical Society–Savannah: "Most of the lifting and lugging is done here [in Cuba] by the Negroes. They are strong, healthy and fleshy. . . . The awful whip is what they have most to fear. . . . Several times I have seen the whip too zealously applied upon their naked bodies . . . but after several blows they do not seem to exhibit so much sensibility. . . . Yesterday morning a Negro was to be garroted for killing his master."

15. *The North Star*, 26 October 1849. According to Turnbull, "'in no quarter, unless, perhaps in the Brazils, which I have not visited, is the state of slavery so desperately wretched as it is on the sugar plantations of the Queen of the Indies'"—i.e. Cuba.

16. Deposition of R. R. Madden, 7 November 1839, CO318/146, NAUK. See also *New York Commercial Advertiser*, 25 November 1839. Says Madden: "On the subject of slavery in Cuba and of the condition of the Negroes held in slavery, I believe I am as

fully informed as any foreigner can be. I have visited a great many estates and made many journeys into the interior."

17. Pedro Argaiz to Secretary of State–Madrid, 1 February 1841, Legajo de Estado 5584, AHN–Madrid.

18. Lord Palmerston to Spanish authorities in Madrid, 20 December 1839, CO318/149, NAUK.

19. *The Liberator*, 15 May 1840.

20. Statement on Cuba, 25 June 1840, Joel Robert Poinsett Papers, Historical Society of Pennsylvania.

21. Larry Rivers, "Florida's Black Heritage," 2006, Black History File #1, Monroe County Public Library.

22. James Innerarity to John Innerarity, 6 March 1843, Reel 25, Panton Leslie Papers.

23. Marvin Dunn, *Black Miami in the Twentieth Century*. Gainesville: University Press of Florida, 1997, 25.

24. "U.S. vs. Flowery," 1 Spr. 109, 8 Law Rep. 258, August 1845, Monroe County Public Library; also here, see *Key West Citizen*, 2 March 1997: "One thousand four hundred thirty-two Africans were brought into Key West as potential slaves for Cuban plantations. The ships they were on had been captured by U.S. cruisers against the slave trade." See "Another Report on the Mystery Ship and its 'Captive' Cargo," referring to ships in 1836 trading between Cuba and the peninsula; in the same file a report on U.S. ship in 1830 captured in Cuba laden with Africans, brought from Key West. Part of the problem was that coral reefs along the Florida coast and the straits were perilous, making simple voyages complex and accidents that led to Africans scurrying in various directions easier. See *A Selection of the Letters of the Late John Ashton Nicholls, Edited by His Mother, Printed for Private Circulation Only*, 1862, 338, Maryland Historical Society–Baltimore: "Shipwrecks are of constant occurrence." See also Kenneth F. Kiple, "The Case Against a Nineteenth-Century Cuba–Florida Slave Trade," *Florida Historical Quarterly* 49/4 (April 1971): 346–55.

25. "Message from the President of the United States. . . . Correspondence in Relation to the Tenth Article of the Treaty of Washington, Providing for the Reciprocal Surrender of Fugitive Criminals," 28th Congress, 1st Session, Senate, 21 February 1844, Monroe County Public Library.

26. *St. Augustine News*, 12 August 1843 and 7 October 1843, Monroe County Public Library. See other file items about "Key Biscayne Murders"—Africans slaying Europeans, then fleeing to the Bahamas.

27. Correspondence between City Council of St. Augustine and Secretary of the Treasury, 14 August 1843, Monroe County Public Library.

28. "Romer Case 1840," Monroe County Public Library.

29. James Westcott to James Buchanan, 31 May 1847, in "Message from the President of the United States Communicating in Compliance with a Resolution of the Senate, Information in Relation to the Fisheries on the Coasts of Florida," 32nd Congress, 2nd Session, Senate, Ex. Doc. No. 45, 24 February 1853, Monroe County Public Library.

30. For more on the unrest surrounding "Escalera" see Reports, 1844, Legajo 64, Numero de Orden 4, Comision Militar, ANC. For more on this see Reports, 1844, Legajo 67, Numero de Orden 1, Comision Militar, ANC. See also Murray, *Odious Commerce*, 160, on "Escalera" as response to U.S. annexationists.

31. Robert Paquette, *Sugar Is Made with Blood: The Conspiracy of La Escalera and the Conflict Between Empires Over Slavery in Cuba*, Middletown: Wesleyan University Press, 1988: 3, 156.

32. *The Colored American*, 10 April 1841: "The papers announce that an insurrection had broken out in Trinidad de Cuba, among the slaves. . . . In the nature of things, [this]

seems to threaten that island, either that they must relinquish their hold upon these poor victims to their rage, or their island will at no distant day be deluged in blood, as a judgment from Heaven." *The Liberator*, 5 May 1843: "Late servile insurrection in Cuba. . . . Number of slaves killed, or who committed suicide . . . about 300." See also *The Liberator*, 28 April 1843 and 9 June 1843: "Insurrection among the Negroes on the south side of the island, in the immediate vicinity of St. Jago de Cuba. . . . Plot appears to have been much more extensive and deeply organized than the outbreak at Cardenas, some five or six weeks ago. . . . An insurrection broke out last week . . . near Cardenas . . . death of many Negroes."

33.   *The Liberator*, 11 March 1842: "Appalling rumor . . . that the blacks of Jamaica had massacred all the white inhabitants" and fear they will now descend on Cuba.

34.   *The Liberator*, 5 May 1843.

35.   *The Liberator*, 26 May 1843, on slave revolt in Cuba: "I have this moment been looking at an American carpenter, who a few minutes since was brought here in a state of insensibility, mutilated in a horrid manner. The poor fellow's horse was killed under him and he wounded. . . . Several families have been massacred."

36.   *The Liberator*, 15 April 1842: "Can slavery continue much longer in Cuba without being followed up by rebellion and bloodshed? It cannot." *The Liberator*, 9 June 1843: While Cuba is in turmoil, in now-abolitionist Antigua "and other English islands" tranquility reigns. "It seems surprising that men of even ordinary intelligence and observation should adhere so pertinaciously [*sic*] to a system which is surely and inevitably working their ruin."

37.   *The Liberator*, 26 July 1844.

38.   *The Liberator*, 10 March 1841, report from Havana: "Vessels of the first class are continually arriving here from Baltimore and are sold to men notorious as slave dealers. . . . In the course of the last week, two highly respectable American gentlemen, General Talmadge of New York and Mr. King of Albany, were impelled by curiosity to visit one of the barracones. . . . On their arrival at the place, they were refused admittance on the supposition of being Englishmen, to which they replied that they were Americans." They were admitted then told "had they been from New Orleans, their request would have been granted [instantly]."

39   *The Liberator*, 1 May 1840. See also *The Colored American*, 2 March 1841: "The British government were about making arrangements with the Spanish Cortes for the emancipation of the slaves of that island. That the citizens of Havana were very much excited in regard to it, and remonstrances were being numerously signed against the measure. By the same we learn, also, that the twenty thousand *colored troops* the British Government have been training in the West Indies, are to be destined to Cuba, to suppress any violence that may occur when such an arrangement shall go into effect."

40.   Statement on Cuba, 25 June 1840, Joel Robert Poinsett Papers, Historical Society of Pennsylvania: "A continual fear is entertained in the island that Negroes from the neighboring British islands may be sent over to cause a rising" in Cuba. "Reported that two hundred thousand Negroes were landed [in] Jamaica, which added to an equal number previously sent there." A "number of Black Regiments" were "drilled" constantly in Cuba.

41.   *The Liberator*, 16 June 1843.

42.   *The Liberator*, 5 December 1845: Auction in Bristol by Mark de Wolfe of "Mount Hope Estate" situated about 20 miles south westerly from the city of Matanzas," including, it was emphasized, "NEGROES." See also Entry, March 1846, Diary of George S. Emerson, Massachusetts Historical Society: En route to Cuba with de Wolfe, "a gentleman of about 50 from Rhode Island, the owner of several estates in

Cuba to which he is now making his yearly visit. . . . He has seen a good deal of the world [and] is good natured."

43. John George F. Wurdemann, *Notes on Cuba, Containing an Account of the Discovery and Early History*. Boston: James Munroe, 1844, 271. See also William Henry Hurlbert, *Gan-Eden: On Pictures of Cuba*. Boston: Jewett, 1854, 198, 199, 200, 201: "Dr. Wurdemann tells us of a planter who having purchased a gang of newly landed Lucumis, thought fit to punish one of them. Soon afterward he was summoned to the help of his overseer, and found the Lucumis dancing their war-dance around a tree on which the Lucumi, who had been punished, was hanging, having taken refuge from what he thought disgrace, in suicide. Matters looked very threatening. But the planter, with great tact, ordered the dead body to be respectfully taken down, placed upon a bier and borne to the *baracon*. He followed it himself, but in hand. . . . At the *baracon*, the planter addressed them in praise of the brave Lucumi nation, and of that particular hero before them, assured them they should be kindly treated. . . . The Lucumis are not merely proud and fierce. They are very intelligent . . . and the Lucumis are by no means the only fierce and intelligent savages imported into Cuba. Whether this constant groundswell into the sluggish waters of slavery is favorable, or not to the safety of the vessel that floats on such a tide, my readers will decide for themselves."

44. *The Liberator*, 26 May 1843.

45. Letter to Martín Van Buren, 4 April 1829, Rodney Collection, Delaware Historical Society–Wilmington: "Few families in America, at the time of the Revolution, of the same extent (and it was a very large one in all its branches) were more united, or more efficient in furthering the cause of independence than was the family of the Rodneys." See also Peter T. Dalleo, "Thomas McKean Rodney: U.S. Consul in Cuba: The Havana Years, 1825–1829," *Delaware History* 22 (1986–1987): 204–18.

46. Peter T. Dalleo, "'Both Pockets Full of Letters': Thomas M. Rodney, John M. Clayton, William R. King and Patronage," *Delaware History* 30/2 (Fall–Winter 2002–2003): 85–119, 95, 96: "In an 1845 case, Rodney wrote about the owner of a captured slave vessel, one John Scorsu, an Italian national in Matanzas, who had real estate interests in Brooklyn, commercial contacts in Baltimore and investments in a slave factory on the Pongo River in West Africa." See also Dalleo, "Thomas McKean Rodney: U.S. Consul in Cuba," 204–18. See also Angel Calderon de Barca to John C. Calhoun, 29 October 1844, in Clyde N. Wilson et al., eds., *The Papers of John C. Calhoun, 1844*, vol. 20. Columbia: University of South Carolina Press, 1991, 155: "Some American citizens arrested upon a charge of conniving at the scheme of revolt of the colored people of that island."

47. Thomas Rodney to John C. Calhoun, 9 July 1844, in Wilson, *The Papers of John C. Calhoun*, vol. 19, 301–2. On the incarceration of U.S. national Robert Bell, charged with conspiracy, see Documents, 1844, Legajo 65, Numero de Orden 13, Comision Militar, ANC. See also Memorandum from Daniel Downing and Samuel Moffat, 26 May 1844, FO72/664, NAUK: "An American in the stocks with me. . . . "

48. *The Liberator*, 12 August 1842. See also Daniel Nason, *A Journal of a Tour From Boston to Savannah Thence to Havana*, 1849, Georgia Historical Society–Savannah: Nason meets "Mr. Leonard W. Kincaid, formerly from Vermont" and now in Cuba, "who was building four stores."

49. James Chapman to John C. Calhoun, 22 December 1848, Wilson, *The Papers of John C. Calhoun,*, vol. 26, 180.

50. Jose Vega Sunol, "Los Asentamientos Norteamericanos en El Norte de Oriente (1898–1933)," *Revista de Historia Holguin* 3/1 (1989): 32–51.

51. Memorandum from consulate in Matanzas, 4 June 1844 in Wilson, *The Papers of John C. Calhoun*, 19:715. See also *The Colored American*, 21 August 1841: "Mr. Cross,

the American Consul at the port, had been incarcerated in prison by the order of the Governor General of Cuba. . . . It is a bold move. . . . A former Consul at that port (late Mr. Shoemaker) also met with the same indignity in the early part of General Jackson's administration, which was promptly taken in hand by them, and brought before the notice of the Spanish government through its Minister at Washington."

52. Report, 1843, Legajo 849, Numero de Orden 28607, Gobierno Superior Civil. See also Report on U.S. Consul concerning his interventions concerning free Negroes and ships, 1844, Legajo 850, Numero de Orden 28629, Gobierno Superior Civil and Report, 1841, Legajo 846, Numero de Orden 28396, Gobierno Superior Civil.

53. Thomas Rodney to John C. Calhoun, 28 March 1844, in Wilson, *The Papers of John C. Calhoun*, 19: 113–14.

54. *The Liberator*, 12 July 1844.

55. Entry, 1844, William Norwood Diary, Virginia Historical Society–Richmond. Robert Campbell, U.S. Consul in Havana to John C. Calhoun, 14 September 1844, in Wilson, *The Papers of John C. Calhoun*, 19:778–79: "There are now in prison at Matanzas . . . sixteen hundred coloured persons bond and free. . . . There have been thirty-nine executions among which was one white (Spaniard) the balance coloured," including "Placido, a coloured poet of more reputation than any other native poet of the island." For more on "Gabriel de la Concepcion Valdes (Placido)," see articles published in Matanzas on him and his execution, 27–29 June 1844, Legajo 42, Numero de Orden 5, Asuntos Politicos, ANC. See also R.R. Madden, *Poems by a Slave in the Island of Cuba, Recently Liberated; Translated from the Spanish... with the History of the Early Life of the Negro Poet Written by Himself*. London: Thomas, Ward, 1840; Frederick S. Stimson, *Cuba's Romantic Poet: The Story of Placido*. Chapel Hill: University of North Carolina Press, 1964. In *The North Star*, 7 December 1849: Placido, stressed this journal of African abolitionists, was a "'Negro and a Man'" and a "revolutionist" who ranked in importance with Haiti's heroic Toussaint.

56. W. Napoleon Rivers, "Placido," *Opportunity* 11/3 (March 1933): 86–88, Box 32, 1:N, National Urban League Papers, Library of Congress.

57. *The Liberator*, 28 August 1846.

58. Report, 11 November 1844, Legajo 42, Numero de Orden 12, Asuntos Politicos, ANC.

59. Report from Consul of Spain in New York, 6 September 1844, Legajo 138, Numero de Orden 19, Asuntos Politicos, ANC: Don Calixto Aguirre and an uprising of Africans in Cuba.

60. Robert Harrison to John C. Calhoun, 23 August 1844 in Wilson, *The Papers of John C. Calhoun*, 19:634: He advised "reorganization and discipline of our Militia. . . . The time is not far distant when every white inhabitant in those States will have to shoulder his musket in defense of everything he holds dearest in life. Your own gallant State . . . from the paucity of its numbers of white citizens compared to the Blacks and the laxity of its Militia discipline, will be greatly exposed and the worst consequences may result therefrom."

61. Jane Landers, *Atlantic Creoles*, 216, 227.

62. John C. Calhoun to Robert Campbell, 1844, in Wilson, *The Papers of John C. Calhoun*, 19:175.

63. *The Liberator*, 10 May 1844: The "servile insurrection in Cuba" led to "many American citizens . . . arrested or placed in irons and in the stocks. . . . There is a strong feeling against Americans."

64. Consul to James Buchanan, Secretary of State, 10 April 1845, Roll 2, T699, *Despatches from U.S. Consuls in Trinidad, Cuba*. See also Report, 1845, Legajo 944, Numero de

Orden 33294-A, Gobierno Superior Civil, ANC, on the departure from Cuba for Philadelphia of a slave of Dr. Daniel Warren. For more on Warren, see Minister of Spain in U.S. to Captain General, 6 September 1839, Legajo 40, Numero de Orden 19, Asuntos Politicos, ANC.

65. Report, 3 December 1842, Legajo 41, Numero de Orden 17, Asuntos Politicos, ANC; alsosee Report, 1842, Legajo 847, Numero de Orden 28458, Gobierno Superior Civil, on U.S. Consul seeks permission to disembark slaves of Mr. Federico Seruges; and Report, 30 April 1844, Legajo 139, Numero de Orden 3, Asuntos Politicos.

66. Report from Spanish legation in U.S., 1842, Legajo 847, Numero de Orden 28499, Gobierno Superior Civil, ANC.

67. Jane Landers, *Atlantic Creoles*, 40. See also Report, 17 May 1844, Legajo 140, Numero de Orden 19, Asuntos Politicos, ANC: Free Negro Antonio Merlin, native of New York, among those expelled from Cuba. See also Report, 11 May 1844, Legajo 138, Numero de Orden 18, Asuntos Politicos: Attempted arrival in Cuba of Francisco Sairas, native of Florida; Report on Emigration Status of Diego Domingo, Free Negro, native of Florida, 6 May 1844, Legajo 140, Numero de Orden, Asuntos Politicos. By 1850 Davidson County, Tennessee, included a number of Negroes born in Cuba. See J. Merton England, "The Free Negro in Ante–bellum Tennessee," *Journal of Southern History* 9/1 (February 1943): 37–58, 40.

68. Royal Order barring the entry to Cuba of any individual of color—free or emancipated, 13 May 1844, Reales Cedulas y Ordenas, ANC. See also Report, 18 October 1844, Legajo 134, Numero de Orden 309, Reales Cedulas y Ordenas; Report, 4 September 1848, Legajo 142, Numero de Orden 7, Reales Cedulas y Ordenas. On Free Negroes from Cuba migrating to Mexico, see Report, 6 March 1841, Legajo 40, Numero de Orden 65, Asuntos Politicos, ANC. On plans to station Free Negroes on the border with Texas as a kind of firewall at the same site and section, see Report, 31 May 1841, Legajo 41, Numero de Orden 7.

69. Jose Maria Calvo and Francisco Chacon, "Report of the Majority of the Committee of the Royal Patriotic Society of Havana," 26 October 1841, in *British Parliamentary Papers*, vol. 22, 416–23.

70. Joseph Crawford to Earl of Aberdeen, 8 May 1844, FO72/664, NAUK.

71. Memorandum from the Captain General, no date [translated by the British], FO72/664.

72. Royal Order, 26 March 1842, Legajo 41, Numero de Orden 36, Asuntos Politicos, ANC. See also Report, 17 October 1842, Legajo 137, Numero de Orden 1, Asuntos Politicos; Report on attempt to circulate in Cuba "La Verdad" and "Patria de Nueva Orleans," 26 February 1848, Legajo 43, Numero de Orden 23, Asuntos Politicos. See also *The Liberator*, 5 January 1849: U.S. national jailed in Cuba for bringing to the island literature calling for republican annexation of the island.

73. *The Liberator*, 28 August 1846: "African Negroes have been taken in by the U.S. Deputy Marshall alleged to have been imported from Cuba."

74. John F. Wurdemann, *Notes on Cuba, Containing an Account of Its Discovery and Early History*. Boston: John Munroe, 1844, 59. See also William Henry Hurlbert, *Gan-Eden: On Pictures of Cuba*. Boston: Jewett, 1854, 185, 189, 190, 191: "I have never seen in any slave country much positive physical suffering, and I saw less in Cuba than I have seen in Carolina. . . . It was my fortune to see in Cuba perhaps the mildest form of agricultural history. . . . The Spanish slave laws resemble those of the East than those of America. . . . There are circumstances of great superiority in the condition of the Cuban over that of the American slave. . . . The Cuban slave is protected by the law in the enjoyment of a certain amount of property. . . . The large proportion of Free Negroes . . . is a standing witness to the advantages enjoyed by

the African race in Cuba. Moreover, the free blacks and mulattoes enjoy privileges which would not be granted them for an instant, in the American slave states. They are enrolled in the militia and some of them have just been called into active service." See also *Provincial Freeman*, 2 September 1854: According to this mainland Negro organ, "We regard the laws of that island as far more favorable to the slave than those of our Southern States. . . . Emancipations are constantly going on. . . . In no part of the [U.S.] do they [Free Negroes] occupy the high social position which they enjoy in Cuba." See also Enrique Manuel Lopez, "The Impact of Slavery and the Legacy of Afro-Cuba Subjugation on Race Relations in Cuba at the Turn of the Century (1866–1912)," Honors thesis, Brown University, 1996, 11: Slavery in Cuba was "much more humane" that that in the United States. See George W. Williams, *Sketches of Travel in the Old and New* World. Charleston, NC: Walker Evans, 1871, 37: "I did not like to see the amalgamation that is going on here. It is lawful for a Cuban to have a colored wife and mongrel children." Williams refers to Cuba in 1856. See also Carlton H. Rogers, *Incidents of Travel in the Southern States and Cuba*. New York; Craighead, 1862, 123–24: "The slaves on this island are exempt from many of the abuses they receive in the Southern States."

75.   Fredrika Bremer, *The Homes of the New World: Impressions of America*, vol. 2. New York: Harper & Bros., 1853, 308: "Spanish law . . . has some excellent and just enactments, as regards the rights and the emancipation of Negro slaves, which those of the American states are still deficient in, to their shame be it spoken!. . . . Slaves here, at all events in the cities, have a much better chance of acquiring money than in the American slave states. . . . It has been astonishing to me, and distressing at the same time, to see the United States stand so far behind Spain in justice and sense of freedom in their legislation for the slave population. . . . The Spaniards of Cuba are not altogether wrong when they, on this subject, look down on the Americans, and call them, as I myself heard, 'barbarians'!" See Demoticus Philalethes, 147, a visitor who speaks of a Cuban slaveholder who educates his Africans: "Our Patriarch would have run the risk of having the Lynch-law applied to him in our Southern States"; unlike Dixie, in Cuba "many Spaniards married to Negresses." See also John Blassingame, "Bibliographical Essay: Foreign Writers View Cuban Slavery," *Journal of Negro History* 57/4 (October 1972): 415–24, 419: "Many travelers felt that Cubans treated their slaves worse than Southerners did. J.G. Wurdemann, a South Carolinian who spent three years in Cuba, concluded that Cuban slaves were 'governed more by the fear of punishment than are the slaves in our Southern States.'" *The Liberator*, 20 August 1858: "I have no doubt . . . that the slaves in Cuba are worked much harder than they were in the British West Indies, or than they now are in the United States." William Cullen Bryant, *Letters of a Traveller; Or Notes of Things Seen in Europe and America*. New York: Putnam, 1850: 393–94: In Cuba "it is generally the natives of Africa by whom these murders are committed," and thus "the whip is always in sight. . . . Nothing can be done without it [whip]" says one visitor. "You cannot make the Negroes work by the mild methods which are used by slaveholders in the United States; the blacks there are far more intelligent." Still, the author added that manumission was easier in Cuba than on the mainland: "It is owing to this, I suppose, that the number of free blacks is so large in the island. . . . The prejudice of color is by no means so strong here as in the United States. Five or six years ago the Negroes were shouting and betting in the cockpits with the whites; but since the mulatto insurrection, as it is called, in 1843, the law forbids their presence at such amusements. I am told there is little difficulty in smuggling people of mixed blood, by the help of legal forms, into the white race, and if they are rich, into good society, provided their hair is not frizzled." See also Alexander Humboldt, *The Island of*

Cuba. New York: Derby & Jackson, 1856, 211: "In no part of the world where slavery exists is manumission so frequent as in the island of Cuba."

76.   Jose A. Gobantes and Francisco de Armas, "Report of the Ayuntamiento of the Havana," 14 October 1841, in *British Parliamentary Papers*, 23:132–38.

77.   *The Liberator*, 18 October 1844. See also Report, 27 March 1841, Legajo 133, Numero de Orden 22, Asuntos Politicos, ANC: Negroes that arrive in Cuba by sea will be incarcerated, then returned to their respective nations. *New York Herald*, 8 October 1844: Consul of Spain in New York City informed to block visits to Cuba by "individuals of color. All people of color are prohibited from entering the territory of this island."

78.   Thomas Rodney to John C. Calhoun, 28 March 1844 in Wilson, *The Papers of John C. Calhoun*, 19:113–14: "Heretofore persons of colour arriving here have been permitted to remain on board their respective vessels on giving bonds of security, but hereafter they will be placed in confinement immediately on their arrival and detained until the vessels to which they belong are ready for sea. . . . The state of affairs has given much trouble to our shipping interest for the stevedores have been arrested and vessels loading have great difficulty in obtaining hands to stow cargo."

79.   Report, 10 December 1841, Legajo 136, Numero de Orden 21, Asuntos Politicos. Report, 10 December 1841, Legajo 135, Numero de Orden 21, Asuntos Politicos, ANC. See also David Turnbull to Earl of Aberdeen, 15 December 1841 in *British Parliamentary Papers*, 23:61: Three free persons of color, Portuguese subjects, working on a U.S. schooner, "express" the "great alarm" that "they should be sold into slavery by the master of the vessel . . . of which they had received the most unequivocal indications." Rebuffed by both the Portuguese and U.S. consuls in Havana, they turn to Turnbull. In the same volume (128–29) see David Turnbull to Earl of Aberdeen, 31 January 1842: A British subject, a Negro, being held in slavery in Cuba "in the town of Gibara . . . by a widow named Norris, the widow of an American who had possessed a coffee plantation . . . and whose name was John Norris." Joseph Crawford to Earl of Aberdeen, 12 June 1843, in *British Parliamentary Papers*, 26:42–43: During the 1812 War, Britain occupied Florida's "Prospect Bluffs" where it "enlisted many of the colored inhabitants" who were given "free papers," and some moved to St. Augustine, from whence they were "sold into slavery" in Cuba and British envoys are now seeking to rescue them. See also *The Liberator*, 11 August 1848: John Lytle, "colored man, born in Philadelphia . . . unlawfully . . . held as a slave for eleven years. He was shipwrecked on the coast of Africa" before falling victim to enslavers headed to Cuba. For more on Lytle, see Joseph T. Crawford to Viscount Palmerston, 22 July 1848, in *British Parliamentary Papers*. 36: 270–71. Eleven years earlier a U.S. ship conveyed free Negroes to Liberia—but the vessel ran aground near "one of the slave factories at Gallinas." The master and the crew—"with the exception of the steward, a Negro," i.e. Lytle—depart. Lytle persuaded to stay with promise of free passage to Havana, then Philadelphia, but upon arrival in Cuba "he was sold along with rest of the unfortunate victims." For more on Lytle, see Legajo de Estado 8040, AHN. Report from British legation in Madrid, 23 January 1839, Legajo de Estado 8028, AHN–Madrid: "Restoration to liberty of a youth named Wellington who was kidnapped in the year 1834 in Montego Bay in Jamaica and sold afterward at Santiago de Cuba." In the same Legajo see Report from U.K. delegation, 20 October 1841: "Wellington" was one of a number of Jamaicans held illegally in bondage in Cuba. British legation, Madrid to Don Francisco Martínez de la Rosa, 2 May 1845, Legajo de Estado 8037: "Emancipated Negroes" including 12 men, 18 women, and 19 children, have "received tickets and had been removed, at the desire of the Spanish authorities to a British colony."

80. Report, 30 April 1844, Legajo 139, Numero de Orden 3, Asuntos Politicos, ANC. See also Plan to establish a depot for arriving free persons of color from Puerto Rico, 4 September 1848, Legajo 142, Numero de Orden 7, Asuntos Politicos.

81. Report, 27 March 1841, Legajo 133, Numero de Orden 22, Asuntos Politicos, ANC: All Negroes arriving aboard boats will be incarcerated, then returned from whence they arrived. Also see Report, 5 April 1841, Legajo 41, Numero de Orden 5, Asuntos Politicos: The authorities in Matanzas bars the arrival of any foreign Negroes. See also Joseph Crawford to Will Cocker, 24 July 1844, FO72/664: "A law of the island to place all coloured persons belonging to the crews of vessels" in jail "during the stay of such vessels unless there is security entered into by bond of the Captain . . . in the sum of [$]1,000 for each person of colour that they shall not land."

82. General Geronimo Valdes to British Consul, 5 April 1841 in *British Parliamentary Papers*, 22:257: For London's objection see Response from British legation, Madrid, 28 December 1840, Legajo de Estado 8037, AHN-Madrid. In the same legajo see British Consulate–Havana to Lord Palmerston, 10 August 1840.

83. Frank Marotti, "Negotiating Freedom in St. John's County, Florida, 1812–1862," 130, 180. Tellingly, some U.S. Negroes in Florida tried to preserve perceived advantages thought to have existed during the Spanish era by retaining a fierce loyalty to Catholicism and clinging to a "Hispanic identity." See also Frank Marotti, *The Cana Sanctuary: History, Diplomacy, and Black Catholic Marriage in Antebellum St. Augustine, Florida*. Tuscaloosa: University of Alabama Press, 2011, 89, 105: In 1839 in St. Augustine "Antonio Alvarez, the Keeper of the Public Archives, swore that free persons of color under the Spaniards 'possessed and enjoyed the same rights as white persons respecting the acquiring of and the alienation of property.'" Yet, by 1845, according to a contemporaneous source, "almost all the Free Negroes . . . went to Cuba."

84. *Convention Between Her Majesty and the Republic of Hayti for the More Effectual Suppression of the Slave Trade Signed at Port-Au-Prince. December 23, 1839*. London: Harrison, 1841.

85. Report, 27 January 1835, Legajo de Estado 8028, AHN–Madrid.

86. Report of Minister of Overseas Commerce and Government, 20 May 1841, Legajo de Estado 8037. See also Report from Madrid, 21 July 1837, Legajo 39, Numero de Orden 21, Asuntos Politicos, ANC, on reputed expedition from Santo Domingo intended to invade Puerto Rico. For more anxiety about Haitian intentions at the same site and section, see Report, 17 May 1841, Legajo 136, Numero de Orden 26.

87. Report of First Secretary at the Palace, 24 May 1841, Legajo de Estado 8037, AHN–Madrid: Place roadblocks in the path of Haitian travelers in the region; more vigilance needed; do not allow travelers from Haiti to disembark in Cuba under any pretext.

88. *Trial of Pedro de Zuleta . . . on a Charge of Slave Trading at the Central Criminal Court*. London: Wood, 1844.

89. Albert G. Robinson, *Cuba and the Intervention*. Boston: Longmans, Greene, 1905, 58.

90. Daniel Webster, "private and confidential" to Robert Campbell, U.S. Consul in Havana, 14 January 1843, in 32nd U.S. Congress, 1st Session, House of Representatives, Ex. Doc. No. 121, "Island of Cuba. Message from the President of the United States in Reference to the Island of Cuba," 31 August 1852, Massachusetts Historical Society. Also at the same site, see all the Diaries of Thomas Coffin Amory, who was in Cuba the same year. For more on the purported invasion of Cuba from Jamaica, see Report, 8 April 1843, Legajo 41, Numero de Orden 52, Asuntos Politicos, ANC. For a contemporaneous account of Spanish diplomats conferring with Webster, see Report of Spanish legation, Washington, circa 1843, Legajo de Estado 8039, AHN-Madrid:

Confirmed is the supposition that London plans to invade Cuba with an army of Africans and virtually all of Webster's points.

91. James W. Cortada, "Spain and the American Civil War: Relations at Mid-Century, 1855–1868," *Transactions of the American Philosophical Society* 70/4 (1980): 1–121, 7.

92. Aaron Vail to Daniel Webster, 30 November 1841, in Kenneth Shewmaker, ed., *The Papers of Daniel Webster: Diplomatic Papers*, vol. 1: *1841–1845*. Hanover: University Press of New England, 1974, 364. See also Kenneth E. Shewmaker, "Daniel Webster and the Politics of Foreign Policy, 1850–1852," *Journal of American History* 63/2 (September 1976): 303–15.

93. Robert Harrison to State Department, 3 October 1843, T31, *Despatches from U.S. Consuls in Jamaica*, NARA–CP. See also Harrison's letters of 14 June 1843 and 24 November 1843 where he averred that London had sent agents from Jamaica to "carry out . . . villainous measures for the insurrection of the slaves in Cuba." This was disquieting since "some of our slaveholding states are only a stone's throw from Cuba," thus governors of Gulf states should be on guard and prepare "their militia for [a] Negro insurrection (which may occur while they are sleeping)." For "sooner or later" London would seek to ignite a slave insurrection on the mainland—and Cuba.

94. Don E. Fehrenbacher, *The Slaveholding Republic: An Account of the United States Government's Relations to Slavery*. New York: Oxford University Press, 2002, 126, 128.

95. Robert E. May, "Lobbyists for Commercial Empire: Jane Cazneau, William Cazneau and U.S. Caribbean Policy, 1846–1878," *Pacific Historical Review* 48/3 (August 1979): 383–412, 389.

96. Benjamin Wright to John C. Calhoun, 4 October 1844, in Wilson, *The Papers of John C. Calhoun*, 20:32–34. On the subsequent fact of James Wright death, see Report, 1845, Legajo 851, Numero de Orden 28722, Gobierno Superior Civil.

97. Prefatory comments, in Wilson, *The Papers of John C. Calhoun*, 19:xxvii. See also Thomas G. Clemson to "My Dear Sir," 7 October 1850, Box 1, *Francis W. Pickens Papers*, Duke University: Though "Havana is delightful . . . I have been long desirous of selling my plantation & Negroes. . . . Perhaps Mrs. Calhoun would like to have them."

98. John Acosta to John C. Calhoun, 18 February 1845, in Wilson, *The Papers of John C. Calhoun*, 21:311: "And while the Cotton, Rice and Tobacco interests of the South, require that these should receive the watchful protection of the Southern man at Liverpool, the important commerce of this City with Cuba, presents equal claims for the North in the appointment of the Consul for the Havana." See also James Hamilton, Jr. to John C. Calhoun, 12 October 1846, in vol. 23 of ibid.: "Dudley Seldon, hitherto a warm supporter of Mr. [Henry] Clay, has now a strong tendency to sustain your claims to the Presidency. He has recently inherited a large Sugar Est[ate] in the island of Cuba, which may have produced a sensible change in his views in regard to the tariff."

99. *The Liberator*, 26 June 1846.

100. *Diary of William Morton*, 1846, Virginia Historical Society–Richmond.

101. Entry March 1846, *Diary of George S. Emerson*, Massachusetts Historical Society: Aboard a ship to Cuba was "Mr. Ballet," the "son of a gentleman of St. Domingo who lost a large fortune in the revolution" and was reduced to "poverty," whereupon "he went to the U.S. and supported himself in Baltimore by giving dancing lessons. He then married Mrs. B and since has lived in Cuba about 20 years. He is now a man of about 60 still lively and with much of the Frenchman about him. . . . Mrs. B. . . . was born in America of West Indian parents." After the couple found some items missing, they were "much troubled" and "all the Negroes were called up and

questioned at length" until one was compelled to confess and was administered a "severe whipping"—republican-style—"which he endured with great stoicism."

102. U.S. Consul to James Buchanan, 15 January 1848, *Despatches from U.S. Consuls in Trinidad, Cuba*: "The antipathy existing between the Creoles and the Old Spaniards is daily increasing and a very revolutionary spirit pervades the former class" which was replete with "secret societies [and] conspiracies." See also *An Invalid, a Winter in the West Indies and Florida*. New York: Wiley and Putnam, 1839: "The Creoles of the place are a lazy, idle class of men, who are content to have nothing."

103. Entry March 1846, *Diary of George S. Emerson*: Aboard ship from the mainland to Cuba is Don A. de Galled y Campos, a young Creole from Havana, though he works at a Philadelphia counting house. He "speaks English remarkably well."

104. Report from Spain's Consul in New York, 1844, Legajo 850, Numero de Orden 28655, Gobierno Superior Civil, ANC. See also Memorandum from Spanish Minister in Washington, 1841, Legajo 846, Numero de Orden 28412, Gobierno Superior Civil.

105. See Jose A. Saco, *La Supresion del Trafico de Esclavos Africanos en la Isla de Cuba*. Paris: Imprenta de Panckoucke, 1845, AAS.

106. Documents on Treaties abolishing the Slave Trade with Mexico, Yucatan and Texas, 7 August 1843, Legajo 143, Numero de Orden 54, Reales Cedulas y Ordenas, ANC. On attempts to conclude a treaty between Texas and Spain at the same site, see Royal Order, 9 September 1841, Legajo 136, Numero de Orden 19, Asuntos Politicos.

107. *The Liberator*, 17 January 1845.

108. Report, 1848, Legajo 943, Numero de Orden 33338, Gobierno Superior Civil, ANC.

109. Letter to Officialdom in Cuba, 23 April 1844, Despatches from Port-au-Prince, Ministerio Asuntos Exteriores–Madrid, They were told that a U.S. captain coming from Kingston said there was a revolution going on in Santo Domingo and, thus, hundreds of refugees were arriving in Jamaica.

110. *The Liberator*, 26 September 1845.

111. Spanish Minister in U.S. to Captain General 21 October 1845, Legajo 121, Numero de Orden 43, Asuntos Politicos. On the same point see Madrid to Captain General, 26 March 1846, Legajo 43, Numero de Orden 9, Asuntos Politicos.

112. *The Liberator*, 3 August 1849.

113. *The Liberator*, 20 February 1846. See also *The Liberator*, 9 January 1846: "The annexation of Cuba is now a cherished object with our slaveholders and having now a decided majority in the Senate by the addition of Senators from Florida to Texas, they are able with the assistance of three or four such free States as New Hampshire, Maine and Illinois to command two thirds of the Senate. . . . Cuba would add some four or six slaveholding Senators and fifteen or twenty Representatives in Congress."

114. *The Liberator*, 19 October 1849.

115. *The Liberator*, 19 December 1845.

116. *The Liberator*, 21 September 1849.

117. *The Liberator*, 27 October 1848. See also Charles Stearns, *Facts in the Life of General Taylor; the Cuba Bloodhound Importer, the Extensive Slave-Holder and the Hero of the Mexican War*. Boston: CS, 1848.

118. *The Liberator*, 26 September 1845: According to Douglass, "One slaveholder from Cuba shook his fist in my face and said, 'O, I wish I had you in Cuba!' 'Ah!' said another, 'I wish I had him in Savannah! We would use him up!'" Yet another pledged to "throw him overboard." For another version, see Frederick Douglass, "Letters to Antislavery Workers and Agencies [Part 1]," *Journal of Negro History* 10/4 (October 1925): 648–76, 663.

119. Andrew Donelson to John C. Calhoun, 8 July 1848, in Wilson, *The Papers of John C. Calhoun*, 25:574.

120. Captain General to the Minister of State, Spain, 27 July 1849, Gobierno Superior Civil, *ANC*.
121. Report from Spanish Ministry in Washington, 8 February 1843, Legajo 41, Numero de Orden 51, Asuntos Politicos: Conspiracy targeting Cuba led by Africans and Creoles under the protection of London. See also *The Colored American*, 27 March 1841.
122. Consul in Vera Cruz to Havana, 22 November 1844, Legajo 140, Numero de Orden 39, Asuntos Politicos. On a similar level, see Report, 6 September 1844, Legajo 138, Numero de Orden 19, Asuntos Politicos.
123. Reports from Consul in Vera Cruz, 27 May 1844–9 January 1845, Legajo de Estado 8039.
124. Report by Consul of Spain in St. Thomas, 1848, Legajo 852, Numero de Orden 28813, Gobierno Superior Civil, ANC.
125. Report by Consul of Spain in Jamaica, 1848, Legajo 853, Numero de Orden 28813, Gobierno Superior Civil.
126. Report, 18 July 1848, Legajo 43, Numero de Orden 28, Asuntos Politicos, on revolutionary plans in Jamaica targeting Cuba.
127. See Report, 1843, Legajo 941, Numero de Orden 33202, Gobierno Superior Civil, ANC;also Report 1842, Legajo 941, Numero de Orden 33173, Gobierno Superior Civil; Report, 1844, Legajo 943, Numero de Orden 33288, Gobierno Superior Civil. Correspondence with Foreign Powers in respect to the Slave Trade, 1840, Legajo 940, Numero de Orden 33134, Gobierno Superior Civil. Report on slave ships embarking from New Orleans, 1844, Legajo 850, Numero de Orden 28645, Gobierno Superior Civil. Correspondence on Slavery, 1834–1844, Legajo 937, Numero de Orden 33052, Gobierno Superior Civil. *The Liberator*, 15 June 1849: "Nefarious slave trade is again very active in Cuba." *The Colored American*, 24 July 1841, on the slave trade to Cuba. Report on slave trading to Cuba with New Orleans tie, 31 July 1843, Legajo de Estado 8028, AHN–Madrid. Report on U.S. slavers near Cape Verde, 9 March 1840, Legajo de Estado 8037; also in this report see British legation, Madrid to Don Evaristo Perez de Castro, 9 March 1840, for elaborate plan involving U.S. vessels shipping Africans to Cuba: "Intended formation of two companies at the Havana, one to carry on the slave trade by vessels directed to keep at a certain distance from the [African] coast and the other company to equip a certain number of small fast sailing vessels to act as pirates upon the commerce of Great Britain." *The North Star*, 2 February 1849: A judge sitting in Galveston handling a case that involved "slaves, natives of Africa, who were brought through Cuba contrary to the laws of Spain and taken to Texas in 1835 in violation of the laws of Mexico."
128. Henry Wheaton, *Enquiry into the Validity of the British Claim to a Right of Visitation and Search of American Vessels Suspected to be Engaged in the African Slave Trade*. Philadelphia: Lea and Blanchard, 1842. See also "Convention Between Her Majesty and the King of the French for the Suppression of the Traffic in Slaves," "signed at London, May 29, 1845," Legado de Estado 8039.
129. Report, 1847, Legajo 945, Numero de Orden 33317, Gobierno Superior Civil. C. J. Dalrymple to Earl of Aberdeen, 21 August 1843 in *British Parliamentary Papers*, 25:142: U.S. schooner "dispatched ostensibly for Rio de Janeiro by an American resident here, Charles Tyng, which, from his connections with the slave dealers may probably be intended" for the slave trade. See also James Hook et al., to Earl of Aberdeen, 5 June 1845, in *British Parliamentary Papers*, 29:29: "Condemned Brazilian slaver" brought to Sierra Leone by a "Spanish slave Captain" from Cuba. "There seems reason to suspect, from New Orleans being her principal port of rendezvous, that some of her cargoes have been taken to the mainland, probably for introduction into Texas."

130. Report, 1845, Legajo 944, Numero de Orden 33297, Gobierno Superior Civil: Britain's consul denounces the U.S. national Robert Wilson—captain of the vessel *Atlanta* bought in Key West—accused of involvement in slaving. At the same site, see also Report, 1847, Legajo 945, Numero de Orden 33325, Gobierno Superior Civil.

131. Letter to Captain General, ca. late 1843, in *British Parliamentary Papers*, 28:65–66.

132. Report from U.K. Commission at Sierra Leone, 31 December 1844, Legajo de Estado 8039: More slave ships captured south of the equator than north and of these, twice as many U.S.-flagged ships as the number two scofflaw, Brazil.

133. Report by British legation, 13 May 1844, Legajo de Estado 8039. See also Richard Burleigh Kimball, *Cuba and the Cubans; Comprising a History of the Island of Cuba*. New York: Hueston, 1850, 75–76: "A few months previous to my arrival, the blacks of the sugar estates of my cousin, Don Rafael, became insurrected. The slaves lately imported from Africa were mostly of the Luccoommee [*sic*] tribe and therefore excellent workmen, but of a violent unwieldy temper and always ready to hang themselves at the slightest opposition in their way."

134. Report by British legation, 5 February 1844, Legajo de Estado 8039.

135. C. J. Dalrymple to Viscount Palmerston, 26 February 1841 in *British Parliamentary Papers*, 21:186: "Rich Negress, Mrs. Lightbourn," a slave trader, her son in charge of a "factory on the River Pongo"; her first spouse may have been "American" and now "she has married a Negro and has a family of eight children" and had close ties to "Baltimore." She was conducting major business, selling Africans at $400 a head, many of whom were headed to Cuba.

136. Reports from Minister in London, 1 June 1843 to 24 January 1846, Legajo de Estado 8039.

137. *Heraldo*, 20 February 1845 in *British Parliamentary Papers*,30:111–12.

138. John F. Crampton to Daniel Webster, 8 July 1842 in *Correspondence on the Proposed Tripartite Convention Relative to Cuba*. Boston: Little, Brown, 1853, Historical Society of Pennsylvania–Philadelphia: Cuba provides "shorter passages from one ocean to another" and "is so placed geographically that the nation which may possess it . . . might either protect or obstruct the commercial routes from one ocean to the other."

139. Joseph T. Crawford to Viscount Palmerston, 9 December 1846 in *British Parliamentary Papers*, 35:33: Ship from New Orleans arrives in Havana with James Edlin aboard, who is headed to British Guiana with an enslaved African aboard purchased in Louisiana. He is curtly informed that he cannot travel on a British ship with a slave—and the slave is then freed.

140. Spanish Vice Consul in Boston, Antonio Vega to Madrid, 4 July 1841, Legajo de Estado 8037, AHN-Madrid: abolitionist society established in New York. Minister of Spain in U.S. to Miguel Tacon, 14 July 1837, Legajo 39, Numero de Orden 18, Asuntos Politicos, ANC: concern expressed about U.S. abolitionists. For more on this issue, see Memorandum from Madrid, 21 July 1837, Legajo 39, Numero de Orden 21, Asuntos Politicos; and Royal Order, 17 September 1841, Legajo 41, Numero de Orden 16, Asuntos Politicos.

141. Memorandum from Don Angel Calderon de la Barca, 14 August 1844, Legajo de Estado 8039.

142. Newspaper clipping, ca. 1845, Legajo de Estado 8039.

143. *An Invalid, a Writer in the West Indies and Florida*, New York: Wiley and Putnam, 1839, 104, 99: Spaniards "are so much opposed to improvements. . . . We do not like the Spanish government." See also B. M. Norman, *Rambles by Land and Water or Notes in Cuba and Mexico*. New York: Paine and Burgess, 1845.

144. Daniel Nason, *A Journal of a Tour from Boston to Savannah Thence to Havana*, 1849, 60, Georgia Historical Society–Savannah: "After residing here five or six weeks I

became of a greasy bronze color, like the natives"—which made him "subject to the constant remarks of my friends—'Why, how black you look!'"

145. Daniel Nason, *A Journal of a Tour from Boston to Savannah Thence to Havana . . .* 1849, Georgia Historical Society–Savannah.

146. James B. Ranck, "The Attitude of James Buchanan Towards Slavery," *Pennsylvania Magazine of History & Biography* 51/2 (1927): 126–42, 139.

147. John E. Baur, "Faustin Soulouque, Emperor of Haiti, His Character and His Reign," *The Americas* 6/2 (October 1949): 131–66, 147.

148. Ben Green to John Clayton, 26 March 1850, Box 40, Folder 399, Duff Green Papers, University of North Carolina–Chapel Hill. In the same collection, John Clayton to Ben Green, 13 June 1849, Box 38, Folder 94: Foiling London's attempt to "obtain by negotiation the cession . . . of the Bay of Samana" was a top priority.

149. *The North Star*, 8 June 1849.

150. *The North Star*, 20 July 1849.

151. *The North Star*, 22 June 1849.

152. *The North Star*, 27 April 1849.

153. *The North Star*, 2 March 1849. See the same periodical of 30 May 1850 as Yulee again demands Cuban annexation.

154. *The North Star*, 7 July 1848.

4. THE U.S. TO SEIZE CUBA TO PREVENT "AFRICANIZATION"?

1. *The North Star*, 12 April 1850.

2. *The North Star*, 24 August 1849.

3. *The North Star*, 28 September 1849.

4. *Frederick Douglas's Paper*, 4 September 1851. For more on this filibustering, see Captain General to Minister of State, Spain, 27 July 1849, Legajo 43, Numero de Orden 32, Asuntos Politicos, ANC; and Captain General to Minister of State, 9 October 1849, Legajo 43, Numero de Orden 39 and Memorandum, 26 October 1849, Legajo 216, Numero de Orden 10. *Correspondence Between the Treasury Department & In Relation to the Cuba Expedition and William Freret, Late Collector*. New Orleans: Alex Levy, 1851, American Antiquarian Society–Worcester; also here, see *A Thrilling and Exciting Account of the Sufferings and Horrible Tortures Inflicted on Mortimer Bowers and Miss Sophia Delaplain for a Supposed Participation with Gen. Lopez in the Invasion of Cuba*. Charleston: Barclay, 1851; and Edward Handiboe, *Will Crittenden, or the Lone Star of Cuba, a Romance*, New York, 1853.

5. Earl Wesley Fornell, *The Galveston Era: The Texas Crescent on the Eve of Secession*. Austin: University of Texas Press, 1961, 194–95.

6. Crist Madan to George Cadwalader, 6 December 1849, Series 7, Box 406, Cadwalader Collection, Historical Society of Pennsylvania. See also *Life of General Narciso Lopez; Together with a Detailed History of the Attempted Revolution in Cuba, from its First Invasion at Cardenas, Down to the Death of Lopez at Havana, by a Filibusterio [pseudo]*. New York: De Witt & Davenport, 1851, New York Historical Society; and Robert Granville Caldwell, "The Lopez Expeditions to Cuba, 1848–1851," Ph.D. diss., Princeton University, 1915; Tom Chaffin, *Fatal Glory: Narciso Lopez and the First Clandestine U.S. War Against Cuba*. Charlottesville: University Press of Virginia, 1996; Basil Rauch, *American Interest in Cuba: 1848–1855*. New York: Columbia University Press, 1948. See also Pamphlet on Lopez, ca. 1850, Historical Society of Pennsylvania–Philadelphia; and Orestes Brownson, *Opiniones de Un Anglo-Americano Acerca de La Espedicion Cubana y Los Anexionistas*. New Orleans: Imprenta de Patria, 1850, American Antiquarian Society.

7. *Frederick Douglass' Paper*, 25 September 1851 and 18 December 1851. See also Report, 1851, Legajo 47, Numero de Orden, Asuntos Politicos, ANC.

8. William Henry Hurlbert, *Gan-Eden: On Pictures of Cuba*. Boston: Jewett, 1854, 230, 227: "Will the conquest of Cuba be attempted? There can be no doubt that slavery, despairing of her northern frontiers, has long been looking to Spanish and Portuguese America as her future domain, into which the power of the Union must be made to force her way. . . . Spain is tyrannical, Cuba is rich, America is ravenously republican. From these propositions it has been deduced that Cuba must soon become a member of our great and glorious confederacy." On the Lopez and Gonzalez expeditions, see Royal Order-Madrid, 31 July 1850, Legajo 43, Numero de Orden 71, Asuntos Politicos, ANC; and Report, 2 August 1850, Legajo 44, Numero de Orden 1; Report, 10 October 1850, Legajo 216, Numero de Orden 22; Report, 14 January 1851, Legajo 218, Numero de Orden 25; Spanish legation in Washington to Captain General, 25 February 1851, Legajo 217, Numero de Orden 17; Report, 17 November 1851, Legajo 46, Numero de Orden 22. The file Report, 10 October 1850, Legajo 216, Numero de Orden 22 also concerns intercepted literature from New York—"La Verdad" and "Horizonte," thought to be favorable to Lopez and Gonzales.

9. J. Preston Moore, "Pierre Soule: Southern Expansionists and Promoter," *Journal of Southern History* 21/2 (May 1955): 203–23. The leading republican, Soule, had a "friendship with William Walker," who spearheaded the campaign against Managua. There was a "presence" in Walker's retinue of "Cuban revolutionists. . . . Soule's influence upon Walker and the domestic policies of the short-lived republic" in Nicaragua "was extensive." Walker's "grandiose purpose" included "conquering Cuba" and thus, "plainly required American approval and support to be lasting." Establishing Nicaragua as a slave state was part of the design. Soule, who had familial ties to Cuba, was called the "patron saint of General Walker." See also Speech of Mr. Soule of Louisiana on Colonization in North America and the Political Conditions of Cuba, Delivered in the Senate of United States, January 25, 1853, Tulane University. See also Amos Aschbach Ettinger, *The Mission to Spain of Pierre Soule, 1853–1855: A Study in the Cuban Diplomacy of the United States*. New Haven: Yale University Press, 1932.

10. *The Liberator*, 23 May 1856: "The fate of Cuba depends upon the fate of Nicaragua and the fate of the South depends upon that of Cuba!" according to a "Southern paper." See also William O. Scruggs, "William Walker's Designs in Cuba," *Mississippi Valley Historical Review* 1/2 (September 1914): 198–211.

11. Mark O. Hatfield, *Vice-Presidents of the United States, 1789–1993*. Washington, D.C.: Government Printing Office, 1997, 181–87.

12. *The Liberator*, 27 May 1853.

13. James W. Cortada, "Spain and the American Civil War: Relations at Mid-Century, 1855–1868," *Transactions of the American Philosophical Society* 70/4 (1980): 1–121, 12.

14. *Frederick Douglass' Paper*, 25 August 1854.

15. Speech of Mr. Joshua Giddings of Ohio in the House of Representatives, March 16, 1854, AAS: A war for Cuba, he argued, would not be "child's play" since it involved confronting Paris and London, which would "surround Cuba with a wall of iron and a sheet of flame. . . . They will doubtless strike at our weakest points." See also Henry Lorenzo James, "The Black Warrior Affair," *American Historical Review* 12/2 (January 1907): 280–98.

16. *Frederick Douglass' Paper*, 23 June 1854.

17. *Frederick Douglass' Paper*, 11 March 1853. For more opposition to the U.S. taking Cuba, see *Frederick Douglass' Paper*, 3 December 1852.

18. *Frederick Douglass' Paper*, , 29 July 1853: "One disaffected slave, one envious monitor,

when the season is dry and the grinding well begun, but to drop a match . . . the swift wind would do the rest" since, he stressed, fire is the "worst *enemy*" of the planter. See also, *Frederick Douglass' Paper*, 18 November 1853: "There are stirrings of insurrection in the island of Cuba. Nothing is more natural"; *Frederick Douglass' Paper*, 9 March 1855: "Probabilities at any time of insurrection, renders Cuba an unceasing danger and permanent cause of anxiety and alarm." See also *Letters of John Ashton Nicholls*, Manchester, U.K., 1862, Maryland Historical Society-Baltimore, 360: Slavery "is very different here [in Cuba]and in some plantations exists in all its greatest horrors and abuse." *North Star*, 20 July 1849: Martín Delany urges a revolt against slavery in Cuba.

19. Fredrika Bremer, *The Homes of the New World*, 287: "Fugitive slaves live in these mountains [near Guanabacoa], and have fortified themselves in their innumerable grottoes and caves, so that any pursuit of them is impossible. They have there built dwellings for themselves and obtained fire-arms and at one time amounted to so large a number—it is said many thousands—that the government of Cuba entertained serious apprehensions from them."

20. *North Star*, 27 April 1848.

21. Entries, 8 & 10 September 1851, Box 1, William D. Valentine Diary, University of North Carolina–Chapel Hill.

22. Reverberations of the faraway Crimea were felt in Cuba, according to the British diplomat, John Backhouse, who was posted there: John Backhouse to "Dearest Mother," 2 April 1854, Box 7, John Backhouse Papers, Duke University: "I have been expecting all along we shan't have to fight the Russians. . . . The President of the U. States has addressed an inflammatory message to Congress on the subject; it has been published in Spanish in newspapers here together with remarks & copies of correspondence all published as a matters of course here. . . . I was amused the other day hearing a Yankee Navy Lieut. talking about the prospects of war with Russia" for the "Yankees seem to be turning their attention afresh to this island." See also John Backhouse to "Dearest Mother," 6 August 1854, in which he casts "blame" on the United States when his mail in Cuba is disrupted. See also George W. Williams, *Sketches of Travel in the Old and New World*. Charleston: Walker Evans, 1871, 22: The writer in 1856 encountered a Briton who "was talking largely of the 'mistress of the world' and said if the United States attempted to buy Cuba, England would whip her as she had whipped Russia!"

23. *The Liberator*, 6 July 1855: Dixie and Russia were deemed to be "identical in principle. . . . The Slave interest regards Russia as its natural ally, England and France, as its natural enemies." See also David Campbell to "My Dear Nephew," 28 February 1854, Box 28, Campbell Family Papers, Duke University: "I think you may set it down as a fixed fact that there is to be a general war in Europe. Russia on one side and England & France on the other are acting the part of great bullies at present."

24. Letter from Edward Everett, 17 September 1853, Lord John Russell Papers, Duke University.

25. Ambrosio Jose Gonzales, "Manifesto on Cuban Affairs Addressed to the People of the United States, New Orleans: Daily Delta," 1 September 1852, Brown University. This document can also be found at the Huntington Library. See also Cuyler Young, "Greatness Renewed. Or, the Rise of the South; with a Southern National Air and the Song of the Cuban Invaders," 1851, *Western Reserve Historical Society–Cleveland*. See also Richard Henry Dana, *To Cuba and Back: A Vacation Voyage*. Boston: Ticknor and Fields, 1859: "The best opinions put the slaves at 650,000, the free blacks at 200,000 and the whites at 700,000." Matanzas, a bastion of republican influence, was said to contain 21,000 residents, including 3,500 "free colored" and "nearly 6,500...

slaves." C. G. Rosenberg, *Jenny Lind in America*. New York: Stringer & Townsend, 1851, 131. See also *Cuba y Su Gobierno, Con un Apendice de Documentos Historicos*. London: Imprenta de C. Wood, 1853, Massachusetts Historical Society.

26. Lynda Laswell Crist et al., eds., *The Papers of Jefferson Davis*, vol. 4: *1849–1852* Baton Rouge: Louisiana State University Press, 1983, 59.

27. Grace Gebelin, "Lopez's Filibustering Expedition to Cuba," M.A. thesis, Tulane University, 1929. See also Anderson C. Quisenberry, *Lopez's Expeditions to Cuba, 1850–1853*. Louisville, KY: Morton, 1906.

28. Letter from Jefferson Davis, 5 May 1848, in James T. McIntosh et al., eds., *The Papers of Jefferson Davis*, vol. 4: *July 1846–December 1848*. Baton Rouge: Louisiana State University Press, 1981, 319. Gonzales and Lopez were also quite familiar with John C. Calhoun. See Clyde N. Wilson et al., eds., *The Papers of John C. Calhoun*, vol. 26: *1848–1849*. Columbia: University of South Carolina Press, 2001, xiii.

29. This lengthy list included John Quitman, a former Governor of Mississippi. Samuel Walker, "The Diary of a Louisiana Planter," 19 December 1859, Tulane University. Quitman, says the writer, "spoke with me freely" about the expedition and, "as I remember a million of money was to be made up before he would consent to take the command. . . . I received from Gaspard Bethancourt, a large number of Cuban securities." The man otherwise known as "Gaspar Betancourt Cisneros" was a "self-professed disciple of Thomas Jefferson from the leading family of Puerto Principe": see Robert Paquette, *Sugar Is Made with Blood*, 103. See also Louise Quitman to "My Dear Brother," 5 August 1850, Box 6, Folder 5, Quitman Family Papers–University of North Carolina–Chapel Hill. Also see Box 7, Folder 83, for Indictment "In the Matter of the United States vs. John A. Quitman, John S. Thrasher & A.L. Saunders," 3 July 1854, Fifth Circuit, U.S. and Eastern District of Louisiana: The parties "have held meetings in this district upon the subject of Cuban affairs, the object and tendency of which is to effect a revolution in the Island of Cuba and that moneys have been collected."

30. John H. Fromberger to "Dear Rodney," 23 April 1851, John H. Fromberger Papers, Delaware Historical Society–Wilmington.

31. *Savannah Morning News*, 10 March 1835.

32. Orville Vernon Burton and Georganne B. Burton, eds., *The Lost Novel of Lucy Holcombe Pickens, The Free Flag of Cuba*. Baton Rouge: Louisiana State University Press, 2002, 10, 11.

33. There was no unanimity on the mainland about Lopez. See William Bland, *The Awful Doom of the Traitor; or the Terrible Fate of the Deluded and Guilty; Being a Full Disclosure of the Character and Selfish Designs of General Lopez Who Decoyed a Multitude of our Best and Bravest Citizens to an Awful and Untimely Grave in the Island of Cuba*. Cincinnati: Rulison, 1851, 10. Here it is said that Lopez fought on the side of the royalists in Venezuela then was co-opted after his father was slain; he moved to Spain and again sided with royalists before decamping to Cuba where he married a wealthy woman and lost her fortune via gambling, at which point he concocted a scheme to regain wealth by seizing Cuba. See also Letter to Gen. George Cadwalader, 30 January 1850, Box 5, Cadwalader Collection: "There is not one planter or proprietor in Cuba or here who does not fear the recklessness of Gen. Lopez, who has only been tolerated by them as chief through me. Please excuse the frank and confidential exposure of my feelings on these matters." Thomas W. Wilson, "An Authentic Narrative of the Piratical Descents Upon Cuba," 1851, American Antiquarian Society: "The press of the United States . . . took a prominent part in advocating the occupation of Cuba by violent means. . . . These despicable scribblers . . ."

34. Dickie Galt to "My Dear Child," 6 January 1851, Box 1, Folder 39, Skinner Family Papers, University of North Carolina–Chapel Hill.

35. Daniel Nason, *A Journal of a Tour from Boston to Savannah Thence to Havana*, 1849: The city [Havana] is a walled city, belonging to Spain and is guarded in day and night by soldiers placed as sentinels in every part of the city." See also *The History of Late Expedition to Cuba, 1850–1853, by One of the Participants*, Boston Public Library.

36. L.M. Perez, ed., "Lopez's Expeditions to Cuba, 1850–1851," *Publications of the Southern History Association* 10/6 (November 1906): 345–62, 346. For U.S. participation in the Lopez invasion, see Nathaniel C. Hughes, Jr., and Thomas Clayton Ware, *Theodore O'Hara: Poet Soldier of the Old South*. Knoxville: University of Tennessee Press, 1998. Lopez's brother-in-law, Antonio de Frias, was a prominent Cuban slaveholder educated in the United States who plotted along with fellow Cuba, Jose Maria Herrera and the U.S. consul, Robert Campbell, to subvert Madrid's rule: See Paquette, *Sugar Is Made with Blood*, 166. See also Rodrigo Lazo, *Writing to Cuba: Filibustering and Cuban Exiles in the United States*. Chapel Hill: University of North Carolina Press, 2005. See also "B. Thrasher": Robert Campbell, 20 July 1850, Robert Campbell Papers, University of Texas.

37. Lewish Pinckney Jones, "Carolinians and Cubans: The Elliotts and Gonzales, Their Work and their Writing," Ph.D. diss., University of North Carolina–Chapel Hill, 1952, 104.

38. Antonio Rafael de la Cova, "Ambrosio Jose Gonzalez: A Cuban Confederate General," Ph.D. diss., West Virginia University, 1994, 1.

39. Jones, "Carolinians and Cubans," 13, 41, 76, 90, 104. See also Finding Aid, Elliott and Gonzales Family Papers, University of North Carolina–Chapel Hill: The marriage date of Elliott and Gonzales here is given as 1856 and Gonzales's birth year is rendered as 1816.

40. Memorandum from Spanish legation in Washington, D.C., 14 August 1849, Box 5, Records of the Spanish Consulate–Charleston, Duke University.

41. Daniel Webster to "Marshals, District Attorneys and Collectors of the United States," 3 September 1850, Box 1, Folder 1, Records of the Spanish Consulate–Savannah.

42. Consul to John Clayton, 16 July 1850, Roll 2, *Despatches from U.S. Consuls in Trinidad, Cuba*. A visiting republican in 1859 concurred. See Joseph Dimock, "Impressions of Cuba," in John Jenkins, ed., *Travelers' Tales of Old Cuba*. Melbourne: Ocean Press, 2010, 64–78, 66: "Though the Spanish nation have an open hatred of everything American . . ."

43. William Adams to Daniel Webster, 9 September 1851, Roll 4, *Despatches from U.S. Consuls in Santiago de Cuba*.

44. Ibid., 24 October 1851.

45. Memorandum from Daniel Barringer, 26 April 1850, Folder 17, Daniel Barringer Papers, University of North Carolina–Chapel Hill.

46. Daniel Barringer to John Clayton, 7 August 1850, Folder 17, ibid.

47. JHF to Daniel Barringer, 23 September 1851, Folder 22, ibid. On the prisoners in Spain, see Letter signed by ninety-one of them to Daniel Barringer, 8 January 1852, Folder 25.

48. Daniel Barringer to "Sir," 5 January 1852, Folder 25, ibid. On the imprisonment of John Thrasher in Ceuta, see Daniel Barringer to Daniel Webster, 14 January 1852, Folder 25.

49. Daniel Barringer to Sir, 12 January 1852, Folder 25, ibid.. For more on this prisoner, see Pedro Lopez to Daniel Barringer, 20 February 1852, Folder 26; and Daniel Barringer to "Sir," 13 February 1852, Folder 26.

50. *Provincial Freeman*, 15 July 1854.

51. Bland, *The Awful Doom of the Traitor*, 10: "A huge Negro fastening us together in pairs with a chain similar to a log-chain and weight, and firmly secured to the ankle. Shortly after our confinement the city was astir and a mingled mass of human beings . . . made up of Negroes, Creoles and Spaniards. They went forth to see fifty-two Americans butchered in cold blood." He deplored the "blows which a giant Negro had rained upon my back. . . . They were about to burn me alive! I shrieked and screamed but the Negroes laughed long and wildly at my cries. . . . After a time I saw the devilish priest moving among the ogre-like blacks" and "at length he gave the command and the Negroes, like demons came rushing with their crimson torches."

52. Cova, "Ambrosio Jose Gonzalez," 211.

53. *Savannah Morning News*, 3 March 1935.

54. Dana, *To Cuba and Back*, 245, 246: "The stranger visiting Havana will see a regiment of one thousand free black volunteers . . . and keeping guard in the Obra Pia. When it is remembered that the bearing [of] arms and performing [of] military duty as volunteers, is esteemed [as] an honor and privilege, and it is not allowed to the whites of Creole birth, except to a few who are favored by the government, the significance of this fact may be appreciated. The Cuban slave-holders are more impatient under this favoring of the free Negroes, than under almost any other act of the government. They see in it an attempt, on the part of the authorities, to secure the sympathy and cooperation of the free blacks, in case of revolutionary movement." See also Leon Beauvallet, *Rachel and the New World: A Trip to the United States and Cuba*. New York: Dix, Edwards, 1856, 321, in which the presence of armed Africans is noted.

55. See Martín Delany's comments in the *Provincial Freeman*, 13 October 1855: "Black military troops must necessarily be the most secure, because the most *reliable* defenders of the country and Spanish interests. More naturally prone to obedience, more loyal and submissive, patient and forgiving and greater lovers of their nativity and homes than the whites; it is but necessary to make them sensible . . . to the American haters of the Negro race with an assurance of equality of rights, and there is not force enough in the United States, to wrest Cuba from the Crown of Spain. With the blacks as guardians and defenders, she must and will stand in defiance of all the schemes and machinations now being planned against Spain in the United States. With the aid of the blacks, Cuba is safe, without it, she must fall prey to American cupidity."

56. Dana, *To Cuba and Back*, 246.

57. Conde de Alcoy to Captain General, 15 January 1853, Legajo 122, Numero de Orden 37, ANC: Rumors of new plans to invade Cuba from New Orleans.

58. Cova, "Ambrosio Jose Gonzalez," 233.

59. Report from David Turnbull in *British Parliamentary Papers. Reports from the Select Committee of the House of Lords to Consider the Best Means which Great Britain Can Adopt for the Final Extinction of the African Slave Trade with Minutes of Evidence, Appendix and Index, Volume 6*, vol. 6. Shannon: Irish University Press, 1968, 68.

60. J. A. Leon, *On Sugar Cultivation in Louisiana, Cuba & the British Possessions. By a European and Colonial Sugar Manufacturer, Part 1*. London: Ollivier, 1848. See also Hurlbert, *Gan-Eden*, 230: "A violent transfer of Cuba from the hands of Spain to those of America would be attended with the most disastrous effects upon her prosperity. The tobacco crop might perhaps be increased, but the sugar interest would be sadly shaken. . . . [I] can see no good flowing from such a consummation, to any American state, unless, perhaps, to *Louisiana*, which might rejoice over the prostration of her greatest rival." Emphasis–original. See also J. S. Thrasher, "Cuba and the United States: How the Interests of Louisiana Would be Affected by Annexation," *De Bow Review* 17 (July 1854): 47. Powerful interests in the Pelican State were so opposed to

the taking of Cuba that—apparently—they aided the British in foiling this scheme. See Mr. Mure to Earl of Clarendon, 6 July 1857, FO313/39, NAUK: Information about slavers embarking from New Orleans may have been leaked to London since "the sugar planters of Louisiana, a powerful & numerous body, are naturally opposed to permit the Cuba planter to import slaves, gaining . . . cheaper labor so that the sugar of Cuba would enter competition with that of Louisiana in the U.S. markets upon more favorable terms." See also Alexander Jones, "Cuba in 1851: A Survey of the Island, Its Resources, Statistics, etc. From Official Documents in Connection with the Present Revolt." New York: Stringer & Townsend, 1851, *Historical Society of Pennsylvania*: The writer suggests that some resident U.S. nationals in Cuba oppose annexation, fearing competition from mainland migrants. Some liked the arbitrage possibilities presented by the fact that Africans cost $300 in Cuba and $800 in Louisiana and did not want to disrupt this trend.

61. Speech by James Hammond, 29 October 1858, in Clyde N. Wilson, ed., *Selections from the Letters and Speeches of Hon. James Hammond of South Carolina*. Columbia: University of South Carolina Press, 1978, 337–38.

62. *Frederick Douglass' Paper*, 28 September 1855: "The Spaniard despises the Creole and the Creole hates the Spaniard."

63. Ibid., 18 March 1852. See also Hurlbert, *Gan-Eden*, 165: "Cuba, in the matter of railways, may compare favorably with many of the American States, and the railways are the result of Creole energy and enterprise . . ."

64. Hurlbert, *Gan-Eden*, 232: "I happened once at a country-house in Cuba to be called upon for my opinion in a controversy as to the propriety of admitting Negroes into railway carriages and coaches. When I said that it seemed to me neither republican nor well-bred to object to the presence, in a public conveyance, of any decent, and well-behaved person of whatever color; 'Ah!' cried the lady in the company, 'I thought you did not look like an American, and now I see that you must be an Englishman!'"

65. George W. Williams, *Sketches of Travel in the Old and New World*. Charleston: Walker Evans, 1871, 38: (In 1856) "there is a marked partiality among the Creoles for the Southerners; they know we are sound on the Nebraska Question. "

66. Charles Sumner to Wendell Phillips, 20 April 1858, in Beverly Wilson Palmer, ed., *The Selected Letters of Charles Sumner*, vol. 1. Boston: Northeastern University Press, 1990, 500–501. After the press reports the "rumor" that Spain will free the enslaved, Senator Sumner retorts: "Should it be verified, our struggle would draw toward its close. That act would be the most important for this continent since the Declaration of Independence." See also Letter to "My Dear Mama," 10 February 1844, William Rufus King Papers: "Spaniards, who however inferior to the Yankees in education . . . possess more good feeling and more good manners than our fellow citizens of the U. States."

67. *Frederick Douglass' Paper*, 1 September 1854. See also Report, 1 January 1854, Legajo 220, Numero de Orden 8, Asuntos Politicos, ANC: Rumors of an uprising in Nuevitas, Cuba led by Free Negroes. Emphasis in original.

68. "Speech of Hon. J. R. Giddings on Cuban Annexation. Delivered in the House of Representatives, December 14, 1852," Western Reserve Historical Society. Annexing Cuba would cause Africans to revolt and "bring the war into Florida, Alabama and other Southern States," guaranteeing an unstoppable "servile war." This Ohioan said he "would rather see Cuba *free*, under British or French rule, than see our fellow-men oppressed, degraded and ruthlessly murdered, under either Spanish or American authority." See also Samuel Sullivan Cox, "Ohio Politics," 1859: "Father Giddings dodges under the bush with his colored friend" ' and Salmon P. Chase to Gerrit Smith, 15 December 1854, in John Niven, ed., *The Salmon P. Chase Papers*,

Volume 2, Correspondence, 1823–1857, Kent: Kent State University Press, 1994, 390. Abolitionist Gerrit Smith endorsed annexation since it would create such conflict that slavery would be destroyed in the process, The words of Giddings can also be found in *The Liberator*, 31 December 1852.

69. Horatio Perry to Franklin Pierce, 10 January 1853, in William R. Manning, ed., *Diplomatic Correspondence of the United States: Inter-American American Affairs, 1831–1860, Volume XI–Spain*, Washington, D.C.: Carnegie Endowment for International Peace, 1939, 685–695. (Emphasis–original)

70. Report from British legation in Madrid, 16 April 1851, Legajo de Estado 8047, *AHN*: An "element of danger" in Cuba is the "vast number of slaves [who] would be ready to join any invaders by whose aid they might achieve their freedom."

71. William H. Robertson to William Marcy, 26 April 1854, in Manning, *Diplomatic Correspondence of the United States*, 768–69. *The Liberator*, 6 July 1855: Citing a New Orleans newspaper, shock was expressed by a republican "passing the royal jail" in Havana: "I observed that the soldiers on duty there were Negroes," and, stunningly, "Negroes [were] placed as guards upon white men" who in turn "complained of Negroes being placed over them." *The Liberator*, 4 May 1855: "the Captain General of Cuba has issued orders for the formation of sixteen companies of colored troops . . . the soldiers are to be free men."

72. Charles Davis to William Marcy, 22 May 1854, in Manning, *Diplomatic Correspondence of the United States*, 789–95.

73. Still, during this time Madrid was objecting to the increase in U.S. slaving. See Consuelo E. Stebbins, ed., *City of Intrigue, Nest of Revolution: A Documentary History of Key West in the Nineteenth Century*. Gainesville: University Press of Florida, 2007, 26, 29, 30. Tellingly, abolitionist books that were banned in the republic were not barred in Spain. See *The Liberator*, 15 May 1857.

74. Hurlbert, *Gan-Eden*, 198: "The wisest Cubans look with extreme dislike upon the constant introduction of new hordes of savages into the island. . . . Is it rumored that Spain thinks of abolishing slavery in Cuba?" See also *A Selection of the Letters of the Late John Ashton Nicholls, Edited by His Mother, Printed for Private Circulation Only, 1862*, Maryland Historical Society–Baltimore, 361: "Cubans," meaning Creoles, "appear to sympathize with the Americans," as opposed to Spaniards.

75. William Marcy to Charles W. Davis, 15 March 1854, in Manning, *Diplomatic Correspondence of the United States*, 170–173. See also Joseph Crawford to Earl of Clarendon, 3 January 1855, in *British Parliamentary Papers*, 41:562–563.

76. Correspondence between F. P. Corbin and Lord Howden, November 1854, Legajo de Estado 8047, AHN-Madrid. In the same file, see Memorandum from Spanish legation in London, 17 November 1853: Rumors about London-Madrid negotiations concerning a treaty to introduce to Cuba African colonists. It was also charged that these rumors too were no more than yet another justification for republican filibustering: Memorandum from Spanish legation in London, 14 August 1854, Legajo de Estado 8047. Nevertheless, the idea that London was bent on "Africanizing" Cuba was spreading like wildfire on the mainland: Clipping, 14 August 1854, Legajo de Estado, 8047; see also Lord Howden to Earl of Clarendon, 13 December 1854, in *British Parliamentary Papers*, 41:449: Pierre Soule informs Lord Howden that he believes that London and Madrid have conspired "to introduce as many Free Negroes as possible into the island of Cuba" which "had given a surprising impetus to the slave trade. . . . For when the slave dealers were fortunate in landing their cargoes unseen, the Negroes were sold as slaves; when the Negroes were openly apprehended the slave dealers averred that they were introduced as colonists. Mr. Soule ended by declaring that this invasion of Negroes was the cause producing

the greatest excitement in the United States, and being regarded as a measure of impending danger, it awakened a feeling that the annexation of Cuba was absolutely necessary for the peaceful existence of the Southern States."

77. Memorandum from Spanish legation in London, 17 November 1853, Legajo de Estado 8047.

78. Cora Montgomery, "The Queen of Islands and the King of Rivers, with a Chart of Our Slave and Free Soil Territory." New York: Wood, 1850, American Antiquarian Society: London seeks to establish a "United St. Domingo and other islands"— including Cuba—in a "Republic of Antilla . . . creating a colored empire" to threaten the United States. If Cuba joined the United States "there can be no doubt whatever that the condition of the white half of the population would be infinitely softened, elevated and improved."

79. *Frederick Douglass' Monthly*, April 1859.

80. Memorandum from Primera Secretaria at the "Palacio," 9 April 1853, Legajo de Estado 8048. On the conflict between Madrid and Washington, see "Message from the President of the United States, Communicating in Compliance with a Resolution of the Senate, Information in Relation to the Abduction of Rey, Alias Garcia, from New Orleans," 14 January 1850, Tulane University. See also A. M. Clayton, "The Relations of the United States and Cuba in 1853 & 1854," Box 2, Folder 23, John Francis Claiborne Papers, University of North Carolina–Chapel Hill: At this point "there were about fifty Americans confined in the state prisons" in Cuba "for alleged violation of the laws against the Slave Trade and I was urged to take violent and rash measures to procure their liberation," said this leading republican.

81. *Frederick Douglass' Paper*, 4 February 1853.

82. A.M. Clayton, "The Relations of the United States and Cuba" in ibid. This document also provides a useful summary of many of the themes in this chapter, as seen contemporaneously.

83. Sam McLean to William Marcy, 22 May 1854, Roll 4, *Despatches from U.S. Consuls in Trinidad, Cuba.*

84. If forced to choose between cooperation on enslavement and opposition to annexation, Spaniards would relinquish the latter and opt for the former—or so said a U.S. diplomat. Sam McLean to William L. Marcy, 26 May 1854, Roll 4: "The subject of annexation is now being entertained by the old Spanish residents of the island, not on account of any particular regard they have for us but for the better security of life and property they would enjoy under our laws, which they think would be jeopardized by a resort to extreme measures or Creole rule." This view was reached after "conversation with one of the wealthiest and most influential Creoles on this side of the island, and with whom I am on intimate terms." See also Sam McLean to William Marcy, 15 July 1854, Roll 4: "Much excitement among the *Spanish* [emphasis–original] part of the population on this side of the island in consequence of the arrest and imprisonment of several wealthy and leading residents of this jurisdiction for participating in the importation of the slaves lately introduced into this neighborhood. The policy of annexation is more freely discussed in places where formerly it would have been thought treasonable to even hint at such a project. . . . Portion of its inhabitants hope will lead to a peaceable transfer of the same to our country."

85. Royal Order, 6 April 1855, Legajo 122, Numero de Orden 56, Asuntos Politicos, ANC.

86. Memorandum of a conversation between Augustus C. Dodge and Juan de Zavala, 25 August 1855 in Manning, *Diplomatic Correspondence of the United States*, 886–91.

87. Report from Spanish legation in London, 22 March 1853, Legajo de Estado 8046, AHN-Madrid: Concerned about Washington's reported plans to absorb Cuba, the

Minister meets with Lord Clarendon—who, in turn, raises the question of slavery and the slave trade.

88. Reports from Spanish Minister in London, 3 October 1852–10 November 1853, Legajo de Estado 8046, AHN-Madrid.

89. Report from British legation in Madrid, 22 March 1853, Legajo de Estado 8046. Also see British legation in Madrid to Lieutenant General, 17 June 1853: A lengthy battle erupts concerning a Negro woman, Nancy, born in Jamaica and brought to Cuba in 1825 as a slave—probably illegally; she died in 1852 leaving children and the issue concerns whether the rights of her previous owner were "forfeited" to London, which means her children should be freed—but the Captain General refuses. For a similar case see British legation to Loftus Otway, 13 August 1852.

90. Joseph T. Crawford to Lord Clarendon, 9 August 1853, Legajo de Estado 8046.

91. British legation to Don Manuel Bertran de Lis, 7 November 1852, Legajo de Estado 8046.

92. See Correspondence from British legation in Madrid, 2 June 1851; 30 March 1851; 10 October 1854, Legajo de Estado 8047.

93. Lord Clarendon to "Sir," 29 August 1853, Legajo de Estado 8046.

94. Joseph Crawford to Lord Clarendon, 2 July 1853, Legajo de Estado 8046.

95. Report by Spanish legation in London, 21 June 1853, Legajo de Estado 8046.

96. Correspondence from Secretary of State, Spain, 16 October 1854, Legajo de Estado 8046.

97. John Backhouse to "My Dear Aunt," 3 August 1853, Box 1, John Backhouse Papers, Duke University: "In the first six months of this year there were more than 6,000 Negroes clearly advertised to have been landed on this island from Africa & more than half that number in the month of June. There were no doubt many other cargoes which we may never hear of. And not one slaver has ever been interfered with by a Spanish ship of war." See also *London Daily News*, 15 November 1853, Legajo de Estado 8046: "In Cuba the Crown of Spain has 25,000 troops, around its shores it has a navy numbering more than 30 vessels of all sorts. . . . Yet in the first six months of 1853 . . . more than 9,000 Africans were introduced. . . . Far be it from us to encourage American schemes of unjust aggression or of lawless outrage. . . . But of evils in this world there may be a choice; and the question as to what power shall ultimately possess Cuba is rapidly becoming a choice of evils. Internal slavery might be prolonged for a while by its transfer to the United States."

98. Memorandum, 8 January 1855, Legajo de Estado 8047.

99. London *Times*, 19 August 1853, Legajo de Estado 8047: "The Cabinet of Madrid professes its cordial gratitude for the support of England and France against the possibility of an attack from the United States. . . . We are still expending several hundred thousands a year to keep in check a trade which probably throws hardly more profit into the coffers of its guilty promoters than it costs us to thwart their operations."

100. Memorandum from Spanish legation in London, 1853 (23 January 1853–12 July 1853), Legajo de Estado 8048; and Memorandum, 1853, 22 February 1852–9 February 1853, Legajo de Estado 6373: The Captain General said it was necessary to counteract the effect of republican publications adverse to Spain by publishing periodicals in English.

101. Memorandum from British legation in Madrid, 28 April 1857 and attached clipping, Legajo de Estado 8048: "The United States are open mouthed to swallow their beautiful neighbour. . . . New Orleans will positively die of thirst or ennui if the consummation is delayed much longer. . . . [Spain] knows well the result of a trial of strength with the lords of Florida and Texas. It knows that nothing whatever prevents

Cuba from being absorbed in the States tomorrow except the public opinion of mankind, chiefly as represented by England."

102. Joseph Crawford to Earl of Malmesbury, 1 January 1853, Legajo de Estado 8048.

103. *The Liberator*, 29 December 1854.

104. Charles Sumner to Lord Brougham, 20 June 1858, in Palmer, *The Selected Letters of Charles Sumner*, 506–7.

105. Charles Sumner to Nassau Senior, 22 June 1858, in ibid., 507–9.

106. Dorothy Dodd, "The Schooner Emperor: An Incident of the Illegal Slave Trade in Florida," *Florida Historical Quarterly* 13/3 (January 1935): 117–28, 120.

107. British diplomat in Brussels to Lord Clarendon, 1 November 1854, in Gavin B. Henderson, "Southern Designs on Cuba, 1854–1857 and Some European Opinions," *Journal of Southern History* 5/3(August 1939): 371–85, 377–78.

108. Robert Durden, "J. D. B. De Bow: Convolutions of a Slavery Expansionist," *Journal of Southern History* 17/4 (November 1951): 441–61, 452. See also "Report of the Massachusetts Committee to Prevent the Admission of Texas as a Slave State," ca. 1845, Western Reserve Historical Society. Worry was expressed that taking Texas would lead to an attempt to take Cuba.

109. David Campbell to "My Dear Nephew," 20 February 1854, Box 28, David Campbell Papers, Duke University; at same site, also seeLetter to "My Dear," 12 December 1857, Box 1, George Frederick Samuel Robinson, First Marquis of Ripon Papers, in which "sale of Cuba" is discussed.

110. *Frederick Douglass' Paper*, 27 October 1854.

111. On the attempt to detain Thrasher in Cuba, see Report, 23 October 1851, Legajo 217, Numero de Orden 4, Asuntos Politicos, ANC.

112. John Thrasher, *A Preliminary Essay on the Purchase of Cuba*, New York: Derby & Jackson, 1859; and *Acquisition of Cuba*, Raleigh, 1859 (documents from North Carolina), both kept at the University of Texas. See also *The Liberator*, 4 March 1859: Fear is expressed that Cuba will "light the flames of a war between the races" that will be difficult to extinguish.

113. Bernard Marigny, *Thoughts Upon the Foreign Policy of the United States, from 1784 to the Inauguration of Franklin Pierce; Statistics of Spain on the Island of Cuba, &c.* New Orleans: Pollee, 1854, 45: "In order to . . . serve her own selfish and Machiavellian policy, [London] wishes to annul the island of Cuba by Africanizing it. . . . The men of that color entertain a natural aversion towards the whites, who for ages back have reduced them to a condition of slavery. Should a revolution break out in that colony, we would probably witness the rise of such men as Toussaint. . . . Whites would be massacred."

114. *James Buchanan, His Doctrines and Policy, as Exhibited by Himself and Friends*, ca. 1854, Brown University.

115. Speech of the Hon. Anthony Kennedy of Maryland on the Cuba Bill, Delivered in the Senate of the U. States, February 1859. Baltimore: Murphy, 1859, Maryland Historical Society–Baltimore. On the split in Dixie on Cuba, see Speech of Hon. John Bell of Tennessee on the Acquisition of Cuba, Delivered in the Senate, 23 February 1858, Virginia Historical Society–Richmond. See also Speech of Hon. Judah P. Benjamin of Louisiana on the Acquisition of Cuba, Delivered in the Senate, February 11, 1859, Tulane University. See also Speech of Hon. James Dixon of Connecticut on the Thirty Million Bill for the Acquisition of Cuba, Senate, 25 February 1859; and Speech of Hon. John Bell of Tennessee on the Acquisition of Cuba, Senate, February 25, 1858, Massachusetts Historical Society: Dixie worried that Cuba will drain resources away from defense of slavery on the mainland. *Frederick Douglass's Paper*, 13 May 1853: William Seward, objected to annexation before abolition.

116. Speech of Hon. William W. Boyce of South Carolina Delivered in the House of Representatives, January 15, 1855, Massachusetts Historical Society (also kept at the Huntington Library). See also Report of Hon. Lawrence O'B. Branch, from the Committee on Foreign Affairs, on the Acquisition of Cuba, to Accompany Bill H.R. No. 678, House of Representatives, January 24, 1859. Washington, D.C.: Congressional Globe Office, 1859, Huntington Library.

117. Speech of Hon. J. R. Giddings of Ohio in the House, March 16, 1854, on the Message of the President of the United States Upon our Relations with Spain, Massachusetts Historical Society.

118. General Lewis M. Ayer, *Southern Rights and the Cuban Question. An Address Delivered at Whippy Swamp on the Fourth of July 1855*. Charleston: Burker, 1855: "We may now be seduced into the quixotic enterprise of conquering Cuba . . . Spain and Brazil are the natural allies of the South and should be so regarded and recognized by us. . . . We, of the South, should extend to Spain, in every possible way, the pipe of peace and the olive branch of friendship."

119. Speech of Hon. Stephen R. Mallory of Florida on the Cuba Bill, Delivered in the Senate of the United States, February 1859. Baltimore: Murphy, 1859, Maryland Historical Society–Baltimore (also kept at the University of Texas). The objection to seeing Cuba as a "sectional" issue was not without merit. See George W. Williams, *Sketches of Travel in the Old and New World*. Charleston: Walker Evans, 1871, 38: "I find quite a number of planters from the United States residing here, and they nearly all hail from the Northern states. It is said they make the hardest masters" and of one it was said, "the Negroes were worked so hard that three hundred died."

120. Speech of Hon. Volney E. Howard of Texas on the Acquisition of Cuba Delivered in the House of Representatives, January 6, 1853. Washington, D.C.: Congressional Globe, 1853, Historical Society of Pennsylvania.

121. Speech by Hon. Lawrence M. Keitt of South Carolina on the Acquisition of Cuba, Delivered in the House of Representatives, January 19, 1859, University of South Carolina–Columbia. See also Speech of Hon. J J. Crittenden of Kentucky on the Acquisition of Cuba, Senate, 15 February 1859, Massachusetts Historical Society.

122. Speech of Hon. M. S. Latham of California on the Rights of Neutrals-Cuba Delivered in the House of Representatives, June 14, 1854. Washington, D.C.: Congressional Globe, 1854, Historical Society of Pennsylvania.

123. "In the Senate of the United States. January 24, 1859," 35th U.S. Congress, Senate, 2nd Session, Rep. Com. No. 351, Massachusetts Historical Society. See also "Speech of J.B. Thompson of Kentucky on the Acquisition of Cuba, Delivered in the Senate . . . February 16, 1859," American Antiquarian Society: "The zeal and ability with which the Senators from Louisiana press the acquisition of Cuba have struck me with some surprise. It seems to me if Cuba were acquired, the whole sugar interest of Louisiana, which is now protected by a tariff, would be prostrated"—and then there is the Catholicism of Cuba.

124. *Frederick Douglass' Paper*, 1 September 1854: Gerritt Smith's view on this matter was criticized sharply; Smith backed annexation on the premise that U.S. slavery was more benign and the slave trade would expire as a result. Smith replied in *Frederick Douglass' Paper*, 9 March 1855: "The type of slavery in Cuba is, in some respects, more terrible than any other part of the world. . . . Plantation after plantation in Cuba has hundreds of males, and scarcely one female. . . . as I pity them, I would have Cuba annexed. . . . I desire the annexation because I believe it will contribute mightily to the overthrow of the whole system of American slavery." *Frederick Douglass' Paper*, 15 December 1854: "The process of emancipation, now going on in Cuba, under treaty stipulations with Great Britain, who is earnestly pressing their fulfillment, is

rapidly working out the extinction of slavery in that island." Smith's view was not "sustained by the facts." See also Gerritt Smith to "Dear Friend," 1 November 1854, University of Kansas: "Is it wicked for the poor slaves of Cuba—the most afflicted and outraged of all slaves—to desire to cast in their lot with our slaves." See also John Thrasher, "Cuba and Louisiana: Letter to Samuel Peters, Esq." New Orleans: Picayune Print, 1854, Huntington Library: If U.S. controls Cuba, the slave trade to Cuba will cease and the then current disparity in prices between Cuba and Louisiana as to slaves—$500 vs. $1,200—would dissipate.

125. Speech of Hon. Jacob Collamer of Vermont on the Acquisition of Cuba; in the Senate of the United States, February 21, 1859, Massachusetts Historical Society.

126. See Walker, "The Diary of a Louisiana Planter," Tulane University: According to a close comrade, John Quitman's "far-seeing mind saw the annexation of Cuba [as] a stronghold for the South when the hour came."

127. Speech of Hon. Robert Toombs of Georgia, the Acquisition of Cuba, in the Senate of the United States, January 24, 1859, in Reply to Hon. W. H. Seward of New York, Maryland Historical Society–Baltimore: "We shall get Spaniards and Englishmen, free negroes, slaves and coolies when we acquire Cuba. Our institutions are sufficient for all. We can Americanize them." For Seward's words, see *Frederick Douglass' Monthly*, March 1859: Obtaining Cuba, "a foreign country, 700 miles long and 70 miles wide containing 1, 500,000 human beings," is a "visionary and mischievous abstraction." See also "Speech of William H. Seward . . . in the Senate of the United States, January 24, 1859." Washington, D.C.: Buell & Blanchard, 1859, Kansas Historical Society–Topeka: Seward objects to $30 million appropriation slated for the purchase of Cuba.

128. *Frederick Douglass' Paper*, 24 March 1854. Emphasis in original.

129. *The Liberator*, 23 January 1857.

130. John Quitman to "My Dear Eliza," 21 September 1850, Box 6, Folder 65, Quitman Family Papers.

131. *The Liberator*, 25 January 1856.

132. Alexander Stephens to Robert S. Burch, 15 June 1854 in "A Letter of Alexander H. Stephens," *American Historical Review* 8/1 (October 1902): 91–97, 97. Emphasis in original.

133. *The Liberator*, 9 September 1859.

134. J. Preston Moore, "Pierre Soule: Southern Expansionist and Promoter," *Journal of Southern History* 21/2 (May 1995): 203–23; Nancy R. and Edward W. Schaefer, "French twists of taste: 19th Century Minister to Paris Grappled with Lust for Cuba, Napoleonic Court Etiquette," *Foreign Service Journal* 74/6 (June–July 1997): 40–45. Basically, the Manifesto that defined U.S. policy to the island declared that Cuba should be acquired—or war declared. See also J. A. Reinecke, Jr., "The Diplomatic Career of Pierre Soule," M.A. thesis, Tulane University, 1914.

135. C. Stanley Urban, "The Africanization of Cuba Scare, 1853–1855," *Hispanic American Historical Review* 37/1 (February 1957): 29–45, 31. See also Occie Clubbs, "Stephen Russell Mallory, Part III," *Florida Historical Quarterly* 26/1 (July 1947): 56–76, 59; and Don E. Fehrenbacher, *The Slaveholding Republic: An Account of the United States Government's Relations to Slavery*. New York: Oxford University Press, 2001, 129.

136. *Washington Globe*, 23 May 1854: "Since the year 1852 the Slave Trade has fearfully increased" in Cuba and U.S. nationals are largely responsible. "American ships are always sought for in Havana for the Slave Trade and command a higher price when purchased or chartered to be used as slavers than the vessels of any other nation. . . . We have acquired a degree of skill in the construction of ships unequalled by any

other nation." For confirmation of the preceding, see *Frederick Douglass's Paper*, 13 May 1852; and *Provincial Freeman*, 26 August 1854: Slave Trade from Africa to Cuba to Texas—"Recently seen [in] the harbor of Sierra Leone filled with condemned American bottoms, built in Baltimore . . . "

137. *New York Daily Times*, 22 April 1853: Slave traders using Baltimore clippers. "Vessels clear for some Cuban port, where they never arrive; and being provided with false papers, and sailing under the American flag, they succeed in reaching the coast, obtaining cargoes of slaves, and landing them in Cuba, with the connivance and complicity of the Spanish authorities." For confirmation of the preceding, see *Frederick Douglass's Paper*, 6 May 1853; *New York Herald*, 18 July 1853. Joseph T. Crawford to Earl of Aberdeen, 30 November 1853, in *British Parliamentary Papers*, 40:776: More ships leaving New York for Africa, then Cuba.

138. *National Intelligencer*, 28 February 1854.

139. *Provincial Freeman*, 15 April 1854: This Louisiana initiative "comes strangely enough from the South, so jealous of all meddling either by word or deed, with their own peculiar condition."

140. British & Foreign Anti-Slavery Society, *Cuban Slavery and the Slave Trade*, London, 1855, Western Reserve Historical Society–Cleveland. On the slave trade to Cuba, see "Case of Augusta Baptista and Albert Stabell, 1855," Term of Court June 1856 to September 1856, Box 9, Entry 24M57 HM 08/00, Record Group 21, Records of the U.S. District Court, District Court of Maryland, Baltimore, Criminal Case Files, 1841–1878, NARA–Philadelphia. In the same collection on a similar point, see "Case of James Johnson et al., 1850," Term of Court: March 1850 to June 1854, Box 7, Entry 24M57, HM 09/00.

141. Don Mariano Torrente, *Memoria Sobre Esclavitud en La Isla de Cuba*. London: Wood, 1853.

142. Memorandum from British legation in Madrid, 27 October 1855, Legajo de Estado 8048.

143. Memorandum from British legation in Madrid, 30 March 1856, Legajo de Estado 8048.

144. Letter to Commander Wise, 12 August 1857, FO313/39, NAUK: The "present state of the slave trade in the Bight of Benin"—"monopoly of that trade . . . is enjoyed by the American flag" with "a conspiracy" just "organized in Cuba with the intention" of expanding this commerce with "American vessels & the American flag . . . Simultaneously with the formation of this company at Havana slaves began to be collected at Wydah" who "belonged to the King of Dahomey" in league with "Domingo Martínez, an old slave merchant." This U.S. firm traded openly at the Havana stock exchange. . . . The Havana company . . . is called the Expedition for Africa, its shares are 1,000 dollars each." See David A. Ross, "The Career of Domingo Martínez on the Bight of Benin, 1833–1864," *Journal of African History* 6/1 (1965): 79–90. In the same file see Mr. Campbell to Earl of Clarendon, 4 February 1857: Near Lagos, U.S. slavers seen, "The property of . . . J. A. Machado of New York." See also Francis Lonsada to My Lord, 31 January 1857, FO313/29, NAUK: "The outfits of slave trading by vessels from" Havana "under the flag of Spain have been but few—the Slave Traders find it less dangerous and in other respects more advantageous to purchase vessels, fit them out and sail from the United States, the agents for such adventurers have of late been chiefly Portuguese who undertake the business in the States and are agents for the slave dealers in Africa." And see file of 5 April 1857: "In the port of New York about 12 vessels are fitted out every year for the Slave Trade and that Boston & Baltimore furnish each about the same number . . . add the slavers of other Eastern ports," and "40 will be below the actual number.

Each slaver registers from 150 to 250 tons. . . . Profits are so immense as almost to surprise belief."

145. John Bartlett to Earl of Clarendon, 3 February 1857, FO313/39, NAUK. See also *Provincial Freeman*, 19 May 1855: Captain James Daman is "on trial for his life" in Philadelphia, charged with "landing a cargo of slaves on the coast of Cuba." *Provincial Freeman*, 19 August 1854: "Final hearing . . . before United States Commissioner Ingraham, in the case of Captain Donald of *Grey Eagle*, charged with having landed six hundred slaves" in Cuba. *Provincial Freeman*, 25 November 1854: Captain James Smith of United States "convicted of having been engaged in the slave trade between the coast of Africa and the island of Cuba." This case is also discussed in *The Liberator*, 26 July 1855. See also *Frederick Douglass's Paper*, 8 September 1854: "New York merchants are constantly sending vessels to Africa to bring cargoes of slaves to Cuba . . . constantly carried on from this port and from Baltimore with a degree of openness and recklessness which makes the government officers accomplices for not taking steps to break it up. . . . Vessels are fitted up almost every week" for this purpose and "there are merchants in our streets today, who are making their tens and hundreds of thousands yearly" from this bestial business. See Anne Farrow, ed., *Complicity: How the North Promoted, Prolonged and Profited from Slavery*. New York: Ballantine, 2005, 127: "On its way to Cuba in 1857, one of the largest New York slave ships. . . . lost 200 of its 1,100 slaves."

146. Report from British legation in Madrid, 28 April 1857, Legajo de Estado 8048: He was doing business "between Benguela and Massomedes" and was based in New York.

147. This point is confirmed in *Provincial Freeman*, 22 April 1854. See also James Buchanan, U.S. legation in London, to "My Dear Sir," 18 March 1854, MSS 1 M 3816A, 965–978, Mason Family Collection, Virginia Historical Society–Richmond: Inquiry as to whether Britain had a "Treaty or understanding directly or indirectly with France," its partner against Russia, "in relation to Cuba. . . . Lord John Russell seems to have . . . proclaimed that there was enough naval force in the West Indies to keep Americans from taking Cuba" during Crimean involvement. On the immediately preceding, see *Correspondence on the Proposed Tripartite Convention, Relative to Cuba*, Boston: Little, Brown, 1853. See also Edmond Gabriel to Earl of Clarendon, 22 January 1856, FO313/13, NAUK: "Vessel believed to be American and bound to the Havanna. . . . Off the coast to the south of Benguela," Angola, with "cargo of more than five hundred slaves . . ." Occurred as Crimea involvement winds down.

148. Letter from Spanish Minister in Port-au-Prince, 12 May 1855, Correspondence from Spanish Legation in Port-au-Prince, MAE: In the same file see Letter from Spanish Minister, 8 May 1855: Haiti is accused of persecuting Cubans and Puerto Ricans in Hispaniola.

149. John Sekora, "'Mr. Editor, if you please': Frederick Douglass, 'My Bondage and My Freedom,' and the End of the Abolitionist Imprint," *Callaloo* 17/2 (Spring 1994): 608–26, 609.

150. H.M. Commissary Judge to Earl of Clarendon, 10 October 1854, in *British Parliamentary Papers*, 41:24–25.

151. Joseph Crawford to Earl of Clarendon, 31 August 1853, Legajo de Estado 8048; in the same file, see also Joseph Crawford to Earl of Malmesbury, 1 January 1853: After reporting that about 8,000 Africans delivered in the past year—"much increased" from previous years—he adds that his official total is more than likely a severe understatement.

152. Sam McLean to William Marcy, 24 June 1854, Roll 4, *Despatches from U.S. Consuls in Trinidad, Cuba*.

153. Hurlbert, *Gan-Eden*, 195, 139. See also Mixed Commission Report, 4 March 1854, FO313/40, NAUK: Charles William Hershey of Nova Scotia sails from New York on what he thinks is a legitimate voyage but soon arrives in "El Mina," Africa where "slaves were brought alongside at sundown," about 450, destined for Havana. See also J. Backhouse to Joseph T. Crawford, 17 November 1854, FO313/40: "700 Negroes . . . landed . . . Bahia Honda"—then "sailed immediately after having discharged her cargo for the United States." The vessel was "built at Baltimore."

154. David Turnbull, *The Jamaican Movement for Promoting the Enforcement of the Slave Trade Treaties and the Suppression of the Slave Trade.* London: Gilpin, 1850, 161: A "young mulatto" was kidnapped from Nassau "with a number of his brothers and sisters by an American named Norris who had married his half sister, the legitimate daughter of his father, a merchant in the seaport town of Gibara," Cuba. "He had there reduced his wife's relatives to slavery, retaining some in his own services and hiring out or selling the rest." See also *The Liberator*, 25 October 1851: "African slavers have discovered a new way of reaching Cuba with their cargoes. . . . Six hundred Negroes are landed on Anguilla island, one of the Bahamas, the slave ship burned to escape detection, and the cargo forwarded to Cuba, in two trips, by a schooner." Of course, the illicit arrival of Africans from the mainland to Cuba was also not unusual. See the case of the enslaved man, Juan Criollo of Cuba—though it was maintained he was actually a free man and native of Charleston: Report, 1853, Legajo 948, Numero de Orden 33475, Gobierno Superior Civil, ANC; also seeReport, 1857, Legajo 950, Numero de Orden 33620, on attempt by Dr. Guillermo Fulton to send slaves from Cuba to the United States. See also *The Liberator*, 6 July 1855: "Mr. Weaver" of Connecticut "bought a slave in Cuba" and "brought him" to his farm—but he promptly fled; *The Liberator*, 27 July 1855: "Abolitionists succeeded in kidnapping and spiriting away another Negro slave, who had just arrived here [Philadelphia] from Cuba with his master, a young Cuban"; *The Liberator*, 1 February 1850: Alexander Asher, fugitive slave from Cuba, just arrived in Boston by way of Nova Scotia. The transmission of enslaved Africans to and from Cuba took on unusual dimensions. See *Frederick Douglass' Paper*, 3 August 1855: "A specimen of suited African twins is now exhibiting in London . . . they were born in Africa . . . sold into slavery in Cuba. During the winter of 1850, Dr. Maginley of North Carolina purchased them as interesting natural curiosities and removed them to the United States. . . . They are inseparably united by the bones of the lower part of the back . . ."

155. Sam McLean to William Marcy, 7 April 1854, Roll 4, *Despatches from U.S. Consuls in Trinidad, Cuba.*

156. *National Intelligencer*, ca. late 1856, in *British Parliamentary Papers*, 43:543.

157. Acting Commissioner, Angola to Earl of Clarendon, 11 February 1857 in *British Parliamentary Papers*, 44:435–437. See Joseph T. Crawford to "Dear Sir," 5 June 1858, FO313/40, NAUK: When Crawford met with a U.S. emissary in Havana, the British diplomat "took occasion to advert to the abuse of the Am. flag and its being so generally prostituted to the carrying on the Slave Trade, that scarcely any other was not used by those who are engaged in that abominable traffic." Joseph Crawford to Edmond Gabriel, 1 November 1858, FO313/39, NAUK: "American brig 'Charlotte' had effected a clearance from the River Congo with a cargo of slaves"; also see Letter to Earl of Malmesbury, 25 August 1858: "Audacious manner in which the slave dealers in the River Congo still carry on their operations under the protection of the American flag. . . . Firm of Figuriere, Reis & Co. of New York . . . embarked 600 slaves . . . taking the vessel to Cuba"; andCommander Wise to Secretary of Admiralty, 9 October 1859: "Chase and captured a brigantine . . . showing American colors . . . about to ship slaves. . . . She is said to belong to a mercantile firm in New

York . . . about 185 tons. . . . She sailed from that port for the Havannah [*sic*]. . . . Orders were to ship 500 slaves up the River Congo & then endeavor to land them" in Cuba. For more on U.S. slaving near the Congo, see Charles Hope to Commander Adams, 20 April 1857, FO313/39; and Mr. Gabriel, Counsel–Luanda to Earl of Clarendon, 30 November 1856, FO313/39: "Two vessels recently escaped from the River Congo carrying off altogether upwards of 1200 slaves. . . . no fewer than four suspicious American vessels have within a short time arrived in River Congo, one of which had on board the well-known Slave Dealer, Joaquin Texeira de Miranda." See also Joseph Crawford to "His Excellency, the Captain General," 17 April 1859, FO313/54, NAUK: U.S. brig headed to Sao Tome: "I have no doubt that said vessel is destined for the Slave Trade." Also in that file, Joseph Crawford to His Excellency, 16 May 1859: Another U.S. vessel headed to Africa with malign intentions; Joseph Crawford to His Excellency, 16 May 1859: Another U.S. vessel has landed in Cuba with Africans aboard. See also *The Liberator*, 22 October 1858: Vessel sails from Montauk, New York, for Africa, seizes 900 Africans, then takes them to Cuba.

158. H.M. Commissary Judge to Earl of Malmesbury, 25 January 1859, in *British Parliamentary Papers*, 46:7. See also "Amended List of Slavers Captured or Destroyed by British Cruisers on the Coast of Africa During the Year 1857," FO 313/39, NAUK: Almost all were sailing from U.S. ports, New York, Newport, Boston, Baltimore—and especially New Orleans. In same file see Earl of Clarendon to Joseph Crawford, 1 August 1857: "Some fifteen vessels had been fitted out at New Orleans for the . . . slave trade." *The Liberator*, 18 September 1857: In Cuba, "the Americans carry on the trade almost exclusively, thanks to the facilities afforded by our deficient laws to evade suspicion on the coast." See also *The Liberator*, 8 October 1858: "Northern men and Northern capital" blamed for slave trade to Cuba.

159. Letter from Captain Rigby, Political Agent at Zanzibar, 15 August 1858, FO313/39, NAUK: "Large American ship . . . shipped twelve hundred slaves for conveyance to Cuba from the ports of the Mozambique." Letter to Earl of Clarendon from Natal, South Africa, 6 July 1757, FO313/39, NAUK: The "Mozambique Channel" is the epicenter of U.S. slaving and "has been renewed on a scale of such magnitude as to lead to the belief that it [has been legalized]." Also, Joseph T. Crawford to "My Lord," 5 December 1859, FO313/29: "Slave trade which is being carried on so extensively & successfully has been revived on the Mozambique and East Coast of Africa . . . [There reside] agents from Boston and from New Orleans" who buy Africans "for about $28 each" then "proceed" to a "port in Madagascar. . . . Preparation" for increase "on even a more gigantic scale in the future" being planned. See also Edward B. Bryan, *Letters to the Southern People Concerning the Acts of Congress and the Treaties with Great Britain in Relation to the African Slave Trade*. Charleston: Walker Evans, 1858. *The Liberator*, 23 February 1855: In Mozambique, 800 Africans "awaiting conveyance to Cuba. . . . Money to be paid by a draft on a commercial house in New York." Memorandum from British legation-Madrid, 2 November 1859, Legajo de Estado 8048: "Active Slave Trade is at present carried on between the East Coast of Africa and the island of Cuba," according to the consul in Zanzibar. In the same file see report from Zanzibar, 25 July 1859, concerning a "large slave ship" that "hoisted American colors" to bar search, then "returned under Spanish colors and commenced shipping a cargo of slaves for Cuba. This vessel was well armed with large guns and carried a strong crew."

160. H.M. Commissioner to Lord John Russell, 5 December 1859, in *British Parliamentary Papers*, 46:11–12. See also *Frederick Douglass's Paper*, 28 September 1855: "The peculiarity of this part of the trade being that it is almost entirely in the hands of the citizens of the United States." See also Laird W. Bergad, "Slave Prices in Cuba, 1840–

1875," *Hispanic American Historical Review* 67/4 (November 1987): 631–55. See also Report, 1858, Legajo 1631, Numero de Orden 82076, Gobierno Superior Civil, ANC: Portuguese consul in Savannah reports that a Spanish ship from Matanzas was on its way to Georgia and from to Africa to obtain "Negros Bozales." For a similar case,see Report, 1858, Legajo 1631, Numero de Orden 82081; and Report, 1858, Legajo 1631, Numero de Orden 82804.

161. Hurlbert, *Gan-Eden*, 195. See also *The Liberator*, 25 July 1856: According to Joseph Crawford, British diplomat in Cuba, when "the profits of a successful venture are so enormous, men will be found sufficiently bold and avaricious, to engage in the hazardous enterprise. . . . Traders calculate that if one vessel out of four proves successful, they can well afford to incur all the losses involved and to assume all the risks. Negroes are readily obtained on the African coast at from $10 to [$30] per head and from $300 to $800 is readily obtained for them when landed, so that a cargo of 500 slaves, costing $15,000, or $30 per head, realizes to the venturesome trader, if sold at an average of $400 per head, at least $170,000 or $180,000, expenses deducted."

162. Speech of the Hon. Stephen Mallory of Florida on the Cuba Bill, Delivered in the Senate of the United States, February 1859. Baltimore: Murphy, 1859, Maryland Historical Society–Baltimore. A similar estimate was made by a visiting republican in 1859; see Joseph Dimock, "Impressions of Cuba," in John Jenkins, ed., *Travelers' Tales of Old Cuba*. Melbourne, Aus.: Ocean Press, 2010, 64–78, 74: "An able-bodied male slave is now valued at an average of $1,200 to $1,500 and some good house servants are held at over $2,000. A slave when first landed, is worth if sound from $300 to $500. . . . The Congoes and those from the Gold Coast are the most numerous. . . . There is a mulatto tribe called Ebroes who make excellent domestic servants."

163. Letter to Juan Maria Ceballos, 8 March 1856, Juan Maria Ceballos Papers, Duke University. See Dimock, "Impressions of Cuba," 64–78, 66. In 1859, it was "estimated that two-thirds of all the shipping entering the port is American. Our trade with the island is immense, and although Cuba is a great market for American goods the difference in favor of Cuba last year was over $5 million." See also the remarks of President James Buchanan: *The Liberator*, 17 December 1858: "Our commerce with [Cuba] is far greater than that of any other nation, including Spain itself."

164. Charles W. Ramsdell, "The National Limits of Slavery Expansion," *Mississippi Valley Historical Review* 16/2 (September 1929): 151–71, 164.

165. Thomas M. Rodney to John H. Fromberger, 25 January 1851, John H. Fromberger Papers, Delaware Historical Society.

166. Francis Lonsada to "My Lord," 30 October 1855, FO313/29, NAUK: "High prices" of sugar in Cuba induces need for more slaves, causing some planters to travel to United States to purchase this labor, thus draining the Republic of laborers. The "increased price of slaves" results no less "and we reckon it 50 to 75 percent in the last three years"—meaning more voyages to Africa.

167. Robert A. Taylor, *Rebel Storehouse: Florida's Contribution to the Confederacy*. Tuscaloosa: University of Alabama Press, 2003, 6, 12, 17.

168. "The Diary of Sidney George Fisher, 1853–1857," *Pennsylvania Magazine of History and Biography* 86/3 (July 1962): 319–49, 345. Also see Anne Lane to William Carr Lane, 14 September 1851, Lane Collection, Missouri Historical Society–St. Louis: "As to Cuba, I think . . . you must give up your hacienda there. No matter if the country be a second Eden, with such a government, and such a population, it must be anything but a desirable residence."

169. Dana, *To Cuba and Back*, 260. See also Leon Beauvallet, *Rachel, and the New World. A Trip to the United States and Cuba*. New York: Dix, Edwards, 1856. See

also Broadside, 1850, Virginia Historical Society–Richmond: "Call for Acquisition" of Cuba by United States: "Whereas ten thousand American ships, laden with products of the Southern and Southwestern States and their returns to the value of three hundred millions of dollars pass annually through the narrow strait between Cuba and Florida" which was "important" to the "security of our southern waters" and, besides, a "question of national necessity and National Supremacy."

170. Turnbull, *The Jamaica Movement*, 18–19: Cuba is compared to "breeding districts of Maryland and Virginia. . . . Planters of Cuba are aware that the Negro population of Virginia has long been doubling itself every twelve years and a half, while the white inhabitants require twenty-five years to accomplish the process of duplication. There is nothing in the climate of Cuba to prevent a similar rate of increase of Negroes" except the "cheapness of labor" from Africa. See also Report, 12 December 1853, Legajo 48, Numero de Orden 39, Asuntos Politicos, ANC: Alarm expressed in Cuba about a possible disappearance of "la raza Blanca" (white race).

171. *The Liberator*, 6 October 1854.

172. H.M. Commissioner to Lord John Russell, 31 December 1859 in *British Parliamentary Papers*,46:13. See also Earl of Clarendon to Joseph T. Crawford, 27 August 1858, FO313/59, NAUK: "Landing of two cargoes of slaves" in Cuba by an "American built brigantine" that "had been abandoned by the slave dealers on the Cuban coast, after she had landed her cargo of slaves." Also see Letter from Earl of Clarendon, 30 November 1859, FO313/39, for list of slavers seized off coast of Africa, including a number of U.S. vessels taken near Angola and Congo. See Report, 5 July 1858, Legajo 223, Numero de Orden 12, Asuntos Politicos, ANC: Details about U.S. slaver, *C. Perkins*.

173. Lord Lyons to Lord John Russell, 25 July 1859, in *British Parliamentary Papers*, 46:231. See also *Frederick Douglass's Paper*, 31 December 1852: "Cuba has been the vilest slave mart on the face of the earth." See also R.W. Courtenay to Secretary of Admiralty, 24 September 1859, FO313/40, NAUK: Vessel "under American colors," recently in Congo with "several hundred Negroes" aboard, cleared for Havana. Also R. W. Courtenay, 27 September 1859, FO313/40: Slaver detained in the River Congo, "fitted out in the Havana but New Orleans appears to be the last port she left under American colors." For similar points, see Letter from Commodore Wise, 27 August 1859; J. W. Pike to Joseph Crawford, 30 August 1859; Letter to Secretary of Admiralty, 6 February 1859. See also Report, 1858, Legajo 1631, Numero de Orden 82086, Gobierno Superior Civil, ANC: Spain's consul in Key West advises that U.S. slaver from New Orleans in the vicinity; also see Report, 1858, Legajo 1631, Numero de Orden 82097: U.S. slaver monitored.

174. Andrew Blythe, U.S. Consul in Havana to "Sir," 29 August 1858, FO313/39, NAUK: "Many complaints have been made to this office by American masters that these British men of war . . . command a system of espionage exceedingly annoying to them."

175. *The Liberator*, 17 December 1858.

176. Mr. Darling to Mr. Eden, 19 June 1858, FO313/39, NAUK.

177. Consul Bunch to Lord John Russell, 5 September 1859, in ibid., *British Parliamentary Papers*, 46:264.

178. *Frederick Douglass's Paper*, 22 September 1851: Douglass lectures on Cuba.

179. *Frederick Douglass's Paper*, 12 August 1853. John Backhouse to "My Dear Aunt," 27 March 1853, Box 7, John Backhouse Papers, Duke University: In Havana, "there are a good many reports about, more or less authenticated, shewing [*sic*] Slave Trade to be very active here at present."

180. Harral E. Landry, "Slavery and the Slave Trade in Atlantic Diplomacy, 1850–1861," *Journal of Southern History* 27/2 (May 1961): 184–207, 201.

181. Leslie Bethell, "The Mixed Commissions for the Suppression of the Transatlantic Slave Trade in the Nineteenth Century," *Journal of African History* 7/1 (1966): 79–93, 83.

182. *Frederick Douglass's Monthly*, May 1859.

183. Joseph T. Crawford to "My Lord," 1 September 1855, Box 7, John Backhouse Papers: John Backhouse was sitting at home with Thomas Callaghan when "suddenly appeared before Mr. Callaghan a black who had laid hold of him and who succeeded in overpowering him, so that he was thrown down and bound hands and feet, the Negro stealing his watch. Almost simultaneously Mr. Backhouse was assaulted by a mulatto man with whom it appears he struggled hard for some time," then "thrown down & stabbed in the left side [leaving] a deep and mortal wound." See also William Cullen Bryant, *Letters of a Traveller; or Notes of Things Seen in Europe and America*. New York: Putnam, 1850: 389: "When we were at Guines [Cuba] we heard that a Negro was to suffer death early the next morning by the *garrote*, an instrument by which the neck of the criminal is broken." He had killed his master. Like other visitors, he was taken by the fact that generally executioners in Cuba were African: "Large black man dressed in a long white frock, white pantaloons and a white cap with a long peak. . . . His hands were tied together by the wrists; in one of them he held a crucifix."

184. By a Citizen of Cambridgeport, *A Journal of a Tour from Boston to Savannah, Thence to Havana*, 48, 54.

185. Leon Beauvallet, *Rachel and the New World: A Trip to the United States and Cuba*. New York: Dix, Edwards, 1856, 367: "Their [African] affection flows only in the direction of beet sugar. It is this ugly culinary root alone which can destroy slavery on the western continent! This beet-root is a bloody abolitionist! And you will see, sooner of later, the black race will be raising statues to it!"

186. Rosa Dimond Phinney was the daughter of Rhode Island's Governor Francis Dimond and resided with her spouse at a Cuban sugar plantation he owned. See Rosa Phinney to "My Dearest Sisters," 27 December 1856, Rosa Phinney Letters, Brown University: "They commenced cutting cane this morning and it is quite lively among the Negroes, it is such a funny sight to see them cutting and filling immense carts as they fast as they cut. . . . We want to see them dance. It was the funniest sight in the world and I laughed myself nearly to death." See also Rosa Dimond Phinney to "My Dear Sisters," 10 January 1857: "Streets were filled with Negroes dressed up in the most outlandish style with masks and bells and kinds of ridiculous things. . . . It was the funniest thing to see the Negros come into front of the windows and dance, all the time singing in the most barbarous manner, they stay until you give them money." See also Bryant, *Letters of a Traveller*, 396: "There is certainly great temptation to wear them out [Africans] in the sugar mills, which are kept in motion days and night."

187. Beauvallet, 367.

188. Demoticus Philalethes, 14: "Cases of poisoning by revengeful slaves are, therefore, very common, and their victims go to the grave, it being believed that they have suffered a natural death; and as the pecuniary interest of the new owners or heirs is in opposition to the discovery of the crime and the punishment of the slave, if found guilty, they, instead of promoting the inquest, endeavour to lessen the suspicions, in order not to lose his value, as they do not receive any compensation if the slave is garroted."

189. Clipping, ca. 1852, Box 1, Appleton Oaksmith Papers, Duke University: Africans attack U.S. slaver in the Congo. See also Letter about Congo, 24 June 1852: "3,000 natives had assembled, all well armed with muskets, clubs and . . ."

5. SLAVERY ENDS IN THE UNITED STATES—AND CUBA?

1. Diary entry, 13 August 1861, in C. Vann Woodward, ed., *Mary Chesnut's Civil War*. New Haven: Yale University Press, 1981, 143. See also Mary Bullard, *Cumberland Island: A History*, Athens: University of Georgia Press, 2003, 151. See also Memorandum, 17 March 1861, Tredegar Iron Works Papers, Virginia State Library-Richmond: Economic relations with Cuba.

2. Antonio Rafael de la Cova, "Ambrosio Jose Gonzales: A Cuban Confederate General," Ph.D. diss., West Virginia University, 1994, 269, 292. Jose Agustin Quintero, son of a wealthy Cuban tobacco planter and British mother, was born in Havana in 1829 and educated at Harvard—and fought alongside the CSA, besides serving as a diplomat in Mexico, 1861–64. He was also close to both Henry Longfellow and Ralph Waldo Emerson: see Philip Thomas Tucker, ed., *Cubans in the Confederacy: Jose Agustin Quintero, Ambrosio Jose Gonzales and Loreta Janeta Belanquez*. Jefferson, NC: McFarland, 2002, 10. See also Memorandum from Thomas Jordan, Chief of Staff of General Beauregard, 15 April 1863, Box 9, Records of Spanish Consulate in Charleston-Duke University: Refuses to grant a discharge from CSA military service to Spanish subject, Valentine Olives.

3. *The Liberator*, 10 May 1861. See also James Morton Callahan, *Cuba and International Relations: A Historical Study in American Diplomacy*. Baltimore: Johns Hopkins University, 1899.

4. *Richmond Times-Dispatch*, 10 February 1862.

5. Wayne Bowen, *Spain and the American Civil War*. Columbia: University of Missouri Press, 2011, 149.

6 Memorandum, August 1861, Legajo 222, Numero de Orden 250, Reales Ordenes y Cedulas, ANC.

7. James W. Cortada, "Spain and the American Civil War," 72.

8. See Edwin F. Pratt, "Spanish Opinion of the North American Civil War," *Hispanic American Historical Review* 10/1 (February 1930): 14–25, 16.

9. See also Alexander Humboldt, *Island of Cuba*, 82. With the showdown between London and Washington over the slave trade, Cuba could easily turn to the "slave breeding states of Virginia, North Carolina and Maryland; and the inducement to them to sell would probably be so great as to draw away from their stock, until they became free states—a far greater gain to the North than Cuba would be to the South." John S. C. Abbott, *South and North; Or Impressions Received During a Trip to Cuba and the South*. New York: Abbey & Abbot [*sic*], 1860,53: In Cuba, it was said, "two thirds" of the population of 1 million are "slaves or free blacks." Many Gulf Coast planters wanted Cuba to be annexed since they were so close to the island and would take their "Negro gangs to Cuba . . . sell their plantations to cotton growers." Thus, "we should probably see such a stampede of slaveholders with their slaves to Cuba as the world has never seen before."

10. Raphael Semmes, *Memoirs of Service Afloat During the War Between the States*. Baltimore: Kelly, Piet, 1869, 139. On an infamous incident involving a leading Confederate in Cuba that almost brought the United States to war with London, see Louis Martín Sears, *John Slidell*. Durham, NC: Duke University Press, 1925. See also Edward Mitchell Whaley, "Short Account of the Experiences of [Whaley] of Edisto Island, South Carolina," 1909, South Carolina Historical Society–Charleston: During the war, he was in Paris and since Dixie was "blockaded," he traveled to Havana where he communed with "the famous house of Upmann Bros., cigar manufacturers. . . . They are Germans and they were very nice to me." He sought to "use my time looking up the officers of the Steamer which had brought

Mason & Slidell," who were Charlestonians. On departing, "the ladies of Havanna [*sic*] presented our boat with a beautiful Confederate flag."

11.   Mary G. Davis Journal Typescript, 1861–1863, Massachusetts Historical Society–Boston. Davis visited Matanzas where she found that coffee plantations were not as profitable as sugar: "Niggers are so high now." There "we broke the ice of new acquaintances with ease and beyond that I found plenty to [see] in birds, flowers and niggers. . . . She took me to see her nigger nursery. . . ."

12.   C. H. Rogers, *Incidents of Travel in the Southern States and Cuba*. New York: Craighead, 1862, 123.

13.   Abbott, *South and North*, 17, 23.

14.   Volume 129, 1862, Brown Brothers Papers, New York Public Library.

15.   See translations of articles published in the United States on the political situation in Cuba, 30 January 1868, Legajo 55, Numero de Orden 321, Asuntos Politicos, ANC.

16.   Howard Temperley, "Capitalism, Slavery and Ideology," *Past & Present* 75 (May 1977): 94–118, 96.

17.   New York Cuban Junta, *Facts About Cuba*, New York, 1870, Box 308, Moses Taylor Papers, New York Public Library.

18.   *The Liberator*, 18 November 1864.

19.   Measures for the Complete Abolition of Slavery, 1865–1867, Legajo de Estado 3552, AHN-Madrid.

20.   Report, ca. 1863, Box 2, Albert G. Riddle Papers, Western Reserve Historical Society–Cleveland. See also Jose Isern, *Pioneros Cubanos en U.S.A., 1575–1898*, 1971, Huntington Library: A useful section on Cubans during the U.S. Civil War is included.

21.   James W. Cortada, "Spain and the American Civil War: Relations at Mid-Century, 1855–1868," *Transactions of the American Philosophical Society* 70/4 (1980): 3–121, 27, 85. Abbott, *South and North*, 52: "The annexation of Cuba to the United States, were it possible, while it would strengthen slavery in the Senate and in the House, would in many respects greatly weaken the institution in continental states. It would be the instant destruction of every sugar plantation in Louisiana. Not one could live a year." See also documents from the Spanish Consulate in Charleston, 1861, Legajo 224, Numero de Orden 29, Asuntos Politicos, ANC. For example, see Clipping from Charleston newspaper: Captain General hailed for allowing CSA vessels to dock in Cuba: "This is practical recognition of the independence of the Confederate States" and "plain common sense"—since "there is far less danger of the United States subjugating the Confederate States, than of France reducing Austria to a provincial condition." This decision will bind Spain and the CSA "as nations having the same domestic and industrial institutions, it is in the interest and desire of the slaveholding South studiously to cultivate" this tie. "There was a time when many wished to strengthen the relative power of the South by the annexation of Cuba" but now with the "dissolution of the Union and independence" of the CSA, the motive for this has "disappeared." The CSA desires "the most cordial relations with Spanish America and Brazil. These are the people most identical with us in institutions—institutions which the rest of the world and the United States hate. . . . We look forward to close and mutually beneficial alliance with Spain."

22.   *The Liberator*, 25 October 1861. Emphasis in original.

23.   Abraham Lincoln to Hon. J. T. Hale, 11 January 1861, in Roy P. Basler, ed., *The Collected Works of Abraham Lincoln*, vol. 4. New Brunswick: Rutgers University Press, 1953, 172.

24.   Don E. Fehrenbacher, *The Slaveholding Republic: An Account of the United States Government's Relations to Slavery*. New York: Oxford University Press, 2001, 131.

25. Minority Report of the Committee on Resolutions, 1860, Papers of the Democratic National Convention, Duke University.
26. Ibid., Wayne Bowen, 28. For a militant response to this troop movement, see "Speech of Hon. Godlove S. Orth of Indiana, Delivered in the House of Representatives, June 14, 1859," Washington: Rives, 1870, AAS.
27. William B. Morse, "The Cuban Question: 1858–1859," AAS.
28. See Consul to Lord John Russell, 17 July 1861, FO72/1013/181, NAUK. In the same file, see also Consul to Lord John Russell, ca. 1861. See also *Charleston Mercury*, 12 September 1861: After the Captain General allows the docking of CSA vessels in Cuba, this Dixie journal asserts, "This is practical recognition of the independence of the Confederate States."
29. Cortada, "Spain and the American Civil War," 85.
30. Wayne H. Bowen, *Spain and the American Civil War*. Columbia: University of Missouri Press, 2011, 125. See also Consul to Lord John Russell, 17 July 1861, FO72/1013/154, NAUK: A CSA steamer—the *Sumter*—landed at Cienfuegos along with a "number of vessels which [it] has captured laden with produce."
31. C. M. Allen to William Seward, 11 February 1864, T262, Roll 7, Consular Despatches–Bermuda, Bermuda Archives.
32. See Gordon H. Warren, *Fountain of Discontent: The Trent Affair and Freedom of the Seas*. Boston: Northeastern University Press, 1981; Norman B. Ferris, *The Trent Affair: A Diplomatic Crisis*. Knoxville: University of Tennessee Press, 1977. See also Arthur Lynn to Lord John Russell, 4 March 1861, Records of the British Consulate in Galveston–Rosenberg Library, Galveston: "A great disquiet exists throughout the manufacturing districts of Great Britain in regard to the future supply of cotton."
33. This was ironic since a leading U.S. envoy stressed that what was driving London's policy regionally was "Cuban Slave Labor." See M. Galody to William Seward, 30 September 1863, Roll 5, T327, *Despatches from U.S. Consuls in Antigua* NARA–CP.
34. Kinley J. Brauer, "The Slavery Problem in the Diplomacy of the American Civil War," *Diplomatic History* 46/3 (August 1977): 439–69, 468.
35. Spanish Consul to "Captain," 23 May 1865, Box 9, Records of Spanish Consulate–Charleston, Duke University.
36. Report from Spanish legation in Charleston, 25 October 1861, Legajo 224, Numero de Orden 29, Asuntos Politicos, ANC: A victory gained by the Confederates on the banks of the Potomac River near Leesburg, albeit with many deaths and injuries. Attached are clippings referencing a "Southern Victory on the Potomac." Also see in same file, Documents from the Spanish legation in New York.
37. See Captain General to Charleston legation, 10 September 1861; Memoranda, 29 September 1861, 10 September 1861, 12 August 1861 and 27 July 1861, Box 21, Records of Spanish Consulate–Charleston, Duke University.
38. Ludwell Johnson, "Commerce Between Northeastern Ports and the Confederacy, 1861–1865," *Journal of American History* 54/1 (June 1967): 30–42, 34. *The Liberator*, 14 January 1859: "Northern enterprise has been extensively engaged in the slave trade between Africa and Cuba and there is no reason to doubt it will brave all dangers." See also Correspondence Concerning Slavery, 1862–1863, Legajo 954, Numero de Orden 33754A, ANC; and Correspondence Concerning the Slave Trade, 1816–1884, Legajo 565, Numero de Orden 27942, Gobieron General. See also Dispositions on the Repression and Penalizing of the Slave Trade, 1866, Legajo Estado 8049, AHN-Madrid.
39. John F. Reiger, "Deprivation, Disaffection and Desertion in Confederate Florida," *Florida Historical Quarterly* 48/3 (1970): 279–98, 280.

40. Memorandum, 28 November 1861, Box 35, Confederate States of America Archives–
     Duke University; also see Report, 27 July 1861: Purchase of arms intended for New
     Orleans via Vera Cruz and Havana.

41. *Charleston Mercury*, 13 September 1861. See also Contract, 1 February 1861, Box
     8, Records of Spanish Consulate–Charleston: Ramon Salas and Charles Poujaud
     "trading together in the city of Charleston under the name & firm of Poujaud &
     Salas" have appointed A. Gonzales & Co. of Matanzas their attorney—indicative
     of developing ties between Charleston and Matanzas. See also Letters to Juan Maria
     Ceballos, 10 July 1856 and 10 August 1856, Juan Maria Ceballos Papers, Duke
     University. See also clippings from Charleston newspapers, datelined Matanzas,
     1861, Legajo 224, Numero de Orden 29, Asuntos Politicos, ANC: Sloop from
     Carolina arrives in Cuba with rice to which the U.S. Consul objects—and is promptly
     rebuffed.

42. Ella Lonn, *Foreigners in the Confederacy*. Chapel Hill: University of North Carolina
     Press, 2002, 6.

43. Henry Ashworth, *A Tour in the United States, Cuba and Canada*, London: Bennett,
     1861, 62.

44. U.S. vs. Schooner Major Barbour, August 1862, A17–75–A17–86, Box 11, ARC ID
     620244, HM FY 2010, Record Group 21, Records of the District Courts of the United
     States, U.S. District Court for the Southern District of New York, Prize and Related
     Records, Civil War Case Files, National Archives and Records Administration–
     New York City. (Hereafter NARA–NYC.)

45. *U.S. v. Schooner Aigburth*, 26 April 1862; and *U.S. v. Joseph Toone*, A 17–214–A
     17–222, Box 24, ARC ID 620244, HM FY 2010, NARA–NYC.

46. *U.S. v. Albion*, December 1861, NARA–NYC.

47. *U.S. v. "Stephen Hart,"* NARA–NYC.

48. Raphael Semmes, *The Cruise of the Alabama and the Sumter. From the Private
     Journals and Other Papers of Commander R. Semmes, CSN and other Officers*, vol. 1.
     London: Saunders, Ottley, 1864, 38. By mid–1861, Dixie was capturing U.S. prizes
     and dragging them to Cuba.

49. Cornelia H. Jenks, *The Land of the Sun*, 98: "There is a hotel called the Carolina
     House, kept by an American, which is quite a place of resort for Americans."

50. Julia Ward Howe, *A Trip to Cuba*. Boston: Ticknor and Fields, 1860, 104, 221, 222,
     224, 227: "Americans should feel a pang in acknowledging that even in the dark article
     of slave laws they are surpassed by a nation which they condemn. . . . The question
     now rises, whether in case of a possible future possession of the island by Americans,
     the condition of the blacks would be improved. There is little reason to think so . . . the
     black and white races are, by all accounts, more mingled in Cuba, than in any part of
     our own country. . . . What a thrill of joy would run through our Southern and South-
     Western states, if every slave father and mother had the power to purchase their own
     offspring for a sum not altogether beyond their reach. . . . Slaves are not sold by
     public auction in Cuba, but by private sale. Nor are they subject to such rudeness and
     insult as they often receive from the lower whites of our Southern cities." See also *A
     Woman's Wanderings in the Western World, A Series of Letters Addressed to Sir Fitzroy
     Kelly, M.P., By His Daughter Mrs. Bromley*. London: Saunders, Ottley, 1861.

51. Delany, *Blake*, 298, 193, 195.

52. Martín Delany, Remarks at Emigration Convention in Cleveland, August 1854,
     in Robert S. Levine, ed., *Martín R. Delany: A Documentary Reader*. Chapel Hill:
     University of North Carolina Press, 2003, 265: "Until the Americans intruded into
     Cuba, contaminating society wherever they located, black and colored gentlemen
     and ladies of rank, mingled indiscriminately in society. But since the advent of these

Negro-haters, the colored people of Cuba have been reduced nearly, if not quite, to the level of the miserable degraded position of the colored people of the United States."

53. Delany, *Blake*, 288.

54. Joseph Crawford to "My Lord," 5 February 1861, FO313/29, NAUK.

55. Bowen, *Spain and the American Civil War*, 115. See also Jose Antonio Piqueras, "La Reina, Los Esclavos y Cuba," in Juan Sisinio Perez Garzon, ed., *Isabel II: Los Espejos de La Reina*. Madrid: Marcial Pons Historia, 2004, 96–97, 108.

56. Report from British Foreign Office, 11 February 1860, Legajo de Estado 8048, AHN-Madrid: "United States capital has been more and more employed in the traffic. The practice is for slave vessels to sail under the American flag. If the flag is rightly assumed and papers correct, no British cruiser can touch them. If no slaves are on board, even though the equipment, the fittings, the water casks," etc., "prove that the ship is on a slave trade voyage, no American cruiser can touch them. The master indeed often taunts the captain of a British cruiser with his impunity from capture. From the East Coast of Africa a most extensive slave trade is carried on almost without interruption." See also Manuel Moreno Fraginals, Herbert S. Klein and Stanley L. Engerman, "The Level and Structure of Slave Prices on Cuban Plantations in the Mid-Nineteenth Century: Some Comparative Perspectives," *American Historical Review* 88/5 (December 1983): 1201–18, 1206. From 1856 to 1863 slave imports to Cuba averaged 13,000 annually—with a high of 25,000 in 1859 alone.

57. *The African Slave Trade to Cuba*, London: British and Foreign Anti-Slavery Society, Ca. 1860s, AAS. See also "Confidential Memorandum. . . . Grievances of British Subjects in Cuba and Puerto Rico, 1845–1857," FO881/692, NAUK.

58. Tiffany Yolanda Jimmece Bryant, "Inter-Subjective and Transnational Racial Effects: The Role of the United States on the Formation and Evolution of the Collective Perception of Racial Relations in Cuba, 1898–1902," Ph.D. diss, , Florida International University, 2010, 87.

59. "Project for the Extinction of Slavery in Cuba and Puerto Rico." New York: S. Hallet, 1865, New York Historical Society.

60. "Stanley" to J. V. Crawford, 10 March 1868, FO313/41, NAUK. Such activity continued during the immediate postbellum era. Also see in same file Charles Francis Adams, U.S. legation in London to My Lord, 5 September 1865: 400 Africans landed 50 miles from Cienfuegos; Governor Rawson, Nassau, to E. Cardwell, 23 September 1865: Slaver with ties to New York lands Africans in Cuba; Stanley to to W. W. Follett-Synge, 22 November 1866: Slaver detained in River Congo basin: "Proof that planters and slave dealers have not yet given up the idea of introducing slaves into that island [Cuba]." See clipping, 10 June 1869, in Port-au-Prince Correspondence, MAE: "Slave ships" headed to Cuba. See also Report from Spanish legation–London, 14 May 1873, Legajo Estado 8049, AHN: London wants cooperation from the United States, France—which agrees—Germany, Spain, and Portugal on suppression of slave trade from East Africa.

61. Secretary of the Navy George M. Robeson to President Grant, 12 March 1870 in John Y. Simon., ed., *The Papers of Ulysses S. Grant*, vol. 20: *November 1, 1869–October 31, 1870*. Carbondale: Southern Illinois University Press, 402. A prominent mainland military leader during the 1898 war also spoke to this issue. See Frederick Funston, *Memories of Two Wars*. New York: Scribner's, 1911, 65–66: "It is a matter of common knowledge that up to as late as 1870 small cargoes of slaves from the west coast of Africa were run into Cuba. Juan Gonzales, the man who served for more than six months as my 'striker' or personal servant, told me that he distinctly remembered his capture, when about ten years of age, by Arabs on the Congo, his sale to the

Portuguese, and the journey in a sailing ship across the Atlantic. He ran away from his master and served in the Ten Years' War, and so gained his freedom. These African Negroes often conversed among themselves in their native dialect, nearly all of them having come from the same region on the Congo." A "surprising fact was that not a few of the older Negroes of Cuba were born in Africa."

62.   Frederick C. Drake and R. W. Schufeldt, "Secret History of the Slave Trade to Cuba Written by an American Naval Officer, Robert Wilson Schufeldt, 1861," *Journal of Negro History* 55/3 (July 1970): 218–35, 228, 229, 232.

63.   *Frederick Douglass's Monthly*, January 1861.

64.   Report, 1861, Legajo Estado 8049, AHN-Madrid.

65.   Report, 22 December 22 1861, Legajo Estado, 8049, AHN-Madrid.

66.   *Frederick Douglass's Monthly*, November 1862. See also Melina Pappademos, *Black Political Activism and the Cuban Republic*, Chapel Hill: University of North Carolina Press, 2011, 102: Most Africans "had arrived in Cuba at least three decades before" the 1898 war and "due to a resurgence in slave trading in the 1860s . . . approximately 12,000 African laborers were imported each year between 1860 and 1866."

67.   See the proposal by a "filibuster" to increase the non-African portion of Cuba's population. Demoticus Philalethes, *Yankee Travels Through the Island of Cuba*, 244: This "brilliant system to increase with a wonderful rapidity the white population of Cuba" by taking $1 million and investing 25 percent of it in "freeing ten thousand newly born Negresses at twenty five dollars a piece. . . . Half a million should be devoted to endow one thousand young and healthy Negresses to marry white men. . . . There would always be a large number of Peninsulars anxious to do it, as their attachment to the blacks is so strong, that almost all the mulattoes are their children" and with the remainder import "Galician or Catalonian women," "giving them two hundred dollars on their arrival [and] many Free Negroes may be induced to marry them."

68.   Larry Eugene Rivers, *Rebels and Runaways: Slave Resistance in 19th-Century Florida*. Urbana: University of Illinois Press, 2012, 13. See also Julie Ann Lisenby, "The Free Negro in Antebellum Florida, 1821–1861," M.A. thesis, Florida State University, 1967.

69.   Susan Greenbaum, *More than Black: Afro-Cubans in Tampa*. Gainesville: University Press of Florida, 2002, 51.

70.   Martín Delany, *Blake*, 295.

71.   Delany cited in Robert S. Levine, ed., *Martín R. Delany*, 161.

72.   *Frederick Douglass' Monthly*, March 1861: "An organized company exists in the city of Havana with a capital of $1,000,000 whose sole business is to import Negroes into the island of Cuba. . . . [A Spaniard] writes to his correspondent [in] New York to purchase a vessel and procure a master. This correspondent is probably . . . a naturalized citizen of the U.S. . . . In this way some seventy vessels are said to have sailed from the port of New York after cargoes of slaves" in the Congo, gleaning a "net profit [of] two hundred and thirty-one thousand, five hundred dollars!"

73.   Warren S. Howard, *American Slavers and the Federal Law, 1837–1862*. Berkeley: University of California Press, 1963, 56.

74.   James W. Cortada, "Spain and the American Civil War: Relations at Mid-Century, 1855–1868," *Transactions of the American Philosophical Society* 70/4 (1980): 3–121, 90.

75.   Memorandum, August 1861, Legajo 222, Numero de Orden 160, Reales Ordenes y Cedulas, ANC.

76.   See Consul to William Seward, 2 July 1862, Roll 7, *Despatches from U.S. Consuls in Trinidad, Cuba*. On slaving to Cuba see also Joseph Crawford to His Excellency, 11

May 1860, FO313/54, NAUK: "560 Bozal Negroes were landed . . . brought in from Africa by a brig under American colors. . . . The whole 560 were sold as soon as they were landed on the beach at $1,000 [each]." In the same file see Joseph Crawford to His Excellency, 7 December 1860: U.S. vessel arrives in Cuba "full of Negroes," i.e. "450 Bozales" destined for slavery. Joseph Crawford to His Excellency, 10 December 1860: "American" vessel headed to Africa for slaving. Joseph Crawford to His Excellency, 18 January 1861: 550 Africans on a "slaver vessel having on board an American and also a Spanish captain" wrecked, taken to island near Cuba and a Spanish vessel comes and takes away the prospective slaves, as Crawford fumes.

77. Petition to Senate and House from Fernando J. Moreno, U.S. Marshal, May 1860, Monroe County Public Library–Key West. See also Donald Gordon Lester, "Key West During the Civil War," M.A. thesis, University of Miami, 1949. *Boston Post*, 15 May 1860: capture of the slave ship *Wildfire*. *Frederick Douglass's Monthly*, June 1860: U.S. vessel arrives in Key West from "south side of the island [of] Cuba. . . . with five hundred and sixty African Negroes on board . . . direct from Africa. . . . This is the second capture made within a very short period of time."

78. "Evidence for the African Cemetery at Higgs Beach, Key West, Florida," by Corey Malcolm, Director Archaeology, Mel Fisher Maritime Heritage Society, and Lawrence B. Conyers, University of Denver, August 2002, Monroe County Public Library. Also here, see Fernando Moreno to "Sir," 10 June 1860: Arrival of another vessel caught "near" Cuba with "411 African Negroes on board . . . manned entirely by foreigners. There were no papers or flag found on board." See also *The Liberator*, 7 September 1860: "Slave brig" with "no papers, flag or name" detained. "She had a slave deck arranged. . . . The brig is a piratical craft, armed with side guns. There were plenty of muskets, pistols and cutlasses on board. The crew was large and was made up of ferocious desperadoes. It is presumed that the brig was fitted to seize by force the first slaver that it met en route for Cuba and thus obtain as many Negroes as she could stow away. The prize was sent to Key West." See also *Frederick Douglass' Monthly*, August 1860: "An American war steamer has captured an American schooner in the waters of the Gulf of Mexico, having on board 400 Africans." See also Joseph T. Durkin, *Stephen R. Mallory: Confederate Navy Chief*. Chapel Hill: University of North Carolina Press, 1954.

79. Report from Key West, 1861, FO313/40, NAUK. See also Report from Spanish consul in Key West, Vicente Cubells, 1860, Legajo de Estado 8048, AHN-Madrid: U.S. ship with 1,000 Africans aboard at issue. See clipping from *Times* of 9 June 1860; and Key West Consul's letter of 11 July 1860: attempted slave trading between Florida, Georgia and Alabama and Cuba; and see in Legajo de Estado 8049, his 26 February 1861 letter reporting that a U.S. ship passed through Key West headed to Angola for slaving. See also Irvin D. Solomon and Grace Erhart, "Race and Civil War in South Florida," *Florida Historical Quarterly* 77/3 (Winter 1999): 320–41, 328: In June 1862 an unnamed slaver was detained in the waters off southern Florida. It had just unloaded almost 800 enslaved Africans in Cuba.

80. Report from Spanish Consul in Newcastle-upon-Tyne, 14 March 1862, Legajo de Estado 8049, AHN-Madrid: Worry expressed that London will put even more abolitionist pressure upon Madrid with the onset of the Civil War.

81. Consul to Lord John Russell, 5 December 1859, in *British Parliamentary Papers* 46:11–12. See also R. R. Burton to Admiralty, 9 January 1860, FO313/40, NAUK: U.S. slaver captured with enslaved Africans aboard, "most of which are under 10 years of age" with "several very much attenuated. . . . The barque sailed from . . . Anguilla near Cuba" and, previously, had "run two successful cargoes of slaves from Mozambique."

82. Lord Lyons to Lord John Russell, 25 July 1859, in *British Parliamentary Papers*, 46:231. *The Liberator*, 1 June 1860: Capture of slaver with 560 Africans aboard; "she had at the time left [the] Congo River. . . . One American on board. . . . His name is William Preston of Philadelphia."

83. Lord John Russell to Joseph Crawford, 31 January 1860, FO313/40, NAUK: In Luanda there was espied an "American brig . . . of New York with 518 slaves but without colours or papers."

84. Farrow, *Complicity*, 126.

85. William Kaufman Scarborough, ed., *The Diary of Edmund Ruffin*, vol. 1: *Toward Independence, October 1856–April 1861*. Baton Rouge: Louisiana State University Press, 1972, 198, 270.

86. J. V. Crawford to Lord John Russell, 30 September 1860 in *British Parliamentary Papers*, 47:14.

87. Consul to Lord John Russell, 28 July 1860, in ibid., 47:181. See also R. R. Burton to Admiralty, 13 April 1860, FO313/40, NAUK: Slaver captured "without colours or papers. . . . Ship had originally been an American packet named 'Roanoke' built at Baltimore, owned by merchants at Philadelphia" and "sold by them" to "slaver merchants of Cuba." Memorandum, 1859, Legajo 431, Numero de Orden 21047, Gobierno General, ANC: U.S. ship destined for Africa with purpose of trafficking in slaves. Memorandum, 1864, Legajo 1633, Numero de Orden 82156, Gobierno Superior Civil, ANC: Frigate from New York proceeding to Matanzas contains "Negros Bozales." Memorandum, 1864, Legajo 1633, Numero de Orden 82133, GSC: U.S. frigate suspected of being slaver; also see similar report, Memorandum, 1860, Legajo 1632, Numero de Orden 82117, GSC. Memorandum, 1861, Legajo 434, Numero de Orden 21047, Gobierno General, ANC: U.S.-flagged ship involved in slave trade to Cuba.

88. Admiralty–London to B. W. Walker, 8 August 1861, ADM123/178, NAUK.

89. Joseph Crawford to Earl Russell, 8 June 1862, ADM123/178, NAUK.

90. Richard Beattie to Senior Officer, 31 October 1862, ADM123/178, NAUK.

91. Lord John Russell to Lord Lyons, 7 November 1862, in *British Parliamentary Papers*, 47:309.

92. Joseph Crawford to Lord John Russell, 16 July 1861, in ibid., 47:142. See also *The Liberator*, 25 September 1857: Slave trade to Cuba "flourishes amazingly."

93. *Raleigh News*, 11 July 1879—refers to 1862.

94. J. V. Crawford to Earl Russell, 14 January 1863, in *British Parliamentary Papers*, 49:151.

95. Taylor Milne, "The Lyons-Seward Treaty of 1862," *American Historical Review* 38/3 (April 1933): 511–26, 516.

96. Debate in Spanish Cortes, 30 January 1862 in *British Parliamentary Papers*, 48:202.

97. Abraham Lincoln to U.S. Congress, 31 May 1864, in Roy P. Basler, ed., *The Collected Works of Abraham Lincoln*, vol. 7. New Brunswick: Rutgers University Press, 1953, 370.

98. *The Liberator*, 24 June 1864.

99. *U.S. v. Erastus H. Booth*, July 1862, Box 4, Entry 67, Nos. 1–266 to 1–332, Record Group 21, Records of the U.S. Circuit Court for the Southern District of New York, Criminal Case File, National Archives and Records Administration–New York City. Hereafter NARA–NYC.

100. *U.S. v. Mary J. Watson*, NARA–NYC.

101. *The Liberator*, 1 December 1864. Nathaniel Gordon, ultimately executed during the war for slaving to Cuba, ran afoul of the authorities earlier after kidnapping an African from Guadeloupe for the purpose of enslavement: see *U.S. v. Nathaniel Gordon*, ARC ID 378437, Record Group 21, NARA–NYC.

102. *U.S. v. John Macomber*, Box 2, RG 21, NARA–NYC.

103. Mary G. Davis Journal Typescript.

104. Memorandum, 1863, Legajo 1293, Numero de Orden 50387, Gobierno Superior Civil, ANC: Arrival from the United States of maids of color; and Memorandum, 1863, Legajo 1293, Numero de Orden 50390, GSC: Arrival from the United States of "La Senora Schefer" bringing a maid of color. See also Memorandum, 1863, Legajo 1293, Numero de Orden 50405, GSC: A request for permission to bring from the United States a free person of color named "Josefa." Memorandum, 1863, Legajo 1293, Numero de Orden 50400, GSC: A request for permission to return from the U.S. a free person of color, "Modesta Rogers." Memorandum, 1863, Legajo 1293, Numero de Orden 50382, GSC: Arriving in Cuba from New Orleans, the "Negro Andres Garcia."

105. Joseph Crawford to Earl Russell, 8 March 1862, ADM123/178, NAUK.

106. Robert Bunch to Earl Russell, 30 September 1865, FO84/1236, NAUK. See also Correspondence Concerning Slavery, 1865, Legajo 965, Numero de Orden 34109, Gobierno Superior Civil, ANC. See also Captain George Howland, 1797–1878, "An Autobiography or Journal of His Life, Voyages and Travels," G.W. Blunt White Library: Writing of 1867, he was en route to Matanzas from New York: "I painted my pretty schooner here and had several offers for her at more than double her cost. They wanted her for a slaver to go to Africa and they made me tempting offers to go in her as masters." See also James W. Cortada, "Spain and the American Civil War," 91: "In 1864 the American consul at San Juan [Puerto Rico] reported that no slaves had arrived on the island since 1859."

107. W. H. Stuart to Governor Rawson, 22 September 1865, in *British Parliamentary Papers*, 50:139: An "American" captain "boasted" of his "tenth voyage" from Africa, with the most recent one "landed . . . twenty-five miles to the westward of Havana." See also Report, 26 November 1867, in *British Parliamentary Papers*, 51:84: Slaver of "American build" sighted near Cuba. See also Documents Concerning Official News from the Government of the United States referencing a Planned Journey of the Steamer "Virgin" with a Cargo of Negroes to Land in Neuvitas, 1866, Legajo 438, Numero de Orden 21242, Gobierno General, ANC; also see Report, 18 May 1868, Legajo 56, Numero de Orden 9, Asuntos Politicos: Slaver found on the coast of Cuba.

108. Report from Spanish legation in Washington, 28 March 1862, Legajo Estado 8049, AHN-Madrid.

109. Letter to Don S. Calderon Collantes, 11 September 1862, Legajo Estado 8049, AHN-Madrid.

110. "The Union Volunteer," 1862, Massachusetts Historical Society.

111. Registers, 1866–1867, Box 21, Records of Spanish Consulate–Charleston.

112. George W. Williams, *Sketches of Travel in the Old and New World*. Charleston, NC: Walker Evans, 1871, 8.

113. Report, ca. 1864, Box 2, Albert G. Riddle Papers.

114. John Kelly Damico, "Confederate Soldiers Take Matters into their Own Hands: The End of the Civil War in Louisiana," *Louisiana History* 39/2 (Spring 1998): 189–205, 196. See also Carl Coke Rister, "Carlota: A Confederate Colony in Mexico," *Journal of Southern History* 11/1 (February 1945): 33–50, 50: A number of former CSA generals wound up in Cuba.

115. Mary Cadwalader Jones, "Chapters from Unwritten Autobiographies. . . . Memories of Fort Sumter," 1865, University of South Carolina–Columbia.

116. Oskar Aichel to "My Dear Wife," 12 November 1863, Oskar Aichel Papers, University of South Carolina.

117. Joseph Howard Parks, *General Edmund Kirby Smith, CSA.* Baton Rouge: Louisiana State University Press, 1954, 483.

118. Eli N. Evans, *Judah P. Benjamin: The Jewish Confederate.* New York: Free Press, 1987, 41.

119. Carol Bleser, "The Marriage of Varina Howell and Jefferson Davis: 'I Gave My Best and All My Life to a Girdled Tree,'" *Journal of Southern History* 65/1 (February 1999): 3–40, 24.

120. William H. Parker, "Recollections," 2 May 1865, in Lynda Laswell Crist et al., eds., *The Papers of Jefferson Davis,* vol. 11: *September 1864–May 1865.* Baton Rouge: Louisiana State University Press, 580.

121. Account of Jefferson Davis in Cuba in ibid., vol. 12: *June 1865–December 1870.* See also James Elliott Walmsley, "The Last Meeting of the Confederate Cabinet," *Mississippi Valley Historical Review* 6/3 (December 1919): 336–49, 345.

122. Letter to Consul, ca. October 1866, Box 2, Records of Spanish Consulate–Savannah.

123. Daniel E. Sutherland, "Looking for a Home: Louisiana Emigrants During the Civil War and Reconstruction," *Louisiana History* 21/4 (Autumn 1980): 341–59, 355.

124. John C. Breckenridge, "A Rebel Leader in Flight to Cuba," *Civil War Times* 6/3 (June 1967): 4–10, 4. See also John W. Blassingame, ed., *The Frederick Douglass Papers, Series One: Speeches, Debates and Interviews,* vol. 3: *1855–1863.* New Haven: Yale University Press, 1985, 383.

125. Cortada, "Spain and the American Civil War," 92.

126. Diary entry, 6 October 1865, vol. 1, Trusten Polk Papers, University of North Carolina–Chapel Hill.

127. Eliza McHatton-Ripley, *From Flag to Flag: A Woman's Adventures and Experiences in the South During the War in Mexico and in Cuba.* New York: Appleton, 1896, 133, 140, 173, 180, 205, 206, 231, 232, 278, 293, 295.

128. Hattie to Mrs. A.H. Elliott, 23 January 1869, Box 5, Folder 94, Elliott and Gonzales Family Papers.

129. Letter from Havana, 14 April 1869, ibid.

130. "Daughter" to "Dearest Mama," 29 April 1869, ibid.

131. James C. Clark, *Last Train South: The Flight of the Confederate Government from Richmond,* Jefferson, NC: McFarland, 1984, 115.

132. 37th U.S. Congress, House of Representatives, 2nd Session, Report No. 148. Emancipation and Colonization, 16 July 1862, in Correspondence from Spanish Legation in Port-au-Prince, Ministry of Foreign Affairs–Madrid.

133. Henry Latham, *Black and White: A Journal of a Three Months' Tour in the United States.* London: Macmillan, 1867, 200, 209.

134. Consul to Lewis Cass, 10 November 1858, Roll 5, T55, *Despatches from U.S. Consuls in Santiago:* "Among the American citizens residing in this district there are only 6 merchants, two or three dentists and thirty engineers . . . mostly from Philadelphia. In the majority of merchant steamers and plantations American engineers are employed, while the Government prefers English engineers for the men-of-war. . . . All the sugar which is produced in this district with the exception of some clayed sugar, which is sent to Spain, is exported to the northern cities of the United States and the trade is [so] active that vessels coming from Halifax and Newfoundland are often obliged to load for New York or Philadelphia."

135. Mr. Hall to William Seward, 18 November 1868 in *Correspondence Relating to the Progress of the Revolution in Cuba. Transmitted to the Senate in Obedience to a Resolution.* Washington, D.C.: Government Printing Office, 1869, Massachusetts Historical Society. See also General Sickles to Mr. Fish, 29 December 1869, in *Correspondence of the Department of State in Relation to the Emancipation of*

Slaves in Cuba and Accompanying Papers Transmitted to the Senate in Obedience to a Resolution. Washington, D.C.: Government Printing Office, 1870, University of Texas–Austin: "I had furnished the Colonial Secretary with a memorandum of the history and results of emancipation in the United States."

136. Mr. Hall to Mr. Washburne, 11 March 1869 and Mr. Sickles to Mr. Fish, 25 September 1869 in *Correspondence Relating to the Progress of the Revolution in Cuba.* In the same volume, see also Mr. Plumb to Mr. Davis, 21 October 1869: In Havana, on the "question of slavery, I have found but one opinion here, that its abolition is now a question only of whether it shall be immediate or extend over a period of, say, five or more years. . . . The measure should be made gradual, freeing at once all born hereafter, and by a system of regulated labor, accomplishing total emancipation within a brief term of years. . . . One of the largest, if not the largest, slaveholder on the island, in conversation with me some time since, stated that he would be entirely willing to accept abolition effected in a term of five years. . . . [I] do not find any expression of belief in official quarters that a declaration of immediate total abolition would be practicable. . . . As a measure to be accomplished within a period of five or eight years, I do [not] think the question of the abolition of slavery on this island would present any serious difficulties, nor would it in this manner be attended, it is believed, with any great disturbance of the labor or the production of the island. . . . Instantaneous abolition . . . would . . . create great apprehension and disorganization, as also political dissatisfaction." See also Memorandum from U.S. on Abolition of Slavery in Cuba, 16 January 1873, Legajo Estado 8049, AHN-Madrid.

137. "Memorandum in Relation to the Abolition of Slavery in the United States," n.d., Legajo Estado 8049, AHN-Madrid.

138. Resolution from U.S. legation in Spain, 1873, Legajo Estado 8049, AHN.

139. Ibid., Secretary of State Fish to General Fish, 26 January 1870 in *Correspondence of the Department of State in Relation to the Emancipation of Slaves in Cuba.* In the same document see General Sickles to Mr. Fish, 26 June 1870: "Spain found herself in this dilemma—to refuse any measure of emancipation was to break the most solemn engagements to the United States, and perhaps incline that government more to the cause of the insurgents, while in committing herself to the abolition of slavery she associates herself with her enemies in Cuba and gave offense to her most trusted partisans. . . . General testimony of these exiles in favor of emancipation, considered with relation to their presumed sympathies with the insurgents and their known desire to see Cuba under the American flag, had great influence in narrowing the scheme of the government to the least possible proportions. . . . Formerly, when the insurrectionary party in Cuba were the allies of the pro-slavery party in the United States the most powerful weapon in the hands of Spain was the proclamation of emancipation that was said to be always ready in the portfolio of the Captain General. . . . It was then said that when Cuba ceased to be Spanish she would be African— never American—for it was supposed that the freedmen, in grateful recognition of this liberty at the hands of Spain, would resent the innumerable wrongs of their servitude upon Cubans. But all this changed after the war, when so large a portion of the Cuban population yielded to the inevitable force of the example of the United States, and accepted the abolition of slavery as the indispensable condition of their unchanged desire for annexation to the American Union. From the moment of Lee's surrender, the old Spanish treaty of emancipation lost its terrors; most of the discontented Cubans became abolitionists and Spain, governed by the most advanced statesmen who have ever held power in Madrid, has appeared to regard all that remains of her dominion in America to be inseparable from the institution of slavery." Also see *Apuntes Sobre La Cuestion de la Reforma Politica y de la Introduccion de Africanos en*

Las Islas de Cuba y Puerto Rico. Madrid: Establecimiento Tipografico de T. Fortanet, 1866.

140. Cortada, "Spain and the American Civil War," 91.

141. Remarks of the Duke de la Torre, 18 April 1866 in *British Parliamentary Papers*, 50:127–49.

142. Broadside, "To the Friends of Human Liberty," ca. 1866, AAS. Also see the similarly oriented "Speech of Hon. Thomas Swann of Maryland, Delivered in the House of Representatives, June 14, 1870," Washington: Rives & Bailey, 1870, AAS.

143. Stephen Macedo, ed., *Universal Jurisdiction: National Courts and the Prosecution of Serious Crimes Under International Law*. Philadelphia: University of Pennsylvania Press, 2004.

144. Gerrit Smith, "Spain . . . Cuba," 1 December 1873, AAS; and Gerrit Smith, "Rescue Cuba Now," 1873: "Strictly speaking, the world has not, as yet, international law. . . . But let me here say that I believe there will be and that too at no distant day a real international law." Also, "The Case of Cuba, with a Letter from John Sherwood, Esq. on the Right of Recognition." New York: American News Co., 1869, AAS: Since Madrid "systematically violated her slave-trade treaties," she deserved no protection from international norms. See Gerrit Smith, Speech, "Let Crushed Cuba Arise!," 4 July 1873, Huntington Library: "Cuba by force of geographical position and indissoluble commercial ties is a part of our country. Is it said that international law forbids helping the Cuban? If it does, then away with international law."

145. George Fitzhugh, "Cuba: The March of Empire and the Course of Trade," *De Bow's Review* 5/1 (1861): 30–42, 33.

146. Richard H. Bradford, *The Virginius Affair*. Boulder: Colorado Associated University Press, 1980, 162.

147. Speech of Mr. Joshua Giddings of Ohio in the House of Representatives, March 16, 1854, AAS.

148. Report, 11 January 1856, Correspondence of Spanish Consulate in Galveston, MAE.

149. Letter from Havana to "Dear Sir," 13 June 1868, Folder 3, Records of Churchill, Brown & Manson Company–G.W. Blunt Library, Mystic, Connecticut.

150. Letter from Matanzas to "Dear Sir," 31 December 1869, Folder 4, ibid.

151. Letter from Matanzas to "Dear Sir," 31 December 1869, Folder 4, ibid.

152. C.W. Tebeau, "Some Aspects of Planter-Freedmen Relations, 1865–1880," *Journal of Negro History* 21/2 (April 1936): 130–50, 136: "So complete is the monopoly of Cuba," said this planter in 1868, "that notwithstanding a tariff of three cents per pound, she is able to supply our markets and prevent the revival of the sugar interests of Louisiana. Abolish slavery in Cuba and you would change all this. You would instantly double, if not quadruple, the value of the sugar lands of Louisiana. You would give Louisiana instead of Cuba the monopoly of sugar raising."

153. "Memorandum of the Wrongs and Acts of Violence Which Since 1868 the Spanish Government in the Island of Cuba have Done to the Person, Family and Property of Inocencio Casanova, a Naturalized Citizen." New York: Macdonald and Palmer, 1871, AAS. See also Mrs. M. F. Squire, *Travels in Central America, Including Accounts of Some Regions Unexplored Since the Conquest*. New York: Leypoldt, Holt and Williams, 1871.

154. Ramon Cespedes to "Most Excellency Sir," 26 December 1873, Roll 1, T800, Notes from the Cuban Legation in the U.S. to the Department of State, 20 January 1844–30 December 1903, NARA–CP. See also Captain General to Spanish Consul in New York, 1868, Legajo 860, Numero de Orden 223, Gobierno Superior Civil, ANC: Investigation of plan to purchase arms by Narciso Herrera Davila.

155. Joseph Moore to J. B. Davis, 21 January 1874, Roll 9, *Despatches from U.S. Consuls in Trinidad, Cuba*.

156. William T. Sherman to Ulysses S. Grant, 1866, in Simon, *The Papers of Ulysses S. Grant*, 16:192.

157. Document from "La Junta Libertadora de Color" in Havana, 1 October 1869, in *Correspondence Relating to the Progress of the Revolution in Cuba*: "The Negroes are the same as the whites. . . . The Cubans wish that the Negroes should be free. The Spaniards wish that the Negroes should continue to be slaves. . . . The Negroes who have any shame should go and fight along with the Cubans. . . . They should burn the estates. . . . The time to fight has come. . . . Fire to the estates and everybody to the mountains to fight against the Spaniards."

158. Miss Holt, "A Teacher's Life, Including a Residence in the Southern States, California, Cuba and Peru," Quebec: James Carrel, 1875, New York Historical Society.

159. Translation of letter from "Insurgents" to "The Citizens of the U.S." 24 April 1869, Roll 6, T55, *Despatches from U.S. Consuls in Santiago*: After high praise for the United States, it was said, "we have been educated in the impious school of slavery & vitiated by the pernicious domestic system of Master and Serfs; Slaves ourselves under the Despotic and Tyrannic Government. . . . Hope to shake off the hated and slavish yoke of Spain & purified by the sacred fire of liberty be numbered as one more star in the American constellation." Letter was signed by Donato del Marmol, "Commanding General of the operations upon Cuba."

160. Francisco V. Aguilera and Ramon Cespedes, *Notes About Cuba*. New York, 4 January 1872, AAS. Also see "Deputation of Earl Granville, K.G. . . . Slavery in the Spanish Colonies," New York: Zarzamendi, 1872, AAS.

161. Leaflet "El Comite Cubano–Puerto Riqueno de Nueva York," November 1868, in Port-au-Prince Correspondence, MAE.

162. "The Cuban History, its History, Government, Resources, Object, Hopes and Prospects: Address of General Napoleon Arango to his Countrymen in Arms," 28 March 1870, Kansas Historical Society–Topeka.

163. New York Junta, *Facts About Cuba* New York: Sun Job Printing Office, 1870, *Kansas Historical Society*.

164. Consul to Hamilton Fish, 10 July 1869, Roll 6, T55, *Despatches from U.S. Consuls in Santiago de Cuba*.

165. Speech of Hon. Jacob A. Ambler of Ohio in the House of Representatives, June 14, 1870, AAS.

166. *Chicago Reader*, 13 January 1984, Box 5, Earl Dickerson Papers, Chicago Historical Society.

167. Cortada, *Two Nations Over Time*, 98. See also Christopher J. Bartlett, "British Reaction to the Cuban Insurrection of 1868–1878," *Hispanic American Historical Review* 37/3 (August 1957): 296–312.

168. Affidavit of Miguel de Aldama, 1 December 1869 in Correspondence Relating to the Progress of the Revolution in Cuba. See also Letters from Cardenas, 25 February 1868 and Havana, 26 March 1868, Box 1, Carlos de Garmendia Papers–Duke University.

169. Affidavit of William C. Tinker, 11 December 1869 in Correspondence Relating to the Progress of the Revolution in Cuba: In the revolutionary precincts in Cuba, slaves were freed. "Large numbers of them were in the army. . . . I talked with numbers of them."

170. L. Lewis to H.H. Harrison, 25 June 1869, Box 4, George Harrison Papers, Duke University.

171. W. L. Hamilton to "Dear Harrison," 19 June 1869, Box 4, ibid.

172. H. H. Kay to "Dear Sir," 22 June 1869, Box 4, ibid. See also Letters of Ann L. Gibbs from Cuba, 1868–1869, Massachusetts Historical Society.

173. Don C. Vosnea to H. H. Harrison, 29 June 1869, Box 4, George Harrison Papers, Duke University; see also C. A. Bragonier, Richmond to P.O. Box in New York, 4

August 1869: "In answer to an advertisement in the Dispatch of this city . . . I . . . have served in the U.S. (regular) army . . . in Texas, Mexico, Florida, Kansas, Dakota & Nebraska." In 1859 Bragonier returned to "my native state (Maryland) & in April 1860 commenced giving instructions in all military drills in Virginia & during the war in the CS Army." He was willing to move to Cuba—"if you can satisfy me that I would receive pay for my services."

174. Mr. Plumb to Mr. Davis, 21 October 1869, Correspondence Relating to the Progress of the Revolution in Cuba: Only "ninety or one hundred . . . foreigners . . . in the ranks of insurgents within the Eastern Department. . . . I doubt if the total number within the island exceeds one hundred and fifty." See also Clinton De Priest to George Coleman, 6 September 1869, Box 4, George Harrison Papers, Duke University: "Please see General Alferro for me. . . . There are here fifteen . . . men who were officers in the last war" who want to "serve as officers in the services of the junta."

175. William Lloyd Garrison to Editors, 25 November 1873, in Walter M. Merrill and Louis Ruchames, eds., *The Letters of William Lloyd Garrison*, vol. 6: *To Rouse the Slumbering Land, 1868–1879*. Cambridge: Harvard University Press, 1981, 283, 286.

176. Jerrell H. Shofner, *Nor Is It Over Yet: Florida in the Era of Reconstruction, 1863–1877*. Gainesville: University Press of Florida, 1974, 268.

177. Jeanie Mort Walker, *Life of Captain Joseph Fry, the Cuban Martyr*. Hartford: Burr, 1875, 214.

178. Clipping, 29 November 1871, Box 221, Blair and Lee Family Papers, Princeton University.

179. Richard H. Bradford, *The Virginius Affair*. Boulder: Colorado Associated University Press, 1980, 66.

180. Walker, *Life of Captain Joseph Fry*, 276. See also Richard Smith Spofford, "The Shame of the Virginius," n.d., Brown University: "Atrocious butchery of Captain Fry and thirty-six of the crew and passengers" by Spaniards.

181. Report from Legation in Washington, D.C., 7 November 1866, Box 9, Records of Spanish Legation–Charleston.

182. Royal Order, April 1866, Legajo 54, Numero de Orden 25, Asuntos Politicos, ANC.

183. A. E. Phillips to Hamilton Fish, 11 June 1869, Roll 6, T55, *Despatches from U.S. Consuls in Santiago de Cuba*.

184. A. E. Phillips to Hamilton Fish, 15 July 1869, Roll 6, T55, ibid.

185. A. E. Phillips to Hamilton Fish, 6 October 1869, Roll 6, T55, ibid.

186. A. G. C., Jr., *To Cuba and Back in Twenty Two Days*. Philadelphia: Tims Printing Office, 28–29, 36, 40–41.

187. See Horne, *Negro Comrades of the Crown*, passim.

188. Memorandum, ca. 1869, Roll 8, *Despatches from U.S. Consuls in Trinidad, Cuba*.

189. El Conde de Valmaseda to Captain General, 21 January 1870, Roll 7, *Despatches from U.S. Consuls in Santiago de Cuba*.

190. Caitlin A. Fitz, "Our Sister Republics," 247.

191. Report, 9 August 1866, Correspondence from Spanish Consulate in New Orleans, MAE.

192. Report, 1863, Legajo 1293, Numero de Orden 50402, Gobierno Superior Civil, ANC.

193. Report, 5 September 1874, MAE.

194. Report, 1863, Legajo 1293, Numero de Orden 50393, Gobierno Superior Civil, ANC.

195. Report, 29 December 1865, Legajo 227, Numero de Orden 19, Asuntos Politicos, ANC.

196. Report, 28 December 1865, Legajo 227, Numero de Orden 18, Asuntos Politicos, ANC.

197. Coded Dispatches from the Spanish legation, 29 October 1866, Legajo 227, Numero de Orden 23, Asuntos Politicos, ANC.
198. Newspaper clipping, ca. 1872, Legajo Estado 8049, AHN-Madrid.
199. George H. Gibson, "Attitudes in North Carolina Regarding the Independence of Cuba, 1868–1898," *North Carolina Historical Review* 43/1 (January 1966): 43–65, 45.
200. "Speech of Hon. Benjamin F. Butler of Massachusetts, Delivered in the House of Representatives, June 15, 1870," AAS.
201. *Evening Mail*, 23 March 1869, in Port-au-Prince Correspondence.
202. Anon., *Rambles in Cuba*. New York: Carleton, 1870, 25–26.

6. TOWARD DE FACTO ANNEXATION OF CUBA

1. For a glimpse of the tensions embedded in these events, see Jose C. Novas, *Twice the Diplomat: Frederick Douglass's Assignments to the Island of Santo Domingo*. New York: Vantage, 2001.
2. Keith Pomakoy, *Helping Humanity: American Policy & Genocide Rescue*. Lanham, MD: Lexington, 2011, 15.
3. Letter from Havana, 14 May 1875, Reel 2, Moses Taylor Papers. See also Lieutenant Jose Muller y Tejeiro, "Battles and Capitulation of Santiago de Cuba," Office of Naval Intelligence, Washington, D.C.: Government Printing Office, *Western Reserve Historical Society*.
4. Gerrit Smith to President Grant, in John Y. Simon, ed., *The Papers of Ulysses S. Grant*, vol. 24: *1873*. Carbondale: Southern Illinois University Press, 2000, 436.
5. Report, 21 March 1843, Correspondence from Spanish Legation in Port-au-Prince, MAE: President Boyer of Haiti and his family flee. In the same file, see *Jamaica Dispatch, Chronicle and Gazette*, 25 March 1843, for more on Boyer and Letters on this same general matter, ca. 1844.
6. [Kingston] *Morning Journal*, 20 April 1843, Port-au-Prince Correspondence.
7. Report, 11 April 1844, in ibid.
8. Report, 1 November 1855. in ibid.
9. See *Frederick Douglass's Paper*, 6 April 1855: A report from Savannah avers that "6,000 or 8,000 men have organized at St. Domingo for a descent and attack upon [Cuba]." For more on filibustering from Hispaniola to Cuba, see *Diario de la Marina* [Havana], 23 April 1859 and 24 April 1859; and *Caceta de la Habana*, 10 April 1859.
10. Report, 25 April 1859, in Port-au-Prince Correspondence.
11. Report, 6 June 1855, in ibid.
12. Report, 12 May 1855, in ibid.
13. Report, 25 May 1855, in ibid. See also the Report of 8 May 1855.
14. Report, 21 February 1860, in ibid.
15. Report, 26 March 1861, Legajo 224, Numero de Orden 25, Asuntos Politicos, ANC.
16. See Memorandum, 14 January 1853, in Port-au-Prince Correspondence: Haitian leaders here—typically—are described as ignorant, barbarian, and brutal. Haiti was warned that Spanish warships in Cuban harbors would be turned against them if they sought to reverse the events in eastern Hispaniola. In the same file see also Spanish Minister to Prime Minister–Madrid, 10 October 1859 and 26 November 1859: More reveling in the problems of Haiti. Republicans knew this—and encouraged this trend: See Pilar to Duke of Valencia, 20 December 1850, Folder 19, Daniel Barringer Papers, University of North Carolina–Chapel Hill: Eastern Hispaniola "became estranged" from Spain "by the Negro Revolution" which delivered "misery & wretechedness" and this region could "not longer endure the degradation" of Haiti. Thus, sadly, "Spanish

blood" in Hispaniola had been "scented by the Negro hordes & large armaments are preparing to renew the invasion" which would mean the "sacrifice" of the "white population of the Dominicans" and "all will be sacrificed to the Negro fury." This will "arouse a spirit for other conquests, their colour will emigrate from other nations and the mountains of Cuba, which rise above the western horizon & are visible from St. Domingo will tempt them to invade and if possible destroy the prosperity of Cuba." If Madrid did not stop the Haitians, then "Cuba will be lost to the Spanish Crown."

17.   See Documents Relative to the Question of Santo Domingo Sent to the Congress of Deputes by the Overseas Ministry, ca. 1861; and Diary of the Cortes, Congress of Deputies; Documents Relative to the Reincorporation of Santo Domingo in the Spanish Monarchy, ca. 1861, in Port-au-Prince Correspondence.

18.   Jane Cazneau to Moses Beach, 24 April 1862, Jane McManus Storm Canzeau Papers, University of Texas–Austin.

19.   Ibid., 7 June 1862.

20.   Ibid., 25 August 1865.

21.   37th U.S. Congress, House of Representatives, 2nd Session, 16 July 1862, in Port-au-Prince Correspondence.

22.   Report, 24 October 1862, in ibid.

23.   Report, 9 July 1862, in ibid.

24.   Report, 8 June 1962, in ibid.

25.   Report, 12 January 1864, in ibid.

26.   Report, 8 April 1863 in ibid. Also in this file see 1864 treaty between U.S. and Haiti; *Le Moniteur Haitien*, 26 November 1864.

27.   Reports, September 1862 and 8 July 1862, in ibid.

28.   Report, 8 July 1862 in ibid.

29.   Report, 24 October 1862, in ibid.

30.   Report, 30 October 1865, in ibid.

31.   *Frederick Douglass' Monthly*, October 1862.

32.   Robert Bunch to Earl Russell, 30 September 1865, FO84/1236, NAUK.

33.   Robert Bunch to Earl Russell, 1 June 1865, in *British Parliamentary Papers*, 129.

34.   Report, 1863, Legajo 226, Numero de Orden 10, Asuntos Politicos, ANC; and Reports from Legation in Washington, D.C., 1864, Legajo 227, Numero de Orden 13, Asuntos Politicos, concerning unrest in Santo Domingo.

35.   Willis D. Boyd, "James Redpath and American Negro Colonization in Haiti, 1860–1862," *The Americas* 12/2 (October 1955): 169–82, 178.

36.   Gerald E. Poyo, "Cuban Revolutionaries and Monroe County Reconstruction Politics, 1868–1876," *Florida Historical Quarterly* 55/4 (April 1977): 407–22, 409. See also Gustavo J. Godoy, "José Alejandro Huau: A Cuban Patriot in Jacksonville Politics," *Florida Historical Quarterly* 54/2 (October 1975): 196–206.

37.   Henry Highland Garnet, Secretary, and S. R. Scottron, Chair, "Slavery in Cuba. A Report of the Proceedings of the Meeting Held at Cooper Institute, New York City, December 13, 1872. Newspaper Extracts, Official Correspondence, etc., by the Cuban Anti-Slavery Committee, 62 Bowery," Huntington Library.

38.   Report, 13 December 1872, Legajo Estado 8049, AHN.

39.   *New York Herald*, 15 December 1872; *New York Evening Mail*, 13 December 1872; *New York Sun*, 10 December 1872.

40.   Diary entry, 19 February 1873, in John Y. Simon, ed., *The Papers of Ulysses S. Grant*, vol. 24: *1873*. Carbondale: Southern Illinois University Press, 2000, 209–10. See also *St. Louis Democrat*, 20 February 1873.

41.   John White to President Grant, 17 November 1873, in Simon, *The Papers of Ulysses S. Grant*, 24:247. See also Americus, *Spain, Cuba and the United States: Recognition*

and the Monroe Doctrine. New York: Alvord, 1870. Letter from John D. Sherwood, Esq., on the Right of Recognition. New York: American News Co., 1869, Kansas Historical Society–Topeka.

42. Henry Turner, Louis Toomer, and John Deveaux to President Grant, 25 November 1873, in Simon, *The Papers of Ulysses S. Grant*, 24:248.

43. Edward A. Johnson, *History of Negro Soldiers in the Spanish-American War and Other Items of Interest*. Raleigh: Capital, 1899, 22, 25–26.

44. Annual Message to Congress, 4 December 1871, in Simon, *The Papers of Ulysses S. Grant*, vol. 22: *June 1, 1871–January 31, 1872*, 272.

45. Speech by Hon. Clinton L. Cobb of North Carolina in the House of Representatives, February 5, 1870, University of North Carolina–Chapel Hill.

46. Message to Congress, 5 December 1876, in Simon, *The Papers of Ulysses S. Grant*, vol. 28: *1876–September 30, 1878*, 68.

47. Annual Message to Senate and House, December 1875, in ibid., vol. 26, 391.

48. George W. Sayler to President Grant, 13 December 1875, in ibid., 26:422.

49. Henry Sanford to President Grant, 18 February 1876, in ibid., 24:374–75.

50. Report by Marshal Serrano, Duke de la Torre, Present Regent of Spain, on the Interrogatories Submitted to Him by the Spanish Government in the Matter of Reform in the Regime of the Antilles. . . . In Reference to the Royal Decree of 25th of November 1865, *Boston Public Library*.

51. James Thomson to President U.S. Grant, 31 January 1876 in Simon, *The Papers of Ulysses S. Grant*, 26: 423.

52. Amos Briggs to President Grant, 14 November 1872 in ibid., 26:301.

53. Henry Highland Garnet, in ibid. "Slavery in Cuba."

54. *The Cuban Question in England. Extracts from Opinions of the Press*. London: Head, Hole, n.d., Kansas Historical Society.

55. J. De Armas y Cespedes, "Position of the United States on the Cuban Question," n.d., Box 308, Moses Taylor Papers. In the same collection, see also *La Revolucion de Cuba: Vista Desde Nueva York*, New York, 1869.

56. Jose de Armas y Cespedes, "The Cuban Revolution: Notes from the Diary of a Cuban," New York, 1869, Box 308, Moses Taylor Papers. In the same collection see also *La Cuestion de Cuba*. Valparaiso: Imprenta del Mercurio, 1974.

57. Fernando Calderon y Collantes to Mr. Fish, 3 February 1876 and response in 54th U.S. Congress, Senate, Document No. 213, Message from the President of the United States, 1896, Brown University.

58. London *Morning Post*, 24 January 1876.

59. Caleb Cushing to Hamilton Fish, 16 January 1876 in 55th U.S. Congress, Senate, 2nd Session, Report No. 885, "Report of the Committee on Foreign Relations . . . Relative to Affairs in Cuba." Washington, D.C.: 1898, Kansas Historical Society.

60. Fernando Calderon y Collantes to Mr. Cushing, 16 April 1878, in ibid.

61. F. L. Norton, "Cuba," 1873, Kansas Historical Society–Topeka. This document can also be found at Johns Hopkins University.

62. W. M. L. Jay, *My Winter in Cuba*. New York: Dutton, 1871, 231.

63. J. B. Russell to "Dear Josie," 17 February 1878, Gilpin Family Collection, Delaware Historical Society–Wilmington.

64. "An American," "The Cuban Question in Its True Light," n.d., Kansas Historical Society.

65. Alrutheus A. Taylor, "Negro Congressmen a Generation After," *Journal of Negro History* 7/2 (April 1922): 127–71, 165.

66. Peter D. Klingman, *Josiah Walls: Florida's Black Congressman of Reconstruction*. Gainesville: University Press of Florida, 1976, 84.

67. Clipping, 25 March 1873, Box 307, Moses Taylor Papers, New York Public Library.

68. London clipping, 20 February 1873, Box 307, ibid.

69. London clipping, 18 April 1873, Box 307, ibid.

70. London clipping, 18 April 1873, Box 307, ibid. Also see contracts between Taylor and assorted Cubans, 19 January 1875 and 10 January 1873.

71. Philip S. Foner and J. Syme-Hastings, "A Tribute to Antonio Maceo," *Journal of Negro History* 55/1 (January 1970): 65–71, 65. For the U.S. Negro tradition of adopting the name "Maceo," see Philip S. Foner, *Antonio Maceo: The 'Bronze Titan' of Cuba's Struggle for Independence*. New York: Monthly Review Press, 1977, 313.

72. Perry E. Gianakos, "The Spanish-American War and the Double Paradox of the Negro American," *Phylon* 26/1 (1965): 34–49, 40.

73. John Ingalls, *America's War for Humanity Related in Story and Picture Embracing a Complete History of Cuba's Struggle for Liberty and the Glorious Heroism of America's Soldiers and Sailors*. New York: Thompson, 1898, 100, 103. See also Johnson, *History of Negro Soldiers in the Spanish-American War and Other Items of Interest*, 123, 127: "If General Weyler evinced any partiality in Cuba it was for the black Creole. During the Ten Years' War his cavalry escort was composed entirely of colored men. . . . He kept black soldiers constantly on guard at the gates of the government palace. . . . Martínez Campos who owed his final defeat at Coliseo to Maceo was a second cousin of this black man."

74. Nathan C. Green, *Story of Spain and Cuba*. Baltimore: International News, 1896, 151, 153, 154, 181, University of South Carolina.

75. See Aline Helg, "Black Men, Racial Stereotyping and Violence in the U.S. South and Cuba at the Turn of the Century," *Comparative Studies in Society and History* 42/3 (July 2000): 576–604.

76. Ambrosio Gonzales to U.S. Grant, 8 January 1876 in Simon, *The Papers of Ulysses S. Grant*, 26:423.

77. Report, 11 February 1878, Roll 8, *Despatches from U.S. Consuls in Santiago de Cuba*.

78. *New Orleans Democrat*, 1 April 1878, Correspondence of Spanish Consulate in New Orleans, MAE.

79. Francis Darr to Carlos del Castillo, 2 June 1873, Reel 1, Moses Taylor Papers.

80. Samuel R. Scottron, President, Cuban Anti-Slavery Society, to "Dear Sir," 21 July 1873, Reel 1, Moses Taylor Papers.

81. Linda McCarter Matthews, "N.G. Gonzales, Southern Editor and Crusader, 1858–1903," Ph.D. diss., Duke University, 1971.

82. George Gage to "Sir," 22 September 1874, Box 12, Records of Spanish Consulate in Charleston.

83. William Stone to John Rawlings, 16 October 1874, in ibid., Box 12.

84. List of Vessels Cleared, 1876, in ibid., Box 13.

85. C. W. Weber et al., to Consul General, 22 December 1876, in ibid., Box 13.

86. Invitation to Luis Bermudez, 16 February 1878, in ibid., Box 13.

87. Report, 15 November 1880, Correspondence from Spanish Consulate in New Orleans.

88. Report, 8 August 1876, Correspondence from Spanish Consulate in New Orleans.

89. Miguel Suarez to Edward Pilsbury, 21 September 1877, Correspondence from Spanish Consulate in New Orleans.

90. Report, 10 January 1877, Correspondence from Spanish Consulate in New Orleans.

91. Letter from J. H. Bailey et al., n.d., ca. 1880, Correspondence from Spanish Consulate in New Orleans, MAE.

92. Sidney Kaplan, "The Miscegenation Issue in the Election of 1864," *Journal of Negro History* 34/3 (July 1949): 274–343, 342.

93. C. L. Marquette, "Letters of a Yankee Sugar Planter," *Journal of Southern History* 6/4 (November 1940): 521–46, 543.

94. U.S. Consul to Assistant Secretary of State, 27 October 1879, Roll 1, T548, *Despatches from U.S. Consuls in Cienfuegos, 1876–1906*, NARA–CP.

95. Report, 12 February 1882, Roll 1, T548, ibid.

96. John Dean Caton, *Miscellanies*. Boston: Houghton, Osgood and Co., 1880, 287, 289.

97. John Wheaton, Collector–Customs House, to Consul, 7 June 1887, Box 4, Records of Spanish Consulate in Savannah.

98. Report, 10 August 1883, Roll 2, T548, *Despatches from U.S. Consuls in Cienfuegos, 1876–1906*, NARA–CP.

99. Maturin M. Ballou, *Due South or Cuba Past and Present*. Boston: Houghton Mifflin, 1888, 47.

100. Rosalie Schwartz, "The Displaced and the Disappointed: Cultural Nationalists and Black Activists in Cuba in the 1920s," Ph.D. diss., University of California, San Diego, 1977, 22.

101. Proclamation by President Arthur, 14 February 1884, Box 16, *Records* of Spanish Consulate in Charleston.

102. List of Spanish Vessels from and to Wilmington, 12 January 1884, Box 16, ibid. See also Consul in St. Mary's, Georgia, to Consul–Savannah, 3 July 1883, Box 2, Records of Spanish Consulate in Savannah: "no report to make relative to vessels clearing for ports in Spain and Colonies."

103. Kathleen Lopez and Rebekah E. Pite, "Letters from Soledad in the Atkins Family Papers at the Massachusetts Historical Society," *Massachusetts Historical Review* 9 (2007): 35–54, 37, 39, 40.

104. G. Wayne King, "Conservative Attitudes in the United States Toward Cuba (1895–1898)," B.A. thesis, University of South Carolina, 1965, 8, 13.

105. Consul to T. F. Bayard, 16 January 1886, Roll 9, T55, *Despatches from U.S. Consuls in Santiago*.

106. Consul to James Porter, 30 April 1887, Roll 10, T55, ibid.

107. *Keys News*, 2 May 2002; and *Miami Herald*, 22 February 2002, in "Biography File," Monroe County Public Library–Key West.

108. Mauricio Delgado to "My Dear Sir," 21 May 1889, in ibid.

109. Clipping, 20 February 2002, in ibid.

110. Note, 1880, in ibid.; Simon, *The Papers of Ulysses S. Grant*, 29:251.

111. *New York Age*, 3 November 1888.

112. *New York Age*, 1 December 1888.

113. Consuelo Stebbins, Vertical File, Monroe County Public Library.

114. Gerald E. Poyo, *'With All and For the Good of All': The Emergence of Popular Nationalism in the Cuban Communities of the United States, 1848–1898*. Durham, NC: Duke University Press, 1989, 84.

115. Sharon Wells, *Forgotten Legacy: Blacks in Nineteenth Century Key West*. Key West: Historic Key West Preservation Board, 1982, 35.

116. Paul Ortiz, "Afterword," in Irvin D. S. Winnsboro, ed., *Old South, New South or Down South? Florida and the Modern Civil Rights Movement*. Morgantown: West Virginia University Press, 2009, 220–44, 224.

117. Marvin Dunn, "The Illusion of Moderation: A Recounting and Reassessing of Florida's Racial Past," in ibid., 22–46, 25.

118. Report, 30 August 1884, Correspondence of Spanish Consulate in New Orleans.

119. Leaflet, n.d., and clipping, 29 May 1994, Hampton Dunn Papers, University of South Florida.

120. Oral History, Sister Earline Fish, 1978, University of South Florida–Tampa.

121. *Tampa Tribune*, 15 May 1987, Hampton Dunn Papers, University of South Florida.

122. *Detroit Free Press*, 16 May 1891.

123. Elliott Duran, *A Week in Cuba*. Chicago: Belford-Clarke, 1891, 55, 56.

124. James W. Steele, *Cuban Sketches*. New York: Putnam, 1881 87, 89, 90: "In Cuba [the Negro] speaks Spanish with the same elimination of harsh sounds," akin to the U.S. Negro's "modified English pronunciation." See also C. A. Stephens, *The Knockabout Club in the Tropics: The Adventures of a Party of Young Men in New Mexico, Mexico and Central America*. Boston: Estes and Lauriat, 1883.

125. Murat Halstead, *The Story of Cuba: Her Struggles for Liberty*. Chicago: Werner, 1896, 51.

126. Rayford Logan, *The Betrayal of the Negro, From Rutherford B. Hayes to Woodrow Wilson*. New York: Da Capo, 1997.

127. Consul to William Wharton, 3 May 1890, Roll 11, T55, *Despatches from U.S. Consuls in Santiago*.

128. *New York Herald*, 23 April 1890.

129. Governor to U.S. Consul, 2 May 1890, Roll 11, T55, *Despatches from U.S. Consuls in Santiago*.

130. Spanish Consul, New York, to Consul–Charleston, 24 November 1890, Box 18, Records of Spanish Consulate in Charleston.

131. Fidel G. Pierra, "Spanish Misrule in America," published by "Cuban Delegation in the United States," ca. 1890, Kansas Historical Society.

132. The National League–Boston, "The Wrongs of the Negro: The Remedy," n.d., Kansas Historical Society.

133. See Nell Blythe Waldron, "Colonization in Kansas from 1861 to 1890," Ph.D. diss., Northwestern University, 1923.

134. Ibid., Linda McCarter Matthews, "N.G. Gonzales," 154, 182, 184, 185, 186, 187.

135. U.S. Congress. Senate. 54th Congress, 2nd Session, Calendar No. 1287, Report No. 1160, "Recognition of Cuban Independence," 21 December 1896, Kansas Historical Society.

136. Pulaski Hyatt to Josiah Quincy, 5 December 1893, Roll 13, T55, *Despatches from U.S. Consuls in Santiago*.

137. Pulaski Hyatt to Edwin Uhl, 1 March 1895, Roll 13, T55, ibid. For a duplicate of this letter, see 54th U.S. Congress, House of Representatives, 1st Session, Document No. 224, "Affairs in Cuba. Message from the President of the United States Relating to Affairs in Cuba Since February 1895 in Response to House Resolution of December 28, 1895, 111–12, Kansas Historical Society.

138. Pulaski Hyatt to Assistant Secretary of State, 31 August 1895, Roll 14, T55.

139. U.S. Consulate–Havana to "My Cousin Jean," 29 July 1896, Jean Yeatman Papers, Duke University.

140. George Bronson Rea, *Facts and Fakes About Cuba: A Review of the Various Stories Circulated in the United States Concerning the Present Insurrection*. New York: Munro's Sons, 1897, xiii, 52, 240. See also *New York Herald*, 18 January 1896; *New York World*, 5 May 1896.

141. Pulaski Hyatt to Assistant Secretary of State, 19 December 1895, Roll 14, T55, *Despatches from U.S. Consuls in Santiago*.

142. Pulaski Hyatt to Assistant Secretary of State, 28 December 1895, Roll 14, T55, ibid.

143. Ibid., Murat Halstead, *The Story of Cuba*, 26, 81, 82, 88, 94, 379, 391–92.

144. 54th U.S. Congress, Senate. 2nd Session, Calendar No. 1287, Report No. 1160, "Recognition of Cuban Independence," 21 December 1896, Kansas Historical Society.

145. Consul to William Wharton, Assistant Secretary of State, 20 August 1890, Roll 4, T583, *Despatches from U.S. Consuls in Cardenas*, NARA–CP.

146. Report, 1896, Roll 5, T583, ibid.
147. Pedro Mora Ledon to "Military Commander" [translation by U.S. Consul], December 1895, Roll 4, T678, *Despatches from U.S. Consuls in Sagua La Grande*, NARA–CP.
148. Pedro Mora Ledon to Walter Barker, 18 December 1895, Roll 4, T678, ibid.
149. Walter Barker to Assistant Secretary of State, 1 February 1896, Roll 4, T678, ibid.
150. Letter to Walter Barker, 19 July 1896, Roll 4, T678, ibid.
151. Consul to Don Ferederico Urda, 21 May 1897, Roll 15, T55, ibid.
152. See Rebecca J. Scott, "A Cuban Connection: Edwin F. Atkins, Charles Francis Adams, Jr. and the Former Slaves of Soledad Plantation," *Massachusetts Historical Review* 9 (2007): 7–34.
153. See José Martí, *Norteamericanos: Apostoles, Poetas, Banditos*. Havana: Centro de Estudios Martíanos, 2009; José Martí, *Jose Martí Reader: Writings on the Americas*. Melbourne: Ocean, 2007; José Martí, *José Martí: Selected Writings*. New York: Penguin, 2002.
154. Ivan Cesar Martínez, *The Open Wound: The Scourge of Racism in Cuba from Colonialism to Communism*, Kingston: Arawak, 1007, 94, 95.
155. John Hyatt, Acting Consul to William Rockhill, Assistant Secretary of State, 8 July 1896, Roll 15, T55.

7. WAR! AND JIM CROW ENFORCED IN CUBA

1. Corporal W. T. Goode, *The Eighth Illinois*. Chicago: Blakely, 1899, 155–56, 165, 192, 225, 234, 239. See also Willard B. Gatewood, Jr., ed., *"Smoked Yankees" and the Struggle for Empire: Letters from Negro Soldiers, 1898–1902*. Urbana: University of Illinois Press, 1971, 205. According to Frank Burns of this regiment: "There is much marrying among American soldiers and Cuban women." See also *Baltimore Afro-American*, 2 September 1899: "A number of colored girls will go to Cuba as trained nurses from the hospital in Chicago"—though it is unclear if a complement of this group also chose to marry islanders.
2. Jack McCallum, *Leonard Wood: Rough Rider, Surgeon, Architect of American Imperialism*. New York: New York University Press, 2005, 124. See also *New York Times*, 26 November 1898.
3. *Miami Herald*, 27 July 1992.
4. Grover Flint, *Marching with Gomez: A War Correspondent's Field Note-Book Kept During Four Months with the Cuban Army*. Boston: Lamson, Wolffe, 1898, 52, 226. See also John Black Atkins, *The War in Cuba: The Experiences of an Englishman with the United States Army*, London: Smith, Elder, 1899; and Horace Edgar Flack, *Spanish-American Diplomatic Relations Preceding the War of 1898*. Baltimore: Johns Hopkins University Press, 1906.
5. *The Parsons Weekly*, 15 October 1898. See also H. Allen Tupper, Jr., *Columbia's War for Cuba*. New York: Success, 1898.
6. Philip S. Foner and J. Syme-Hastings, "A Tribute to Antonio Maceo," *Journal of Negro History* 55/1 (January 1970): 65–71, 65.
7. Remarks of J. H. Peck, ca. 1890s, File, Cuban Revolution, 1895–1898, Tony Pizzo Papers, University of South Florida.
8. See Archivo General, *Inventario General del Archivo de la Delegacion del Partido Revolucionario Cubano en Nueva York (1892–1898)*, vol. 1. Havana: Sociedad Editorial Contemporanea, 1918, New York Historical Society. See also Raimundo Cabrera, *Cuba and the Cubans* Philadelphia: Levytype, 1896.
9. This analysis derives from Jesse Hoffnung-Garskoff, "The World of Arturo Alfonso

Schomburg," in Miriam Jimenez Roman and Juan Flores, eds., *The Afro-Latino Reader: History and Culture in the United States*. Durham, NC: Duke University Press, 2010, 70–91, 75. See also Robert C. Nathan, "Imagining Antonio Maceo: Memory, Mythology and Nation in Cuba, 1896–1959," Ph.D. diss., University of North Carolina–Chapel Hill, 2007.

10.   Elinor de Verney Sinnette, *Arturo Alfonso Schomburg: Black Bibliophile & Collector*. Detroit: Wayne State University, 1980, 26.

11.   Michele Reid-Vazquez, *The Year of the Lash: Free People of Color in Cuba and the Nineteenth Century Atlantic World*. Athens: University of Georgia Press, 2011, 90, 94. See also Tony Casado, *Antonio: An Autobiography*. Newton, KS: Mennonite Press, 1987.

12.   Jesse Hoffnung-Garskof, "The Migrations of Arturo Schomburg: On Being Antillano, Negro and Puerto Rican in New York, 1891–1938," *Journal of American Ethnic History* 21/1 (Fall 2001): 3–49, 7, 9, 10, 20, 22, 23, 24.

13.   Franc R. E. Woodward, *"El Diablo Americano": Strange Adventures of a War Correspondent*. New York: Burslem, 1895, 67, 68, 92, 93, 110, 131.

14.   Philip S. Foner and J. Syme-Hastings, "A Tribute to Antonio Maceo," *Journal of Negro History*, 55 (Number 1, January 1970): 65–71, 65. See also *Colored American Magazine*, November 1900.

15.   Johnson, *History of Negro Soldiers in the Spanish-American War and Other Items of Interest*, 13. See also Louis S. Diggs, *Forgotten Road Warriors: The History of an All African American Maryland National Guard Unit from Baltimore, Maryland that was Activated During the Spanish-American War*, 2005, Maryland Historical Society.

16.   Trumbull White, *United States in War with Spain and the History of Cuba*. Chicago: International, 1898, 254.

17.   Philip S. Foner, *The Spanish-Cuban-American War and the Birth of American Imperialism*, vol. 1: *1895–1898*. New York: Monthly Review Press, 1972, 5–6. See also José Martí, "Our America" in *Obras Completas*, vol. 2. Havana: Editorial Nacional de Cuba, 1963, 113, 99; and Fernando Ortiz y Fernandez, "Cuba, Martí and the Race Problem," *Phylon* 3/3 (1942): 253–76.

18.   Arturo Schomburg, "General Antonio Maceo," *The Crisis* 40/5 (May 1931): 155–56, 174, 176.

19.   William Seraile, ed., *Bruce Grit: The Black Nationalist Writings of John Edward Bruce*. Knoxville: University of Tennessee Press, 2003, 160. See also Richard Harding Davis, *Cuba in War Time*. New York: Russell, 1897.

20.   Webster Merritt, *A Century of Medicine in Jacksonville and Duval County*. Gainesville: University Press of Florida, 1949, 154.

21.   Canter Brown, Jr., and Larry Eugene Rivers, *For a Great and Grand Purpose: The Beginnings of the AMEZ Church in Florida, 1864–1905*. Gainesville: University Press of Florida, 2004, 47, 109, 113, 155.

22.   Charles E. Wynes, "John Stephens Durham, Black Philadelphian: At Home and Abroad," *Pennsylvania Magazine of History and Biography* 106/4 (October 1982): 527–37, 535.

23.   Paul S. George, "Colored Town: Miami's Black Community, 1896–1930," *Florida Historical Quarterly* 56/4 (April 1978): 432–47, 438.

24.   Corporal W. T. Goode, *The Eighth Illinois, Chicago*, 124, 145. See also "Statement on the Situation in Cuba. By the Home Mission Board of the Southern Baptist Convention," Atlanta, 1903, University of North Carolina–Chapel Hill.

25.   *Chicago Defender*, 4 July 1914. See also Father William Montgomery, "Mission to Cuba: The Oblate Sisters of Providence in Latin America, 1800–1970," Ph.D. diss., Catholic University of America, 1997.

26. Norma Jean Sawyer, *Key West*. Charleston: Arcadia, 2002, 4. See also Benjamin D. Brotelmarkle, *Crossing Division Street: An Oral History of the African–American Community in Orlando*. Cocoa, Florida: Florida Historical Society Press, 2005; David R. Colburn, *Racial Change and Community Crisis: St. Augustine, Florida, 1877–1980*. New York: Columbia University Press, 1985.

27. *The Crisis*, 36 (Number 7, July 1929): 230–231.

28. "Captain Floyd and Cuba Libre," *The Crisis* 36/7 (July 1929): 230–31, 247.

29. Edwin S. Redkey, *Black Exodus: Black Nationalist and Back-to-Africa Movements, 1890–1910*. New Haven: Yale University Press, 2003: 203.

30. Nancy Raquel Mirabal, "De Aqui, De Alla: Race, Empire and Nation in the Making of Cuban Migrant Communities in New York and Tampa, 1823–1924," Ph.D. diss., University of Michigan–Ann Arbor, 2001, 168. See also Enrique Collazo, *Los Americanos en Cuba*. Havana: Instituto Cubano del Libro, 1972.

31. Roger D. Cunningham, *The Black-Citizen Soldiers of Kansas, 1864–1901*. Columbia: University of Missouri Press, 2008, 176, 185–86. See also *Pittsburgh Courier*, 2 April 1927: Andy Razaf, famed composer of such songs as "Ain't Misbehavin'" —and often defined as a U.S. Negro—spent time on the island as a child "when his Grandfather Waller led a regiment of Kansas soldiers." See also *New York Times*, 2 July 1899.

32. Willard B. Gatewood, "Kansas Negroes and the Spanish-American War," *Kansas Historical Quarterly* 37/3 (Autumn 1971): 300–313, 307, 311.

33. *Baltimore Afro-American*, 2 July 1898.

34. William Seraile, ed., *Bruce Grit: The Black Nationalist Writings of John Edward Bruce*. Knoxville: University of Tennessee Press, 2003, 50.

35. Hal S. Chase, "Shelling the Citadel of Race Prejudice: William Calvin Chase and the Washington 'Bee,' 1882–1921," *Records of the Columbia Historical Society* 49 (1974): 371–91, 385.

36. Foner, *The Spanish-Cuban-American War and the Birth of American Imperialism*, 417.

37. Harris Moore Bailey, Jr., "The Splendid Little Forgotten War: The Mobilization of South Carolina for the War with Spain," *South Carolina Historical Magazine* 92/3 (July 1992): 189–214, 198.

38. Willard B. Gatewood, "Black Americans and the Quest for Empire, 1898–1903," *Journal of Southern History* 38/4 (November 1972): 545–66, 547, 549.

39. W. H. Crogman et al., *Progress of a Race or the Remarkable Advancement of the Afro-American Negro*. Atlanta: Nichols, 1898. See also Louis R. Harlan, "Booker T. Washington in Biographical Perspective," *American Historical Review* 75/6 (October 1970): 1581–99, 1591. In his graduation exercise of 1875, Washington opposed annexation in a debate, arguing that Spain had a right to Cuba—which was applauded.

40. Brian G. Shellum, *Black Officer in a Buffalo Soldier Regiment: The Military Career of Charles Young*. Lincoln: University of Nebraska Press, 2010, 73.

41. Booker T. Washington, *A New Negro for a New Century*, 24.

42. Willard B. Gatewood, "Alabama's 'Negro Soldier Experiment,' 1898–1899," *Journal of Negro History* 57/4 (October 1972): 333–51, 344.

43. George W. Reid, "Four in Black: North Carolina's Black Congressmen, 1874–1901," *Journal of Negro History* 64/3 (Summer 1979): 229–43, 229.

44. *Richmond Daily Planet*, 20 August 1898.

45. Piero Gleijeses, "1898: The Opposition to the Spanish–American War," *Journal of Latin American Studies*, 35 (Number 4, November 2003): 681–719. See also Frank Freidel, "Dissent in the Spanish-American War and the Philippine Insurrection," *Proceedings of the Massachusetts Historical Society*, Third Series, 81(1969): 167–184.

46. Ann Field Alexander, *Race Man: The Rise and Fall of the 'Fighting Editor,' John Mitchell, Jr.* Charlottesville: University of Virginia Press, 2002, 89, 92, 95, 99, 100, 101.

47. *The Nation*, 5 May 1898.

48. *Baltimore Afro-American*, 16 April 1898.

49. *The Colored American*, 13 August 1898.

50. *Baltimore Afro-American*, 10 December 1898.

51. Johnson, *History of Negro Soldiers in the Spanish-American War and Other Items of Interest*, 123.

52. *La Fraternidad*, 21 February 1899.

53. Lisa Brock, "Back to the Future: African-Americans and Cuba in the Time(s) of Race," *Contributions in Black Studies: A Journal of African and Afro–American Studies* 12/1 (1994): 9–32, 17.

54. Esteban Montejo, *The Autobiography of a Runaway Slave*. London: Macmillan, 1993, 236. For a portrait of Cuban soldiers of African descent, see Burr McIntosh, *The Little I Saw of Cuba*. New York: Tennyson Neely, 1899.

55. Ibid., Tiffany Yolanda Jimmece Bryant, "Inter-subjective and Trans-national Effects: The Role of the United States in the Formation and Evolution of the Collective Perception and Racial Relations in Cuba," Ph.D. diss., Florida International University, 2010, 178.

56. G. M. Brown, *Ponce de Leon Land and Florida War Record*. St. Augustine: Brown, 1902.

57. Nancy Raquel Mirabal, "The Afro-Cuban in Ybor City and Tampa, 1886–1910," *OAH Magazine of History* 7/4 (Summer 1993): 19–22.

58. Michele Alishahi, "For Peace and Righteousness: Blanche Armwood and the Struggle for Freedom and Racial Equality in Tampa, Florida, 1890–1939," M.A. thesis, University of South Florida, 2003, 35. See also John R. Durham, "Blanche Armwood: The Early Years, 1890–1922," M.A. thesis, University of South Florida, 1988.

59. Gary R. Mormino, "Tampa and the New Urban South: The Weight Strike of 1899," *Florida Historical Quarterly* 60/3 (January 1982): 337–56, 346.

60. Susan Greenbaum, *Afro-Cubans in Ybor City: A Centennial History*. Tampa, 1986, University of Miami.

61. Franc R. E. Woodward, *El Diablo Americano: Strange Adventures of a War Correspondent in Cuba*. New York: Burlsem, 1895, 42.

62. Anon., *Rambles in Cuba*. New York: Carleton, 1870, 76.

63. "Message from the President of the United States Transmitting the Report of the Naval Court of Inquiry upon the Destruction of the United States Battleship *Maine* in Havana Harbor, February 15, 1898, Together with the Testimony Taken Before the Court," Spanish American War, Monroe County Public Library.

64. Brent Weisman, "Soldier and Patriots: Buffalo Soldiers and Afro-Cubans in Tampa, 1898," U.S.F. Anthropology Studies in Historical Archaeology, 1999, University of South Florida. See also Robert P. Ingalls, *Urban Vigilantes in the New South: Tampa, 1882–1936*. Knoxville: University of Tennessee Press, 1988.

65. *Cleveland Gazette*, 21 May 1898.

66. Nancy Raquel Mirabal, "The Afro-Cuban Community in Ybor City and Tampa, 1886–1910," *OAH Magazine of History* 7/4 (Summer 1993): 19–22.

67. *Tampa Weekly Tribune*, 5 October 1892, Tony Pizzo Papers, University of South Florida.

68. Evelio Grillo, "Black Cuban, Black American," in Roman and Flores, 99–112, 100, 102, 103, 108. see f.n. 9.

69. Adrian Burgos, Jr., *Cuban Star: How One Negro League Owner Changed the Face of Baseball*. New York: Hill and Wang, 2011, 20.

70. Rob Ruck, *Raceball: How the Major Leagues Colonized the Black and Latin Game*. Boston: Beacon, 2011, 12.

71. Jules Tygiel, *Baseball's Great Experiment: Jackie Robinson and His Legacy*. New York: Oxford University Press, 1997, 16.

72. Adrian Burgos, Jr., "Playing Ball in a Black and White 'Field of Dreams': Afro-Caribbean Ballplayers in the Negro Leagues, 1910–1950," *Journal of Negro History* 82/1 (Winter 1997): 67–104, 71.

73. *Tampa Weekly Tribune*, 9 June 1898. See also Willard B. Gatewood, "Alabama's Negro Soldier Experiment, 1898–1899," *Journal of Negro History* 57/4 (October 1972): 333–51, 342: "Birmingham's editor also argued that . . . the Negro soldier . . . could stand the climate" in Cuba "better than the white."

74. *Baltimore Afro-American*, 30 April 1898.

75. Ibid.

76. *Tampa Weekly Tribune*, 11 August 1898.

77. The Diary of Private William C. Kniffen of the 9th Illinois Volunteer Infantry, 1898, Camp Cuba Libre Papers, University of South Florida. See also Herschel V. Cashin, *Under Fire with the 10th Cavalry*. New York: Bellwether, 1970 [originally published 1899].

78. *Cleveland Gazette*, 18 March 1899.

79. Oral history, Samuel Swain, 1978, University of South Florida.

80. Remarks of Mayor Gillett, Council Chambers, 2 April 1898, File on Spanish-American War, Hampton Dunn Papers, University of South Florida.

81. Brent R. Weisman, ed., "Soldiers and Patriots: Buffalo Soldiers and Afro-Cubans in Tampa, 1898," Florida Division of Historical Resources, Bureau of Historic Preservation and the Historic Preservation Advisory Council, 5. In the same collection, see Susan Greenbaum, "Patriots in Exile: Afro-Cubans in Tampa, 1886–1909," 84–149.

82. Willard B. Gatewood, "Negro Troops in Florida, 1898," *Florida Historical Quarterly* 49/1 (July 1970): 1–15; and William Schellings, "Florida Volunteers in the War with Spain, 1898," 47–59.

83. Gary R. Mormino, "Tampa and the New Urban South: The Weight Strike of 1899," *Florida Historical Quarterly* 60/3 (January 1982): 337–56, 347, 349.

84. Willard B. Gatewood, "Alabama's 'Negro Experiment,' 1898–1899," 347.

85. T. G. Steward, *Buffalo Soldiers: The Colored Regulars of the United States Army*. Amherst, NY: Humanity Books, 2003, 97, 100.

86. Sylvia Hilton, "The United States Through Spanish Republican Eyes in the Colonial Crisis of 1895–1898," in Sylvia Hilton and Steve J. S. Ickringill, eds., *European Perceptions of the Spanish American War of 1898*. New York: Peter Lang, 1999, 53–70, 56.

87. Markus M. Hugo, "Uncle Sam I Cannot Stand, for Spain I Have No Sympathy: An Analysis of Discourse About the Spanish-American War in Imperial Germany, 1898–1899," in Hilton and Ickringill, *European Perceptions of the Spanish American War*, 71–94, 78.

88. Joseph Smith, "British War Correspondents and the Spanish-American War, April–July 1898," in ibid.

89. Frank Schubert, "Seeking David Fagen: The Search for a Black Rebel's Florida Roots," *Tampa Bay History* 22 (2008): 19–34. See also George F. Hoar, *Cuba and the Philippines: Both Entitled to Independence*, Chicago: Anti-Imperialist League, 1900; and "Republic or Empire. Address by the Hon. George S. Boutwell, President

of the Anti-Imperialist League and of the New England Anti-Imperialist League, Delivered before a Mass Meeting at the Cooper Institute, New York, New York, May 24, 1900," Massachusetts Historical Society.

90. "Report by Mr. Elliot on the Question of the Negroes in the Southern States," "confidential," April 1899, FO881/7148, NAUK.

91. *Tampa Tribune*, 12 May 1898. See also Gary R. Mormino, "Tampa's Splendid Little War: A Photo Essay," *Tampa Bay History* 6 (Fall–Winter 1982): 47–55.

92. *Tampa Tribune*, 8 May 1898. See also Office of Naval Intelligence, *War Notes No. 1. Information From Abroad. Battles and Capitulation of Santiago de Cuba (Completed) by Lieutenant Jose Muller y Tejeiro. Second in Command of Naval Forces of the Province of Santiago de Cuba*. Washington, D.C.: Government Printing Office, New York Historical Society. Translated from the Spanish.

93. *New York Times*, 19 January 1899.

94. Willard B. Gatewood, "Black Troops in Florida During the Spanish American War," *Tampa Bay History* 20 (Spring/Summer 1998): 17–31, 18. See also Maura Barrios, "José Martí Meets Jim Crow: Cubans in the Deep South," paper, n.d., University of South Florida–Tampa.

95. *Baltimore Afro-American*, 2 July 1898. See also Marvin Fletcher, "The Black Volunteers in the Spanish American War," *Military Affairs* 38/2 (April 1974): 48–53.

96. Herschel Cashin, *Under Fire with the Tenth U.S. Cavalry*. Chicago: American Publishing House, 1902, 80, xiii.

97. See the remarks of John Marshall of the 8th Illinois infantry, speaking from Santiago in the *Illinois Record* [Springfield], 3 September 1898: "We are camped on the battlefield about two miles out. Dead Spanish soldiers are being burned on the hill about a quarter of a mile from us. Others are buried all over the place, some with their feet and hands sticking out, buzzards picking the flesh off their bones. . . . The stench is almost unbearable. The Spanish prisoners are being made to clean it."

98. *The Parsons Weekly*, 15 October 1898.

99. "From Cabin to Cottage," ms. , Jackson Cox Papers–University of Texas. See also "Charge of the Colored Troops," 1898, Brown University, for depiction of U.S. Negro troops in Cuba.

100. Theodore Roosevelt, *The Rough Riders: An Autobiography*. New York: Library of America, 2004, 85, 106, 112, 116, 227. Dale Walker, *The Boys of '98: Theodore Roosevelt and the Rough Riders*, New York: Doherty, 1998, 225, 226.

101. Willard B. Gatewood, "Black Americans and the Quest for Empire, 1898–1903," 562.

102. *Baltimore Afro-American*, 31 August 1912.

103. Booker T. Washington, *A New Negro for a New Century: An Accurate and Up-to-date Record of the Upward Struggles of the Negro Race*. Chicago: American Publishing House, 1900, 66. See also Burr McIntosh, *The Little I Saw of Cuba*. New York: Neely, 1899, 115: "Nearly all who came to the ford attempted to avoid the water as much as possible, all excepting the colored troops. The moment these men saw the water, every one of them let out a yell and rushed into it with a shout of delight."

104. Frank F. Excdall, "Fighting' Fred Funston of Kansas," *Kansas Historical Quarterly* 22/1 (Spring 1956): 78–86, 84.

105. *Topeka Capital-Journal*, 21 August 1998.

106. Lester D. Langley, "Fightin' Fred Funston and the Rebellion in Cuba," *Prologue* 18/1 (Spring 1986): 7–23, 13.

107. 55th U.S. Congress, Senate, 2nd Session, Report No. 885, "Report of the Committee on Foreign Relations . . . Relative to Affairs in Cuba." Washington, D.C.: Government Printing Office, 1898, 12, Kansas Historical Society.

108. Frederick Funston, *Memories of Two Wars*. New York: Scribner's, 1911, 28, 34, 35, 65.

109. Thomas W. Crouch, *A Yankee Guerrillero: Frederick Funston and the Cuban Insurrection, 1896–1897*. Memphis: Memphis State University Press, 1975, 73, 121. See also James J. O'Kelly, *The Mambi-Land, or Adventures of a Herald Correspondent in Cuba*. Philadelphia: Lippincott, 1874, 60: In the slave quarters, "the greatest number were men, most of them natives of Congo." See also Samuel Hazard, *Cuba, with Pen and Pencil*. Hartford, CT: Hartford Publishing, 1871.

110. "The Adventurous Career of Frederick Funston," *Current Opinion* 56/6 (June 1914): 427–28, 427. See also Thomas W. Crouch, "Frederick Funston of Kansas: His Formative Years, 1865–1891," *Kansas Historical Quarterly* 40/2 (Summer 1974): 177–211.

111. Report, n.d., ca. 1898, Leonard Wilson Collection, Western Reserve Historical Society.

112. E. Dupuy de Lome to Mr. Secretary, 18 December 1897, Reel 29, Volume 39, U.S. Department of State, *Notes from the Spanish Legation in the U.S. to the Department of State, 1790–1906*, University of North Carolina–Chapel Hill: "Numerous expeditions" of vessels enmeshed in "filibustering expeditions" from Florida, supplying the "Cuban insurgents." In the same collection see also Juan du Bose to John Sherman, 13 February 1898: "Well-known insurgent leader Sanchez Agramonte, accompanied by several filibusters, has left New York today going in the direction of Long Island." Also in same collection see undated Memorandum from Legation, ca. early 1898: Agramonte and his comrades "not only violated the neutrality laws by committing the hostility of landing bodies of armed men, conveying munitions of war on the shores of Cuba but also violated the navigation laws."

113. Lester D. Langley, "Fightin' Fred Funston and the Rebellion in Cuba," *Prologue* 18/1 Spring 1986): 7–23, 9.

114. "Guide to North Florida Living," May–June 1983, Hampton Dunn Papers.

115. *Fort Myers News-Press*, 15 February 1976.

116. Woodward, *El Diablo Americano*, 93.

117. F. A. Lord, Wilmington consul to Consul–Charleston, 23 September 1895, Box 19, Records of Spanish Consulate–Charleston: "Captain and crew" headed to Cuba in "steamer for having munitions of war aboard. . . . It is openly talked here that they are offering one thousand dollars down and one hundred dollars per month for volunteers." In same collection see Report by Spanish Consul–New York, 16 November 1895: Captain Samuel Hughes of New York accused of embarking on "expedicion filibuster." Robert Batten, Collector General's Office–Kingston to Spanish Consul in Jamaica, Box 19: As to Captain Hughes, when his vessel was detained in Jamaica found "concealed" were "two new Remington rifles and one box marked Bridgeport containing 500 ball cartridges."

118. David Charles Turpie, "The Failure of Reunion: The South and Republican Foreign Policy, 1898–1902," Ph.D. diss., University of Maine, 2010, 16, 35, 82, 90, 99, 109, 110, 141, 142, 143. 146, 147. See also "Speech of Hon. Henry Cabot Lodge of Massachusetts in the Senate of the United States," April 13, 1898, filed under "Intervention in Cuba," Massachusetts Historical Society. See also Thomas G. Dyer, *Theodore Roosevelt and the Idea of Race*. Baton Rouge: Louisiana State University Press, 1980; and Wallace Finley Dailey, ed., *Pocket Diary 1898: Theodore Roosevelt's Private Account of the War with Spain*. Cambridge, MA: Harvard College Library, 1998, Brown University. Howard C. Hill, *Roosevelt and the Caribbean*. Chicago: University of Chicago Press, 1927.

119. "Speech of Hon. B. R. Tillman of South Carolina in the Senate of the United States, Friday, April 15, 1898, Independence of Cuba, No Reconstruction or Carpet Bag Government Under Pretense of Patriotic Motives," University of South Carolina. See also "United States Congress. Speeches on Cuba," ca. 1898, Brown University.

120. Matthew C. Butler to R. A. Alger, 26 September 1898, Matthew C. Butler Papers, University of South Carolina.

121. 55th U.S. Congress, Senate, 2nd Session, Report No. 885. See also Major E.L.N. Glass, *The History of the Tenth Cavalry, 1866–1921.* Fort Collins, CO: Old Army Press, 1972.

122. Joseph Fry, *John Tyler Morgan and the Search for Southern Autonomy.* Knoxville: University of Tennessee Press, 1992, 187. See also Bertha Davidson, "Arkansas in the Spanish–American War," *Arkansas Historical Quarterly* 5/3 (Autumn 1946): 208–19; and Harold J. Sylvester, "The Kansas Press and the Coming of the Spanish-American War," *The Historian* 31/2 (1969): 251–67. See also Arthur S. Wolverton, "History of War with Spain," n.d., Kansas Historical Society.

123. Gatewood, "Alabama's 'Negro Soldier Experiment,' 1898," 348.

124. 55th U.S. Congress, Senate, 2nd Session, Report no. 885, Kansas Historical Society.

125. 54th U.S. Congress, Senate, 1st Session, Report No. 141, 20 January 1896, Brown University.

126. *Tampa Weekly Tribune*, 31 August 1899.

127. Willard B. Gatewood, "Virginia's Negro Regiment in the Spanish-American War: The Sixth Virginia Volunteers," *Virginia Magazine of History and Biography* 80/2 (April 1972): 193–209, 205, 206.

128. Speech of Hon. St. George Tucker of Virginia in the House of Representatives, Monday, March 2, 1896, University of North Carolina–Chapel Hill.

129. Office of Custodian of American History to General William McDowell, 29 May 1897, Box 53, Baldwin–McDowell Papers, New York Public Library.

130. Richard Harding Davis, *Cuba in War Time.* New York: Russell, 1898, 130. See also Richard Harding Davis, *The Cuban and Porto Rican Campaigns.* New York: Scribner's, 1898.

131. Bailey, Jr., "The Splendid Little Forgotten War," 198. See Tony Pizzo to Winston Churchill, 5 March 1951, Tony Pizzo Papers, for reminiscing about Churchill's time in the region. Office of Winston Churchill to Tony Pizzo, 24 January 1952: "His visit took place, if his memory is correct, in 1895."

132. Philip Brown to "Dear Sir," 10 March 1897, Box 53, Baldwin–McDowell Papers.

133. Philip F. Brown to Francis Wayland Glen, 25 February 1897, Box 53, Baldwin–McDowell Papers.

134. London clipping, 20 February 1873, Box 307, Moses Taylor Papers.

135. John Mason to "My Dear Brother," 29 November 1898, Besse Mason Papers, Duke University.

136. John Mason to "My Dear Mother," 17 November 1898, ibid.

137. John Mason to "My Dear Mrs. English," 19 August 1898, ibid. See also *Papers of the Military Historical Society of Massachusetts, Volume XI, Naval Actions and Operations Against Cuba and Porto Rico, 1593–1815.* Boston: Stillings Press, 1901.

138. John Mason to "My Dear Brother," 1 August 1898, Besse Mason Papers. See also *The U.S. Yankee on the Cuban Blockade 1898.* New York: Members of the Yankee's Crew, 1928, Massachusetts Historical Society. For more on the war, same collection, see Guild Family Papers.

139. Diary entry, 10 July 1898, Diary of Harry S. Bowman, Maryland Historical Society.

140. Lecture, n.d., Box 3, George Kennan Papers, New York Public Library.

141. Letter to William McDowell, 27 September 1898, Box 53, Baldwin–McDowell Papers. Unfortunately, Spain's vice-consul in North Carolina—a U.S. national—did not speak Spanish well, either. See F. A. Lord, Wilmington consul to Spanish Consul, Charleston, 9 January 1895, Box 19, Records of Spanish Consulate in Charleston: "I regret to inform you of my very small knowledge of Spanish. At my father's death,

who had been Vice Consul for nearly fifty years, there being no one in this place who knew Spanish, I was appointed Vice Consul." This handicapped his work in this port for he was "afraid to ask [for] help" in interpreting "for fear of divulging some news abroad which I alone should know." See F. A. Lord to "Dear Sir," 1 September 1896, Box 20, Baldwin–McDowell Papers.

142. Ibid., Esteban Montejo, *The Autobiography of a Runaway Slave*, 237, 239. See also Micol Seigel, *Uneven Encounters: Making Race and Nation in Brazil and the United States*. Durham, N.C.: Duke University Press, 2009, 153: In 1899 a "white minstrel quipped, 'Der ain't no niggers since de war broke out; I'm a Cuban now,' you'll hear them shout."

143. *Tampa Weekly Tribune*, 5 January 1899.

144. Paula Giddings, *Ida: A Sword Among Lions*. New York: Amistad, 2008, 390.

145. *Tampa Weekly Tribune*, 8 October 1903.

146. *Tampa Weekly Tribune*, 19 April 1900.

147. See Typescript of diary in Cuba, 12 September 1898, P. J. McCook Papers, Massachusetts Historical Society: "News has come lately of disturbances in the country districts. The trouble was caused originally by an organization called the 'Black Hand' composed of rabidly anti-Spanish natives. . . . Their natives resemble in many ways those of the southern Ku Klux Klan of 'carpet bag days.'"

148. Laurence E. Prescott, *Without Hatreds or Fears: Jorge Artel and the Struggle for Black Literary Expression in Colombia*. Detroit: Wayne State University Press, 2000. The author connects the perception that there was more activism by Africans in Cuba than in Colombia—though slavery was abolished decades earlier in that latter nation—to the more active U.S. presence on the island.

149. *Tampa Weekly Tribune*, 24 November 1898.

150. *Tampa Weekly Tribune*, 16 August 1900.

151. *Baltimore Afro-American*, 17 June 1899.

152. Johnson, *History of Negro Soldiers in the Spanish-American War and Other Items of Interest*, 30–31.

153. Report on A. C. Goggins, n.d., Box 1, Florida Negro Papers, University of South Florida.

154. David Starr Jordan, "Lest We Forget: An Address Delivered Before the Graduating Class of 1898." Palo Alto, CA: Leland Stanford Jr. University, 10 August 1898, Massachusetts Historical Society.

155. *Tampa Weekly Tribune*, 18 August 1898. For detailed narratives about particular battles, "Squadron Bulletins" and the like from the 1898 war, see Box 1, Folder 14, Freebee, Gregory, McPherson Papers, University of North Carolina–Chapel Hill. See also *Views of Admiral Cervera Regarding the Spanish Navy in the Late War, 1898, Office of Naval Intelligence, United States*, Cornell University.

156. Report, ca. 1899, Box 53, Baldwin–McDowell Papers, New York Public Library.

157. Richard Harding Davis, *Cuba in War Time*. New York; Russell: 1898, 31.

158. Trumbull White, *United States in War with Spain and the History of Cuba*. Chicago: International, 1898, 279. See also 54th U.S. Congress, Senate, 2nd Session, Document No. 84, 1897, "Message from the President of the United States Transmitting in Response of the Secretary of State Covering a List of Persons Claiming to Be Citizens of the United States Who Have Been Arrested on the Island of Cuba since February 24, 1895 to the Present Times," Tulane University.

159. Letter to "Dear Friend," 6 January 1899, Arthur Kennickel Papers, Georgia Historical Society–Savannah. See also Charles F. Gauvreau, *Reminiscences of the Spanish-American War in Cuba and the Philippines*. Rouses Point, N.: Authors Publishing Co., 1915, University of Central Florida–Orlando.

160. Caroline L. Wallace, *Santiago de Cuba Before the War or Recuerdos de Santiago*. London: Tennyson, 1898, 10, 31.

161. *Scrapbook of Cartoons, Clippings, etc. Related to the Spanish-American War of 1898*, ca. 1899, University of North Carolina–Chapel Hill.

162. Davis, *Cuba in War Time*, 78.

163. *The Colored Citizen* [Washington, D.C.], 11 November 1898.

164. Scrapbook on 1898 war, Box 1, Elmer Roberts Papers, University of North Carolina–Chapel Hill.

165. Philip S. Foner, *Antonio Maceo: The 'Bronze Titan' of Cuba's Struggle for Independence*. New York: Monthly Review Press, 1977, 260.

166. Rafael Lopez Valdez, *Racial Discrimination from Colonial Times to the Revolution*. Havana: Instituto Cubano de Amistad con Los Pueblos, 1971, Box 26, Folder 6, William L. Patterson Papers, Howard University. See also Alejandro de la Fuente, *A Nation for All: Race, Inequality and Politics in 20th-Century Cuba*. Chapel Hill: University of North Carolina Press, 2001,

167. Clipping, 20 February 1899, Box 1, Elmer Roberts Papers, University of North Carolina–Chapel Hill.

168. See Enver Michel Casimir, "Champion of the Patria: Kid Chocolate and the Redemption of Cuban National Pride," M.A. thesis, University of North Carolina–Chapel Hill, 3.

169. *Baltimore Afro-American*, 25 November 1899.

170. "Confidential" message to Elihu Root, 23 February 1900, Box 28, Leonard Wood Papers, Library of Congress, Washington, D.C.

171. Ibid.

172. Leonard Wood to U.S. President, "Confidential," 28 October 1901, Box 29, Leonard Wood Papers.

173. Clipping, 20 April 1900, Reel 1, ibid.

174. State Department to Archibald Grimke, 25 April 1898; Archibald Grimké to State Department, 7 April 1898, Box 24, Archibald Grimké Papers–Howard University.

175. Carolyn Fluehr-Lobban, "Antenor Firmin: Haitian Pioneer of Anthropology," *American Anthropologist* 102/3 (September 2000): 449–66, 450.

176. Jana K. Lipman, *Guantánamo: A Working-Class History Between Empire and Revolution*. Berkeley: University of California Press, 2009, 118–19, 121, 127.

177. Christine Skwiot, *The Purposes of Paradise: U.S. Tourism and Empire in Cuba and Hawai'i*. Philadelphia: University of Pennsylvania Press, 2010, 209. See also James J. A. Fortier, ed., *The Spanish-American War of 1898: Liberty for Cuba and World Power for the United States*. New Orleans: State Museum, 1939; and John Kendrick Bangs, *Uncle Sam Trustee*. New York: Riggs, 1902.

178. William King to Fisher Harris, 18 January 1898, Box 1, Fisher Harris Papers, Duke University.

179. See "Senator Platt's Speech on Cuba," 15 July 1901, Massachusetts Historical Society.

180. Philip W. Kennedy, "Race and American Expansion in Cuba and Puerto Rico, 1895–1905," *Journal of Black Studies* 46/3 (March 1971): 306–16. See also Allen H. Merriam, "Racism in the Expansionist Controversy of 1898–1900," *Phylon* 39/4 (1978): 369–80.

181. See Juan C. Santamarina, "The Cuba Company and the Expansion of American Business in Cuba, 1898–1915," *Business History Review* 74/1 (Spring 2000): 41–83.

182. Marshall E. Schott, "Louisiana Sugar and the Cuban Crisis, 1895–1898," *Louisiana History* 31/3 (Summer 1990): 265–72.

183. Carmen Diana Deere, "Here Come the Yankees! The Rise and Decline of United States Colonies in Cuba, 1898–1930," *Hispanic American Historical Review* 78/4

(November 1998): 729–65, 742, 752.

184. Alenjandro de la Fuente, "Race and Inequality in Cuba, 1899–1981," *Journal of Contemporary History* 30 (January 1995): 131–68, 135. See also Rubin Francis Weston, *Racism in U.S. Imperialism: The Influence of Racial Assumptions on American Foreign Policy, 1893–1946.* Columbia: University of South Carolina Press, 1972, 140–41: In 1899 a U.S. census of Cuba based supposedly on skin color—as opposed to the mainland's "1 drop rule"—found "whites" with a 57 percent majority, while the "Negro element in the population had decreased from a high of 58.5% in 1841 to a low of 32.1 percent in 1899." Meanwhile, Negroes were deemed to be "50 percent of insurgents in 1898 and 80 percent in 1906." See also Victor H. Olmsted, *Cuba: Population, History and Resources.* Washington, D.C.: U.S. Bureau of the Census, 1909, 143–44: "The number of whites steadily increased up to the census of 1899 when there was a diminution of 35, 535, as compared with the number in 1887. The colored increased up to 1861; in 1877 there was a decided decrease, amounting to 117, 149; by 1887 the number had increased by 42, 901 but this increase was followed by a decrease of 23, 355 by 1899. . . . The colored formed 43.8 per cent of the population in 1775, and the proportion diminished slightly in the succeeding 18 years. But between 1792 and 1817 it increased greatly, the colored becoming largely in the majority and forming 55 percent of the total. A small increase followed in 1827, succeeded by a larger increase in 1841, when the proportion of colored reached its maximum, 58.5 percent. After that date it diminished rapidly and in 1861 was but 43.2 [percent]. . . . The diminution of the proportion of colored inhabitants during the last half-century is doubtless but another illustration of the inability of the colored race to hold its own in competition with the whites, a truth which is being demonstrated on a much larger scale in the United States." Needless to say, the lack of precise definitions of "colored" and "white" and the like in the Cuban context makes many of the preceding assertions questionable.

185. B. R. Tillman, "Address [on] The Negro Problem and Immigration," Delivered by Invitation before the South Carolina House of Representatives, January 24, 1908. Columbia, SC: Gonzales and Bryan, State Printers, 1908, Kansas Historical Quarterly.

186. Gatewood, "Black Americans and the Quest for Empire, 1898–1903," 554.

187. Booker T. Washington, "The Negro in the New World," *Journal of the Royal African Society* 10/38 (January 1911): 173–78, 177.

8. RACE/WAR IN CUBA?

1. See "Finding Aid," Elliott and Gonzales Family Papers. See also Lewis Pinckney Jones, "Carolinians and Cubans," Ph.D. diss., University of North Carolina–Chapel Hill, 1952.

2. Linda McCarter Matthews, "N. G. Gonzales: Southern Editor and Crusader, 1858-1903," 195, 196, 228, 236: There was also anti-Semitism emerging at the trial of Gonzales' murderer. When a witness, August Kohn—who was Jewish—was sworn in, the defense attorney was quick to ask: "Do you swear before God and the Living Christ? Do you swear before Christ?" See also Narciso Gonzales, *In Darkest Cuba: Two Months Service Under Gomez Along the Trocha from the Caribbean to the Bahama Channel.* Columbia, SC: State, 1922.

3. Alessandra Lorini, "Cuba Libre and American Imperial Nationalism: Conflicting Views of Racial Democracy in the Post-Reconstruction United States," in Manisha Sinha et al., *Contested Democracy: Freedom, Race and Power in American History.* New York: Columbia University Press, 2007, 191–214, 207.

4. "Battle of Santiago," n.d., Horace Porter Papers, Johns Hopkins University.

5. *Cleveland Gazette*, 22 October 1898.

6. Robert Porter, Special Commissioner for the United States to Cuba and Porto Rico, "Report on the Commercial and Industrial Condition of the Island of Cuba." Washington, D.C.: Government Printing Office, 1898, New York Historical Society.

7. Charles M. Pepper, *Tomorrow in Cuba*. New York: Harper & Bros., 1899, 141–43, 149, 152, 156, 157, 158, 159.

8. *Baltimore Afro-American*, 10 December 1910.

9. Adjutant General's Office, *Military Notes on Cuba*. Washington, D.C.: Government Printing Office, 1898, New York Historical Society.

10. Ibid., Tiffany Yolanda Jimmece Bryant, "Inter-Subjective and Transnational Racial Effects," 226.

11. Louis A. Perez, Jr., *Cuba Under the Platt Amendment, 1902–1934*. Pittsburgh: University of Pittsburgh Press, 1986.

12. *Washington Bee*, 19 May 1899. See also Herbert H. Sergeant, *The Campaign of Santiago de Cuba*, Chicago: McClurg, 1907.

13. *Wisconsin Weekly Advocate*, 18 January 1900. The articles cited from the Negro press from 1898 to 1900 can mostly be found in Gatewood, *"Smoked Yankees" and the Struggle for Empire*.

14. Allen Alexander Wesley to Booker T. Washington, 5 October 1898, in Louis R. Harlan, ed., *The Booker T. Washington Papers*, vol. 4: *1895–1898*. Urbana: University of Illinois Press, 1975, 486–87. Wesley graduated from Fisk University and served as a surgeon in Cuba with the U.S. military.

15. Grace W. Minns to Booker T. Washington, 24 May 1901, 123, in ibid., vol. 6: *1901–1902*, 1977.

16. Interview, 29 April 1899, in ibid., vol. 5, *1899–1900*, 1976, 83–88.

17. *Baltimore Afro-American*, 9 April 1910.

18. *Pittsburgh Courier*, 17 October 1936.

19. Governor Joseph F. Johnston to Booker T. Washington, 28 June 1899, in Harlan, *Booker T. Washington Papers*, 5:140; and Booker T. Washington to Governor Johnston, 5 July 1899, 5:148: "There is not one in the party who under any circumstances could be mistaken for a white."

20. William Archer, *Through Afro-America: An English Reading of the Race Problem*. New York: Dutton, 1910, 249, 251, 252.

21. *Baltimore Afro-American*, 26 July 1902.

22. *Baltimore Afro-American*, 29 January 1910.

23. *To Cuba via the Palace Steamer Prince Arthur Plying Between New Orleans and Havana*, ca. 1904, Tulane University.

24. D. E. Sickles to Elihu Root, 2 April 1901, Box 29, Leonard Wood Papers.

25. Melina Pappademos, *Black Political Activism and the Cuban Republic*. Chapel Hill: University of North Carolina Press, 2011, 22.

26. H. Leon Prather, *We Have Taken a City: Wilmington Racial Massacre and Coup of 1898*. Rutherford, NJ: Fairleigh Dickinson University Press, 1984.

27. Frank Carter to Senator Butler, 5 June 1898, Box 9, Folder 101, Marion Butler Papers, University of North Carolina–Chapel Hill.

28. Frank Carter to Marion Butler, 6 June 1898, Box 9, Folder 101, ibid.

29. See "Report of Major General John R. Brooke, Commanding Division of Cuba," Havana, 1898, Harvard University, on separation in voting rolls between the "Spanish element" and the "colored."

30. Henry Bagley to "My Dearest Mother," 17 January 1899, Box 3, Folder 34, Bagley Family Papers, University of North Carolina–Chapel Hill.

31. Henry Bagley to "My Dearest Ones," 21 March 1899, Box 3, Folder 34, ibid.

32. Octavius Coke to "My Dear Mama," 14 July 1899, Box 1, Octavius Coke Papers, University of North Carolina–Chapel Hill.

33. William P. Upshur to "Dear Mother," 14 October 1906, Box 2, Folder 12, William P. Upshur Papers, University of North Carolina–Chapel Hill

34. William P. Upshur to "Dear Father," 14 March 1905, Box 2, Folder 11, ibid.

35. William P. Upshur to "Dear Father," 26 March 1907, Box 2, Folder 13, ibid.

36. William P. Upshur to "Dear Mother," 19 March 1905, Box 2, Folder 11, ibid.

37. William P. Upshur to "Dear Father," 14 October 1906, Box 2, Folder 12, ibid.

38. William P. Upshur to "Dear Mother," 23 February 1907, Box 2, Folder 13, ibid.

39. William P. Upshur to "Dear Mother," 10 February 1906, Box 2, Folder 12, ibid.. See also "Crawley" to "My Darling Little Wife," 24 January 1899, Folder 1, C.C. Vaughan Papers, University of North Carolina–Chapel Hill, on more complaints about inability of Cubans to understand the English language. Searching, tense, and fundamental debates over language were a hallmark of the early U.S. presence in Cuba. See Report by Lincoln de Zayas, 15 October 1907, Box 1, Folder 4, Frank Parker Papers, University of North Carolina–Chapel Hill. In the same collection see Report by H. W. Wheeler, 30 October 1907; Frank Parker to Adjutant General, 3 January 1908; Henry McCain, Adjutant General, War Department to Frank Parker, 30 March 1909. See also Letter to "My Darling Wife," 24 January 1899, Folder 1, C.C. Vaughan Papers, University of North Carolina–Chapel Hill. The apotheosis of this unfortunate trend arrived when Julio Garcia of Havana hanged himself in Port Gibson, Mississippi, because of his difficulty in learning and communicating in English, see *Chicago Defender*, 30 December 1922.

40. William P. Upshur to "Dear Father," 20 February 1906, Box 2, Folder 12, William P. Upshur Papers, University of North Carolina–Chapel Hill.

41. See e.g. "Trip to Havana with My Daughter Frances," December 1907, Ms. 728, John Semmes Papers, Maryland Historical Society. See also Trumbull White, *Our New Possessions*. Chicago: Ayer, 1898.

42. Report, 5 December 1904, Roll 2, T800, *Notes from the Cuban Legation in the U.S. to the Department of State*. See also Office of the Chief of Staff, *Military Notes on Cuba*. Washington, D.C.: Government Printing Office, 1909. See also Joseph Bucklin Bishop, *Issues of a New Epoch*. New York: Scott-Thaw, 1904.

43. James Weldon Johnson, *Along This Way: The Autobiography of James Weldon Johnson*. New York: Viking, 1933, 3, 58, 59, 63, 65, 67.

44. Salim Washington, "Of Black Bards, Known and Unknown: 'Music as Racial Metaphor in James Weldon Johnson's 'The Autobiography of an Ex-Colored Man,'" *Callaloo* 25/1 (Winter 2002): 233–56, 244: The protagonist is "the guest of a 'dark colored' woman and her Cuban husband. Johnson . . . worked in a Cuban cigar factory as a youth, as did his protagonist."

45. James Weldon Johnson, "Placido," *The Crisis* 23/3 (January 1922): 109–10. See also Richard Jackson, "The Shared Vision of Langston Hughes and Black Hispanic Writers," *Black American Literature Forum* 15/13 (Autumn 1981): 89–92.

46. *Chicago Defender*, 11 October 1913.

47. Alejandro de la Fuente, *A Nation for All*, 166.

48. Melina Pappademos, ibid., 144.

49. "Sociedad de Beneficial, Instruccion y Recreo , La Union Martí–Maceo to Booker T. Washington, 4 March 1912, Reel 649, Booker T. Washington Papers, Library of Congress.

50. Leaflet, 16 July ca. 1912, Booker T. Washington Papers: The speaker, Reverend W. McHenry Wintes, "D.D., L.L.D.," was a "graduate of 1902 class, Oxford University. . . . He is the Cuban that spoke before the Hon. W. McKinley and Cabinet before

the Spanish and American war pleading for his people in Cuba. Dr Wintes speaks fluently in seven languages."

51. *Chicago Defender*, 29 July 1922.
52. *Chicago Defender*, 19 July 1913.
53. *Chicago Defender*, 23 August 1913.
54. *The Crisis*, 11 November and 13 March 1912.
55. *The Crisis*, 18 November 1912.
56. *Philadelphia Tribune*, 26 June 1915.
57. Hallie E. Queen, "The Colored Citizen of Puerto Rico," *The Crisis* 13 (November 1916): 13–14.
58. Andrew Zimmerman, *Alabama in Africa: Booker T. Washington, the German Empire and the Globalization of the New South*. Princeton: Princeton University Press, 2010, 63.
59. *Baltimore Afro-American*, 28 October 1916.
60. *Baltimore Afro-American*, 8 January 1916.
61. *Pittsburgh Courier*, 9 March 1912.
62. *Chicago Defender*, 5 February 1916.
63. *Baltimore Afro-American*, 9 March 1912.
64. *Baltimore Afro-American*, 20 April 1912.
65. William Seraile, *Bruce Grit: The Black Nationalist Writings of John Edward Bruce*. Knoxville: University of Tennessee Press, 2003, 51.
66. *Baltimore Afro-American*, 25 May 1912.
67. *Baltimore Afro-American*, 12 October 1912.
68. *Baltimore Afro-American*, 8 February 1913.
69. *Baltimore Afro-American*, 5 October 1912.
70. *Chicago Defender*, 29 November 1913. See also *Baltimore Afro-American*, 3 October 1914.
71. *Philadelphia Tribune*, 20 March 1920.
72. *Philadelphia Tribune*, 2 October 1930.
73. Theresa Runstedtler, *Jack Johnson, Rebel Sojourner*. Berkeley: University of California Press, 2012, 151, 153, 208.
74. Claude McKay, "Soviet Russia and the Negro," *The Crisis* 27/2 (December 1923): 61–65, 63.
75. *Chicago Defender*, 19 January 1924.
76. *Chicago Defender*, 18 November 1922.
77. *Chicago Defender*, 23 March 1912.
78. *Chicago Defender*, 10 February 1912.
79. *Chicago Defender*, 23 March 1912.
80. *Chicago Defender*, 30 June 1917.
81. *Chicago Defender*, 6 June 1931.
82. *Chicago Defender*, 17 January 1920.
83. *Chicago Defender*, 24 May 1924.
84. *Chicago Defender*, 22 July 1911.
85. Ibid., Andrew Zimmerman, *Alabama in Africa*, 202.
86. *Baltimore Sun*, 4 January 1910.
87. Pamela J. Smith, "Caribbean Influences on Early New Orleans Jazz," M.A. thesis, Tulane University, 1986.
88. Leslie A. Heaphy, *The Negro Leagues, 1869–1960*. Jefferson, NC: McFarland, 173, 176.
89. Janet Bruce, *The Kansas City Monarchs: Champions of Black Baseball*. University Press of Kansas, 1985, 92. See also Jim Bankes, *The Pittsburgh Crawfords*. Jefferson, NC: McFarland, 78.

90. Louis A. Perez, *On Becoming Cuban: Identity, Nationality and Culture*. Chapel Hill: University of North Carolina Press, 1999, 266.

91. Jesse Hoffnung-Garskof, "The Migrations of Arturo Schomburg," 35.

92. Clipping, 3 October 1971, Box 1, Geoffrey Mohlman Papers, St. Augustine Historical Society. See also Jack Orr, *The Black Athlete: His Story in American History*. New York: Lion Books, 1969, 56. Recounted is the story of U.S. Negroes seeking to "pass" by terming their teams, e.g. "Cuban Giants," and speaking a language that was supposed to pass for Spanish.

93. *Philadelphia Tribune*, 27 January 1912.

94. *Philadelphia Tribune*, 26 February 1927.

95. *Chicago Defender*, 25 May 1912.

96. *Chicago Defender*, 1 June 1912.

97. Leland H. Jenks, *Our Cuban Colony: A Study in Sugar*. New York: Vanguard, 1928, 114, 115, 116, 182.

98. Arturo Schomburg, "General Evaristo Estenoz," *The Crisis* 4/3 (July 1912): 143–44. According to a visiting mainlander, "The people of Puerto Rico are complaining that they are not as well off as they were prior to 1898 so far as the cost of living is considered." See W. C. Olds to Daniel Augustus Tompkins, 24 April 1908, Box 2, Daniel Augustus Tompkins Papers, Duke University.

99. *The Crisis* 4/5 (August 1912): 175–76.

100. James B. Clarke, "The Cuban Revolution," *The Crisis* 4 (October 1912): 301–2.

101. Theodore Roosevelt to William Howard Taft, 22 January 1907, William Howard Taft Papers, Duke University.

102. *Granma*, 27 May 2012.

103. Bernardo Ruiz Suarez, *The Color Question in the Two Americas*. New York: Hunt, 1922, 43.

104. Enrique Manuel Lopez, "The Impact of Slavery and the Legacy of Afro-Cuban Subjugation on Race Relations in Cuba at the Turn of the Century (1866–1912)," Honors thesis in History, Brown University, 1996.

105. Renee Caridad-Delphin, "Rhetoric and Reality: An Examination of the Cuban 'Race War of 1912,'" Senior Prize Essays from the Department of History, 2001, RU 170, Box 10, Folder 97, Yale University. See also Julio le Reverand, ed., *Historia de Cuba*, vol. 3. Havana: Editorial Pueblo y Educacion, 1975, 258–59.

106. Jules Robert Benjamin, *The United States and Cuba: Hegemony and Dependent Development, 1880–1934*. Pittsburgh: University of Pittsburgh Press, 1977, 199. See also Rafael Fermoselle, *Politica y Color en Cuba: La Guerrita de 1912*. Montevideo: Editorial Geminis, 1974; and Rafael Fermoselle-Lopez, "Black Politics in Cuba: The Race War of 1912," Ph.D. diss., American University, 1972. At NARA–CP, see also File 837.00/467, RG 59.

107. J. M. Gomez to Frank Parker, 13 May 1912, Box 1, Folder 7, Frank Parker Papers, University of North Carolina–Chapel Hill.

108. *Baltimore Afro-American*, 30 April 1910.

109. Report, 17 February 1912, Correspondence from Spanish Legation in Havana, MAE.

110. *Baltimore Afro-American*, 30 March 1912.

111. Report, 21 March 1912, Correspondence from Spanish Legation in Havana, MAE.

112. Report, 8 April 1912, ibid.

113. Report, 22 May 1912, ibid.

114. Report, 25 May 1912, ibid.

115. Report, 6 June 1912, ibid.

116. Report, 7 June 1912, ibid.

117. Report, 6 June 1912, ibid

118. A.M. Beaupre, U.S. Government to Don Manuel Sanguily, June 1912, ibid.

119. Report, 12 June 1912, ibid.

120. Report, 19 June 1912, ibid.

121. President William Howard Taft to "Diplomatic and Consular Officers of the United States," 11 May 1909, Folder 1, Charles Magoon Papers, University of North Carolina–Chapel Hill. See also F.B. Cullen, *The Serpent's Trail or Memoirs of Harold Bagote, Physician: A Tale of the South and of Cuba*. New York: Broadway, 1910.

122. Harry F. Guggenheim, *The United States and Cuba: A Study of International Relations*. New York: Macmillan, 1934, 211.

123. Fernando Ortiz, "American Responsibilities for Cuba's Troubles," Speech at Town Hall, New York City, 8 November 1931, Reel 3, International Committee for Political Prisoners Papers, New York Public Library.

124. Jesse Hoffnung-Garskof, "The Migrations of Arturo Schomburg," 25.

125. Report, 25 June 1912, Correspondence from Spanish Legation in Havana, MAE.

126. Clipping, 12 June 1912, ibid. See also Various Reports, June 1912, Lgajo 113, Numero de Orden 16, 17 & 31, Secretariat of the Presidency, ANC.

127. *Philadelphia Tribune*, 25 May 1912.

128. *Philadelphia Tribune*, 1 June 1912.

129. *Philadelphia Tribune*, 8 June 1912: "The Americans must be taught by the strong arm of the law that they shall not be permitted to introduce into Cuba the anti-Negro sentiments prevailing in the United States. . . . Inhabitants of the United States generally have no adequate idea of racial conditions in Latin America. . . .To govern these alien peoples equally and peaceably Americans must leave their Alabama prejudices at home."

130. *Philadelphia Tribune*, 15 June 1912.

131. *Pittsburgh Courier*, 14 June 1912.

132. *Pittsburgh Courier*, 5 July 1912.

133. *Baltimore Afro-American*.

134. Letter to General Estes G. Rathbone, Havana, 10 July 1899, Box 1, Folder 2, Elmer Roberts Papers: "Need" in Cuba "for an American-owned newspaper" that is a "skillful advocate of annexation." Also discussed was "buying *La Lucha*," which has a "constituency already organized to receive the ideas that it was designed to convey." Hiring a "Cuban figurehead" was a must.

135. *Havana Post*, 22 January 1913.

136. *Havana Post*, 8 May 1913.

137. *Havana Post*, 11 January 1913.

138. *Havana Post*, 13 July 1913; see also same periodical 25 June 1913: "Negro kills baby to get its blood," inspired by "voodooists. . . . " and 19 July 1913: "Negro terrifies little children" in Camaguey.

139. *Havana Post*, 23 April 1913.

140. *Havana Post*, 23 April 1913. As on the mainland, apprehension about Japan arose in Cuba along with heightened racial chauvinism. See *Havana Post*, 6 May 1913: Wilson careful of Jap feelings . . ." See also Gerald Horne, *Race War! White Supremacy and the Japanese Attack on the British Empire*. New York: New York University Press, 2003.

141. Fred Foltz, Lieutenant Colonel of Cavalry to Adjutant General, "confidential," 21 August 1912, Box 1, Folder 7, *Frank Parker Papers*.

141. Pablo Mendieta to "My Dear Captain Parker," 28 January 1913, Box 1, Folder 8, ibid.

143. Juan Gonzales to Frank Parker, 15 July 193, Box 1, Folder 8, ibid.

144. Theresa Runstedtler, 212, ibid.

145. Jason M. Yaremko, *U.S. Protestant Missions in Cuba: From Independence to Castro*. Gainesville: University Press of Florida, 2000, 79.

146. *Baltimore Afro-American*, 20 July 1912.

147. *Baltimore Afro-American*, 25 May 1912.

148. *Baltimore Afro-American*, 12 October 1912.

149. *Havana Post*, 24 March 1913.

150. Louis A. Perez, *On Becoming Cuban: Identity, Nationality and Culture*. Chapel Hill: University of North Carolina Press, 1999, 322.

151. *Chicago Defender*, 21 February 1914.

152. *Havana Post*, 5 January 1912.

153. *Havana Post*, 23 April 1913.

154. Gerald Horne, *Black and Brown: African Americans and the Mexican Revolution, 1910–1920*, New York: New York University Press, 2005.

155. Ibid., Theresa Runstedtler, 223, 79.

156. *Chicago Defender*, 3 April 1915. See also Albert G. Robinson, *Cuba Old and New*. New York: Longmans, Green, 1915.

157. *Chicago Defender*, 21 April 1923.

158. *Chicago Defender*, 20 April 1918.

159. Oral History, Frank Grillo [Machito], May 1980, Institute for Jazz Studies, Rutgers University–Newark.

160. *Chicago Defender*, 12 December 1931.

161. *Norfolk Journal & Guide*, 28 January 1933.

162. Enver Michel Casimir, "Champion of the 'Patria': Kid Chocolate, Athletic Achievement and the Significance of Race for Cuban Natural Aspiration," Ph.D. diss., University of North Carolina–Chapel Hill, 2010.

163. *Chicago Defender*, 22 July 1916.

164. Megan J. Feeney, "Hollywood in Havana: Film Reception and Revolutionary Nationalism in Cuba before 1959," Ph.D. diss., University of Minnesota, 2008, 355.

165. *Pittsburgh Courier*, 3 October 1936. Thousands viewed the body of this native of Raleigh when she passed away in 1936; this was preceded by her organizing and heading the Red Cross on the island.

166. Benjamin Allen, "A Story of the Growth of E. Atkins & Co., and the Sugar Industry in Cuba," 1925, Massachusetts Historical Society. See also Christopher Harris, "A Study in Personal Influence: Edwin F. Atkins and the Evolution of America Cuba Policy, 1894–1902," M.A. thesis, Harvard University, 1998.

167. April Merleaux, "Sugar and Civilization: Race, Empire and the Cultural Politics of Sweetness in the United States, 1898–1939," Ph.D. diss., Yale University, 2010, 74, 83, 88, 241, 293. See also "Statement of Edwin F. Atkins to Senate Finance Committee on Behalf of E. Atkins & Co. and Various Sugar Companies Operating in Cuba Affected by the Sugar Schedule," August 1921, Massachusetts Historical Society. The company began operation on the island in 1835. See also *New York Times*, 8 April 1929. See also Barry Carr, "Identity, Class and Nation: Black Immigrant Workers, Cuban Communism and the Sugar Insurgency, 1925–1934," *Hispanic American Historical Review* 78 (1998): 83–116.

168. *Savannah Morning News*, 24 March 1935.

169. *Savannah Tribune*, 8 June 1910.

170. W. C. Olds to Daniel August Tompkins, 24 April 1908, Box 2, Daniel August Tompkins Papers–Duke University.

171. William P. Upshur to "Dear Mother," 27 February 1916, Box 2, Folder 16, William P. Upshur Papers, University of North Carolina–Chapel Hill.

172. William P. Upshur to "Dear Mother," 20 December 1916, Box 2, Folder 16, ibid.

173. William P. Upshur to "Dear Mother," 12 January 1917, Box 2, Folder 16, ibid.

174. James Weldon Johnson, "Self-Determining Haiti: Four Articles Reprinted from 'The

Nation' Embodying a Report of an Investigation Made for the NAACP." New York: The Nation, 1920, University of Miami.

175. Amy Jacques Garvey, *Garvey and Garveyism*. New York: Octagon, 1986, 39.

176. "West India Negroes in Cuba," *Opportunity* 3/27 (March 1925): 66–68; Box 31, I:N, National Urban League Papers, Library of Congress.

177. *Pittsburgh Courier*, 23 January 1936. See also Biography of Alonzo Holly, n.d., Box 1, Florida Negro Papers, University of South Florida.

178. Remarks of the Reverend John S. Simmons, 20 April 1936, Box 1, Florida Negro Papers.

179. *Norfolk Journal & Guide*, 2 November 1929.

180. Robert A. Hill, ed., *The Marcus Garvey and Universal Negro Improvement Association Papers*, vol. 2: *27 August 1919–31 August 1920*. Berkeley: University of California Press, 1983, 69.

181. Robert Harris et al., eds., *Carlos Cooks and Black Nationalism from Garvey to Malcolm*. Dover, MA: Majority Press, 1992, xi.

182. Report by Special Agent, 22 February 1920, in Hill, *Marcus Garvey and Universal Negro Improvement Association Papers*, 2:220.

183. Captain Joshua Cockburn to Marcus Garvey, 5 December 1919, ibid., 161–62.

184. Report by Special Agent, 11 April 1920, ibid., 2:290.

185. *Norfolk Journal & Guide*, 9 August 1921.

186. Editorial Note, in Robert A. Hill, ed., *The Marcus Garvey and Universal Negro Improvement Association Papers: The Caribbean Diaspora, 1910–1920*, vol. 11. Durham, NC: Duke University Press, 2011, clxxxix. See Affidavit of Thomas Harvey, 1953, Box 18, UNIA Papers–Emory University, Atlanta. Isaac Wynter was leader of the Garveyites in Cuba.

187. Tony Martín, *Race First: The Ideological and Organizational Struggles of Marcus Garvey and the Universal Negro Improvement Association*. Westport, CT: Greenwood, 1976, 49.

188. Robert Trent Vinson, *The Americans are Coming! Dreams of African American Liberation in Segregationist South Africa*. Athens: Ohio University Press, 2012, 1, 83.

189. *Negro World*, 1 May 1920.

190. *Negro World*, 29 April 1920.

191. *Negro World*, 1 May 1920.

192. Amy Jacques Garvey, *Garvey and Garveyism*, 62. See also *Heraldo de Cuba*, 21 March 1921: front page article on Garvey visit to Cuba.

193. Hugh Mulzac, "Memoirs of a Captain of the Black Star Line," in John Henrik Clarke, ed., *Marcus Garvey and the Vision of Africa*. New York: Vintage, 1974, 127–138, 133.

194. See Frank Guidry, *Forging Diaspora: Afro-Cubans and African Americans in a World of Empire and Jim Crow*. Chapel Hill: University of North Carolina Press, 2010..

195. Remarks of R. H. Bachelor of Guantánamo, Convention Report, 4 August 1924, Hill, *The Marcus Garvey and Universal Negro Improvement Papers*, vol. 5: *September 1922–August 1924*. Berkeley: University of California Press, 1986, 650–51.

196. *New York Times*, 2 February 1925.

197. Rupert Lewis, "The Question of Imperialism and Aspects of Garvey's Political Activities in Jamaica, 1929–1930," in Rupert Lewis and Maureen Warner-Lewis, eds., *Garvey: Africa, Europe, the Americas*. Trenton: African World Press, 1994, 79–98, 87.

198. *Chicago Defender*, 8 February 1930.

199. Clipping, 30 January 1931, Reel 3, International Committee for Political Prisoners Papers, New York Public Library.

200. Clipping, 31 January 1931, Reel 3, ibid.: "There is no racial problem . . . in Cuba" said

Delgado as he accused Garvey of "sowing racial discord." Garvey was "dangerous," it was said.

201. "Tomas Fernandez Robaina, Marcus Garvey in Cuba: Urrutia, Cubans and Black Nationalism," in Lisa Brock and Digna Castaneda Fuertes, ed., *Between Race and Empire: African Americans and Cuba before the Cuban Revolution*, Philadelphia: Temple University Press, 1998, 120–128, 124.

202. Bernardo Ruiz Suarez, 16, 23, 34, 43, 50, 51, 57, 63, 64, 93–95, ibid.

203. Report from U.S. Embassy–Madrid and attached articles *El Sol*, 13 October 1927, Roll 1, M509, *Despatches Relating to Political Relations Between the U.S. and Cuba*, NARA–CP. See also Frederick B. Pike, *Hispanismo, 1898–1936: Spanish Conservatives and Liberals in their Relations with Spanish America*. South Bend, IN: Notre Dame University Press, 1971.

204. *Philadelphia Tribune*, 6 March 1926.

205. *Baltimore Afro-American*, 13 September 1925. Cited is the book by Luis Araquistain, *La Agonia Antillana: El Imperialismo Yanqui en el Mar Caribe*.

206. *Federal Surveillance of Afro-Americans (1917–1925): The First World War, the Red Scare and the Garvey Movement*, Report, 18 July 1919, Reel 12, #155, University of North Carolina–Chapel Hill.

207. *Baltimore Afro-American*, 27 July 1912.

208. Norma Jean Sawyer and La Verne Wells-Bowie, *Key West*. Charleston: Arcadia, 2002, 10, 49.

209. "Bahama Village," *Key West Citizen*, 16 June 1991, Monroe County Public Library.

210. Interview, Tom Hambright, 10 February 2010, Monroe County Public Library.

211. "Manuel Cabeza," Clipping, 28 May 2000, Biography File, Monroe County Public Library.

212. Jason M. Yaremko, 79, ibid.

213. Ambrose E. Gonzales to R. H. Sullivan, 21 February 1923, C.B. Berry Papers, South Carolina Historical Society.

9. THE RISE OF THE REDS—ON THE MAINLAND AND THE ISLAND

1. *Baltimore Afro-American*, 22 August 1931.

2. *Baltimore Afro-American*, 12 September 1931.

3. *Baltimore Afro-American*, 27 March 1943.

4. Gerald Horne, *Powell vs. Alabama: The Scottsboro Boys and American Justice*. New York: Franklin Watts, 1997.

5. *Baltimore Afro-American*, 16 December 1916.

6. *Baltimore Afro-American*, 19 November 1920.

7. *Baltimore Afro-American*, 29 November 1918.

8. *Baltimore Afro-American*, 30 May 1919.

9. *Baltimore Afro-American*, 5 November 1920.

10. *Baltimore Afro-American*, 19 November 1920.

11. *Baltimore Afro-American*, 21 January 1921.

12. *Baltimore Afro-American*, 16 October 1920.

13. Arturo Schomburg, "My Trip to Cuba in Quest of Negro Books," *Opportunity* 11/2 (February 1933): 48–50, Box 32, 1:N, National Urban League Papers, Library of Congress.

14. *Chicago Defender*, 6 September 1930. For a summary of the Sims-Bethune and Pickens cases, see *New York Amsterdam News*, 10 September 1930. See also Joyce A. Hanson, *Mary McLeod Bethune & Black Women's Political Activism*. Columbia: University of Missouri Press, 2003.

15. *Chicago Defender*, 13 September 1930. See also ibid., Rosalie Schwartz, "The Displaced and the Disappointed: Cultural Nationalists and Black Activists in Cuba in the 1920s," Ph.D. diss., University of California, San Diego, 1977, 194, on Club Atenas: "The founding members, sixty–eight of them, included engineers, lawyers, students, property owners, tobacco workers, a telegrapher, a tailor, a professor, a dentist and several journalists."

16. *Baltimore Afro-American*, 13 September 1930.

17. *New York Amsterdam News*, 5 March 1930.

18. *Baltimore Afro-American*, 8 March 1930.

19. *Norfolk Journal & Guide*, 4 October 1930.

20. *Baltimore Afro-American*, 20 September 1930. For more on this important meeting, see *New York Amsterdam News*, 20 September 1930.

21. *New York Amsterdam News*, 1 October 1930.

22. *Baltimore Afro-American*, 27 September 1930. See also the 28 January 1933 edition of the same periodical, on Maceo's daughter residing in New Orleans. See also 16 September 1933 edition: "The best end Cuba has produced in American football is young Maceo," grandson of the famous general. *New York Amsterdam News*, 24 September 1930: Like most U.S. Negroes, Pickens was enthralled by General Maceo.

23. Mary McLeod Bethune, Letter, *The Crisis* 37/12 (December 1930): 412.

24. *New York Amsterdam News*, 5 November 1930.

25. Gustavo Urrutia, trans. Langston Hughes, "Negro Tourists in Cuba," *The Crisis* 39/2 February 1931): 52–53.

26. Gustavo Urrutia, "The Students of Yesterday," *The Crisis*, 39/4 (April 1931): 123.

27. Schomburg, "General Antonio Maceo," 174.

28. Press release, 19 September 1930, Box 1, C325, Folder 9, NAACP Papers, Library of Congress.

29. William Pickens to Dr. Miguel Céspedes y Casado, Havana, 26 September 1930, Box 1, C325, Folder 9, ibid.

30. Jose Garcia Ynerarity to R. W. Bagnall, 18 December 1930, Box 1, G221, Folder 14, ibid.

31. *Baltimore Afro-American*, 4 September 1926.

32. Director of Branches to Jose Garcia Ynerarity, 15 December 1930, Box 1, G221, Folder 14.

33. Jose Garcia Ynerarity to Claude Barnett, 1 October 1930, Box 203, Folder 4, Claude Barnett Papers, Chicago Historical Society.

34. Jose Garcia Ynerarity to Claude Barnett, 11 October 1933, Box 203, Folder 4, NAACP Papers, Library of Congress.

35. *Baltimore Afro-American*, 2 January 1926.

36. *Baltimore Afro-American*, 29 August 1931.

37. William Pickens to Jose Garcia Ynerarity, 10 January 1931, Box 1, G221, Folder 14, NAACP Papers, Library of Congress.

38. William Pickens to Gustavo Urrutia, 10 December 1930, Box 1, C325, Folder 9, ibid.

39. Ibid., Rosalie Schwartz, "The Displaced and the Disappointed," 219.

40. Du Bois quoted in Philip S. Foner, *The Spanish-Cuban-American War and the Birth of American Imperialism*, vol.2, 99.

41. E. San Juan, Jr., "African American Internationalism and Solidarity with the Philippine Revolution," *Socialism and Democracy* 24/2 (July 2010): 32–65, 46.

42. Report, ca. 1930s, Reel 3, International Committee for Political Prisoners Papers, New York Public Library.

43. Mary McLeod Bethune, "The Customs of Cuba as I found Them," n.d., Box 2, Folder 14, Mary McLeod Bethune Papers, Tulane University. See also *Baltimore*

Afro-American, 9 April 1932: "One drop of blood doesn't make a Negro down in Cuba. . . . Seventy percent of Cubans have some colored blood. . . . Cubans do not bother to make microscopic examinations of the hair, blood, eyes, lips and nails in order to determine the race to which an individual belongs."

44. "Translation from Diario de la Marina," 31 August 1930, Box 2, Folder 14, Mary McLeod Bethune Papers, Tulane University.

45. Gustavo Urrutia to Mary McLeod Bethune, 26 November 1930, Box 2, Folder 7, ibid.

46. *Philadelphia Tribune*, 12 February 1931.

47. Walter White to Gustavo Urrutia, 19 April 1932, I: D72, NAACP Papers.

48. Ibid., Rosalie Schwartz, "The Displaced and the Disappointed," 224.

49. Margaret Ross Martín, "The Negro in Cuba," *The Crisis* 41/1 (January 1932): 453–55, 454. See also *Baltimore Afro-American*, 4 October 1930: "[William] Pickens finds White servants in Cuba's colored clubs. . . . In Cuba where there is no law against race mixture, about all the mixing is done by white men marrying colored women. . . . There is no segregation by law in Cuba, although Cuba has more colored people in proportion than the United States. . . . Americans have started discrimination which has grown worse in Havana. . . . Voluntary segregation in most social clubs; the colored club, the Spanish club and the 'white' club. The reason why 'white' and Spanish are different is the fact that the Spaniards make themselves exclusive from the newer whites in club life"—which disrupted "white" unity, a key to the mainland. Whereas in Cuba one was deemed to be "white" if one was "famous, rich or powerful—whatever your color," a pattern more indicative of the Americas as a whole and not the United States.

50. *Chicago Defender*, 11 March 1933.

51. *Chicago Defender*, 29 September 1934.

52. *Chicago Defender*, 10 November 1928. For more on the KKK in Cuba, see *New York Amsterdam News*, 1 November 1933; and File "Ku Klux Klan," Tony Pizzo Papers, University of South Florida. .

53. *Baltimore Afro-American*, 4 July 1919.

54. *New York Amsterdam News*, 1 November 1933. For more on the KKKK, see Alejandro de la Fuente, 78, 204.

55. *Chicago Defender*, 21 October 1933.

56. Bernardo Ruiz Suarez, 64, 94.

57. Walter White to "Whom It May Concern," 20 February 1934, I: G40, NAACP Papers.

58. James R. McGovern, *Anatomy of a Lynching: The Killing of Claude Neal*. Baton Rouge: Louisiana State University Press, 1982.

59. E. P. Sanchez to Walter White, 21 November 1934, I: G40, NAACP Papers.

60. *Bandera Roja*, 16 June 1934; and *Diario de la Marina*, 1 November 1933. See also John Gronbeck Tedesco, "Reading Revolution: Politics in the U.S.-Cuban Cultural Imagination, 1930–1970," Ph.D. diss., University of Texas, 2009.

61. James Mortellaro to Tony Pizzo, 18 December 1979, Tony Pizzo Papers.

62. *Baltimore Afro-American*, 25 October 1930. See also *New York Amsterdam News*, 10 September 1930: Pickens scoffed at the widely cited idea that the island's population was "70 percent white and thirty percent of other races." "Those figures should be at least reversed," he charged, since "the population seems to be eighty or ninety percent colored, as 'color' goes in the United States."

63. *Chicago Defender*, 30 July 1932.

64. Carter G. Woodson, "Attitudes of the Iberian Peninsula," *Journal of Negro History* 20/2 April 1935): 190–243, 212.

65. Frances Strauss to Langston Hughes, 19 September 1930, Box 120, F2263, Langston Hughes Papers, Yale University.

66. Langston Hughes translation of poem by Nicolás Guillén, *Opportunity* 8/8 (August 1930): 240, Box 32, 1:N, National Urban League Papers, Library of Congress. See also Guillén poem translated by Hughes in *Opportunity* 11/3 (March 1933): 88.

67. Edward Mullen, ed., *Langston Hughes in the Hispanic World and Haiti*. Hamden, CT: Archon, 1977, 25, 29.

68. Langston Hughes to Samuel Feijoo, 5 October 1945, Box 224, F3712, Langston Hughes Papers. Hughes was not alone in his admiration of Cuban poets. See Lisa Brock, "Back to the Future: African-Americans and Cuba in the Time(s) of Race," *Contributions in Black Studies: A Journal of African and Afro-American Studies* 12/1 (1994): 9–32, 15: "If one examines 'Crisis,' the NAACP magazine, and 'Opportunity' the Urban League organ, for example, scarcely a decade went by without Placido being remembered either in an essay on his life or in a literary critique of his poetry."

69. Juan M. Leiseca to Langston Hughes, 6 March 1930, Box 224, F3712, Langston Hughes Papers.

70. Note, n.d., Box 485, F12326, ibid.

71. Langston Hughes, "A Cuban Sculptor," *Opportunity* 8/11 (November 1930): 334, Box 32, 1:N, National Urban League Papers. See also Langston Hughes, "Havana Dreams," *Opportunity* 11/6 (June 1933): 181.

72. Langston Hughes, "Oye Muchacho!," *Revista de la Habana*, nos. 7–8 (1930), Box 429, F9565, Langston Hughes Papers.

73. Mark Weiss, ed., *The Whole Island: Six Decades of Cuban Poetry*. Berkeley: University of California Press, 2009, 45.

74. *Baltimore Afro-American*, 3 December 1932.

75. Langston Hughes, "The Trip to Havana, 1930," Box 492, F12436, Langston Hughes Papers. See also *New York Amsterdam News*, 5 March 1930.

76. "Ward Line, United Fruit Refused to Sell Passage to Cuba," ca. February 1930, Box 485, F12326, Langston Hughes Papers.

77. William Campbell to Langston Hughes, 14 March 1930, Box 120, F2266, ibid.

78. Report, ca. 1930, Box 485, F12326, ibid.

79. *Baltimore Afro-American*, 9 May 1931.

80. *New York Amsterdam News*, 5 August 1931.

81. Gerald Horne, *Negro Comrades of the Crown: African-Americans and the British Empire Fight the U.S. Before Emancipation*. New York: New York University Press, 2012.

82. *Chicago Defender*, 17 April 1915.

83. *Chicago Defender*, 23 March 1929.

84. *Chicago Defender*, 11 March 1933.

85. *Afro-Cubans in Ybor City: A Centennial History*, 1986, University of South Florida.

86. Walter T. Howard and Virginia M. Howard, "Family, Religion and Education: A Profile of African-American Life in Tampa, Florida, 1900–1930," *Journal of Negro History* 79/1 (1994): 1–17, 2.

87. Clipping, 26 February 1989, Tony Pizzo Papers.

88. Enrique A. Corderop, "Preliminary Research Report Part Two: the Afro-Cuban Community in Tampa, Florida" *History 4900*, 1984, University of South Florida.

89. Letter from Jose Rivero Muniz, 14 October 1961 in *Florida Historical Quarterly* 40/3 (January 1962): 313–14.

90. "Celebrations and Amusements Among Negroes of Florida, January 19, 1937," Box 1, Florida Negro Papers, University of South Florida.

91. "Forum," 6 January 2002, Tony Pizzo Papers. See also Enrique A. Corderop, "Preliminary Research Report, Part Two, the Afro-Cuban Communisty in Tampa, Florida," *History 4900*, 1984, University of South Florida.

92. Oral history, Lydia Lopez Allen, et al., 1994, University of South Florida.

93. Robert W. Saunders, *Bridging the Gap: Continuing the Florida NAACP Legacy of Harry T. Moore*. Tampa: University of Tampa Press, 2000,

94. Oral history, Robert Saunders, 2002, University of South Florida.

95. "A Study of Negro Life in Tampa Made at the Request of the Tampa Welfare 1927," Tony Pizzo Papers.

96. Report, 26 August 1938, Box 4, Florida Negro Papers

97. Remarks of Paul Diggs, 12 August 1938, Box 6, ibid.

98. Raul Canizares, *Walking the Night: The Afro-Cuban World of Santería*. Rochester, VT: Destiny Books, 1993, 122.

99. Rosalie Peck and Jon Wilson, *St. Petersburg's Historic African American Neighborhoods*. Charleston: History Press, 2008, 39.

100. Saunders, *Bridging the Gap*, 56.

101. Martín Richardson and John A. Simms, eds., "Federal Writers' Project, American Guide (Negro Writers' Unit), Jacksonville," 1936, Box 2, Florida Negro Papers.

102. Saunders, *Bridging the Gap*, 40. See also Ericka Lynise Burroughs, "Robert William Saunders and a Memoir of the Civil Rights Movement in Florida," M.A. thesis, University of South Florida, 1996.

103. Oral history, Lydia Lopez Allen, 1994, University of South Florida.

104. Interview, Thomas Moreno, 1 June 1937, Box 2, Florida Negro Papers.

105. *Norfolk Journal & Guide*, 13 December 1930.

106. "The Florida Negro," ca. 1938, Box 1, Florida Negro Papers.

107. Verne E. Chatelain to Dr. Carita Doggett Corse, 24 February 1938, Box 8, Florida Negro Papers.

108. "Reminiscences of Old Aunt Sarah, a Former Slave of Grandmother's," n.d., Box 7, ibid.

109. Rosalie Schwartz, "The Displaced and the Disappointed: Cultural Nationalists and Black Activists in Cuba in the 1920s," Ph.D. diss., University of California, San Diego, 1977, 243.

110. Langston Hughes to Manuel Marsal, 7 May 1932, Box 224, F3712, Langston Hughes Papers.

111. *Baltimore Afro-American*, 3 March 1934.

112. William Patterson, "Scottsboro Protest Must Grow," *Labor Defender*, February 1934, New York University. See also, Gerald Horne, *Black Revolutionary: William Patterson and the Globalization of the African-American Freedom Struggle*, Urbana: University of Illinois Press, 2013.

113. Envoy, Port-au-Prince to Secretary of State, 3 January 1933, RG 59, Decimal Files, 1930–1939, 838.00b/10, m1246, Roll 6, NARA–CP.

114. U.S. Embassy–Havana to State Department, 25 May 1934, RG 59, Decimal File, 1930–1939, 837.00B/145, NARA–CP.

115. Remarks on DOI, *Labor Defender*, November 1933, New York University.

116. *Baltimore Afro-American*, 5 January 1935.

117. *Chicago Defender*, 2 August 1930.

118. *Chicago Defender*, 11 July 1931.

119. *Baltimore Afro-American*, 13 October 1934.

120. *Baltimore Afro-American*, 23 March 1935. See also Josephine Herbst, "The Soviet in Cuba," *New Masses* 14 (19 March 1935): 9–12.

121. Memorandum, 7 June 1933, Box 176, Sumner Welles Papers, Franklin D. Roosevelt

Presidential Library, Hyde Park, New York.

122. *Norfolk Journal & Guide*, 24 February 1934.

123. *New York Herald Tribune*, 12 November 1934.

124. *Washington Post*, 12 November 1934, Box 1, C325, Folder 9, NAACP Papers.

125. Brief on Cuba, *Labor Defender*, January 1935, New York University.

126. On Domingo Ferrer, *Labor Defender*, February 1935, ibid.

127. *Chicago Defender*, 14 October 1933.

128. "Discussion Outline #7, June 1932," "Cuba and the Tasks of the International Labor Defense," Box 3, Clarina Michelson Papers, New York University.

129. *Baltimore Afro-American*, 5 January 1935.

130. Speech of James Ford in Havana, 13 November 1938, Box 1, James Ford Papers, New York University.

131. James Ford, "World Problems of the Negro People (A Refutation of George Padmore)," Box 5, CPUSA Papers, New York University.

132. Darien J. Davis, "Nationalism and Civil Rights in Cuba: A Comparative Analysis, 1930–1960," *Journal of Negro History* 83/1 (Winter 1998): 35–51, 35.

133. James Ford, "World Problems of the Negro People (A Refutation of George Padmore)." New York: Harlem Section of CPUSA, n.d., Box 5, CPUSA Papers, New York University. See also Alejandro de la Fuente, *A Nation for All*, 192.

134. Bernardo Ruiz Suarez, *The Color Question in the Two Americas*, 64.

135. Speech by James Ford at Club Atenas, 22 November 1938, Box 1, James Ford Papers.

136. Report, 8 December 1934, Reel 268, Records of the CPUSA.

137. Reports, 1 August 1935; 9 June 1936, 5 August 1935, Box 77, Harvey Klehr Papers, Emory University.

138. Meredith L. Roman, "Another Kind of Freedom: The Soviet Experiment with Antiracism and Its Image as a Raceless Society, 1928–1936," Ph.D. diss., Michigan State University, 2005.

139. Theresa Runstedtler, *Jack Johnson, Rebel Sojourner*, 195.

140. Cesar J. Ayala and Rafael Bernabe, *Puerto Rico in the American Century*. Chapel Hill: University of North Carolina Press, 2007, 138.

141. *Pittsburgh Courier*, 1 December 1934.

142. Gustavo Urrutia to Herbert Seligman, 15 April 1932, I: D72, NAACP Papers.

143. Alejandra Bronfman, *Measures of Inequality: Social Science, Citizenship and Race in Cuba, 1902–1940*. Chapel Hill: University of North Carolina Press, 2004: 145.

144. *Norfolk Journal & Guide*, 21 May 1932.

145. *Chicago Defender*, 10 February 1934. On the impact of Scottsboro in Cuba, see e.g. Frank Walter, "Scottsboro Again Echoes over the World," 29 February 1934, "International Press Correspondence," New York University.

146. *New York Sun*, 14 September 1933. See also Schwartz, "The Displaced and the Disappointed," 193: "The colored population in Camaguey and Oriente tended to maintain a stronger distinction between blacks and mulattoes, than did their counterparts in Pinar del Rio, Havana and Matanzas."

147. *New York Sun*, 25 August 1933. See also "Negro Workers and the Cuban Revolution," *The Negro Worker* 4/1 (May 1934): 27–29.

148. Notes on Trip to Cuba in 1930s, Box 6, Elinor Langer Collection on Josephine Herbst, Yale University: "Big black man with tattered black shoes, stands, looking. . . . Turns looks mournfully at me . . . black boy in park, foot in bloodstained rag, other foot in sock tied with rope to sole of a shoe flapping. . . . Negro woman from Barbados asks have I any work, willing for anything, wash, clean, cook. Says she just walks and walks. No work. What work is goes to natives. 'Hunger runs the sugar mills' says a Negro worker from Jamaica."

149. Charles Alexander, "Negro Workers in Cuba," *The Negro Worker* 10/11 (October–November 1931): 18–19, 18: "From nearly all the West Indian islands Negro workers emigrate to Cuba. The majority of them come from Jamaica, from which island many of them fled. . . . Negro workers starving in Cuba. . . . Negro workers come from Barbados, St. Vincent, Trinidad, St. Lucia, Grenada and other West India islands."

150. Right Reverend John Hurst to Walter White, 8 April 1922, I: C351, NAACP Papers. See also Curtis B. Haley, Jr., ed., *General Minutes and Yearbook, 1929–1930: Methodist Episcopal Church, South*, University of North Carolina–Chapel Hill.

151. *Baltimore Afro-American*, 4 February 1939: Eight Bishops from the African Methodist Episcopal church just returned from Cuba "for the purpose of establishing branches" there. *Baltimore Afro-American*, 12 October 1940: Bishop Reverdy C. Ransom nonetheless issued a "recent criticism" of the "neglect" of the AME church to Cuba. *Baltimore Afro-American*, 7 September 1940: Sue Bailey Thurman, spouse of the leading theologian, Howard Thurman, and a major thinker in her own right tours Cuba with a focus on Africans. .

152. Report of Tom Johnson to Politburo, 14 May 1931, Reel 167, Records of the CPUSA, Library of Congress: "In Tampa, Florida we have organized recently a unit of Cuban cigar workers of 13. . . . Unquestionably among these Cuban cigar workers we have great influence." On Tampa's turbulent labor history, featuring prominent roles for Communists and anarcho-syndaclists, see File, Strikes, Tony Pizzo Papers.

153. NAACP Resolution, 31 December 1930, Box 1, C325, Folder 9, NAACP Papers.

154. Margaret Ross Martín, "The Last Word in Cuba," *The Crisis* 40/5 (May 1933): 105–6. See also J. B. Matthews, "Cuba: A Colony in Revolt," *The Crisis* 41/1 (March 1934): 11–12.

155. *New York Amsterdam News*, 5 August 1931.

156. *New York Amsterdam News*, 26 August 1931.

157. *Norfolk Journal & Guide*, 19 August 1933.

158. Carleton Beals and Clifford Odets, "Rifle Rule in Cuba," New York: Provisional Committee for Cuba, 1935, University of Kansas. On the other hand, Manning Johnson, another Negro member of the delegation—who eventually became a stool pigeon—received a tremendous ovation when he called for "the rallying of the American masses to take the bloody hand of the Mendieta–Batista government from the necks of the poor Cuban people and to take the feet of American imperialism out of Cuba." See *Daily Worker*, 12 July 1935, Box 1, Folder 6, Celeste Strack Papers, Southern California Library for Social Studies and Research, Los Angeles. See also *New York Herald Tribune*, 3 July 1935.

159. Clifford Odets, "What Happened to Us in Cuba," *New Masses*, 16 (July 1935): 9–10.

160. *New York Amsterdam News*, 13 September 1933. See also Harold Preece, "War and the Negro," 1935, Box 2, Solomon & Kaufman Research Files, New York University: "Cuba presents the same unpardonable example of ingratitude to a brave people. The Cuban people were among the first to rise against the Spanish overlords. . . . Ask any of the scabrous, underfed Negroes frequenting the Havana wharves, how these promises have been kept."

161. *Baltimore Afro-American*, 10 November 1934.

162. William O. Spears to Mrs. Spears, ca. 6 March 1927, Box 1, Folder 7, William O. Spears Papers, University of North Carolina–Chapel Hill.

163. "The Richmond Rambler," 30 July 1934, Box 2, Folder 16, ibid.

164. William O. Sears to "My Darling," 11 November 1933, Box 2, Folder 14, ibid.

165. William O. Spears to "My Darling," 17 November 1933, Box 2, Folder 14, ibid.

166. William O. Spears to "My Darling," 22 November 1933, Box 2, Folder 14, ibid.

167. William O. Spears to "My Darling," 7 December 1933, Box 2, Folder 14, ibid.

168. William O. Spears to "My Darling," 7 March 1934, Box 2, Folder 14, ibid.
169. William O. Spears to "My Darling," 9 May 1934, Box 2, Folder 16, ibid.
170. William O. Spears to "MY Darling," 15 May 1934, Box 2, Folder 16, ibid.
171. William O. Spears to "My Darling," 12 May 1934, Box 2, Folder 16, ibid.
172. William O. Spears to "My Darling," 16 May 1934, Box 2, Folder 16, ibid.
173. William O. Spears to "My Darling," 1 June 1934, Box 2, Folder 16, ibid.
174. William O. Spears to "My Darling," 19 June 1934, Box 2, Folder 16, ibid.
175. William O. Spears to "My Darling," 19 June 1934, Box 2, Folder 16, ibid.
176. Kenneth Janken, *Rayford W. Logan and the Dilemma of the African-American Intellectual.* Amherst: University of Massachusetts Press, 1993. See also Material on Santiago, 1933, Box 24, Folder 6, Rayford Logan Papers, Howard University.
177. *Baltimore Afro-American*, 19 August 1933.
178. *Baltimore Afro-American*, 28 July 1934.
179. *Baltimore Afro-American*, 30 September 1933.
180. *Baltimore Afro-American*, 19 August 1933. On Ford in Cuba, see *Atlanta Daily World*, 29 January 1934.
181. *Baltimore Afro-American*, 26 August 1933.
182. *Pittsburgh Courier*, 25 November 1933.
183. *Baltimore Afro-American*, 9 September 1933.
184. *Baltimore Afro-American*, 26 August 1933.
185. *Baltimore Afro-American*, 2 September 1933.
186. *Baltimore Afro-American*, 16 September 1933.
187. *Baltimore Afro-American*, 23 September 1933.
188. *Norfolk Journal & Guide*, 21 October 1933.
189. *Norfolk Journal & Guide*, 30 December 1933.
190. *Atlanta Daily World*, 23 January 1934.
191. *Pittsburgh Courier*, 27 January 1934.
192. *Baltimore Afro-American*, 23 September 1933.
193. *Baltimore Afro-American*, 16 September 1933.
194. *Baltimore Afro-American*, 23 September 1933.
195. Memorandum on Telephone Conversation, 22 November 1933, Box 14, Francis White Papers, Herbert Hoover Presidential Library, West Branch, Iowa.
196. Rafael Iturralde et al. to Secretary of State Henry Stimson, 22 April 1929, Box 2, Arthur Garfield Hays Papers, Princeton University.
197. Memorandum of Activities Relating to Cuban Affairs, 13–20 February 1917, Box 1, John Foster Dulles Papers, Princeton University.
198. *Baltimore Afro-American*, 9 September 1933.
199. *Baltimore Afro-American*, 16 September 1933.
200. *Baltimore Afro-American*, 30 September 1933.
201. Press Release, 8 January 1931, Box 1, C325, Folder 9, NAACP Papers.
202. Joaquin Ordoqui-Mesa, Ofelia Dominguez-Navarro, and Pablo de la Torriente to Walter White, 15 April 1935, Box 1, C325, Folder 9, NAACP Papers: In Cuba "hundreds of thousands of students, teachers, doctors, lawyers and workers" are "in daily peril." For more on this, see File on Cuban Political Situation, 1934–1935, Box 28, Sumner Welles Papers,, Franklin D. Roosevelt Presidential Library, Hyde Park, New York.
203. Report, 14 May 1935, Box 437, Folder 5, Council on Foreign Relations Papers, Princeton University.
204. *Baltimore Afro-American*, 23 September 1933.
205. *Pittsburgh Courier*, 30 September 1933.
206. William O. Spears to "My Darling," 9 May 1934, Box 2. Folder 16, William O.

Spears Papers.

207. *Pittsburgh Courier*, 23 September 1933. This story is repeated in *Philadelphia Tribune*, 21 September 1933.
208. *Pittsburgh Courier*, 28 October 1933.
209. *Pittsburgh Courier*, 27 January 1934.
210. *Atlanta Daily World*, 30 December 1936.
211. James Ford Remarks at Club Atenas, 22 November 1938, Box 1, James Ford Papers.
212. *Philadelphia Tribune*, 18 January 1934.
213. *Pittsburgh Courier*, 5 November 1938.
214. *Pittsburgh Courier*, 2 January 1937.
215. Interview with Fulgencio Batista, 10 November 1938, Box 170, Sumner Welles Papers.
216. *Baltimore Afro-American*, 6 January 1934.
217. *Chicago Defender*, 18 January 1936.
218. *Chicago Defender*, 18 January 1936. See also *Baltimore Afro-American*, 9 August 1941: Intermarriage is found to mostly take place between "white men and colored women."
219. ANP to Mr. Thorndike, 23 August 1933, Box 203, Folder 3, Claude Barnett Papers, Chicago Historical Society
220. Colonel Batista to ANP, 10 October 1933, Box 203, Folder 3, ibid.
221. Associated Negro Papers to Jose Garcia Ynerarity, 24 October 1933, Box 203, Folder 4, ibid.
222. Martín Kaye and Louise Perry, "Who Fights for a Free Cuba?" New York: Workers Library, 1933, University of Central Florida–Orlando.
223. *Pittsburgh Courier*, 14 March 1936.

10. WAR! AND PROGRESS?

1. Langston Hughes article on Spain, October 1937, Box 314, F5103, Langston Hughes Papers, Yale University. On the Valencia trip see *New York Amsterdam News*, 30 October 1937.
2. *Baltimore Afro-American*, 23 October 1937 and 30 October 1937.
3. Notes for a Radio Talk, 1937, Box 479, F11925, Langston Hughes Papers.
4. Poem, 25 October 1948, Box 377, F6422, Langston Hughes Papers.
5. Langston Hughes, "Going South in Russia," *The Crisis* 41 (Number 6, June 1934): 162–63.
6. Manuel Caballero, *Latin America and the Comintern, 1919–1943*. Cambridge: Cambridge University Press, 1986, 160.
7. Langston Hughes, "Negroes Salute Spain," n.d., Box 485, F2318, Langston Hughes Papers.
8. *Atlanta Daily World*, 8 February 1938. On this point see also *New York Amsterdam News*, 16 October 1937.
9. *Chicago Defender*, 19 September 1936.
10. *Chicago Defender*, 8 February 1936.
11. *Chicago Defender*, 15 August 1935.
12. Memorandum, ca. 1930s, Legajo 31, Numero de Orden 57, Secretariat of the Presidency, ANC.
13. Memorandum, 12 April 1935, Legajo 30, Numero de Orden 17, Secretariat of the Presidency, ANC.
14. *Chicago Defender*, 1 July 1937.
15. Gerald Horne, *Black and Red: W. E. B. Du Bois and the Afro-American Response to the Cold War, 1944–1963*. Albany: State University of New York Press, 1986.

16. Langston Hughes, article on Spain, October 1937, Box 314, F5103, Langston Hughes Papers.
17. Danny Duncan Collum, ed., *African Americans in the Spanish Civil War: "This Ain't Ethiopia, But It'll Do."* New York: G. K. Hall, 1992.
18. *Baltimore Afro-American*, October 1937, Box 314, f5103, Langston Hughes Papers.
19. *Baltimore Afro-American*, 12 February 1938. See also Cary Nelson, *The Aura of the Cause: A Photo Album for North American Volunteers in the Spanish Civil War.* Waltham, MA: Abraham Lincoln Brigade Archives, 1997, 193.
20. *Baltimore Afro-American*, 26 February 1938.
21. Pearl Jiminez, "An Interview with Nicolás Guillén, Cuba's Outstanding Poet," *Opportunity* 24/1 (January–March 1946): 7, 29.
22. *Atlanta Daily World*, 5 November 1941.
23. *Baltimore Afro-American*, 17 April 1943.
24. *Daily World*, 25 July 1976, in Philip S. Foner, ed., *Paul Robeson Speaks: Writings, Speeches, Interviews, 1918–1974.* New York: Brunner Mazel, 1978, 124.
25. See the thick file 1937–1938, Legajo 39, Numero de Orden 14, Secretariat of the Presidency, ANC.
26. *Baltimore Afro-American*, 22 January 1938.
27. *Baltimore Afro-American*, 24 April 1943.
28. Serapio Paez Zamora to Claude Barnett, 27 November 1943, Box 203, Folder 3, Claude Barnett Papers.
29. Claude Barnett to Serapio Zamora, 1 February 1944, Box 203, Folder 3, ibid.
30. Davis, "Nationalism and Civil Rights in Cuba," 35.
31. *Baltimore Afro-American*, 26 August 1939.
32. *Baltimore Afro-American*, 30 September 1939.
33. *Baltimore Afro-American*, 13 July 1940.
34. *Baltimore Afro-American*, 26 August 1939.
35. *Baltimore Afro-American*, 23 October 1937. See also Andre Simone, "Meet Cuba's Batista," *New Masses* 48 (28 September 1943): 17–19.
36. Roi Ottley, *New World A-Coming.* New York: Arno Press, 1968, [originally published 1943], 50.
37. *Chicago Defender*, 27 January 1934.
38. *Chicago Defender*, 16 June 1934. The others were the Soviet Union, France, and Argentina.
39. *Baltimore Afro-American*, 10 September 1938. From 1930 to 1938 the number of readers doubled to an average of 79, 952 copies sold weekly, giving it "twice as much circulation as the second paper." See Carl Murphy et al., "The Afro: Seaboard's Largest Weekly," *The Crisis* 45/2 February 1938): 44–46, 50.
40. Dispatch, 7 September 1938, Box 203, Folder 3, Claude Barnett Papers.
41. *Baltimore Afro-American*, 19 November 1938.
42. Ibid.
43. *Baltimore Afro-American*, 26 November 1938.
44. *Baltimore Afro-American*, 3 June 1939.
45. *Pittsburgh Courier*, 17 June 1939: Batista "saved Cuba from the Jews" then fleeing Europe and seeking admittance to Cuba.
46. *New York Amsterdam News*, 19 November 1938.
47. *New York Amsterdam News*, 2 March 1940.
48. *Baltimore Afro-American*, 19 December 1942.
49. *New York Amsterdam News*, 10 December 1938. See also Cristobal Davis, "Cuba: A Fascist Link Weakens," *New Masses* 25 (14 December 1937): 5–6.
50. *New York Amsterdam News*, 11 February 1939.

51. *New York Amsterdam News*, 20 August 1938.
52. *Baltimore Afro-American*, 19 December 1942.
53. *New York Amsterdam News*, 22 February 1941.
54. *New York Amsterdam News*, 19 December 1942. See also Andre Simone, "Meet Cuba's Batista," *New Masses* 48 (28 September 1943): 17–19.
55. Remarks, ca. 1940, Box 4, Folder 49, George Messersmith Papers, Delaware Historical Society.
56. Remarks, ca. 1940, Box 4, Folder 5, ibid.
57. Remarks, ca. 1940, Box 4, Folder 51, ibid.
58. Remarks, ca. 1940, Box 4, Folder 53, ibid. For more on Cuban thugs, see Sam Dlugin, "Blood on the Sugar (The Terror in Cuba)," New York: ILD, n.d., University of Central Florida.
59. Remarks, ca. 1940, Box 4, Folder 54, George Messersmith Papers.
60. Albert Cannon to "Dear Aunt," 1940, Albert Cannon Family Papers, South Carolina Historical Society.
61. "Race Prejudice in Cuba," *The Crisis* 42/3 (March 1935): 73–74, 82.
62. *Baltimore Afro-American*, 30 January 1942.
63. Dispatch, 28 December 1936, Box 203, Folder 3, Claude Barnett Papers.
64. Dispatch, 2 December 1936, Box 203, Folder 3, ibid.
65. Joseph North, "Cuba's First Negro Mayor," *New Masses* 36/11 (September 1940): 6–7. See also *Baltimore Afro-American*, 9 August 1941: In Santiago the "main commercial enterprise is the Bacardi rum factory, which hires numerous colored folk but which . . . keeps them in inferior positions and pays them barely a subsistence wage."
66. *Baltimore Afro-American*, 19 July 1941.
67. *Baltimore Afro-American*, 7 November 1942.
68. *Baltimore Afro-American*, 26 December 1942.
69. *Baltimore Afro-American*, 13 February 1943.
70. *Baltimore Afro-American*, 12 July 1941.
71. Mercer Cook, "Cuba Observes Centenary of Negro Major General Guillermo Moncada," *Opportunity* 19/9 (September 1941): 264–266, 264.
72. Mercer Cook, "Miguel Angel Céspedes," *Opportunity* 19/11 (November 1941).
73. *Baltimore Afro-American*, 8 May 1943.
74. *Baltimore Afro-American*, 2 September 1944.
75. *Baltimore Afro-American*, 9 August 1941.
76. Jesse O. Thomas, "Jim Crow Flies to Cuba," *Opportunity* 19/10 (October 1941): 307–8.
77. Cook, "Miguel Angel CéspedesCéspedes," 339–341.
78. *Baltimore Afro-American*, 19 July 1941.
79. Vincent Byas, "Views on the Cuban Negro," *Opportunity* 20/2 (February 1942): 44–46.
80. Thomas Schoonover, *Hitler's Man in Havana: Heinz Luning and Nazi Espionage in Latin America.* Lexington: University Press of Kentucky, 2008; Max Paul Friedman, *Nazis and Good Neighbors: The United States Campaign Against the Germans of Latin America in World War II.* Cambridge: Cambridge University Press, 2003.
81. Gerald Horne, *Black Liberation/Red Scare: Ben Davis and the Communist Party.* Newark, DE: University of Delaware Press, 1994.
82. "Political Situation in Cuba—Strained Relations Between the United States and Cuba," 2 August 1943, Box 142, Sumner Welles Papers. In the same file is a copy of *Cuba Today*, August 1943, which fingers Red leaders who were said to be Negroes.
83. Dr. Jose J. Yremols to Sumner Welles, 28 May 1940, Reel 68, *Records of the U.S.*

Department of State Relating to United States Political Relations with Latin America and the Caribbean, 1930–1944, Department of State Decimal Files, 711.12–711.39, University of North Carolina–Chapel Hill.

84. *Baltimore Afro-American*, 13 September 1941.
85. *Baltimore Afro-American*, 23 October 1943.
86. *Baltimore Afro-American*, 27 December 1941.
87. *Baltimore Afro-American*, 14 November 1942.
88. *Baltimore Afro-American*, 20 March 1943. See, for example, Alex Poinsett, *Working with Presidents: Louis Martin and the Rise of Black Political Power*. Lanham, MD: Madison, 1987.
89. *Cleveland Call & Post*, 3 April 1943.
90. *Baltimore Afro-American*, 28 June 1941.
91. *Baltimore Afro-American*, 31 July 1943. For more on this point, see also *New York Amsterdam News*, 31 July 1943. See also *Pittsburgh Courier*, 13 November 1943, on Cuban student Renee Comas studying chemistry at Hampton.
92. *Atlanta Daily World*, 3 July 1942.
93. *Atlanta Daily World*, 20 October 1945.
94. *Atlanta Daily World*, 4 April 1945.
95. *Baltimore Afro-American*, 23 March 1946.
96. *Baltimore Afro-American*, 30 March 1946.
97. William Levi Dawson to Jose F. Carneado, 1 March 1946, Box 31, Folder 12, William Levi Dawson Papers, Emory University.
98. *Baltimore Afro-American*, 16 August 1941.
99. *Baltimore Afro-American*, 30 August 1941. See, for example, Benjamin Mays, *Born to Rebel: An Autobiography*, New York: Scribner's, 1971.
100. *Atlanta Daily World*, 14 August 1941.
101. *Baltimore Afro-American*, 24 November 1945.
102. *Baltimore Afro-American*, 31 July 1943.
103. *Baltimore Afro-American*, 13 September 1941.
104. *Baltimore Afro-American*, 4 October 1941.
105. *Baltimore Afro-American*, 5 July 1941.
106. *New York Amsterdam News*, 21 June 1941.
107. *Atlanta Daily World*, 29 June 1942.
108. *Pittsburgh Courier*, 4 January 1941. This plaint also targeted Arnulfo Arias of Panama who "refused to permit the immigration of Negroes from either Cuba or the West Indies," *Philadelphia Tribune*, 25 October 1941.
109. *New York Amsterdam News*, 28 June 1941.
110. W. E. B. Du Bois, "A Chronicle of Race Relations," *Phylon* 3/1 (1942): 66–86, 66.
111. *Atlanta Daily World*, 20 August 1941.
112. *Atlanta Daily World*, 24 August 1941.
113. *New York Amsterdam News*, 26 March 1938.
114. *Baltimore Afro-American*, 17 March 1951.
115. *Baltimore Afro-American*, 27 September 1941.
116. *Baltimore Afro-American*, 2 August 1941.
117. *Baltimore Afro-American*, 13 September 1941.
118. *Baltimore Afro-Americans*, 19 December 1942.
119. *Baltimore Afro-American*, 16 January 1943.
120. *Chicago Defender*, 31 July 1943.
121. *Baltimore Afro-American*, 15 May 1943.
122. *Baltimore Afro-American*, 27 March 1943.
123. *Baltimore Afro-American*, 4 September 1943.

124. *Baltimore Afro-American*, 2 September 1944. See also "Programa Socialista," La Habana: Partido Socialista Popular, 1945, University of Texas–Austin. See major section on "igualdad racial" (racial equality) and "derechos de la mujer" (rights of women).

125. *Atlanta Daily World*, 13 October 1940.

126. *Baltimore Afro-American*, 3 April 1943.

127. *Pittsburgh Courier*, 21 July 1945.

128. Remarks, 24 November 1941, Box 7, Ogden Reid Papers, Yale University.

129. *New York Amsterdam News*, 16 November 1946.

130. *Pittsburgh Courier*, 1 November 1947.

131. Remarks, 6 July 1952, Box 7, Ogden Reid Papers.

132. *Chicago Defender*, 16 November 1945.

133. *Baltimore Afro-American*, 12 July 1947.

134. *Baltimore Afro-American*, 16 November 1946.

135. *Pittsburgh Courier*, 25 January 1947: Other than Jesús Menéndez , "leader of 500,000 sugar plantation workers," the four included "Blas Roca, General Secretary of the Communist Party . . . Lázaro Peña, General Secretary of the Confederation of Cuban Workers and Garcia Aguero, Communist Senator."

136. Louis Ray Sadler, "The Rocambole Conspiracy: A Planned Invasion of Cuba from the United States in 1947," M.A. thesis, University of South Carolina, 1971, 2.

137. John J. Munro, "The Anti-Colonial Front: Cold War Imperialism and the Struggle Against Global White Supremacy, 1945–1960," Ph.D. dissertation, University of California–Santa Barbara, 2009, 102, 121: Ms. Cooper Jackson confirmed the Castro meeting in a brief conversation with me on the sidelines of a book signing for the author, Erik McDuffie, at New York University in October 2011.

138. *Pittsburgh Courier*, 19 July 1947.

139. *Baltimore Afro-American*, 16 December 1944.

140. *Baltimore Afro-American*, 17 March 1945.

141. *Baltimore Afro-American*, 6 December 1947.

142. Michael T. Martín and Lamont H. Yeakey, "Pan American Asian Solidarity: A Central Theme in Du Bois' Conception of Racial Stratification," *Phylon* 43/3 (1982): 202–17, 210.

143. *Philadelphia Tribune*, 7 May 1946.

144. *Pittsburgh Courier*, 10 August 1940.

145. *Baltimore Afro-American*, 31 March 1945.

146. Claude Barnett to Serapio Zamora, 21 November 1944, Box 203, Folder 3, Claude Barnett Papers.

147. Claude Barnett to Angel Suarez Rocabruna, 31 August 1946, Box 203, Folder 3, ibid.

148. Unclear correspondent to Claude Barnett, n.d., Box 203, Folder 3, ibid.

149. Gerald Horne, *Fighting in Paradise: Labor Unions, Racism and Communists in the Making of Modern Hawaii*. Honolulu: University of Hawaii Press, 2011.

150. *Baltimore Afro-American*, 31 January 1948.

151. David Anderson to U.S. State Department, 24 December 1948, Reel 9, *Confidential U.S. State Department Central Files, Cuba: Internal Affairs and Foreign Affairs, 1945–1948*, University of North Carolina–Chapel Hill.

152. *Chicago Defender*, 24 July 1948.

153. Roi Ottley, *New World A-Coming*, 243.

154. *Baltimore Afro-American*, 9 August 1947.

155. *Baltimore Afro-American*, 23 August 1947.

156. *Chicago Defender*, 16 August 1947.

157. *Pittsburgh Courier*, 3 April 1948.

158. *Baltimore Afro-American*, 28 August 1948.
159. Speech at Howard University by Pedro Portoondo Cala, ca. 1948, Box 18, Folder 21, Charles Hamilton Houston Papers–Howard University.
160. *Philadelphia Tribune*, 10 August 1946.
161. Mona Z. Smith, *Becoming Something: The Life of Canada Lee*. New York: Faber and Faber, 2004, 36.
162. Dunn, *Black Miami in the Twentieth Century*, 154.
163. John Rolin Newman, Jr., "Negro League Baseball," M.A. thesis, University of South Florida, 2000, 27.
164. Adrian Burgos, Jr., *Cuban Star: How One Negro League Owner Changed the Face of Baseball*. New York: Hill and Wang, 2011, 46, 229,
165. *Baltimore Afro-American*, 16 July 1949.
166. Chris Lamb, *Blackout: The Untold Story of Jackie Robinson's First Spring Training*. Lincoln: University of Nebraska Press, 2004, 148. See also *Pittsburgh Courier*, 28 September 1946.
167. *Baltimore Afro-American*, 8 March 1947. See also Bill L. Weaver, "The Black Press and the Assault on Professional Baseball's 'Color Line,' October 1945–April 1947," *Phylon* 40/4 (1979): 303–17, 312.
168. *Baltimore Afro-American*, 15 March 1947.
169. *Chicago Defender*, 15 October 1949.
170. *Pittsburgh Courier*, 5 May 1951.
171. *Baltimore Afro-American*, 15 March 1947.
172. Tana Porter, ed., *African Americans in Central Florida: How Distant Seems our Starting Place*, n.d., Orange County Regional History Center–Orlando.
173. Gregory W. Bush, "From Old South Experiences to New South Memories: Virginia Key Beach and the Evolution of Civil Rights to Public Space in Miami," in Winnsboro, ed., *Old South, New South or Down South*, 198–219, 201.
174. Abel A. Bartley, "The Triumph of Tradition: Haydon Burns' 1964 Gubernatorial Race and the Myth of Florida's Moderation," in ibid., 176–197, 190.
175. *Baltimore Afro-American*, 28 August 1948.
176. Franklin Williams to Gloster Current, 6 December 1949, Box 1, James C. Clarke Papers, University of Central Florida.
177. Ben Green, *Before His Time: The Untold Story of Harry T. Moore, America's First Civil Rights Martyr*. New York: Free Press, 1998. See also Joseph North, "Behind the Florida Bombings: Who Killed NAACP Leader Harry T. Moore and His Wife?." New York: New Century, 1952.
178. *New York Amsterdam News*, 23 July 1949.
179. *Baltimore Afro-American*, 5 January 1946.
180. *Baltimore Afro-American*, 22 December 1945.
181. *Baltimore Afro-American*, 24 May 1947.
182. *Baltimore Afro-American*, 21 August 1948.
183. *Philadelphia Tribune*, 10 April 1951.
184. William Levi Dawson to William Levi Dawson, 1 March 1946, Box 31, Folder 12; and Christine Ray Davis to Jose Garcia Inerarity, 22 September 1952, Box 5, Folder 27, William Dawson Papers, Howard University: "Major Davis and I wish to thank you sincerely for your wonderful hospitality during our brief visit to Havana."
185. *Atlanta Daily World*, 16 June 1949.
186. *Chicago Defender*, 24 July 1948.
187. *Baltimore Afro-American*, 5 April 1947.
188. *Norfolk Journal & Guide*, 27 April 1946.
189. *Norfolk Journal & Guide*, 6 January 1951.

190. *Atlanta Daily World*, 29 December 1949.

191. *Baltimore Afro-American*, 5 April 1947.

192. *Atlanta Daily World*, 15 January 1950.

193. *Chicago Defender*, 2 July 1955.

194. Jim Haskins and N. R. Mitgang, *Mr. Bojangles: The Biography of Bill Robinson*. New York: Morrow, 1988, 262.

195. *Chicago Defender*, 21 August 1937.

196. *Baltimore Afro-American*, 17 September 1949.

197. *New York Times*, 20 January 2002.

198. Alan Lomax, *Mister Jelly Roll: The Fortunes of Jelly Roll Morton, New Orleans Creole and "Inventor of Jazz."* New York: Duell, Sloan and Pearce, 1950, 62. See also Carolyn M. Harrison, "The Impact of American Jazz in the West Indies–Jamaica, Trinidad and St. Lucia," M.A. thesis, Rutgers University–Newark, 2005.

199. Lief Bo Petersen and Theo Rehak, *The Music and Life of Theodore 'Fats' Navarro*. Lanham, MD: Scarecrow, 2009, 7, 10.

200. Carl Woideck, *Charlie Parker: His Music and His Life*. Ann Arbor: University of Michigan Press, 1996, 138.

201. Bill Cole, *Miles Davis: A Musical Biography*. New York: Morrow, 1974, 44, 53, 54.

202. Jack Chambers, *Milestones: The Music and Times of Miles Davis*. Toronto: University of Toronto Press, 1983, 16.

203. Fats Navarro, Vertical File, Institute of Jazz Studies, Rutgers University–Newark.

204. Gene Santoro, *Myself When I Am Real: The Life and Music of Charles Mingus*. New York: Oxford University Press, 2000, 77.

205. Nel King, ed., *Charles Mingus, Beneath the Underdog: His World as Composed by Mingus*, New York: Knopf, 1971, 185, 189, 191.

206. Oral History, Frank "Machito" Grillo, May 1980, Institute of Jazz Studies.

207. Gig B. Brown, "Know What I Mean: The Life and Music of Julian 'Cannonball' Adderley," M.A. thesis, Rutgers University–Newark, 1999, 6.

208. Donald L. Maggin, *Dizzy: The Life and Times of John Birks Gillespie*. New York: HarperEntertainment, 2004, 216. In 1980 I organized a fund-raising concert in Manhattan on behalf of liberation movements in the nation that was soon to become Zimbabwe that featured Machito.

209. Oral History, Mario Bauza, 13 December 1978, Institute of Jazz Studies.

210. Vertical File, Mario Bauza, n.d., Institute of Jazz Studies.

211. *New York Times*, 12 July 1993.

212. *Cubop! The Life and Times of Mario Bauza*. New York: Caribbean Cultural Center, 1993, Institute of Jazz Studies.

213. Ruth Glasser, "From 'Indianola' to 'No Cola': The Strange Career of Afro-Puerto Rican Mission," in Roman and Flores, *The Afro-Latino Reader*, 157–75, 169.

214. Paquito d'Rivera, *My Sax Life: A Memoir*. Evanston: Northwestern University Press, 2005, 158.

215. Chano Pozo: Max Salazar, "The Fast Life and Death of Chano Pozo," ca. 1978, Institute of Jazz Studies. See also *Baltimore Afro-American*, 17 September 1949: Kid Gavilan suffers "neck wounds in a street fight with three men Sunday" in New York and is "treated at Harlem Hospital."

216. Dizzy Gillespie with Al Fraser, *To Be or Not . . . to Bop: Memoirs*. Garden City, NY: Doubleday, 1979, 320.

217. Mark J. Lommano, "Topics on Afro-Cuban Jazz in the United States," M.A. thesis, Rutgers University–Newark, 2007, 21, 22, 53.

218. Babs Gonzales, *I Paid My Dues: Good Times . . . No Bread*. New York: Lancer, 1967, 127.

11. RACE TO REVOLUTION

1. Digna Castañeda Fuertes , "Epilogue," in Lisa Brock et al., eds., *Between Race and Empire*, 281–85, 282.
2. *The Prison Letters of Fidel Castro*. New York: Nation Books, 2007.
3. *New York Amsterdam News*, 6 September 1952.
4. *Baltimore Afro-American*, 22 March 1952.
5. Roger Baldwin to "Dear Rowland," 15 February 1957, Box 834, American Civil Liberties Union Papers, Princeton University.
6. *Norfolk Journal & Guide*, 8 March 1952.
7. Clipping, 10 November 1950, 2B3/102, *Media Morgue*, NYHT, CDL, University of Texas–Austin.
8. Jose Gomez Sicre to Drew Pearson, 26 August 1952, G231, Drew Pearson Papers, University of Texas.
9. Memorandum from Thomas Krock, n.d., G231, ibid.
10. Darien J. Davis, "Nationalism and Civil Rights in Cuba," 42.
11. *Miami Herald*, 25 March 1954.
12. Memorandum from Carlos Hevia, n.d., G231, Drew Pearson Papers.
13. Oral History of the American Left, Howard Johnson, 17 October 1979, New York University.
14. Agenda, 1950, "William Patterson vs. Subversive Activities Control Board," Part II, Reel 27, *Records of the Subversive Activities Control Board*, NARA–CP.
15. *National Guardian*, 24–31 August 1953; see also Van Gosse, *Where the Boys Are: Cuba, Cold War America and the Making of a New Left*, New York: Verso, 1993,
16. Press Release, 10 August 1953, Box 22, PE036, Printed Ephemera, New York University.
17. "Proceedings of the 16th National Convention of the Communist Party, USA, February 9–12, 1957." New York: New Century, 1957, University of Kansas.
18. William L. Patterson to Roger Baldwin, 13 March 1957, Box 41, Frances Grant Papers, Rutgers University.
19. Special Agent–Chicago to Director, FBI, 11 April 1958, 100–23825–5201, Ben Davis FOIA Files, Gerald Horne Papers, New York Public Library.
20. *Chicago Defender*, 17 July 1954.
21. *Norfolk Journal & Guide*, 13 October 1956: Studying at Shaw University in Raleigh, Ramon Pez Ferro of Cuba and Bertha Maza Socarra. *Chicago Defender*, 20 April 1957: Olga Williams, a "junior from Havana" wins honors at Bethune-Cookman. *Atlanta Daily World*, 9 April 1957: Cuban students at Bethune-Cookman. *Baltimore Afro-American*, 23 January 1954: Talladega College students return from Havana after "study tour." *Atlanta Daily World*, 12 January 1954: "Unsegregated [sic] harmony impresses touring Talladega students." *Baltimore Afro-American*, 10 May 1958: Five co-eds from Florida A& M University tour Havana.
22. *Atlanta Daily World*, 21 September 1958: Gerade M. Ebanks of Havana to teach at Morehouse College.
23. Ben Carruthers to Claude Barnett, 30 April 1952, Box 203, Folder 3, Claude Barnett Papers. Chicago Historical Society
24. *Atlanta Daily World*, 26 January 1955.
25. *Chicago Defender*, 21 April 1951.
26. *Baltimore Afro-American*, 5 November 1949.
27. *New York Amsterdam News*, 2 September 1950.
28. *Baltimore Afro-American*, 2 August 1958.
29. *Norfolk Journal & Guide*, 12 July 1958.

30. *New York Amsterdam News*, 2 August 1958.

31. *Pittsburgh Courier*, 27 September 1958.

32. *Norfolk Journal & Guide*, 9 August 1958.

33. *Chicago Defender*, 20 August 1958.

34. *New York Amsterdam News*, 8 July 1950.

35. *New York Amsterdam News*, 4 November 1950.

36. *New York Amsterdam News*, 9 February 1952.

37. *New York Amsterdam News*, 6 September 1952.

38. Mary L. Dudziak, "Josephine Baker, Racial Protest and the Cold War," *Journal of American History* 81/2 (September 1994): 543–70.

39. Richard Lentz and Karla K. Gower, *The Opinions of Mankind: Racial Issues, Press and Propaganda in the Cold War*. Columbia: University of Missouri Press, 2011, 71.

40. *Philadelphia Tribune*, 24 February 1953.

41. *Pittsburgh Courier*, 4 October 1952.

42. *Pittsburgh Courier*, 15 May 1954.

43. Claude Barnett to Slaughter's Hotel, Richmond, 16 July 1952, Box 203, Folder 3, Claude Barnett Papers.

44. Pedro Portuondo Cala to Claude Barnett, 23 June 1952, Box 203, Folder 3, ibid.

45. David F. Garcia, "Contesting that Damned Mambo: Arsenio Rodriguez and the People of El Barrio and the Bronx in the 1950s," in Roman and Flores, *The Afro-Latin@ Reader*, 187–98, 191.

46. Carmen Gomez Garcia, "Cuban Social Poetry and the Struggle Against Two Racisms," in Brock, *Between Race and Empire*, 205–48, 233, 234. On left-led resistance in the United States on this front, see Gerald Horne, *Communist Front? The Civil Rights Congress, 1946–1956*. London: Associated University Presses, 1988.

47. Keith Ellis, "Nicolás Guillén and Langston Hughes: Convergences and Divergences," in Brock, 129–67, 153. See also Helena Benitez, *Wilfredo and Helena: My Life with Wilfredo Lam, 1939–1950*. Lausanne: Acatos, 1999.

48. W. E. B. Du Bois to Fernando Ortiz, 18 May 1951 Reel 67, #298; and Fernando Ortiz to W.E.B. Du Bois, Reel 67, #299, W.E.B. Du Bois Papers, Duke University.

49. Searapio Paez Zamora to Claude Barnett, 7 November 1955, Box 203, Folder 3, Claude Barnett Papers.

50. Claude Barnett to President Batista, 2 September 1957, Box 203, Folder 3, ibid.

51. F. Tabernilla Palermo, Office of the President, to Claude Barnett, 14 November 1957, Box 203, Folder 3, ibid.

52. Claude Barnett Memoir, Box 406, ibid.

53. Claude Barnett to Jose Valera, 3 May 1958, Box 203, Folder 3, ibid.

54. Neill Macaulay, *A Rebel in Cuba: An American's Memoir*. Chicago: Quadrangle, 1970, 35.

55. Oral History, Francisco Rodriguez, Sr., 11 August 1978, University of South Florida.

56. Oral History, Otis Anthony, 2009, University of South Florida.

57. Oral History, Francisco Rodriguez, 1978, University of South Florida.

58. Oral History, Francisco Rodriguez, 18 June 1983, 1978, University of South Florida.

59. Ibid..

60. "Communism and the NAACP," 10 February 1958, Group III, Box A76, NAACP Papers.

61. Letter to Roy Wilkins, 19 November 1957, Group III, Box A275, ibid.

62. "Thurdston" to Roy Wilkins, 25 February 1957, Group III, A275, ibid.

63. See R. Saunders to Gloster Current, 10 December 1956, Group III, A275, ibid.

64. Telegram to Gloster Current, 7 February 1957, Group III, Box A276, ibid.

65. NAACP–Tampa to Roy Wilkins, 16 June 1956, Group III, Box A275, ibid.

66. Robert Saunders to Francisco Rodriguez, ca. 1954, Group II, Box B116, ibid.
67. Francisco Rodriguez to Herbert Hill, 22 November 1954, Group II, A343, ibid.
68. Herbert Hill to Francisco Rodriguez, 26 May 1958, Group III, C25, ibid.
69. Robert Saunders to Reverend Dee Hawkins, 18 June 1956, Group III, Box A275, ibid.
70. Statewide Minister's Conference, 24 October 1958, Group III, C25, ibid.
71. *Daytona Beach Morning Journal*, 29 April 1958; and *Miami News*, 28 April 1958.
72. Robert Saunders to Roy Wilkins, 23 August 1956, Group III, Box A275, ibid.
73. Nelson Wardell Pinder, Oral History, 24 July 2006, Orange County Regional History Center–Orlando, Florida.
74. Robert Saunders to Robert Carter, 13 February 1958, Group III, Box A275, NAACP Papers.
75. "A Study of the Need for Negro Public School Teachers in the State of Florida from 1953 to 1960," Group II, Box A226, ibid.
76. Brochure, 24 June 1956, Group III, C24, ibid.
77. Robert Saunders to All branches, 25 November 1957, Group III, C25, [citing *La Gaceta*], ibid.
78. Robert Saunders to All branches, 9 November 1956, Group III, C25, ibid.
79. 18th Annual Session of the Florida State Conference of Branches, Shiloh Metropolitan Baptist Church, Jacksonville, 25 October 1957, "Freedom Fund Dinner" speaker: Rodriguez, Group III, Box C25, ibid.
80. Annual Report for 1958, Group III, C25, ibid.
81. *Pittsburgh Courier*, 30 March 1957.
82. Memorandum, 15 February 1955, Reel 22, #898, *Confidential U.S. State Department Central Files, Cuba: Internal Affairs and Foreign Affairs, 1955–1959*, University of North Carolina–Chapel Hill.
83. Richard Salvatierra, "El Negro Norteamericano," *Bohemia* 44 (11 May 1952): 10–12, Biblioteca Jose Martí. At the same location, see "El Negro de Los Estados Unidos y La Segregacion Racial," *Life en Espanol*, September 1956.
84. Jose Vega Sunol, *Norteamericanos en Cuba: Estudio Ethnohistorico*. Havana: Fundacion Fernando Ortiz, 2004, 300.
85. Memorandum for the Record by John Hoagland, 18 January 1957, Box 17, Personnel Series, John Foster Dulles Papers, Dwight D. Eisenhower Presidential Library–Abilene, Kansas.
86. See Boxes 3 and 4, R. Henry Norweb Papers, Western Reserve Historical Society–Cleveland: Norweb was ambassador to Cuba in the 1940s.
87. Memorandum for the Record by Clyde Roberts, Jr., 4 June 1956, Box 16, John Foster Dulles Papers.
88. Undated clipping, ca. 1950, Box 826, ACLU Papers.
89. L. Mendel Rivers to Hon. W. Muckenfuss, 18 July 1858, Box 1, Mendel Rivers Papers, College of Charleston.
90. *Congressional Record*, 20 March 1958, Box 64, Robert Alexander Papers, Rutgers University.
91. *Chicago Defender*, 15 December 1958.
92. Oral History of the American Left, Jose Alvarez, 15 March 1983, New York University.
93. *Hoy* [Cuba], 28 August 1960.
94. Renee Romano, "No Diplomatic Immunity: African Diplomats, the State Department and Civil Rights, 1961–1964," *Journal of American History* 87/2 (September 2000): 546–679, 555.
95. J. Edgar Hoover to Gordon Gray, 8 September 1960, Box 2, FBI Series, White House Office, Office of the Special Assistant for National Security Affairs: Records, 1952–1961, Eisenhower Presidential Library.

96. Richard Wiebe to Editor, "The Crisis," 18 June 1961, Box III, A93, NAACP Papers.

97. Roy Wilkins to Juan Betancourt, 26 April 1961, Box III, A93, ibid.

98. Jerome Wilson to H. Daniel Lang, 8 March 1961, I: E42, National Urban League Papers.

99. Report, 5 July 1960, 100–23825–5, Ben Davis FOIA File, Gerald Horne Papers.

100. Report, 25 September 1960, 100–23825–5, ibid.

101. Announcement, 12 October 1961, Box 53, George Murphy Papers, Howard University.

102. *Granma*, 13 December 2009. See also Danielle Pilar Clealand, "Uncovering Blackness: Racial Ideology and Black Consciousness in Contemporary Cuba," Ph.D. diss., University of North Carolina–Chapel Hill, 2011; and Devyn Spence Benson, "Not Blacks But Citizens! Racial Poltiics in Revolutionary Cuba, 1959–1961," Ph.D. diss., University of North Carolina–Chapel Hill, 2009.

Index